THROUGH ASIA

THROUGH ASIA

BY

SVEN HEDIN

WITH NEARLY THREE HUNDRED ILLUSTRATIONS FROM SKETCHES AND PHOTOGRAPHS BY THE AUTHOR

VOL. I

GYAN

Published by

GYAN

Gyan Publishing House
5, Ansari Road
Daryaganj, New Delhi-110002
Phone: 011-47034999, 9811692060
E-mail: books@gyanbooks.com

Distribution Network
gyanbooks.com
India, USA, Canada, UK, Australia, France

ISBN : 978-81-212-1489-6 (Set)
ISBN : 978-81-212-2904-3 (HB)
First Published, 1898

2nd Impression 2021

Printed at: Gyan Press, Delhi.

Through Asia, Vol. I
Author: Sven Hedin

THROUGH ASIA

BY

SVEN HEDIN

WITH NEARLY THREE HUNDRED ILLUSTRATIONS FROM SKETCHES AND PHOTOGRAPHS BY THE AUTHOR

VOL. I.

METHUEN & CO.
36 ESSEX STREET, W.C.
LONDON
1898

Sven Hedin

TO

HIS ROYAL HIGHNESS

THE PRINCE OF WALES

THIS RECORD OF

NEARLY FOUR YEARS' TRAVELS

IS

BY HIS PERMISSION

RESPECTFULLY AND GRATEFULLY

DEDICATED

PREFACE

THIS work does not claim to be anything more than a plain account of my journeys through Asia during the years 1893 to 1897. It has been written for the general public, and presents nothing more than a description of my travels and the more memorable of my experiences—not by any means the whole of my experiences. To have recorded everything that I set down in my note-books would have swelled out the book to twice its existing length. Nevertheless those portions of my journey which I have merely touched upon, or have passed over altogether in silence, will not, I trust, be altogether lost. If this book is received with the indulgence which I venture to hope for it, I propose to issue a supplementary volume, to contain a multitude of matters of varied interest and of not less importance than those contained in these pages.

For these reasons the great bulk of the scientific observations I made find no place in the present volumes. All the same I believe the geographer will be able to discover in them something or other that will be of interest to him.

In this place I will content myself with a bare mention of the scientific labours, upon which the chief part of my time, energy, and attention were constantly expended—the drawing of geological sections of the meridional border ranges on the east side of the Pamirs and of the mountain-chains of the Kwen-lun system; the collecting of anthropometrical measurements from a number of Kirghiz; an inquiry into the periodical migrations of the nomads; a study of the etymology of the geographical nomenclatures; measurement of the volume of every river I crossed; bathymetrical soundings in the lakes; and the collection of botanical specimens, more especially of algæ from the lofty alpine regions of the Pamirs and Tibet. Moreover I devoted special attention to the taking of meteorological observations regularly three times a day. These Dr. Nils Ekholm has kindly undertaken to work out for me. Another important task was the collection of voluminous materials dealing with the geographical character and extent of the Desert of Gobi, as also with the complicated river-system of the Tarim, which I was enabled to study at many different points all the way from the Pamirs and the highland regions of Tibet down to the termination of the stream in the far-distant lake of Lop-nor. Further, I noted the periodical fluctuations in the volumes of the Central Asiatic rivers; how during the summer they swell to flood-like dimensions, and then during the winter dwindle away to, in many cases, paltry rivulets, or even dry up altogether; and how these fluctuations occur with unvarying regularity—the ebb and flow, as it were, that accompany the heart-beats of the mighty continent.

The astronomical observations, which I made for the purpose of checking and controlling my instrumental calculations, consisted of determinations of latitude and time in seventeen several places. The instrument I employed was a prismatic circle, and the object I observed the sun or failing that the moon. Mr. Rosén, who has kindly calculated my results, is satisfied that the errors in the latitudinal observations are in every instance less than fifteen seconds, and in the temporal determinations in all cases under one second. The longitudes of certain of the stations were already known with scientific exactitude; these data I employed as bases for the determination of the longitudes of the remaining places. By this means too I was enabled to check more effectually the accuracy of my chronometers, a circumstance the more needful seeing that these latter were frequently subjected to the rough vicissitudes of travel through difficult regions. I brought home latitudinal observations for seven fresh places, and longitudinal observations for six.

As soon as I passed beyond the fairly well-known regions of the Russian Pamirs, I took up, in the summer of 1894, the strictly topographical division of my labours, and with diopter, plane-table, and calculation of paces measured the environs of the lake Little Kara-kul; next I mapped the glaciers of that king of the Central Asiatic mountain-giants, Mus-tagh-ata. After that I surveyed every route I travelled over during the years 1894, 1895, 1896, and the early part of 1897. These important labours were never for a single day remitted. Throughout the whole of the long red line, which marks my travels through Asia, there is not a single break right away to the day (2nd March, 1897) when I rode in at the gate of Peking, and recorded my last entry on the five hundred and fifty-second sheet of my field-book or surveying journal.

In making these measurements I used only a compass and a base-line. The latter varied from 200 (656 feet) to 400 (1312½ feet) metres, and was in every case accurately measured with the metre-measure. After measuring my base-line, I carefully noted the time it took the caravan, properly laden and travelling at its ordinary average pace, to traverse it from the one end to the other; at the same time I was scrupulous to make all due allowance for the inclination of the ground and other inequalities of the surface.

As a rule I laid down my maps on the scale 1 : 95,000. Across the level expanses of the deserts, however, I worked to the scale 1 : 200,000; and in mountainous regions, where the road wound through defiles, where numerous side-valleys joined the main valley, and where the morphological character of the surface underwent frequent and varying changes, I used the scale of 1 : 50,000. The aggregate distance of the route I mapped in this way amounts to 1049 Swedish miles, or 6520 English miles; that is to say, nearly four and a half times the distance from London to Constantinople, two and a half times the distance from New York to San Francisco, and one and a half times the distance from Cairo to Cape Town, in other words, more than one-quarter of the earth's circumference. If to this be added more than 8000 miles which I travelled by carriage or rail in the better known portions of the continent, we get for the entire extent of my travels a grand total of 14,600 miles, or more than the distance from the North Pole to the South Pole. The rate of travel of my caravans, calculated from the results of the whole of the journey, averages a little over two and three-quarter miles an hour.

Out of the above-mentioned 6520 miles no less than 2020 were through regions which no European had ever before visited. Over certain portions of the remaining 4500 miles one traveller had preceded me, over other portions two travellers, but in no case more than three. Despite that, my observations along even those stretches may claim to possess a certain degree of originality; for being able to speak Jagatai Turki with fluency, I was independent of the errors and wilful deceits of interpreters, and consequently was in a position to gather a good deal of information of a more or less important character which will be new to most readers. For one thing, I was able to record a vast number of geographical names, none of which had hitherto appeared on any map, European or Asiatic.

As a curiosity, I may mention that the 552 sheets upon which my route is laid down measure 121 yards in length; and this does not include the maps I made of the glaciers of Mus-tagh-ata. For the present these sheets and such other cartographical materials as I brought home with me are lodged at the famous geographical institute of Justus Perthes in Gotha, where they are all being worked out in detail; and the results will be eventually published in *Petermann's Mitteilungen.*

Although fully conscious of the mistakes of my journey, and of the shortcomings of this my book, and whilst aware that a more experienced traveller would have reaped a richer and a more valuable harvest from the fields upon which I laboured, I nevertheless comfort myself with the reflection that I believe I really did my best as far as lay in my power.

A word or two as to the accessories of the book. The two principal maps have been prepared at the Lithographical Institute of the (Swedish) General Staff, under the superintendence of Lieut. H. Byström; my original place-determinations being embodied upon Curzon's map of the Pamirs, and Pievtsoff's map of Central Asia, as foundations for the two maps respectively. Their primary purpose is to illustrate and make clear the routes I followed. Hence they do not claim to be accurate in matters of minute detail; indeed they could not be so, seeing that my cartographical data have not yet been completely worked out.

In consequence of the generosity of my publishers, I am fortunately enabled to impart a fuller measure of life and reality to certain exciting and characteristic incidents of my story by means of pictures drawn by

Swedish artists. The illustrations to which I allude must not however be regarded as mere products of the artistic imagination. For each of them I supplied sufficient material in the nature of sketches and photographs, and where such were wanting I furnished precise and detailed descriptions. In a word, each individual picture has come to life as it were under my own eye and under my own controlling hand; and I cannot help expressing my admiration of the quickness of apprehension and the lively interest which the several artists have manifested in their work.

For the original calculation of the altitudes, which occur throughout these pages, I am indebted to the kindness and skill of Dr. Nils Ekholm. For the conversion of the metric heights and other measurements into feet, miles, etc., and for the conversion of the Celsius scale into the Fahrenheit scale, as well as for the transliteration of the place-names, the translator is responsible.

Finally, it gives me pleasure to acknowledge a special debt of thanks to Mr. J. T. Bealby, B.A., sometime of the editorial staffs of the *Encyclopædia Britannica*, *Chambers' Encyclopædia*, etc., for the ability and experienced and conscientious care with which he has rendered my original Swedish into English. In the translation of a portion of the book Mr. Bealby was assisted by Miss E. H. Hearn.

SVEN HEDIN.

STOCKHOLM, *1st May*, 1898.

CONTENTS

INTRODUCTION

A WINTER JOURNEY OVER THE PAMIRS

THE MUS-TAGH-ATA AND ITS GLACIERS

ACROSS THE TAKLA-MAKAN DESERT

LIST OF ILLUSTRATIONS

INTRODUCTION

CHAPTER I.

RÉSUMÉ OF CENTRAL ASIAN EXPLORATION

A NEW era is approaching in the historical development of geographical discovery. The pioneers will soon have played their part; the "white patches" on the maps of the continents are gradually decreasing; our knowledge of the physical conditions of the ocean is every year becoming more complete. The pioneers of the past, who cleared the way through increasing danger and difficulty, have been followed by the explorers of the present day, examining in detail the surface of the earth and its restless life, always finding new gaps to fill, new problems to solve.

Although many regions have already been the object of detailed investigation, there are several still remaining in which the pioneer has not yet finished his work. This is particularly the case with the interior of Asia, which has long been neglected. Immense areas of the almost inaccessible Desert of Gobi, and endless wastes in the highlands of Tibet, are to this day as little known as the Polar Regions.

It was with the view of contributing my little to the knowledge of the geography of Central Asia that I set out on the journey which this book describes. I had prepared myself for it by years of work in my study; and in 1890–91 I made a reconnaissance into Russian Turkestan and Kashgar, in order to examine the suitability of those territories as a base of operations for exploring unknown country.

After my return from Kashgar, my chief concern was to procure the necessary means for carrying out my undertaking. To His Majesty King Oscar of Sweden and Norway I accordingly addressed the following particulars of my plan, which I give here, as they will best show how far and in what manner I succeeded in fulfilling the task I set myself. Somewhat abbreviated, my memorandum ran as follows :—

In the heart of Asia, between the two highest chains of mountains on the earth, the Kwen-lun and the Himalayas, is the most stupendous upheaval to be found on the face of our planet—the Tibetan highlands. Its average height is 13,000 feet, and in the north it attains as much as 15,000 feet. Its area, therefore, of 770,000 square miles (two and a half times that of the Scandinavian peninsula) is on a level with the highest peaks of the Alps. According to the Chinese maps its northern parts, which constitute one of the least known tracts of Asia, appear to consist of a system of uninhabited lake-basins possessing no outflow. Farther south the Tibetan and Mongol nomads lead a wandering shepherd life; and it is only in the extreme south of the region that there is any population.

Tibet lies aside from the great highways used by travellers of the nineteenth century. Only a few of the more adventurous Europeans have done their share towards collecting the scanty material upon which our present knowledge of the country is based. Its desolate scenery, its lofty, inaccessible mountains, and its extreme remoteness, situated, as it is, in the heart of a vast continent, have deterred travellers, and driven them to find scope for their activity in other parts of the world—in the Polar Regions, among the oceanic islands, or where the coast has provided a certain point of departure to unknown regions lying within comparatively easy reach. And yet there is scarcely any part of the world in which the explorer is so richly rewarded for his pains, or finds such an inexhaustible field for observation of every kind, as in Tibet; the country whence the light of holiness streams forth upon the world of Lamaism, just as its waters, in the form of mighty rivers, stream forth to give life and nourishment to the countries which surround it. Many important problems in physical geography still await their solution in Tibet and in the Desert of Gobi, each of which would be a distinct gain to science. In a strictly geographical sense, Tibet is one of the least known regions in the world. Even the maps of Africa cannot now show a white patch of such vast extent as occurs under the name of Tibet on our maps of Central Asia. In this respect the Polar Regions alone are comparable with Tibet. The itineraries furnished by the Roman Catholic missionaries, at a period when the country was more easily accessible than it is at the present time, cannot be followed on the map with absolute certainty, and from a geographical standpoint are often of little value.

But even this country, jealously closed as it is by fanaticism, has been compelled to open its doors to the persistency of European inquiry. The western and eastern parts in particular have been traversed by English, Russian, and French travellers. In modern times the only explorers who have gained entrance to Lhasa (Lassa) have been a few Indian pundits, trained by British officers. The jealous apprehensions of the Chinese Government, the religious fanaticism of the Tibetans, and the wild nature of their country—these are the factors which have kept Tibet in isolation longer than any other country in Asia. At a time when the influence of neither Russia nor England was so great as it is now, more than one European succeeded in crossing the country, and even in reaching the capital. The first European to enter Lhasa was a monk, Odorico di Pordenone, who travelled from China to Tibet in the first half of the fourteenth century. In 1624 the Spanish Jesuit Antonius de Andrade went from India to Tibet; and in 1661 the two Jesuit missionaries, Grueber and D'Orville, made their remarkable journey from Peking to Lhasa by way of Koko-nor (Koko-nur), Tsaidam, and the country of the Tanguts. They remained in the capital for two months, and then returned by way of Nepal to Agra, and thence to Europe. In the eighteenth century the mysterious city was visited by several missionaries. Desideri lived in Lhasa from 1716 to 1729, and Della Penna from 1719 to 1735, and again from 1740 to 1746; they, however, have left no writings, except a few letters. Between the years 1729 and 1737 the bold Dutchman Van der Putte travelled from India, by way of Lhasa and Koko-nor, to Peking, whence he returned through Farther India to Lhasa. On his return home he burned all his papers, under the impression that nobody would believe his wonderful narrative. In 1811 Manning reached Lhasa; and in 1845 the two French missionaries, Huc and Gabet, made their celebrated journey from Peking by way of Koko-nor, Burkhan-buddha, and Tan-la to the capital of Tibet, a journey which Father Huc described in an interesting book. Since then no European has succeeded in penetrating to Lhasa. Every subsequent expedition which started with that city as its goal has been compelled to turn back, its mission unaccomplished.

As I mentioned before, the outlying parts of the country have been visited by several European travellers, not all of whom, however, have done scientific work or brought home valuable information. The extreme west of Tibet was explored in 1856 and 1857 by the brothers Schlagintweit, in 1865 by Johnson, in 1868–70 by Shaw, in 1868–70 by Hayward, and in 1870 and 1873–74 by Forsyth and his many associates, in 1885–87 by Carey and Dalgleish, in 1888–90 by Grombtchevsky. Kishen Singh, an Indian pundit, who was a member of Forsyth's expedition, succeeded in penetrating somewhat farther into the country than the others. One of the most remarkable journeys ever made in Tibet was that of the pundit Nain Singh, who had taken part in Schlagintweit's and Forsyth's expeditions, and was sent by Captain Trotter in July 1874 from Leh in Ladak to Lhasa. His caravan consisted of twenty-six sheep, carrying light loads. Only four of them survived the journey, which extended to a thousand miles and lasted four months. The animals subsisted on such herbage as they were able to find on the way. At the town of Niagzu, on the boundary between Ladak and Tibet, they met with both forest and pasture. The tract east of Lake Panggong was uninhabited, except by a few shepherds and their flocks. The natives called themselves Changpas or Northmen; but to the inhabitants of Turkestan they were known as Taghliks or Mountaineers. The Tibetan plateau stretched away east for 800 miles, to the sources of the Chinese rivers and the Burkhan-buddha Mountains. As far as eye could reach, it appeared to consist of a grass-grown plateau region diversified by hills and valleys, with snow-clad mountains in the distance. Occasionally a shepherd's tent was seen; and antelopes, wild asses, and wild sheep abounded. The results of the journey were 276 determinations of latitude, the mapping of 1200 miles of unknown country, 497 observations for altitude with the boiling-point thermometer, and a series of meteorological observations.

Among those who have travelled in eastern Tibet the Russian General Przhevalsky (Prjevalsky) ranks first. The 17th (29th) November 1870 he started from Kiakhta with three Russian followers, and passed through the Desert of Gobi by way of Urga and Kalgan to Peking. After a trip to Dalai-nor, he left Kalgan in May 1871, and travelled west, through the mountain chains of In-shan and Muni-ula, then up the Yellow River (Hwang-ho) until he reached the country of Ala-shan, and its capital Dyn-yuan-in. He afterwards returned to Kalgan. Then after a good rest he went back to Dyn-yuan-in, where we find him in June 1872. Here began the most remarkable part of his travels, the country which he next traversed being little known. He first explored the highlands of Kan-su, a well-wooded mountain region lying north-east of Koko-nor; then, having made the circuit of the lake, and crossed the Southern Range of Koko-nor, the expedition reached the great swamps of Tsaidam, whence it ascended into the higher regions of Tibet, the home of the wild yak. Several of the mountain-chains of the Tibetan highlands were crossed on the way to the Yang-tse-kiang, which was reached on January 10th

(22nd), 1873. Although it was Przhevalsky's intention to penetrate as far as Lhasa, which he approached within twenty-seven days' journey, he was constrained to abandon the plan owing to his caravan animals becoming exhausted and his provisions running short. Przhevalsky's first journey terminated at Irkutsk in Siberia, at which place he arrived on October 8th, 1873.

For three years the expedition had struggled against difficulties which seemed almost insurmountable; had defied the summer heat of the Mongol desert, the winter cold of the Tibetan highlands; had spent months in a small frail tent, often at a temperature of forty degrees below zero (Fahr. and C.), living on game killed by members of the expedition. The energy and endurance which Przhevalsky showed are worthy of every admiration. It is evident, he was swayed by a clear understanding of the great importance of his undertaking. Although surrounded by a hostile population, and exposed to every kind of danger, he disregarded both, and amid the pestilential smoke from the argal (dry dung) fire in his tent went on working out his memoranda and sorting his collections. It was a geographical achievement which has rightly placed Przhevalsky's name in the forefront of Asiatic exploration. The most wonderful thing is, that this journey, which amounted to 7350 miles, cost very little more than 6000 roubles (say £600), a proof that it *is* possible to travel inexpensively in Asia, if you only know how to set about it.

Przhevalsky's second journey lasted from August 1876 to July 1877. Although it extended to less than 2650 miles, the cost was more than 19,000 roubles (or about £1900); but this time his equipment was more complete and his escort more numerous. The results of this journey also were of extreme importance. The region which he added to the domain of geographical knowledge was one of the least known in Central Asia. Previously our sole conceptions of its nature were derived from hearsay, from Chinese maps, and from tradition.

From Kulja his route led through the Ili valley to

Yulduz, afterwards south by way of Korla, and along the lower Tarim, to Lop-nor (Lob-nor) and the Altyn-tagh. When Przhevalsky saw that it was impossible to reach Tibet, and particularly Lhasa, the object of his desire, by way of Lop-nor and the desolate region south of the Altyn-tagh, he determined to try what he could do by way of Gutshen and Khami; but he was taken ill on the road, and was constrained to return to Russia.

The crowning feature of this expedition was the discovery of the new Lop-nor, and of the great chain of mountains Altyn-tagh, which has so greatly altered the appearance of our maps of Central Asia. He also discovered the existence of the wild camel, a discovery afterwards confirmed by other travellers, viz., Carey, Younghusband, and others.

Przhevalsky's third expedition lasted from March 1879 to November 1880, and covered some 4750 miles. On this occasion he was accompanied by twelve natives, and had a sum of 23,500 roubles (£2350) at his disposal. He chose Saisansk on the Russian frontier as a point of departure, and travelled, by way of Bulun-tokhoi and the Urungu river, through Dzungaria to Barkul, and thence over the Tian-shan Mountains to Khami. After that he crossed the Desert of Gobi, touching his former route at a couple of points. This time he penetrated much further to the south, namely, across the Yang-tse-kiang and the Tan-la Mountains as far as 32° N. lat.

Przhevalsky's fourth and last journey began in October 1883, and ended in the same month two years later. With twenty followers, most of them Cossacks, he accomplished a distance of 4850 miles; the cost of the expedition being 42,250 roubles (£4225).

From Kiakhta he crossed the Gobi by the same route he had taken on a previous occasion, and went on further through the highlands of Kan-su as far as the two lakes of Tsaring-nor and Oring-nor, the twin sources of the Hwang-ho. This was the culminating point of the fourth journey. After a deviation to the Yang-tse-kiang, he continued on through Tsaidam, thence over the Altyn-tagh to Lop-nor and Khotan, at the northern foot of the Kwen-lun Mountains, and finally down the Khotan-daria and over the Tian-shan Mountains.

The extensive journeys in 1878–82 of the intrepid Indian pundit Krishna, commonly called A—K, were of the greatest importance for the geography of Northern Tibet. In the spring of 1878 he was ordered by the Indian Government to explore the territory bordered on the north by Przhevalsky's journeys, on the east by the routes of the French missionaries Desgodins and Durand and of the Englishman Gill, on the south by the Sang-po (Brahmaputra river) and the Himalayas, and on the west by the meridian which runs through Lhasa and Lop-nor. In more recent years this region has only been crossed by Huc and Gabet, and by Bonvalot and Prince Henry of Orleans.

Disguised as a merchant, and provided with plenty of money and instruments, A—K went, by way of Sikkim, to Lhasa, reaching that city in September 1878. There he stopped for a whole year, waiting to find a large and well-armed caravan with which he might travel northwards, as the Tangut robbers make the roads in that direction very unsafe. On September 17th, 1879, a Mongol caravan arrived. A hundred of its members, Mongols, with a few Tibetans, were going back at once. All were mounted and all armed with spears, swords, and firearms. A—K seized the opportunity. Great caution was observed during the march; patrols were sent on ahead, and a watch kept at night. The route which was followed at first coincided with that of Nain Singh in 1875, when he journeyed from Tengri-nor to Lhasa. South of Tan-la A—K touched the route taken by Przhevalsky on his third journey. The highest pass in the Tan-la, 16,400 feet, marked the watershed between the upper Mekong and the Yang-tse-kiang. After five months on the plateau he reached the Anghirtakshia Mountains over a pass 15,750 feet in altitude. A halt was made at Tenghelik in Tsaidam; but just as the caravan was on the point of starting again it was attacked by two hundred robbers, who relieved

A—K of all his goods and baggage animals. He managed, however, to retain his notes and instruments, and in spite of his reverses determined to persevere with the solution of the problems which had been set him. He wintered on the western shore of the Kurlyk-nor until March 1880. Thence he intended to steer his course towards Lop-nor; but his Indian servant deserted him, carrying off most of his possessions. He himself was obliged to take service with a Mongol, who was going to Sa-chow. There he was well treated by a lama, but was compelled by the Chinese governor to turn back. This turning-point is of importance. It was from that region Przhevalsky made his journey towards Tsaidam and Tan-la in 1879–80; and in the same quarter Count Széchenyi's expedition through China came to an end. With one faithful follower A—K started on his return journey; but was again compelled to take service with "Chinese Tatars." Finally, however, he reached Darchendo (Tatsien-lu) in safety, and at the mission-station there received every help from the bishop; and thence returned by way of Batang and Darjiling to India.

In 1888–89 the American Rockhill made a journey into eastern Tibet. Starting from Peking with only one follower and a few horses, he proceeded to the Koko-nor and Alak-nor, crossed the Yang-tse-kiang, and eventually got back to Shanghai. He could speak Chinese and Tibetan, and travelled in disguise. He did some first-rate mapping, measured heights, made notes, and says that previous European maps are incorrect and unreliable in respect of both orography and hydrography.

Several other travellers, induced by the desire for research or by ambition, have of late undertaken journeys into inner Tibet and towards Lhasa. Many have failed; while others can show good results. The most successful expedition was that of Bonvalot and Prince Henry of Orleans, which crossed Asia from north-west to south-east. The expedition followed Przhevalsky's route along the Tarim as far as the Lop-nor and the Altyn-tagh. On November 17th, 1889, they set out from the Lop-nor, and on the 23rd crossed the Altyn-tagh, leaving Przhevalsky's and Carey's routes behind them. They then struck a direct course to the south across unknown country and without guides. This march lasted till February 17th, 1890, and extended to two days' journey south of the Tengri-nor. The Tibetan plateau, on which they were travelling for three months, nowhere falls below the altitude of thirteen thousand feet. Some of the mountain-chains of the Kwen-lun system were crossed by passes at more than 18,000 feet in altitude, and numerous lakes were discovered. The country was barren in the extreme, totally devoid of trees or bushes; it did not even provide sufficient provender for the camels and horses of the caravan, which, in consequence of the fatigue, the privations, and the severe cold, gradually died off until very few were left. From December 4th to January 30th not a human being was encountered. Two days' journey south of the Tengri-nor the expedition was stopped by the Tibetans, and in spite of negotiations lasting nearly seven weeks it failed to obtain permission to continue its march to Lhasa. The travellers were therefore obliged to make a considerable circuit, and reached Tongking in September.

In May 1890 the Russian Captain Grombtchevsky endeavoured to penetrate into western Tibet from Polu, but being unsuccessful, he turned aside to Khotan, and spent July and August in exploring the Tisnab valley, the upper Yarkand-daria, and the watershed between these two rivers. After a visit to the Pamirs, he proceeded, by way of Kashgar, to Tashkend (Tashkent), where I met him at the end of the same year. He had covered a distance of more than 4700 miles, and his researches form a connecting link between those of Kuropatkin (1877), Forsyth (1873–74), Przhevalsky (1885), and Pievtsoff (1889–90). He met the last-named in Niya, where the two travellers were able to compare notes and place-determinations.

In 1889 and 1890 General Pievtsoff, accompanied by Przhevalsky's companions, Roborovsky and Kozloff, and by the geologist Bogdanovitch, made a journey into East Turkestan, crossing the Tian-shan Mountains, proceeding up the Yarkand-daria to Yarkand, thence to Khotan, and wintered at Niya. From the northern foot of the Kwen-lun Mountains they made several expeditions on to the Tibetan plateau, and explored, in particular, that part of it which lies to the north of the Arka-tagh. The return journey was by way of the Lop-nor, Kara-shahr, and Dzungaria. Pievtsoff's journey is one of the most important that has been undertaken in these parts, and no traveller has made such reliable place-determinations as he.

In the Altyn-tagh and the tracts south of them Przhevalsky's route in his fourth journey was crossed at several points by that of the Englishman Carey. Accompanied by Dalgleish, who was afterwards murdered, Carey crossed the Altyn-tagh, the Chamen-tagh, and the uninhabited plateau between these two ranges of mountains, before he was able to reach the Kwen-lun proper and the Tibetan highlands. He passed over these chains at a point rather more to the west than that chosen by Przhevalsky, and afterwards intersected Przhevalsky's route on the plateau between the Chamen-tagh and the Kwen-lun Mountains. Carey afterwards proceeded to the east along the foot of the Kwen-lun, went a short distance between this range and the Koko-shili, and crossed the pilgrim road from Mongolia to Lhasa immediately south of the point where it climbs over a pass in the Kwen-lun Mountains. At the river Ma-chu he turned northwards, and traversed a portion of A—K's route. This journey took place in 1885–87.

Captain Younghusband, whose name is well known from his travels in the Pamirs, travelled in 1888 from Peking, *viâ* Barkul, Ak-su, and Kashgar, to India; and Captain Bower, between June 1891 and March 1892, crossed Tibet and China from Leh to Shanghai.

The expeditions which I have here summarized are the most important within the regions which I propose to visit.

It would lead me too far were I to endeavour to render an account of the great problems that still await solution in the interior of Asia. The discovery of new chains of mountains, lakes, and rivers, of the traces of an ancient civilization, of antiquities which might possibly throw light on the great migrations of the races through Asia, the identification of old disused caravan roads, and finally the mapping of an entirely unknown region—all this possesses an irresistible attraction for the explorer; but I can only touch upon one or two questions of peculiar interest.

In the Asiatic highlands the geologist has unique opportunities of studying phenomena of the greatest possible interest, interesting not only on account of the processes of evolution which the mountain chains are actually undergoing there, but also for the reason that those mountain chains themselves are so little known. The tableland of Tibet rises like an enormous platform up to a mean height of thirteen thousand feet above the lowlands of Hindustan on the one side, and the desert of the Tarim basin on the other, the latter being one of the lowest depressions in the interior of any continent. Lake Lop-nor has an absolute altitude of not more than two thousand five hundred feet, and at Luktchin, south of Turfan, a depression has been found which actually lies a considerable distance below the level of the sea. On the side next the Tarim basin the Tibetan highlands are bounded by the Himalayas and the Kwen-lun, whose western extremities meet in the Pamirs and the regions south of it. While the older geographers and discoverers bestowed their attention upon little else save the topographical appearance, or at most the surface elevations, of a country, modern geographical discovery claims from its surveyors reliable knowledge of the original causes of the present condition of the surface of the earth, and the genetic connection, origin, age, and relation of the mountain chains to each other. There are important questions still to be solved in High Asia on these points, and a long period of time must necessarily elapse before these problems can be brought within measurable distance of solution. During the last twenty-five years only four geologists of standing have devoted any attention to the region of the Kwen-lun system, namely, Stoliczka, Von Richthofen, Loczy, and Bogdanovitch.

But vast gaps still divide the regions which they have severally investigated. It is my intention during this projected journey to contribute as far as lies in my power to the filling in of these gaps, where every observation, every contour-line, is of the utmost value.

Another problem of intense interest is the Lop-nor question, which was raised by Baron von Richthofen. I will mention here some of the points set forth in his article entitled "Bemerkungen zu den Ergebnissen von Oberst-lieutenant Prjewalski's Reise nach dem Lop-noor und Altyn-tagh" (*Verhandlungen der Ges. für Erdkunde*, V., 1878, pp. 121 *et seqq.*).

Marco Polo was the first to make the Lop desert known to Europeans, and on D'Anville's map of Asia Lop-nor with its rivers is found for the first time, though in latitude 42° 20′ N. Shortly before Przhevalsky's journey the lake was supposed to be situated in an enormous basin, and at a greater distance to the south than to the north of the mountains which bounded it. Przhevalsky, however, found that the lake lay much farther south than was supposed from the maps and Chinese accounts, and the result of this and his other expeditions was, that the maps of the interior of Asia came to present quite a different appearance from what they had heretofore. The territory between Korla and Altyn-tagh was quite unknown; as was also the fact, that the lower Tarim ran for such a long distance in a south-easterly direction. The discovery of the Altyn-tagh possessed equal importance as a contribution to the knowledge of the physical geography of Asia as for the comprehension of the position and direction of the ancient trading-routes. It now became clear why the ancient silk caravans from China to the West kept so near the south of Lop-nor, necessitating their passing through the much-dreaded desert between Sa-chow and the lake.

Basing his deductions partly on certain geological laws, and partly on a large map of China and Central Asia published in Wu-chang-fu in 1862, Von Richthofen says:—

"The most remarkable thing about Przhevalsky's Lop-nor is, that he discovered a freshwater lake, where we are constrained to assume the presence of salt water. It is an absolute impossibility that a *lake-basin*, which for a series of geological periods has acted as a reservoir for the deposition of salt from a great river, should contain fresh water and be the resort of fish. This would be inconceivable even though the whole course of the Tarim lay through regions which in the general estimation were quite free from salt. But as a matter of fact all the regions whence the lake gathers its drainage are so saline that freshwater springs are quite an exception, and occur only close to the foot of the mountains. Now the water of the Tarim must contain a greater quantity of salt than almost any other large river in the world. The concentration of these saline ingredients by evaporation must take place to a very great extent in the last reservoir of the Tarim, and the continuation of the process from time immemorial must therefore have caused an unusually large deposit of every kind of steppe salt. From the remotest ages the Chinese have called Lop-nor 'the Salt Lake.' . . . Contrary to all theoretical conclusions and historical accounts, we now have from the first European eye-witness, who is furthermore gifted with uncommon powers of observation, the distinct assurance that the last basin of the Tarim is a freshwater lake. There must therefore exist peculiar circumstances to account for this apparent contradiction."

It might perhaps be supposed that during the winter, when the evaporation is slight, the fresh water rises and spreads above the salt water; but the inconsiderable depth of the lake sufficiently nullifies this supposition. Another explanation is that the Tarim, which often changes its channel, has abandoned its former reservoir in favour of another, the present one, which is supposed to be of comparatively recent formation.

The most probable explanation is that, besides the two reservoirs visited by Przhevalsky (the Kara-buran and Kara-kurchin, *i.e.*, Kara-koshun), there is yet a third, into which an arm of the Tarim debouches. No Chinese map shows a southern branch of the Tarim; but a large lake is indicated on latitude 41° N., *i.e.*, in the direct line of any continuation of the Tarim, and is called on the maps Lop-nor. The circumstance, among other things, that Przhevalsky did not find the name of Lop-nor in use also points to the same conclusion. On the other hand, he did hear the name in use for that part of the Tarim which lies east of where the real Lop-nor should be.

Another important argument is implicit in the fact that the Tarim, at its confluence with the Ughen-daria, has a breadth of three hundred to three hundred and sixty feet, and a strong current; but below the junction of all its various tributaries a breadth of only one hundred and eighty to two hundred and ten feet, and a slow current. It is possible that, when Przhevalsky journeyed amongst these tributaries, or rather anastomosing arms, the most easterly branch discharged a part of its water eastwards through another and separate channel into the inaccessible salt desert, and that the traveller overlooked this channel. Von Richthofen concludes his investigation with the words, "However highly we may value what Przhevalsky has done towards the exploration of the Lop-nor, we cannot consider that the problem, for the sake of which he underwent such great hardships, is as yet definitively solved."

The three expeditions of Carey and Dalgleish, Bonvalot and Prince Henry of Orleans, and Pievtsoff, each of which has visited Lop-nor since Przhevalsky, have not added to our knowledge of this remarkable lake, for the reason that they all followed the same route that he took.

The solution of the Lop-nor question is still a desideratum for all who are interested in the geography of Asia.

The future traveller to Lop-nor must not content himself with proving the existence of the basins discovered by Przhevalsky; he must make a systematic and accurate investigation of the districts north of them, in order to try and find the lake into which the Tarim, according to Von Richthofen, empties a portion of its waters. This lake, too, is marked on the Chinese maps, which as a rule are remarkable for their great topographical accuracy.

CHAPTER II.

THE PLAN AND OBJECTS OF MY JOURNEY

FOR several years I have been occupied in studying the geography of Central Asia, partly at home and partly at the University of Berlin, under Baron von Richthofen, the celebrated authority on Chinese geography. I have also prepared myself by two journeys to Persia and Central Asia, in the years 1885–86 and 1890–91 respectively, the latter after the conclusion of Your Majesty's mission to Shah Nasr-eddin of Persia. During these journeys I had the opportunity of becoming accustomed to Asiatic travel, to association with the natives, and of learning one or two of the most important languages. In the hope of being able to make these preparatory studies of use in the cause of science, I have ventured to seek Your Majesty's protection and support for the execution of a scheme which, if all goes well, will reflect honour on our country, and contribute to disperse the clouds which still rest over a great part of Central Asia. An expedition into that part of the world which was the cradle of the Aryan race, and from whose dim interior the Mongols streamed out over the whole of Asia and part of Europe, and where there is such a host of geographical questions still awaiting solution, is one of the most important undertakings within the domain of geographical discovery. The object of my prospective journey is to traverse Asia from west to east, from the Caspian Sea to Peking, and in particular to explore the intermediate regions which are least known.

The Swedish expedition should, if possible, leave Stockholm in the month of May of the present year (1893).

Its equipment should be completed in Turkestan and Ladak, and nothing need be taken from Stockholm except instruments and firearms. Accompanied by one assistant, whose duty it would be to take astronomical observations, I propose to travel through Russia to Baku, across the Caspian Sea to Usun-ada, and thence by rail to Samarkand. It is my intention to drive through West Turkestan in a tarantass by way of Tashkend, Kokand, Margelan, and Osh, and thence over the pass of Terek-davan—all places well known to me—to Kashgar in East Turkestan, the termination of my former journey in 1890–91. In Kashgar I shall hire a horse caravan to take us, by way of Yarkand and the Kara-korum pass, to Leh, where there are an English agent and English merchants. The journey to Kashgar will take two months to accomplish, thence to Leh one month, so that, if all goes well, the beginning of August should see us in Leh.

It was also my intention originally, from the region around Lop-nor, to try and penetrate over the Kwen-lun Mountains into Northern Tibet. But in December of last year, whilst on a visit to St. Petersburg, I met General Pievtsoff, who in 1889–90 made the expedition previously mentioned into East Turkestan. General Pievtsoff advised me against attempting to carry out my plan along the lines which I then unfolded to him. He had had unfortunate experience of the difficulties which travellers encounter in those regions, having endeavoured unsuccessfully to penetrate into the country with horses and camels. Train animals perish in great numbers owing to the difficulties of the country, the inclement weather, the rarefied air, and the almost entire absence of pasturage. General Pievtsoff advised me to make Leh, in Ladak, the starting-point for my proposed expedition into Tibet. There one can procure not only the necessary provisions and articles essential to an adequate equipment, such as tents, saddles, furs, felt carpets, household utensils, boxes for collections, etc., but also reliable men, natives of the adjacent provinces of Tibet. Above all, he told me, that tame yaks were also procurable at Leh, animals to which the rarefied atmosphere is natural, and which find their way with inconceivable sureness of foot in places which seem quite impassable. In regions which to all appearance are absolutely barren, they are further able to find mosses and lichens, which they lick from the rocks. The expedition will require a caravan of fifteen yaks, and an escort of six well-armed natives.

According to Pievtsoff, the autumn is the best time of year for travelling in Northern Tibet. The expedition ought therefore to leave Leh in the middle of August, and strike an east-south-easterly line towards the lake Tengri-nor, about the same direction as that taken by the pundit Nain Singh in 1874. Somewhere north of Tengri-nor, in an uninhabited tract, I propose to encamp, and disguised, and accompanied by one or two followers, endeavour to penetrate to Lhasa, returning thence to the chief encampment at Tengri-nor. This somewhat adventurous method of trying to enter the capital of Tibet I shall naturally not resort to unless circumstances are favourable, and the reaching of Lhasa seems likely to prove of undoubted value in the interests of geography. From Tengri-nor we shall strike through Tibet and endeavour to reach East Turkestan over the Kwen-lun Mountains; the town of Cherchen would then be our nearest goal. And there we ought to arrive in February of next year.

After exchanging the yaks for camels, we shall proceed northwards through an entirely unknown part of the Desert of Gobi, until we reach the course of the river Tarim. In the desert there are no roads and no springs, nothing but barren, moving sand-hills. The inhabitants of the Niya oasis on its southern confines, however, told Przhevalsky, that in the winter it is possible to traverse the desert, for there are in that season occasional falls of snow, which render it possible to procure water. It is my intention to study the aspect of this desert and the movements of its sand-hills.

We shall then follow the east bank of the Tarim, in order to discover whether the river does or does not send off a branch to the east, so as to form a lake in 41° N. lat., to the north of Przhevalsky's Lop-nor. The investigation of the Lop-nor problem should be completed by June 1894, and our expedition will then have accomplished its most important as well as its most difficult objects.

From Lop-nor we shall steer a direct course to the east, and proceed through the unknown portion of the desert known as Kum-tagh; then go on by way of Su-chow (Su-chau) to Ala-shan, where we ought to discover inscriptions and memorials of the earliest times of the Uigurs; then across the Yellow River, through Ordos, where we shall keep north of the Great Wall; and finally through the two northern provinces of China, Shan-si and Pe-chi-li, to Peking, where we ought to arrive in November 1894.

It is easier to devise a scheme of this character at one's writing-table than it is to carry it out. My programme must therefore be regarded as the ideal which I shall endeavour to attain. If the whole plan cannot be realized, still I will hope that at least I may have strength and energy to execute a considerable portion of it. It is evident, especially in a land so little known as Tibet, that it is impossible to determine on a particular route beforehand, as unforeseen circumstances must inevitably arise, and perhaps necessitate a radical change in any predetermined scheme.

In Peking the expedition may be regarded as at an end. From that city I shall send my Swedish companion home with the collections, notes, and general results. Should my funds hold out, I shall probably seize the opportunity to make acquaintance with southern Mongolia and the Desert of Gobi proper. I propose therefore to return home by way of Khami and Turfan, as in any case I should be responsible for the safe return of my followers to their own country.

The expedition, starting from Osh in Fergana, where Russian means of communication cease, and caravans have to be resorted to, will, I reckon, cover a distance of about 5300 miles. The cost of the whole expedition I estimate at about 30,000 kronor (£1670).

The scientific work which should be done may be comprised under the following heads:—

1. The construction of a topographical map of the entire route traversed. The determination of geographical latitudes and longitudes wherever possible. The determination of fixed altitudes with the hypsometer or boiling-point thermometer and three aneroids, and the indication of them on the map.

2. Geological investigations, the sketching of profiles and contours, and the collection of petrological specimens.

3. Anthropological researches and measurements among the peoples we come in contact with. The photographing of various racial types. Study of the religious beliefs of the semi-savage tribes, and their mode of living, etc. Linguistic studies.

4. Archæological researches. The description, measurement, and sketching of the ruins of noteworthy towns, burial-places, etc.

5. The photographing of towns, places of geological interest, etc.

6. Meteorological observations. Periodical determinations of the temperature of the atmosphere, of the earth, and of river and lake water; ascertaining the amount of moisture in the atmosphere, the direction of the winds, etc.

7. Hydrographical investigations. The depth of lakes, the volume of water in the rivers, together with their variations at the different seasons of the year, the velocity of currents, their direction, etc.

8. The collection of plants, particularly algæ.

9. The keeping of a diary during the entire period of the expedition.

This was the scheme which I laid before the King, and which was stamped with his approval. Now that my work is at an end, and I am able to compare the journey I planned with the real journey I carried through, I congratulate myself, that on the whole the two routes coincided fairly well across East Turkestan, Tibet, and Mongolia, although there were noteworthy deviations, caused by the course of events. In the first place, the route I actually followed was much longer than the one projected, and included regions which I at first considered altogether inaccessible. Furthermore, I altered my plans at the very outset, and instead of crossing over the Caspian Sea, which I already knew well, I went from Orenburg through the Kirghiz steppe. The Pamirs, which were not included in my original programme, became the object of three extended excursions, during which the eastern or Chinese Pamirs, in particular, were explored in many directions. The Takla-makan, the great western extension of the Desert of Gobi, was crossed in two directions; and there I had the great satisfaction of making important archæological discoveries. Finally, I made several expeditions into the country between Kashgar, Ak-su, and Khotan.

After the expedition through the desert to the Tarim and Lop-nor, and back again to Khotan, there only remained one of the chief objects of the programme, namely Tibet, unaccomplished. Then I heard of Dutreuil de Rhins's and Littledale's expeditions to pretty nearly the same parts as those I intended to visit, and that both had tried to reach Lhasa, and failed. I therefore thought it would be better to work those parts of Northern Tibet which were still a complete *terra incognita*. Everywhere there, with the exception of the point where I should intersect Bonvalot and Prince Henry of Orleans' route, I should be the first European pioneer, and every step would be an accession of geographical territory, every mountain, lake, and river a discovery.

After I had successfully accomplished this undertaking, although not without great difficulty, instead of following the route I had mapped through Mongolia to Urga, I preferred to strike a more southerly line, namely through Tsaidam, the country of the Tanguts, the territory of Koko-nor, and the province of Kan-su, where on several occasions I could not help following or crossing the routes of other travellers. In Ala-shan I chose a route which had not hitherto been travelled over, and it was not until I reached Ordos, Shan-si, and Pe-chi-li that I entered regions which have long been well known. Between Peking and Kiakhta I travelled through Mongolia proper, and afterwards hastened homewards through Siberia.

Of other discrepancies between my original plan and my journey as actually carried out, I will only mention that at the last moment I decided to go alone. This was partly for the sake of economy, and partly because I did not like the idea of being involved in dangers and hardships which I could endure myself, but in which a companion might not have cared to risk his life.

Moreover, instead of making one continuous journey, as I had originally intended, I found it advisable to break it up into several expeditions. This was rendered possible through the boundless hospitality shown me by the Russian consul-general in Kashgar, M. Petrovsky. He has since been specially honoured by the King of Sweden and Norway for his invaluable services to my undertaking.

After crossing the Pamirs in the winter and spring of 1894, I employed the summer and autumn for a new expedition into the east and middle Pamirs, Kashgar being my point of departure. In the spring and summer of 1895 I traversed the Takla-makan Desert and the north of East Turkestan; and finally, in the summer and autumn of the same year I made a third excursion into the southern Pamirs. In the same way I subsequently made Khotan a new base of operations, leaving there in the beginning of 1896 for my long journey round East Turkestan to Lop-nor. It was only when I left Khotan in the end of June 1896 that I really burned my boats behind me, cutting off every connection with the West until I reached the extreme East —Peking. This arrangement made the journey longer both as regards distance and time; but, on the other hand, the results were much greater, and after each expedition, thanks to the Russian post, I was able to send home my collections. I do not think I am wanting in modesty, if I say that I now look back with satisfaction on the many important geographical discoveries made during this journey, and on the solution of problems which had long been the subject of controversy among geographers.

The breaking up of my journey into several shorter expeditions was a happy thought. After each such expedition I was able to rest, and recover strength necessary for a new campaign. I also worked out the results of my journey provisionally, and prepared for the work awaiting me during my next expedition; and each time I started off with new interests and new points of view.

In this account of my travels I have aimed to depict the reminiscences and impressions which I gathered during my long and lonely wanderings in the heart of Asia. It is clear that the results of a journey which occupied three and a half years are too voluminous to be comprised in a single book; and I have thought it wiser to separate the scientific data from matter which is of more general interest. I propose, therefore, to give a description of the journey, the countries I passed through, the peoples with which I came into contact, and the adventures I and my men experienced in unknown and uninhabited regions. The scientific results, which require a longer time for their working out, and which are of more special interest, will be published separately at some future date.

Thanks to King Oscar's protection and generous aid, I had no difficulty in raising the 30,000 kronor or £1670 I required. More than half the sum was given by the king, the Nobel family, and friends of geography in Gothenburg through Mr. Westin. The other half was contributed by Baron Åkerhielm, a former minister of state, and Messrs. E. Cederlund, Treschow, Andersson, J. Bäckström, C. von Platen, Carl Lamm, Sager, and Davidsson, and Mrs. Emma Benedicks and Mrs. Clara Scharp.

Five of these are no longer living; but to the others I desire to take this opportunity of expressing my sincerest thanks.

On my arrival at Peking I was, however, obliged to borrow 4000 kronor or about £220, so that the cost of the entire journey, instruments and equipment included, amounted to 34,000 kronor or rather less than £1900.

Amongst other contributions I must mention a Husqvarna double-barrelled rifle from Mr. W. Tamm, an express carbine from Consul-General J. W. Smitt, an aluminium craniometer from Professor G. Retzius, and an artificial horizon from Baron Nordenskiöld.

My luggage from Stockholm was not very great, as the bulkier part of my outfit was to be obtained in Asia. I had the following instruments: a prismatic circle (Wegener) with two horizons, two chronometers (one Frodsham from the Royal Academy of Science in Stockholm, and one Wirén from the observatory in Tashkend), three French aneroids, a number of thermometers and other meteorological instruments from Fuess in Berlin, among them black-bulb insolation thermometers, psychrometers, spring thermometers, maximum and minimum thermometers. I also took with me a plane-table with stand, together with compasses, a camera by Watson, and a kodak by Eastman, with a complete supply of films and plates, chemicals, and other necessaries. Furthermore I took two ordinary watches, a field-glass, and a small aluminium telescope; about forty pairs of glasses and snow-spectacles; finally, geologists' hammers, metre measures, a water-colour box, drawing materials, and a number of sketch-books and note-books, etc.

My weapons consisted throughout the entire journey of the two above-mentioned rifles, a Russian Berdan rifle, a Swedish officer's revolver, and half-a-dozen other revolvers, and two cases of ammunition.

The library was naturally reduced to the smallest possible compass, and consisted only of a few important scientific books and the Bible. On the other hand, I took with me a very complete collection of itineraries laid down during the last ten years in the interior of Asia; and also Russian and English survey maps of the Pamirs, maps of the Desert of Gobi and of Tibet.

Thus equipped and provided with a Chinese passport, I left my dear old home in Stockholm on October 16th 1893; and on board the "Von Döbeln" steamed eastwards towards my unknown fate.

It was a cold, dark, autumn evening such as I shall never forget; heavy rain-clouds hung over the city of Stockholm, and her lights soon vanished from sight. More than a thousand and one nights of loneliness and longing were before me; everything I held dear was behind me. Yet that first night was the bitterest of all; I never suffered so much from home-sickness again.

Only those who have left their country for a lengthened period, and with the clouds of uncertainty before them, can conceive the feelings which such a break occasions. But, on the other hand, the whole wide world was before me, and I determined to do all that lay in my power to solve the problems which I had set myself.

CHAPTER III.

ACROSS RUSSIA TO ORENBURG

AN unbroken railway journey of 1400 miles, the distance which separates Orenburg from St. Petersburg, is hardly an unmixed pleasure. Still less is it so at a period of the year when rain, snow, and wind take away all desire on the part of the traveller to while away the time of waiting by promenading the platform; while smoky or overheated stoves make it unpleasant to remain in the carriage.

The four days and nights which it takes to cross European Russia in this manner are, however, neither long nor dull. After leaving Moscow, there is always plenty of room in the train. You can arrange your corner of the carriage as comfortably as circumstances will allow, and let your gaze wander away over the endless fields and steppes of Russia. You may smoke your pipe in perfect peace, drink a glass of hot tea now and then, trace the progress of your journey on a map, watch how one government succeeds another, and while away the time generally in conversation. In the dominions of the Tsar it is considered the most natural thing in the world for everyone to address his fellow-passengers. If no other pretext presents itself, you may always begin a conversation by asking your neighbour's destination. My fellow-travellers, in most cases, were going to places in the governments of Ryazan, Penza, and Samara. When they asked me in return, where I was going, and were told in answer "Peking," they were not a little surprised, and often were not quite clear where the place was.

Endless steppes, arable land, bearded peasants with fur

caps and long coats, white churches with green onion-shaped domes and surrounded by rustic houses, windmills which now, at any rate, had no need to complain of want of wind—these were the chief objects to be seen from the carriage windows. Hour after hour, day after day, the same picture was unrolled before our eyes. The only tract of forest we passed through was in the east of Tamboff, but the trees were all low, except an occasional pine which lifted its head above the rest.

On we hastened eastwards through the governments of Ryazan, Tamboff, Penza, Saratoff, and Simbirsk, until at last we reached the greatest river in Europe. We crossed it at Syzran by one of the longest bridges in the world, 1625 yards in length. The Volga resembled a large lake rather than a river. The opposite bank was lost in the mist; the muddy brownish-grey masses of water rolled sluggishly on under the vast span of the railway bridge, every whit as lifeless as the landscape through which they flowed. Two or three rowing-boats, and a paddle steamer moored to the bank, were the only signs of life we saw. Then on again we were whirled across the never-ending steppe. On the boundary between the governments of Samara and Orenburg we began to detect signs of the proximity of the south-western extension of the Urals. The country became more broken, and the railway often curved in and out between the hills. For considerable distances the line was bordered by wooden palings, intended to protect it from the snow. The farther east we travelled the more desolate became the landscape. We never saw human beings except at the stations. The steppe was occasionally dotted with herds of cattle, sheep, and goats. The sky was grey and dull; and the fields had the yellow tint of faded grass. Such were the borderlands between Europe and Asia.

At the end of four days of railway travelling I arrived, considerably shaken and jolted, at the important town of Orenburg, situated near the point where the Sakmar joins the river Ural. The town was not very interesting. Its low stone houses are arranged in broad streets, unpaved and full of choking dust, and overtopped by the neat churches, of which the still unfinished Kazansky *sobor* (Kazan cathedral) is the largest.

The outskirts of the town, however, were not destitute of artistic sights; for there the Tatars and Kirghiz held their mart, partly in the open air, partly in low wooden sheds. In one place were sold all kinds of carts and conveyances, telegas and tarantasses, brought the most part from Ufa; in another vast quantities of hay, piled up on carts, drawn by teams of four Bactrian camels; in

A STREET IN ORENBURG

another horses, cattle, sheep, fowls, geese, turkeys, and various other live stock. Of the 56,000 inhabitants of Orenburg, 8000 were Mohammedans, the greater number being Tatars, the rest Bashkirs and Kirghiz. The principal *mesjid* (mosque) of the Tatars was particularly beautiful, having been built at the expense of a rich merchant. Among the Mohammedans there were a number of merchants from Khiva and Bokhara, who sold cotton imported from Central Asia.

In time of war Orenburg furnishes eighteen, and in time of peace six, Cossack regiments of a thousand men each. The regiments take it in turn to serve, so that in time of peace each six regiments serve for three years. Sometimes the men of the other twelve till the land which the Crown grants them in exchange for their services. As a rule the Government provides them with nothing more than a rifle; horse and uniform they have to furnish themselves. The six regiments on service are usually quartered at Tashkend, Margelan, Petro-Alexandrovsk, Kieff, Warsaw, and Kharkoff. The Cossacks of Orenburg always amount to a considerable force, and are only exceeded in numbers by the Cossacks of the Don and by the Kuban Cossacks. The Ural Cossacks, at the time of my visit, had only three regiments on duty, one in Samarkand and two on the Austrian frontier. The men are well-to-do, as they own the exclusive right of fishing in the lower Ural river, while above their chief town, Uralsk, they have built dams to prevent the sturgeon from going up to Orenburg. The Cossacks' chief bears the title of "Ataman." The Ataman of the Orenburg Cossacks was at that time General Yershoff, the governor of Orenburg.

In conclusion, if I add, that Orenburg is situated on the threshold of Asia, at the extreme east of Russia; that it can boast of barracks, a hospital, a poor-house, schools, and hotels, of which the best was significantly called "Europe"; that it has a theatre, in which the plays of Turguenieff and Ibsen have the best "runs"; that it is the seat of the governor and vice-governor of the government of Orenburg, and that the military governor of the province of Turgai (between the Ural river and Lake Aral) also resides there,—I think I have mentioned all that is of importance with regard to this town.

Its climate is essentially continental. In summer the heat is dry, close, and oppressive, and the atmosphere is filled with dust. In winter the thermometer often falls forty degrees (Fahr.) below zero; the cold, however, is not particularly noticeable, as the atmosphere is usually still. From time to time snowstorms choke the streets, and as the snow, which falls in vast quantities, is not cleared away with any great expedition, it is often impossible to go out for a whole day at a time. But the bulk of the snow removed, the sledging is perfect; the handsome black horses trot briskly along the streets, their bells jingling, and the sledge gliding easily over the surface. During spring and autumn the climate is very variable; and when the thaw sets in the streets become veritable swamps.

The distance between St. Petersburg and Orenburg is 1400 miles, and between Orenburg and Tashkend 1300 miles, so that I now had before me a drive nearly as long as the four days' railway journey. Thirteen hundred miles in a tarantass, in the month of November, across steppes and wastes, over roads probably as hard as paving-stones, or else a slough of mud, or impassable from snow!

I did not look forward to the prospect of driving a distance farther than from Stockholm to Rome, or than from Berlin to Algiers; but I had already (1890–91) made the railway journey to Samarkand, and wished to take this opportunity of seeing the boundless Kirghiz steppes and the Kirghiz Kara-kum Desert (the Black Sand), in order to compare it with the desert of the same name in the Transcaspian Region.

It is possible, for those who prefer it, to travel by the post. But this means a change of conveyance at every station; and as there are ninety-six stations, the inconvenience and waste of time caused by the repeated unstrapping and re-arranging of one's luggage may easily be imagined. It is better to buy your own tarantass at the beginning of the journey, stow away your baggage once for all, stuff the bottom of the conveyance with hay, and make it as comfortable and soft as possible with cushions and furs—a tarantass has neither springs nor seats—and only change horses at the stations.

Before starting, a stock of necessary articles, notably provisions, has to be laid in, for as a rule nothing eatable is to be obtained at the stations. On payment of fifteen kopeks (kopek = $\frac{1}{4}$*d.*) the traveller may demand the use of a samovar, and sometimes a piece of black bread may be bought. In addition to provisions, you should always be provided with rope, twine, nails, screws, etc., so that you may be able to repair any damage that may happen to the equipage, and last but not least cart grease, for at every third station the process of greasing the wheels has to be gone through. Upon quitting Orenburg you leave behind every trace of civilization; you plunge into tracts of absolute desolation, and are entirely dependent upon yourself.

For the first 180 miles we were still on European soil, through the government of Orenburg; the next 330 lay through the province of Turgai, and the remainder of the distance through the province of Syr-daria, alongside Lake Aral and the Jaxartes or Syr-daria (river). The road passed through six small towns, namely Orsk, Irghiz, Kazalinsk, Perovsk, Turkestan, and Chimkent, and many villages; but as a rule the white-painted station-houses, with their square courtyards for horses and vehicles, stood quite isolated in the desert, their nearest neighbour being probably a Kirghiz winter *aul* (tent-village). In the heart of the steppe some of the stations were primitive in the extreme, the station-house being merely a Kirghiz *yurt* (tent), surrounded by a hedge of rushes laced through branches of trees. But even these, like the rooms in the better stations, were embellished by a portrait of the Tsar, as well as provided with a leather sofa, chairs, and a table. In one corner hung an *ikon* (sacred image), with its censer, and there was a Testament on the table for the edification of the traveller. Every station between Orenburg and Orsk possessed a copy of the Bible, presented by the great traveller Przhevalsky.

The master of the posting-station, *staresta* or *starshina*, also called *piser* or clerk, is always a Russian, and spends his life with his family in a state of terrible loneliness and isolation. The only break in their solitary existence is the advent of the post-courier, or when some traveller comes rolling along in his tarantass. But this touch with the outer world is short-lived. The traveller's one thought is to get away from the lonely house as quickly as possible. He orders fresh horses, drinks his glass of tea while they are being put to, and hastens away as fast as he can drive. The staresta receives from one hundred and fifty (£15) to two hundred and eighty (£28) roubles a year in salary, and has under him four *yamshtchiks* or drivers, nearly always Tatars or Kirghiz. Neither is their lot to be envied; for they have to be ready to climb into their seat in all weathers and at all times, and drive their *troika* (team of three horses) over the same road which in rain or darkness, in scorching heat or wind, in cold and snow, they have traversed a thousand times before. They undoubtedly have a habit of dropping asleep as soon as they get well started; but in so doing they only follow the example of their passengers, and it is easy to forgive them. Each yamshtchik receives from sixty (£6) to sixty-five (£6 10*s.*) roubles a year, and a monthly allowance of fifty-four lbs. avoir. of bread and half a sheep. Provisions, and everything else that may be wanted at the station, are brought at intervals by a special messenger, whose chief occupation it is to travel up and down the whole long line of posting-stations.

The whole of the posting-road between Orenburg and Tashkend is private property. No *gosudarstvenny sbor*, or "fee to the crown," is paid at any of the stations between Orenburg and Orsk, for the station-masters own their own horses and vehicles. For a part of the road between Tokan and Terekli, which is owned by a merchant of Orenburg, Miakinoff by name, a fee to the crown of ten kopeks (2½*d.*) per horse is demanded for each stage. Payment of the entire distance to Terekli is made in Tokan. From Terekli to Tashkend a merchant named Ivanoff, belonging to the latter place, is the owner of the post-road. He pays the station-masters and yamshtchiks, and provides horses and vehicles, receiving payment for the entire distance at either of the terminal stations.

Everywhere I went people talked of the good old times, when this road was the only road leading to Russian Turkestan; when numbers of travellers were continually going backwards and forwards; and when every station had its nine or ten troikas (some thirty horses). General

Skobeleff's campaign against the Turkomans and Annenkoff's railway to Samarkand introduced a new order of things. The mail-post to Tashkend and the large majority of travellers prefer the new route, because it is shorter, cheaper, and more convenient; and the days of the old posting-road through the Kirghiz steppe are numbered. Travellers are now a rarity. The towns have lost both in importance and size. The once flourishing vehicular traffic between Turkestan and Russia has been diverted to other routes. The caravans which carried cotton and wool to Orenburg have grown fewer and fewer. The local post, combined with political and strategical interests, alone prevents this road from becoming entirely disused.

During my short stay in Orenburg the vice-governor, General Lomachevsky, placed at my disposal an honest old *chinovnik*, Solovioff by name, who had seen forty-five years' service in the town. With his help, I was able to procure everything I required both well and cheaply. I bought a perfectly new tarantass, roomy and strong, and provided with thick iron rims round the wheels, for seventy-five roubles (£7 10*s.*); I subsequently sold it in Margelan for fifty (£5). It was an easy matter to stow myself and my luggage (about six cwt.) away in it; and for nineteen days and nights without a break it was my only habitation.

CHAPTER IV.

ACROSS THE KIRGHIZ STEPPES

ON November 14th a *buran* (snowstorm), the first of the winter, raged in Orenburg, and the thermometer at mid-day sank to 21°2 Fahr. (−6° C.). As everything was ready, however, I did not postpone my departure. My trunks and ammunition-cases were all sewn up in matting, and lashed with strong rope on the back of the tarantass and in front of the driver's seat. Bags which were likely to be in constant use, cameras and boxes of provisions, together with carpets, cushions, and furs, were all crammed inside. The wheels were well greased, and the first troika of horses harnessed. It was, however, evening before everything was quite ready for a start. General Lomachevsky and the inmates of the hotel kindly bade me God-speed. The heavy carriage rolled through the gates of the courtyard, and its jingling bells began to echo merrily through the streets of Orenburg. Before dark we reached the edge of the barren steppe. The wind howled and whistled round the hood of the carriage, and drove clouds of powdery snow in our faces. By degrees, however, the wind went down, and the stars came out and lighted up the thin mantle of snow with which the whole country was covered.

In Neshinka I was overtaken by the post, which goes to Tashkend twice a week. As it only conveys the local mails, there were but two troikas; the mail-bags, however, weighed in the aggregate between 16 and 17 cwt. The first postilion only goes as far as Orsk. From that place another courier conveys the post to Irghiz, a third takes it to Kazalinsk, a fourth to Perovsk, a fifth to Turkestan, and the last to Tashkend. We joined company as far as Orsk, and shortly afterwards our three heavily-laden troikas set off from the station-house. The road to Kamenaya Osernaya was hilly and heavy, but later on the country became leveller, the snowstorm abated, and the road was often bare. On the way to Gherial we met the first wayfarers we had fallen in with; namely a caravan of a hundred camels or so, conveying bales of cotton from Orsk to Orenburg. The train with its Kirghiz attendants made a very picturesque appearance in the desolate landscape. About this time the axle of one of the post-telegas came to grief, and the vehicle had to be left behind. My luggage, too, owing to the incessant chafing and shaking, got loose and had to be re-fastened. The sky was cloudy; it was blowing, but not snowing. The temperature was 27°5 Fahr. (-2°5 C.). The river Ural was not yet visible, but we crossed several of its tributaries by means of small wooden bridges. There were numerous small stanitsas (forts) in the neighbourhood, garrisoned by Orenburg Cossacks.

At Krasnogornaya, which we reached at daybreak, we stopped for breakfast. The postilion, a stalwart, shaggy old Russian, bemoaned that it was a fast day, when all flesh, with the exception of fish, is forbidden. Great therefore was his surprise and delight when I offered him a tin of preserved sturgeon. He made alarmingly short work of it, and consumed eleven glasses of tea in a quarter of an hour. He told me, that during the past twenty years he had made the journey to and fro between Orenburg and Orsk (175 miles) thirty-five times a year—that is to say, a distance which exceeds the space between the earth and the moon by more than six thousand miles.

In Verkhne Osernaya, a large village, with a church in the middle, prettily situated near a ravine, the women were offering for sale shawls woven of goats'-wool. They resembled Kashmir shawls, and could be pulled through a ring.

Steppes! Nothing but steppes, though there were mountains in the distance. The road followed the frozen, snow-sheeted river Ural. Except for an occasional Kirghiz yurt (tent), the landscape was desolate in the extreme, and the distances between the stations long. But the incessant jolting over the hard-frozen ground and the monotonous jingling of the horses' bells had a somnolent effect, and time after time I dropped off to sleep.

At Podgornaya the country became more broken. Our next stopping-place was in the Guberla Mountains. There

MY TARANTASS WITH A TROIKA (TEAM OF THREE HORSES)

I took a four-in-hand (*chetvorka*) and drove up hill and down dale, twice crossing the broad river Guberla. Along this stage an accident once happened to a Russian officer, his driver being killed; since then railings have been put up at all the more dangerous places.

At some of the better stations we met great droves of cattle, chiefly oxen, being driven to Orenburg, and thence farther on into Russia. After forty-eight hours' travelling we eventually reached Orsk, a place of 20,000 inhabitants, situated on the left bank of the river Ural and on the right bank of the Or. It stands therefore on Asiatic ground, and is entered by a narrow wooden bridge thrown across the majestic stream of the river Ural. The houses cluster round an isolated and commanding hill, crowned by a clock-tower, from which a watch is kept at night in case of fire. The view is very extensive. Low mountains are visible in the vicinity. The country is only flat towards the south-west, where runs the road towards Tashkend. The *sobor* (governor's house), institutions and schools, post, telegraph, and bazaars are situated between the river Ural and the hill; there too the merchants and burghers have their houses. On the south side of the hill dwell the poorer classes, the peasantry, Tatars, and Kirghiz.

It was intended to erect the chief church of the town on the top of the hill, and the foundations are even partially laid; but the necessary funds were not forthcoming, and the work was discontinued. The church would have been visible for many a mile in both Europe and Asia.

During the spring the Ural rises to a great height, and sometimes inundates the lower parts of Orsk, as well as forms vast lakes in the vicinity. The inhabitants then climb their hill to admire the transformation of the steppe into a sea. When the ice begins to melt in the spring, it destroys the bridge, which is simply built on poles, so that it has to be rebuilt every year. At such times the post is carried across the river in boats.

Between the river Ural, the Caspian Sea, Lake Aral, the Syr-daria, and the Irtysh stretches the vast level plain of the Kirghiz steppe. Thinly inhabited by Kirghiz nomads, the steppe is also the home of a few species of animals, such as wolves, foxes, antelopes, hares, etc., and there too certain prickly steppe plants struggle against the inclement conditions of the region. Where there is sufficient moisture, *kamish* or reeds grow in great quantities; and even the driest sandy wastes are diversified by the tufted bushes of the saksaul (*Anabasis Ammodendron*), often attaining six or seven feet in height. The roots, which are excessively hard, provide the chief fuel of the Kirghiz, and are collected during the autumn for winter use. At nearly every aul (tent-village) you see big stacks of them, and we frequently met large caravans conveying nothing else.

Every now and then the steppe was traversed by water-courses, although at this season of the year they were generally dry. They ran into small salt lakes, on whose shores innumerable birds of passage congregate in spring and autumn. It is by the side of these streams that the Kirghiz pitch their auls, consisting of black tents (*uy*) and sheds made of kamish. Their winter auls, on the other hand, are huts built of clay or earth. In the summer they move northwards, with their herds of cattle, to escape the oppressive heat, and to find pasturage which is not scorched up by the sun. Many Kirghiz own as many as 3000 head of sheep and 500 horses, and are then considered to be in very good circumstances. The winters in northern Turgai are bitterly cold. During the months of January and February snowstorms rage with unmitigated violence; the Kirghiz then seek their old winter settlements, and protect the sheep in pens hedged round with reeds. In a word, the climate is typically continental.

The Kirghiz are a half-savage people, but capable, healthy, and good-natured. They love to call themselves *Kaisak*, *i.e.* brave fighting men, are content with their lonely life on the steppes, worship freedom, recognize no authority, and despise those who live in towns or labour at agriculture. In the struggle for existence their lot is a hard one. Their herds are their chief means of subsistence, providing them with food and clothing. The scanty vegetation and the soil itself furnish materials for their dwellings. The long, glowing roots of the saksaul protect them against the cold of winter. Their language is not very rich; when they talk together, they eke out mutual comprehension by very vivacious gestures. They cherish a devoted love for their desolate steppe, where their forefathers lived the life of freedom, and find it beautiful and varied, although the stranger seeks in vain for an object on which to rest his eye. It is true that, like the sea, the steppe is grand and impressive; but it is utterly monotonous and melancholy. I drove across it day in, day out at a giddy speed; but the landscape always remained the same. The tarantass was always the centre of a vast expanse without boundary or horizon, so vast indeed that it seemed almost possible to discern the globular shape of the earth. Spring is the only season in which it can afford the stranger any pleasure to visit these regions. The air is then perfumed with the delicious scent of flowers; for vegetation develops with incredible rapidity, in order to make the most of the short space of

KIRGHIZ CAMEL RIDER ON THE STEPPE

time before the burning sun of summer comes to scorch everything up.

As might be supposed from the physical conditions of the region in which they live, the sense of locality and power of vision displayed by the Kirghiz are developed to a high degree of keenness and exactitude. In a country across which the stranger may travel for days and days, without, so far as he can perceive, anything to vary its uniform flatness, and across which there is not the slightest indication of a road, the Kirghiz finds his way, even at night, with unerring certainty. Nor do the heavenly bodies serve him as a guide. He recognizes every plant, every stone; he notices the places where the tufts of grass grow more thinly or more closely together than usual. He observes irregularities in the surface which a European could not discover without an instrument. He can discriminate the colour of a horse on the horizon long before the stranger, with the best will in the world, is even able to discover its presence; and he can tell whether a cart, which when seen through a field-glass appears to be a mere dot in the distance, is advancing or receding.

At Orsk my vehicle was well greased, the baggage re-stowed, and I again crept into my moving domicile. The driver whistled to his horses; the troika set off with lightning speed southwards, and—farewell to Europe! At the first station, Tokan, I paid forty-four roubles (£4 8*s.*) to defray the cost of the entire journey of 320 miles to Juluz; after that I had only to show the receipt. Between Orenburg and Orsk (175 miles; thirty-four roubles, or £3 8*s.*) each stage was paid for separately.

From Orsk the posting-road followed the right bank of the river Or, through an almost imperceptibly diversified country to the station of Buguti-sai, near which there was a Kirghiz village. The inhabitants did not seem to be particularly charmed by my visit, as I had my two cameras with me. They kept asking me if the bigger one was a gun; and nothing would induce them to group themselves in front of it. I did however succeed in getting some of them to sit to the smaller one.

After a long rest at Buguti-sai, we finally left the valley of the Or. The moon threw a silvery glamour over the lonely steppe, sheeted here and there with snow; but there were neither people nor settlements to be seen. The silence was unbroken except by the sound of the horses' bells, the shouts of the driver, and the crunching of the snow as the wheels of my heavy tarantass pounded over it.

The station-houses were all exactly alike—plain wooden houses, generally painted red, with a flight of steps in the middle of the front wall, leading up to the principal door. On one side of the steps was a pole for a lantern, and on the other a sign-post giving the distances to the two nearest stations. From the entrance-passage you passed into the station-master's room on the right, and on the left into the parlour for travellers. The latter was furnished with two sofas, two tables, a mirror, a good many chairs, and a large stove, in which the dried roots of the steppe plants were always burning. The fuel was kept piled up by the side of enormous hay-stacks, a short distance from the house. In the large square yard at the back were a

THE "TOWN" OF KARA-BUTAK

number of carts and sledges; and there also were the stables and a room for the drivers.

At the station of Tamdi I rested for some hours during the night, and in the morning saw on the ice of the Tamdi stream the tracks of a number of wolves, which had been bold enough to enter the yard and steal three of the staresta's geese. The thermometer showed 4°1 Fahr. (− 15°5 C.), and the thin snow crackled under the wheels of the tarantass when we drove off in the early morning. Every blade of grass was feathered with hoar frost, and it was bitterly cold.

The first Russian "town" we passed on Asiatic soil was Kara-butak, which, like Rome, is built on seven hills, though it is somewhat smaller than the latter, as it only consists of thirty-three houses, inhabited by thirty odd Russians, about a hundred Tatars, and a few Kirghiz. The only claim which Kara-butak possesses to notice lies in the fact that it is a small fort, erected twenty-five years ago by General Obrutcheff, to keep in check the Kirghiz, who were then harrying the Russian frontier.

HARNESSING A TROIKA

The *vayenny natyalnik*, or commandant, in command of eighty-four men, told me that his life there was no better than transportation, and that he could not endure it for longer than one year. His only distractions were reading, shooting-matches with the soldiers, and sport. It had been very different in the days when there was a daily post. There were several large Kirghiz settlements in the vicinity; and several others all the way to Irghiz; but south of that place they became rarer and rarer, until they ceased altogether on the border of the Desert of Kara-kum.

The road to Irghiz ran for the most part close beside the Irghiz river, at that time of the year almost dried up. We crossed it between the stations of Kum-sai and Kara-sai. On we went day and night across the monotonous steppe, drawn by the swift post-horses. By this time I had become so used to travelling in a tarantass, that I found no difficulty in sleeping at night, rolled up in my rugs and furs at the bottom of the vehicle, and only awoke when we suddenly pulled up before a new station-house. Having shown my receipt to the staresta, and put to fresh horses, we were soon on the road again. An awakening of this kind in the middle of the night, with the thermometer only five degrees Fahr. above zero (– 15° C.), is anything but exhilarating; you are stiff and bruised and sleepy, and long for a glass of tea. At last the sun rises above the horizon, floods the steppe with its golden rays, melting the rime frost which during the night has decked the grass with its delicate white down, and driving the wolves from the posting-road.

A few more stations and we reached Irghiz, standing on an eminence overlooking the river of the same name, west of the point where it runs into the salt lake Chalkar-tenis. Irghiz is a *ukreplenye* (fort) and its commandant a *uyäsdny natyalnik*, or chief administrative officer of the district. The place has a small church, and about a thousand inhabitants, including the garrison of a hundred and fifty men, of whom seventy were Orenburg Cossacks. The greater number of the inhabitants were Sart merchants, who come there periodically to barter with the Kirghiz. They bring their wares from Orenburg, Moscow, and Nizhni-Novgorod. Irghiz was founded in 1848 by the Russians, and, like Kara-butak and Turgai, is entirely Russian. It was one of the forts erected immediately after the occupation of the steppe, in 1845, for the pacification of the Kirghiz. Before the Russian occupation Irghiz was called Yar-mollah (the Holy Grave on the Terrace), and was merely an unimportant Kirghiz burial-place and resort for pilgrims. After the Russian conquest of Turkestan this place, like others in the same region, increased in importance, and the larger caravans began to make it a halting-place. Fewer caravans visit it now; still there were some lying outside the village. The reason why we never met with them on the posting-road was that they take shorter and quicker routes. The traffic with the Kirghiz flourishes more particularly at Troitsk and Uralsk, for it is in the neighbourhood of those towns that the richest nomad auls exist.

Off we went again with our four-in-hand. The sun set about five o'clock; and as he lingered for a moment, like a fiery cannon-ball, on the distant horizon, a subdued purple radiance was diffused across the steppe. At that hour the light produced very extraordinary effects. Having nothing with which to make comparisons, you are liable to fall into the strangest blunders with regard to size and distance. A couple of inoffensive crows hobnobbing together a short distance from the road appeared as large as camels, and a tuft of steppe grass, not more than a foot in height, looked as big as a vigorous tree. After the sun disappeared, the purple tints changed to violet and light blue; and in a few minutes these gave place to still darker shades, which finally merged into the darkness of the night. The night, however, did not get very black; for the air was pure and clear, the stars shone out like electric lamps, and the moon poured her silver glamour over the scene.

At Ak-sai at 1 a.m. on November 21st I noted the lowest temperature −3·1 Fahr. (−19·5 C.) we had during the journey. The countless facets of the hoar frost shimmered in the moonlight, and the windows of the station-house were transfigured with the lace-like trees and flowers of frost.

The stage to Terekli was the longest of the whole journey, amounting to 22½ miles; in the course of it we crossed the boundary between the provinces of Turgai and Syr-daria. At Juluz, the first station belonging to the merchant Ivanoff, which had a comfortable room for travellers, I paid twenty-five roubles (£2 10*s.*) for the 150 miles to Kazalinsk.

CHAPTER V.

FROM LAKE ARAL TO TASHKEND

FOUR miles north of Terekli we plunged into the Desert of Kara-kum (the Black Sand). Vegetation grew scantier and scantier, and in a short time we were immersed in an ocean of sand. This region was at one time covered by the waters of the Aralo-Caspian Sea, a fact evidenced by the prevalence of shells of *Cardium* and *Mytilus*, which are said to have been found far in the desert.

It was a moonlight night when I arrived at the little station of Konstantinovskaya, where the travellers' "room" was merely a Kirghiz *kibitka* (tent), not very inviting at that period of the year. From this place to Kamishli-bash, a distance of eighty miles, Bactrian camels are generally used, as horses are not strong enough to drag the conveyances through the *barkhans* or sand-hills, which occur along that portion of the route.

I had not been waiting many minutes at Konstantinovskaya when I heard a well-known gurgling sound, and the fantastic silhouettes of three majestic camels became visible in the moonlight. They were harnessed all three abreast to the tarantass, and when the driver whistled set off at a steady trot. Their pace was swift and even, and they often broke into a gallop.

Ere long I noticed that the surface gradually sloped towards the south-west. A thick bank of vapour hung over Lake Aral in the same direction; while in the north and east the sky was clear. Between the stations of Alti-kuduk and Ak-julpaz the road ran close by the side of the lake, often not more than half-a-dozen paces from it. The fine yellow sand was so hard and compact that the camels' hoofs left scarcely a perceptible trace; but farther up it rose into sand-hills, and there the tarantass sank in up to the axles.

Lake Aral lies 157 feet above the level of the sea; and its area is 27,000 square miles, ten times the size of Lake Wener, or nearly the same size as Scotland. The shores of the lake are barren and desolate, its depth inconsiderable, and the water so salt that it cannot be used for drinking purposes except at the mouths of the rivers; but far out in the lake there are said to exist certain fresh-

THE STATION OF KONSTANTINOVSKAYA

water belts. Close to the shore at the north-east end is the station of Ak-julpaz, and near it a low ridge of sand, on the top of which the Kirghiz have made a burying-place, with square tombs built of slabs of stone. Eight years ago the station stood on the actual shore. But at certain seasons it was threatened by inundation and became entirely cut off from the posting-road; it was therefore moved about half a mile further inland. When there is a high wind from the south-west, the water is driven up the bay towards the desert, and overflows the shore for great distances, filling up all the hollows and depressions of the ground. In these pools sturgeon and other fish may be caught with the hand. At the time of which I write the bay was frozen over, and at a distance of some miles from the shore I saw a caravan crossing the glassy ice. The same passage is also used in summer, for the water is then extremely shallow, not more than seven feet at its deepest, and in most places only two or three feet. During the warm season of the year, when the sand is dry, it is blown by the wind in the direction of the lake, continually changing the coast-line, filling up the creeks and forming sand-spits, islets, and sand-banks. The coast is bordered by

MY TARANTASS DRAWN BY THREE CAMELS

a number of salt lagoons, called by the Russians *solonets*, which however are generally dry in summer. They are former creeks or bays which have been cut off from the great lake by the drift-sand. The fishing in these lagoons is first-rate; the Ural Cossacks, who engage in it, lay their nets at a distance of ten or a dozen miles from the shore. When the water is frozen they use sledges or camels to reach their fishing-holes in the ice; at other times they row out in boats of a moderate size.

The climate in these tracts is good. The summer heat is tempered by the proximity to Lake Aral, while in the winter the cold is seldom severe; but, on the other hand, rain and thick mists are common phenomena. At the time of my visit it rained continuously, so that in many places the road was covered with broad pools. The water splashed and spouted up as the camels tramped through it; the conveyance threatened every moment to stick fast in the moist, tenacious sand; and the rain pattered ceaselessly on the tilt. When, at nine o'clock on the evening of November 23rd, the temperature rose

THE KIRGHIZ STEPPE, NEAR LAKE ARAL

to 31°1 Fahr. (-0°5 C.), the air seemed to be quite warm.

As a rule, the camels were obedient and docile, and the driver was able to keep on his seat; but one or two of the teams became cantankerous, and insisted on going their own way, so that the postilion was obliged to ride the middle animal. The reins are fastened to a piece of wood inserted through the nostrils, and in this cruel manner the beasts are compelled to obey.

Strange as it had been to drive with camels, it was with a feeling of relief that I again saw three black horses being harnessed to the tarantass. My joy was short-lived, however; for before we got half-way to the next station the vehicle stuck fast in a salt marsh, and, in spite of our utmost exertions, could neither be dragged backwards nor forwards. The driver shouted and lashed with his whip, the horses flung out, and stumbled, and broke their traces. But it was all no use. The driver had to unharness one of them, and ride back to the station for help.

After a couple of hours' waiting in the rain, wind, and darkness, wondering whether the wolves would come and pay me a visit, I was joined by a couple of Kirghiz, who harnessed two fresh horses in front of the troika, thus making a *patyorka*, or team of five. Their united exertions at length succeeded in extricating the vehicle from its sandy bed, into which it had sunk deeper and deeper. When at last we got under way again, and rolled off across the steppe, large cakes of wet sand and clay hung dripping from the wheels.

At Yunyskaya, the last station before we reached the Syr-daria, I stopped a while during the night of the 24th; but as I was drinking my tea, a violent buran (snowstorm) came on, smothering everything in fine driving snow. The tarantass was covered over with tarpaulins, and there was no alternative but to wait till daybreak. The road was so bad the last two stages before reaching Kazalinsk, that I was obliged to drive after the patyorka or team of five, and engage an extra man to ride on the near leader.

Kazalinsk stands on the right bank of the Syr-daria, 110 miles by river, and 50 miles by road, from Lake Aral. It consisted of 600 houses, of which 200 were inhabited by Russians, and had 3500 inhabitants, of whom 1000 (their families included) were Ural Cossacks. The rest of the population was made up of Sarts, Bokharans, Tatars, Kirghiz, and a few Jews. The richest merchants were natives of Bokhara; the Kirghiz, on the other hand, being poor. Their more wealthy kinsmen live on the steppe, and derive their riches from their herds. In the month of May, when the pasturage is good, countless sheep are driven to Orenburg to be sold.

At the time of the Russian advance upon Khiva, Kazalinsk had a certain claim to importance as a depôt and fortified place. The Lake Aral fleet of five small steamers made this place their station, and the garrison consisted of a whole battalion. The town has now a garrison of only twenty-four men, and two launches; the other vessels having been moved to Charjui on the Amu-

MY TARANTASS DRAWN BY A PATYORKA (TEAM OF FIVE HORSES)

daria. There is no longer any life or movement in the place. The whirring sails of the windmills, and the numerous fishing-boats in the lake, were the only objects which gave relief or colour to the monotony of the scene. The streets of the town were at that season of the year impassable, even to the wearer of waterproof boots reaching to the knee. The Russian houses were built of bricks, and were low and white; those of the Sarts, Bokharans, and Kirghiz of dried clay, and were grey and dilapidated, and often surrounded by long and dreary-looking walls. There were two schools, a church, and some public buildings, the residence of the chief of the district (*uyäsdny natyalnik*) being the most important. Each was surrounded by a grove of fine silver poplars, in the tops of which a host of crows kept up an incessant chatter.

The Ural Cossacks have the exclusive right of fishing in the river. They confine themselves principally to its estuary; the previous year (1892) they had taken 14,000 sturgeon. At the time of my visit the river was expected to freeze every day; and as it often becomes frost-bound in a single night, the fishermen had already beached their boats. Higher up the adjacent land does not rise much above the level of the current, so that a hard frosty night often inundates extensive tracts of country. The water, flowing over the ice, freezes again thicker than before, and so compels the stream to find another course. Sometimes this puts a stop to traffic, for the inundated tracts can be crossed neither on horseback nor with *arba* (cart), and the post-troikas are compelled to make long detours into the steppe.

Accompanied by seven Cossacks, I made a short excursion for the purpose of examining the current, etc., of the river. Near the fort, on the right bank, we found a depth of not less than forty-nine feet. The volume of water was just now the lowest that had been observed for fifteen years. In the months of July and August the stream is highest, and it gradually sinks during the autumn. The water was a yellowish-grey colour, but good to drink.

The climate of Kazalinsk is also influenced by the proximity of Lake Aral; although in the winter the thermometer sinks as low as – 22° to – 31° Fahr. (– 30° to – 35° C.). The snowfall is inconsiderable, and the snow disappears quickly; for this reason sledging is not common. At the time of my visit there was a good deal of mist and fine rain. I paid forty-nine roubles (£4 18*s.*) there for the 240 miles, and for four horses, to Perovsk, and in the latter town for the 385 miles, and for three horses, to Tashkend sixty-one roubles (£6 2*s.*).

THE SYR-DARIA, NEAR KAZALINSK

As I had nothing further to do in Kazalinsk, I continued my journey up beside the stream with the patyorka. The alluvial soil of yellow clay was as flat as the top of a table, and at short distances clay mounds, with a bunch of kamish (reeds) on the top, have been built to guide the yamshtchiks (post-drivers) in the winter, when everything is buried under the snow, and it is impossible to discern any trace of the road. These mounds are the beacons and sea-marks of the desert ocean. The scene was as

ANOTHER VIEW OF THE SYR-DARIA, NEAR KAZALINSK

desolate as ever, neither people nor habitations being met with during the whole day's journey, except a couple of Kirghiz on horseback, driving a hundred camels or so into the steppe. The noble Syr-daria was the only other object which arrested the attention.

The road followed the bank of the Jaxartes (Syr-daria) as far as the unimportant garrison-town of Karmakchi, generally called by the Russians Fort No. 2. It consisted of seventy Mohammedan (native) and nine Russian houses. At this place we again turned into the steppe, to make the detour round the extensive marshes of Bokali-kopa, which are annually inundated by the Syr-daria. In this region we passed the two poorest stations of the whole journey, namely Alexandrovskaya and Semionnovskaya, each consisting of not more than three Kirghiz yurts, one for the staresta, one for travellers, and one for the post-drivers and their families. The former place contained also four-legged inhabitants, a number of big rats, running unconcernedly backwards and forwards across the felt carpets. The station was surrounded by a reed wall, outside which tarantasses and telegas stood in a row.

For several stages the road had run through a barren waste, where nothing grew except a few thinly scattered saksauls. We now entered a region which bore traces of recent inundation, and where the kamish (reeds) grew high and thick.

All the way from Fort Perovsk, which is situated on the banks of the Jaxartes, and in every way resembles Kazalinsk, except in being cleaner, to the station of Chumen-arik vegetation was very abundant. It consisted of kamish, saksaul, and prickly shrubs, which grew in thickets, forming a veritable jungle, and through which the road often wound in a sort of narrow tunnel. This was a favourite haunt of tigers, wild boar, and gazelles; and there were geese, wild-duck, and above all immense numbers of pheasants. These last were so bold, that they sat by the side of the road, and calmly contemplated the passer-by; but the moment we stopped to fire they rose with whirring wings. Their delicate white flesh was indeed a welcome addition to my bill of fare, the more so as my provisions, so far as delicacies were concerned, had very nearly come to an end. The Kirghiz shoot the pheasants with wretched muzzle-loaders, and sell them generally for six ($1\frac{1}{2}d.$) or seven kopeks ($1\frac{3}{4}d.$) apiece. They charged me, however, ten or twelve (*3d.*) kopeks. In Orenburg a pheasant costs as much as a rouble and a half (*3s.*); in St. Petersburg two or three. Officers and lovers of sport from Tashkend often visit this sportsman's El Dorado, and always return with a good bag.

The station-house at Julsk was built only ten yards or

so from the river bank, and is annually threatened with inundation. Between that place and Mesheh-uli the country was rather broken. We crossed some narrow sand-belts, then some canals and dried-up watercourses by means of wooden bridges. All this part of the road was strewn with dried reeds, to prevent vehicles from sinking into the mud during the rainy season. At the time of my journey the ground was hard and lumpy, owing to the frost. Here the Kirghiz again became numerous. We frequently passed their auls, and saw their herds grazing among the thickets.

A MISERABLE STATION NEAR THE SYR-DARIA

On November 29th the sunset was very beautiful. The heavens in the west glowed as from the reflection of a prairie fire, and against it the gnarled and tufted branches of the saksaul stood out in inky blackness. The whole steppe was lit up by a magic fiery glow, while in the east the sombre desert vegetation was bathed in gold.

A railway journey is certainly a very much more convenient mode of locomotion than driving in a tarantass. In the former you have no need to trouble yourself about the friction of the wheels, or the safety of the axles; in a tarantass, on the contrary, you must always be prepared for contingencies of the kind, and be continually inspecting the vehicle. My astonishment may easily be imagined, when, on examining the carriage at Mesheh-uli, I found that the front axle was snapped right across, and only held by four screws. The staresta gave me the comforting consolation that I should find a blacksmith at the town of Turkestan, about 120 miles further on, and he thought that the evil moment might be postponed if the driver went very slowly downhill.

Yani-kurgan, a Kirghiz village, with a caravanserai and the ruins of an old Kokand fortress, was situated immediately on the bank of the Syr-daria. The road in places was miserable, and I sat on thorns, expecting the axle to give way every minute, which would have been anything but pleasant in the middle of the steppe. The endless monotony of the landscape was at this stage somewhat relieved by the Kara-tau Mountains, which became visible on the left, looking like a low wall.

At Tash-suat, where the Syr-daria flowed in a broad, stately stream, visible to a great distance, we left the river on the right hand, and directed our course for the old city of Turkestan. The vegetation once more became extremely scanty; but along the hard, level road, which not even the continuous fall of rain had succeeded in spoiling, we met a number of caravans travelling at a steady pace.

At last we came within sight of the gardens of Turkestan, with its tall poplars, long grey, clay walls, in part new, though mostly old and ruinous, and its magnificent saints' tomb dating from the time of Tamerlane (fourteenth century). We were soon driving through the empty bazaar—it was a Friday (December 1st), the Mohammedan Sabbath—to the station-house, where a Kirghiz smith at once set to work to mend the broken axle of the tarantass.

Turkestan, which was conquered in 1864 by General Chernyayeff, is at all times a ruinous and uninteresting town; but in the rain and mist it became actually disagreeable. The only object that could at all justify a delay of a few hours is the colossal burial mosque, erected in 1397 by Tamerlane in memory of a Kirghiz saint, Hazrett Sultan Khoja Ahmed Yasovi. Its *pishtak* or arched façade is unusually high, and is flanked by two picturesque towers. The mosque is further embellished by several melon-shaped domes. All the tiles have fallen off the façade; but on the longer wall and the back wall of the rectangular building they are still intact. Their iridescent shades of blue and green resemble the tiles one sees at Samarkand. The mosque abuts upon the quadrangular clay fortress wall, which Khodiar Khan caused to be built; and within this also the Russian barracks are situated. Guided by some Sart boys, I threaded my way through a labyrinth of narrow lanes, and up the dark chilly staircase leading to the summit of one of the towers, whence there was a splendid view over Turkestan and the neighbouring country. In my case, however, it was considerably veiled and restricted by the heavy rain that was falling. The usual melancholy impression of the East made itself felt even here. The monuments of ancient architecture fettered me by their beauty and impressed me by reason of their age; but the modern houses were nothing better than miserable mud huts, with flat roofs, divided from each other by narrow crooked lanes.

As I said before, it was the Mohammedan Sabbath, and I went to see the mosque just as service (*namaz*) was about to begin. Numbers of Sarts in gay-coloured coats and white turbans gathered outside; then, removing their hard, clattering heavy boots at the entrance, they solemnly filed into the huge mosque. The middle of the floor was occupied by a large copper bowl, flanked by a number of *tughs*, *i.e.*, tufts of black horsehair on long sticks. The walls were plastered white, and inscribed with proverbs. I was politely motioned out by an old *akhun* (attendant) when the summons to prayer was called at the entrance; but I went up into one of the galleries, whence, unseen and unsuspected, I could observe the long rows of kneeling and bowing Sarts—a striking picture, which put me in mind of the nights of Ramadan in Constantinople.

The first two stages from Turkestan were extremely dirty and rugged; it was without comparison the stiffest piece of road on the whole journey. Between Ikan and Nagai-kura we literally stuck fast in the mud. I am not superstitious; but it was the thirteenth stage from Tashkend, and we had still thirteen versts (8½ miles) to Nagai-kura. It was impossible to move the horses. The shaft horse reared and became unmanageable; while the other two had apparently made up their minds to kick the tarantass to pieces. It was midnight, and pitch dark. There was nothing for it but to send the yamshtchik back to Ikan for a couple of extra horses. Meanwhile I went to sleep and slept for three hours, only awaking when the "five-in-hand" were hard at work hauling us out of the mud. It had taken us 6½ hours to do a paltry fourteen miles.

The country from Aris to Buru-jar was very much broken; and it was considered advisable to keep on the team of five. The pace downhill was terrific, the horses fairly laid themselves flat with the ground, so that the air whistled past our ears. Now and again we sped past a village, a horseman, or a caravan, or a big lumbering arba (high-wheeled Turkestan cart), with its wheels literally fast embedded in the mud.

At intervals along the road there were small pyramids of sun-dried clay, intended to serve as sign-posts in the winter. You would suppose that the telegraph-posts would be sufficient for that purpose; but the road wound now to the right, now to the left of them, and after a heavy fall of snow they are altogether buried from sight. The post-couriers, therefore, who are not under any circumstances allowed to stop or wait, often have an adventurous time of it when crossing the steppe in a snowstorm. From one telegraph-post it is often impossible to discern the next, and they may easily lose their way whilst going from one to the other. It not infrequently happens that the post-troikas, when overtaken by a snowstorm, are forced to spend the night in the snowdrifts, and wait till the storm abates or day breaks.

The Aris is quite a respectable river. It was formerly crossed on high-wheeled arbas; but a few weeks before my arrival a ferry had been started. The equipage with its patyorka was placed on long boats lashed together, and was hauled across the river by the ferrymen pulling at a thick rope stretched from bank to bank.

Beyond Buru-jar numerous ravines and steep slopes were encountered. Going downhill the yamshtchik held in the middle or shaft-horse as hard as he could, for on

CROSSING THE RIVER ARIS.

that animal rested the entire weight of the carriage; but as soon as it became too much for him, he let him go, and the momentum carried down the tarantass at a terrific pace, so that it was as much as ever the horses could do to keep their feet. The other two horses, which were harnessed in front of the troika with loose traces, had to keep a sharp look-out so as not to be run into by the shafts; if the near horse, with its rider, had gone down he would almost certainly have been run over by the heavy tarantass. All went well however, although our lives often seemed to be in jeopardy; the horses were sure-footed, and the men reliable and careful. At one of the stations one of the side horses of the troika became unmanageable, kicked and reared, and would on no account let himself be harnessed. It took six men to hold him, two on each side, one at his head and one at his tail; and when, at last, he was harnessed and let go, he started off at a furious pace, so that his eyes blazed and sparks flew from his hoofs. Just as darkness was coming on, we reached the town of Chimkent, the first place that was familiar to me from my former journey. The streets were silent and deserted; everything was quiet, although lamps and candles were shining through the windows.

We were now nearing Tashkend (Tashkent), where the governor-general of the province resides. Two more long stages through mud a foot deep, and there was only a short piece of the road left. The way seemed to be endless; although the road was now very good. I had had enough of tarantass driving; and it was with a feeling of real pleasure that I turned into the streets of Tashkend shortly after midnight on December 4th, and secured a couple of comfortable rooms at the Ilkin Hotel.

Thus ended my nineteen days' drive; in the course of which I had covered 1300 miles and passed over 11½ degrees of latitude. I had watched the days growing longer, although mid-winter was approaching, and had left behind me a region that was swept by snowstorms, and where winter was in full career. At the beginning of the journey the thermometer was three to four degrees below zero Fahr. (–19°5 C.), and I had now reached a land where spring seemed to be approaching, for the soft, balmy air made it a pleasure to be out of doors, and the thermometer showed 50° to 55° Fahr. (10° to 12° C.).

GENERAL VIEW OF TASHKEND

CHAPTER VI.

FROM TASHKEND TO MARGELAN

I SPENT nearly seven weeks in Tashkend; but as I have already described the town in my former book, I will only record here one or two special reminiscences. The governor-general, Baron Vrevsky, received me with boundless hospitality; I was his daily guest, and enjoyed the opportunity of making acquaintances who were of great assistance to me in my journey across the Pamirs.

During Christmas and New Year I was a guest at many festivities. Christmas Eve, the first and pleasantest during my travels in Asia, I spent at the residence of Baron Vrevsky in almost the same manner as at home in the North. Many of the Christmas presents laid out awaiting their future owners were accompanied with French verses; and in the middle of one of the rooms of the palace stood a gigantic Christmas tree, made of cypress branches, and decorated with a hundred tiny wax candles. We spent the evening in the customary ways, in conversation, by a smoking samovar in the drawing-room, which was tastefully furnished with all the luxury of the East. Portraits of King Oscar, the Tsar, and the Emir of Bokhara, each signed with the autograph of the original, adorned the walls. The fair sex could not have been represented more worthily than by the Princess Khavansky, the governor-general's charming daughter, who did the honours at all entertainments, private as well as official, with grace and dignity.

Christmas Eve was kept *en famille;* but for New Year's Eve Baron Vrevsky invited some thirty guests to his house. As midnight approached, champagne was served round, and in silence and with uplifted glasses we awaited the striking of the clock. As the New Year came in, the words "*S' novom godom*" ("A Happy New Year to You!") were spoken to right and to left by each person.

On January 2nd the usual official dinner was given in the banqueting-hall of the palace. The guests were all civil and military officials of high rank, the emissary of the Emir of Bokhara, the three chief kadis or judges of the Sarts in Tashkend, and so forth. Every year the Emir of Bokhara sends a special emissary to convey to the governor-general the compliments of the season. This year it was the handsome black-bearded Tajik, Shadi Beg Karaol Begi Shigaol, whom the Emir sent to welcome me, when I crossed the frontier between Samarkand and Bokhara two years previously.

According to custom, Shadi Beg brought with him presents amounting in value to over eleven hundred pounds. In this case they consisted of eight horses, with handsome saddle-cloths embroidered in gold and silver, of red and blue satin, carpets, cloths, ornaments, and several hundred costumes, chiefly from Bokhara, but some also from Kashmir and China.

Among the guests was a man who had played a prominent part in the modern history of Central Asia, namely Jura Beg. When a young man he was in the service of Emir Nasrullah of Bokhara, and on his death had seized the native province of Shahr-i-Sebs, the ancient Kesh, where Tamerlane was born. There he ruled as beg for some years; but was ousted by a rival, and thrown into prison. The people, who were not satisfied with the rule of the new beg, liberated Jura Beg and re-constituted him their prince. When the Russians, under General Kaufmann, took Samarkand in 1868, Jura Beg hastened with a considerable force to the relief of the famous city, and besieged it obstinately, reducing the Russians to great distress, from which they were only saved at the last moment by a relief expedition.

A "BIT" OF TASHKEND

General Kaufmann thereupon made a compromise with Jura Beg, by which the latter was to retain his position as beg of Shahr-i-Sebs, upon his pledging himself not to molest the Russians. When, however, a few years later, some Cossacks were killed in his territory, he was treated so harshly by General Kaufmann, that he was constrained to flee from Shahr-i-Sebs, where he had ruled for ten years. He then wandered about in the mountains, with his friend Baba Beg, and finally went to Kokand, to seek aid and hospitality from the last khan, Khan Khodiar.

VIEW FROM THE MOHAMMEDAN PORTION OF TASHKEND

The latter, however, took him prisoner, threw him in chains, and sent him to his enemy, General Kaufmann.

Kaufmann received him with kindness, but kept him under military surveillance. The Russians in Tashkend treated him in a manner befitting his dignity, and he enjoyed comparatively a large measure of freedom. When General Skobeleff initiated his campaign against the Khanate of Kokand, Jura Beg, who knew the country and hated Khodiar Khan, offered his services. During this campaign, which proved the death-blow of Kokand, Jura Beg greatly distinguished himself, and was made a Russian colonel, and given the order of the Cross of St. George. He is now, in manner, and speech, and dress, completely Russianized, lives in a well-appointed house in Tashkend, receives a yearly pension of £300 from the Russian Government, and £500 from the Emir of Bokhara, who, however, is his sworn enemy. He leads a life of ease and leisure, studies learned Oriental works, and is content with the great change which has taken place in his existence. But the story of his adventurous and exciting life, which he told me during the evenings I spent at his house, is indeed pathetic—a powerful Asiatic prince to become a Russian colonel!

To return to the dinner. It was truly sumptuous, with glittering candelabra and resplendent star-decorated uniforms. The only thing that served to remind the stranger that he was in Central Asia was the presence of the Oriental guests in their costly gay-coloured khalats (coats) and turbans. When the champagne was served, the governor-general rose and read aloud a telegram from the Tsar, and proposed his health. Standing, and with their faces turned towards the Tsar's portrait, all the guests listened to the Russian National Anthem. Baron Vrevsky then proposed the health of the Turkestan army and the Emir of Bokhara, and was himself the subject of a speech by the governor of the province of Syr-daria.

It was not however social enjoyments which kept me so long in Tashkend. I was busily engaged the whole time with preparations for the continuation of my journey eastwards. I worked off large arrears of correspondence, took a number of photographs in the Sart quarter of the town, adjusted my instruments at the observatory, and collected a good deal of information, both written and oral, regarding the Pamirs. All my instruments were in good preservation, except the quicksilver barometer, which had come to grief on the journey from Orenburg, and had to be thoroughly repaired by the German mechanic at the observatory. The only other thing which was the worse for the continual jolting of the

A STREET IN TASHKEND

tarantass was the ammunition. When I opened the two cases in which it was packed a sorry sight met my eyes. The paper cases of two or three hundred cartridges were ground to powder, and the tin boxes in which they had been packed were crumpled together like paper. That none of the many sharp corners had struck a cap, and caused a serious explosion, was little short of a miracle; my journey would then have had a speedier conclusion and a different termination. Having put the ammunition

KIRGHIZ YURTS (TENTS) IN TASHKEND

in order again, and made it up to the original amount, I had it all re-packed.

Lastly, I had a great deal of shopping to do. I laid in a stock of tinned provisions, tea, cocoa, cheese, tobacco, etc., sufficient to last several months; I also bought sundry small articles, such as revolvers, and the ammunition for them, clocks, compasses, musical-boxes, field-glasses, kaleidoscopes, microscopes, silver cups, ornaments, cloth, etc., all intended as presents for the Kirghiz, Chinese, and Mongols. In the interior of Asia textiles almost take the place of current coin; for a few yards of ordinary cotton material you may buy a horse or provisions to last a whole caravan several days. Finally, on the special recommendation of the governor-general, I was enabled to purchase the latest and best ten-verst maps of the Pamirs, a chronometer (Wirén), and a Berdan rifle, with cartridges and twenty pounds of shot.

When at length my preparations were all completed, I bade farewell to my friends in Tashkend, and started again on January 25th 1894 at three o'clock in the morning.

I had not got farther than Chirchick, where I had to pay 37 roubles (£3 14*s.*) for the ninety odd miles to Khojent and for eight horses (for two carriages were now necessary), when I was delayed for want of horses. There was so much traffic that, although the stations keep as many as ten troikas, they are often short of horses; and when a traveller is unfortunate enough to clash with the post, for which the station-masters are responsible, there is nothing for it except to possess one's soul in patience.

It had turned considerably colder again, and at nine in the morning the thermometer registered only 12°2 Fahr. (−11° C.). The face of the country was hidden under snow; but the road was hard and lumpy, and made the tarantass shake to such an extent that it was more like an instrument of torture than a means of locomotion. The quicksilver barometer was again in the utmost danger; and to protect it I was obliged to lay it on a cushion on my knees, and nurse it like a baby. Through the thick, chilly mist, in which everything was enveloped, I caught occasional glimpses of the camel-caravans we met or overtook.

The town of Biskent possesses a certain interest in the recent history of Central Asia, as being the birthplace, about the year 1825, of Yakub Beg, who in 1865 conquered the whole of Kashgar. He was one of the most remarkable rulers that have ever lived; and his memory in the interior of Asia, where he was usually called "Bedawlet" or "the Happy," will long remain green. Ever since he was murdered in Korla, in the year 1877, the country has been in a state of great confusion. His son Hak Kuli Beg marched with his father's army, which was fighting against the Chinese, to Kashgar, where he too was murdered, according to report by his brother Beg Kuli

Beg. The latter still lives in Biskent, where he owns several houses and farms, and draws a Russian pension. He is a strong shapely man, fifty years of age or so, with a jet black beard and hard features. Surrounded by his eight sons, he is awaiting with impatience the first sign of dissension in Kashgar, when he will hasten thither to take possession, if possible, of his father's throne. At least, that is what he told me himself. Poor fellow! long may he live on in that hope, for he does not know what great

A VIEW FROM TASHKEND

political changes have taken place in East Turkestan since the days of Yakub Beg!

After several delays, caused by want of horses, I at last, on the 27th, reached Khojent, where my sole errand was to take measurements of the Syr-daria. I shall say a few words about these further on; of the town itself I have already given a description in my former book. Suffice it, therefore, to say a word or two only about the large bridge which spans the Syr-daria. It is divided into two parallel roadways for the convenience of traffic, is provided with a black railing, and is built on piles resting on three wooden caissons filled with stones.

The owner, who is a private person, made a profitable contract with the Government for thirty years. During the first twenty he was to be allowed free possession of his bridge; but for the following ten he was to pay 3000 silver roubles (£300) a year to the Government. Of these ten years six have still to run. The cost of building the bridge was put down at £5000; but it has had to be rebuilt twice. When the ten years have run out, the bridge is to be handed over to the Government in good condition.

Of Kokand, which I reached on January 29th, I am now able to add a few details, for the completion of my former description. There are thirty-five *madrasas* or Mohammedan theological colleges in the town. I mention in particular the madrasa Hak Kuli, which was founded in the year 1221 of the Hejra (1806). The madrasa Khan has eighty-six rooms and three hundred pupils. The madrasa Jami, with its large quadrangle shaded by poplars, willows, and mulberry trees, its minaret, its beautiful cloisters with vari-coloured paintings on the chequered ceiling, and its carved wooden pillars, between which a number of young mollahs (theological students) were sitting reading, likewise has eighty-six rooms, but only two hundred pupils.

I also went to see the Hakim Ayim, which was built twenty-three years ago by Khodiar Khan's mother; it has a library with a picturesque balcony or *kitab-khaneh* within the quadrangle. She gave land and gardens at the same time, the income from which amounts to 1500 tillahs (about £560) yearly, and is devoted to the maintenance of the college and the students. The madrasa Sultan Murad Beg was built by Khodiar Khan's younger brother, and has ninety-nine rooms and a hundred and fifty pupils. The Madrasa-i-Mir is the oldest college in Kokand, having been founded by Narbuta Khan and restored in the year 1212 of the Hejra (1797); it has fifty-seven rooms and one hundred and forty pupils.

THE MAIN ENTRANCE TO A BAZAAR

At the time of my visit there were five thousand students at the different madrasas in Kokand maintained by donations, while three hundred were living at their own expense. Besides the institutions which I have just mentioned, there were, connected with Mohammedan instruction, forty-eight *mekteb-khaneh* or schools for six hundred boys and two hundred girls, and thirty *khari-khaneh* or schools founded with money left for the purpose, and situated near the testators' graves. In these some three hundred and fifty pupils are educated. Finally, there were three Jewish schools, with sixty pupils. The population of Kokand was about 60,000, of whom 35,000 were Sarts, 2000 Kashgarians and Taranchis, 575 Jews, 500 Gypsies (Lulis), 400 Dungans, 100 Tatars, 100 Afghans, 12 Hindus, as usual money-lenders, and 2 Chinese. To this add 350 Russians and a garrison of 1400 men. The rest were Tajiks. A dozen or so of Chinese are in the habit of visiting the place every spring with carpets from Kashgar. The town consisted of 11,600 houses and possessed nine cotton factories. During the last few years Kokand has shown a tendency to prosperity; the Russian quarter in particular has increased steadily. In addition to the Russian administration, there is also a native administration for the maintenance of order. The burgomaster is called *kur-bashi*, and under him are four *aksakals*, each of whom has the supervision of a "large" quarter (*katta-mähälläh*); under them again there are ninety-six *allik-bashis*, each presiding over a *kishkintai-mähälläh* or "little" quarter.

In Kokand I visited a couple of *hammam* (hot baths), naturally without making use of them; for they offered the opposite of what we understand by a bath, and were rather hot-beds for the propagation of skin diseases. They were entered through a large hall, with carpet-covered benches and wooden columns; this was the room for undressing in. From that you passed through a number of narrow labyrinthine passages to dark, steamy, vaulted rooms of different temperatures. In the middle of each there was a platform on which the bather is rubbed and washed by a naked shampooer. A mystic twilight prevailed in these cellar-like crypts, and naked figures with black or grey beards flitted about through the steam-laden atmosphere. The Mohammedans often spend half their day in the bath, smoking, drinking tea, and sometimes even taking dinner. The moral condition of the town is terribly degraded; the female dancers, who perform at weddings and other ceremonies, contribute to this in no small degree.

Instead of driving direct by the post-road to Margelan, I chose the detour of two hundred versts (130 miles), by way of Chust and Namangan, so as to obtain further opportunities of completing my soundings of the river Syr-daria.

After sending my baggage direct to Margelan in a couple of arbas (carts), I left Kokand on January 30th in my old tarantass, and directed my course northwards to Urganchi, a largish *kishlak* (winter village), where the fair was in full swing and the streets full of people. The road led through an unbroken succession of villages, and on either side of it were *ariks* or channels, tributaries of the irrigation system which waters the oasis of Kokand. At the village of Gurum-serai wayfarers are ferried across the Syr-daria in a large boat. Thence a miserable road leads by way of Pap to the little town of Chust, whose only claim to importance lies in its cultivation of cotton, rice, and grain. After that the road passed over small hills composed of yellow loess and conglomerates. The going was now first-rate everywhere, and we made good progress. At Tura-kurgan we crossed the stream of Kazan-sai, which in summer brings down great quantities of water from the Chotkal Mountains; though it never attains the volume of the Syr-daria, as the water is distributed through a number of ariks, which irrigate the rice-fields.

Namangan is surrounded by villages and gardens, and is the residence of a *uyäsdny natyalnik* (chief of a district). The Seid Kuli Beg, Khoja Ishan, and Serdabi madrasas were the only buildings in the town of even passing interest to the traveller. The square market-place, Ispär-khan, which extended in front of the madrasa last named, was the rendezvous for the smiths and vendors of hardware.

It was no easy matter to get out of Namangan. Through the frozen mud of the streets the wheels of a thousand arbas had cut two deep ruts, which we had no choice but to follow. We had to drive slowly all the way to the Naryn, the source proper of the Syr-daria, jolting and shaking the whole time. The Naryn was crossed, close to the confluence of its principal tributary, the Kara-daria, by a simple wooden bridge, which is destroyed every summer by the rising of the waters, and has to be rebuilt annually. From the village of Balikchi, on its left bank, the driver took me to Min-bulak on the Syr-daria. Somewhat higher up, this river sends out a curious bifurcating arm, the Musulman-kul, and this again forms a reed-grown marsh, Sari-su, which was entirely frozen over, the ice being covered with snow. The landscape was still desolate, but somewhat diversified in places. Occasionally I saw a flock of grazing sheep, but what it was they were eating I could never quite make out. On February 4th, *viâ* Yaz-auan, I reached Margelan, the chief town of Fergana, where the governor, General Pavalo-Shveikovsky, received me with great courtesy. During the twenty days I spent in his house, occupied in completing the last preparations for my journey across the Pamirs, he showed me the greatest kindness, and gave me much valuable advice.

CHAPTER VII.

THE SYR-DARIA

BUT before I leave Fergana and set forth on the adventurous winter journey across the Pamirs, I will give a short summary of my survey of the Syr-daria river.

The first series of soundings, which I made on November 25th 1893 at Kazalinsk, gave a volume of 20,000 cubic feet in the second; the depth of the river varied between 6½ ft. and 10 ft.; the average depth being 8 ft., and the average velocity 2 ft. 6 in. in the second. The temperature of the water was 31°3 Fahr. (0°4 C.). The air was quite still, and the observations were made from a boat at six points in a direct line across the river, the boat being anchored for each sounding and measurement.

Two months later, on January 27th 1894, I made a similar series of observations at Khojent. The temperature of the air at 1.30 p.m. was 26°8 Fahr. (– 2°9 C.). A slight wind was blowing from the east, and in the water the thermometer showed 32°9 Fahr. (0°5 C.). Along the right bank there was a thin sheet of ice nine or ten yards wide; under the left a belt eighteen yards in width; both had formed in the shelter of the bridge. Above and below this there was no ice to be seen, except a few small flakes drifting on the water, which was much clearer here than at Kazalinsk. Thanks to the bridge, which was 574 ft. in length, of which 144 ft. were over dry land, it was easy to get the width of the river, namely 430 ft. The observations were made, like those at Kazalinsk, at six points from a boat, which was kept in position sixty-five yards below the bridge by a rope. The depth was measured with a pole 20 ft. long, and the velocity as usual with a stationary and a free float.

As might be expected from the rugged character of the Fergana valley, the greatest depth, and consequently the greatest velocity, of the river were not far from the right bank, where there is a steep, detached mountain ridge; whereas the left or south bank is comparatively low. All the same it is sufficiently high above the current to make it difficult for the inhabitants of Khojent to get their water-supply from the river, when the little stream Ak-su, which flows through the town, fails.

The mean depth was 12 ft. 8 in. (maximum 18 ft. 11 in.); the area of a vertical section 1720 square feet; the mean velocity of the current 2 ft. 6 in. (maximum 3 ft. 1 in.) in the second; and the volume 12,900 cubic feet in the second. The space between the bridge and the surface of the water was 20 ft. 3 in.; but on the piers there were marks which showed the water to have been nearly 14 ft. 9 in. higher the previous summer.

It may seem remarkable that I found upwards of 7000 cubic feet less water at Khojent than at Kazalinsk; but this fact admits of a natural explanation. In the first place, the river Chirchick near Tashkend had at its lowest level a volume of 3500 cubic feet; then, further down the Syr-daria receives several tributaries from the mountains Kara-tau and Talas-tau, one of which, the river Aris, being, as I have said before, of very considerable size. Finally, it must be borne in mind that the river is deprived of very little water for the irrigation canals during the winter, that the evaporation during the cold season is inconsiderable, that at its lowest level little or no water is absorbed by the marshes at the sides of the river, and that, finally, the observations at Khojent were made two months later than those at Kazalinsk.

The Syr-daria has never been sounded during the summer; but we may fairly conclude, that at that season of the year the conditions are reversed; that is to say, that the volume of water at Chinaz (near Tashkend) is considerably greater than at Kazalinsk.

In January 1891 on my return journey from Kashgar to Issyk-kul, I had an opportunity of observing what enormous masses of snow accumulate during the winter on the mountains south of Issyk-kul. When these masses melt in the spring and summer, the Naryn becomes a large river, foaming torrentially along its rocky bed down to the valley of Fergana. The Kara-daria also becomes a river of considerable dimensions, although the snowfall in the part of the Tian-shan Mountains where its sources are situated is not so great as in the tracts south of Issyk-kul. Like the Chirchick, the Kara-daria also contributes a large volume of water to the Syr-daria, so that at Chinaz the latter is a noble river during the spring and autumn months, though it does not out-rival its sister river, the Amu-daria. It rolls swiftly through the heated steppe, and empties its waters into Lake Aral. The whole of its water does not, however, reach the destination which the formation of the country would naturally seem to prescribe for it. Chinaz lies 610 ft. above the level of Lake Aral; but from that point the river flows a distance of 882 miles, and the fall is therefore only 8⅓ inches in every mile. The water has plenty of time to evaporate, a process which takes place the more rapidly as during the summer the air is excessively hot and dry. But other factors are at work to despoil the river. Part of the water is absorbed by the soil; another part is used for irrigation; a third and very considerable portion leaves its bed and forms, particularly on the right bank, extensive swamps and lakes. The largest swamps extend between Kazalinsk and the mouth of the river. Others occur east of Perovsk; more particularly between Perovsk and Karmakchi, where the reed-grown Bokali-kopa is nearly 2000 square miles in area. In this way, then, the river loses much of its flood; hence it may easily be conceived, that in summer the volume of water is much greater at Chinaz than at the mouth of the river.

Between Min-bulak and Khojent the Syr-daria was crossed by fifteen ferries, the traffic being conveyed across by twenty-seven barges hired from a Russian. The greatest amount of traffic crosses at the Shakhand ferry; there the earnings in summer amount to 1200 roubles (£120) a month; but in winter to only 300 or 400 roubles (£30 to £40). An arba (cart) laden with goods pays twenty-five kopeks ($6\frac{1}{4}$*d.*), a loaded camel fifteen ($3\frac{3}{4}$*d.*), a horse five ($1\frac{1}{4}$*d.*), and a foot passenger two ($\frac{1}{2}$*d.*).

At Gurum-serai, one of the most important of the ferries, I made another series of observations. The sky being clear and the atmosphere still, the temperature of the air at 4.30 p.m. was 23°2 Fahr. (–4°9 C.), and the mean temperature of the water 35°4 Fahr. (1°9 C.). The width of the river, which was measured trigonometrically, was 640 ft. The right bank was low and flat; the left very steep, 10 ft. high, and much excavated by the current. The greatest depth, viz., 9 ft. 5 in., occurred at a distance of only 33 ft. from the left bank; but, remarkably enough, the greatest velocity (4 ft. 1 in. in the second) occurred at a distance of only 16 ft. from the right bank. In the middle of the river there was a sandbank, over which the velocity was inconsiderable. But on both sides of it, that is between the sandbank and the river-banks, where the deeper places were, the velocity was much greater.

The mean depth was 5 ft. 3 in.; area of vertical section 3070 square ft.; mean velocity 2 ft. 7 in. in the second; and volume 7850 cubic feet in the second. The great difference of 5050 cubic feet between Khojent and Gurum-serai is striking, particularly as the river just at this part does not take up any tributary worth mentioning; but, as I shall point out shortly, this is explicable from modifying conditions of temperature and rainfall.

On the way from Namangan to Margelan I crossed the lower Naryn at the kishlak (winter village) of Jidda-köpö, and the lower Kara-daria between the two villages of Chuja and Balikchi. Respecting the two tributaries of the Syr-daria, it is generally stated that the Naryn is the more voluminous and the Kara-daria the swifter. In point of fact, the Kara-daria is always the swifter, for within a distance of ninety-one miles from Usghen (3220 ft.) to Chuja (1310 ft.) it falls 1910 ft., or 21 ft. in every mile. The Naryn, on the other hand, in a distance of eighty-seven miles, that is to say, from a point near the ruins of the fortress of Ketmen-tube (2800 ft.) to Jidda-köpö (1310 ft.), falls only 1490 ft., or 17 ft. in every mile. Although these differences in altitude are not very great, they are so far appreciable, that the Kara-daria, even in its lower reaches, is somewhat swifter than the Naryn. The other assertion, on the contrary, is not always right, for during the winter the Kara-daria is always much larger than the Naryn, sometimes even twice as large. This is due to the fact that the Naryn flows through a more northern and colder tract, and because it is on all sides surrounded by chains of high mountains, in which severe cold obtains; while the Kara-daria has a more southerly course, through the eastern extension of the Fergana valley, where the winter temperature is considerably milder, and high mountains protect it from the cold north winds.

The volume of the Naryn diminishes also owing to a large quantity of its drainage supply being locked up in the form of ice. This is particularly the case with regard to the small streams and tributaries which flow through the high side-valleys. In the tract through which the Kara-daria flows the winter temperature, on the contrary, is not so low, and the river, therefore, receives during the cold period of the year a comparatively large quantity of water, although here again the snowfall is less. The Kara-daria is thus deprived of a smaller quantity of its water through the formation of ice than the Naryn. In the spring, as soon as the ice and snow on the mountains surrounding the Naryn begin to melt, the river rises, and in a short time becomes much larger than its sister stream, which has not been able to collect any great provision of ice and snow within its bounds during the winter.

The pile bridges that the Sarts have built across the Naryn and the Kara-daria greatly simplified the task of sounding those two rivers. On February 2nd, at two in the afternoon, the weather being favourable and the temperature 21°9 Fahr. (−5°6 C.), I made the following observations in the Naryn.

The mean depth was 5 ft. 10 in. (maximum 8 ft. 7 in.); the area of the vertical section 840 square feet; mean velocity 3 ft. 8 in. (maximum 4 ft. 6 in.); and the volume of water 3070 cubic feet. The greatest depth and the greatest velocity occurred on the right side of the river; and there, too, the stream was loaded with large quantities of packed ice. The greatest quantity of drift-ice I found in a current only 12 yards from the right bank; thus it did not follow, as might be expected, the swiftest current, which was 25 yards out from the same bank.

About one mile to the south, I crossed the Kara-daria about a couple of hours later, and I then made the following observations in that river:—mean depth 5 ft. 3 in.; maximum depth 10 ft. 11 in.; area of vertical section 1220 square feet; mean velocity 3 ft. 10 in. (maximum 4 ft. 6 in.); volume of water 4700 cubic feet.

Together, therefore, the Naryn and the Kara-daria carried 7770 cubic feet of water, or almost precisely the quantity I found in the Syr-daria at Gurum-serai.

Comparing the two streams, it will be found that the Kara-daria is 9 ft. broader than the Naryn, but as a rule is shallower, while the maximum depth is greater. In both rivers the maximum depth is near the right bank, and in both the greatest velocity of the current occurs to the left of the greatest depth. In both the right bank is much more eroded than the left. It is also higher and steeper; the left bank sloping up gently and gradually from the water's edge. The same thing is true of the Syr-daria at Khojent.

These conditions seem to be dependent upon the tendency which the river shows to shift its channel to the right. In 1892 there was unmistakeable proof that the Naryn in its lower reaches also exhibited the same tendency. Nearly seven miles above Utch-kurgan the Naryn quits its transverse valley and flows through the level valley of Fergana. As soon as the river leaves its deep, sharply-defined, rocky bed, it becomes broad and shallow, and is filled with shoals and islets of sand; and only confines itself to one bed for short distances, and that when the water is lowest.

About a mile below Utch-kurgan the Yanghi-arik, the largest irrigation canal that carries water to the rice-fields of the district of Namangan, branches off from the right bank of the river. At the same time the Naryn itself shows a tendency to break through and join the Yanghi-arik; which, if accomplished, would naturally prove very disastrous to the agriculturists in that fruitful region. To prevent this, the Russian Government in 1893 built four dams in the river at right angles to the right bank, so as to force the water back to its proper channel. The highest dam up the stream was 141 ft. long, the lowest 942 ft.; the first three were 33 ft. broad, the fourth and lowest 20 ft. They were all constructed of piles, stones, and fascines. The work was done in two months by a Russian officer with 200 to 400 Sart workmen, and cost about 18,000 roubles (£1800). In the dead water below each dam large quantities of sand and mud quickly accumulated, in places to such a degree that it was possible to plant trees, with the view of imparting a greater power of resistance to the structure. This fact plainly shows that at this point the river manifests a strong tendency to trend to the right.

On the way from Min-bulak to Margelan I observed in several places traces of former river-beds. The largest was the Sari-su, which flowed into the reed-grown marsh of the same name. At the time of my visit it was entirely frozen, a sheet of glittering ice. It is very probable that the continuation of the Musulman-kul arik, farther east, is an old bed of the Syr-daria.

South of the Syr-daria, between the meridians of Kokand and Margelan, there is an unbroken string of marshy lakes—Atchi-kul, Dam-kul, and Sari-su. In the spring these are fed with water from the river through the old discarded river-beds; the surplus water from the ariks (irrigation canals) of Andijan also flows into them. South of these marshy tracts stretches the desert. North of the Syr-daria, on the other hand, there are no swamps or ancient river-beds; though in the lower course of the river there are marshes and lagoons, for the greater part situated on the right bank. Here again we find plain indications, that the river is trending to the right or north-east. For a distance of close upon 400 miles, from Kazalinsk to Tash-suat, the post-road runs close beside the right bank. Several station-houses, which were originally built at a certain distance from the river, have now been reached by it; and some of them have had to be abandoned and new ones built at a greater distance from the bank.

On further comparison between the Naryn and the Kara-daria, I found that the Naryn carries a large quantity of drift-ice; while in the Kara-daria, on the contrary, there is not a trace of it. The water of the Naryn was almost clear and transparent; that of the Kara-daria turbid and impure. The water of the Naryn had a mean temperature of 32°2 Fahr. (0°1 C.); in the sister river the thermometer showed 37°9 Fahr. (3°3 C.). The quantity of sedimentary matter is naturally partly dependent on the varying nature of the country through which the rivers flow, partly on the volume of the streams, and their rate of fall, possibly also on the temperatures of their waters.

Finally, I must add a few words as to the influence which the volume of water in the Naryn and the Kara-daria had on the Syr-daria at Min-bulak, Gurum-serai, and Khojent. I wished to take another series of soundings at Min-bulak; but unfortunately the ferry was so arranged that it was impossible to keep the boat still on the river. The width was 590 ft. Eleven yards from the left shore the depth was 4 ft. 11 in., and the velocity of the current not less than 4 ft. 10 in. in the second; 22 yards from the right bank the depth was 4 ft. 9 in., and the velocity only 1 ft. 10 in. In about the middle of the river the depth was 8 ft. 2 in.

The differences of temperature and colour of the water in different places furnished materials for some interesting conclusions. On the right bank of the Syr-daria the thermometer showed 34° Fahr. (1°1 C.); sixty-five yards out 34°7 Fahr. (1°5 C.); sixty-five yards from the left bank 35°8 Fahr. (2°1 C.); whilst close under the same bank it was 36°1 Fahr. (2°3 C.). Here the river was steaming at 11 a.m., the temperature of the air being 14°5 Fahr. (−9°7 C.). That is to say, thick columns of vapour rose into the air; and the ferryman told me, that early in the morning the mist is so dense that the ferry-boat vanishes from sight a few yards from the shore. The phenomenon appeared to be very common at this time of the year. On the right bank, where the cold water flowed, the river did not steam at all. There, on the contrary, a strip of water, sixteen yards in breadth, was of the same clear, light-green colour as the water of the Naryn; but outside this belt, the water suddenly became muddy, and continued so right across to the left bank, exactly as in the Kara-daria. This proves that at the distance of 4½ miles below their confluence the two currents have not commingled, or rather that the warm muddy water of the Kara-daria spreads over the cold clear water of the Naryn, except for a narrow belt near the right bank. The fact that lower down the latter increases a whole degree in warmth in such a short distance is naturally due to its close contact with the warmer water of the Kara-daria.

At Gurum-serai the temperature of the water, as I mentioned before, was everywhere 35°4 Fahr. (1°9 C.), and the same muddy colour prevailed across its entire breadth; moreover the river was quite free from ice. Even without the aid of calorimetry these phenomena prove that the current of the Kara-daria is more powerful than the current of the Naryn, and that in the intervening 55 miles all the drift-ice has time to melt. That the conditions were the same on January 30th and February 2nd is proved by the volume of water being the same in both cases. At Khojent, on the contrary, the conditions were very different. In the first place, the volume of the water was 5050 cubic feet greater than at Gurum-serai. The temperature of the water was only 32°9 Fahr. (0°5 C.), that is to say, more than two degrees and a half colder than at Gurum-serai, which is 110 miles distant from Khojent. Finally, the water was much clearer than at Gurum-serai, and carried a not inconsiderable quantity of drift-ice. For this reason, the bulk of the current flowing through the bed of the Syr-daria at Khojent on January 27th consisted of Naryn water; for it possessed generally the same characteristics as the latter: it was cold, clear, and charged with drift-ice.

Shortly afterwards the temperature of the air sank. On January 30th at nine in the morning, at Chust, I read 11°7 Fahr. (−11°2 C.). At Namangan on February 1st, at eight in the morning, 14°9 Fahr. (−9°5 C.); and the following day, at the same place and time, 12°9 Fahr. (−10°6 C.).

The temperature had, without doubt, fallen in the mountains, and to a very great extent. The tributaries of the Naryn, and even the Naryn itself in part, began to freeze; the river was thus much reduced and became less than the Kara-daria. The Syr-daria dropped rapidly, and at Gurum-serai its volume was 5000 cubic feet less than on any previous day.

It is, no doubt, astonishing, that the volume of a river can decrease to so great an extent in such a short space of time; but it is a common phenomenon, and admits of easy explanation. The chief of the district of Namangan told me, that the Naryn often rose there ten feet during the course of five days, and fell again afterwards just as rapidly. This phenomenon always takes place after violent and continuous rain in the neighbouring mountains. As I have mentioned previously, it cannot be affirmed positively, that the Naryn is always the larger of the two rivers, for their respective volumes change with the seasons, *i.e.*, with the changes of temperature and the rainfall in the country through which they respectively flow.

The Syr-daria does not freeze at any point of its course through Fergana; but at Chinaz it often forms ice so thick that it will bear the post-troikas.

A WINTER JOURNEY OVER THE PAMIRS

CHAPTER VIII.

UP THE ISFAÏRAN VALLEY

ON the borderlands between East and West Turkestan the earth's crust is thrust upwards into a lofty plateau or mountain-knot of gigantic dimensions. From it radiate some of the most stupendous mountain-ranges in the world, eastwards the Kwen-lun, south-eastwards the Himalayas, and between these two the Kara-korum Mountains, stretching into Tibet. From the same elevated region the Tian-shan highlands branch off towards the north-east, and in the opposite direction, towards the south-west, the Hindu-kush Mountains. It is here that several authorities place the home of the first parents of our race. The traditions of a dim and distant antiquity declare, that the four sacred rivers of Paradise, mentioned in the Bible, had their origins in these sublime altitudes. The people of High Asia still revere the Pamirs, calling them the Roof of the World, and regarding them as the coign of vantage from which the towering mountain giants look abroad over the whole world.

Until quite recently the Pamirs were, politically, subject to the Khans of Kokand. But when Khodiar Khan, the last ruler of that country, was deprived of both kingdom and crown by his powerful neighbour on the north, Russia, she also laid claim to the sovereignty of the Pamirs. For some time however, as they were both difficult of access and almost uninhabited, she bestowed but little attention upon them. This indifference on the part of the Russians gave encouragement to the adjacent states to annex one portion after another of the former territories of the

Khans. The Afghans occupied Badakshan and Shugnan, overran Roshan and Wakhan, and in the last-mentioned district built strong posts of observation all along the river Pänj. The Chinese took possession of the frontier districts on the east; and the British established themselves in Chitral and Kanjut. But the Russians were not unobservant of what was going on. In the year 1891 Colonel Yonnoff, with a force of something like 1000 Cossacks, and a long train of pack-animals, carrying commissariat and ammunition stores, and even machine-guns, started from Margelan, and marched right over the Pamirs to the Hindu-kush, as far as the Baroghil pass, where he came into collision with a small Afghan outpost. A short time afterwards he built, on the river Murghab, the fort Shah Jan, a name which was subsequently changed to Fort Pamir. There he left behind a permanent garrison of two or three hundred Cossacks to watch over the interests of his country.

This was the origin of the Pamir Question, the subject of so much animated discussion in the immediately succeeding year. And thus the region of the Pamirs, hitherto shrouded, and almost forgotten, among the arctic-like severities of the heart of Asia, became the object of the liveliest interest, the focus of political and strategic movements of a momentous character.

Certain portions of the Pamirs were however left unclaimed, abandoned to the few Kirghiz who were content to stay there and struggle for existence against the bitter cold. These nomads acknowledged no man's sovereignty, and paid no tribute; although each of their neighbours around them laid claim to it, and possessed frontier garrisons strong enough to enforce their claim. But they were all fully conscious of the fact, that a movement in that direction by any one of them would be the signal for hostilities; and though all the three powers were ready to fight, none wished to incur the grave responsibility of taking the first decisive step.

During the course of my stay with Baron Vrevsky, governor-general of Russian Turkestan, we had many conversations together about the Pamirs, the outcome of which was, that I conceived the idea of crossing that region on my way to Kashgar. But no sooner did I mention my purpose than, almost with one accord, well nigh every voice was raised to dissuade me from it. The officers who had taken part in Colonel Yonnoff's reconnaissance across the Pamirs prophesied, that I should have a dangerous journey, and advised me to wait two or three months longer. One of these gentlemen, a captain, who had spent the previous winter on the Murghab, earnestly represented, that I should be exposing myself to the greatest possible dangers, and running a grave risk from the severities of the winter climate. Nobody, he said, not even a native of the Far North, could form any conception of the intensity of the cold and the fury of the snowstorms which rage on the Pamirs in the depth of winter. Even in the middle of summer, during a snow-buran (hurricane), the thermometer frequently drops to 14° Fahr. (- 10° C.). In the winter of 1892–93 the temperature fell to -45°4 Fahr. (-43° C.) in the end of January, and snowstorms were an everyday occurrence. These burans or snow-hurricanes come on with startling suddenness. One minute the sky will be perfectly clear; scarcely one minute later, and down swoops the storm. In an instant the path is obliterated. The atmosphere grows dark with whirling snow-flakes. It is impossible to see a yard before you. All you can do is to stand perfectly still, wrap your furs about you, and thank God if you escape with your life.

One piece of advice the captain insisted upon above all else: that I should never on any account separate myself from my caravan during the march. If at such a moment a buran were to sweep down upon me, I should be hopelessly lost. It would be impossible to get back to my followers, even though they were no more than a dozen paces away. The air becomes thick and black with blinding flakes. Nothing can be seen—nothing; you have hard work to see even the horse you ride. To shout is useless. Not a sound can be heard, not even the report of a rifle. All echoes are completely drowned in the roar of the hurricane. The unhappy traveller who has the ill-fortune to be thus caught, alone, without tent or provisions, furs or felts, may resign himself to the inevitable: his fate is sealed. Neither Colonel Yonnoff nor Captain Vannofsky envied me my journey in the smallest degree; and yet both were experienced travellers, well acquainted with the fascinating perils of travel on the Pamirs. Both were of one mind in warning me to prepare for a hard campaign.

And yet there were two men who did not see my project in such dark colours, namely General Vrevsky and Major-General Pavalo-Shveikovsky, the governor of Fergana. Instead of throwing cold water on my plan, they encouraged me in it, and promised to do all that lay in their power to render it as practicable and as easy as possible. Both kept their promise in a most gratifying way.

A week before the day I had fixed for starting from Margelan, the governor of Fergana, at the suggestion of Baron Vrevsky, sent *jighits* (Sart couriers) to the Kirghiz who were wintering in the valleys of the Alaï Mountains, commanding them to give me a friendly welcome, to provide *yurts* (tents) at certain places and times arranged for, to furnish me with supplies of food and fuel, to send people on in advance to clear the road through the snow, and hew steps in the ice which coated the narrow and dangerous mountain-paths of the Alaï Mountains, and in general to render all needful assistance in guiding the caravan and getting forward the baggage from station to station. Mounted messengers were likewise despatched to the Murghab; besides which I also carried letters to the commandant of that post, and to the Chinese officer at Bulun-kul near the frontier. The jighits were further directed to accompany me the whole way. In a word, I met with nothing but the most generous assistance at Margelan in completing the equipment of my caravan, and in making preparations for my journey.

The route which I mapped out before starting led over the Alaï Mountains by the pass of Tenghiz-bai, then up the Alaï valley alongside the Kizil-su (river), climbed the Trans-Alaï range, and went down by the pass of Kizil-art to the lake of Kara-kul, over that lake, through the pass of Ak-baital, and so on to Fort Pamir on the Murghab. The entire distance amounted to over 300 miles, and was divided into eighteen short day's marches, with five days extra for rest, as set forth in the subjoined table:—

From Margelan to Utch-Kurgan	23 miles.
To Austan	15 "
" Langar	26½ "
" Tenghiz-bai	17 "
" Daraut-kurgan	16 "
" Kizil-unkur	14½ "
" Kur-gur (Kashka-su)	17 "
" Jipptik	16½ "
" Archa-bulak	13 "
" Bor-doba	18 "
" Kok-sai	18 "
" Kara-kul (north shore)	16½ "
" Kara-kul (south shore)	13 "
" Mus-kol	18 "
" Ak-baital	12 "
" Rabat, No. 1	15 "
" Chicheckli	16½ "
" Fort Pamir	17 "

At each of the stations Austan, Daraut-kurgan, Archa-bulak, Kara-kul, and Rabat No. 1, I proposed to rest one day, so as not to overtask the horses. This programme was carried out on the whole with tolerable fidelity. A few deviations in points of detail, rendered necessary by circumstances, were the only changes that were made.

I hired horses from an old Sart trader at the rate of a rouble (about 2*s.*) a day for each—seven baggage animals and one saddle-horse for myself. It would have come cheaper to buy them, and sell them again in Kashgar. But according to the agreement I made, I incurred no responsibility for loss or injury to the animals, and was under no obligation in the matter of feeding them or attending to them. These duties were performed by two men, who took with them three additional horses carrying supplies of forage. A jighit named Rehim Bai, an active, weather-beaten little fellow, who had braved wind and sun and cold throughout many a long journey in Central Asia, was appointed my right-hand man. In addition to his experience of Asiatic travel, he was an excellent cook, and spoke Russian. I gave him 25 roubles a month,

EN ROUTE FROM MARGELAN TO THE ALAÏ MOUNTAINS

together with rations and "lodging." He had to provide himself with a horse and winter felts. But on this journey he came near to losing his life, and left me at Kashgar.

When Rehim fell ill, his place was taken by one of the two horsemen who accompanied him, Islam Bai, whose home was at Osh in Fergana. Islam proved the better man of the two, and throughout the entire journey served me with a fidelity and devotion which merit the warmest praise. The following pages will best show how great is the debt of gratitude I owe to this man. When he first came to me, I was a perfect stranger to him, and he had no conception of the real object of my journey. Nevertheless he willingly left his peaceful home in Osh, to share with me all the dangers and perils of a protracted journey through the heart of Asia. We travelled side by side through the terrible Desert of Gobi, facing its sand-storms in company and nearly perishing of thirst; and when my other attendants fell by the side of the track, overcome by the hardships of the journey, Islam Bai with unselfish devotion stuck to my maps and drawings, and thus was instrumental in saving what I so highly prized. When we scaled the snowy precipices, he was always in the van, leading the way. He guided the caravan with a sure hand through the foaming torrents of the Pamirs. He kept faithful and vigilant watch when the Tanguts threatened to molest us. In a word, the services this man rendered me were incalculable. But for him, I can truthfully say, that my journey would not have had such a fortunate termination as it had. It gratifies me to be able to add, that King Oscar of Sweden graciously honoured him with a gold medal, which Islam Bai now wears with no small degree of pride.

I left behind at Margelan a quantity of stores and equipments for which I had no further need, including the venerable Orenburg tarantass, which I had hitherto used, and my European trunks. In place of these last I bought some Sart *yakhtans*, that is, a kind of wooden box, covered with leather, and so constructed that they could be conveniently slung on horseback like a pair of panniers. I purchased the needful saddles, furs, and Pamir boots made of felt and untanned leather, and laid in a stock of extra provisions. I also took with me two steel spades to dig out the snow with when putting up the tent; and ice-axes and pickaxes to help us up the steep ice-coated precipices. When we crossed over the frozen lake of Kara-kul, I intended taking soundings, and for this purpose provided myself with a new hempen cord, 500 yards long, with ten-yard lengths knotted off, and a sinker at the end. The plane-table stand was so constructed that, with the addition of a Caucasian *burkha* (cloak or mantle), it could be converted into a temporary tent in case we were surprised by a snowstorm.

On 22nd February 1894 the string of horses started in charge of the jighits for Utch-kurgan. One horse was laden with photographic materials, packed in two yakhtans (boxes). A second carried my topographical and other instruments, books, and the medicine-chest; the third the ammunition-chests; the fourth and fifth the commissariat supplies; the sixth and seventh my weapons and personal belongings. Last of all, at the tail-end of the caravan, were the three horses carrying forage for the others, one of them almost buried from sight under two enormous bags stuffed with straw.

Two guides on foot went on first, and directed the horses wherever necessary. The jighits rode. As the long imposing-looking caravan filed away out of the yard of the governor's palace, I stood and watched it with not a little pride. I did not accompany it, but spent that night at Margelan, the last I was to see of European civilization for many a month to come. That evening everybody in Margelan assembled within the governor's hospitable walls to bid me farewell. What a contrast to the evenings which immediately followed!

At eight o'clock on the following morning, after a last word in dear old Swedish with General Matveyeff and Lieutenant Kivekäs, both light-hearted sons of Finland, and a hearty send-off from the hospitable governor and his charming family, I said good-bye to Margelan, and cantered away after my caravan. I caught it up at Utch-kurgan. The distance was only 23 miles; and yet even in that distance the contour of the ground rose 1100 feet, up to an altitude of some 3000 feet above sea-level.

Utch-kurgan is a large village picturesquely situated on the river Isfaïran, at the point where it emerges from the northern declivities of the Alaï Mountains. I was received with a flattering welcome. A mile or two outside of the village I was met by the *volastnoi* (native district chief) of the place, accompanied by his colleague, the *volastnoi* of Austan, a place higher up in the mountains. The former

THE STATION OF AUSTAN

was a Sart; the latter a Kirghiz. Both wore their gala *khalats* (coats) of dark blue cloth, white turbans, belts of chased silver, and scimitars swinging in silver-mounted scabbards. At their heels rode a numerous cavalcade of attendants. These dignitaries escorted me to the village, where a large crowd had assembled to witness my entry and enjoy the rare pleasure of a real *tamashah* (spectacle). After *dastarkhan* (refreshments) had been offered round, the caravan started again, escorted by the troop of horsemen.

The valley of the Isfaïran grew more sharply contoured as we advanced, and narrowed at the end to a width of only a few hundred yards. At the same time the path ascended, following in part the bed of the stream; though in places it ran along the face of steep, well-nigh precipitous slopes. The river has cut a deep channel through the coarse-grained conglomerates, and its waters, dark green in colour, but clear as crystal, danced merrily along among the boulders.

A few hours' ride brought us to our second halting-station, Austan. There the volastnoi of the place had got ready for us a comfortable yurt (tent) of white *kashma* (thick Kirghiz felt), decorated on the outside with broad strips of coloured cloth, and furnished inside with Kirghiz carpets and—a crackling fire. Having rigged up a temporary meteorological observatory, and piled the baggage outside the tent, the men tethered and fed their horses, and then gathered round a fire in the open air. Here Rehim Bai got the first opportunity to exhibit his skill as cook. By the time I had completed my observations daylight had gone, and I set about arranging my bed for the night, not a very irksome task however, seeing that the bed consisted simply of a piece of sacking stretched upon two poles, the ends of which rested on a couple of yakhtans (boxes).

The next day was dedicated to rest. The Kirghiz *kishlak* (winter village) of Austan, numbering about a hundred *uy* (tents), lay about three-quarters of a mile higher up the valley, surrounded by clumps of stunted white poplars. But the day was not spent in idleness: I made a short excursion from camp, and carried out several scientific observations. The Isfaïran brought down a volume of 280 cubic feet in the second. The temperature of the air at seven o'clock in the morning was 31°1 Fahr. (–0°5 C.); maximum during the day 51°1 Fahr. (10°6 C.). The boiling-point of water was at 206°3 Fahr. (95°7 C.); consequently the altitude above sea-level may be taken as 4510 feet.

In the hurry of my departure from Margelan I had forgotten one thing—namely, a watch-dog, to lie outside the yurt at nights. The oversight was made good in a curious way. On 25th February, whilst we were doing the next stage to Langar, an expansion of the valley 26½ miles farther on, a big Kirghiz dog, yellow and long-haired, came and joined himself of his own accord to our troop. He followed us faithfully throughout the whole of the journey to Kashgar, and kept grim *karaol* (watch) outside the tent every night. He was christened Yollchi, or "Him who was picked up on the road."

Immediately after leaving Austan, the track climbed steeply up the left side of the valley. The horses clambered up one after the other in a long string. Ere many minutes were passed, we had ascended so high that we could hear nothing of the brawling torrent below except a soft lisping murmur. The path was very tiring; it wound in and out of the heaps of mountain detritus, squeezing itself through the narrow passages between them. Sometimes it skirted the edge of a terrace, which swung back round a side-glen. Sometimes it threaded its way between gigantic fragments of rock. Every now and again it ran steeply down the side of the valley, and for a little distance followed the bed of the stream; then up it would suddenly mount again as abruptly as it had plunged down.

The parallel ridges of the Alaï were cleft transversely by the deep valley of the Isfaïran, so that the ruptured ends abutted upon it *en échelon*, like the side-wings of a stage-setting. The scenery was both wild and grand.

THE ISFAÏRAN VALLEY

Gigantic talus-slopes or landslips, resulting from the action of wind and weather upon the more friable rocks of the mountains above, stretched down to the bottom of the valley. The course of the stream was marked by a few scattered trees and bushes growing close to the margin. Upon the mountain sides above many a venerable and stunted *archa* (Asiatic juniper) hung its shaggy head over the yawning precipices.

Time after time we had to cross over the stream on wooden bridges, which sagged and swayed at every step we took. One of these was known by the significant name of Chukkur-köpriuk, that is the Deep Bridge. Seen from the lofty crest along which the path ran, it looked like a little stick flung across the narrow cleft far down below. Headlong down the mountain side plunged the track; then over the bridge and as steeply up again, zigzag, on the opposite side. At every ten or a dozen paces the panting horses stopped to catch their breath. Again and again their burdens fell forwards or backwards, according as they descended or ascended, and had to be hitched right again. The voices of the men urging on the horses, and shouting warnings to one another, echoed shrilly among the hollows of the precipices. In this way we made our way slowly and cautiously along the narrow, breakneck path.

Shortly after crossing the Deep Bridge, the road became paved with ice-slides, and bordered with snow-clad slopes, which terminated a little lower down in a vertical wall, at the foot of which the clay-slates cropped out in sharp-edged slabs or flakes. The first horse of the string, the one which carried the bags of straw, together with my tent-bed, was led by one of the Kirghiz guides. But, despite the man's care, when he came to this spot the animal slipped. He made frantic efforts to recover his feet. It was in vain. He slid down the declivity, turned two or three summersaults through the air, crashed against the almost perpendicular rocks which jutted up from the bottom of the valley, and finally came to a dead stop in the middle of the river. The bags burst and the straw was scattered amongst the rocks. Shrill shouts pierced the air. The caravan came to a standstill. We rushed down by the nearest side-paths. One of the Kirghiz fished out my tent-bed, as it was dancing off down the torrent. The others encouraged the horse to try and get up. But he lay in the water with his head jammed against a large fragment of rock, and was unable to respond to their exhortations. The Kirghiz pulled off their boots, waded out to him, and dragged him towards dry land. It was however wasted labour. The poor brute had broken his back; and after a while we left him lying dead in the middle of the river, whither he had struggled back in his dying agonies. The straw was swept together, sewn up again, and packed on one of the other horses, which carried it till we reached our night-quarters at Langar.

As soon as we got back to the track, we went to work with spades and axes, and cleared away the ice, and then strewed sand over the place from which we had cleared it.

The horses were led across this dangerous spot one by one, and with every precaution for their safety. I need scarcely say that I traversed it on foot.

Before we reached the end of our day's journey we were suddenly overtaken by the twilight. The shades of night crept thicker and thicker together in the deep narrow gorge, choking it with gloom. But after a while the stars began to peep forth; and their keen glitter, piercing the obscurities of the ravine, gave us a faint light by which to continue our perilous journey. I have encountered a fair share of adventures and dangers in High Asia; but the three hours' travelling which still lay before us till we reached Langar were, I believe, the most anxious of any I had hitherto experienced. The first ice-slide was merely the forerunner of others to come. They now followed one another in quick succession, each more perilous than the last. Thus we walked, and crept, and slid slowly on, beside the black abysses gaping for their prey. This occasioned in-

VIEW BETWEEN AUSTAN AND LANGAR

numerable delays, for many and many a time we had to stop to cut steps in the ice and strew them with sand. Each horse required two men to get him over these places, one to lead him by the halter, whilst another hung on to his tail, ready to lash him if he stumbled or slipped. Notwithstanding this, several of them did fall; but luckily they managed to recover their feet. One fell and slid several yards down the snowy slope, but fortunately stopped in time. His pack was loosened and carried up the path; the animal was helped to get back,

MAKING A ROAD IN THE ALAÏ MOUNTAINS

and his burden was once more lashed tightly on his back. I myself crawled several hundreds of yards on my hands and knees, whilst one of the Kirghiz crept close at my heels, and held me in the more perilous passages. A fall in any of those places would have meant instant death.

In a word, it was a desperate journey—dark, cold, awe-inspiring. The only sounds that broke the unearthly silence of the gorge were the piercing screams of the men whenever one of the horses fell, their shouts of warning when they drew near to one of these perilous passages, and the constant roar of the torrent, which churned its way down through the foam-white rapids.

It was an Asiatic river spirit dashing a storm of music from her quivering harp!

When we at length arrived at Langar, weary, frozen, hungry, we had been toiling through the snow for twelve hours at one stretch. How welcome the two tents we found ready pitched for us there, with a brightly blazing fire in each!

CHAPTER IX.

OVER THE TENGHIZ-BAI PASS

FROM Langar we travelled almost due south towards the pass of Tenghiz-bai. But before I go on to relate how we surmounted it, I must say a word or two about the principal passes which connect the valley of Fergana with the valley of the Alaï. There are five of them, namely these, going from east to west:—

Talldik . . .	11,605 feet in altitude.
Jipptik . . .	13,605 „ „
Sarik-mogal . . .	14,110 „ „
Tenghiz-bai . . .	12,630 „ „
Kara-kasik . . .	14,305 „ „

This gives a mean altitude of 13,250 feet for the Alaï passes. It is noticeable that their absolute elevation increases as the chain advances westwards; the difference in altitude between the passes and the valley, or the relative altitude of the passes, likewise increases from east to west.

The easiest of these passes is the one mentioned first, namely, Talldik. It has recently been levelled, and is now practicable for carriages and artillery. But it is closed by the snows the greater part of the winter. The second and third are very difficult, chiefly because of the avalanches, the violent winds, and the furious hurricanes of snow. The depth of snow on Tenghiz-bai varies very greatly from year to year. In normal seasons it does not amount to any great quantity, and for this reason it is the pass that is mostly used during the winter. It is the route followed by the post-couriers (jighits) who carry the mails between Margelan and Fort Pamir.

Nevertheless it is no unusual thing for the Tenghiz-bai pass to be closed during the last two or three weeks of February. In 1893 it was only closed for ten days. In 1892 it was impassable for a period of two whole months. And in 1891 the depth of the snow was so great, though for a shorter period, that junipers twelve or thirteen feet high were completely buried from sight in the snowdrifts.

February is the month in which avalanches fall and snowstorms rage with the greatest frequency. At that season the boldest Kirghiz hesitates to put foot inside the pass, unless the weather is perfectly still and serene. All the same, hardly a winter passes without a fatal mishap of some kind. The numerous skeletons of horses, and even of human beings, which litter the track, might serve as milestones during the summer months.

The Kirghiz of the aul (tent-village) of Daraut-kurgan, in the valley of the Alaï, told me a pathetic story of a man, who came to that place from Utch-kurgan early in the year 1893, in order to spend Ramadan (the Mohammedan month of fasting) with some friends. On the way home he was overtaken, on 23rd March, in the pass mentioned by a violent buran (snow-hurricane), and was forced to stay there four days and nights squatting on the ground, with no other protection than his sheepskin coat. His horse died. His provisions gave out. When the snowstorm ceased, he found the way blocked in both directions. Nevertheless he pushed on, and by dint of creeping, climbing, and wading came, after two days and two nights of terrible labour, to the district of Kara-kiya, where he fell in with some of his own countrymen, who took charge of him, and fed him and nursed him. As soon as he had recovered a little, he continued his journey to Utch-kurgan. But he died the very first night after getting home, overcome by the hardships and privations he had undergone.

I was also told that a caravan of forty men was overwhelmed that same winter in the Terek-davan pass by an avalanche, and killed to the last man.

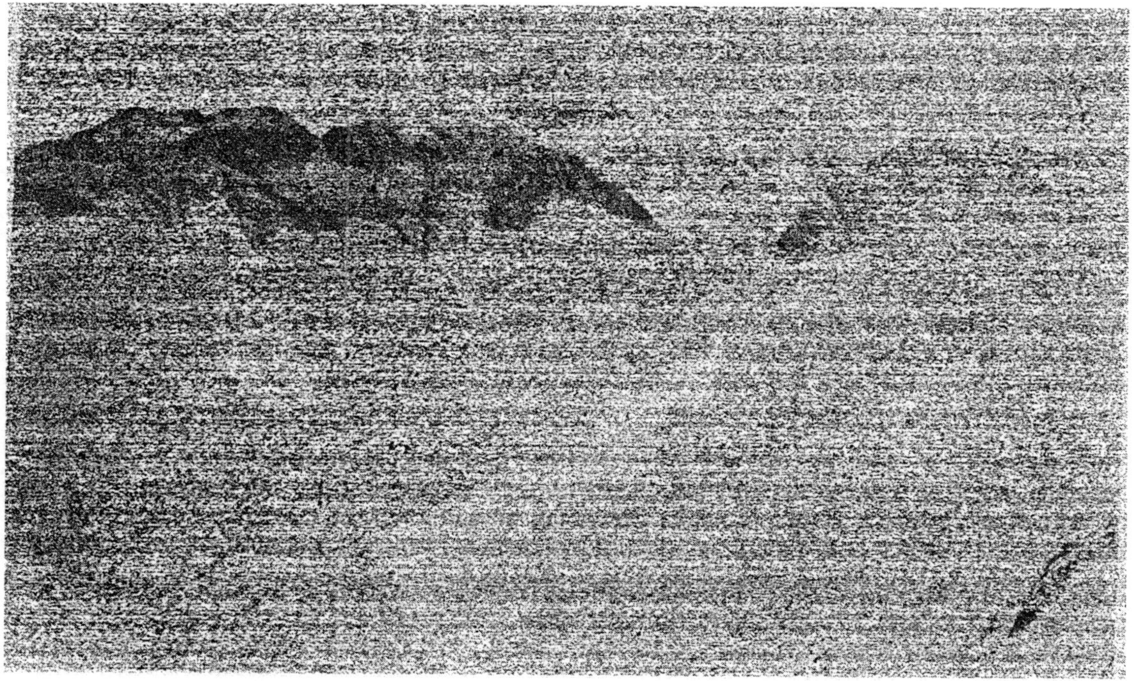

A PORTION OF THE ALAÏ MOUNTAINS AS SEEN FROM THE PASS OF TENGHIZ-BAI

On the night of 26th February I sent eight Kirghiz on in advance into the pass with spades, pickaxes, and hatchets to hew a road for the horses. The caravan followed up after them early the next morning. The first difficult place we came to was at Kara-kiya. There we found the Kirghiz hard at work hewing steps—actual steps—in the ice. For the last fall of snow, which lay on the surface, had melted during the day, and then frozen during the following night.

The mountain horses or ponies of the Kirghiz are truly wonderful little animals. Their ordinary load is usually about thirteen stone (180 lbs.). With this load on their backs they are able to slide great distances down the mountain slopes. They climb like cats up the steep declivities; and although the narrow, slippery mountain-paths are generally coated with ice, and run along the edge of precipices, they balance themselves on them with almost inconceivable sureness of foot. The name Kara-kiya, meaning the Black Gorge, is a very appropriate name for the place. It is a narrow tunnel or pass shut in by perpendicular walls of rock, and shrouded in the deepest shadows. Into those cavernous depths no ray of sunshine ever penetrates. At this spot the Isfaïran was spanned by two bridges. Underneath the upper one the torrent plunged with the force and noise of a thundering cascade. In this region the hand of Nature has worked with sublime effect. Landscapes alternately wild, awe-inspiring, and full of romantic charm followed one another in quick succession. The eye commanded a truly wonderful perspective both up and down the glen.

Above the bridge of Haidar-beg the valley bore the name of Chettindeh, and the stream was spanned by four small wooden bridges. The last of these was a miserable contrivance. Its supports were so rotten that my men were in a state of the greatest anxiety, as they carefully led the horses across it one by one. A short distance further on the glen was completely choked by a newly fallen *kutshka* (avalanche or snow-slide), which blocked both stream and path. The former came boiling from underneath the ice like a river emerging from an underground tunnel; whilst a new path, or rather staircase, had to be hewn across the sloping talus of ice-blocks. As luck would have it, we chanced at this very spot to meet a dozen or so Kirghiz from Kara-teghin, travelling on foot to Kokand and Margelan in search of work. They stopped and helped us to repair the road. But even then, after all our efforts, the path was so steep that each horse had to be actually pushed up by half-a-dozen men.

The glen narrowed rapidly towards its upper end, rising with extraordinary steepness and becoming indistinguishable from the mountain slopes. At the same time the relative altitudes decreased in proportion as the absolute altitudes increased. The last portion of the way was tough work; avalanche succeeded avalanche at short intervals. Almost every horse in the string fell once, some of them twice; and as they were unable to get up again in the snow with the loads on their backs, the baggage had to be taken off them and then lashed on afresh. In this way we were delayed time after time. The last ice-slide we encountered was so difficult to cross that the horses could not by any possibility get over it loaded; accordingly the Kirghiz unloaded them and carried the baggage across on their own backs. Indeed they carried it all the way to Rabat (Rest-house)—a little hut built of stones and timber overlooking the glen below. There also a *uy* (tent) had been pitched. I had walked the greater part of the day, and was thoroughly tired. The altitude was 9350 feet; and during the night I began to feel the symptoms of mountain-sickness—a splitting headache and an acceleration of the heart's action. These symptoms, which were caused by the sudden change from a relatively low to a relatively high altitude, continued all the following day; but passed off after about forty-eight hours, leaving no ill effects behind them.

On the following morning the Kirghiz road-makers and Jan Ali Emin, aksakal (chieftain) of the Kara-teppes, who had been in charge of the work, returned to Rabat. At the same time, I and my men, fully realizing the risks

THE TENGHIZ-BAI PASS

[*Face page* 123.

of the undertaking, started on our journey up the pass, which was now buried deep in snow. The difficulties of the road were almost inconceivable, and our labours trying in the extreme. But by dint of persevering we managed to surmount all obstacles, and came to a trough-shaped depression on the summit of the range, where the snow was fully six feet deep. A deep and narrow pathway had been trampled through the snowdrifts. But it was like a shaking bridge laid across a bog. One step off the path, and the horses plunged up to the girth in the snow; and it took all our combined efforts to dig them out again, and get them back upon the "bridge." All this occasioned serious loss of time.

We now became aware of a group of sombre-looking peaks, split and weathered by wind and frost, towering above the eternal snows away in the south-west. It was a detached spur of the Kara-kir, pointing the way like a sea-beacon up to the dreaded pass of Tenghiz-bai. The track mounted up to the last summit by an endless series of zigzags, putting the horses' strength and climbing powers to the severest proof. But at length we reached the top of the pass safe and sound, and with all our baggage intact. There we rested an hour for tea, made meteorological and other observations, took photographs, and admired the entrancing scenery.

The spot at which we rested was shut in on every side by snowy crests, with bare, black pinnacles protruding here and there through their mantles of snow. Looking northwards, we had the valley of the Isfaïran below us. We turned towards the south-west, and a magnificent panorama fascinated the eye. In the far-off distance were the sharply accentuated crests of the Alaï Mountains, and on the opposite side of the valley the system of the Trans-Alaï, its summits melting into the clouds, its flanks glistening with snowfields of a dazzling whiteness.

The mountain saddle upon which we stood formed the watershed between the basins of the Syr-daria and the Amu-daria. After recovering our breath in the clear rarefied mountain air, we started to make our way at a leisurely pace down into the region where the head-streams of the latter river have their origin. The descent on this side was every bit as steep as the ascent had been up the northern face. The path was smothered under innumerable landslips and avalanches. Some of them had carried down with them in their fall vast quantities of earth and *débris;* so that we did not perceive them until the horses suddenly dropped up to the girth in the soft and treacherous ground. I measured one of the largest of these avalanches, which had fallen the day before. It was a quarter of a mile across and had a depth of nearly seventy feet. The Kirghiz were not slow to congratulate one another upon having so fortunately escaped its clutches. The gigantic ice-slides rush down the mountain-side with such overwhelming force and momentum, that, under the enormous pressure, their lower strata or under-surface become converted into ice, and anything living which should have the misfortune to be buried under it would be literally frozen fast in the middle of a block of ice as hard and as vitreous as glass. Once clasped in that icy embrace, a man would be hopelessly doomed. But in all probability the unhappy wretch who was thus swept away would be stunned by the fall, and would freeze to death before his consciousness returned.

Thoroughly exhausted by the exertions of the day, we halted in a little side-glen called Shiman. Here the snow was several feet deep, and the Kirghiz were obliged to clear a space before they could get the tent erected. We passed the night hemmed in by a high breastwork of snow.

The next day we continued our march down the glen of the Daraut-kurgan. Every ten minutes or so we forded the stream, which raced along under arches and bridges of snow. Each time we did so, the horses were obliged to leap down the perpendicular bank of ice into the water, and then leap up again on the opposite side. Every time they did this, I was in a fever of anxiety lest any mishap should befall the animals which carried the ammunition and the photographic apparatus. However everything passed

THE ALAÏ AND TRANS-ALAÏ MOUNTAINS SEEN FROM THE PASS OF TENGHIZ-BAI

off all right. The only incident was one of the commissariat horses plunging down a steep snow-slide, and rolling into the torrent. But we followed him down, unloaded him, hauled up the yakhtans with a rope, re-loaded the animal, and then ploughed slowly on through the snow-drifts till another horse stumbled and fell.

At mid-day it began to snow. A thick mist came on, hiding everything from view, and preventing us from seeing where we were going to. One of the Kirghiz went on first and sounded the depth of the snow with a long staff, as

OUR CAMP AT DARAUT-KURGAN

sailors do when navigating unfamiliar waters. But there was this difference; whereas sailors aim to avoid the shallows, we sought for them, and for the firm ground underneath them. Several times our guide dropped out of sight altogether in the snow, and had to crawl out, and try again in another place.

The glen we were following emerged into the valley of the Alaï near the spot where Khodiar, the last independent Khan of Kokand, had built the fort of Daraut-kurgan, a building with low clay walls, and a tower at one corner. Another hour's travelling brought us to the Kirghiz aul (tent-village) of Daraut-kurgan, consisting of about a score of tents (households) under the authority of the hospitable chieftain, Tash Mohammed Emin.

The origin and meaning of the name Daraut-kurgan are differently explained by different Kirghiz. Some maintain that it is composed of three words *darah*, *utt*, and *kurgan*, the first common to both Persian and Kirghiz, and meaning "valley," the other two both Kirghiz words meaning "grass" and "stronghold" or "fort" respectively. Others declare that the name is a corruption of the Persian *dar-rau*, meaning "immediate" or "make haste on the road"; and go on to explain, that Daraut-kurgan is intended to warn the traveller to make haste and get through the dreaded pass as quickly as he can.

To add to our difficulties, it began to blow a gale from the west. The snow still continued to fall, and the mist did not lift. The Kirghiz said that a violent snowstorm was raging up in the Tenghiz-bai pass; we might thank our stars we had got through it in time. And indeed it was a stroke of fortune to escape in the way we did. A day earlier and we might have been crushed under the avalanche; a day later and we might have been annihilated by the buran (snow-hurricane).

CHAPTER X.

UP THE ALAÏ VALLEY

BEFORE I proceed with my itinerary, I should like to say a few words about the Alaï valley, the huge trough-like depression which separates the Alaï chain from the Pamir plateau. Bounded on the north by the Alaï Mountains, and on the south by the Trans-Alaï, it is terminated at its eastern extremity by the massive mountain-knot of Mus-tagh-tau. Thence it stretches seventy-five miles westwards, and is continued in the valley of Kara-teghin. Its breadth varies from three to twelve miles; the altitude sinks from 10,500 feet in the east to 8200 feet at Daraut-kurgan in the west. It is drained by the Kizil-su, which traverses it throughout its entire length, gathering up on the way the rainfall of the surrounding mountains. After quitting the Alaï valley, the river enters the valley of Kara-teghin, winds through it under the name of the Surkhab, and finally joins the Amu-daria, bearing a third name, the Wakhsh, at the point of confluence. The volume of the Kizil-su amounted to 780 cubic feet in the second at Daraut-kurgan. Add to this the volume of 175 cubic feet in the second contributed by its affluent, the Kara-su, and we get a total volume of eighty-two and a half million cubic feet in the twenty-four hours. The volume is greatest in the middle of summer, when the snows melt at the fastest rate. Indeed for about six weeks at midsummer the flood is so powerful that it is impossible to ford the river at Daraut-kurgan. During that time all communication between the auls on the opposite banks is completely interrupted.

The volume of the stream is very much greater during the night than during the daytime. This is owing to the fact that the water from the snows, which are melted by the sun during the day, does not get down to the valley before darkness sets in. The flood begins to rise at about eight o'clock in the evening. At six in the morning it begins to fall again. It reaches its lowest level at eight, and maintains the same level all day long. In March, when I saw it, the water was as bright and as clear as crystal. But during the summer it is tinged a brick-red colour by the sands and clays it passes through in its upper course. It is from this circumstance it gets its name of Kizil-su, which means the Red River. A similar circumstance has given the same name to its neighbour over on the other side of the mountains, namely the stream which flows from the Terek-davan pass eastwards to Kashgar and Lop-nor.

In the northern, middle, and eastern districts of the Pamirs—the districts through which my route ran—the downfall of snow is very unevenly distributed. Three sharply separated zones, dependent upon the configuration of the surface, may be distinguished. (i.) In the north, the valley of the Alaï, which becomes filled every winter with enormous masses of snow. (ii.) In the east, the region of Sarik-kol, which receives a very much less quantity of snow. (iii.) Lying between these two, the tracts around the lakes Kara-kul and Rang-kul, neither of which has any outflow; there the snowfall is almost insignificant. It may be assumed, that as a general rule the moisture-laden winds, which blow towards the lofty plateau of the Pamirs, discharge the greater portion of their precipitation upon the border-ranges, before they reach the central parts of the region. In these tracts it is only in sheltered spots, where the force of the wind is broken, for example, close to and around the passes, that any great quantity of snow falls. In all other places the thin, dry snow is quickly swept away by the wind.

One immediate consequence of the unequal geographical distribution of the snowfall is the unequal distribution, as well as the unequal size, of the rivers and glaciers. Both occur only in those regions where there is a plentiful snowfall. In the central parts of the plateau they are few and

MY CARAVAN IN THE ALAÏ VALLEY

of inconsiderable dimensions. Taking the results of my observations and measurements as a basis, I calculate that on an average one cubic yard of snow out of the total quantity on each square yard of land-surface goes to feed the rivers in the form of water. The snow as it lies is of extraordinary density, and only about one-fourth of its volume melts and becomes converted into water. If we estimate that the aggregate snowfall of the Alaï valley and the mountain-slopes which surround it covers 2,870,000,000 square yards, we may reckon the aggregate volume of water which they yield at 19,500,000,000 cubic feet, or a solid cube of water measuring 2700 feet on each of its sides. This estimate can scarcely be considered excessive, when it is borne in mind, that the volume of the river during the period of high flood, in the middle of the summer, is out of all comparison greater than during the colder seasons of the year. If we assume a volume of eight hundred and eighty cubic feet in the second as the mean for the whole of the year, the figures work out at an annual aggregate volume of close upon 27,800,000,000 cubic feet. A calculation made upon such insufficient data can obviously be nothing more than an approximation. It is self-evident that the excess precipitation must be set down to the summer rains.

During the winter violent westerly winds blow up the valley of the Alaï with great constancy and regularity. Easterly winds also occur, but are very rare. The high mountain chains on the north and south of the valley shelter it against northerly and southerly winds; although it does occasionally blow from the south-east. During the summer the air is stiller, and the wind blows seldom, and then with but little force. The west wind is called Kara-teghin *khamal*, the east wind Irkestam *khamal*, and the south-east wind Murghab *khamal*, after the various districts from which they blow.

In the valley of Fergana the spring rains come in the middle of March. In the Alaï valley, on the other side of the mountains, the same month is the season of the *sarik-kar* or yellow snow, the name given to the last of the winter snows. Why it is so called the Kirghiz were never able to explain satisfactorily. But it is a fact, that the name is in common use all over the Pamirs. The most probable explanation is perhaps this. By that time in certain quarters the snow has already melted, exposing the surface of the ground. The dust which rises from those places is probably caught up by the wind and blown upon the freshly fallen snow, staining it a dirty yellow colour.

I need scarcely add, that the beginning of the winter snows, and their disappearance in spring, vary in the various districts. In the higher regions it snows all the

AMID THE SNOWS OF THE ALAÏ VALLEY

year round. In the Alaï valley the first snow falls in the end of October, and the last traces disappear about the middle of April.

But to return to our journey. During the night between 28th February and 1st March the wind howled and whistled through the tent hour after hour, and at length rent several narrow slits between the separate pieces of felting. In the morning, when I woke up, the floor of the tent was braided with ribbons of drifted snow; one of them ran diagonally across the pillow on which my head rested. But what cared I about wind and snow? I slept like a bear in his winter lair. The storm continued to rage all the next day. The wind, which blew from the west, whirled thick clouds of snow, as fine as powder, past the yurt (tent) from morning till night. In fact every minute the tent itself threatened to go, although we lashed it down with extra ropes, and supported it with additional stakes.

On the 2nd March we travelled as far as the winter village of Gundi. But before starting in the morning we took the precaution to send men on in advance to clear the path and trample a passage through the snowdrifts. And fortunate we did so, for the old track was completely obliterated by the storm. We kept as close to the southern foot-slopes of the Alaï Mountains as we possibly could,

THE AUL OF GUNDI

because in many places on that side the snow had been swept clean away.

At Gundi we met with a misfortune. We had just got the tent pitched and arranged, and had carried in the yakhtans, and the more perishable portions of the baggage, when Rehim Bai managed to give the quicksilver barometer a knock, which smashed the delicate glass tube and set the glistening beads of quicksilver rolling along the ground. My costly and sensitive instrument, which I watched over as tenderly as a mother watches over her infant, alas! it was now useless, and might just as well be flung into a snowdrift. I could no longer record its readings three times a day as I had conscientiously done hitherto. Rehim Bai was dismayed at what he had done; but, as he really was not to blame for what had happened, I let him off with a mild wigging. What was the use of heaping reproaches upon him? That would not mend the barometer. Besides, I still had three other aneroid barometers and hypsometers.

With the idea of affording me some consolation for my loss, the men arranged a concert for the evening. One of the Kirghiz came into my tent, and squatting down began to play the *kaumuss*, a three-stringed instrument played with the fingers. The music was monotonous and of a melancholy cadence; but it harmonized well with the surroundings, and the moods they inspired. In a word, it was typically Asiatic. I sat and listened to it with pleasure, giving my imagination captive to the music, the soft moaning of the night wind, the gentle crackle of the fire. How many and many a night did I not spend thus during the long years that followed, listening to the dreamy sounds of that primitive Kirghiz instrument! How many a dark, solitary winter afternoon did I not while away in this foolish fashion! In course of time I grew accustomed to the kaumuss, and derived as much pleasure from it as the Kirghiz did themselves. In fact, I grew fond of it. Its soothing music carried my mind away into the fairy realms of day-dreams; my thoughts flew far away to my home amid the dark pinewoods of Sweden. And how sweet and pleasant a thing it is to dream yourself back amongst those who are near and dear to you! Many a night I was lulled to sleep by the measured tones of the kaumuss, played as an accompaniment to some melancholy Asiatic song.

March 3rd. The storm had subsided, though the sky was still enveloped in clouds. The peaks of the Trans-Alaï range shimmered with the loveliest tints of grey, and white, and pale blue. Two hours of travel brought us to the little aul (tent-village) of Kizil-unkur, and another two hours to the pass of Ghaz, a low saddle among the southern spurs of the Alaï Mountains. All the way, even as far as Kashka-su, the river Kizil-su flowed close to the foot of the Alaï, as far from the Trans-Alaï as it could get. Our path lay close alongside the right bank of the stream, which boiled along at torrential speed in a sort of narrow cañon, now forcing its way between mounds of red sand, now cutting a deep trench through the conglomerate strata.

Then we gradually worked away from the Kizil-su. The further we advanced towards the east, the deeper lay the snow. The track was entirely blotted out by the latest storm, and the snowdrifts were so thick that all

THE KIZIL-SU

day long four camels went on in front to trample down a path, or rather a furrow, through them, along which the horses toiled at a painfully slow and heavy pace. The wind continued to sweep down on us in furious gusts, frequently smothering the whole caravan in dense clouds of driving snow.

At length we came to the little brook of Kashka-su, on the other side of which was the aul of the same name. To get to it, we had to ride over the torrent on a bridge of ice and snow. There we found awaiting us a most comfortable yurt (tent). Not only were Kirghiz carpets spread on the ground, they were also hung round the walls; whilst the fire which blazed in the middle of the tent scattered showers of sparks in every direction, and crackled and shot out chips of burning wood to such a degree that a man was told off to watch lest it should burn holes in the carpets.

The 4th March it snowed all day long. The landscape was shrouded in a thick mist, so that not a single feature could be seen. Sky and earth were one indistinguishable veil of white haze. The only relief to the eye was the long dark line of the caravan, shading off to a dull grey towards the head of the column and gradually fading away in the distance. Two camels led the way, their riders being instructed to find out where was the firmest

CAMELS TRAMPLING A PATH THROUGH THE SNOW

ground. Accordingly they cruised up and down every rise and swelling of the path. But the snow was so deep that several times they dropped into it till scarce a vestige of them could be seen. Then, having scrambled out, they tried another place. The horses struggled on as best they could in the track of the camels, their packs and stirrups jolting and trailing against the banks of snow on each side of them.

At length we caught sight of a yurt on a hill-side—a black spot amid the universal whiteness. A short distance further on we saw men engaged in putting up another tent. They were only about two hundred yards distant; but between us and them there was a ravine into which the snow had drifted to the depth of eight or ten feet, and it took us more than an hour to get all the baggage-animals safely over. The first which ventured to try to cross dropped through the treacherous surface, and was near being smothered in the deep snow. It was as much as ever the men could do to free the horse from his packs and haul him back again on to firm ground. Then they set to work to dig out a path; but the snow was so deep that they were unable to get through it. At length the Kirghiz hit upon an ingenious device for overcoming the difficulty. They took the felt coverings of the tent and spread them over the snow. But there were not sufficient pieces to stretch right across, so, after a horse had advanced as far as he could get, the felts were lifted from behind him and laid down again in front of him. In this way, but at the cost of extreme labour and great waste of time, we managed to get all the animals safely across.

That district was called Jipptik. But the aul (tent-village) of that name was two miles further on, and the tents had been shifted solely for our accommodation. Notwithstanding that, it was anything but a comfortable camp. The fuel was insufficient in quantity, and worse than that—damp, so that the tent was filled with eddies of pungent smoke. The tent itself was very speedily surrounded by high ramparts of snow.

March 5th. The night was bitterly cold. The thermometer registered a minimum of –4°9 Fahr. (–20°5 C.); close at the head of my tent it was 14° Fahr. (–10° C.) at eight in the morning. Everything inside the tent was frozen—canned provisions, milk extract, ink. Outside the tent, the poor horses, which had passed the night in the open air, hung their heads dolefully, and tried to scrape away the snow, which crackled in the frosty air every time it was touched. The day, however, was fair, and about one hour before noon the sun peeped through. Then the majestic outlines of the Alpine Trans-Alaï began to glimmer through the fast vanishing mist, the topmost crests being still wreathed in gauzy veils of cloud. Every now and again we caught a glimpse of Kaufmann Peak (23,000 feet high)—a pyramidal summit, which glittered like silver in the sunshine, and appeared to be overtopped by scarce any of its neighbours.

We waited some time for a band of Kirghiz, who, it had been arranged, should come to meet us from Archa-bulak and clear a track for us through the snow. But after waiting some time and seeing nothing of them, our friend Emin, chief of the Kara-teppes, rode on in advance to see what had become of them, as well as to reconnoitre the ground. I confess it was not an encouraging sight to see his horse floundering through the snowdrifts, his flanks decorated with fringes of rime, whilst the breath gushed from his nostrils like light puffs

OUR HORSES ENDEAVOURING TO FIND GRASS IN THE SNOW

of steam. For an hour and a half we watched him creeping like a black speck across the endless sea of white snows. Most of the time nothing was visible except the rider and the horse's head.

After an absence of a couple of hours Jan Ali Emin returned, and reported that it was impossible to advance further; the snow was many feet deep, and his horse had been down several times. We held a consultation, as the outcome of which Emin and Rehim Bai rode over to the aul of Jipptik to beg assistance. The rest of us stayed behind in camp, literally snowed up on every side. At length, after some further waiting, we perceived a long string of horses and camels approaching from the north, the direction of the foot-hills of the Alaï. They were people from the aul, bringing us hay and fuel. When they came up, they strongly advised us to remain where we were till the following morning.

Early on the 6th March we began to make preparations as if for a military campaign. Before daylight four men started on camels to trample a path through the snowdrifts. The Kirghiz told me, that some winters the snows were a great deal worse than they were that winter. Sometimes they were piled up higher than the top of the tent, and intercommunication between the auls had to be kept up by means of yaks specially trained to do the work of snow-ploughs, in that with their foreheads

JAN ALI EMIN RIDING THROUGH THE SNOW

and horns they shovel narrow tunnels or passages through the snowdrifts.

The task we had immediately before us was to cross the river Kizil-su—by no means an easy thing to do. Except for a deep rapid current in the middle, about ten or a dozen yards wide, the stream was sheathed in ice, and the ice covered with heavy masses of snow. Moreover the edges of the ice were unsafe, being greatly eaten into by the water. It was not at all a pleasant sensation to sit on my horse's back when he came to the edge of the ice above the ford and gathered himself together for a leap into the water. If he slipped or fell, I felt I was certain to get a cold bath, which in the temperature that then prevailed would have been anything but agreeable; worse than that—it would have been dangerous, seeing that I was hampered with thick, heavy furs, which were a great impediment to freedom of movement. And even when the horse had made the leap in safety, and was wading through the ford, I only just escaped being seized with giddiness, for the river boiled and foamed about him, and raced along so swiftly as almost to lift the animal off his feet. Unless I had kept a firm hand on him, he would have been swept off the ford into deep water, where he would have lost foothold and been carried away by the current. Nevertheless it is generally in the summer that mishaps of that sort occur.

Once over the Kizil-su, we struck obliquely across the valley towards the outer slopes of the Trans-Alaï

CROSSING THE KIZIL-SU

Mountains, leaving the river behind us on the left. The ground was difficult travelling, owing to the great number of natural springs which gushed up in every direction. The water which oozed from them was partly frozen into huge cakes of ice; and where the temperature was somewhat higher, it trickled away unfrozen underneath the snow. This gave rise to soft, treacherous expanses of snowy brash, into which the horses sank at every step. From the character of the echo given by their hoof-beats we were able to tell what sort of surface was hidden underneath the snow. A dull, heavy sound meant hard frozen ground; a clear metallic ring indicated firm ice; whilst a muffled, hollow sound told us that we were riding over cakes or arches of ice.

Gradually as we advanced the surface became more uneven. We entered amongst the low foot-hills of the Trans-Alaï range, leaving the pass of Talldik behind us on the north. The snows grew deeper and deeper. After marching ten hours we decided to halt, although the region around was desolate in the extreme—not a blade, not a living creature to be seen. The men cleared the snow away from the side of a low hill, and there stacked the baggage for the night. The camels that were bringing the yurt from Jipptik lagged behind on the road, and we had to wait a full hour till they came up. In the meantime we kindled a fire, and gathered

CROSSING THE KIZIL-SU (A SECOND VIEW)

round it close together in a circle, and tried to warm our frozen limbs with tea. There were forty-seven degrees of frost Fahr. (–26° C.), and the least touch made the snow crackle like parchment. I did not get under the shelter of the tent until late that night.

I have already said that the governor of Fergana had sent orders to the Kirghiz to have a tent and fuel prepared for us at each stage of our journey against the day fixed for our arrival. The reason there was no tent ready for us when we reached Urtak, as this particular place was called, was due to the following untoward circumstances. Khoja Min Bashi, *volastnoi* (district chief) of Utch-teppe, which belongs to the administrative district of Osh, had intended to meet me himself, and with that end in view set out to cross the Alaï Mountains. But in the pass of Att-yolli, near Talldik, he had been overtaken by a snow-hurricane, and so prevented from continuing his journey. In the same storm forty sheep were buried in a snowdrift, their shepherd narrowly escaping with his life. When he found himself stuck fast, the volastnoi managed to get six other men sent forward in his place with the tent and fuel. But they had had hard work to force their way through the pass, and after nine days' toil, and the loss of one horse, were compelled to abandon both tent and fuel. Four of them, struggling on, succeeded at length in getting through to Jipptik, where

MARCHING UP THE ALAÏ VALLEY

they borrowed another tent and fresh fuel from the chieftain of the Kirghiz of that place. When we at last met them in Urtak, they were very uneasy about the two comrades they had left behind. One of the four had got a frost-bitten foot; whilst another was suffering from snow-blindness. He had been walking for three days through the dazzling snows, and consequently had overstrained his eyes. His companions did their best to screen their eyes with tufts of horsehair stuck between their caps and foreheads, also with pieces of leather strap through which they had cut narrow openings. Both invalids were tended with the greatest care, and at the end of a couple of days were all right again.

It was unusually late that night before we got to bed—fully an hour after midnight before all sounds were hushed in camp. At that time the thermometer registered – 25°6 Fahr. (– 32° C.). It was my usual practice to sleep alone in the tent, as it was not altogether pleasant to have the Kirghiz too close: they are seldom the sole occupants of their furs or felts. But intense cold is a pretty effective safeguard against the inconvenience I am alluding to. With such a low temperature I had not the conscience to let the men lie under the open sky. Accordingly as many of them crowded into the tent, and stowed themselves away on the carpets, as could possibly squeeze in, till we lay as tightly packed as herrings in a barrel. Notwithstanding this, the temperature inside the tent sank to – 12°6 Fahr. (– 24°8 C.). The minimum during the night was – 30°1 Fahr. (– 34°5 C.). The next morning when we woke a shower of ice flowers and icicles fell over us from the tent-roof. But I never saw the stars glitter with such matchless brilliancy as they did that night.

CHAPTER XI.

OVER THE TRANS-ALAÏ.

IT was eleven o'clock in the day when we got started on the 7th March. We were all exhausted by the toilsome march of the previous day, and it was late when we turned in. Everybody therefore was glad to wait till the sun warmed the air before we set off again. Our Kirghiz guides led us through a series of low hills close alongside the Kara-su. This river gets its name of the Black Water from the circumstance that it has its origin, not in the snows of this highland region, but in natural springs; besides which, its water was so clear that in its deeper reaches it appeared to be almost black. We crossed over the stream two or three times on the brittle ice crust which spanned it from side to side. Underneath us we could hear the water gurgling and gulping with a clear metallic sound. There were not above two or three places where we could see the river flowing unhindered between the stones with which its bed was encumbered.

The snowdrifts grew deeper and deeper; so that the caravan could only make its way through them at a painfully slow pace. Towards the east we could see the termination of the Alaï valley, where the offshoots of the Alaï and the Trans-Alaï Mountains met together above a trough-shaped depression. The outlines of the latter chain now stood out in sharper relief, and its crest flashed back the dazzling coruscations of light which played about its snow-mantled shoulders. The chief tints were white and blue; and far, far above it sparkled the pure turquoise blue of the Asiatic sky. White gossamer clouds like bridal veils hovered about the summit of Kaufmann Peak and the neighbouring altitudes. But what icy cold—what frigid brides!

The horses toiled on through the snow. The men had to be constantly on the alert, for the packs were always slipping round underneath the horses. Very often every man in the company was wanted to lend a hand to get them put straight again. At the more difficult places the characteristic cries of the Kirghiz *Bismillah* (In God's name!) or simply *Haidah* (Get on!) rang out shrilly upon the mountain air.

Our canine friend Yollchi thoroughly enjoyed himself. He tumbled like an acrobat over the snowdrifts. He rolled over and over in the snow, thoroughly cooling his thick, shaggy hide. One moment he would playfully catch up a mouthful of snow, the next he would race off swift as an arrow ahead of the caravan. The creature was half wild when he joined us; and I never succeeded in making him properly tame. Having been reared amongst the Kirghiz, he could never by any bribe be induced to come inside my tent. For the Kirghiz are Mohammedans, and look upon the dog as an unclean animal. The very dust off his feet would pollute the inside of a tent. I tried my best to wean Yollchi from such superstitious notions. But do what I would, I could not get him past the tent door—neither by fair means nor foul. He had never once in his life set foot inside a tent, and obviously had made up his mind that he had no manner of business in such a place.

The climate in that part of the world is not without its peculiarities. Whilst the sun is well-nigh burning one side of your face, the other side will be freezing. At noon, if the sky is clear, and there is no wind, it gets so hot that you are glad to fling off your sheepskins. But the moment the sun gets behind a cloud, or the shadow of a mountain comes between the sun and yourself, you begin to shiver with cold. After shedding your skin once or twice, your face gets as hard and dry as parchment, and you turn as brown as a Hindu. At noon on 5th March the thermometer registered 14° Fahr. (– 10° C.) in the shade, while the black-bulb insolation thermometer showed 125°6 Fahr. (52° C.).

It began to darken whilst we were still two hours from the next camp. The horses travelled so slowly, and my back ached so from the heavy furs I wore, that, bidding Min Bashi accompany me, I left the caravan, and set off in the darkness to make my way as best I could over the pathless country. Min Bashi went on first. I followed in the track, or rather furrow, which his horse ploughed through the snow. It was a wearying ride, and, but that the stars shone brightly, would have been as dark as pitch. At last, however, we came to the solitary little hut of Bor-doba. Had there been a worthy Boniface in charge, he would have been vastly amazed to hear two snow-smothered horsemen ride up to the door at that late hour of the night, fasten their horses outside, stamp the snow off their clothes and boots, and without further ceremony march into the house. To prevent any misconception as to the style of "house" it was, I will state at once, that this rabat (rest-house) was merely an earthen hut, with a wooden roof supported by rough beams, and that the only provision for sleeping was a square bank of earth in the middle of the floor. This and a few similar huts have been put up by the direction of the governor of Fergana, for the convenience of the mounted post-messengers who travel backwards and forwards between Margelan and Fort Pamir. This particular hut stood at the foot of a desolate hill, and from that circumstance gets its name of Bor-doba, a corruption of Bor-teppe, the Grey Hill. We both dropped straight off to sleep, and slept until the bustle and noise caused by the arrival of the caravan awakened us. Then we had tea made and warmed ourselves over a glorious fire.

On the way to Bor-doba we saw the tracks of eight wolves, which had crossed over the valley in a scattered troop from the Alaï Mountains to the Trans-Alaï. Further on they all struck into our track, which led through a narrow opening between two hills. The Kirghiz told me, it was an old and well-known wolf-trail.

The next morning at daybreak, when my men went out to see after the horses, they caught sight of seven wolves sneaking away in the direction of Kizil-art.

Wolves are very common in those regions. During the summer they haunt the Alaï valley, and levy tribute upon the Kirghiz flocks of sheep. The Kirghiz sheep-dogs can see them more than a mile off; but are frequently outwitted by the wolves, who will hang about a flock for weeks at a time, persistently spying out for a favourable opportunity to seize their prey. They are extremely bloodthirsty and murderous; and, if by any chance they light upon an unprotected flock, will kill every sheep

BOR-DOBA

in it, leaving not a single animal alive. Not many weeks previously a single wolf had in the course of one night bitten to death 180 sheep belonging to a Kirghiz of Utch-teppe. But woe betide the wolf that has the ill-luck to be wounded by the Kirghiz, and falls alive into their hands. They force open his mouth, thrust a short, thick piece of wood between his jaws, and lash them all firmly together. Another heavy piece of wood is fastened to one of his feet, to prevent him from running away. Then they torture him to death. On one occasion I was instrumental in putting an end to a horrible scene of this kind.

When the great winter snows fall in the Alaï valley,

the wolves go up to the Pamirs, and range the districts around Lake Kara-kul, preying principally upon the magnificent arkhari or argali (*Ovis Poli*), *i.e.*, the wild sheep of Central Asia, as well as upon the *kiyick* (goat) and hares. In hunting the wild sheep the wolves display remarkable craft and intelligence. Having enclosed the sheep in a wide ring, they begin to howl, so as to make their presence known, and gradually close in upon their prey. When they get near enough, they cut off two or three of the sheep and force them to take refuge on a narrow, outjutting crag, from which there is no return except into their jaws. If the crag is too steep for them to scale it, they patiently wait at the bottom until the wild sheep's slender legs become numbed from sheer weariness, and they roll down the precipice into the jaws of their ravenous persecutors. In the vicinity of Kara-kul we often saw flocks of arkhari quietly grazing a couple of miles from us. The Kirghiz used to discover them at a marvellous distance, so far off in fact that I, with my most powerful field-glass, could only just discern something of their movements. In various parts of the Pamirs travellers come across their skulls, bleached by the sun and still adorned with their huge curled horns. These are no doubt the sole remains of wolves' feasts.

According to the Kirghiz, two wolves can sometimes be dangerous to a solitary man. They told me many blood-curdling stories about wolves and their depredations up in those lofty regions of Asia. A few years ago a man was attacked and killed by wolves in the pass of Talldik, and when a day or two afterwards the Kirghiz went to fetch down his body, there was nothing left except the bare skeleton. On another occasion a Kirghiz perished in a buran in the Kizil-art pass. A week later the man's corpse was found in the snow; but the horse which he rode had been entirely devoured by wolves. Only the previous winter one of my Kirghiz guides and a jighit (Sart messenger) were surrounded by a dozen wolves. Fortunately they were armed, and shot two of them. These were immediately devoured by the rest, after which they all took to flight.

At Bor-doba we rested a day. I employed it in making scientific observations. For one thing, we cut a vertical section three feet deep through the snow, and found it was deposited in six separate layers, showing different degrees of purity and consistency. The bottom layer was 8¼ inches thick, of a dirty appearance, and almost as hard as ice. The top layer, 17 inches thick, was soft and pure as wool. It is reasonable to suppose that the different layers or strata of snow corresponded to different periods of snowfall, and that those which lay underneath were pressed together by the weight of the superimposed layers; so that during the winter of 1893–94 about six vertical feet of snow must have fallen in the place where we made our section. The temperature of the air at three o'clock in the afternoon was 7°5 Fahr. (−13°6 C.); the black-bulb insolation thermometer gave a reading of 115°9 Fahr. (46°6 C.). Nevertheless at a depth of 1¼ inches in the snow the temperature was only −8°5 Fahr. (−22°5 C.). This tends to prove that the differences in the daily range of temperature were scarcely sensible at even that slight depth, or distance, from the direct action of the sun's rays. (The minimum of the preceding night was −18°8 Fahr. or −28°2 C.) As we went down towards the surface of the solid ground, that is deeper, measuring from the crust of snow, we found that the temperature gradually increased. For instance, at a depth of 17 inches it was 12°2 Fahr. (−11° C.); at 23 inches 17°6 Fahr. (−8° C.); at 25½ inches 18° Fahr. (−7°8 C.); at 27½ inches 21°7 Fahr. (−5°7 C.); and on the ground, or at a depth of 36 inches, 24°1 Fahr. (−4°4 C.).

The ground was frozen as hard as a stone. But with pickaxes and hatchets we made a hole two feet deep and put down a thermometer; it registered 30°4 Fahr. (−0°9 C.). Taking the whole series of observations together, I came to the conclusion, that the solid earth freezes to a depth of a little over three feet and a quarter; which agrees with the results I obtained in other parts of the

Pamirs. From what the Kirghiz told me, I inferred that the frozen ground thaws through to the bottom during the summer.

On the morning of 9th March all the Kirghiz fell upon their knees in the snow and prayed to Allah to vouchsafe them a safe journey through the dreaded pass of Kizil-art. I fully prepared myself for a terrible journey, for in the pass of Kizil-art the snow-hurricanes are wont to swoop down upon the unsuspecting traveller out of a perfectly cloudless sky; but to my surprise I found it much easier than the pass of Tenghiz-bai, especially as we were favoured with the best of weather. Bor-doba lies at such a great altitude that the climb thence to the pass, which

SOME OF OUR PACK-HORSES

crosses the highest ridge of the Trans-Alaï, was not especially steep. The torrent, which races down from the pass in spring and summer, was now frozen up, and its bed choked with sheets of ice, which, being polished bright by the wind, reflected the blue sky like a mirror. For the most part the range consisted of reddish sandstones and clay-slates; the former varying from brick colour to blood red in tint, the latter being dark green, light green, and grey. The bottom of the valley was thickly strewn with *débris* and disintegrated rocks, brought down from the higher regions of the mountains.

The gradients grew steeper as we approached the summit of the pass, and the snows lay deeper. But we reached the top (14,015 feet) without any mishap; though, when we got there, we were assailed by an icy northern wind, which penetrated sheepskins and felt boots alike.

On the very highest point of the pass stood the burial-cairn of the Mohammedan saint Kizil-art, a mound of stones, decorated with the religious offerings of pious Kirghiz, namely *tughs* (*i.e.* sticks with rags tied round them), pieces of cloth, and antelopes' horns. Arrived at this shrine, my men again fell upon their knees, and thanked Allah for having preserved them on the way up to the top of the dreaded pass. They told me, that Kizil-art was an *aulia* or saint, who in the time of the Prophet travelled from the Alaï valley to the countries of the south to preach abroad the true faith. In the course of his journey he discovered this pass, to which he gave his own name. He is said to be now buried on the highest point of it. Others of the Kirghiz gave a much more probable explanation of the name, namely that the cairn has simply been built in commemoration of the saint. Further, they fully believe that, if the holy Kizil-art had not discovered the pass, it would be impossible, even at the present day, to travel across the Pamirs from this direction. Tradition has also preserved the memory of his six brothers, all of them holy men like himself. Their names were Mus-art, Kok-art, Khatin-art, Kolun-art, Ghez-art, and Ak-art. The suffix "art" is one out of several Kirghiz words meaning "pass," and each of these six names is applied to a pass in the mountains of the Pamirs.

CHAPTER XII.

LAKE KARA-KUL

ON the southern side of the range there was at first a good deal of snow; but it soon began to get thinner. At the end of a march of eight hours' duration we came to the little caravanserai of Kok-sai. The name of this place is indelibly engraven upon my memory. It was there I recorded the lowest temperature it has been my lot to observe in the course of all my journeyings through Asia. The quicksilver thermometer fell to – 36°8 Fahr. (– 38°2 C.), that is, almost as low as the freezing-point of mercury.

South of the pass of Kizil-art the landscape changed its character entirely. There was a far smaller quantity of snow. Over large areas the surface of the earth was bare and exposed, in others buried under sand and the *débris* of disintegrated rocks. The mountains were softer and more rounded in outline, and their relative altitudes were less; whilst their several ridges or crests were separated from one another by broad, shallow, trough-shaped valleys. The region around Lake Kara-kul, between the passes of Kizil-art and Ak-baital, possesses no drainage outlet towards the Amu-daria; and the products of disintegration are not carried away by the streams, but remain and help to level up the natural inequalities of the surface. In other words, the distinction holds good here which Baron von Richthofen lays down as obtaining between regions which have no drainage outlet and peripheral regions which have a drainage outlet.

All day long on 10th March we rode towards the south-east, crossing in the early part of the day an open trough-shaped valley, girdled by low, snow-clad mountain-ridges of moderate height. In the valley itself there was very little snow. What there was lay in thin, scattered patches. Before us on the right the valley opened out wider, and swelled up into a series of low, rounded hills. On the left a spur ran out south-westwards across the valley, terminating in a single isolated cone. Continuing on up this gradually rising ground, we came, at the end of another four hours' march, to the little pass of Uy-bulak, from the summit of which we had a grand panorama towards the south-east. Far down under our feet we could see the north-east corner of Great Kara-kul, cased in a panoply of ice and mantled with snow. All round it stood a ring of giant mountains, draped from head to foot in one unbroken garment of dazzling snow. Within the pass the snow was once more 15 to 16 inches deep, and coated with a curiously hard, dry crust, tough as parchment, and so strong that the horses frequently went over it without breaking it. It was just as though we were travelling over a huge, tight-stretched sheepskin.

From Uy-bulak and the foot of the mountains a broad steppe sloped downwards at an almost imperceptible angle towards the northern shore of the lake. Except in a few places, it was almost entirely covered with snow, which, under the force of the prevailing westerly and north-westerly winds, had assumed a strangely odd appearance. It resembled a number of small parallel dunes, or the wrinkled folds that come into cream when it is poured out on the ground and left to freeze. Several clumps of *teresken*, a hard, dry scrubby shrub, which yields excellent fuel, were scattered about the steppe.

The sun set at six o'clock. At the moment of his disappearance the shadows of the mountains on the west side of the plain raced across it so swiftly that it was difficult for the eye to follow them. Then they slowly mounted up the flank of the mountains on the east side, till nothing but the topmost pyramidal peaks were left glowing in the evening sunshine. A quarter of an hour later, and the entire region was dimmed with the twilight. The mountains on the east stood out like pale, chilly spectres against the background of the rapidly darkening sky; whilst those in the west were like a black silhouette thrown upon the brighter—light blue and mauve tinted—atmosphere behind them.

We halted not far from the shore of Great Kara-kul, taking shelter in an earthen hut, where we passed the night in warmth and comfort.

On the morning of 11th March I set off to cross the lake towards the south-west, taking with me a specially selected portion of the caravan, namely two Sart jighits, two hardy Kirghiz, all of us being mounted, with two pack-horses carrying the baggage. We also took with us provisions and fuel to last two days, as well as a *teghermetch* (a small conical Kirghiz tent), an iron bar, axes, spades, and the sounding apparatus and line. Before leaving the rest of my people, I arranged with them to meet us at the next camping-station, not far from the south-east corner of the lake.

Kara-kul is a saline lake, with an area of 120 to 150 square miles, and is shut in by mountain-chains of considerable elevation. But on the north, east, and south-east the mountains recede sufficiently far from its shores to leave room for a strip of steppe-like plain, two or three miles in breadth. Its Kirghiz name, which means the Black Lake, is so far appropriate, in that in summer its waters do appear dark when contrasted with the mountains which hem it in, for even in that season broad patches of snow often continue to lie on the ground. Its maximum length is about twelve miles; its maximum breadth about ten. A peninsula jutting out from the southern shore, and an island lying almost due north of the peninsula, divide the lake into two basins—an eastern, which is extremely shallow, and a western, much the larger, and going down to abysmal depths. The object of my first day's investigations was the eastern basin.

About two and a half miles from the shore we came to a halt. The iron bar and axes were immediately brought into requisition. It cost us an hour's hard labour to break

GREAT KARA-KUL SEEN FROM UY-BULAK

through the ice, for it was pretty nearly three feet thick. The ice was hard and transparent, and brittle as glass. The last stroke of the iron bar made a hole through which the water gushed and boiled up till it filled the pit we had made in the ice to within an inch or two of the top. It was clear as crystal, but of a greenish-black colour, and bitter to the taste. We let down the sounding-cord, which was divided off into lengths of ten yards. But very little more than the first length passed my hands. With the help of the measuring-tape I found that the lake had a depth of nearly 41¼ feet. The temperature of the water was 31°3 Fahr. (–0°4 C.) in the hole, and 29°8 Fahr.

MAKING A SOUNDING-HOLE IN LAKE KARA-KUL

(1°2 C.) at the bottom of the lake. As soon as we had finished the hole, which was nearly four feet across, the ice began to crack in every direction all around with loud reports, whilst a series of curious sounds issued from underneath it in quick succession.

We went on another two and a half miles, and made another sounding-hole. Then we struck across the ice towards the little island I have mentioned, hewing a third hole on the way. We landed beside a narrow creek, and rode across the island, till we found a suitable camping-ground. The Kirghiz said, the island had never before been visited by human beings. We pitched the small yurt (tent) we had brought with us, and immediately in front of the entrance made a fire of teresken faggots. Then, having taken our supper, we spent a raw, cold, disagreeable night, with the temperature down to – 20°2 Fahr. (– 29° C.), at an altitude of 13,000 feet above the level of the sea.

We woke up early the following morning, frozen, numbed, and out of humour. We rode across the ice about three miles due west from the island, then stopped and set about sounding the depth of the western basin. The normal tension of the ice was of course the same in every quarter. Our riding over it naturally disturbed the equilibrium, by increasing the downward pressure. As we moved along, every step the horses took was accompanied by peculiar sounds. One moment there was a growling like the deep bass notes of an organ; the next it was as though somebody were thumping a big drum in the "flat below"; then came a crash as though a railway-carriage door was being banged to; then as though a big round stone had been flung into the lake. These sounds were accompanied by alternate whistlings and whinings; whilst every now and again we seemed to hear far-off submarine explosions. At every loud report the horses twitched their ears and started, whilst the men glanced at one another with superstitious terror in their faces. The Sarts believed that the sounds were caused by "big fishes knocking their heads against the ice." But the more intelligent Kirghiz instructed them there were no fish in Kara-kul. Then when I asked *them* what was the cause of the strange sounds we heard under the ice, and what was going on there, they answered with true Oriental phlegm, "Khoda billadi" (God alone knows!). Anyway, if the faithless Lady Ran* were hatching mischief against us, she strangely miscalculated her power. The ice did not break; it would have borne the whole of the city of Stockholm.

That day too we were favoured with splendid weather—not a speck of cloud, not a breath of wind. There

* The goddess of lakes in the old Scandinavian mythology.

TAKING A SOUNDING THROUGH THE ICE OF GREAT KARA-KUL

were nearly three inches of hard snow on the ice, which prevented the horses from slipping. How different all this was from the discouraging accounts given me in West Turkestan. There they told me, that Kara-kul was never free from snow-hurricanes, that every flake of snow which fell was instantly swept away, and that I might look to have the entire caravan blown bodily across the glassy surface of the lake. Besides all this, they assured me I should have to put up a tent and hew my sounding-hole inside it; instead of which we did the work in the open air and in bright sunshine.

During the course of the day we rode across the lake from the north side to the south, making four other holes on the way.

The results of the soundings are embodied in the subjoined table; the Roman numerals indicating the bore-hole, the first column the depth of the lake in feet, the second and third the temperature at the bottom of the lake on the Fahrenheit and Centigrade scales respectively, and the fourth the thickness of the ice.

Eastern Basin.

	Ft.	In.		Fahr.		C.		Ft.	In.
I.	41	3	...	34°2	...	1°2	...	2	11¾
II.	42	9	...	34°9	...	1°6	...	3	5¾
III.	62	10	...	35°2	...	1'8	...	2	6

Western Basin.

	Ft.	In.		Fahr.		C.		Ft.	In.
IV.	726	5	...	38°1	...	3°4	...	1	7
V.	748	5	...	38°3	...	3°5	...	1	6
VI.	756	3	...	38°3	...	3°5	...	1	4½
VII.	256	3	...	35°8	...	2°1	...	1	8¾

These figures show that the eastern basin is shallow; whilst the western is very deep. A glance at the map, or better still at the lake itself, suggests that the contour of the lake bottom and its shores should be what the actual measurements proved it to be. The eastern basin is bordered by a tract of steppe-land, which slopes gently down towards its shore. The western basin is overhung by high, steep mountains. The lake is fed by several small brooks, which have their origin in natural springs in the vicinity, and from the melting of the snows on the mountains around. The springs are especially plentiful at the eastern end of the lake, and form large pools or marshes. One other deduction may be drawn from the table given above, though it is so self-evident as scarcely to need particularizing. It is this: with every increase in the depth of the lake, the temperature rose and the ice grew thinner.

Shortly after passing a little promontory, we saw before us the long fjord, or gulf, which cuts deep into the southern shore. It presented a striking picture; for, whilst the declivities came down at an angle of twenty degrees on

A SMALL ISLAND IN LAKE KARA-KUL

the west, there was on the east a flat shelf sloping up gently towards the foot of the mountains, and in the background, at the head of the fjord, a semicircle of the snow-clad giants of the Pamirs. Judging from what I could see of the configuration of the ground, I hardly think that the southern half of the fjord can exceed 160 feet in depth.

We cut our last sounding-hole right in the middle of the mouth of the fjord. As soon as we got through the ice, three of the men begged to be allowed to ride on in advance with the horses to Ak-tam, the place near the south-east corner of the lake where we had agreed to spend the night, so that they might get the tent ready against my arrival. I and the jighit Shir remained behind, to take the soundings. By the time we had finished, it was dark; yet not so dark but that we could see to follow the trail of the other men who had gone on to camp. We tracked them obliquely across the fjord; but lost the trail when we touched the shore. We rode a long time across the peninsula which I have mentioned before, scrambling over sand and stones and other products of disintegration. In a little the crescent of the moon appeared above the horizon, and shed down its cold, pale beams upon the desolate scene. And desolate indeed it was—not a sound to be heard, not a vestige of a living creature to be seen. Every now and then we stopped and shouted—no answer. Once we came across the trail in a scanty snowdrift. But the next moment the moon was shrouded in the night-mist, and we lost it again. After riding for fully four hours, we came to the shore of the eastern basin. But we saw no sign of horsemen, no signal fire, no appearance of a camp.

The other men had, it was evident, travelled another way. The question was—which way? We rode on another hour, trusting to chance to guide us. But it was all to no purpose: we could not find those we sought. We determined therefore to halt for the night. The spot where we came to this resolve was a level expanse of sand, dotted with thin patches of snow. We tethered the horses together by a halter to prevent them from running away. The poor creatures, which had had no food all day, hungrily scraped at the sand with their hoofs; but they found nothing except the tough, hard roots of teresken. At these they tugged greedily. Having made the best preparations for spending the night that our resources admitted of, we sat close together, and talked till an hour after midnight, firing one another's fears with gruesome wolf stories. Shir said however that, if danger threatened us from that quarter, the horses would be our best protectors, as they would be certain to give us warning.

Having thoroughly tired ourselves with talking, we squatted down Kirghiz-fashion in our sheepskins, *i.e.*, on our knees with our backs to the wind. I made a pillow of the portfolio or satchel which contained my maps, sketch-book, thermometers, and so forth. But I was not a Kirghiz. I found it impossible to sleep in that attitude. Every now and then Shir dropped off and began to snore; but I could not sleep a wink. I tried the position we Europeans are accustomed to, but was soon chilled through by the cold, and had to rise and move about to get warm again. From time to time the horses nuzzled against us, as if to remind us that we had forgotten to give them their supper.

Fortunately for us the night wind was not too fresh, and the temperature only fell to 4°1 Fahr. (– 15°5 C.).

THE STONE HUT AT AK-TAM

About six o'clock in the morning day broke, and we mounted into the saddle, hungry and stiff with cold. We rode southwards for an hour, till we came to a place where there was a little scanty yellow grass, left by the last flock of sheep which browsed over the spot in the autumn. Whilst the horses grazed for an hour or two, I and Shir got a good sleep, for the sun was up and kept us warm.

Having mounted again, we pushed on still towards the south. On the way we met a solitary Kirghiz, travelling on foot from Rang-kul to the Alaï valley. As with most of his race, his eyes were as sharp as a hawk's; he had discovered us nearly two miles before meeting us.

I and Shir found our comrades at the end of another hour's riding. Our first concern was to thaw our stiffened limbs and warm ourselves with hot tea; then, whilst the horses were eating their fodder, we despatched our breakfast, consisting chiefly of mutton and tinned provisions.

March 14th. The country rose from the Kara-kul very gradually towards the south. Before we had travelled far, we rode into a broad valley, stretching between two parallel mountain ranges, which ran north and south, and were sheathed in snow. As a rule a larger quantity of snow falls every year in this valley than around Great Kara-kul, though the depth seldom exceeds four inches. Thick clouds hung about the mountain-tops; everywhere else the sky was perfectly clear. About noon however the wind got up, and it soon blew with great violence. For close upon five hours we rode steadily towards the south-south-west; but coming to a bifurcation of the valley, we turned to the left and struck out towards the south-south-east. Just where the valley divided, we saw, conspicuously crowning a low hill, the masar or tomb of the Kirghiz saint Oksali, built of slabs of stone and decorated with horns and tughs (sticks with rags and pieces of cloth tied round them).

The valley into which we turned was the valley of Mus-kol, which led up to the pass of Ak-baital. There was but little snow on the ground; but as we advanced, the surface became more and more thickly strewn with disintegrated *débris*.

Upon my arrival in camp, I was met by four Kirghiz, wearing their gala *khalats* (coats). They had been sent from Fort Pamir to welcome me, and had been waiting five days, with a tent and supplies of food and fuel. They told me that my long delay had begun to make the Russian officers at the fort uneasy. As a matter of fact, we had been seriously delayed by the enormous quantities of snow we met with in the Alaï valley.

The word Mus-kol signifies "ice valley." Soük-chubir, the place where we encamped, might very well mean Cold Siberia, for the usual name for that region in

Turki is Chubir (Siberia). Whether this last interpretation is correct or not, and it is not quite certain that it is, both names may with good show of reason be said to be appropriate. For the region thereabouts is characterized by an excessive winter cold; while the valley is distinguished for a remarkable natural phenomenon, which I will now proceed to describe.

The little stream which traverses the valley of Mus-kol has its origin for the most part in natural springs. During the winter the water gradually freezes and spreads across the valley in huge "cakes" or sheets of ice. They resemble small frozen Alpine lakes, and their surface is so glassy bright that it reflects every dimple of the sky and every angle of the mountain crests. In certain seasons these ice-sheets do not entirely melt away during the course of the summer. The largest I saw was nearly two miles long and more than half a mile broad. We rode half-way across it in order to examine its thickness. The lateral strain upon the ice, and the pressure of the water from beneath, give rise to long narrow ridges, which are sometimes thrust up to the height of several feet, and are cleft by fissures going right through them from top to bottom. With the axes and iron bar we cut a transverse section through one of these ridges, and found it was merely a crust about eleven inches thick. Below it was a hollow arch, 9½ inches in height; and then came the water, three feet deep, going down to the sandy floor of the valley. The water was clear as crystal and of a light green colour; the thermometer gave its temperature as 31°6 Fahr. (−0°2 C.) Looking down through the open section we made, I perceived that the still, transparent water was arched over in both directions by a long tunnel, and that the under surface of the ice-arch was decorated with frost-work, crystal pendants, and stalactites, all shimmering with the loveliest hues of blue and green.

There were three of these ice-lakes. On the edge of the smallest of the three, close beside the spot where we pitched our camp for the night, were two typical ice volcanoes. Two springs gush out of the level ground. Late in the autumn, when the temperature permanently falls, the water which wells from them freezes. Meanwhile the springs continue to bubble up all the while the water continues to freeze. In this way two cones of ice are formed. One was 16½ feet high, and had a circumference of 225 feet; the other measured 26¼ feet and 676 feet in height and circumference respectively.

Four deep fissures radiated from the crater of the smaller volcano, which was about fifty-five yards distant from the other. At the time of our visit they were all half filled with ice. The cone was built up of an innumerable number of thin layers of light green ice, each layer representing a separate freezing. The mouth of the crater was closed by white ice, full of air-bubbles; but there was not at that time the least sign of water oozing out. It was an "extinct" volcano.

The larger volcano consisted of a double cone, one superimposed upon the other. The bottom one, which was built up entirely of white ice, was low and flat, its sides inclining at an angle of not more than five degrees. The upper cone, which was a dome of pure, transparent ice, rising at an angle of thirty degrees, and measuring 70 feet in diameter, was seamed throughout by a network of intersecting fissures, some concentric, others radiating from the centre outwards. Here again the mouth of the crater was frozen over, compelling the water to seek a new outlet through a side-fissure or "parasite" volcano. Although the water trickled out at a lively rate, it gradually froze before reaching the ice-lake, and so became set into a sort of "ice-flow." Its temperature was 31°5 Fahr. (–0°3 C.).

In the small ice-lakes it begins to freeze in the very beginning of November, and the last of the ice does not thaw and get down to Lake Kara-kul before the middle of June. In one of them it never does melt entirely away, being favoured by a shady, sheltered position; so that, when the new ice begins to form in the end of September, some of the old ice is still left.

We were surrounded on all sides by glacial landscapes; only unfortunately mists and snowstorms prevented me from taking photographs of them. Looking towards the west, along the longer axis of the ice-lake, it was easy to imagine we were gazing down a narrow fjord or sea-gulf; the horizon was wreathed in mist and seemed to lie at an immense distance away. To right and left were mountain-chains; but it was only the slopes nearest to us which emerged out of the haze.

On March 15th we rode all day long up the valley of

A REST ON THE PASS OF AK-BAITAL

Mus-kol, traversing it right through from one end to the other. At its upper extremity, to which the ascent had been very gradual, we halted for the night, close to the northern entrance of the pass of Ak-baital. The next day brought us a hard climb of ten hours' duration right over the pass, which rises to the pretty respectable altitude of 15,360 feet. A sharp snowstorm, waxing for a time into a hurricane, gave us a chilling welcome in the pass. The ascent was tough work for the horses, chiefly in consequence of the extreme rarefaction of the air. They had to exert themselves to the uttermost, and frequently stopped to gasp for breath; and despite our utmost care often fell. The pass consisted of two distinct ridges, separated by a stretch of almost level ground, which took us a good half-hour to ride over. It was covered with snow to the depth of 12 to 16 inches. On the summit of the pass we rested a short while, although there was a keen sou'-wester cutting through it. The temperature there was 12°2 Fahr. (−11° C.), and water boiled at 184°3 Fahr. (84°6 C.).

The caravan started down the eastern side of the pass,

KORNEI-TARTI
Breaking up Camp

which was at first extremely steep, in a thick mist. But, the steep upper slope passed, the country fell away at an easy gradient all the way to Kornei-tarti, our next camping-ground. In the Ak-baital pass another of our overworked horses fell dead. One of the Kirghiz bought the skin from Islam Bai, the leader of the caravan, for two roubles (4*s.*).

Kornei-tarti, meaning "the Trumpet Blast," is a narrow glen, half choked with detritus, partly products of denudation, partly large stones and rocks, through which meandered a little brook; though at the time of my journey this last was covered with a hard crust of ice. The bottom of the glen was one unbroken expanse of snow; but on the mountain-sides there was little, except in the declivities which faced north. Of vegetation there was not a trace. We went on steadily steering for the south-east and east-south-east, the country retaining the same characteristics as before. At Ak-gur (the White Grave), where a conspicuous spur jutted out into the glen, we were met by Kul Mametieff, a Tatar, whom the commandant of Fort Pamir had sent to act as my interpreter. He was dressed in full uniform, and wore half-a-dozen medals on his breast, and brought with him a letter eloquent of friendly greetings from his master. We continued to ride on till we came to Togolak-matik (Round Cauldron Valley), or the junction of the valley of Rang-kul with that of Ak-baital.

On the 18th we accomplished the last stage of this portion of our long journey, namely the lower extremity of the valley of Ak-baital, and the part of the valley of the Murghab which we had to traverse to get to the Russian outpost on the Pamirs. The first thing we noticed, upon catching sight of the fort at a distance, was the Russian flag flying from its north-west corner, proclaiming the sovereignty of the Czar over the "Roof of the World." When we drew nearer, we saw that the ramparts were beset with soldiers and Cossacks to the number of 160, drawn up in line. They gave us a cheer of welcome; and at the main entrance I met with a hearty reception from the commandant, Captain Saitseff, and his officers, six of them in all. They conducted me to the room in their own quarters which had been ready for me a whole week. A yurt was set apart for the use of my men.

As soon as I got my baggage stowed away, I went and had a good bath, and then joined the officers at mess. It was a meal not soon to be forgotten. I delivered the greetings I had brought from Margelan. I had a thousand and one questions to answer about my adventurous ride across the Pamirs in the middle of winter. Then, when the Cossack attendants served round the fiery wine of Turkestan, the commandant rose, and in a neat speech proposed the health of Oscar, King of Sweden and Norway. If ever a toast was responded to with real sincerity and gratitude, it was when I stood up to return thanks for the honour done to my king. If ever there was a place where joy reigned supreme, it was surely here on the "Roof of the World," 11,850 feet above the level of the sea, far removed from the bustle and noise of the busy world, in the very middle of Asia—a region where our nearest neighbours were the wild sheep of the mountain crags, the wolves which prowl over the snowy wastes, the imperial eagle which soars through the endless spaces of the sky.

THE AUTHOR AND THE RUSSIAN OFFICERS AT FORT PAMIR

CHAPTER XIII.

POPULATION OF THE RUSSIAN PAMIRS

THE greater part of our route across the Pamirs led, as we have seen, through uninhabited regions. The Russian districts of the Pamirs had in October 1893 a population of not more than 1232 persons. But the Alaï valley and the valley of Sarik-kol possessed, relatively speaking, a denser population. Administratively the Alaï valley is divided into two portions, the western half belonging to the *uyäsd* (district) of Margelan, the eastern half to the *uyäsd* of Osh. The information which I derived from the Kirghiz chiefs who dwell in those regions is not perhaps absolutely reliable; but it is sufficiently near the truth to deserve consideration.

Scattered through the Alaï valley there were, they told me, fifteen kishlaks or winter settlements, aggregating a total of 270 yurts (households or families), who in part remained there the whole year through, in part migrated to the higher regions during the summer. The number of tents in the larger auls was estimated as follows: in Daraut-kurgan 20, Kok-su 120, Kizil-unkur 50, Altyn-darah 5, Tuz-darah 45, Kashka-su 20, and Jipptik 10. Ethnologically the inhabitants of these settlements were said to fall into the following groups: Teit-Kirghiz dwelt at Daraut-kurgan, Altyn-darah, and Tuz-darah; at Kashka-su, Teit and Chal-teit; at Jipptik, Choy-Kirghiz; at Kok-su, Naiman Kirghiz; in Kara-teghin, Kipchaks, Naiman Kirghiz, and Kara-teit. The greater portion of these people migrate every summer to the neighbourhood of Lake Rang-kul, where, after the snows have disappeared, the grassy steppes furnish good pasturage for their sheep.

THE KIRGHIZ BEG OF THE AUL OF MURGHAB

A portion of them also winter, as we have seen, in the Alaï valley. There too, in the end of May or beginning of June, the prosperous Kirghiz of Fergana bring *their* flocks to graze on the plentiful grass which springs up along the borders of the Kizil-su. They pitch their *yeylaus* or summer camps on the banks of the river, and amuse themselves with their *baigas* or games on horse-back, feast, marry—in a word, make summer holiday. The greater portion stay only a couple of months, none longer than three months. The rest of the year they spend in their kishlaks or winter-quarters in Fergana.

During the summer there are about 150 yurts at Kashka-su.

The Kirghiz who go up to the Pamirs from Osh and Andijan travel by way of the Talldik and Jipptik passes; those who belong to Margelan and Kokand prefer the pass of Tenghiz-bai. This last is also the route which nowadays is chosen by the large number of Tajiks who travel on foot every summer to Fergana in search of work. The Alaï valley is also an important link in the chain of communication which connects East Turkestan with Kara-teghin and Bokhara, and so with the pilgrim road to Mecca and Medina; so that during the warmer months of the year many a trading-caravan and pilgrim-train passes up and down the valley.

The portion of the Pamirs which belongs to Russia is divided between two *volasts* (arrondissements), embracing in all seven *eminstvos* (communes):—

1. The volast of the Pamirs consists of five eminstvos: Kara-kul with 131 inhabitants in October 1893, Murghab with 253, Rang-kul with 103, Ak-tash with 239, and Alichur with 256.

2. The volast of Kuh-darah includes only two eminstvos, namely, Sarez with 95 inhabitants and Kuh-darah with 155. The inhabitants of the volast of the Pamirs were almost exclusively Teit Kirghiz; of Kuh-darah almost exclusively Tajiks. The total population, grouped by sex and age, embraced 320 men, 369 women, 342 boys, and 201 girls, a total of 1232.

These statistics were given me by Captain Saitseff. His predecessor, Captain Kuznetsoff, took a census of the district under his authority in October 1892, with the following result:—a total of 1055 people—255 men, 307 women, 299 boys, and 194 girls. Captain Saitseff's figures thus show an increase of 177 during the year. But the increase was partly due to immigration. The Kirghiz who dwelt on the other side of the Chinese and Afghan frontiers were attracted into Russian territory by the improved conditions of living, the result of the Russians' wise and humane treatment of the native populations of Asia. The regions most frequented during the winter months were those around Rang-kul, Kosh-aghil, and Ak-tash. There were also several auls (tent-villages) in the Alichur Pamirs, some even in the Pshart valley, south of Kara-kul. The little aul of Murghab lay a short distance east of the fort.

Captain Kuznetsoff estimated that the 1055 Kirghiz occupied 227 yurts (tents), and that their live-stock consisted of 20,580 sheep, 1703 yaks, 383 camels, and 280

TAJIKS FROM ROSHAN

horses. The Tajik population of the western Pamirs he estimated at 35,000.

The eastern slopes of the Pamirs, that is the tracts lying east of the Sarik-kol range, belong to China. With regard to them, there exist of course no reliable statistics. The beg of Su-bashi (south of Little Kara-kul) told me, that in the environs of that lake there were some 300 Teit-Kirghiz dwelling in about 60 yurts. He himself was chief of 286 yurts, most of which however lay on the east of the great mountain of Mus-tagh-ata. All the Kirghiz of the Pamirs, irrespective of the tribe to which they belong, are called by their kinsmen in Fergana by the one common appellation of Sarik-kolis, or people of Sarik-kol.

The statistics which I have just given demonstrate how thinly the Pamirs are inhabited. Nor could anything different be expected, considering the characteristics of the region—the intense cold, the frequency and fury of the snowstorms, the few pasture-grounds and their scanty supplies of grass. Of the two self-contained internal drainage-basins, Kara-kul and Rang-kul, the latter only has a settled Kirghiz population. The Kara-kul Kirghiz are true nomads. At the period of my visit to the lake their tents were pitched some little distance away on the south and south-west; its shores were entirely unoccupied. The grazing-grounds in the vicinity are frequented during the spring, summer, and autumn. But there is no grass during the winter; it is cropped too close by the sheep in the latter part of the autumn. Sometimes the Kirghiz from Rang-kul migrate to the steppes round Kara-kul for the summer grazing.

CHAPTER XIV.

GEOGRAPHICAL SUMMARY

BARON VON RICHTHOFEN divides the whole of the Asiatic continent into three distinct regions of very unequal extent—the Central, in which the rivers drain into inland lakes; the Peripheral or border lands, in which the streams make their way down to the seas which wash the coasts of the continent; and the Transition or Intermediate tracts, which partake of the characteristics of the other two. The subdivision also holds good when applied to the Pamirs. Here too there are three similar geographical districts—a central district draining into lakes Kara-kul and Rang-kul, a peripheral draining to the Amu-daria (and so into Lake Aral) and to the Tarim (which empties into the lake Lop-nor).

The most remarkable feature in the region of internal drainage is the process of levelling-up which goes on unceasingly. The detritus which results from the disintegrating action of the weather, and the more or less mechanical agency of wind and water and gravity, is constantly being carried down from the mountains all round its borders towards the lower parts of its depressions, and being deposited there. In this way the natural inequalities in the configuration of the ground are being gradually smoothed away. Although, broadly speaking, this process is going on in the tracts around Lake Kara-kul, it is also true that there are very great differences in the relative altitudes in that same quarter. For instance, the lake lies at an elevation of 13,000 feet above sea-level. It has been sounded to a depth of 756 feet, a remarkable depth considering that Kara-kul is a saline lake in the centre of Asia. And near its western margin the mountains tower up to an altitude of 4000 feet above the surface of the lake. Here there is an enormous field for the process of levelling-up to work in. But the soundings which I took in the lake proved that it *is* also operative there, for the bottom was covered with fine mud.

The mountain-chains which encircle the depressions of Kara-kul and Rang-kul attain to relatively great heights, and the passes which cross them are seldom much lower than the crests. The pass of Kalta-davan, for instance, has the same absolute altitude as Mont Blanc, namely 15,780 feet, the pass of Kizil-art is 14,015 feet; of Ak-baital 15,360 feet; and Chuggatai 15,500 feet. The lake of Rang-kul, which lies 12,240 feet above sea-level, marks the lowest point of the depression. The area which falls between the passes just named amounts to about 2100 square miles, an area which is approximately equal to that of the basin of Issyk-kul.

The traveller who journeys from Fergana to East Turkestan cannot help observing that the character of the country which stretches from Kizil-art on the north to Ak-baital on the south, and is bordered by the Chuggatai range on the east, is totally different from the tracts which immediately surround it. It is not a highland region; but a high-level plain, bounded on the north and south by latitudinal chains, and on the east by a meridional chain. Surveying the region from the summit of the Kizil-art pass, I was struck by the low angle of inclination and the soft rounded forms of the mountain-slopes; and noticed that the hills which diversified it were piled up, as it were, on the level ground, instead of striking off as sharply defined ranges in definite directions. The entire region bears witness to the enormous power of the forces of denudation exercised unceasingly over a vast period of time. *Débris* and fragments of rock, from the size of pebbles to the largest boulders, strew the ground in every direction. The lower flanks of the mountains are buried under detritus and mounds of disintegrated materials. On every hand, in fact, I saw convincing proofs of the destructive power of frost and rain and snow. Hard bare rock was nowhere visible, except near the crests of the ranges, in places where the wind is able to work unchecked.

The valleys of this high-level plain or plateau are broad and almost level. They rise at such a gradual inclination towards the outer ring of mountains that they often seem to be perfectly horizontal. Each of them is as a rule traversed by a little mountain-stream, which is fed partly

A TRANSITIONAL LANDSCAPE ON THE PAMIRS
One of our Camps

by natural springs, partly by the melting snows, and which empties itself into one of the two lakes, Kara-kul or Rang-kul. The scenery is frequently grand, but always depressingly monotonous, more especially in winter. In that season there is not a living creature to give animation to the desolate wilderness. A powerful field-glass will sometimes enable you to see a distant flock of arkhari (wild sheep), or kiyick (goats). Of human beings or human dwellings there is not a glimpse. Pastures are few, and the grass scanty. In a word, the landscape, with its barren, naked surfaces, puts you in mind of a typical lunar landscape.

Unlike similar tracts of Asia which possess no drainage outlet, the depression of Kara-kul does not suffer from accumulations of sand. The explanation of this no doubt is that the finer products of denudation are swept up by the constant violent windstorms which prevail in that region, and are carried away to be deposited in parts of the continent where the atmospheric conditions are permanently calmer. Sandstorms and duststorms are indeed by no means a rare visitation of the Pamir plateau. It is very probably to them that the so-called "yellow snow" owes its origin; for an examination of the snowdrifts to which that name is given reveals the presence of extremely fine particles of yellowish soil.

The most powerful agencies of disintegration in this part of the world are the winds and the enormous and sudden variations of the temperature. I saw striking evidences of their power on the little island in Lake Kara-kul, in huge blocks of syenite and clay-slate ground, scooped out, polished into the most fantastic shapes. The variations of temperature are enormous, not only in winter, but also in summer. At Fort Pamir, at seven o'clock in the morning of 11th January 1894, the thermometer recorded a temperature of $-36°$ Fahr. ($-37°8$ C.); one hour after noon it was $53°6$ Fahr. ($12°$ C.) in the sun—a difference of nearly $90°$ Fahr. ($50°$ C.) in the course of only six hours! The amount of radiation is almost inconceivable. At a time when the temperature of the air was just at the freezing-point, the black-bulb insolation thermometer actually registered $133°$ to $136°$ Fahr. ($56°$ to $58°$ C.). These stupendous forces labour on unrestingly century after century, wearing down the solid structure of the continent—in this an imperfect image or analogue of the earth itself, which is but the last surviving wreck of substances which have been in process of formation and re-formation through countless æons of time.

This region of exclusively internal drainage is girdled round by a zone of what Von Richthofen calls Transitional areas. On the north it is bounded by the Alaï Mountains, on the east by the chain of Sarik-kol, on the south by the Hindu-kush, whilst its western limit is marked by the line of 73° E. long. According to Von Richthofen, the definitive characteristic of a region belonging to the Transitional zone is the fact, that the erosive power of the water, and the resultant action of the violent alternations of temperature, have in more recent times broken a new path for the drainage streams, so that instead of seeking an interior, land-locked basin, they are now able to find an outlet to the rivers which eventually discharge into the sea; or *vice versâ*, they cease to send their waters oceanwards, but turn them instead towards an interior basin which makes no contribution to the seas around the continent. A Transitional region is therefore one which retains the typical features of the region to which originally it definitively belonged.

The Transitional zones of the Pamirs bear a very close general resemblance to the self-contained drainage-basin of the Kara-kul. Erosion is not yet sufficiently far advanced to enable the streams to carry off all the products of disintegration which cumber the valleys, the contours are soft and rounded, the valleys themselves broad and shallow. The tendency of the active disintegrating forces operative in the Pamirs is to convert it into a Peripheral region. For instance, in the south-west the little brook of Kok-uy-bel, a feeder of the Murghab, which in its turn goes to augment Lake Aral, has extended its remotest arteries to within about six miles of the brook of Mus-kol, which discharges into Lake Kara-kul. The springs which give origin to the Kok-uy-bel lie only a trifle higher than the level of the lake; so that, geologically speaking, the Kok-uy-bel may perhaps to-morrow be converted into an outlet from the lake, through which its waters would gradually flow away till it became empty. Simultaneously with this change, the Kara-kul depression would begin to lose the characteristic features of an independent area of internal drainage, and would gradually assume those of a Peripheral region.

A typical Peripheral region is one which through the agency of erosion has lost its former character of a high-level plain or plateau, and assumed the more definitely marked aspect of a region in which Nature's fingers have carved and moulded with powerful effect. Its outward contours are very much steeper and wilder, the relative altitudes greater; the plateau is cleft almost to its foundations by gigantic trenches or fissures radiating outwards; the valleys or glens, which cut into it, are deep and narrow, revealing the internal structure of the mountains; whilst along their bottoms the torrents foam and race through confined, gorge-like channels, over huge boulders of stone which have crashed down from the heights above.

On the west side of the plateau the turbulent head-streams of the Amu-daria, namely the Murghab, Ghunt, and Pänj, in many places force their way between vertical walls of rock, as though they were traversing a tunnel through the mountains. Such places are absolutely impassable, except to the native inhabitants of those regions, namely the clever Tajiks. There are places above certain of the streams where these people have driven wooden pegs into the sides of the perpendicular crevices, and with the sureness and nimbleness of apes clamber up from peg to peg, bearing heavy burdens lashed upon their backs. It is surprising what skill they show in availing themselves of every jutting piece of rock, every ledge and cornice, every crack and chink in the precipitous cliff-wall.

The border regions of the Pamirs are distinguished for the striking geographical homologies they present. On the north the river Kizil-su flows between the two parallel mountain-chains of the Alaï and the Trans-Alaï. On the east the Sarik-kol valley, between the Mus-tagh and Sarik-kol ranges, is traversed by the Ghez-daria and the Yarkand-daria. On the south the Wakhan is hemmed in by the Wakhan chain and the Hindu-kush, which both run in the same direction. The Pänj too on the west likewise flows between parallel ranges of mountains, though they are of a less imposing altitude. The valleys through which these several streams descend from the Pamirs to the lower regions exhibit features of a Transitional character. On the one hand, whilst they resemble the deeply trenched valleys on the outer borders of the plateau, with their large rivers in full flood all the year round; on the other hand, they possess many features in common with the level plains of the central areas of depression. Although strictly speaking, according to Von Richthofen's definition, the Ghez-daria and Yarkand-daria belong to the central area of depression, the districts through which they flow, and which their muddy streams to some extent help to mould and level up, exhibit the characteristics of a Peripheral zone. The drainage-basin of the Ghez-daria embraces four lakes, the two largest being Bulun-kul and Little Kara-kul. The Ghez-daria, as well as the Kara-su, an affluent of the Yarkand-daria, are fed principally by the snows and glaciers of Mus-tagh-ata; so that in spring and summer their currents swell to streams of very respectable dimensions. On 28th April the Ghez-daria had a volume of 850 cubic feet in the second, and we had some difficulty in crossing it. Later on in the summer it cannot be forded at all. These two strong torrents have made an irresistible assault upon the Mus-tagh range: both have cut their way through it. The Yarkand-daria is the chief contributary of the river Tarim; indeed it furnishes the greater portion of the volume of its waters.

Summarising in broad general terms, we may say that the Pamirs may be grouped in two sharply contrasted divisions—an eastern half, which is principally a plateau-land such as I have described, and a western half, consisting of a system of latitudinal mountain-chains disposed parallel to one another. There can be no doubt that at one period the entire region was strictly a plateau, and that it is being rapidly broken down by the agency of erosion. Indeed it is not more than a generation ago when the Pamirs were universally considered to be a plateau pure and simple. We know now, that they form a gigantic quadrilateral, embracing within its confines surface configurations and types of scenery of the most diverse description.

On the Pamirs, as in other parts of the world, the boundaries of different climatic regions are determined by the outstanding physical features. Over the central areas of the region the amount of snowfall is exceedingly small; but the cold is intense, the night temperatures being below freezing-point all the year round, with the exception of a couple of weeks in the middle of summer. In the Alaï valley, on the contrary, the climate is relatively milder, but at the same time the snowfall is enormous. Even in the valley of Sarik-kol the quantity of snow which falls every year is by no means inconsiderable. It follows therefore, as a direct consequence of the unequal distribution of the snowfall, that the rivers of the Pamirs carry down very unequal quantities of the drainage-water. For instance, at the time of my journey the Kizil-su had a volume nearly four times as great as the Murghab (or Ak-su), the chief head-stream of the Amu-daria; besides, the measurement of the latter was taken a month later than the measurement of the former. The volume of the Kizil-su was 950 cubic feet in the second; the volume of the Murghab only 250 cubic feet.

The ethnological and linguistic divisions of the Pamirs coincide pretty accurately with the physical divisions. The population of the plateau proper are almost entirely Kirghiz, relatively few in number. Further west, the Peripheral districts of Darvaz, Roshan, and Shugnan are inhabited almost exclusively by Tajiks, and the population there is relatively much denser. Nor is this a merely accidental difference. The Kirghiz are nomads. Their wealth consists of flocks of sheep, yaks, camels. As the seasons change, they move from one pasture-ground to another. Hence they naturally prefer the level stretches of the plateau to the deep, narrow glens and steep mountain-sides of the Peripheral regions. The Tajiks, on the other hand, are a settled population, their conditions of life being totally different from those under which the nomad Kirghiz live.

The separate linguistic areas are almost necessarily coincident with the ethnological areas. The Kirghiz give their own Turki names to the geographical features with which they are brought into relation. The Tajiks call the same objects by names borrowed from *their* language, which is Persian. By way of illustration, I may mention that nearly all the rivers which flow towards the west are generally known by their Kirghiz names in the upper part of their course, and by their Persian (Tajik) names in their lower course. Thus we have the Ak-su known lower down as the Murghab, the Gurumdi known as the Ghunt. In one district there are two small streams flowing together side by side. One has a Kirghiz (Turki) name—Kok-uy-bel, because the glen through which it flows is frequented by Kirghiz. The other bears the Persian name of Kuh-darah, because there is a Tajik village close beside the entrance to its valley.

CHAPTER XV.

FORT PAMIR

FROM this brief geographical summary I pass to the little Russian outpost of Fort Pamir, and a brief account of the very pleasant time I spent there between 19th March and 7th April 1894.

Fort Pamir, situated on the right bank of the Murghab, at an altitude of 11,800 feet above sea-level, was built as a check upon Chinese and Afghan aggressions upon the territories of the former Khans of Kokand. Although the Russians conquered the khanate in 1875 and 1876, for some time they bestowed but little thought upon the region of the Pamirs. It was only thinly populated and very difficult of access, and possessed nothing to invite attention. General Skobeleff, for as far-sighted as he was, never seems to have given it a thought. But when the neighbouring powers began to stretch out their hands towards it, Russia awoke to the necessity for energetic action. Colonel Yonnoff's famous expedition was the first result of the change of policy on the part of the St. Petersburg authorities. It was an expedition which opened up political questions of a grave and delicate character; which however were satisfactorily terminated by the labours of the Anglo-Russian Boundary Commission in the summer of 1895.

As regards Fort Pamir, I may mention that it was built by the men of the fourth battalion of the Russian army of Turkestan in the year 1893, between the 2nd July (O.S.) and the 30th October. The outer wall, which forms an oblong, was constructed of sods and bags of sand, and encloses a fair-sized courtyard, around which are ranged the officers' quarters, and a

NORTHERN FACE OF FORT PAMIR

long earthen structure, covered in with beams, and containing barracks, kitchens, hospital, bath-rooms, workshops, and so forth. The commissariat stores and ammunition are kept in yurts. There is also a little meteorological station, where observations are taken three times every day. In the corners of the longer side which faces the north are two platforms, each furnished with a battery of Maxim-Nordenfeldt machine-guns. The fort occupies a commanding position on a terrace of conglomerate, which overlooks, but at some distance away, the right or northern bank of the Murghab. Between the two extends a marsh or morass, out of which gush a great number of springs of clear water. Fort Pamir is a striking testimonial and proof of the energy and spirit of the officers who built it. For it was anything but an easy task to erect such a structure at that high altitude and at such an immense distance from the resources of civilization. Every inch of timber and every ounce of other building material had to be transported on horses' backs all the way from Osh in Fergana, pretty nearly by the route I have described. The months in which the work was done were unusually stormy; furious hurricanes of blinding snow, mingled with fine sand, being of frequent occurrence. Part of the time both officers and men dwelt in Kirghiz yurts, which were again and again blown over by the wind.

Within the last few years a new route has been opened to Kashgar, and the merchants of that town now resort to the southern Pamirs, where they traffic with the Kirghiz, bartering the wares they bring with them for sheep. They then drive the sheep down to the market-towns of Fergana, where they make a good price of them; and so return home to Kashgar by way of the passes of Terek-davan and Talldik, with a substantial profit in their pockets.

The commandant of Fort Pamir, Captain V. N. Saitseff, was a settler of long standing in Turkestan. As aide-de-camp to General Skobeleff he took part in the campaign against Khiva in 1873, and in that against Kokand in

1875–6. Besides being commandant of the fort, he was also governor of the Kirghiz population of the Pamirs.

Of Fort Pamir I have none but the happiest recollections. I reached it at the end of a long, toilsome journey through an uninhabited and difficult mountainous waste, and was received in that little outlying fragment of mighty Russia with open arms, more like an old friend or long-standing acquaintance, by a group of officers who, I have no hesitation in saying, were as amiable, as courteous, as generous a set of men as it is possible to meet with. And without undue self-love, I can flatter myself, that my arrival formed a not unpleasing diversion in the lonely and monotonous life which the garrison of the fort are compelled to lead during the greater portion of the year. For all winter through, ever since September of the previous year, not a soul had been near the fort except the Kirghiz. As soon therefore as the Russian officers learned from the mounted couriers I sent on in advance, that I was approaching, they hurried up to the battery platforms, armed with every field-glass that could be got in the fort, and swept the horizon northwards until my caravan came into sight. And when I rode in through the gate, I was received with the warmest of welcomes by every man of the garrison.

Fort Pamir often reminded me of a ship at sea. The outer walls might be likened to the bulwarks; the wide, open, sweeping valley of the Murghab to the sea; and the courtyard to the deck. Up and down this latter we used to walk day after day, stopping every now and again to gaze through our powerful field-glasses towards the far-distant horizon—a view which never varied in its dull lifelessness, except on one day in the week. That was Tuesday, when all eyes were early on the alert for a single, solitary horseman, the post-courier (jighit), who brought the eagerly-expected mails from far-off Russia. His arrival was the great event of the week.

When his horse trots in through the gate, every man of the garrison hurries out to receive him. The commandant's adjutant makes haste to open the mail-bags. Everybody

INTERIOR OF FORT PAMIR, LOOKING SOUTH

stands around in anxious expectation. The adjutant draws forth the letters, newspapers, post-parcels from those they love, now alas! so far off. He distributes them to the happy recipients. Joy reigns supreme, except in the bosoms of the unhappy beings for whom this Asiatic Father Christmas has brought no heart-warming gift. For three post-days in succession I was counted amongst the unenvied ones. This was because of the alteration in my route. All my letters were sent on to Kashgar, with the result that for a period of four whole months I never received a single letter from home. The contents of the mail-bags distributed, the rest of the day is spent in greedily devouring the welcome home news. Evening comes. Officers and men meet for dinner, each in their own quarters. But all alike pursue one common topic of conversation—the events which have been happening recently in the great world of politics and human action from one end of the world to the other.

Our day was generally spent in the following manner. Every man had tea (first breakfast) in his own room. At noon precisely a signal by roll of drum called us all together for a substantial breakfast. After that we had tea again in our own private quarters. At six o'clock a fresh drum-signal reminded us that dinner was ready. After dinner we broke up into little groups, to each of which coffee was served round. We then talked until late into the night; and towards midnight I and the commandant used to have a snack of supper.

Drill filled up most of the morning hours. The soldiers and Cossacks were also during the course of the day instructed in certain of the sciences which have a bearing upon military matters. But my time was for the most part occupied in more peaceable pursuits, for one thing photography. In the evening, when I developed my plates, I was usually surrounded by half-a-dozen closely interested spectators, who never tired of watching how, as by a wizard's "pass," the frigid mountain scenery and its half-wild inhabitants imparted life and meaning to the photographic plates.

Amongst other things we measured the volume of the water carried down by the Murghab, and set up a gauge-post in the river, upon which one of the officers might observe the rise and fall of the current during the coming spring and summer. We also measured the depth to which the crust of the earth is frozen in winter; and industriously compared notes upon what we had seen and observed. The soundings I made in Kara-kul awakened the liveliest interest. Nobody had expected that the lake would go down to anything like a depth of 756 feet.

One of my friends in Margelan told me that Fort Pamir was an earthly paradise. I asked him "Why?"

He replied, "Because there are no women there!"

Although I am very far from sharing his opinion, I am bound to confess, it would not be easy to find a circle in which contentment, cheerful spirits, and the tone of light and easy comradeship are better preserved than they were at Fort Pamir. Nobody cared a rush about appearances. The officers went about in threadbare uniforms, and with their boots unpolished. Nobody wasted time on the niceties of the toilet. Directly we heard the dinner-bell, or rather drum, we went straight into the mess-room without stopping to don such superfluous articles as collar and cuffs. No need to furbish up all the pretty sayings a polished man of the world feels it obligatory upon him to whisper in the ear of the lady he takes in to dinner. In a word, everybody at Fort Pamir was perfectly free, subject to no irksome social restraints. Cossacks prepared and cooked the food we ate. Cossacks waited at table. Cossacks rubbed us down in the bathroom, acted as house and chamber-maids, even washed our dirty linen. There was not the faintest glimpse of a petticoat to be seen inside Fort Pamir. The only creatures of the female sex within its walls, so far as I was able to ascertain, were a female cat, a couple of bitches, and some hens. But to call Fort Pamir a paradise because no woman brightened it with her lovely smile—that is a doctrine I certainly cannot subscribe to.

Captain Saitseff enjoyed the full sympathy and esteem

THE JIGHITS' TENTS AT FORT PAMIR

of his officers, and maintained the strictest discipline and good order amongst the men under his command. The long dreary winter, during which the little garrison had been straitly shut up within the walls of their fort, like a band of Polar explorers compelled to winter in their ice-bound vessel, had not occasioned the least slackening of discipline, the least indifference or discontent amongst either officers or men. Nevertheless the immediate approach of spring, which was indicated by the increased

RUSSIANS AND KIRGHIZ AT FORT PAMIR

warmth of the sun's rays, by the melting of the snows on the mountains, and of the ice on the lakes and rivers, seemed to re-awaken several dominant interests. It was a season when every day brought fresh opportunities for scientific observation. Already the birds had begun their summer migrations. Small flocks of ducks and geese of a great variety of species were on the wing from their winter-quarters in India to their summer haunts in Siberia. The Murghab was apparently one of their favourite resting-places, where alas! several of them entered upon a rest that was destined to prove unexpectedly long. The Cossacks spread their nets in the river. Others of the garrison took their sporting-rifles and stalked the wary arkhari or wild sheep (*Ovis Poli*), and not seldom brought home a pretty well filled bag.

The relations between officers and men were in all respects excellent. On one occasion, when thirty time-expired men were setting off to return to their homes in Osh, it was quite touching to see how, in orthodox Russian fashion, their superiors kissed each man three times on the cheeks. Their rifle on their shoulder and

THE CONGLOMERATE TERRACE ON WHICH FORT PAMIR STANDS

their knapsack on their back, the men set out right cheerfully to tramp the long 280 miles which should bring them to their more genial homes in the warm valleys of Fergana.

Sunday was given up to all kinds of games and dancing. The music was but poor, being limited to a concertina, two drums, a triangle, and a couple of cymbals; but the performers went to work with a will, and made the very most of their resources, whilst the cleverest of the Cossacks danced their national *kamarensky* with such spirit that the dust whirled up around them in clouds. Then, when the sun set, and the west wind, which at regular intervals during the day had swept past the fort with an angry howl, subsided, there rose upon the rarefied mountain air a succession of Russian songs, sung by some seventy fresh, strong voices. They were partly folk-songs with a melancholy cadence, partly soldiers' ditties of a livelier character. The last Sunday of my stay at Fort Pamir was closed by a musical evening of this kind. The atmosphere was still and calm, the air cold; the stars glittered with indescribable brilliancy; and the gentle murmur of the Murghab stole upon the ear in the pauses of the singing. The soldiers sang with much feeling, as though their hearts were touched by memories of their far-off native land; and their officers and myself listened with genuine sympathy, as their fresh, warm voices melted away into the lofty regions of immeasurable space.

LANDSCAPE NEAR FORT PAMIR, LOOKING NORTH-WEST

Russian Officers returning from a Hunt

THE MUSTAGH-ATA AND ITS GLACIERS

CHAPTER XVI.

FROM THE MURGHAB TO BULUN-KUL

ON 7th April 1894, after partaking of a substantial breakfast, I bade adieu to Fort Pamir, though I was escorted a good distance on my way by the commandant and his officers. Arrived at the little torrent of Ak-baital, we found some of the Cossacks awaiting us with tea. Then, having thanked my Russian friends for the splendid hospitality they had shown me during those never-to-be-forgotten days—a last shake of the hand from the saddle, a last wave of the cap, and away I spurred towards the north, followed by the interpreter of the fort, the Tatar, Kul Mametieff, whom the commandant sent with me as a guard of honour.

Just as daylight was fading, we came to the twin lakes Shor-kul and Rang-kul, which are connected by a narrow sound. There we took up our quarters for the night, camping in a *yulameika*, a tall, conical tent with no smoke-vent. Meanwhile my right-hand man, Rehim Bai, had fallen ill, and all the way to Kashgar was totally unfitted to discharge his regular duties. We had to transport him thither like a bale of goods on the back of a camel. His place was taken by the man of whom I have spoken before—Islam Bai; and it was during this part of my journey that I first learned to know and value that excellent man's many excellent qualities.

The snow lay in scanty patches; but both lakes were sealed with thick sheets of ice. Strange to say, however, the sound between them was open water, and swarmed with wild-duck and wild-geese. The configuration of the ground—grassy plains sloping gently down towards the lakes—suggested that the lakes themselves were shallow.

Next day I sent the caravan by the nearest road to the little fort of Rang-kul; whilst I myself with four men started across the ice of Rang-kul to take soundings. We only chopped out two holes, and found that the lake was as a matter of fact extraordinarily shallow, the two measurements giving 5 feet and 6½ feet respectively. The ice, on which was a thin sprinkling of snow, was 3 feet and 3¼ feet thick where the two sounding-holes were hewn. There was a small open channel close alongside the shore. The temperature of the water in the sounding-holes was 31°6 Fahr. (–0°2 C.); at the bottom, which was covered with loose slime and mud, mingled with decayed vegetable matter, it was 37° (2°8 C.). The vegetable matter consisted almost exclusively of algæ and sedges. The word *ranga* is used to indicate the sedge *Carex physoides*. All the same, it is more likely that the lake derives its name from the wild-goat which frequents that region, and which is known as the *rang* and the *kiyick*.

The word Shor-kul means "salt lake," and its waters were both salt and bitter. It was pretty evident that, while Rang-kul was fed by fresh springs and streams, Shor-kul derived its supplies from Rang-kul through the little sound already spoken of; and that evaporation went on to a very much greater extent in the former, leaving the saline concentrates behind it. In the eastern end of Rang-kul there was a long narrow island, barely a dozen feet high, but with perpendicular shores of soft greyish-blue clay, much eaten into by the waters of the lake. Vast numbers of wild geese are said to breed there every spring as soon as the ice melts.

The soundings taken, we rode straight across the lake, and on to the fort, garrisoned by about two-score Cossacks under a commandant. We stayed there two days. We left the fort on the 11th April, riding almost due east towards the little pass of Sarik-gai, which crosses a spur of the northern mountains. On the west side of the hill we were approaching, the wind, mostly coming from the west, had heaped up enormous masses of sand, shaping them into gigantic dunes or billows with a slightly corrugated surface. On the other side of the pass we descended into the broad, open, level valley of Naisa-tash, in which were two Kirghiz auls (tent-villages). We took up our quarters in the one which stood farthest east. It consisted of five yurts (tents), occupied by nineteen individuals of the Chighit tribe, ten of them being men. They spend the winter and summer beside Lake Rang-kul; but cross over into the valley of Naisa-tash for the spring grazing. Their wealth in live-stock embraced 400 sheep, 40 yaks, 7 camels, and 3 horses.

On the following day, April the 12th, we were to cross the provisional frontier-line between the Russian and Chinese Pamirs. Ever since we left Rang-kul we had seen glittering immediately ahead of us the snowy crests of Sarik-kol. That lofty range we had to climb over. Out of the several passes which lead over it I chose the one known as Chuggatai, 15,500 feet in altitude. We struck off towards the north-east. The inclination increased the further we advanced, until at the foot of the pass it became very steep and difficult. The track too was not at all easy, being strewn with large blocks of gneiss and clay-slate, still draped for the most part with snow. On the summit of the pass, which had a high, sharp pitch like a house-roof, we halted to rest; and whilst resting were surprised by a violent hailstorm, which came out of the south-west. The temperature was 5° Fahr. below freezing-point (– 2°8 C.).

The descent towards the north, on the other side of the range, was equally as steep as the ascent had been; and it cost us a wearisome march to reach the first aul of Chuggatai—a little collection of four yurts with twenty-four inhabitants. But we pushed on to another aul of six yurts a short distance lower down. There we made our first camp on Chinese territory.

I speedily learned that all sorts of wildly extravagant rumours were flying about the neighbourhood concerning me. It was said, that I was a Russian, coming at the head of three-score Cossacks, armed to the teeth, to make a hostile raid into Chinese territory. My arrival had therefore been looked forward to with not a little apprehension. But when the Kirghiz saw me ride up alone, accompanied by only a small band of their fellow-believers, their fears quickly subsided, and they gave me a very friendly welcome. All the same, they lost no time in sending off a mounted messenger to Jan Darin, commandant of the little Chinese fort of Bulun-kul.

The next morning therefore I was not surprised to see the emissaries of the Chinese officer ride up, bringing greetings of welcome. They were also charged to find out who I was, and what was my business. The head of the "embassy" was one Osman Beg of Taghdumbash, a fine-looking Kirghiz, with a handsome, intelligent countenance. He commanded a *lanza* or troop at Bulun-kul. His companions were Yar Mohammed Beg, chief of the frontier-guard stationed at Kiyak-bash, and a mollah or priest. All three wore white turbans and parti-coloured khalats (long Kirghiz coats). Their mission accomplished, they rode back to Bulun-kul, to make their report.

The aul (tent-village) was situated near the junction of the Chuggatai and Ak-berdi valleys. At that point the stream has cut its way to a great depth into the thick conglomerate strata, so that the huge boulders of coarse crystalline rock, which overhung the current, threatened every moment to topple down the precipitous banks into the river. The valley of Ak-berdi was also eroded to a great depth, and was obstructed with blocks of conglomerate. Consequently, agreeably to what I have said above, the chain of Sarik-kol forms the boundary line between two widely differing areas of physical conformation. On the inner side it is flanked by a region of Central depression, with broad, shallow, level valleys, possessing no drainage outlet towards the ocean. On its outer side, that is towards the east, it overlooks a Peripheral region, where the valleys are deep and narrow, and the effects of the erosive action of the outward flowing streams assume grandiose proportions.

On the 13th April we made only a very short stage,

as far as the point where the valley of Ak-berdi runs out into the valley of Sarik-kol. The accommodation provided for me there consisted of one miserable yurt, covered with ragged felts. For precaution's sake it was put up at a distance of three *kitchkerim* or "shouts" (*i.e.*, the distance to which the human voice can be heard when raised in a loud shout) from the fort. We had scarcely got our baggage stowed away in something like order, when a *yuz-bashi* (chief of one hundred men) came to announce that the acting commandant of Bulun-kul, the Kirghiz officer Tura Kelldi Savgan, together with Chao Darin, his Chinese colleague of Tar-bashi, a little fort at the mouth of the Ghez valley, were on the way to pay me a visit. I had barely time to get outside the yurt, when up they trotted, with half a score Chinese soldiers at their heels. A gay spectacle they made too, with their grey trousers, shoes, and scarlet tunics, decorated with large Chinese ideographs (language signs) in black. Every man was armed with a rifle, and rode a white horse, bearing a red saddle and big stirrups which rattled noisily. I invited them to step inside the tent, and bade my men serve round an extra dainty dastarkhan (lunch), consisting of sardines, chocolate, preserved fruits, sweet cakes, and liqueur—delicacies which I had brought with me from Margelan specially to tickle the Chinese palate. Chao Darin conceived a particularly strong affection for the liqueur, and inquired how much a man could drink without getting intoxicated. My cigarettes too met with much appreciation; although my Chinese friend Chao Darin preferred his own silver-mounted water-pipe.

Conversation was carried on between myself and the mandarin under considerable difficulties. At that time I was not sufficiently master of the Kirghiz tongue to be able to speak it fluently. I therefore expressed myself to Kul Mametieff in Russian. Kul Mametieff conveyed my meaning in the Turki language to the mandarin's interpreter, a Sart from Turfan, and *he* in his turn passed on the message in Chinese to Chao Darin.

Tura Kelldi Savgan was a pleasant man, with a good

deal of vivacity of manner, at once a smart and cautious diplomatist. As soon as they learned of my intention to make an attempt to climb Mus-tagh-ata, they objected to Kul Mametieff going with me, on the ground that he was a subject of Russia. But when I showed them my pass, and the letter I carried from Shu King Sheng, the Chinese ambassador at the Court of St. Petersburg, addressed to the Dao Tai of Kashgar, they withdrew their opposition, but stipulated that, immediately we came down from the mountain, Kul Mametieff should take the shortest road back to the Russian Pamirs. On the other hand a Kirghiz *allik-bashi*, a non-commissioned officer who nominally commanded fifty men, was bidden go back at once, having no pass. I then proposed to send Rehim Bai on a camel direct to Kashgar, for his illness was assuming a critical phase, and he was in urgent need of rest and comfortable quarters. But to this Tura Kelldi Savgan would not agree; for if, said he, Rehim Bai were to die on the road, his death would involve the Chinese authorities in difficulties. It was only by promising to return to Bulun-kul when I came back from my ascent of Mus-tagh-ata, and not make for Kashgar by any other route, that I finally succeeded in overcoming the last of their scruples. Even then I had to leave behind in their hands one of my men as a hostage, together with one-half of my baggage. This compact made, I announced that it was my intention to return their visit without delay; but both officers declared, that they had no authority to admit a European inside the fort in the absence of the commandant, Jan Darin, who had gone to Kashgar. But Jan Darin would soon return, they said.

In this laborious way we parleyed backwards and forwards for five mortal hours. When at last they rose to go, I thought to make a good impression upon them by presenting them with a Tula *kinshal* (dagger) and a silver drinking-cup. They protested, it was not at all the right thing for me to offer *them* presents after such a *recherché* dastarkhan; that it ought to be the other way on, seeing that I was their guest. But in the end they suffered themselves to be persuaded, saying they hoped to have an opportunity to return my presents when I came back from my trip up the Mus-tagh-ata. Having taken their leave in due form, they galloped off in a whirlwind of dust, through which their white horses, their scarlet uniforms, their glittering weapons were for a long distance dimly visible. And we never saw a glimpse of the gentlemen again; although they indicated their presence by forbidding the Kirghiz of the neighbourhood to furnish me with supplies of mutton, fuel, and other necessaries.

The rest of the day was spent in making preparations for the ascent of Mus-tagh-ata. I decided to take only four men with me, namely Kul Mametieff, Islam Bai, and the two Kirghiz, Omar and Khoda Verdi. Four pack-horses were got ready to carry the necessary baggage—provisions, bed, furs, presents, medicine-chest, photographic apparatus, scientific instruments, and several other indispensable articles. Everything else was left behind in the care of Khoja, the Sart, who was also charged to look after Rehim Bai. The more comfortable quarters I succeeded in getting for the invalid had done him no good. The winter journey over the Pamirs had completely broken him down. His cheeks were white and hollow, his eyes big and with a vacant glassy stare in them. His friends would scarcely have recognized him, he was so changed. He offered a he-goat to Allah, and declared that he felt a little better in consequence.

In the evening we were honoured with a visit from some of the Chinese soldiers from the fort. They begged to be allowed to peep into one or two of my commissariat boxes and yakhtans (packing-cases). We afterwards learnt that up at the fort they believed all my boxes were packed full of Russian soldiers, who in that way were being smuggled across the frontier. The fact that each and every trunk I had was only capable of holding at the most about one-half of a soldier did not in any way help to allay their suspicions. I opened two or three, and after that they appeared to be easier in their minds. During the night the Chinese placed sentries all round my tent; but they had the good feeling to post them at a distance and out of sight. It was plain, they had received orders to keep us under surveillance, and find out what was my real purpose in visiting this remote corner of the vast Chinese empire.

Whichever way we turned, we had a magnificent view before us. Due east, on the opposite side of the little lake of Bulun-kul, rose the sublime snow-clad mountain mass of Ak-tau, the "White Mountain," the northern continuation of Mus-tagh-ata. On the left of it was the beginning of the Ghez valley, and on the right the broad trough of Sarik-kol. In the near foreground, and only a short distance from our camp, was the little Kirghiz aul of half-a-dozen yurts; whilst the mountain-slopes around were dotted with long-haired yaks, grunting as they grazed. To the south lay the beginning of the narrow glen called Kum-yilga, the "Sand Ravine."

CHAPTER XVII.

MUS-TAGH-ATA

IT was the 14th April when we set off to climb the great Mus-tagh-ata. Immediately after we started, we were met by a violent storm from the east, which drove clouds of fine drift-sand straight into our eyes. Having passed the two little lakes of Bulun-kul and taken a distant glance at the fort, we turned up the broad valley of Sarik-kol. For fully an hour we were followed by a big black yak. We wondered whether he was trained to play the part of spy; but eventually he grew tired of keeping up with us, and stopped.

The valley of Sarik-kol is a gigantic trench, piercing to the heart of the stupendous Pamir plateau. Sometimes narrow, sometimes expanding to a considerable width, its bottom is littered with huge boulders of gneiss and other rocky *débris*, all polished smooth by the action of water. At one place we came to a colossal erratic block of gneiss split clean in two, in such a way that we were able to ride between the two halves as though we were going through the gateway of a mediæval town. The valley itself was hemmed in on both sides by lofty mountains, the flanks of which were thickly strewn with crumbled and disintegrated rocks. Scantily supplied with pasture grounds, it was uninhabited except for a single solitary yurt. On the whole it sloped up gradually and easily towards the foot of Mus-tagh-ata.

We soon perceived that we were no longer travelling in the Russian portion of the Pamirs. When we came to the end of our day's march, we found no yurt ready pitched for us by Kirghiz sent on in advance. We were now, plainly enough, on the Chinese side of the frontier. We were no longer to be indulged with such luxuries and comforts. How many a night after that did we not sleep under the open sky! Such was our fate on this the first night of our trip. We endeavoured to make the best of circumstances, by looking about for a hollow that was in some degree sheltered from the wind. We found one in a part of the valley called Kayindeh-dala (the Birch Plain). A singularly inappropriate name, for the ground was stony and barren, and there was not a single specimen of the graceful green lacework which drapes the birch to be seen. Very possibly however the name is a survival from a time when those trees did grow in the locality.

We encamped under the shelter of a huge block of gneiss, which leaned over a little towards the south. Round the front of it somebody had built up a low wall of stones, which afforded some measure of protection against at any rate the worst of the wind. We piled the baggage all round us, spread out our carpets, and made our camp as comfortable as we could; and when shortly afterwards our ears were greeted with the bubbling of the soup over the fire of teresken faggots we were as happy as kings. But the wind whistled in through the crevices between the stones, and dust and sand kept swirling round us in eddies, so that our teeth gritted every time we took a mouthful of food. Once during the evening it snowed a little, but about ten o'clock the weather changed with marvellous suddenness. The atmosphere became calm, and the sky clear. Then the moon came forth and poured her light into our grotto, and lit up the desolate scene, deepening the oppressive silence and making the valley appear ten times more dreary and awe-inspiring than it was before.

April 15th. The farther we went towards the south, the more broken grew the surface. We came to the little Alpine lake of Bassyk-kul, with its fantastic shore-line, leading me to think that its deep inlets must have been carved out by the most capricious of the brownies. The middle of the lake was crusted with ice, brittle and porous;

but close in beside the shore we saw open water. It was pure, limpid, and sweet to the taste. At a short distance from the lake, I observed an old Chinese inscription engraved on a block of gneiss, that was deeply embedded in the ground and surrounded by a rough wall of stones. Close by were two other gneiss boulders, both bearing signs of having been subjected to the smoothing, polishing action of glacial ice. On one of them I just discerned traces of an inscription similar to that on the stone already mentioned, but most of the lettering had been obliterated by the wind and its powerful ally, the drift-sand. The place where the stones were was called Tamga-tash or the Signet Stone.

A low hill in the vicinity gave us a distant view of the Little Kara-kul, a beautiful Alpine lake embosomed in deep mountains, whose reflections played upon its surface, constantly changing its waters from blue to green and from green to blue. The ice was all gone, except for a small strip near the southern shore. A fresh breeze was blowing off the lake, ruffling its surface with foam-tipped waves, which chased one another in endless succession, and finally broke against the shore with a rhythmical and harmonious murmur.

The path gradually approached closer to the lake, until it was only separated from it by a chain of low hills, the surviving remnant, as I discovered on a second visit, of an ancient moraine. That I should come back again to that lake, I little dreamed at the time I first saw it; and yet I did come back, and its lovely shores grew dear to me! How many a lonely evening did I not lie and listen to the mysterious tidings which those melodious wavelets whispered, and which there was none to interpret! And how many a time did I not feast my eyes upon those giant mountains, which mirrored their snowy crests in the transparent waters of the lake of Little Kara-kul! But I shall have occasion to relate my recollections of the place in a subsequent chapter, and therefore I hasten on with my journey.

In some places the cliffs, along which the path ran, had

crumbled away, and we were obliged to scramble down as best we could, and ride through the water along the ridge of commingled *débris* and gravel. On the south of the lake we struck into the broad valley watered by the stream Su-bashi, where large herds of shaggy yaks were busy plucking the young spring grass. In the meantime the wind had quickened up into a veritable storm. Dense clouds of dust and sand, and even fine particles of abraded rock, blew straight into our faces, with such violence that we were sometimes compelled to stand still and turn our backs to the storm. When we came to the fort that guards the valley, we found the Chinese as busy as bees unpacking and inspecting a fresh consignment of stores which had just come in for the garrison. But we were met by a stalwart horseman, Togdasin Beg, chief of the Kirghiz of Su-bashi. He received me politely and in a friendly spirit, and conducted me to his large and handsomely appointed yurt. This man subsequently became one of my best friends amongst the many I made in Asia.

As soon as we got our tent in order, we were honoured by a stream of visitors, who kept coming all the evening. First there were all the Kirghiz of the neighbourhood. Then we had the Chinese soldiers of the garrison, amongst them some Dungans (Chinese Mohammedans). All the sick too of the valley came to me begging for medicine. One old woman said she had the Kokand sickness. Another patient suffered from toothache. A third had a pain in his nose. One of the Dungan soldiers experienced an uncomfortable feeling in his stomach when a storm was blowing. And so they went on. I treated them one and all in the same simple fashion, by prescribing for each alike a small dose of quinine. And on the principle that the bitterer the remedy the more efficacious it is—a principle which is thoroughly believed in by all Asiatics—they went away universally satisfied.

The next day we were entertained at tea by the notables of the Kirghiz auls and by certain of the Chinese soldiers. In the evening Togdasin Beg came to my tent by invita-

TOGDASIN BEG

tion, and was entertained with a liqueur and the harmonies of a musical-box, which so enraptured him, that he declared he felt twenty years younger. He said he had never enjoyed anything so much since the days when the great Yakub Beg ruled over Kashgar. Somewhere about twenty years earlier, he told me, the Sultan of Turkey sent a large musical-box as a present to Yakub Beg.

Ever since I left the Alaï valley my thoughts had been constantly running upon the ascent of Mus-tagh-ata, and I neglected no opportunity of gathering from the Kirghiz all the information I could at all bearing upon the project. But every man I talked to, without exception, assured me that it would be utterly impossible to reach the top. The precipices and yawning chasms would prove insuperable obstacles to progress. The flanks of the mountain were sheathed in ice as bright and smooth as glass. On them and on the summit storms roared without cessation; and if I were so venturesome as to defy the giant, he would bid the winds sweep me away like a grain of sand.

But Mus-tagh-ata is truly a magnificent mountain. Whenever the Kirghiz pass it, or first catch sight of it in the course of a journey, they fall upon their knees and say their prayers. They declare that it is the abode of three score and ten saints. Nay, they assert that it is one gigantic masar or burial-mound of saints. Within its interior dwell amongst others the souls of Moses and Ali, the son-in-law and nephew of the prophet Mohammed. When Ali lay at the point of death, he prophesied to those about him, that as soon as the breath was gone out of his body, a white camel would come down from heaven and carry him away. As he said, so it came to pass. When he was dead, the white camel appeared, took the holy man on its back, and hastened with him to Mus-tagh-ata. The Kirghiz are firmly convinced that Moses' soul also abides in that mountain; and for that reason they sometimes call it Hazrett-i-Musa or the Holy Moses.

The Kirghiz of Su-bashi told me this story about the holy mountain. Many hundred years ago an aged *ishan* (holy man) went up the mountain by himself. And when he came a certain way up it, he found a lake and a little stream, with a white camel grazing on the shore. There was also a large garden planted with plum-trees, and under the plum-trees there walked to and fro a number of venerable old men dressed in white garments. The holy man plucked some of the fruit and ate it. Then came one of the venerable inhabitants of the garden, and said to him, that it was well he had done so; for if he had despised the fruit, as all those aged men had done, he would have been condemned like them to stay on the mountain, walking up and down the garden, to the end of time. Then came a rider on a white horse, and caught up the holy man, and galloped with him down the steep mountain-side. And when the ishan came to himself, he found that he was down in the valley, and could only remember dimly all the marvellous things he had seen.

There is also another legend associated with this part of the world, dating from the time when the famous Khan Khoja ruled over all the lands that lie between Kashgar and Manas in Dzungaria. The Chinese sent two emissaries to Khan Khoja, offering him peace; but he refused to accept it. One of the emissaries he killed, and cut off the ears and nose of the other, and so sent him back to the Emperor of China. This put the Emperor beside himself with rage. He bade his men fill three big cooking-pots with nails. Then he had the nails counted, and took a vow, that he would send against Khan Khoja as many soldiers as there were nails in all three pots. Khan Khoja had an army of 70,000 men, and for one whole month he lay encamped near Manas over against the innumerable host of the Chinese. But at last battle was joined, and Khan Khoja was defeated with the loss of 38,000 men; whereupon he marched back to Kashgar with the remnant of his army, and from Kashgar pushed on to Bulun-kul, where another battle was fought. Again the Khan was defeated, and again he retreated, going as far as the lake of Little Kara-kul. There he was once more hard pressed by the Chinese; but at the critical moment, when things again began to look desperate for him, a band of forty horsemen, giants in size and mounted on raven-black horses, galloped down Mus-tagh-ata and, flinging themselves upon the Chinese, decided the battle in Khan Khoja's favour.

Now there was in his army the *palevan* (hero) Chum Kar Kashka Bater, and he was counselled by his master, never, so long as he was engaged in fight, to look behind him. If he obeyed, he would always be victorious; but if he disobeyed, he would perish. In three fights Chum Kar obeyed his master, and so overcame his adversaries. But in the fourth he glanced behind him; and in the moment he did so, was struck by an arrow and slain. The hero's masar, or tomb, stands on a dominant buttress of the west flank of Mus-tagh-ata. One of the glaciers of the mountain commemorates the hero's name to the present day.

But the Chinese soon gathered another army, numbering as many men as the stars in the sky, and came and fell upon Khan Khoja near the lake of Little Kara-kul. Thereupon the forty horsemen withdrew and rode back up Mus-tagh-ata—an ending, by the way, strangely at variance with all the imaginative tales I am acquainted with! Khan Khoja's evil star still remained in the ascendant. He was worsted again, and fled to Rang-kul and Kornei-tarti. But the Chinese pursued after him and compelled him to give battle once again. His army was routed and scattered like chaff, so that at last the Khan was left alone with none but his trumpeter to bear him company. Then the Khan bade the trumpeter sound his trumpet. Instantly the scattered fragments of his forces were gathered around him. But they were far too weak to stand against the Chinese, who drove them before them, pursuing them over hill and valley until they had slain nearly all of them. When Khan Khoja at length came to Yeshil-kul (the Green Lake), he had but fifty faithful followers left. There he went up alone into a high mountain; but when he looked down, his men were surrounded by their enemies, the Chinese. Khan Khoja gave them a sign with his hand, and they flung themselves into the lake. Then lo and behold! a new marvel happened. They would not sink; and the Chinese shot at them as though they had been shooting wild-duck or other game. But Khan Khoja took up a handful of dust, muttered a prayer over it, and cast it over the lake. In a moment the heroic fifty disappeared beneath the waves. The Khan himself fled to Badakshan; but the Shah of Badakshan cut off his head and sent it to the Chinese. His body was taken possession of by certain of his friends, and by them sent to Kashgar, where it lies buried in Hazrett-Apak.

The Kirghiz tell further, that on the top of Mus-tagh-ata there exists an ancient city named Janaidar, which was built in the days when universal happiness and universal peace reigned throughout the world. But since that time there has been no intercourse between the people of Janaidar and the inhabitants of the earth. Consequently the former still enjoy an existence of unblemished happiness. In the city of bliss there are fruit-trees which bear magnificent fruit all the year round, flowers which never wither, women who never grow old and never lose their beauty. The choicest pleasures of life are as common there as bread; death, cold, and darkness are banished from its confines for ever.

In a word, Mus-tagh-ata resembles Mount Demavend in northern Persia, and other strikingly conspicuous mountains, in being invested with a halo of mystery and made the centre of a tissue of fantastic legends and stories. The half-wild Kirghiz look upon it as a holy mountain, and regard it with profound reverence and fear. No wonder then the European does not escape the magic glamour of its spell!

Mus-tagh-ata, the loftiest mountain of the Pamirs, and one of the loftiest mountains in the world, towers up to the height of 25,600 feet, and like a mighty bastion overlooks the barren wastes of Central Asia. It is the culminating point in a meridional chain, the Mus-tagh or Ice Mountains, a chain that is worthy to rank with the stupendous ranges which converge upon the Roof of the World—the Himalayas, Kwen-lun, Kara-korum, Hindu-kush. The unchallenged pre-eminence of Mus-tagh-ata over the peaks which cluster around it is proved by its name, which means the Father of the Ice Mountains. And the name is very appropriate; for truly, like a father, it lifts its white head amongst its children, which in their turn are all clad in white robes of snowy purity and sheathed in breastplates of ice. The silvery sheen of the great mountain flashes like the gleam of a lighthouse to a vast distance across the desert ocean. Many a time have I gazed wonderingly upon it from afar off. Many a month have I wandered on its rugged flanks. Many a night and many a day have I been, as it were, spell-bound by the weird mystery of its fascinations.

Upon questioning the Kirghiz of Su-bashi as to the possibility of climbing the patriarch of the snows, I found they were not so discouraging in their opinions as were their kinsmen in the inner parts of the Pamirs. They were all quite willing to accompany me, and ready to further my purpose to the utmost of their ability. All the same, they prophesied, that the attempt would be a failure. Hunters who had lost their way whilst pursuing game into the higher reaches of the mountain had become giddy through breathing the "heavy" air. Even the agile and sure-footed wild sheep had been known to recoil in terror from the brink of the icy precipices, when driven out towards them by a posse of hunters. Nor was the imperial eagle able to swing himself up to the topmost pinnacles; his wings grew numb before he could reach them.

As a consequence of all this we planned a formal and elaborate campaign against the giant, and resolved, cost what it would, to conquer him. Our plan was to lie in ambush and keep a close watch upon him, and seize the first careless moment, *i.e.* take advantage of the earliest favourable days as regards weather, to deliver our attack. We decided to establish a third depôt at the highest possible point, and therefrom make our reconnaissances and take measures for advancing further.

CHAPTER XVIII.

AN ATTEMPT TO CLIMB MUS-TAGH-ATA

IN the course of a long exploring journey, the traveller's plans are often upset by annoying difficulties and hindrances, causing him to deviate from the route he laid down beforehand, and compelling him to abandon objects which he had set his heart upon attaining. I encountered a reverse of this character in my attempt to scale Mus-tagh-ata. It was my desire, as it was also my intention, to climb to the summit of the mountain, examine its geological structure, its coat of ice-mail, and the gigantic glaciers which plough their slow way down its rugged sides. But alas! Instead of carrying out this plan, and achieving the proud consciousness of standing far above the heads of all peoples and princes in the world, and having five continents under my feet, with only a few Asiatic mountain-peaks above me, I was compelled to return, with my strength broken and my eyes bandaged, and seek a warmer climate.

However, on the morning of 17th April I found a picturesque troop awaiting me when I stepped outside my yurt. It consisted of half-a-dozen weather-worn Kirghiz, enveloped in sheepskins and carrying alpenstocks in their hands, with nine yaks, big, black, good-natured, phlegmatic creatures, and two sheep. Some of the yaks were loaded with the needful provisions, spades, a pickaxe, hatchets, ropes, furs, felts and felt carpets, the photographic apparatus, and other stores. The indispensable scientific instruments and field-glasses were carried by the Kirghiz in satchels. The remaining yaks bore saddles on their backs. As soon as we were mounted, and had taken leave of Togdasin Beg, the caravan put itself into motion, and slowly began the ascent, in a south-south-east direction. The yak is guided by means of a cord drawn through the cartilage of the nose. All the same the animal goes pretty much his own way, no matter how strongly his rider may protest. It is his wont to march doggedly on, with his muzzle close to the ground, breathing so hard that you can almost imagine your ears are buzzing with the sharp drone of a steam-saw tearing its way through timber some distance away.

At a place called Kamper-kishlak, or "Old Woman Village," we passed a glacier, with light green ice in its crevasses, and a gigantic boulder of gneiss, split in two, immediately underneath its terminal moraine. According to tradition, the place derives its name from the fact that once, when the Shah of Shugnan waged war against the Kirghiz, the latter all fled, with the exception of one old woman, and she hid herself between the two halves of the huge piece of rock.

The ascent was very steep, and nowhere afforded firm footing, the slopes being thickly strewn with gneiss blocks of every conceivable size and shape. The mountain is indeed built up almost exclusively of gneiss and crystalline slates; although in the mounds of detritus higher up I picked out fragments of black porphyry and micaceous schists, the latter showing signs of having been subjected to great pressure. I also found the last-mentioned rock in solid masses at the altitude of 16,500 feet.

Coming towards evening to a place that was free from snow, as well as sheltered from the wind, we halted there at an altitude of 14,560 feet, and pitched our simple camp. It consisted merely of a few felt carpets, supported by the alpenstocks and tied with a rope. Then one of the sheep was slaughtered, whilst the Kirghiz prayed "Allahu akhbar bismillah errahi man errahim"—"God is great. In the name of God the Merciful, the Righteous!" and before the flesh was cold it was plunged into the melted snow which filled the cooking-pot. The fuel with which our fire was made was nothing better than yak-dung. But later on in the evening we were joined by another Kirghiz, who brought us two yak-loads of teresken, and then we very soon had a splendid fire roaring away. Around it we gathered to eat our plain evening meal. The lively flames darted backwards and forwards like a giddy dancer, now skimming the lips of one of the spectators with a coquettish kiss, now singeing the beard of this or the other frozen Kirghiz, in a way that gave rise to a good deal of merriment. The moon rose from behind the shoulder of

MUS-TAGH-ATA SEEN FROM THE NORTH

Mus-tagh-ata encircled by a bright halo; the fire gradually died down; and we slept the sleep of the just under the open sky on Hazrett-i-Musa's (Holy Moses') mountain.

The following day, the 18th April, the weather was unfavourable, the sky being wreathed with clouds; besides which, it was cold and windy. Nevertheless we made up our minds to go on. The Kirghiz preferring to walk, we took only three yaks with us to carry our belongings. By innumerable sharp zigzag curves we worked our way up the mountain-side, which grew steeper and steeper with every yard. The yaks kept plodding on, showing extraordinary sureness of foot; but their halts were many and long. At length the clouds lifted, and revealed to our gaze a panorama for which the only appropriate epithet is magnificent. The valley of Sarik-kol lay spread out before us like a map. To the north we caught a glimpse of Little Kara-kul and Bulun-kul. On the south-west the view was shut in by the mountain-chains on each side of the Murghab; whilst far down underneath our feet, towards the west, the tomb of Chum Kar Kashka crowned what appeared to be a little knoll of insignificant height; though we knew that, seen from the valley below, it was in reality a big mountain.

At length we came to the glacier of Yam-bulak, and there made halt to rest awhile. We were then 15,900 feet above the level of the sea; and consequently stood higher than the tops of all the mountains of Europe. The glacier moves with the majesty of a king out of its castle portals—that is to say, a deep, wide dislocation of the strata; but no sooner does it get plenty of open ground before it, than it spreads out to twice or three times its former width, at the same time growing of course thinner. All its moraines—terminal, lateral, new and old—together with the glacial stream, and its deposits of steely blue mud—from the splendid coign of vantage we occupied we had a bird's-eye view of them all.

Having attained the altitude of 17,500 feet, we found water boiled at 180°5 Fahr. (82°5 C.), that the aneroid indicated 15.6 inches, and the thermometer read 23°9 Fahr. (−4°5 C.). There we were overtaken by a buran so furious that we were compelled to stop where we were for several hours. Even when we did venture to make a fresh start, we were obliged to proceed with the utmost caution; for the freshly-fallen snow completely hid the treacherous cavities and projecting rocks which diversified the surface.

When, after sundry hardships and adventures, we at length returned to camp, we found pleasing evidence of

Togdasin Beg's friendliness; for he had sent us a yurt, together with a fresh supply of provisions and fuel.

The 19th April we were visited by a snowstorm even at the altitude of our camp. Since then, it was evident, we might possibly have to wait some time for favourable weather, I sent Kul Mametieff down into the valley to bring up a sufficient supply of provisions to last us several days.

Meanwhile, taking Islam Bai and two of the Kirghiz with me, I made a little excursion to the edge of the Yam-bulak glacier. The rest of the Kirghiz, who the day before had complained of a splitting headache and feelings of nausea, were allowed to stay behind in camp and rest. It was altogether a most interesting and instructive trip. We obtained an accurate topographical chart, profiles, various measurements, and a dozen photographic views. Armed with rope, ice-axes, and alpenstocks we started from the side of the glacier, and ventured some 350 yards across its surface, until stopped by a crevasse sixty feet deep. I inferred from certain protuberances of the ice about 100 feet in height, that the minimum vertical thickness of the glacier was probably 150 to 170 feet. During this venturesome expedition we leapt over several yawning crevasses, though not without observing the well-known precautions of ice-craft.

That evening I determined to move the yurt round to the southern face of the mountain, and make another attempt to get to the top from that side. But my plans were unexpectedly thwarted. For like an evil spirit my old inflammation of the eyes (iritis) suddenly seized me, causing me excruciating agony. I applied the remedies I had with me, but all to no purpose. The next day the pain was so intense, that I was obliged to leave my men and ride down to Su-bashi. Thus ended my ambitious hopes. The members of the expedition were paid off, and the company dissolved. And Mus-tagh-ata, which glittered in the glorious sunshine, a magnificent sight for those who had eyes to see withal, was for the time being left to enjoy his solitary state in peace.

But despite the warmer climate and the rest I granted myself, the inflammatory symptoms rather increased than got better; so that at the end of a couple more days, I decided it would be wiser to go back to Bulun-kul, where I had left the half of my baggage, with six horses, in charge of two men. When I set out from the aul I was followed by the sincere sympathies of all its inhabitants; nay, even some of the Chinese soldiers came to express their sorrow at my ill-fortune. As the caravan filed off, they all stood silently by, as though assisting at a funeral. And this melancholy impression was still further deepened, when at the end of about an hour we were overtaken by a band of soldiers, who had been prevented by their military duties from coming to see me off. They now wished me *bon voyage*, and escorted me on my way for about half-an-hour, singing songs in my honour, but songs of such a doleful character that I really began to fancy the caravan *was* a funeral procession, and that the singers were the hired mourners and I myself the corpse.

And in truth it was a melancholy journey—that which we began on the morning of the 25th April. I had taken strong doses of salicylic acid and morphia, and felt both deaf and brain-sick. My left eye was covered with a bandage totally impervious to the light; whilst my right eye, which was well, but extremely sensitive to the light, was protected by glasses doubly darkened. In spite of my condition, by dint of riding ten hours at a stretch, we accomplished the entire distance to Bulun-kul in one day. Upon reaching Little Kara-kul we were assailed by a snowstorm, which continued to increase in violence as the day wore on, so that by the time we arrived at Bulun-kul it was not only quite dark, but the country was again clothed in its winter vestments. Without a moment's delay I despatched a messenger to Jan Darin, who had now returned from Kashgar, begging him to oblige me with a decent yurt. The answer brought back was, that Jan Darin was drunk, and could not be disturbed. I had, therefore, to make the best I could of the miserable yurt of which I have before spoken, although the snow swirled in through the holes in the sides. Notwithstanding this, I intended stopping there two or three days, because the inflammation continued to get worse.

But my plan was roughly knocked on the head; for about noon on the 26th a messenger came from Jan Darin, saying that, if I hadn't gone by an early hour on the following morning, he would help me on my way with his soldiers. We had no choice, therefore, but to obey orders. But I will hasten to add, in exculpation of the Chinese, that throughout the whole of my journey, this was the solitary occasion on which I met with insolent treatment

OUR CARAVAN IN THE VALLEY OF THE GHEZ-DARIA

at the hands of a rude and unpolished mandarin, for during the course of the succeeding years I saw the Chinese character from a very different side, and found them a truly amiable race of men.

On the 27th April I sent Kul Mametieff back to Fort Pamir. He was subsequently honoured with a medal by King Oscar of Sweden and Norway. In addition to that, His Majesty paid a similar compliment to more than one of the Russian officers stationed at the fort, in recognition of the distinguished services they had rendered me; so that it would scarcely surprise me to learn that the Russians take me for a prince in disguise!

At Tar-bashi (the Head of the Narrow Passage) we

turned off eastwards, so as to descend the deep valley of the Ghez, which eats its way far into the heart of the Mus-tagh chain. I am sorry to say I know little about the road we followed, for I rode with my eyes almost completely blinded by bandages. I can only say, that we reached our first night's station, Utch-kappa (the Three Stone Huts), down steep, breakneck paths. The next day we had to traverse an extremely difficult gorge of the Ghez-daria. The current was very strong and clung close to the foot of the high crags which shut in the valley on the right. The path wound down the face of the almost vertical cliffs, being protected on the outer or river side by a breastwork of stakes and poles latticed together with withes. My men thought they would prefer to go down by the bed of the stream. But the leading horses came within an ace of losing their foothold in the deep, swift current; and that sent the men back to the path. On we struggled, slowly, contending against serious difficulties, until two of the horses stumbled and refused to advance another step. This compelled us to return once more to the river-bed. We proceeded with the utmost caution, and finally succeeded in getting through the gorge.

I judged it wisest to trust my packing-cases only to the best of the horses, and this necessitated unloading and loading up again, which wasted a good deal of time. Each packhorse was taken through by two mounted men, who held themselves in readiness to whip him on if he happened to heel over. It was a very queer feeling came over me when I moved down into the turbulent current, neither seeing the bottom, nor yet knowing whether it was covered with loose gravel or big cobble-stones, whether it was deep or shallow. One thing, however, was imperative, namely to keep fast to the ford, or I should get a bath; and a bath in such a place, seeing that I was riding with my feet in the stirrups, would have been dangerous, for only a few paces distant the cliffs closed in upon the river, and drove it plunging down a cataract.

From that point onwards we crossed and re-crossed the stream several times, sometimes wading through fords, sometimes being obliged to trust ourselves to bridges of a more or less precarious character. One of these bridges formed the prominent feature in a very picturesque piece of scenery; for one end of it rested on a big round boulder which choked the bed of the river. The valley descended at a very steep inclination, and the river tumbled down one cataract after another. But as we went down, the narrow passages of the gorge, such as the one I have already described, were choked with thick mist, completely shutting out the prospect, although the bare cliff walls gave back the echoes with a singularly penetrating sound. The ground was extraordinarily

THE GHEZ-DARIA

rough and stony. Gigantic blocks of gneiss were half embedded in the stupendous conglomerate precipices which overhung the path; but so loosely fixed, that every moment I fancied they must break away and crash down upon our heads. In truth I was considerably relieved when we had passed the last of these perilous places.

By this the temperature had completely changed. We now perceived for the first time that the season was spring. The minimum during the previous night was 31°8 Fahr. (–0°1 C.). At midday it was 46°4 (8° C.), by two o'clock in the afternoon it had risen to 52°9 (11°6 C.); by three o'clock to 55°4 (13° C.); by four o'clock to 58°1 (14°5 C.); and by eight o'clock in the evening to 59° (15° C.); the temperature steadily rising as we descended. We rested for a while at Köuruk-karaol (the Bridge-Watch), where on the 29th April the minimum was as high as 39°2 (4° C.).

The district which we had now reached was in ill-repute, because of the Chinese and Kashgarian robber-bands which infested it. I therefore judged it prudent to post sentries during the night, with orders to keep an eye especially on the baggage and the horses. My men advised me to have my weapons handy and ready for use. But the night passed as quietly as other nights had done: the robbers did not molest us.

The following day we again had a difficult crossing. One of the packhorses, ridden by Khoja the Sart, stumbled and fell, and narrowly escaped drowning. In a moment every man of my company was in the water, heedless of clothes. But it cost them a vast amount of labour to rescue the animal and the stores it carried. Khoja went head over heels into the water, and got an involuntary bath. As on the previous day, we were obliged to cross the stream time after time, sometimes by means of fords, at others over what were in many cases dangerous bridges. At length, however, the valley began to widen out, and as it did so, we began to come across patches of scrub. At noon the thermometer showed 66°2 Fahr. (19° C.). We were getting to lower elevations and a warmer climate. Everything was shrouded in a thick yellow mist; moreover my eyes pained me a good deal, so that I saw but little of the picturesque country we were passing through.

The 30th April was the last day we spent amongst the mountains. Before the morning was over they began to decrease rapidly in elevation, till they were little better than insignificant hills, and finally they fell away and became lost in the distant haze which hung over the trumpet-shaped entrance to the valley. The surface grew leveller, and yielded a good supply of grass, which caused the horses to lose all sense of discipline. The poor animals, whose bellies had been sadly pinched during the journey across the snowy mountains and barren wastes of the Pamirs, snatched greedily at the appetising pasture as they went along. We crossed three more small bridges, the last of them a particularly dangerous one. We narrowly escaped losing one of our horses there, which put its foot through the thin planking. The baggage having been taken off the animal's back, all hands set to work to haul him up again. That done, the men mended the bridge by filling up the hole with turf. After that we left the Ghez-daria on the left, and travelled on to Tash-melik (more correctly Tash-balik — Stone Fish), where there was a small Chinese fort, the commandant of which would not allow us to proceed until he had first seen and examined my pass. The last night of our journey was spent at the village of Terem (Arable Land), and on the evening of the 1st May we reached Kashgar. There I was warmly welcomed by my old friend Mr. Petrovsky, Russian consul-general, and his secretary Mr. Lutsh.

BRIDGE OVER THE GHEZ-DARIA

CHAPTER XIX.

REMINISCENCES OF KASHGAR

I REMAINED fifty days in Kashgar, waiting till my eyes got well. This time I employed in working out the results of my journey up to that point, in arranging and tabulating my observations, and plotting out my maps. The rest was indeed very welcome, in fact absolutely necessary. I thoroughly appreciated the hospitality of my friend's house, where I was surrounded by all the comforts and conveniences of civilization. Consul Petrovsky is the most amiable man in the world, in every way a right excellent host. His intellectual conversation was as instructive as it was elevating. For he is a thorough man of science to his finger-tips. During the years he has been stationed at Kashgar he has made many discoveries and observations of the greatest value for history and archæology. Some day he intends to publish them to the world. His library contains a selection of the best books that have been written on subjects connected with Central Asia. He has also a laboratory fitted with the most costly instruments and scientific appliances. It would be absolutely impossible to have a better base than Mr. Petrovsky's house for a series of exploring journeys in the interior of Asia.

I have already described Kashgar and the vicinity in my former book, *Genom Khorasan och Turkestan.* Suffice it therefore to say here, that the old town stood there on the banks of the Kizil-su every whit as grey and solitary as when I first saw it in 1890. I add however a few words about the Europeans and Chinese with whom during this visit I was brought into contact.

The members of the consulate embraced Mr. Petrovsky and his wife, his secretary, two military officers, a revenue officer, and a troop of half a hundred Cossacks.

Adam Ignatieff, a Roman Catholic Pole, who went out to Kashgar ten years ago as a missionary, was still there, a standing guest at Mr. Petrovsky's table. He was a fine old man, with a smooth-shaven face and snow-white hair, was dressed entirely in white, wore a rosary round his neck with a cross dependent from it, and looked like a cardinal out of office. We used to rally him over the dinner-table; but he met all our allusions, even the most embarrassing, with a jovial smile, and resented nothing so long as he got his full number of drams. The only person who put faith in his pretensions to missionary zeal was himself. For during all the ten years he had been in Kashgar he had not made a single proselyte; indeed he had made no serious attempt at conversion. He boasted that he had converted one old Sart woman on her deathbed; but the malicious declared that the old woman was already dead when he converted her.

During the following winter Adam Ignatieff often used to visit me in the evening; and many was the lonely hour he thus helped to shorten by his conversation. We would both sit over the fire till well on into the night, and he would relate to me the various episodes of his adventurous life. He told me how, during the Polish Rebellion, he had helped to hang a Russian priest; for which deed he was banished to Siberia, and remained there about thirty years. He was of noble blood, and belonged to the family of Dogvillo. But he was then living half a wastrel in Kashgar, a lonely man, forgotten, friendless, with none to care for him or take any interest in him, with none to shed a tear over his grave, when the end of his days should come. Nevertheless he was always cheerful, always friendly and jovial, perfectly contented with his lot. And so we used to sit, talking over the fire, like a couple of hermits.

I also found in Kashgar another old friend in Father Hendricks. He was in all respects a remarkable man, who had been domiciled in the town quite as long as Adam Ignatieff. A Dutchman by birth, he had been twenty-five years in Asia, spoke twelve different languages, and followed closely and with interest the affairs of the world; he was in short a man of wide culture, endowed with no small share of talent—in this respect the exact opposite of Adam Ignatieff. He made his home in a Hindu caravanserai, a miserable hovel without windows, and lived in a state of the greatest poverty, apparently long ago forgotten by his friends in Europe, for it was seldom, if ever, that he received any letters. It was however a real pleasure to talk to him. He was both amusing and ready witted, sang French songs with the same verve that he recited his Latin masses, and was a thorough original, if ever there was one. To see him striding at a smart pace through the Mohammedan bazaars, with his long cloak, his broad-brimmed hat, his staff, his long beard, and his big spectacles, always put me in mind of a greyfriar monk. Solitary, solitary, solitary—such was the burden of his life's song. A solitary man, he recited punctually every day the masses which none came to listen to; solitary he sat on the platform beside the door of his hovel and read, heedless of the bustle of the caravans that came and went; solitary he dressed the scanty fare which his poverty permitted him to eat; solitary he wandered about the roads of an evening—always and everywhere a solitary, lonely being. It was always a pleasure to me when I fell in with him. Many an hour we sat together philosophizing over life, for I too was just as lonely a man as he.

There was also a third missionary in the town, a Mohammedan, who had been converted to Christianity and baptized by the name of Johannes or John. He had studied the Koran in Erzerum in Turkish Armenia, and from the minarets of that city cried to the Faithful, "*La illaha il Allah, Mohammedeh rasul Ullah*" (There is no God but Allah, and Mohammed is His Prophet). After being converted to Christianity, he spent two years at a mission school in Sweden. At the time of my visit to Kashgar he chiefly occupied himself with translating the Bible into Turki and the dialect of Kashgar, and with playing Swedish Psalm tunes on a violin in the evening.

Such were the happy destinies of the champions of the Cross in that remotest of Chinese cities! I felt truly sorry for them. Their energies were wasted, their labours fruitless, their lives empty, hard, and of none account.

During my first visit in Kashgar I had the good fortune to come in contact with two pleasant English gentlemen, the famous traveller Captain Younghusband and Mr. Macartney. The former had in the interval returned to India. The latter still dwelt in Kashgar, occupying a comfortable house in a splendid situation close to the garden of Chinneh-bagh. On more than one occasion he entertained Father Hendricks and myself with splendid hospitality. Mr. Macartney was the Agent of the Indian Government for Chinese affairs in Turkestan. He had had a first-rate training, and spoke fluently the principal languages of Europe and the Orient, being especially distinguished in Chinese. In fact, he was too good for his post. He was capable of rendering his country substantial services in a more distinguished sphere of action.

I will now turn to the more eminent of the Chinese with whom I had relations during my stay in Kashgar.

The highest official in each of the nineteen provinces of China is the governor; and with him are associated the vice-governor, the head of the provincial treasury, the judge, and the procurators. Now, whereas the first four exercise authority over the whole of the province, the functions of the last official, the procurator or *Dao Tai* (the Man who Shows the Right Way), are limited to a smaller district or subdivision of the province. For instance, in the province of Sin-chiang (Sin-kiang), which embraces the whole of East Turkestan, Ili, a part of Dzungaria, and a part of Gobi, there are several dao tais. Urumchi, the capital of the province, has one; Ak-su has another; there is a third at Kashgar; and so on.

The dao tai's sphere of authority is therefore less extensive than the spheres of his colleagues; but within his own sphere his actual authority is in several respects superior to theirs, seeing that he enjoys the power to check and regulate their action, as well as to make representations to the central government, if he considers them lacking in the performance of their duty. The position he occupies is in many ways similar to that which was occupied by the Russian provincial procurators in the time of the Empress Catharine II.; but with this fundamental difference, that, whereas the functions of the Russian procurators were limited to protesting, the Chinese dao tai possesses, under certain circumstances, the power to command.

My friend Shang, Dao Tai of Kashgar, exercised authority over a very extensive region, stretching northeastwards towards the boundary of the procuratorship of Ak-su, and embracing Kashgar, Maral-bashi, Yarkand, Khotan, Keriya, and Cherchen. His duties are principally civil; but they also extend into the domain of military affairs, in that he acts as paymaster to the troops and inspector of commissariat. The district of Sarik-kol, on the Eastern Pamirs, is administered, like the similar frontier districts of the Russian and Afghan Pamirs, by military officers. The Dao Tai of Kashgar is able to exercise a certain measure of influence upon the conduct of affairs in Sarik-kol; for he is authorised to give advice and furnish intelligence, but is not allowed to issue direct commands.

When a young man, Shang was nothing more than a simple clerk to a mandarin; but having distinguished himself at the time of the first revolt in Dzungaria (1864), he rapidly mounted the ladder of promotion, till he attained his present high position. Although no Adonis, he was from top to toe a thoroughly high-principled gentleman. On ordinary days he was wont to flit his saffron yellow body about in a little blue cart; but for ceremonious occasions and functions of high solemnity he came out in magnificent attire, namely a robe of blue and black silk, in the ample folds of which golden dragons played hide and seek, whilst golden lions of fantastic shape climbed up a bewildering tangle of interlaced garlands. A mystic button on his silk skull-cap proclaimed that he was a *darin* or mandarin of the second class. To complete his gala costume, he wore round his neck a long chain of hard fruit-kernels, polished and carved on the outside.

Upon arriving in Kashgar, one of my first duties was

SHANG, DAO TAI OF KASHGAR

of course to go and pay my respects to this high and influential official. He received me in a singularly polite and cordial fashion. He lived in a straggling *yamen* (official residence), consisting of a labyrinth of square courtyards, with mulberry-trees planted in the middle and wooden verandahs running round the sides. The pillars which supported the verandahs were decorated with Chinese ideographs, and the walls of the building with mural paintings, representing for the most part dragons and other fantastic animals. The Dao Tai himself received me at the first door, and with an affable smile conducted me as far as the audience chamber, where we took our seats on opposite sides of a little square table, and drank tea together and smoked out of silver pipes. Soldiers, armed with long-shafted halberds, kept watch beside the door, and a group of respectable yellow-skinned functionaries, with well-preserved pigtails and buttons in their black silk caps, stood like a circle of lighted candles all round the room, keeping as silent and motionless as statues all the time the audience lasted. The Dao Tai himself wore the insignia of his lofty dignity. With the view of repaying honour with honour, I had put on my best "dress" suit of broadcloth, and went to his palace riding a horse as white as fresh-fallen snow and escorted by a troop of Cossacks.

For two hours we conversed together, or rather competed which should excel the other in paying compliments. The Dao Tai asked me how I liked his tea. I answered "Chao" (good), that being the only Chinese word I knew. Thereupon he clapped his hands and said, "By the memory of my fathers, what a marvellously learned man my guest is!" A little later he told me, that the river Tarim, which flowed *out* of Lop-nor into the desert, reappeared again several thousand *li* (quarter of a mile) distant, and formed the great river Hwang-ho of China. At this I gave him as good as I got: "What a well-informed man your Excellency is! You know everything."

But I also let him hear a little plain truth as well. I told him how I had been received at Bulun-kul, the first place I entered on the Chinese side of the frontier; expressing my astonishment that I should have been treated with such discourtesy in face of the pass and letters of introduction I carried, and declaring my intention of making representations on the subject in higher quarters. Upon hearing this, the Dao Tai's face clouded, and with some show of emotion he begged me not to lodge a complaint; he would himself teach Jan Darin a lesson. I promised, therefore, that for that once I would let the matter drop; for of course I never had any intention of doing what I said. But I have found that the only way to deal with the Chinese is to be positive in your statements and peremptory in your demands, if you wish to avoid being made ridiculous by their fantastic exaggerations.

Towards the close of our interview the Dao Tai reminded me, that Kashgar possessed two chiefs—himself and the Russian consul-general. The Mohammedans declare that Mr. Petrovsky is the true successor of the Jagatai Khans (who ruled over Kashgar from the death of Jenghiz Khan to past the middle of the sixteenth century). He pointed out that, since I had taken up my quarters for a time with the Russian chief, it would only be right that I should also grant his Chinese colleague the honour of entertaining me, for at any rate a few days. I thanked him very, very much for the honour, but declined.

The next day the Dao Tai returned my visit, coming with all the pomp and circumstance of Oriental display. At the head of the procession rode a herald, who at every fifth step sounded a gigantic gong. He was followed by several men armed with switches and whips, with which they dusted the jackets of everybody who had not the good sense to get out of their way. The great man himself rode in a little covered cart, with three windows and two high wheels, drawn by a mule, which was shaded by an awning, held up by rods fixed to the shafts. On both sides of this state chariot walked attendants bearing huge parasols and lemon-coloured standards, inscribed with Chinese ideographs in black ink. The rear of the procession was brought up by a troop of soldiers, mounted on beautiful white horses, but wearing such fantastic uniforms as would have astounded even Doré.

CHAPTER XX.

A CHINESE DINNER-PARTY

I CANNOT part from my Chinese friends in Kashgar without adding a brief account of a Chinese dinner-party, which I shall never forget. I had scarcely recovered from dining at the house of Tsen Daloi, a kind of mayor of the city, when I had the honour to be invited, along with the staff of the Russian consulate, to a similar function at the palace of the Dao Tai.

I recollect something about an ancient Greek deity who swallowed his own offspring. I have read in Persian legend about the giant Zohak, who devoured two men's brains every day at a meal! I have heard rumours of certain African savages, who invite missionaries to dinner, and give their guests the place of honour inside the pot. I have been set agape by stories of monstrous big eaters, who at a single meal could dispose of broken ale-bottles, open penknives, and old boots. But what are all these things as compared with a Chinese dinner of state, with its six-and-forty courses, embracing the most extraordinary products of the animal and vegetable worlds it is possible to imagine? For one thing, to mention no more, you need to be blessed with an extraordinarily fine appetite — or else be a Chinaman — to appreciate smoked ham dripping with molasses.

When a Chinaman issues invitations to dinner, he sends out one or two days beforehand a tiny card of invitation contained in a huge envelope. If you accept the invitation, you are supposed to keep the card; if you have not time, that is if you decline, you are expected to send it back. If the banquet is appointed for twelve o'clock, you need not go before two p.m. Should you however appear punctually, you will find your host taking his midday siesta, and see neither guests, attendants, nor signs of dinner. When things are sufficiently advanced in your host's house, he sends off another messenger, who comes and shows you his master's calling-card. This is to be interpreted as a signal, that you may now begin to dress yourself, though you need not bustle about it.

We too of the consulate made a truly gorgeous show as we rode in procession to the great man's palace. The place of honour at the head of the procession was filled by a Sart from West Turkestan, the aksakal (chief) of all the merchants, subjects of Russia, who dwelt in Kashgar. He wore a red velvet khalat (coat), decorated with two or three Russian gold medals. Close behind him rode a Cossack, carrying the silk banner of the consulate, red and white, with a little blue cross stitched diagonally across the corner. Consul-general Petrovsky and I rode in a sort of landau, escorted by two officers and by Adam Ignatieff, in the long white coat with the cross and rosary round his neck. Last came a dozen Cossacks in white parade uniforms, curbing in their snorting horses with a tight rein.

Thus arrayed in holiday magnificence, we rode, under a broiling hot sun, at a gentle pace through the narrow, dusty lanes of Kashgar, across the market-place of Righistan, with its hundreds of tiny stalls, shaded by thatched roofs, each supported by a slanting pole, past mosques, madrasas (Mohammedan theological colleges), and caravanserais, across the "flea" bazaar, where old clothes are on sale, coming occasionally into collision with a caravan of camels or a string of donkeys laden with small casks of water, and entered at length the Chinese quarter of the city, full of quaint shops, with up-curling roofs, painted dragons, and red advertisement signs. Finally we drove in at the great gates of the Dao Tai's yamen (residence), and were there received by his Excellency in person, surrounded by a band of beardless and wrinkled military attendants dressed in their gayest attire.

We had not got further than the preliminary "appetiser" when the presence of Adam Ignatieff started his Excellency off on the subject of the missionary activity of Europeans in China. He spoke in terms of great admiration of the Christian missionaries, praising their self-abnegation and disinterested zeal for the well-being of their fellow-men; but, speaking with marked emphasis, he went on to add, that he felt bound to look upon them as the authors and instigators of discord, setting members of the same family at variance, undermining the time-honoured ordinance of domestic subordination, dividing the population into two hostile camps. I ventured to remind him of the murder of two Swedish missionaries in Sung-po, of which I had just heard; but the Dao Tai professed total ignorance of the affair.

Our host then conducted us and his Chinese guests to a little pavilion in the garden, where dinner was to be served. Chinese etiquette prescribes, that the host shall touch his forehead with the cup each guest drinks out of, and thereupon present it to him; similarly with the chopsticks each guest eats with. The Dao Tai also shook each chair, to prove that it was in a sound condition, and passed his hand over the seat as if to brush away the dust. This performance over, we took our seats round the big, red, lacquered table. Next came in a string of servants, each bearing a little round porcelain dish with some preparation of food upon it. They put down the dishes along the centre of the table. There were dozens of them; and the first supply was followed by others, time after time. In front of each guest stood still smaller dishes containing spices, sauces, and soy.

If the guests neglected to help themselves, the host occasionally sent them portions of the delicacies which lined his own dishes—such as the skin, fins, and cartilage of different varieties of fish found in the seas and rivers of the Chinese empire, fungi, salted mutton fat cut into long strips, lizards (salamanders), ham with a great variety of widely different adjuncts, besides a multitude of strange preparations, the real constituents and names of which remained mysteries to me. As for tasting them, I really had no confidence in their suspicious appearance, still less in the rancid odours they gave off. The culminating triumph of the feast was smoked ham in molasses, washed down with tea and Chinese brandy, strong and boiling hot. The greater part of the numerous dishes served at the banquet had been brought from China proper, and consequently, owing to the vast distance, at a very considerable cost. Evidently his Excellency, who at ordinary times lived very plainly himself, was desirous to show us every mark of respect. But I am sorry to say we scarcely did justice to the skill of the Chinese cuisine, although a Brillat-Savarin would no doubt have gone into raptures over it.

The only person who worthily upheld the honour of Europe was Adam Ignatieff; but he did wonders, exciting the amazement of the rest of us, and even the admiration of the Chinese themselves. With punctilious conscientiousness he partook of every one of the forty-six courses, and, with the rosary still round his neck and the cross on his breast, drank seventeen cups of brandy, stuff which to my throat was as hot and burning as sulphuric acid poured upon iron-filings. And at the end of the three hours that the banquet lasted, he rose every whit as sober as when he took his seat at the beginning.

The conclusion I came to about Chinese state banquets was, that you require a certain amount of time to become accustomed to the many unfamiliar dishes which are put before you. All the same, several of them were excellent, some even quite delicious. Undoubtedly the most delicious of all was the soup made from the edible nests of the swallow, or more correctly swiftlet, a dish which is seldom served in this far off region because of its extremely high price.

On one of the walls there were painted two or three black flourishes. I enquired what they signified, and was told they meant "Drink and tell racy stories." There was no need for any such admonition; for the spirit which reigned over the company was so hilarious, and we transgressed so wantonly against the strict rules of Chinese etiquette, that the Dao Tai and his compatriots must surely have blushed for us a score of times, had not their skins been from infancy as yellow as sun-dried haddocks.

We were entertained all through the dinner by the melodies of a Sart orchestra, consisting of drums, flutes, and singers; whilst the monotonous music was occasionally enlivened by a couple of dancing boys, as though we were not dizzy enough without their gyrations.

As soon as the last of the six-and-forty courses had disappeared, the guests, following the rigorous law of custom, instantly rose to take their leave. That moment was one which I had long been anxiously waiting for; for I was dying for a cigar, and a glass of sherry with iced water, to banish the recollection of one of the most extraordinary banquets it has ever been my lot to be present at.

As we drove home, the streets, the market, the bazaars were silent and empty. The only persons we saw were a few solitary wanderers—a dervish or a leprous beggar. The sun set behind the airy contours of the Terek-davan pass. The twilight lasted only just long enough to make the bare announcement that a new night was approaching. Then the Orient lay down and dreamed again on its own grave.

I shall not easily forget the many happy hours I spent in Consul Petrovsky's society. It is always a pleasure to me to go over them again in my thoughts. For, as I have already said, he was really an extraordinary man, both in the matter of experience and general culture. I owe him a very deep debt of gratitude, not only for his unstinted hospitality, but also for the extremely valuable advice he gave me, drawn from the store-house of his wide experience. He has lived twelve years in Kashgar, and no man possesses a more intimate knowledge of that region than he does. To many it may seem like transportation for a well-educated man to have to spend so many of the best years of his life in a place like Kashgar. But it was nothing of the sort to Mr. Petrovsky. He had learned to like the place; and he had an inexhaustible fund of interest in its historical and archæological treasures which he had unearthed. There was one thing about Mr. Petrovsky which had for me an especial attraction. He was always cheerful, always in excellent good humour; for, when you come to think of it, what is there that can give greater or truer pleasure than to associate with people who see life and the world in bright colours, and are perfectly contented with the lot destiny has shaped for them? At the same time he was both philosopher and critic. With biting wit and scathing irony he would lash the minor follies of the world, more especially everything that savoured of toadyism and servility. Throughout all my travels I have met no man who made a deeper or more real impression upon me than Mr. Petrovsky; nor is there any I would so gladly meet again and yet again.

In a word, I had a splendid time of it in Kashgar. I was quartered in a cosy little room in a pavilion in the consulate garden, and after breakfast used to stroll backwards and forwards under the shady mulberry and plane trees, along a terrace which commanded a wide view of the desolate regions through which I was shortly to journey on my way to the Far East. I had constant company in a colony of swallows, which had built their nests under the projecting eaves, and which were quite at home, flying freely in and out of the open doors and windows, for, the summer air being warm, the doors and windows stood wide open all day and all night long. On Easter morning I was awakened by the clear melodious echoes of a church bell, which the day before had arrived from Narynsk, and was hung in the chapel of the Russian consulate. I spent my time there working all day, and wrote two or three geographical papers. Altogether, it was in every way a delightful existence, and just suited me down to the ground. I heard the wind whispering in the tops of the plane trees. What it really said I knew not;

but I loved to dream that it was bringing me greetings from home. Little did I know then that I had still three whole years of hard travel before me in the heart of Asia!

My life was however anything but solitary. Apart from the staff of the consulate, the place swarmed with Orientals — Sarts and Kirghiz — who came in and out on business or pleasure. Then there was a crowd of Mohammedan servants, and a Chinese interpreter, to say nothing of hens and chickens to the number of three hundred, turkeys, geese, and ducks, a monkey,

GARDEN OF THE RUSSIAN CONSULATE IN KASHGAR

four parrots, and more than a dozen dogs. I was on good terms with the whole menagerie, with the sole exception of the monkey. His favour I could not succeed in winning, even when I resorted to such tempting delicacies as apples and pears.

During my seven weeks' stay in Kashgar I often discussed my plans of travel with Mr. Petrovsky, especially how my journeys ought to be arranged, so that I might visit each region in the season most favourable for reaping a successful harvest of observations. The result of our conversations was a total alteration of the original idea with which I left Europe. Instead of exploring all the regions I had set my mind upon in one continuous and unbroken journey, as I had at first intended, I decided to carry out my purpose in a series of longer or shorter expeditions, all starting from Kashgar as a centre. By that means I should be able to carry my observations to a place of safety as I made them, to develop my photographic plates, pack and send off home my collections, as well as have an excellent base at which to make preparations for each fresh expedition.

I intended my first journey to be to Lop-nor, that being the object upon which my heart was most set. But in the beginning of June the weather underwent a sudden change. Summer—the Asiatic summer—was upon us almost before we were aware of it. The sky glowed like a gigantic furnace. The temperature rose to 100°4 Fahr. (38° C.) in the shade; the black-bulb insolation thermometer showed 150°8 (66° C.). The queen of the night was powerless to infuse coolness into the superheated atmosphere of East Turkestan. And every afternoon the desert wind blew in across the ancient capital of Yakub Beg, dry, burning, impregnated with fine dust, filling the streets with a stifling, impenetrable haze. And as the summer advanced, the heat would increase, as well as grow more intense the nearer we travelled towards the middle of the continent. I thought of the superheated atmosphere, heavily charged with dust, vibrating above the dunes of drift-sand; I thought of the whirlwinds which every afternoon drive up and down the banks of the Tarim; I thought of the 1000 miles of long, difficult marches across the unending waterless deserts, and—I shuddered. It was only the other day, as it were, that I had been living in nearly forty degrees (Fahr. and C.) of frost high up on the Pamirs. I should be all the more sensitive to the burning heat of the desert. At the eleventh hour therefore I resolved to spend the summer in the higher regions, and continue my observations in the eastern Pamirs, and wait for the winter or the spring before starting for Lop-nor.

CHAPTER XXI.

FROM KASHGAR TO IGHIZ-YAR

WE left Kashgar on the evening of 21st June 1894. The caravan consisted of half-a-dozen pack-horses, laden with provisions, instruments, khalats (Kirghiz coats), cloth, coloured handkerchiefs, and bag-caps, intended as presents for the Kirghiz; these articles being valued amongst them almost as much as money. Besides these things, I had my tent-bed, winter clothing, felts, weapons, and ammunition. The only reading I took with me consisted of certain scientific books, and half a year's issue of a Swedish journal, as old as the hills, but none the less delightful on that account, when every line conjured up dear old Sweden before my mind's eye.

My companions were the Evangelical missionary Johannes; Islam Bai, from Osh in Fergana, the successor of Rehim Bai; the Taranchi Daod (David) from Kulja, who acted as my interpreter of Chinese; and Ekbar-khoja, caravan *bashi* (leader), from Fergana. It was from the last-named I hired my horses. In addition, I was to be provided every day with two Kirghiz guides, to point out the road. The Dao Tai's good offices exceeded all expectation. Not only did he give me two big bright-coloured letters of introduction of a general character, he also supplied me with an official proclamation to the commandants of Sarik-kol and Tagharma, to the effect that I was of a rank equivalent to a mandarin of "the second button," and was accordingly to be received and treated as such. In sharp contrast to their former behaviour towards me, the Chinese local authorities were now anxious to do all in their power to serve me.

The sun's rays were still very hot, although it was nearing sunset, when the caravan moved off between the poplars and willows which line the broad highroad, one of the great public works of Yakub Beg. It being market-day, the road was enlivened with a brisk traffic. There were mandarins of different "buttons," driving along in their little blue carts, each drawn by a mule bedizened with trappings and bells; there were small troops of Chinese officers and soldiers in gay uniforms, all mounted. But not the least striking features were the huge, picturesque *arbas* (carts) crowded with Sarts or Chinese on their way to Yanghi-hissar or Yarkand. Each vehicle was arched over with a tunnel-like roof of straw, and drawn by four horses, hung all over with bells of various sizes; one horse being harnessed between the shafts, the other three a considerable distance in front, pulling by means of long, roughly-made ropes. These clumsy but serviceable vehicles are the diligences of East Turkestan. By them, for the extremely modest fare of ten Kashgar tengeh (about 2*s.* 3*d.*), you can ride all the way from Kashgar to Yarkand, a distance of four long days of travel. We met one caravan of merchandise after another. Along the sides of the roads were swarms of beggars and cripples of every kind and degree, water-sellers with their big earthenware jars, bakers and fruit-dealers, displaying their wares on tiny stalls; whilst a swarm of sun-browned urchins paddled in the muddy water that stagnated in the ditches by the roadside. We passed a line of saints' tombs; the monument which the Russian consul-general, Mr. Petrovsky, erected in 1887 to the memory of the murdered Adolf Schlagintweit, now undermined by the spring floods; and Yakub Beg's ruined castle of Dovlet-bagh (the Garden of Riches). We crossed the Kizil-su, a reddish-brown mud-stream, crawling underneath the double-arched bridge. Finally, leaving the Chinese town, Yanghi-shahr, on the left hand, we struck the desolate, lifeless country, which stretched away southwards and eastwards, flat and boundless, as far as the eye could see. By that time, nine o'clock in the evening, it was quite dark. We therefore stopped in the village of Yiggdeh-arik, and rested and took our suppers, till the moon should get up. It was two o'clock in the morning when we arrived at Yappchan, the object of our first day's march.

On 22nd June the temperature was so high (91°6 Fahr. or 33°1 C. at 1 p.m.) that we preferred to stay in the shade; but towards evening it grew cooler, and we resolved to start again. We had not advanced very far, when we were met by a beg, followed by two attendants. He had been sent by the *amban* (Chinese governor) of Yanghi-hissar, bearing greetings from his master, with expressions of welcome into his district. He was at the same time ordered to furnish me with provisions, and do everything that lay in his power to help me in my journey. After escorting us a piece of the way, the beg rode back again, in order to find out and get ready a suitable place for tea. The avenues of trees and cultivated fields became more and more interspersed with belts of sand as we advanced. Two hours after leaving Yappchan, I saw sand-dunes nearly twenty feet high. They stretched from north-west to south-east and from north to south; but were so overgrown with vegetation that they offered no impediments to traffic.

After stopping a short time for tea in the village of Soguluk, where a party of Chinese were making a fearful hubbub, we continued our journey in the dark towards Yanghi-hissar, and arrived there early the next morning. An apartment had been allotted to us in the Hindu caravanserai; and the caravan created quite a commotion when it filed in at the gate, for all the guests of the "hotel" were sleeping in the courtyard under the open sky.

Later on that same morning, the 23rd June, I was awakened by a mandarin of inferior rank, who brought fresh greetings and protestations of eternal friendship from the amban, together with a sheep, two pullets, a sack of wheat, another of maize, a bundle of grass, and a faggot of firewood. All day long I had three begs sitting outside my door, ready to run my errands at the slightest hint. And in this friendly spirit I continued to be treated by the amban during the whole of the forty-eight hours I remained in his town.

In return for his obliging kindness, I presented him with a revolver and a knife. Thereupon he sent me a complete Chinese dinner, consisting of a number of remarkable, but delicious, dainties, arranged on dishes and in tiny cups, grouped round a whole roasted pig, which was placed on a big tray with a leg to it. At the same time he expressed his regret that, being indisposed, he could not give himself the honour of helping me to consume the good things he had sent. This message furnished me with the welcome opportunity to reply, that, as I was quite unable to do justice to such a bounteous spread all by myself, I felt called upon to send it back to him. For I strongly suspected, that all these unusual attentions were merely an artifice to put me under such strong obligations of gratitude towards the astute amban, as almost to compel me to conform to his wishes. His real object was to turn me aside from the route I had chosen for getting up to the high plateau, namely the glens of Keng-kol and Tar-bashi. That route lay through his district; and it ran counter to the wishes of his worship the amban that I should travel through the country over which he exercised rule. He feared, and with justice, that I should map it out, and so open it up to European travellers, from whose presence it had hitherto been tolerably free. Indeed, he directly advised me to follow the route *viâ* Yarkand, alleging that the mountain-torrents were now so greatly swollen, that I should run very serious risk, and if my baggage were to suffer injury or get lost, he would be held responsible for it by the Dao Tai.

Meantime I had learned from other quarters, that donkey-caravans had actually crossed the torrents. Moreover, the time of year was the reverse of favourable for going all the way round by Yarkand, where pestilence always rages in the summer. When the amban learnt, that it was still my intention to pursue my original plans, he sent offering to supply me with guides. Then, finding no other pretext for keeping up communications with me, he inquired the best way to proceed in order to make water run uphill for purposes of irrigation. I replied to his inquiry by making a paper model of a windmill, and adding explanations of its purpose and the way to use it.

On the outskirts of Yanghi-hissar I noted the first indications of the proximity of a mountainous country, in certain minor irregularities of the ground. For example, a narrow ridge, about half-a-mile long and from 60 to 80 feet high, stretched away eastwards from the town. It was so evenly and regularly formed, that it might easily have been mistaken for an old fortified wall or rampart, had it not been built up of sand and conglomerate. On the north of this ridge lay the greater part of the town, with its houses and bazaars embowered in gardens. On the south of it there was nothing more than a single row of clay huts, with low flat roofs. Along the foot of the ridge was the cemetery, every tomb being surmounted by a small dome. When the sun was at its fiercest, the place gave off the offensive smell of a charnel-house.

But the prospect from the town was both fine and extensive. Mus-tagh-ata shut in the south-west like a steel-blue wall, its white battlements inviting us to cooler climes. Between Yanghi-hissar and Mus-tagh-ata the face of the country was dotted with low hills. But in the opposite quarters, that is towards the east and north, there was nothing but the desert, as level and unbounded as the ocean. The town possessed nothing whatever to interest a stranger, its few mosques and madrasas (theological colleges) being totally destitute of architectural pretensions. One of the latter was built, I was told, sixty years ago by Halim Akhun. Its façade, ornamented with blue and green tiles, and flanked by a couple of small towers, overlooked an open square with a muddy pond in the middle. There was also a typical Central Asiatic mosque, small in size, with a colonnaded verandah along the front showing simple decorative designs, painted inscriptions, and streamers; and associated with this was the masar (saint's tomb) of Kara-chinak. The court-yard of the mosque was planted with venerable poplars, with stems of a mighty girth. By an ingenious contrivance one of them was made to do duty as a sort of minaret. Lastly I will merely mention the masar of Supurga Hakim; it had a green cupola and four small towers.

On the whole the town was a rural sort of place, abundantly filthy, its streets narrow and dusty, its bazaar protected against the burning heat of summer by wooden roofs and straw mats. The men went about for the most part naked from the waist upwards. The small boys were entirely naked. The little girls had their heads and feet bare, but wore one garment—a bright red skirt. The women, who seldom go veiled, frequently sat at the stalls in the bazaars, or in the open squares, with baskets of fruit at their feet. As a rule they were not blessed with good looks. Like their sisters in other parts of East Turkestan, they wore their black hair in two long thick plaits.

The Chinese quarter of the town, which, like the Chinese quarter of Kashgar, was called Yanghi-shahr (the New Town), lay close beside the Mohammedan quarter, and was defended by a lofty crenelated wall with towers and a moat. It was there that the amban of the town had his yamen (residence), with its train of bare-headed Chinese in long, white tunics and wide, blue trousers.

The Indian caravanserai, where we put up during our stay in the place, was built round a square courtyard, with a pillared verandah along each of its sides. Its principal inhabitants were half-a-score Hindus from Shikarpur, importers of cloth from India by way of Leh, Kara-korum, Shahidula, and Yarkand. But their chief business was money-lending; and by exacting exorbitant rates of interest they had so completely got the people into their power, that the greater portion of the proceeds of the harvest flowed into their pockets.

But I must not linger longer in Yanghi-hissar. The mountain breezes are wooing me; and there is a great deal to do before I can permit myself to indulge in rest. I was unable to persuade our host, Odi from Shikarpur, to accept any return for the hospitality he showed me. But I in some sort satisfied my conscience by making him a present of the amban's sheep and firewood, together with a knife which I added out of my own stores. Kasim Beg escorted us as far as the canal of Mangshin-ustang, which has a volume of 280 cubic feet in the second. There he dismounted, bowed, and took his leave; his place being taken by another beg, Niaz, who accompanied us throughout the whole of the journey. About six o'clock in the evening we were assailed by an extremely violent whirlwind, which came out of the north-west, and filled the air with dense clouds of dust and sand. The gust only lasted five minutes; and was shortly afterwards followed by a heavy pelting rain, which wetted us to the skin before we were able to reach shelter in a hut by the roadside. But it brought a compensating advantage, in that it purified the air and settled the dust.

From the village of Kara-bash (Black Head) we directed our march due south, leaving on our left the highroad to Yarkand. For a pretty considerable distance eastwards the country was diversified with ranges of low hills of sand, clay, and conglomerate. The route we followed was excellent riding, being a perfectly level steppe, diversified by a few scattered knolls. We rested two hours in Sughet (the Willow Tree), then started again in the night; but it was so pitch dark that we had to be guided through the narrow lanes of the village by a man carrying an oil-lamp. It was about two in the morning when we arrived at the kishlak (winter village) of Ighiz-yar (the High Terrace). There we took up our quarters in a finely situated court-yard.

The amban of Yanghi-hissar had despatched a man on before into the mountains to prepare the way for us. We met this man, Emin Beg, on the 25th June, returning with the intelligence that the torrents had really become much swollen during the past few days, but that nevertheless they were not so high as to offer any serious impediment to the progress of the caravan. As a reward for his welcome news, I invited him to take tea with me, and let him enjoy the rare treat of listening to a tune on the musical-box. One of the inhabitants of the place strummed a *setar* (zither), and a mollah read aloud passages from the Koran to a group of the Faithful.

One *tash* (five miles) south of the village there is an iron-mine known as Kok-bainak. The ore occurs in strata of loose earth or clay, and is dug out and carried to Ighiz-yar to be smelted. Both the appliances and the process of extraction are of the most primitive description; the furnace being only about six feet high, with three feet interior diameter. It is housed in a little hut built of planks and sun-dried clay. After the furnace is half filled with charcoal, the ferruginous earths are thrown in, till they cover the charcoal to the depth of six or eight inches. The fuel is then lighted, and half-a-dozen men squat on their haunches in front of as many holes made near the bottom of the furnace, and blow into it with goat-skin bellows, in order to intensify the draught. They keep up at that nearly all day long, from time to time examining, by means of an iron rod inserted through a hole in the side of the furnace, how the smelting is progressing. Towards evening the molten metal comes running out at the bottom of the furnace. After every burning the furnace of course requires to have the slag and ashes raked out, so that it may be clean and ready for a fresh batch of ore. The metal thus obtained is of such a miserably poor quality that it cannot be forged. It is only fit to be converted into the more primitive agricultural implements. It is no use for horse-shoes. One entire day's smelting yields 5 *chäreck*, which are sold in Yanghi-hissar for 30 tengeh (6*s.* 8*d.*). One chäreck is equal to 12 *jing;* and one jing equals 1½ Russian pounds or 1¼ pounds avoir. The owner of the furnace, the *yuz-bashi* (chief of one hundred men) or village chieftain of Ighiz-yar, manages the business himself, personally superintending the smelting, and paying each of his seven workpeople at the rate of only six *da-tien* a day; the *da-tien* being a Chinese bronze coin equal to less than half a farthing in value.

CHAPTER XXII.

THROUGH THE GORGE OF TENGHI-TAR

OUR spirits were high when we left Ighiz-yar early on the morning of 26th June; for immediately before us we saw the valley of Tazgun opening its arms to welcome us. The mountains themselves, now brown, now grey, were barely visible, their contours being blurred by the great amount of dust which obscured the atmosphere; but at their feet we could just discern two of the kishlaks or winter villages, snugly ensconced amid groves of green trees. But as we drew near to the entrance of the valley, the outlines of the mountains gradually came out more distinctly into view, at the same time seeming to creep closer together. The valley of Tazgun is very narrow, so narrow even at its entrance, that it could easily be defended by the little fort of Ighiz-yar-karaol, with its garrison of only twenty-four men. On the other side of that post the population are exclusively Kirghiz nomads, who climb up to their summer grazing-grounds on the plateau by paths which strike upwards from several of the side-glens of the Tazgun valley. Passing one of these glens, Mahmud-terek-yilga (the Glen of Mahmud's Poplar), I caught a glimpse at its head of a mountain covered with glittering snow. The air was pure and mild; so we pitched upon a shallow grotto in the syenite cliffs of Tokai-bashi for our camping-ground for the night.

Our camp was near the junction of two glens, Käptch-kol and Keng-kol. We struck up the latter; and as the torrents which coursed down both glens contributed about equal volumes to the river Tazgun, we now had to deal with a current only half the volume of that in the Tazgun valley. The glen of Keng-kol (the Broad Glen) did indeed contract as we advanced; yet not so much but that there was space for several small meadows and pasture-grounds, frequented in summer by the Kipchak Kirghiz, who spend the winter lower down near the entrance to the valley. There were still a few isolated poplar trees to be seen, for the vegetation was by no means meagre. The cliffs on each side of the glen consisted of syenite, porphyry, and black clay-slates, very much weathered, so much so indeed that in many places the bottom of the glen was completely covered by their *débris*. Otherwise the surface was soft soil.

At the aul of Keng-kol (11,000 feet) we were hospitably received by the aksakal (white-beard, *i.e.* chieftain) of the place, Abdu Mohammed, who gave up to me a portion of his own large yurt. We were detained at that place all day long on the 29th June by violent showers of rain. The aul (tent-village) numbered twenty-one inhabitants, who spend there the three summer months of every year. Every evening the sheep and goats are driven to the aul to be milked; and are then shut up for the night in large fenced-in folds, guarded by fierce, long-haired dogs, to protect them from the wolves, which abound in that district. Whenever the dogs bark during the night, a man hurries out towards the point where danger threatens, and by loud shouts endeavours to frighten the wolves away.

About noon a troop of men and women, dressed in holiday attire, came to the aul. They were on their way to the funeral of a boy in another aul lower down the valley. But some of them thought they would have a pleasanter time of it with us; and therefore stayed behind when their companions continued their journey. The company in my host's yurt was thus augmented by a dozen men, eight women, and seven children; and yet it was so roomy, that we were not at all crowded. They were a lively set of people too, as a single picture will show. One man played the *dutara* (a two-stringed instrument of music); others sat about in little groups chatting. Some of the women, wearing enormous white head-dresses, ate bread and drank milk out of big wooden bowls. The children ran about and played. Our hostess was engaged in suckling her infant, a boy of about one month old, leaning over his cradle to do so. The head of the family, old Abdu Mohammed, was the only individual who heeded the obligations of religion. He alone punctually observed the hours of prayer. None of the rest heeded them, but went on laughing and talking. There was the usual fire in the middle of the tent.

There was a good deal of humus and luxuriant herbage in the vicinity of the aul of Keng-kol, which was situated on the right bank of the stream. Immediately opposite to it, on the other side of the river, the bare rock cropped out in several places, consisting of clay-slates, alternating with a hard species of crystalline rock. The stream was at that time very insignificant; but the water was limpid, cold, and wholesome. In consequence of the recent rains, it was expected to rise soon to flood-level. The rainy season in that valley is coincident with May and June. Snow never falls except during the four winter months.

During the following days the ground became more broken and variable, as well as wilder, in character. Our route led out of the glen of Keng-kol into that of the Charlung, one of the tributaries of the Yarkand-daria. The pass connecting the two glens, like the two streams which flowed down from it in opposite directions, was called Kashka-su (the Many-coloured Stream).

The little glen, which led up to the pass out of the Keng-kol valley, was extremely narrow, and rose at a steep angle. Owing to the great variations in the contour of the ground, I was obliged to take frequent measurements, in order to calculate our rate of marching and the distance marched. I found that, to ascend this glen, it took the packhorses 4½ minutes to climb a quarter of a mile; and our day's march varied from 12 to 20 miles.

Although the black clay-slates cropped out visibly on

both sides of the pass, on its culminating ridge there was not a trace of bare rock to be seen. The contours were on the contrary gently rounded off, the ground being covered with humus and luxuriant grass. At the time of my visit the latter was being grazed by large troops of horses belonging to Sart merchants of Yarkand. The top of the pass afforded a splendid view of the deep-cut glens on both sides of the ridge, and of the snow-clad mountain-peaks in the far distance. The two streams which carried off the rainfall on each side of the watershed were about the same size. The feeders of both have eaten their way deeply into the flanks of the mountain, giving origin to many fan-shaped corries or gullies. The altitude of the pass was 13,000 feet above sea-level.

The path on the other side of the pass went straight downwards, due south, towards the little aul of Koi-yolli (the Sheep-Path), consisting of six yurts, and so on to the karaol (watch-house) of Chihil-gumbez, a collection of stone and clay houses, stables, and yurts, besides a cemetery with a small chapel crowned with a cupola (*gumbez*). The inhabitants numbered only thirteen; and, like those of Keng-kol and Charlung, were Kipchak Kirghiz. The watch-house stood at the junction of three routes, those namely which come from Yarkand, from Keng-kol, and from Tagharma. A great many caravans and mounted men pass the place in the course of the year; indeed I was told that the daily average of travellers was ten.

On 1st July we went over another pass, Ter-art (the Leather Pass), 13,250 feet, which closely resembled Kashka-su, except that the ascent and descent were even steeper. On the crest of the ridge the clay-slates stood out almost vertically in sharp fantastically-shaped snags, flakes, and slabs. The spaces which intervened between the separate summits were frequently filled with mounds of detritus, which in their fall had exposed the planes of fracture of the inky-black argillaceous rocks. The descent on the other side was through a remarkably wild and striking ravine, traversed by a little rippling mountain-brook. Its sides were walled in by bare clay-slates; the bottom littered with huge masses of conglomerate, consisting of broken schists and white coarse-grained syenite, embedded in yellow soil and sand, through which the torrent had carved out a deep channel for itself. Rushes and grass grew between the blocks of syenite. Another rivulet came down a side-glen, Borumsal, greatly quickening the vivacity of the Ter-art. Eventually the glen widened out; but after it did so, became every now and again almost blocked by terraced ridges of conglomerate several hundred feet thick. About three o'clock in the afternoon the south-west wind brought up a slight mist; this gradually thickened, and towards evening changed into a drizzling rain, which searched through everything, so that we were glad to find shelter in the aul of Pasrabat (the Low-lying Station), a place of three yurts, 9460 feet above sea-level, inhabited by thirteen Kessek Kirghiz.

But although so small, Pasrabat is so far important, that it lies on the road connecting Kashgar, Yanghi-hissar, and Yarkand with Tash-kurgan, the principal Chinese stronghold in the Eastern Pamirs. For this reason it boasts of a small fort. The stream of Pasrabat runs into the Taghdumbash-su, which in its turn becomes an affluent of the Yarkand-daria.

Several times during the night I was awakened by the rain, which beat with a loud pattering upon the roof of the tent, and occasionally came through upon me, sprinkling me all over. The next morning the neighbouring glens were again shrouded in thick mist. As soon as I got up, I had an animated discussion with the Kirghiz, as to whether we should go on or stay where we were. They advised me to push on, being afraid that, if the rain continued, though only one day longer, the mountain-torrents would rise so high as to be impassable. But my *karakesh* (owner of horses) was of opinion, that the day was already too far advanced; we should not get to the biggest stream we had to cross between Pasrabat and our next station until after dark. Accordingly we decided to remain where we were.

This gave me an opportunity to take certain observations as to the volume of water carried down by the stream. By this the rainfall of the past day or two had begun to come down from the mountains, and the flood had already risen very considerably. Yesterday it was clear as crystal; to-day it was grey and muddy, and boiled along tumultuously among the stones. The breadth of the torrent increased to 53 feet, its depth to a maximum of 21·6 inches, its volume to 250 cubic feet in the second. At midday the temperature of the water was 50°9 Fahr. (10°5 C.). The variations which the current underwent during the course of the day will show how sensitive these mountain-brooks are to precipitation and temperature. By three o'clock in the afternoon the water had sunk ·6 of an inch. This was owing to the fact, that the highest rills which fed the stream froze during the night. But at five o'clock, by which time that morning's rains had got down to Pasrabat, the stream rose 1·38 of an inch. At seven o'clock it was 6·3 inches above the height of my first measurement; but in consequence of the steepness of the banks, the breadth had not increased more than about 3¼ feet. The noisy brawling of the current, now of a brownish-grey colour, sounded duller and heavier than in the earlier part of the day; for the stones and pieces of rock which protruded above the surface in the morning, checking the flow of the water, and causing it to splash up into the air, were now entirely submerged. Now that the outpour of the rains had got down as far as our camp, the volume was more than twice as great as in the morning, being 495 cubic feet in the second. At the same time the temperature was 49°5 Fahr. (9°7 C.). By eight o'clock the current had risen yet another ·8 of an inch, and the temperature had fallen to 48°9 Fahr. (9°4 C.), and another hour later the figures were ·4 of an inch and 48°4 Fahr. (9°1 C.) respectively. All this goes to show that, as the volume of the water increased, it took a proportionally longer time for it to attain to the temperature which prevailed in the lower valleys.

At seven o'clock next morning the flood stood at about the same level as when I took my first observation; but during the night the temperature had fallen to 45°5 Fahr. (7°5 C.).

That day, July 3rd, we had an unusually trying day's march. At first the glen was of medium breadth, and tolerably rich in grass, bushes, and willow trees. Every now and again the conglomerates stretched pretty far up the mountain sides, forming rampart-like walls, with covered galleries, excavations, and grottoes, but so precipitous that they looked as if every moment they would crash down into the glen. But after we passed the end of the side-glen of Yam-bulak (the Grotto Spring), the main glen became very narrow, and its bottom choked with disintegrated *débris*. The torrent too dwindled a good deal, having lost two or three of its principal contributaries.

At Yam-bulak there was a hut by the wayside, and our eyes were charmed by the sight of the fresh white flowers of the wild rose. Beyond that point the glen was called Tenghi-tar, a very suitable name, although a pleonasm; for *tar* means "narrow" and *tenghi* "narrow glen-path." Here the coarse crystalline rocks predominated again; the sharp pinnacles and needles of the mountains in the argillaceous formation being replaced by more rounded domes and flattened tops. The glen was, as I have said, choked with *débris*, nevertheless vegetation thrived; the beech, wild-rose, and hawthorn being the most noticeable species.

Finally the glen contracted to a wedge-shaped trough carved, as it were, out of the mountain-side. The path grew more and more difficult. We wound a hundred, a thousand times in and out round the fallen boulders; and every now and again crossed the stream, its water once more clear and limpid. The glen was closed by an upheaval of gneiss, overlain sporadically by conglomerate strata. At a spot appropriately named Issyk-bulak, a triple hot spring gushed out from beneath a large block of conglomerate. The water, though not particularly copious, burst forth with a splash, and had a disagreeable sulphurous odour. It coloured the stones upon which it fell brown and yellow; nevertheless luxuriant green grass and other vegetation grew only a little way lower down. A column of steam rose above the springs, the water having a temperature of 127° Fahr. (52°8 C.) at the point where it emerged. The torrent, which raced down the glen, passed within eight yards of the springs. Ten yards above them its water was 54°5 (12°5 C.); but ten yards below them as much as 66°2 (19° C.).

Two minutes further up the glen we discovered another hot spring, very similar to the first, except that it was much smaller and its temperature 125° (51°7 C.). Above this spring the temperature of the glen torrent was only 54° Fahr. (12°2 C.). My reason for quoting these trivial details of varying temperature in the stream is this. In winter the torrent never freezes below the hot springs all the way to Yam-bulak; whilst above them it always freezes.

Above the hot springs the glen contracted still more, and at length became a veritable ravine, only a few yards wide, the air cold and clammy as in a cellar, the rocky sides perpendicular, the stream filling up nearly its entire width, dashing itself against the boulders, flashing up above them in spray, plunging down small waterfalls. Near the entrance to the gorge lay the carcass of a dead horse, a warning to us to keep a watchful eye upon our own animals. And indeed there was need of it; for the ascent was painfully steep. But, as some compensation for that, the scenery was grand and wild. When we shouted, and we had to shout pretty loud to make ourselves heard, the echoes were dashed from side to side against the hollow cliffs. Above our heads there was only a narrow strip of sky visible. Every minute almost the gorge appeared as if it would come to a sudden stop, the cliffs seemed to meet and join. But no; it was only a fresh bend in the glen. We turned the corner, and lo! another splendid prospect opening itself out before us. And so this remarkably picturesque gorge went winding on, a narrow sinuous gap excavated through the granite and quartzite rocks by the furious little torrent.

It was anything but an easy task to get our heavily laden pack-horses safe and sound through this long and difficult defile. For the greater part of the way we were obliged to ride up the bed of the torrent; and the tossing spray prevented us from watching the horses' feet. The inhabitants of the district had filled up the lowest pools with blocks of stone, large and small, thus making a sort of bridge or causeway. But at the best, these pieces of road-making were only so many new pitfalls of peril. The water had scooped out and carried away all the smaller, softer materials which had been used to fill up the spaces between the bigger blocks; so that the causeways were now full of gaping holes, into which the horses frequently slipped and nearly broke their legs. Two or three of them actually fell off the causeways. Then away dashed the men into the stream, to get them up again and rescue the cases and bales. All the way up my heart was in my mouth, for fear the horse I rode should give me an unwelcome bath. One spot in particular I recollect quite well. It was a very ugly place. A number of big round stones, with brightly polished, slippery surfaces, formed a kind of sill stretching obliquely across the bed of the torrent. A couple of men climbed up each on to a large boulder, and seizing hold of the packing-cases, and hauling away at them, helped the horses to clamber over.

At length however the path grew better. For at a spot called Tarning-bashi-moynak (the Pass at the Head of the Gorge) the glen was divided into two widely differing halves by a mountain-spur, which projected from the left. At its foot the torrent shot down to such a great depth that it was quite impossible to advance. We therefore climbed up and over the crest of the projecting spur, getting a magnificent view of the glen both ways, up and down, from the top. In striking contrast to the deep narrow gorge we had left, the glen ahead of us widened out into a broad, level valley, with gently sloping hillsides and rounded eminences above them, plenty of vegetation, and a practicable path along-

CATTLE AND SHEEP NEAR KARA-YILGA

side the stream. A little higher up the rock formation on the left hand was again conglomerates; but on the right syenite, its surface so smoothly polished that I could not help fancying it had been worn away by water or glacial ice. Upon looking back, I perceived that the spur before mentioned was overtopped by a double-crested mountain, covered with perpetual snow. The Kirghiz called it Kara-yilga-bashi (the Head of the Black Valley). The portion of the glen above Tarning-bashi-moynak was called Tar-bashi (the Head of the Narrow Gorge), showing how sharply the Kirghiz are wont to discriminate between regions of dissimilar formation and character.

By this we had nearly reached our camping-place for the night, Bulak-bashi (the Head of the Springs). The yuz-bashi (chieftain) of the place, an old beg, received us with the friendliest courtesy, and at once ordered a comfortable yurt to be got ready for our accommodation. At this place I observed a very remarkable phenomenon in connection with the stream of Tar-bashi. When we arrived, its current was low, and perfectly limpid; but at half-past three in the afternoon we suddenly heard a distant rumbling sound. The noise grew rapidly louder and louder. Then, foaming like a white surf-roller, down rushed the flood, born of the melted snow and ice in the higher altitudes, and of the recent rainfall in the lower. How lucky we had got through the gorge! Otherwise the whole caravan would infallibly have been swept away. But we only just cleared it in time! This was what the Kirghiz were anxious about at Charlung.

Since leaving Ighiz-yar we had crossed over the broad, far-stretching easterly spurs of the Mus-tagh range — a confused jumble of crests, peaks, and intervening valleys. From the valley of Keng-kol we had crossed over into the glen of Charlung, and from the glen of Charlung into the glen of Pasrabat, climbing up and down two passes of relatively minor significance on the way. At the place where the Tenghi-tar, one of the head-feeders of the stream which descended the glen of Pasrabat, broke obliquely through the crystalline mountain-chain, we had traversed an extraordinarily romantic gorge, which, having cut out its channel to a great depth, recalled the characteristics of the typical Peripheral region of which I have before spoken. Above the gorge the glen had widened out; the enclosing mountains assuming at the same time a gentler inclination and falling to a relatively lower elevation—a typical Transitional region in miniature. We now began to enter upon a typical high-plateau or Central region. I had ascertained, that the volume of water in the mountain-streams generally increased towards four o'clock in the afternoon, and went on increasing until well on in the evening; proving that the snows which are melted by the midday sun do not get down to the glens until several hours later. The streams were lowest about noon and a couple of hours afterwards, and attained their maximum during the night. But these general variations are subject to irregular oscillations, caused by the irregularity of the rainfall. It is these deluge-like floods which do the real work of erosion, a fact evidenced further by their thick, muddy-looking water. During the early part of the day the stream gradually deposited the detritus it caught up on its way down, and so became clear again.

Bulak-bashi was a place of six yurts, inhabited by thirty Kessek Kirghiz. They are stationary there all the year round, being commissioned to keep karaol (watch) upon the passes, to lodge and help Chinese travellers journeying over them, and to carry to and fro the Chinese post. Both at Bulak-bashi and at Pasrabat there were therefore three postmen stationed, each three being paid 25 *chäreck* (nearly 6 bushels) of wheat from Yanghi-hissar and 20 *chäreck* (nearly 5 bushels) from Tash-kurgan. Since leaving Yanghi-hissar we had passed six watch-houses—Ighiz-yar, Tokai-bashi, Kashka-su-bashi, Chihil-gumbez, Pasrabat, and Bulak-bashi. Two of the men belonging to the aul last-named were looked upon as *bais*, *i.e.* rich men; each owned about one thousand sheep, two hundred goats, one hundred yaks, thirty horses, and the same number of camels. The winters were said to be

A KIRGHIZ AUL IN THE EASTERN PAMIRS

very cold in that glen; and whilst the head-feeders of the stream remain frozen, which they usually do for two or three months, the stream itself dries up. Snow falls during five months in the year; but seldom lies more than knee-deep. The rainy season properly so-called begins in the middle of May; there is rainfall also in the summer and autumn.

The 5th July was one of our heavy days: we crossed over the main chain of the Mus-tagh system. The night before was still and sparkling bright. The thermometer dropped below freezing-point; and even at a late hour in the morning the edges of the brooks and pools of stagnant water were fringed with ice. The upper extremity of the glen widened out more and more. The mountains which fenced it in, outliers of the principal crests we had on both sides of us, grew flatter and flatter. The gneiss rarely cropped out in continuous masses. The little brooks came rippling down the glens on both sides of the valley one after the other, as though emerging from the side-wings of a stage. The valley-stream, being at this point nearer its sources, attained its greatest volume about noon, and its waters were not yet muddy. As we passed several of these small side-glens, we saw at their upper ends the main mountain-ranges clothed with glittering mantles of snow. The only places immediately overlooking the valley itself on which snow still remained were the slopes which faced north, north-east, and north-west. The floor of the valley was in great part a carpet of luxuriant herbage, on which several herds of yaks were grazing, and in part was littered with *débris* and fragments of rock from the mountains above.

A short time afterwards we came to an oval cauldron-shaped valley or *cirque*, surrounded by a ring of mountains partly covered with snow. Immediately ahead of us rose a ridge of considerable altitude; and soon, to the north, we perceived the pass of Yanghi-davan (the New Pass), which leads to Yam-bulak, but is only used when the Tenghi-tar route is impassable. In the middle of that open, dish-shaped valley lay two small lakes, each about

500 yards long. They are fed by the melting of the snows around, and their waters, clear as crystal, are the source of the Chichekli-su, a little brook which runs down into the glen of Shindeh, and so on to Pasrabat and the Yarkand-daria. The name Chichekli is likewise given to the low saddle which serves as the watershed between the glen of Tar-bashi and the glen of Chichekli.

From the cauldron-shaped portion of the glen the track swung up a relatively easy slope to the pass (15,065 feet) of Kityick-kok-moynak (the Little Green Pass). A little further on was another pass, the Katta-kok-moynak (the Big Green Pass), equally easy, although it attained 15,540 feet in altitude. Between the two a small fan-shaped valley gathered up a number of mountain-rills, and out of them formed an affluent to the Chichekli-su. Both passes were on the top of low rounded domes, where, except for a few scattered patches of gneiss, the bare rock was not visible, being effectually covered with humus.

CHAPTER XXIII.

THE PLAIN OF TAGHARMA

THE passes just mentioned formed the culminating points of the route. On the other side, that is towards the west, the path descended very abruptly, going down alongside a little brook, which, like the Tenghi-tar on the east side, has excavated a deep, narrow passage through the solid rock. It cost us an hour's hard work to get down. The more sheltered spots still harboured patches of ice and snow, across which we sometimes rode. The glen, which was called Därshett, gradually widened out, and at last we perceived the end of it—a rocky gateway giving access to a broad plain. Against the far-off background of the plain stood out in clear relief a bluish-white mountain-wall, denticulated at the top. It was the Mus-tagh chain. But we still had a detached spur of no great elevation to surmount. On the other side of it there burst upon our view the wide, level plain of Tagharma, deliciously green, and bathed in the brilliant afternoon sunshine. On our right lay the Chinese stronghold of Besh-kurgan (the Five Forts), surrounded by a rectangular wall and garrisoned, it was said, by a *lanza* or troop of 120 men. As soon as we had crossed the river Tagharma, we were met by the begs and yuz-bashis. They greeted us politely, and told me they had been directed by letters from the Dao Tai to place themselves at my disposal.

The plain of Tagharma is in reality an elevated steppe, carpeted with the greenest of green grass, and abundantly watered by running streams, which gather their water from the snowfields on the mountain-summits around, and unite to form the Kara-su (the Black Water), a tolerably large stream, or the Tagharma-su (the Apple-Mountain Water), which effects a junction with the Yarkand-daria by way of Tash-kurgan. A large number of Kirghiz dwelt on the plain; the yeylaus (summer camps) of the district enjoyed an excellent repute.

The 6th July was a day of rest. The heat was very oppressive at noon, the thermometer registering 89°6 Fahr. (32° C.) inside the tent, and 127°4 (53° C.) outside in the sandy soil. The black-bulb insolation thermometer rose as high as 160°4 (71°3 C.). Not only does the plain itself, in virtue of its great extent, absorb an enormous quantity of heat, it is also open towards the south and slopes in that direction. The sky was as pure as crystal, except that a very few light fleecy clouds hovered about the mountain-tops. The atmosphere trembled and vibrated with the heat that was radiated upwards. A fine gossamer-like haze hung over the surface of the ground. Our camp was situated at an altitude of 10,620 feet.

The rainfall in the plain of Tagharma presents a strong contrast to the rainfall in the glens by which we had penetrated through the mountain-spurs of the Mus-tagh. In the former the quantity of rain which falls is inconsiderable. When it does rain, it comes in gusts lasting about a couple of hours at a time. The season for it to come is the spring. The amount of snowfall is also small, and is spread over barely three months. The winters are extremely cold; but owing to the clear, dry atmosphere, the newly-fallen snow disappears very quickly.

The great amount of radiation, and the plenteous natural irrigation, foster vegetation to an extraordinary degree. The plain was carpeted with luxuriant grass, thick in bottom growth, diversified by moist verdant tussocks, and enlivened by the music of running brooks and springs. Herds of grazing yaks and sheep roamed all over it; and here and there the eye caught glimpses of the cosy Kirghiz auls. In the valleys farther east we had experienced frost at night. On the plain of Tagharma even the nights were warm. And not warm only: they were also silent and tranquil—not even the soft whispers of the brooks reached our ears. But the mosquitoes were very troublesome, keeping us awake a long time.

The Kirghiz, who inhabit the plain of Tagharma, remain there winter and summer alike. They counted eighty yurts, fifty being occupied by Kessek Kirghiz and thirty by Teit Kirghiz. On an average there were four persons to each yurt. Besides these, there were twenty families of Tajiks at Besh-kurgan and Sarala. But the majority of the Kirghiz were poor. All together, they owned scarcely more than 2000 sheep and 200 yaks; several of them possessed barely half-a-dozen sheep, some none at all. On the other hand the Tajiks were reputed rich. These people are not nomads, but permanent dwellers in houses of clay. Their chief occupation is agriculture; their principal crops being wheat and barley. At the same time they breed sheep and other domestic flocks, a single individual frequently owning as many as one thousand sheep. The Kirghiz say they were much better off a score of years ago, when Yakub Beg was ruler in Kashgar. In his time they enjoyed much greater freedom, and were allowed to drive their flocks and herds westwards to the grazing-grounds on the Pamirs; whereas now the Chinese jealously forbid them to cross the Russian frontier. Our host, Mohammed Yussuf, was beg of all the Kirghiz of Tagharma.

Wild animals were numerous in that region, and embraced the wild goat, hare, and other rodents, the wolf and fox, the partridge, wild-duck, wild-geese, and several species of *Natatores* and *Grallatores.*

On 7th July we continued our journey, aiming west and north-west for the foot of the Mus-tagh-ata *massiv*, having on our right hand that part of it which is called Kara-korum (the Black Stony Region). Our route lay alongside the Kara-su, which derives its waters from glacial streams and natural springs combined, and, after gathering up the drainage of the plain of Tagharma, effects a junction with the Yarkand-daria. We passed the ends of several old moraines and a great many erratic blocks of gneiss, proving that glacial action was once far more prevalent in this region than it is at the present time.

In the middle of the plain, at a place called Gedyäck (the Violin), there was a picturesque *tu*, that is a mound of stones, with a branch of a birch-tree fixed in it and hung round with the skulls and horns of wild sheep and tekkes (wild goats), the tails of horses and yaks, pieces of white rag, and other religious offerings of the Kirghiz. Several smaller birch poles were stuck into the stone-heap round about the larger one; and the whole vicinity was littered with horses' and antelopes' skulls. Immediately in front of the mound was a fair-sized block of gneiss which had been hollowed out by water or ice. The cavity was black with smoke; and the explanation given me was, that pilgrims were in the habit of leaving in it offerings of lighted candles or oil lamps, when they came to the *tu* to repeat their prayers. In that same spot too a little side-glen, called Kayindeh-masar (the Holy Tomb of the Birch), opened upon the plain from the west. The name is derived from the burial-place of an important saint, situated in the middle of a little grove of birch trees. It is also one of the principal burial-places of the Kirghiz; a legend running to the effect that it was the resting-place of the hero Khan Khoja in one of his warlike excursions. The *tu* has been built in the middle of the public road, as an intimation that there is a burial-place in the vicinity; also as a sign that the great saints' masar of Mus-tagh-ata rears aloft its snow-white head immediately above it.

Away to the right we now saw for the first time several of the glaciers with which we were to become more intimately acquainted during the course of the summer.

On 8th July there remained but one day's march between us and Su-bashi, our first goal. After that we proposed to surmount the easy pass of Ullug-rabat (the Large Station), which divides the valley of the Sarik-kol into two portions, a northern which sends off its drainage waters to the Ghez and a southern which drains into the Yarkand-daria. It was a splendid day. The mountain-peaks on our right stood out bold and clear-cut, their glittering snowfields contrasting sharply against the limpid, light blue sky; the only flaw upon its pearly purity being a few light feathery clouds far off towards the south. In a word, the still, soothing peace of the Sabbath rested upon the whole face of the country, so that it was pure joy simply to sit still in the saddle and quietly observe it.

We reached the summit of the pass at one o'clock, and from a cairn of stones there (13,875 feet altitude) were able to get a general survey of our surroundings. The large glaciers radiated westwards from the central *névé*, the ice at their fractured edges and in the crevasses glistening a beautiful translucent blue. The spaces between the glacial arms were filled up with stupendous crags and pinnacles of rock, coal black in colour below the snow-line. We were too close in to the mountain to be able to see the majestic dome which crowns it. That can only be seen to advantage a long way west of the place in which we were then; for instance, its noble proportions can be seen clearly and distinctly from the Murghab. There was an almost equally fine view to the north, where the valley of Sarik-kol inclined a little towards the north-west, so that the Mus-tagh chain shut in the view on that side. The dominating feature on the south and west was the Sarik-kol chain, curving in towards the Pamirs; but in certain places it was obscured by the undulating country between—a country diversified by knolls of sand, gravel *débris*, and earth, gradually merging one into the other, overgrown with scanty patches of tussock-grass. In the immediate foreground, on the north, was the tolerably level plain of Su-bashi, having at its upper end the karaol (watch-house) of Irik-yak, garrisoned by seven Kirghiz, whose duty it was to watch the two passes Mus-kurau and Tock-terek. The latter possessed two approaches, in one of which, that called Kara-tock-terek, there was an isolated hill of fine-grained granite, which has been subjected to great pressure, and showed a fluidal structure, interspersed with veins of pegmatite or coarse-grained granite. The glacial current, which came down at the same point and flowed into the Tock-terek, was very turbid, owing to the quantity of detritus and glacial mud it held in suspension. It had also a bigger volume than the stream it joined. The latter, not being of glacial origin, was clear.

At the bottom of the northern slope of Ullug-rabat we came upon an aul of nine yurts, and shortly after that upon another of five, both standing on the brink of the stream, and both owning large flocks of sheep pasturing in the neighbourhood. At the first aul (tent-village) I was met by Togdasin Beg, who gave me a flattering welcome. He led me to his own aul, where the yurt I occupied before still stood in the same place; at the moment, however, it was occupied by nearly a dozen dirty, ill-smelling Chinese soldiers, who gaped their fill at me, shouted, laughed, and touched and poked their fingers at my several packages. Then came the secretary of Shi Darin, the commandant, requesting to see my passport. He saw it and was satisfied. Thereupon I invited him to partake of tea. He did so, and made himself tolerably agreeable.

Togdasin Beg asserted, that the garrison numbered 66 men, but I question whether there were more than a dozen; at any rate I never saw more, and if there had been more, they would certainly have come to my yurt, for their curiosity was insatiable. Togdasin had simply counted the horses, and then jumped to the conclusion that there was a corresponding number of men. But in that part of the world the Chinese have a most extraordinary way of enumerating their troops. They are not content with counting the soldiers only, but reckon in also their horses, rifles, shoes, breeches, and so forth; so that the resultant total is a long way above what it ought to be. They apparently go on the supposition, that the rifle is at least as valuable as the man; and by an analogous train of reasoning, they argue that a man is of little use if he has to travel on foot, that he cannot go about naked, and so on. Hence they count in the whole kit, rifle, breeches, and all. By this peculiar process of arithmetic they fancy they deceive the credulous Kirghiz, as well as the Russians on the other side of the frontier, into believing that their garrisons are very much stronger than they are in reality. Woe to the Kirghiz who should presume to count the soldiers of the Celestial Empire by the same common rule as that by which he counts his sheep! A short time before my visit in that quarter a Kirghiz yuz-bashi (chief of 100 men) was asked by Mi Darin, commandant of Tash-kurgan, how many men there were at Su-bashi. The chief replied, "Thirty." Thereupon Mi Darin wrote to his colleague Shi Darin, asking if the statement was correct. Shi Darin promptly sent for the yuz-bashi, and beat him, asking him how he dared to count the garrison, or even presume to think about its size.

The Chinese troops at Su-bashi were armed with half-a-dozen English rifles and an equal number of Russian; except for these, their principal weapons were Chinese bows and lances. The European rifles were in bad condition, not having been cared for. I myself saw two or three of the troops stick their rifle-barrels downwards into a muddy brook and use them as jumping-poles to get across with. Less than a dozen of their horses were really serviceable animals; the others were nothing better than sorry caravan horses. Drill, rifle-practice, or other military duties are seldom performed. Togdasin told me, that the entire garrison, the commandant included, spend days and days smoking opium, gambling, eating, drinking, and sleeping. These frontier garrisons are relieved at irregular intervals from Kashgar, Yarkand, and Yanghi-hissar; and three or four times a year are supplied with provisions by means of caravans from the same towns. The Kirghiz pay no taxes to them; but are under the obligation to supply half-a-dozen sheep every month, for which the Chinese pay at the rate of about one-half or one-third of their real value.

CHAPTER XXIV.

AMONG THE KIRGHIZ

I GRADUALLY learned to have much sympathy with the Kirghiz. I lived amongst them for four months a solitary European, and yet never once, during all that time, felt lonely. The friendship and hospitality they showed me never wavered. They shared with willing pleasure in the hardships of my nomad existence; and some of them were at my side in every sort of weather, took part in all my excursions, all my mountain ascents, all my expeditions across and to the glaciers. In fact, I won a certain measure of popularity in the valley of Sarik-kol. The people came from far and near to visit me at my camping-stations; bringing me presents of sheep, wild-duck, partridges, bread, yaks' milk and cream. And almost invariably, when I drew near to an aul, I was met by a troop of horsemen and escorted to the beg's yurt, given the place of honour near the fire, and offered dastarkhan (refreshments).

But the little ones entertained me most. Many of them were such sweet, pretty little things, as they ran about with a coloured cap on their head, and not a stitch else on them, unless it were their father's huge skin boots, that I sometimes found it hard to tear myself away from them. At the first glance of such a strange apparition as my spectacles and my strange clothes they generally fled and hid behind their mothers, or concealed themselves in their favourite hiding-places in the yurt; but the offer of a lump of sugar quickly won their confidence. On their part too the Kirghiz soon understood that I regarded them as friends, and felt at home amongst them. I lived con-

KIRGHIZ MOTHER WITH HER BOYS

stantly in their yurts, ate the same food they did, rode their yaks, wandered from district to district as they did,—in a word, became to all intents and purposes a full-blooded Kirghiz. They often used to say to me: "*Siz indi Kirghiz bo oldiniz*" (You have become a Kirghiz now).

Three months earlier I had experienced nothing but kindness at the hands of Togdasin Beg, chief of the Kirghiz of Sarik-kol, and their intermediary with Jan Darin at Bulun-kul. On this the occasion of my second visit, he welcomed me like an old acquaintance, showing me every attention and honouring me with the choicest delicacies of the Kirghiz *cuisine.* He asserted, that a day or two's rest in his yurt was absolutely indispensable for me, before I went on to visit his neighbour Mus-tagh-ata, a chieftain who from a sublimer tent commands authority over a greater race of subjects. I was very glad to accept his insistent hospitality, for I wanted to engage men and yaks for the summer. For 11th July my host planned a grand surprise. Being anxious to show me the full glory of Su-bashi and the neighbouring yeylaus (summer camps), he made arrangements for a *baiga* or "mounted games"; which, although as but a drop in the ocean when compared with a parade of imperial troops, nevertheless for romantic and fascinating effects probably exceeded anything household troops can produce.

During the course of the morning the flower of the manhood in the district rode towards the higher-lying auls in the plain of Irik-yak, where the games were to take place. On they rode, troop after troop. Towards noon I too went in the same direction, escorted by a bodyguard of 42 Kirghiz wearing their best khalats. And what varieties of colour! Khalats of every conceivable shade, check girdles, daggers and knives, baldrics with jingling vade-mecums—a piece of steel for striking fire, an awl, tobacco pouch, etc., head-coverings of every variety, mostly however small round black close-fitting caps (*calottes*), embroidered in red and yellow and blue. Closely surrounded by this gay holiday throng, I involuntarily felt in my plain grey travelling suit like a dervish amongst better folk. The sole ornament which gave a little brightness to my outward man was my compass chain, which, without much stretch of the imagination, the Kirghiz might easily have taken to be pure gold. Of the elders none made such a brave show as Togdasin Beg and Togda Mohammed Beg, chieftain of the Kirghiz who dwelt on the east side of Mus-tagh-ata. The former wore an orange-yellow gala khalat, edged with gold brocade, which I had brought him as a present from Kashgar the day before. Chance seemed to have played the chief part in determining the choice of attire in the case of the latter; for the colours were decidedly loud—a long navy blue khalat, girdled by a broad light blue sash, and a violet bag-cap with a gold ribbon round it. The wearer was a tall and strikingly typical Kirghiz, with oblique, narrow eyes, prominent cheek-bones, thin black beard and coarse moustaches, and rode a big coal-black horse of some foreign breed. Add to this the scimitar which dangled at his side in a black scabbard, and you have a picture of a true Asiatic Don Quixote.

We drew near to the upper villages, in and about which the bands of horsemen grew thicker and thicker. I was conducted to the place of honour in the middle of the plain, where I found awaiting me Khoat Beg, a fine old chieftain one hundred and eleven years old, surrounded by five of his sons—grey old men they were too—and a score of other horsemen. Although the aged patriarch's back was a little bent under the burden of his years, he nevertheless sat his saddle with as firm a seat and as proud a bearing as any amongst them. He wore a violet khalat, lined with fur, brown skin boots, and a brown turban. He had striking features, a large Roman nose, short white beard extending under the chin, and deep-sunk, grey eyes, which seemed to live more in the memories of the past than in the actual observations of the present. His people manifested the greatest veneration towards him; some of the begs hastening to throw themselves from their horses in order to pay their respects to him, all which he took with the imperturbable majesty of a god. The old man had formerly been Chong Beg (principal chieftain) over the Sarik-kol Kirghiz, a dignity which had passed from father to son in his family through seven generations before him, partly as independent chiefs, partly under foreign domination.

When not absorbed in his own meditations, the old man was very talkative, and plainly enjoyed telling what he could remember of past times and his own family circumstances.

A KIRGHIZ BAIGA

He had seven sons and five daughters, forty-three grandchildren, and sixteen great-grandchildren. Nearly all of them lived together in one community, a large aul (tent-village) which in summer was pitched beside Lake Kara-kul, and in winter near Bassyk-kul. His eldest son, Oshur Beg, an unusually facetious old man, who gradually attached himself to me, told me, that his father Khoat Beg in the course of his long life had had four Kirghiz wives, two of whom still lived, old women of ninety, besides one hundred Sart wives, whom he bought at different times in Kashgar, and whom he successively discarded when he grew tired of them.

Khoat Beg took such a strong fancy to my spectacles, that he asked me to give him them; but as I could not do without them, I told him that, as he had managed to get along without such things for one hundred and eleven years, I thought he might do without them a little bit longer. I afterwards made him presents of cloth, caps, and handkerchiefs. Later on in the autumn the old chief was to go with one of his sons to Yanghi-hissar, climbing a pass which came within about 350 feet of the altitude of Mont Blanc. He was going to look at some land he owned there, as well as to indulge in a little merry-making before the beginning of the long winter sleep.

A he-goat, in the literal sense of the word a scape-goat, was dragged in front of us. A Kirghiz sliced the animal's head off with a single sweep of his knife, and let the blood flow until it ceased of itself. The carcass was, so to speak, the prize of the subsequent mimic warfare, the object of the contestants being to obtain possession of it.

A man came forward, caught up the sheep across his horse, and rode away with it. We waited a few minutes. Then we saw a troop of horsemen approaching at a furious gallop. Eighty horses' hoofs rang on the hard ground—the grass gnawed off to the very roots by the sheep. The din was deafening. Wild, shrill shouts mingled with the jingling of the stirrups. On they came, enveloped in a cloud of dust. The foremost horseman flung the dead goat immediately in front of my horse's forefeet. Like a horde of Huns or a band of robbers they dashed past us, away across the plain. But wheeling smartly round, they were soon back again at the spot where we stood. The person who is thus honoured with having the dead goat flung down before him is expected to testify his sense of the favour conferred in some tangible fashion, either by offering dastarkhan—which is what the Kirghiz usually do—or by the present of a handful of silver *tengeh* (about 2¾*d.* each), which was what I offered on this occasion.

We had barely time to draw back before the wild

troop were upon us again. They flung themselves upon the still smoking carcass of the goat, and began to struggle for it as though they were fighting for a bag full of gold. All I could see of them was an indistinguishable confusion of horses and men enveloped in a cloud of dust. Some of the horses fell; others reared; others shied. Holding fast to their saddles, the riders leaned over towards the ground and snatched at the carcass as they swept past it. Some fell off and were nearly trampled under foot. Others clung underneath their horse's belly. All grasped at the goat, tugging and hauling in the wildest disarray. The stragglers in the gallop, the new arrivals, all plunged headlong into the *mêlée* as though they would ride right over the mass of struggling horsemen. The men shouted. The horses whinnied. The dust rolled up in clouds. The contestants were allowed to practise certain artifices, such as pulling at another man's bridle, striking his horse over the nose with his whip-stock to force him back, or even dragging one another out of the saddle.

The confusion was still worse confounded by a couple of champions who rode yaks with sharp horns. As these strong-necked animals pushed their way into the *mêlée*, they kept tickling the horses with their horns. This made the horses plunge and kick. The yaks, irritated by the kicks, thrust themselves in all the more stubbornly, till the contest began to look remarkably like a bull-fight. At length one of the men got a firm hold upon the goat's skin. He snatched the body up, clasped it tight between his knee and his saddle, and, bursting out of the throng, galloped away like the wind, describing a wide circle round the plain. Hard after him raced all the others. They disappeared from sight in the distance. Two or three minutes passed. Again the dull thud—thud of scores of horses' hoofs beating the ground. Straight down upon us they charged, oblivious of all hindrances. Another moment and they would have ridden over us and crushed us. We could not get out of their way. But, when within two or three yards of us, they wheeled sharply off, still going at a headlong pace. Once more the goat, now bruised into an indistinguishable mass of flesh, was flung at our feet, and then the struggle began again. This went on time after time.

I remarked to Khoat Beg, that it was a good thing for us old folk to be safe outside the scrummage. The old chief laughed, and said, he fancied it must be well-nigh a hundred years since he was my age. I let him surmise that in point of fact he was nearly four times as old as I was.

Meanwhile Togdasin Beg became so excited by the mimic battle, that he flung himself into the thick of it, and actually succeeded in gaining possession of the goat, and made his horse leap to one side. But getting a few Chinese hieroglyphics wealed across his face and nose in crimson, he became as quiet as a lamb, and pulling his horse in beside ours, was content to sit still and remain an onlooker.

Whilst the sport lasted, most of the participators in it took off their khalats, indeed some of them had the right side of the upper part of their body naked. With but very few exceptions every man came out of the contest with some sort of wound or scratch. Several of them had their faces so bloody that they rode off to the nearest brook to wash themselves. Nor were limping horses a rare sight. Caps and whips lay scattered all over the ground, and, the game at an end, I saw their owners wandering about over the battlefield looking for them. To tell the truth, it amazed me there were no serious mishaps. The reason of there being none is that from their earliest years the Kirghiz grow up on horseback, and so become habited—become skilled in all that belongs to horsemanship. This exciting and dangerous sport being concluded, the chief men present were invited to dastarkhan in the tent of the nearest beg. There we were entertained by the musicians of the neighbourhood to a "chamber concert."

I had been obliged to dismiss my interpreter, the Taranchi Daod. He turned out to be a self-willed

KIRGHIZ CHILDREN

individual, and was not very accurate in his Chinese interpretations. Immediately after arriving at Su-bashi he added to these accomplishments by beginning to gamble with the Chinese, and in one day lost 40 tengeh. When therefore I sent back the karakesh (horse owner) I hired at Kashgar, together with his horses, Daod received his orders to go with him. Thus of the men who left Kashgar with me the only one remaining was my faithful Islam Bai. I now further engaged two trustworthy Kirghiz, namely Yehim Bai and Mollah Islam, both of whom did excellent service during the journeys of the summer. In addition to these men, I employed others for shorter periods, as well as horses.

CHAPTER XXV.

LITTLE KARA-KUL LAKE

I HAD chosen Little Kara-Kul lake as a suitable starting-point for my summer's cartographical labours and excursions, and accordingly journeyed thither on July 12th, to take possession of a yurt which had been put up by agreement on its southern shore.

On the way, near a few small auls, we witnessed another baiga, which was, if possible, more turbulent than the previous one. A rider came tearing past with a live goat on his saddle, chopped its head off at one blow, and with the dripping body dangling against his horse's side began to career wildly round the auls. Hard after him followed the rest. But the man had a first-rate horse, and it was not until the third round had been completed that he was caught, and the goat taken from him and dashed at my feet, raising a cloud of dust. One or two of the men got ugly tumbles, and a yuz-bashi scraped his face against the ground, but went on, however, scarred and bloody, as if nothing had happened. After taking dastarkhan (refreshments) we rode down to the lake, followed by the tumultuous troop, who still continued their mimic contest; and we were not sorry when soon afterwards they disappeared, and we were left to settle down in peace in our lonely tent.

This was pitched close to the shore, and in front of it spread the blue waters of the little lake, disappearing in the mist. Togdasin Beg and a few other friends came with us and were invited to tea. They stopped until it began to grow dark; and the festive feeling was enhanced by a musician, who performed on a stringed instrument called a *kaumuss*. The victor of the baiga came to see me, and presented me with a can of *kumiss* (fermented mare's-milk); it was sour and cold, and tasted excellent. The only drawback to our camping-ground was the myriads of mosquitoes swarming over the flat shore of the lake, which was intersected in all directions by pools and arms from the glacier stream.

July 13th was our first working day by the lake. As we found that the south shore, permeated as it was by stagnant water, would probably be unhealthy for a lengthened stay, we decided to move to a suitable spot on the east side; and accordingly the next day the men packed up our goods and chattels, and we moved over. I myself took a couple of Kirghiz with me and mapped the outline of the lake with the plane-table and diopter, continuing the work till I reached the new camping-station. On the way I paid a short visit to old Khoat Beg, who was encamped there with six yurts.

At the south-east corner of the lake, in a narrow opening in the rock, we saw the Sarik-tumshuk-masar (the Saint's Grave on the Yellow Cape), decorated with yaks' tails and rags. A clear spring gushed out at the base of the steep schistose rocks with a temperature of 47°1 Fahr. (8°4 C.).

Our steps now bore directly along the shore, where the ruptured ends of the stratified schistose rocks fell sheer into the lake, often necessitating our riding in the water.

On our left stretched the lake, its surface varying from a pretty light green to deep navy blue, blotched here and there with streaks of dirty yellow mud brought down by the streams. On the west shore rose the huge rocky wall of the Sarik-kol chain, with its out-jutting promontories just visible through the hazy atmosphere.

When I arrived at the new camp, everything was in order; the yurt had been put up close to the shore, on a little patch of luxuriant grass between it and the mountain, and there our horses were contentedly grazing.

Yolldash (the Travelling Companion), a wretched Kirghiz dog, which, like the late Yollchi, had joined our expedition as a volunteer, and was greatly valued by my men, had already made himself at home and was guarding the tent. When we first made his acquaintance, he was travelling with some Chinese horsemen, who had visibly reduced him to the brink of starvation. However, when the dog saw us, he thought that, no matter who we might be, we should surely be better than the Chinese, so he turned back with us. I thought the creature so starved and miserable, that I wanted to send him away. But my men begged so hard for the new member of the expedition, that I gave way; and he followed us faithfully for a long while. He had a fine time of it now, ate as much as he liked, and enjoyed the sole right to the remains of our meals. He soon picked up, and grew into an unusually good and handsome dog. He was the best of watchdogs and the best of companions, and when, later on, we made a second visit to the Russian Pamirs, he became a great favourite among the officers on account of his liveliness. By degrees he grew to be such a companion to me that I could not do without him, and when, about a year later, he died of thirst in the Takla-makan Desert, the parting was really bitter.

We bought a sheep, which we now proceeded to kill, and all had a good meal. Islam roasted a *chisslik* (steak or chop); the Kirghiz provided us with yaks' milk; rice and tea we had ourselves, so that we could not have fared better.

That evening the sunset was beautiful, and threw a peculiar light on the clouds and western mountains, which were illumined with various shades of grey and yellow. The wind had been in the north, but towards evening went round to the east; and the waves, which broke against the stony beach with a sleepy, melodious murmur, were crested with dancing white horses. The moon soon rose over this beautiful picture; and, the temperature being pleasantly warm (62°6 Fahr. or 17° C.), we were able to enjoy our new camp, which was called Yanikkeh, to the utmost.

The following are a series of notes from my diary just as I wrote them down.

"July 14th. After the first meteorological observation of the day had been taken, we made a little botanical trip in the neighbourhood, and collected algæ from two or three lagoons along the shore.

"About one o'clock a violent squall passed over the country, with sharp gusts of wind and rain, which however did not last long. The white-crested waves were driven up to a considerable height, and dashed noisily against the beach. The sky was heavy and black with rain-clouds, chasing each other to the south. During the forenoon the mountains had been shrouded in the usual dust-haze, but the rain cleared the air, so that we could now see the

WEST SHORE OF LITTLE KARA-KUL

white snowfields of Mus-tagh-ata shining through the broken clouds with dazzling brilliance. The surface of the lake passed through the most wonderful changes of colour; near the western and southern shores it was such a bright green that the boldest impressionist would not have dared to paint it as it actually was. Farther out it was striped with violet; while near the eastern shore the water was dark blue. Grey and gloomy stood the mountain-giants, keeping guard over the little Alpine lake which lay cradled between their lofty crests. There was a flat stretch of fine pasture along the south shore; but on our side, with the exception of the little meadow where we were encamped, the mountains rose sheer from the lake.

"It was not till the afternoon that the weather permitted a short topographical excursion in the neighbourhood; even then we were overtaken by sharp showers of rain, and heard the thunder rumbling among the clefts of Mus-tagh-ata. We wandered through a typical moraine landscape, where wide tracts were strewn with mounds of grit and boulders of all sizes; nearly all the latter being of different kinds of gneiss and schist, chiefly crystalline mica-schist.

"These collections of gravel and grit sometimes formed continuous ridges, sometimes isolated cones. Not seldom they formed *cirques*, fifty to two hundred yards in diameter, with a rampart round, the last sometimes completely closed, sometimes with a single opening. Some of these *cirques* had a cone, others a cavity, in the middle.

"Several boulders were very highly polished, or striated; and everything tended to show that we were in a tract from which a glacier had once receded. One of these boulders particularly attracted my attention and was chosen as a topographical fixed-point on account of its dominant position. Its surface, two yards long and one broad, was smooth and polished, and on it was roughly but characteristically depicted six *tekkes* (wild goats). The brown gneiss rock had been scratched away with a sharp stone or perhaps an iron tool, and the design stood out in relief in dull grey. The Kirghiz could tell me nothing about the picture, except that they thought it was very old.

"We discovered that the north end of the enormous moraine fell sheer down to a river, which was almost entirely fed by the melting of the glaciers and snowfields. The stream was called the Ike-bel-su (the River from the Two Passes) and flowed through the Sarik-kol valley, then broke through the Mus-tagh chain, and under the name of the Ghez-daria (as I have already mentioned in a previous chapter) reached the plains near Kashgar.

"From the summit of the moraine we had a splendid view over the upper reaches of the river, rolling down its current as if issuing from a rocky portal between the lofty snow-covered mountains. On through the valley it wound, sometimes narrow and foaming, sometimes calm and broad, with grass-grown banks, on which were two or three Kirghiz auls.

"When we again returned to camp over another part of the moraine-ridge, we found that the Kirghiz had procured another big yurt; and in it my men settled down with the kitchen paraphernalia.

"Immediately south-east of the camp there was a dominant mountain of black schist, called Kara-kir (the Black Peaks); and, as it seemed to promise a splendid point of vantage for surveying the neighbouring country, I wished to ascend it as early as possible, which we did on July 15th.

"The panorama which unfolded itself to my view when we reached the top exceeded my most sanguine expectations. The long moraine-ridge, with its labyrinth of cones and grit-mounds, appeared from that elevated point of view to dwindle to insignificance, and the green-banked ribbon of the Ike-bel-su winding through the grey scenery formed a particularly marked feature in the landscape. But the sublime grandeur of the Mus-tagh-ata, whose white crests were visible between the clouds, completely dwarfed everything else. Fantastic, inky-black rocks broke up through the expanses of snow, some attaining an altitude of 20,000 feet; and above them again towered the spotless dome. The east side of the mountain was so precipitous and irregular, that I perceived at once, from its shape, it must be quite inaccessible. The northern versant presented a confused medley of rocks, snow-fields, and glaciers. On the other hand, the western declivities were particularly even and rounded, towards the summit the angle being only twenty-two degrees; while on the east side the inclination varied from thirty to forty-eight degrees.

"The Tegherman-tash-su (the Millstone Brook), which fell into the Ike-bel-su, was divided at its mouth into five arms, flowing over a talus slope or sort of sloping delta, partly formed by its own glacial *débris* and mud.

"In the south-west we saw the broad, level valley of

Su-bashi, with its river also forming a delta, and its marshes and innumerable miniature lakes laced like beads on a mat.

"In the west also there was a grand panorama. The bright surface of Little Kara-kul, lying between the massive mountain-chains, immediately underneath our feet, appeared quite small in comparison with their overwhelming masses. Its light green surface contrasted forcibly with its own dark green grassy shores, and with the grey mountain-walls broken here and there by moraine deposits. Sometimes the grass trenched a little upon the lake; but it was nowhere broad, except on the southern shore. The light fleecy clouds were reflected in the water, as their shadows glided over it. The turbid yellow flood of the Su-bashi, which debouched on the south, wound through the lake like a dirty ribbon. Immediately in front of us, near the west shore, there was a little island, the only one in the Kara-kul, if we except a few small green plots which have become detached from the grassy southern shore. On the other side of the lake the Sarik-kol chain faded away towards the north and west.

"The northern shore of Little Kara-kul was a moraine-wall, a continuation of that already described; that is the reason why the outline of that shore was so very irregular. The moraine was intersected by a stream which issued from the lake, which was also conspicuous from its green grassy banks; farther down it united with the Ike-bel-su. In the north-west, beyond the Kara-kul, we could see the two basins of Bassyk-kul.

"About midday we were again overtaken by a storm of rain and hail, but continued our way till we were sent home by really bad weather. I now felt that I had pretty well taken my bearings; I had my programme clear, and knew how and on what plan the mountain should be attacked.

"Every evening after dark I held a *levée* in my tent. The Kirghiz came from far and near, and always brought with them welcome gifts of sheep, partridges, new bread, fresh yak's milk and cream; in return for which they received money, pieces of cloth, caps, knives, etc., which I had brought from Tashkend for the purpose. In a short time we had a whole circle of friends, and felt quite at home in the place. During our later excursions, we never passed an aul without going into one of the yurts, and we were always pretty sure to find one or two old acquaintances. Our chief friend and protector, however, was Togdasin Beg, who often came to see us, and procured everything for us that we wanted, such as yaks, horses, tents, and the like.

"The whole day on July 16th there was a thick fog. In the morning the lake presented a curious sight, as the mist completely hid the farther shore from view, and we seemed to be standing on the brink of a boundless sea.

"I bade a couple of my Kirghiz undress and wade out into the shallow water, to collect some of the algæ which grew along the shore. Yolldash was also carried out, and given a thorough and much-needed bath. The water was not so cold but it could be used for bathing purposes. At one o'clock it was 63°7 Fahr. (17°6 C.), but it cooled off considerably during the night. At seven in the morning of the same day it was 53°2 Fahr. (11°8 C.). On clear days the water soon became warm in the shallow places, though naturally only the upper layers. By midday on July 16th, for example, the radiation rose to 138°2 Fahr. (59° C.), although the atmosphere was not clear; but at the depth of four inches the water was only 82°4 Fahr. (28° C.), which shows how impervious even such a thin layer of water is to the direct heat of the sun.

"We made an excursion to the confluence of the Kara-kul stream with the Ike-bel-su. At the north end of the lake we found a large semicircular creek, or bay. It was shallow, and grassy near the shore, although the moraine came down to within 50 or 100 yards of it. Near the mouth of the river the grass was broader and more luxuriant; but the mosquitoes swarmed over it in thick clouds, by no means enhancing our comfort.

"The Kara-kul stream issued from the lake through a trumpet-shaped creek, studded with erratic blocks projecting above the surface of the water; shortly afterwards it widened out into a small basin, called the Su-karagai-kul (the Water-Pine Lake). North of this, but not connected with the river, was another small sheet of water called the Angher-kul (the Duck Lake). Both basins were bordered with grass and marshland, interspersed between the moraines through which the river cut its way.

"A little farther on, the gradient suddenly became so steep that the river broke into cataracts over the stony *débris* which littered its bed, though its banks were in places still lined with narrow strips of grass. On it foamed, its channel becoming more and more deeply eroded, until it emptied itself into the Ike-bel-su. Near its mouth the velocity decreased all of a sudden, as if the river had encountered a serious check. Sometimes its water was as clear as crystal, sometimes foaming white, sometimes deep blue, until finally it mingled with the main stream, which was turbid and grey from the glacial-mud, and possessed twenty times its force. The bed of the Ike-bel-su was excessively deep, the river having energetically carved its way through conglomerates 150 to 300 feet high. It was absolutely impossible to cross it. I put down the breadth at 27 yards, and the velocity was 5½ feet in the second.

"A deafening roar echoed between the perpendicular walls; the water dashed a yard into the air every time it encountered an obstructing stone, and the spray rose in clouds; but the foam was hardly distinguishable, being as grey as the flood itself.

"A few yards below the confluence of the Kara-kul, its clear blue water, which was pressed towards the left bank, totally disappeared. Its effect was only visible a short distance, while its foam disappeared at once. With such violence and momentum did the enormous masses of water plunge on their way that we could feel the ground vibrating under our feet.

"The Kara-kul river had a temperature of 61°9 Fahr.

(16°6 C.); the Ike-bel-su of 57°9 Fahr. (14°4 C.). Thus the water which came direct from the glaciers was four or five degrees colder than that which lingered in the lake under the sun's rays, although the lake itself received similar cold glacial streams. After depositing its glacial mud in Lake Kara-kul, the stream became perfectly clear.

"Between the two watercourses the great moraine-bed sent out a tongue, thickly studded with chains of hills, ranged sometimes in rows, sometimes in circles, crescents,

OUR CAMP AT YANIKKEH, EASTERN SHORE OF LITTLE KARA-KUL

and amphitheatres. They belonged to the terminal moraine, which was still standing, showing how far the tongue of the Ike-bel-su glacier, which has now disappeared, reached at one time.

"On my return I had a visit from Oshur Beg, Khoat Beg's son, who brought me two live wild-geese caught at Bassyk-kul, and bread, milk, and butter.

"July 17th. There was a south wind blowing this morning, and the water on our shore was not quite clear, the waves having brought sedimentary matter from the mouth of the river. The beach round the creek exhibited plain indications of the effect wrought by the waves under the influence of the south wind. The water washed up an even wall of sand all round the creek, leaving also a belt of dry seaweed. We started out on an excursion, but were overtaken by such a violent north-north-westerly gale that we were obliged to turn back. This region is notorious for its winds. Those which come from the north and south are the most violent, as they sweep unhindered through the meridional valley. In accordance with the configuration of the country, the east winds are more irregular and squally, while from the west, or Pamirs, it seldom blows at all.

"Yes indeed, the wind often put our patience to the test; it curtailed or prevented the carrying out of many plans, and the whole summer long we were very much dependent on the caprices of the weather. On unfavourable days there was nothing for it but to sit in the yurt and write, or work out my sketch-maps. It was always refreshing to hear the monotonous song of the waves on the beach. To-day, too, the lake was greatly perturbed; long white-topped waves crossed it diagonally, and cast up sand and seaweed on the beach, so that the water was muddy for ten yards or more out into the lake, before the fresh green-blue colour supervened again. A thick mist came on by degrees, enshrouding the Kara-kul, so that nothing except the two points on either side of our creek were visible, and they seemed to be much farther off than they were in reality. When one white crest after the other came rolling in from out of the mist I had the feeling of standing by the open sea.

"Along the beach, near our camp, there were two small lagoons, one behind the other. The outer lagoon was connected with the lake, whence a deep narrow channel conveyed water to it every time the waves broke. The inner lagoon was separated from the outer by a strip of land six or seven yards broad, intersected by a narrow but deep channel, so that even there the water was churned up by the wind. The outer lagoon was separated from the lake by a grass-grown wall of earth a yard in height, which threatened to give way under the continual beating of the waves. It was evident that the lake had at one time overflowed our present camping-ground. The bottom of the lagoon was covered with fine sand and algæ, and in its sheltered waters were tadpoles and water-spiders.

"In the afternoon it rained hard, but about six o'clock suddenly cleared. All at once we heard a rushing sound, as if a gale of wind were approaching from the north-west. The noise grew louder and louder, came nearer and nearer. On the now calm and shining surface of the lake a dark blue band became visible on the opposite shore. It rapidly approached our side. The wind howled and lashed the water, and the next moment a hailstorm broke over us. It only lasted a few moments; but the ground was white with hailstones a quarter to half an inch in diameter. They soon melted in the sharp shower of rain which followed.

CHAPTER XXVI.

LITTLE KARA-KUL LAKE

(Continued)

"IT was not necessary to stay long by the Little Kara-kul to perceive clearly its geological formation. I soon saw that it was a moraine lake, formed by the damming of the valley by the moraine of the Ike-bel-su glacier, the remains of which are now pierced by the rivers that issue from the lake. The basin, or part of the valley dammed by the moraine, is filled with glacier and spring water, which bring down with them large quantities of sediment, and this, in conjunction with the drift-sand, is gradually choking the network of lake streams. The day will no doubt come when they will be effaced altogether, and the Kara-kul river will flow through the valley in a continuously eroded bed. The lake was undoubtedly much larger at one time, when the river flowed at the top of the moraine, and had not yet succeeded in digging down through it. The number of boulders still cumbering the bed of the river and lying in its broad mouth—fragments of the former medial moraine—testify to this; as do the lagoons just described. That the whole valley was once cut off by the now defunct glacier we have unmistakeable proof in the number of gravel-mounds, ridges, and boulders which lie scattered about on every side.

"The material, consisting of fine-grained mica-schist, crystalline schist, pretty, fine grey gneiss, coarse-grained gneiss with felspar crystals, and red varieties of the same, etc., is similar to that which I found in the higher regions of the Mus-tagh-ata. The gneiss boulders, which are spread over large areas, could only be brought thence, and the force which brought them such long distances from the solid mountain could only be ice. Indeed they exhibit unmistakeable signs that this was the case: they are rounded or hollowed out like bowls, and are much striated, or polished by attrition.

"July 18th. I had now completed my work on the east shore of the Kara-kul, and determined to move on to another camping-ground. I therefore ordered the men under Islam Bai's supervision to break up camp, and move the tent and baggage to a suitable spot on the shore of the lake, Bassyk-kul. Meanwhile I myself went on a topographical trip, accompanied by one of the Kirghiz, intending to make for the new camp in the evening.

"We crossed the bed of the moraine higher up than formerly, and then went down to the aul of Keng-shevär, a place of four yurts lying on the left bank of the Ike-bel-su. The tents were surrounded by splendid pasturage, and several of our friends lived there and received us with great cordiality. According to custom, the oldest inhabitant of the aul came forward to meet the guest with both hands to his forehead, and then showed me the way to his yurt, which had been hastily set to rights. A piece of carpet and one or two cushions were placed on the seat of honour opposite the entrance, and there I was invited to sit down by the fireside. The other inhabitants of the aul dropped in one by one and seated themselves round the fire, on which was boiling an iron pot containing tea. Tea and milk were served in bowls of wood or Chinese porcelain, and conversation was soon in full swing. Sometimes the men's wives, with their high, white, turban-like head-gear, and some of the young girls were also present; but they did not take part in the conversation. They only affected importance with regard to the fire, which they fed with *tesek* (dried yak-dung), and attended to the management of the household generally. These visits were always pleasant, and had further the great advantage, that I was able to glean valuable information as to ways and tracks, climate, the migrations of the Kirghiz, their manner of living, and the like.

"Our hosts told us, that they spend the summer only at Keng-shevär; in the winter, this part being exposed to wind and snow, they move on to the Shuveshteh kishlaks (winter villages), which are situated farther up and are more sheltered from wind and weather.

"The Ike-bel-su presented quite a different appearance seen from this little tent-village to what it had at the outlet of the Kara-kul stream, being 200 feet broad and the velocity about three feet in the second. At the only place where it was possible to ford it, we let a Kirghiz ride over, and found that the maximum depth amounted to 3¾ feet, but the bed was tolerably level and did not vary much. The volume was 2440 cubic feet in the second, which is remarkable for a river chiefly fed by glaciers. The water was said to be lowest about four o'clock in the afternoon; but it rises towards the evening, as the glacial streams, which do not reach the river before that time, then give up their tribute. There were several low islets in the river, more or less grass-grown, of which one divided it into two arms. In winter the bed is dry or has, at most, a few narrow rivulets of frozen water; but by the beginning of August the stream falls so considerably that it is possible to ride over it at several points without danger. A little way below the aul a projecting spur of the moraine forces the river to make a sharp bend to the right. The result of this is a little lake-like basin, into which the water eddies; after that it continues its way in a deep wide channel, breaking through the moraine-wall with a roar that can be heard at some distance.

"Opposite Keng-shevär, on the other bank, there was an aul with seven yurts. As its inhabitants pastured their sheep during the day on the left bank, the animals had all to be brought back across the stream in the evening, and it was very amusing to see what a difficult business it was. A number of men on horseback took each a couple of sheep across their saddles and rode in a long string through the river; but, as there were many sheep, it took a considerable time before the whole flock was safely landed on the other side.

"But we had to think of getting back before dusk came on and put an end to our map-making. We therefore set our course over the moraine, where we again found many pretty cirques with vegetation in the middle. In such situations grass grows comparatively well, as it is sheltered by the ring-like formation of the moraine, which also retains any rain that may fall. We reached the new camp on the shore of the Lower Bassyk-kul by way of the Angher-kul. In the middle of the former lake there was

MUS-TAGH-ATA FROM BASSYK-KUL, LOOKING SOUTH-SOUTH-EAST
Erratic Blocks (Gneiss) and Moraines in the foreground.

an island, with a moraine cairn sticking up in it. Our two yurts were pitched on a patch of grass, and around us lay a new domain to be explored.

"Our first day at Bassyk-kul was anything but a success. The wind blew; it poured with rain from morning till night, the heavy drops pattering incessantly on the tent-covering. Open-air work was out of the question; but happily I had so much back work to make up that the involuntary confinement was rather welcome than otherwise. Togdasin Beg paid me a visit, and was regaled with tea and Chinese brandy, the latter specially brought for such occasions, and was furthermore entertained with tunes on the musical-box, which never failed to arouse the Kirghiz' intense astonishment and liveliest interest. Our mountain friends were most impressed, however, by the Husqvarna rifles. They found the mechanism so complicated, that they declared no human hands could have constructed it, and that it must have been made by Allah himself.

"Togdasin Beg told me, that the Chinese garrison in the Sarik-kol valley was following all my movements with some uneasiness, and was kept informed daily by Kirghiz spies of what I was doing and where I was going. They wondered, if I were a *oruss* (Russian) or *Ferenghi* (European), how long I meant to stay, what my real motive was in making maps, and why I hacked pieces of stone out of the rocks. They had been ordered to watch the frontier towards the Russian Pamirs, and now a stranger, whom they supposed to be a Russian, had made his appearance, and was proceeding, unhindered, to find out how the land lay. Thanks, however, to the passport which the Dao Tai had given me they never molested us.

"Heavy blue-black rain-clouds swept down the many lateral valleys which strike off from the Sarik-kol chain towards the open country, in which were the two Bassyk-kul lakes. Everything was enveloped in a thick Scotch mist, darkening the otherwise magnificent landscape with gloom. Every now and again a fragment of the glacier or mountain-side became visible through the mist, which clung to the surface of the ground and drifted off to the south. The Kirghiz assured me that such continuous rain as that of to-day was unusual. The patch of grass on which we were encamped was transformed into a swamp, and we were constrained to dig deep ditches round the yurt, with branches running towards the lake, to protect ourselves from the wet. In the evening it cleared up, and the atmosphere became perfectly still. The lakes lay like dark mirrors, in which all the fantastic projections of the mountains were clearly reflected.

"During the ensuing days I explored the country round our new camping-ground, and mapped the west shore of Little Kara-kul. First of all we followed the shore-line, and where the rocks fell sheer into the lake we rode through the water, on the disintegrated terraces at their base. Then we made short excursions from the lake to the neighbouring mountains, where we often had decidedly disagreeable passages to traverse. There was one point which was especially favourable for studying this remarkable and beautiful Alpine region. Each of the twenty-one glaciers of the Mus-tagh chain was visible with the field-glass, clearly lit up, so that every detail was distinct. The slopes of the chain were draped with dazzling white snow, except the rocky pinnacles which projected highest. In places however, particularly in the lower regions, the snow was tinged a dirty yellow, due to dust brought thither by the wind. On the summits the snow formed a continuous covering, closely following the relief of the underlying mountains; but in several places its lower edge was broken, the snow having slid down over the precipices. Otherwise the tendency of the snow is to gravitate towards the gathering-basin of the glaciers, whence it is gradually dispersed by the ice-streams. These are sometimes narrow and compact, sometimes hive-shaped, sometimes thin and spreading, but always covered with gravel and boulders, which rest on the belts of ice between the transverse crevasses and give the glaciers a striped appearance. Some of the ice-streams are so covered with moraines that it is only with difficulty they can be distinguished from their surroundings.

"A trip to the isthmus between the two small lakes showed that they were separated from each other by a decayed, and often broken, moraine-wall, beside which we found erratic gneiss blocks measuring as much as 1000 cubic metres or 35,300 cubic feet, and with beautifully polished surfaces. It was plainly the oldest of the terminal moraines of the former Ike-bel-su glacier.

"On one occasion when we were returning from a trip of this kind, Yehim Bai, who was carrying the topographical instruments, lost a brass diopter, and I gave him to understand that, if the missing instrument were not found, he would be in disgrace. He forthwith started off to go over the ground again, and see if he could find it. An acquaintance, whom he eventually met, told him, that an extraordinary metal thing had been found and taken to the Chinese commandant, Jan Darin, at Bulun-kul, who thought he could put a spoke in my wheel by retaining it. I sent off a messenger at once, to inform Jan Darin that he would have to settle the matter with the Dao Tai, if he did not return me the instrument. I received the diopter back immediately.

"I spent a whole day in investigating the country between the Lower Bassyk-kul and the Ike-bel-su. A small stream issued from the lake, and flowing through fairly luxuriant grass-land, littered with fragments of the moraine, joined the main stream a little way north of the river Kara-kul. The Ike-bel-su had decreased considerably in volume the last few days, owing to the fall in the temperature; but here too it raced between perpendicular or oblique conglomerate walls, in the sides of which round gneiss blocks were partially embedded, looking as if every moment they would topple down into the river.

"On July 24th I examined the upper basin of the Bassyk-kul. About the middle of the south shore a promontory, formed by a spur of the mountain, fell almost sheer into the lake, so that none but foot-passengers could get round it. We, being mounted, were obliged to make our way through a pass over the ridge.

"This little pass, called Bassyk-kulden-kiasi-davan (the Mountain-Path Pass of Bassyk-kul), was situated not more than two hundred feet above the lake, but had steep approaches, and its summit commanded a fine view. At our feet basked the little lake, washing the promontory on three sides; we also saw its small islands and shoals, its submarine moraine elevations and erratic blocks, still half immersed in the water, and the small deltas which form

BASSYK-KUL AND BASSYK-KULDEN-KIASI-DAVAN

at the mouths of the streams that entered it from the western valleys. On the isthmus between the lakes was the crumbling moraine-wall, in the middle not more than eight or ten feet above the level of the water. Just at that low spot there was a marsh; nevertheless all visible connection between the two lakes was entirely wanting. The Kirghiz told me, that even in the spring and summer, when the increase of water from the western valleys is sometimes considerable, the rise of niveau is never very perceptible, and no water ever flows over from the upper

THE LOWER BASSYK-KUL AND THE MUS-TAGH CHAIN

to the lower basin. Hastily surveyed, it might be supposed that the lake possessed no outlet, and that it was therefore salt. The water, however, was perfectly fresh and clear. A glance at the map reveals a satisfactory explanation of this. The lower lake, it is true, does not receive any visible affluent, but out of it flows a tiny stream. The lake must therefore receive an invisible influx, and this naturally comes from the upper basin, whose surplus water percolates under the isthmus moraine to the lower lake, and thence finds its way to the Ike-bel-su. Bassyk-kul was situated 12,221 feet, and Little Kara-kul 12,201 feet, above sea-level.

"Several subsidiary chains branched off from the main Sarik-kol range, and their *yilgas* or side-glens all opened towards the lake. The most important were the Kara (the Black), Yellang (the Bare), and Khamaldi (the Gusty) yilgas. The last-named had its own stream, running into a creek; while the streams from the first two united with several other small watercourses, and formed one, which again just before reaching the lake divided into two arms with a delta between. The sediment brought down by these several streams has been deposited in long narrow tongues and islets of mud; and beyond them again lay a group of moraine islands.

"In the three glens which I have just mentioned there was more or less good pasturage; the yaks, however, have to put up with the inferior qualities, as the better grass is reserved for the sheep. Here the Naiman Kirghiz of Khoat Beg's aul spend the three coldest winter months. Through the Kara-yilga a path leads up to the Sarik-kol pass, Kok-ala-chukkur (the Green-Chequered Depths), and thence to Lake Rang-kul. It can however only be traversed by yaks or by people on foot, and is seldom used, except occasionally by Kirghiz going to the Russian Pamirs without permission from the Chinese authorities.

"At four o'clock it again began to rain; and the wind blew from the north. We rode back towards the west shore of the lake by following the little Kara-yilga stream, which was now dry, with the exception of small pools in the deeper holes. An hour and a half later we observed a most extraordinary phenomenon. A slight rushing sound was heard from up the bed of the stream. Then a brownish grey wave of water appeared suddenly round a bend, and foamed down among the stones, first slowly and gradually, filling the deeper parts, and winding between the steep excavated banks, along which there was a narrow belt of vegetation. This onrush of water takes place regularly every evening at this time of the year; it is glacier water from the Sarik-kol chain, which only reaches the lake towards evening.

"On July 25th we broke up camp at Bassyk-kul and

went to Keng-shevär, whence I intended beginning the exploration of Mus-tagh-ata. On our way thither, we passed an unusually fine circular moraine, about a hundred yards in diameter, situated on the south shore of the Bassyk-kul. In the middle there was a tiny round pool, surrounded by a ring of white salt deposit, which in its turn was girdled by a belt of vegetation; outside of all was the moraine-wall, with its one opening towards the lake. Although the pool was on a level with the lake, and quite near its shore, so that it was fair to assume a subterranean connection between them, the water in the *cirque*, which was called Shor-kul (Salt Lake), was absolutely salt. The Kirghiz told me that sheep which drink of it get cramp and die.

"At Tamga-tash we met Togdasin Beg, bringing me a sheep and a can of yak's milk as presents. He accompanied us to Keng-shevär, and stopped the night there. The sheep was killed in the evening, and the inhabitants of the aul were invited to the feast; but we were disturbed during the proceedings by a violent whirlwind, which threatened to carry away the yurt. All the guests scrambled to their feet and seized hold of the tent-poles, while two or three other men anchored the tent with ropes and supports."

CHAPTER XXVII.

AMONGST THE GLACIERS OF MUS-TAGH-ATA

THE following day we rode up the northern flank of Mus-tagh-ata, and crossed the huge ridge on the left side of the Ike-bel-su. The gradient was steepish before we reached the top, which rose and fell in long sweeping undulations, but otherwise was fairly level, the surface being covered with sand, gravel, and small boulders, with here and there a few tussocks of grass and clumps of *Ranunculaceæ*. On the other side of the summit, we again reached the Kara-kul watershed, whence a brisk little rivulet from the glen of Köntöi flowed down to the lake through a broad shallow bed. Beside this stream, at a height of 13,530 feet, were the Kotch-korchu yeylaus (summer grazing-grounds), which we chose as our first starting-point for exploring the glaciers.

The Kirghiz belonging to the aul had come there three months previously, and intended to remain three more; the six winter months they spend in the Köntöi-yilga. There exists among the Kirghiz a traditional agreement by which each family or clan possesses its own kishlaks and yeylaks; a rule which cannot be broken without a general convocation being held. The inhabitants of this place, like most of the Sarik-kol Kirghiz, belonged to the Kara-teit tribe. Their aksakal, or chief, Tugul Bai, was ninety-six years old, sound in mind and body, and with pleasing manners. The active life they lead in the open air hardens the Kirghiz to such an extent that as a rule they live to a very great age.

To-day again there were torrents of rain and the thunder echoed among the mountains. Shortly afterwards we heard a rushing sound, which our hosts explained was always audible after heavy rain; it was the rain-water streaming over the precipices.

My first business at Kotch-korchu was to pay and dismiss the two Kirghiz, Nur Mohammed and Palevan, who had done good service hitherto, but knew nothing of the glacier world up above, neither had they any yaks. In their stead I engaged a couple of Kirghiz belonging to the place, and had their yaks out on parade in the evening; yaks being the only riding-animals which can make their way at all in these high glacial regions.

On July 27th, mounted on a splendid black yak and accompanied by a couple of Kirghiz as guides, I steered my course eastwards towards the first glacier to be explored, Gorumdeh. We rode quietly along over country sloping towards the north, and cut through by three small glacier streams. Leaving on the right some angular inky-black rocks, we discovered behind them a small glacier, excessively steep at its upper end, but of no very great extent. Farther to the east there were several similar prominent outcrops of rock, huge ragged masses of mountain, between which the glaciers thrust out their finger-like projections towards the north. The largest of these was called Gorumdehning-bashi (the Head of the Stony Tract); its stream, which gathered up glacier water from all the other brooks, flowed through a deeply excavated channel and farther down united with the Ike-bel-su.

I contented myself with mapping the left lateral moraines of the Gorumdeh glacier whilst riding up. For this purpose I only used the compass. The distances I measured by adding up the yak's steps, allowing for the errors due to our irregular course, and after having previously measured how many steps on the uneven ground corresponded to a hundred yards.

The lower part of the Great Gorumdeh glacier was so encumbered with gravel and other detritus that it was often difficult to distinguish it from the neighbouring rocks. How steep this stream of ice was will be understood, when I state that the point of the tongue inclined at an angle of fully nine degrees. But after that the slope of the glacier-trough decreased considerably, and the large full-flowing stream that issued from underneath the terminal moraine meandered fairly quietly down, often without forming cataracts.

The Lesser Gorumdeh glacier was split into two branches by an island of rock, the outer branch being hedged on the left by eight or ten more or less parallel lateral moraines. Between the outermost of these, which

THE GORUMDEH GLACIERS, LOOKING SOUTH

was thirty to forty-five feet high, and the soft grass-grown ridge on which we were riding, there was a stream, which higher up traversed a small triangular lake between the ridge, the moraine, and the solid rock of Mus-tagh-ata.

The right-hand wall which bounded the Lesser Gorumdeh glacier on the west was crowned with extensive snow-fields, which from time to time slip down to its foot and there form new miniature glaciers. In this way they have heaped up a remarkable terminal moraine, about forty-five feet in height, at the base of the mountain. From this also a stream finds its way down the northern declivities to Little Kara-kul.

On our way back to the yurt we were in several places astonished by the brilliant colouring of the Alpine flora. The flowers seemed to flourish in spite of the niggard soil of the moraines, and were conspicuous by their almost glaring hues. The higher we ascended the purer and more vivid the colouring. No doubt the slight absorption of light by the atmosphere at those lofty altitudes has a direct influence on vegetation.

Another day was devoted to the Great Gorumdeh glacier. From a grassy ridge we rode our yaks out over the rugged moraines, and terrible difficulty we had to get across them. Rock succeeded rock, and the yaks often stepped through the holes between them, though luckily without falling. I could not help admiring the cleverness of these animals in picking their way; though riding them is by no means pure enjoyment. You require some practice before you can feel thoroughly at home in the saddle. One moment the heavy animal balances himself on the sharp edge of a rock; the next he jumps incontinently over a yawning chasm, and somehow manages to secure a foothold on the opposite side. Sometimes, again, he pulls himself together, and with rigid, immovable legs, proceeds to glissade down a precipitous gravel slope, where a two-legged being would inevitably come to grief. Riding a yak, however, in spite of the animal's undeniable good points, is a trial of patience, by reason of his absolute sluggishness of temperament. He often comes to a dead stop, and has to be reminded of his duties with a cudgel. To any application of the whip he is absolutely insensible, whilst he looks upon a moderate blow as a sort of caress, and answers it with a cheerful grunt. Nothing short of a bludgeon would convince the beast I rode, that we were not out on a mere pleasure trip. In spite of blows he plodded on at his usual phlegmatic pace.

I now ascertained that the moraine belt on the left side of the Great Gorumdeh glacier was much broader than I had thought yesterday, and for a couple of hours we rode over a succession of broad ridges. Finally we reached a little moraine tarn, with green muddy water, into which flowed a many-branched babbling brook that came foaming down one of the outermost moraines, forming a delta of muddy sediment and *débris* at its foot, over which its arms again divided.

This stream seemed to issue from one of the smaller glaciers; but although its volume was as much as 70 or 100 cubic feet in the second, the tarn had no visible outlet, nor did it rise above a certain level, as the surplus water that issued from underneath the moraines flowed into the general glacier-basin. The tarn could not exist at all between moraine-walls of such coarse material were it not that the sedimentary matter which it brings down itself forms a sort of foundation for the water to rest upon.

From the tarn we rode up in a southerly direction, between two gigantic moraine-walls. The trough between them was overgrown with sparse tufts of grass, wild rhubarb, and other plants, and was well named Gul-tcha-yeylau (the Pasture of the Wild Sheep); for here, and far out on the glacier, we found the tracks of wild sheep.

As the moraines farther on became worse and worse, consisting exclusively of cyclopean blocks of naked rock, we left our yaks, and made our way on to the glacier on foot. After passing the last lateral moraine, which by-the-by was still in course of formation, we reached the firm ice. At first it was covered with gravel and boulders to such an extent that the clear ice-pyramids only peeped out at intervals. The lateral moraine, carried on the back of the glacier, was 500 yards in breadth, and ceased somewhat abruptly where the white ice began. This formed a chaos of pyramids and mounds, which, however, had no sharp edges, but were much rounded, and caked with a layer of soft, wet ice, chalky white and resembling snow. This was, of course, the result of ablation, or the destructive influence of the atmosphere and warmth upon the ice, which was then working everywhere

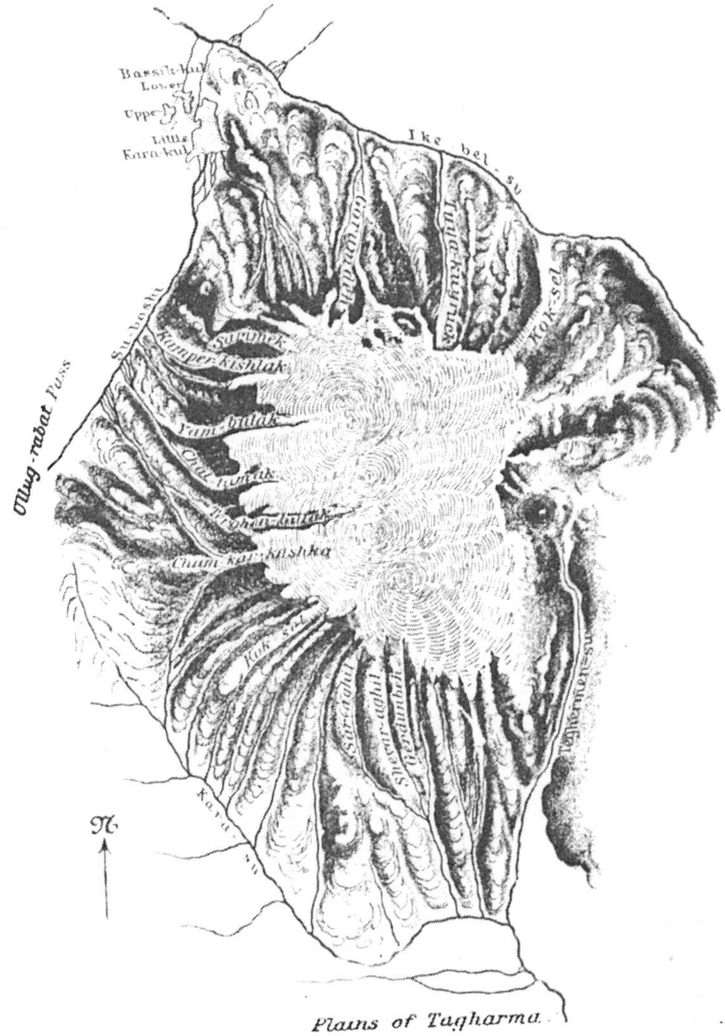

SKETCH MAP OF MUS-TAGHATA

with great activity. The sound of trickling, dripping water was audible in all directions among the boulders and stones, in the crevasses, and in small pools on the surface of the ice. The glaciers rumbled and cracked; every now and again we heard the ringing echo of smaller boulders and gravel falling into the gaping fissures, and in the distance the rushing sound of the glacial torrents, which, now that the sun was high, were fed abundantly from every side. The material brought down from the mountain consisted for the most part of the same grey gneiss which we had previously observed down by the lakes. Gigantic blocks such as those that lay beside Bassyk-kul were, however, absent. The smaller fragments of stone, by reason of their greater power of absorbing heat, had sunk down in holes in the ice, and lay at the bottom in a little pool of water. The larger blocks, on the other hand, protected the underlying ice from melting, and therefore formed glacier tables resting on low platforms of ice.

A glance northwards, that is to say, down the glacier, showed us, to the left, the grey masses of the lateral moraine, with only occasional glimpses of the ice showing through; to the right the white corrugated surface of the naked glaciers, with the two medial moraines gradually merging into one, the biggest I saw on the Mus-tagh-ata; and in the background the deep depression which marked the continuing line of the glacier, and through which probably the Gorumdeh formerly streamed to the Ike-bel-su glacier, although the old terminal moraine has been entirely swept away by the glacier-stream.

Lastly we went down to a place near the tongue of the glacier, which was split into two portions by a small lake of clear water. The highest altitude we reached on the glacier was 14,700 feet above sea-level.

To the south was the vast *firn* or root of the glacier, a gathering basin into which the snow slid down from the surrounding precipices, leaving step-like platforms behind it.

On July 29th we again broke up camp and got under way for a new base of operations, namely, a spot more conveniently situated for the investigation of the glaciers which streamed out towards the west.

We started in a south-south-westerly direction, and made our way up the grass-grown slopes. The weather was cold and misty, with an occasional snowstorm. At length we reached the pass of Sarimek (the Pass of the Yellow Elbow), an important feature in the country, as it forms the passage over a gigantic spur of the Mus-tagh-ata which stretches to the north-west, dividing the glaciers and streams of the northern declivities from those of the western. The pass was strewn with gravel and small boulders, and on its southern face were fissured rocks of an unusually hard, dark crystalline schist, inclined at an angle of thirty-eight degrees to the north.

If, standing on this pass, we turned towards the massive knot of Mus-tagh-ata, the following picture from left to right, or from north to south, unfolded itself to view: First of all, the rocky buttresses, foreshortened, with a small snow-clad glacier; then, between two arms of the mountain, both in part thickly carpeted with snow, there was another small glacier, fairly clean at the top, but at its lower extremity strewn with fine gravel, so that the blue ice in the fissures was only visible here and there. In the middle of the glacier transverse crevasses predominated, at its lower end longitudinal crevasses. The tongue of the glacier was girdled by gigantic moraines crumpled up into several ridges. Between the third rocky buttress and that part of Mus-tagh-ata which we were on in April, and high up on the mountain-side, there was a deep gorge, into which the Sarimek and Kamper-kishlak glaciers poured their streams, while they in their turn were separated by a huge snow-clad wall of rock. The former glacier was encumbered with moraines; the latter was shining white. Finally, in the south, the pass of Ullug-rabat; and in the west the entire Sarik-kol chain, with its thinly-scattered snowfields. It was partly hidden by particularly beautiful white cirrus-clouds, which contrasted strikingly with the steel-blue, wintry sky over the Pamirs in the background.

The descent from the pass was very steep; we rode down the gully of a stream which issued from the right-hand side of the Sarimek glacier, and raced merrily along its stony bed, tumbling down falls and cataracts as it went. We left the terminal moraine with its imposing front, crossed some streams, and reached a small patch of water-soaked greensward, where I collected several new species of plants. A herd of kiyick, or wild goats, were peace-

SARIMEK AND KAMPER-KISHLAK GLACIERS, LOOKING SOUTH-EAST

fully grazing there; but upon catching sight of us, they instantly sprang up the mountain-side. We then crossed five more brooks, fed with glacier water. Between them low elongated ridges ran down to the Sarik-kol valley, forming black and gloomy continuations of the rocky buttresses which, like radii or ribs, divided the glaciers one from another.

Some of the men, who had gone on ahead with the caravan, were already camped when we arrived, having chosen a piece of lush, well-watered grass, that afforded splendid pasturage for the yaks.

That evening it snowed hard, and the next morning the mountains were covered with a thin sheet of snow. The Kirghiz said, that winter was already coming in the mountains, and that it would get colder and colder every day.

On July 30th winter was upon us in full severity. It snowed the whole day, heavily and ceaselessly; sometimes the entire landscape was enveloped in dense clouds of driving snow, so that not a trace of the mountains, or of the valley lying deep down below them, was to be seen. It was dark, cold, and gusty, and the inhospitable mountain received us at Yam-bulak-bashi much as it had done the April previously. There was no prospect of any excursion that day, for we could not see many steps in front of us for the snowstorm, and my winter wardrobe, consisting of a sheepskin coat, fur cap and waistcoat, and *valenkis* (Russian felt boots), was not yet unpacked. In order not to be hampered with too much paraphernalia, I had this time only brought a small yurt with me; and in this I sat the whole day, writing and drawing, with a cup of hot tea every now and then to keep me warm. The men crowded together in their great sheepskin coats, and sat crouched under the shelter of a block of gneiss, listening to Mollah Islam, who was reading aloud out of an old book of tales. As the snowstorm increased in violence, I made them come into the tent, and let them continue their reading. Towards evening it ceased to snow; but heavy grey clouds swept through the deep valleys, trailing their long fringes and draperies behind them. Every now and again flying fragments became detached from them, and sprinkled the rocks with their white powder. In the evening we had a visit from the aksakal of the aul of Yam-bulak, and half-a-dozen other Kirghiz, who came to bid us welcome, and brought a sheep with them as a present. They were regaled with tea and bread, as usual, and were given an equivalent for their sheep.

When the weather eventually cleared, all the mountains re-appeared in a garb of dazzling white, and we were surrounded by a thorough winter landscape. The white mantle, however, did not reach down to the bottom of the Sarik-kol valley, because at this time of the year the snow changes to rain at a lower altitude.

The weather being favourable on July 31st, we were able to start on our scramble over the Yam-bulak glacier. Its surface was perfectly white, being covered with soft,

THE YAM-BULAK GLACIER AND ITS PORTAL IN THE MUS-TAGH-ATA

wet, sticky snow. Small glacial streams, with a temperature of 31°5 Fahr. (0°29 C.) rippled cheerily over the ice. We struck a south-south-easterly line across the uneven ice-sheet towards the right-hand lateral moraine, which was from three to seven feet thick, and sent out long crescent-shaped offshoots towards the central parts of the glacier. There were also a few small glacier-tables or ice-pillars 14 inches in height; and a crevasse, 6 feet wide and 32 feet deep, which would have put an end to further advance, had it not hung so far over at the edges that we were able to get across it. The ice in its sides was of the purest blue, and heaps of snow lay at the bottom. The glacier was for the most part covered with a thin layer of soft, wet slush, caused partly by the newly fallen snow, partly by the destructive agency of ablation. The beautiful transparent blue ice was only visible in the fissures, and in the channels where the small glacial streams flowed over the surface of the glacier. These streams, with their delightfully babbling, crystal-clear

ON THE YAM-BULAK GLACIER, LOOKING EAST

water, were none of them large; for usually they were soon swallowed up by some gaping crevasse.

After we had advanced some 440 yards on the glacier, probably a third of the whole way across, the ice became perfectly impracticable, a maze of hummocks and pyramids, crevasses and streams, these last running in deep trenches, sunk between the irregularities of the ice and partly hidden by snow-bridges.

Looking upward from this point towards the rocky part of the mountain, situated between its perpendicular buttresses, *i.e.* towards the east, we perceived even then that the glacier trended in three different directions, namely to the east, the south, and the west; or in other words, forwards and to both sides. Immediately after leaving the upper reaches of the mountain, it streamed over a fairly steep fall, and then across broken ground. Its lower part was therefore excessively cut up and fissured by transverse crevasses. The offshoots of the right-hand moraine, consisting of gneiss and innumerable varieties of schist, reached as far as the spot where we were standing. There, too, we again found some glacier-tables, one on

VIEW FROM THE YAM-BULAK GLACIER, LOOKING WEST

a pillar nearly four feet high and leaning over very much to the south-west, where the sun, as usual, had most power to undermine it. There also, from a very narrow outlet, a glacier stream issued: we heard the water purling softly at the bottom, fifty feet or more down.

On our return to the moraine, where we left the yaks tied to the boulders, we came across a place where the marginal moraine was broken off, so that the edge of the glacier lay naked and flayed, so to speak. Its sides rose up to a height of forty feet at an angle of sixty-four degrees, and down the glassy face ran numerous tiny streamlets, the head-waters of the Yam-bulak-bashi. In a couple of small moraine-pools at the edge of the glacier the water was a grey-green colour, and had a temperature of 31°2 Fahr. (0°46 C.).

Our expedition proved that the glacier differed very much in appearance from what it was in April. The crevasses were not so deep, being partly filled with material which had fallen in; nor were their edges so sharp; while the surface was in general softer and more rounded. Shortly put, everything tended to prove, that the glacier was in a condition of great activity, and that all the agents of ablation were at work to level down its outer form and fill up its depressions.

We afterwards followed the right lateral moraine to the tongue of the glacier; but had not reached it when a violent gale sprang up from the south, accompanied with hail, which stung us in the face, and compelled us to seek shelter under some overhanging rocks. The hail was followed, as usual, by torrents of rain, and it was only after waiting an hour that we were able to proceed.

Immediately in front of the tongue of the glacier we made a halt: it was a confused jumble of pyramids, ridges, and huge fragments of ice, all greatly weathered. The face resembled four icebergs, two large ones in the middle and two smaller ones on either side, separated from each other by crevasses, and set up, as if on purpose, facing the south-west sun, which beats on them and destroys them. From the right-hand side a little stream flowed through a glacier portal only 24 inches high, which, at a distance, looked like a narrow fissure between the sill or ground-moraine and the ice. The water in the stream was grey and muddy from the abraded materials it held in suspension. It foamed and bubbled along the ice and among the moraines. Here too a number of small brooks and streamlets assembled on their way down to the glacier river, and fell in cascades of perfectly clear water, not broader than a man's arm. They spurted out from the top of the glacier-wall in veritable fountains and waterfalls, the fine spray which streamed off them being coloured with all the tints of the rainbow. One of the small terminal moraines seemed to indicate that it had advanced since our last visit in April.

In the evening the sides of the mountain were lashed by a violent hailstorm, which pelted the roof of the yurt, and compelled us to shut the smoke-vent and put out the fire. The hailstones were about a quarter of an inch in diameter, and as they were followed by snow, which fell in big, close flakes, the slopes and the moraines were

THE GLACIER STREAM OF THE YAM-BULAK GLACIER, LOOKING EAST

soon covered again with their wintry mantle. Yolldash, who was guarding the entrance of the tent, howled dismally out in the cold. The bad weather continued the whole of the next day, August 1st, though mostly in the shape of rain, so that the snow quickly disappeared; but it was a day lost, and there was nothing for it but to stick to the tent and work out my last sketch-maps.

August 2nd was devoted to the Kamper-kishlak glaciers. The smaller of these ended at a considerable altitude, and had piled up in front of itself an enormous terminal moraine, 750 to 1000 feet in height. This bore rather the appearance of a huge mound of gravel, for the material which resulted from attrition gradually fell and slipped down the steep mountain-sides. The moraine-mound inclined at an angle of thirty-five and a half degrees.

It was now a question of getting up on the top of the great Kamper-kishlak glacier, the left side of which we were following, though riding on the moraine. The ascent was so steep that we were obliged to leave the yaks and proceed on foot, till we reached the solid mountain—hard crystalline schist—on the left side of the rocky buttresses. The sky was entirely clouded over; but the usual hailstorm did not whiten the ground, as the hailstones rolled, hopping and jumping, into the numberless crevasses of the moraine, and when the shower cleared off, the wet boulders quickly dried in the arid air.

The glacier extended down its bed in the shape of a long flat, narrow spoon, turned alternately up and down, and surrounded on all sides by moraine-ridges. On the whole its surface was level, with elongated, flattened undulations. No transverse crevasses were seen; but, on the other hand, there were two or three very long narrow ones running lengthwise down the middle of the tongue, and the whole of the left side of the ice was jagged by small fissures set close together at the edge. When we got down upon the ice again from the rocks, it became clear to me at once how the lateral moraine had been formed. Had I taken but one step, I should have slid twenty through the loose *débris*, which continued falling, like a landslip, down upon the lateral moraine.

Once over the fissures at the edge, it was an easy matter to walk on the ice, which was sheeted with a thick layer of snow. This, however, sometimes concealed longitudinal crevasses, which we had to feel for with our alpenstocks. A block of gneiss, some 140 cubic feet in extent, had dropped through the ice by reason of its weight, instead of forming a glacier-table. After we walked about six hundred and sixty yards across the glacier (its full width was some three-quarters of a mile), farther advance was cut off in every direction by a deep crevasse, a dozen feet wide and forty-five in depth. Its sides were a deep blue, and from them hung long icicles.

On August 3rd we started on a new excursion, namely, back again to the Yam-bulak glacier, to put in rods, by which, after a certain time had elapsed, we could tell at what rate the ice was moving. It was by no means easy to find a stick long enough for this purpose, for there was not a tree or a bush to be found in the whole of the Sarik-kol valley, except half-a-dozen stunted birches at Kayindeh-masar, which, of course, could not be touched, as they were growing on holy ground. At length Yehim

BUILDING A KIRGHIZ YURT

Bai succeeded in finding a bundle of *oks*, or poles used to support the dome-shaped roof of the yurt.

Equipped with these, we succeeded in getting nearly 580 yards across the ice, and putting in nine poles, some in small moraine-ridges, others in the ice itself, and their position was marked on a map drawn to the scale of 1:4480. It would have been better to have placed them in a straight line across the glacier; but this was impracticable, as the whole of the left side was absolutely inaccessible, and formed a projecting hump as compared with the right side. This is because the left half of the glacier is completely shaded by the mountain crests to the south of it during its entire passage between the enclosing walls of rock. Not a ray of sunshine, therefore, reaches this part of the glacier until after it has emerged from the mountain's arms. The right half, on the other hand, even when in the gorge, is exposed to the direct rays of the sun, and therefore melts incomparably the quicker. This fact was plainly perceptible in the shape of the glacier, even after its issue from the passage, as the right half was about 130 feet lower than the left. After it emerged, the glacier-tongue spread out to two or three times its previous breadth, and became correspondingly thinner, so that the process of melting goes on over a more extended surface, and the tongue soon shrinks to a comparatively narrow point.

The inevitable hailstorm came on at four o'clock. First of all, in the deep valley below us we saw light clouds, like smoke, hurrying before the north wind. Then they swiftly ascended the mountain-side, and before we knew where we were had enveloped us in their disagreeable vapour. It grew dark and cold. The hailstones rattled on the ice, and we could do no work, only seat ourselves under the shelter of a lofty ice-pyramid, and wait. When we got back to the tent, a long time afterwards, we were very tired and half frozen.

The new day which broke promised fine weather by way of a change, and we had a glorious trip to the Kamper-kishlak glacier, the right side of which we had still to examine. On that side the glacier sent out a massive "spine," which almost touched the left flank of the lateral moraine of the Sarimek glacier. It consisted of a sheet of ice, nearly 100 feet thick, broken off almost perpendicularly at its face, and on the whole was remarkable for its great purity. There were no moraines on the front wall of the glacier worthy of the name; but there were occasional blocks of gneiss and mica-schist, the largest measuring as much as 850 cubic feet. This rudimentary terminal moraine was fed in a niggardly way by the fragments of rock we had seen scattered about over the surface of the glacier.

At the base of the glacier-wall there was a large grotto, a dozen feet high and nearly as many deep, which had manifestly been caused by the relative warmth of the earth. Four small glacial streams and several little rills dropped from the edge of the ice in pretty cascades. The largest had a fall of sixty feet, and had eaten into the edge of the ice, so that it did not come all the way from the top. Another had cut nearly twenty feet into the ice, and as the brash had got heaped up on top of it, the streamlet resembled a spring issuing from a hole in the level wall. It was a beautiful sight, to stand underneath the big waterfall, and watch it shoot out into the air as if from the gutter of a house, split into a thousand drops that glittered like pearls in the sun. The ice was everywhere as soft as a sponge, so that we could actually make "snowballs" of it. Water was dripping, trickling in every direction; no matter which way we turned we heard the sound of bubbling and running water. The ice was courting destruction in venturing down to tracts whose climate it could not endure. Beneath the face of the glacier were large detached blocks and heaps of extremely rotten ice, which had broken off and were melting rapidly. When the grotto, just mentioned, has become sufficiently hollowed out, and the superincumbent mass of ice too heavy, the latter will crash down, and contribute to the hastier decay of the glacier.

Keeping immediately alongside the ice, we then rode round the face of the glacier, and continued up its right side. At one point at the foot of the glacier, where a cascade splashed noisily into a pool of its own making, the Kamper-kishlak approached so close to the lateral moraine of its neighbour, the Sarimek glacier, that we could scarcely get through the narrow passage.

The surface of the glacier sloped at an angle of twenty-five and a half degrees, and was thus extraordinarily steep as compared with the glaciers of the Alps, which often have an inclination of less than one degree in their lower regions. The two contiguous glaciers of Sarimek and Kamper-kishlak approached each other at right angles, and between them, near the rocky spine which divided their common *névé*-basin, a brook issued and helped to fill up the intervening space with mounds of gravel and patches of *grass*. The latter, however, was only in demand by the wild-goats of the mountain.

We found that the left half of the Kamper-kishlak glacier, like that of the Yam-bulak, was much higher than the right half, and was further encumbered with huge moraines, while the right side had hardly any. This circumstance shows plainly that the stream of ice was trending towards the left wall of rock, where it pressed close against the foot of the mountain and derived its moraine material from near at hand. On the left side the ice lay underneath the moraine; while on the right the moraine lay underneath the ice.

CHAPTER XXVIII.

MY SECOND ATTEMPT TO ASCEND MUS-TAGH-ATA

THE whole time we had been at this considerable elevation, an elevation not exceeded by many of the Alpine peaks, I had kept an eye on the Mus-tagh-ata, watching for a suitable opportunity to make an ascent; but the weather had invariably rendered it impossible. At one time it snowed and hailed; at another there was an icy north wind, which took away all desire to ascend to still higher regions, where the wind whirled up the fine snow in thick clouds like dust. At yet another time the clear sky and bright sunshine would tempt us to make a start; but suddenly bad weather would set in and upset all our plans for the day. Two or three times we actually had the yaks ready, and the loads distributed among their bearers, and were about to start, when a storm delayed us; and in order not to waste the day entirely we gave up the Mus-tagh-ata, and went some shorter excursion to the glaciers.

By this it was the 5th of August, and, as we had already discovered, to our cost, that winter was an early guest in those altitudes, and that we had not much time to spare, we determined to be ready for a campaign the following day. The 5th was given up to rest. Solemn silence reigned in the yurt, and I was the prey of a presentiment, that we should soon be hovering between heaven and earth. Our yaks, which had been worked very hard of late, were discharged, and returned home with their owners; whilst Mollah Islam procured fresh ones, in excellent condition, in their stead. Saddles, alpenstocks, rope, provisions, and instruments were collected and packed in the evening. The day had been fine; but at dusk the usual hailstorm came on, accompanied by a gale of wind. The mountain, with its snowy wastes and white icefields, which a while ago had glittered in the still bright evening air, was again enveloped in thick clouds, and towards evening the wind-gods whirled in a frantic dance round one of their loftiest thrones.

Leaving Islam Bai to take care of the camp, I set off, on August 6th, at half-past six in the morning, accompanied by Yehim Bai, Mollah Islam, and three other Kirghiz, and a train of seven splendid yaks.

The day was brilliantly fine; so absolutely clear was the atmosphere that the smallest details of the mountain could be distinguished even from its foot, and the summit seemed quite near, although the declivities deceptively hid the highest parts. Not a breath of wind stirred the air; not a cloud marred the serene purity of the heavens. At first we rode slowly, in the light of the rising sun, up the gradually ascending slopes of the Yam-bulak-bashi, then up the steeps in the shade of the rock, till the sun got so high, that it beat full in our faces.

We made good progress, and by ten minutes past seven had reached the height of 14,760 feet. The steep declivities were now littered with gravelly material, of the same varieties as the solid rock higher up. The gravel was so closely packed that no vegetation was able to insinuate its roots. Two of the yaks had already "struck," and as they delayed us very much we left them behind. The Kirghiz preferred to walk, and took it in turns to lead the big handsome yak I was riding, which climbed up the sloping *débris* without any apparent effort. By eight o'clock we had reached the altitude of Mont Blanc, and a short distance above that, at 16,250 feet, we reached the snow-line. At first the snow lay in smallish patches, with the *débris* exposed between them, then in a continuous sheet, through which individual fragments of rock protruded here and there. The snow was compact and coarse-grained, but had no hard crust. After we had ascended another six or seven hundred feet, the snow was caked

MUS-TAGH-ATA SEEN FROM THE WEST

with a thin crust, and lay so solidly packed that the men's soft leather boots left no footprint behind; but then, it is true, they were not provided with wooden soles. The snow crunched under the yaks' pointed hoofs; but the animals never once stumbled. The higher we went the deeper grew the snow, though it never formed drifts worthy of the name. From a quarter of an inch its depth increased to four or five, and at the highest point we reached it was just under fourteen inches. The continual wind, the excessive evaporation, and the dome-like shape of the underlying surface, which exposed the snow to the action of the wind, made it difficult for snowdrifts to accumulate. The snow crystals glittered in the sun with a thousand dazzling facets, and although I wore double snow-spectacles, I suffered somewhat from snow-blindness. The men, who had no glasses, complained that everything seemed to be going round, and that sometimes the landscape appeared to be quite black.

We stopped to rest more and more frequently. I employed the time in making sketches, and in taking our bearings with the compass. We followed the edge of the rocky wall on the right-hand side of the glacier; and therefore had a glorious view over its entire surface, which glittered below us. Up in the *couloir*, where the rocky walls gradually became lower, according as the surface of the glacier rose higher, and where they diverged somewhat from each other, until they finally merged into the rounded ridge which connected the two culminating summits of the mountain, there was a splendid view of the distant trough-shaped depression.

In the middle part of the glacier longitudinal crevasses predominated; the largest ran exactly midway between the walls of rock, and stretched down towards the tip of the glacier's tongue. At three places in particular, where the ice glided over a natural depression, they were intersected by transverse crevasses; and the chequered system, with ice cubes and ice pillars, was the result. In one place the crevasses appeared to start from a common centre and radiate in all directions, as they were broad and gaping in the middle, but grew narrower towards their extremities. The glacier was probably about five-eighths of a mile broad, and its breadth everywhere tolerably equal. It appeared to be considerably steeper than it really was; but in this it was the eye that was at fault. The mountain summit was high above us, whilst the tongue of the glacier stretched a long way below us; and in the clear, attenuated mountain air the distance between these two points ap peared to be quite short. No traces of striation or glacial scratches were perceptible on the perpendicular rocks, which towered 1300 feet above the surface of the glacier. This negative testimony does not, however, count for much; as, if at any time such indications did exist, they would long ago have been obliterated by the weathering of the rocks, a process which is ceaselessly going on in these parts, mainly because of the enormous and sudden changes of temperature. The part of the mountain on which we then were had consequently a ragged, serrated edge, consisting of an unbroken series of rocky projections and undulations, which had nothing whatever to do with the glacier, as they were exclusively the result of weathering.

The side of the mountain sloped here at an angle of twenty-two degrees towards the plain of Su-bashi, a gradient which was easily perceptible in the rarefied air. The snow became purer and more dazzling, and the icy crust crackled audibly. We advanced slowly, doubling one rocky projection after another, and skirting the bays or recesses between them, faithfully following the outline of the edge of the rocks; while new perspectives of exactly the same kind continued to appear one after the other the higher we ascended. At an altitude of 16,700 feet Mollah Islam and two of the other Kirghiz left their yaks in the snow, declaring that it would be better to walk. However, they did not get more than six hundred feet higher when they fell down from exhaustion and headache, and were soon dead asleep in the snowdrifts.

I went on with the two remaining Kirghiz and the two yaks. My beast was always led by one of them; the

THE YAKS TAKING A REST ON THE LOWER SLOPES OF THE MUS-TAGH-ATA

other yak they rode turn and turn about. They too complained of splitting headache, and were ready to drop from breathlessness. I did not suffer much from either of these symptoms, though I had a slight headache, which increased when we got higher up; but I was only attacked with breathlessness when I got off the yak to make observations. The slight exertion of remounting the animal gave me violent palpitation of the heart, and I was almost choked by breathlessness. On the other hand, the yak's movements, which were now much more laboured, did not affect me in the least. I had suffered much more at a far lower altitude on Mount Demavend, in Persia, but on that occasion I was on foot. The secret lies in avoiding bodily exertion as far as possible; for instance, you can ride up to a very considerable altitude without suffering much from that species of discomfort. In this ascent however all the Kirghiz were ill, a couple of them even declared they were going to die; while I, on the contrary, kept comparatively brisk the whole time. But the Kirghiz, in spite of my remonstrances, persisted in leaving their yaks behind, and what with struggling through the snow and climbing up the steep declivities, they exhausted the strength which they so greatly needed to withstand the enervation caused by the rarefaction of the air.

Meanwhile, a fresh wind sprang up from the south-west, driving the snow, which was as fine as flour, and without a crust, into eddies; while the sky became hidden by thick clouds. As we were all now rather done up, we determined to halt and take observations. Bread and tea were brought out, and fuel to boil the water for the latter; but we had only to look at the food, and we were seized with such a choking sensation that none of us would touch it. We suffered only from thirst, and looked longingly at the snow, which the yaks licked up in large mouthfuls.

The view which presented itself from this point (20,660 feet) was inconceivably grand. We could see right across the Sarik-kol chain far away to the picturesque snow-decked mountains of Trans-alaï and the Murghab. Only a few summits in the nearer parts of the Sarik-kol Mountains seemed to exceed 16,500 feet in height. But in the Mus-tagh chain, which is a continuation of Mus-tagh-ata, there were on the north a couple of peaks which did not fall far short of the "Ice Mountains' Father" himself in altitude. The whole of the Sarik-kol valley was spread out like a map under our feet, clearly visible from Ullug-rabat to Bulun-kul. Every lake, except the Upper Bassyk-kul, which was hidden by intervening rocks, shone blue-green in the prevalent grey of the moraine landscape, but from our position looked like insignificant pools. The Yam-bulak glacier pointed its icy finger down the valley, and far beyond its outer extremity we were able to distinguish the concentric semicircles of its former terminal moraine, long since dead. We could not have obtained a better view anywhere of the glacier streams, and their beds between the outstretched arms of the mountain, than from the spot where we stood.

The large rivers of the Yam-bulak and Chum-kar-kashka glaciers ran parallel to the very end of the valley, which was as grey as steel from their alluvium.

There still remained four other rocky buttresses above us, and behind them the northern summit of the mountain, now appearing quite near. The parts between it and the farthest visible point of the mountain had a flatter perspective.

We now held a council of war. The day was drawing to an end, and it was beginning to be cold in the wind (33°3 Fahr. or 0°7 C. at 4 p.m.). Moreover the Kirghiz were so done up that they could go no farther; the yaks stood panting, with their tongues hanging out. We had reached the foot of a dome-shaped elevation, which gradually merged into the flat crown of the summit. On its slopes the snow lay in more massive and more compact layers; and there were cracks and displacements in it which pointed to a tendency to avalanches. The Kirghiz warned me against attempting this precipitous snow-slope. They declared it was ready to fall; and that the yaks, owing to their weight, might easily be the cause of an avalanche, in which case we should reach the foot of the mountain quicker than we bargained for, though in a mutilated condition. They furthermore told me, that from the valley below avalanches were sometimes seen falling on this very slope. The snow then soared up in enormous clouds, rolled together, and slipped over the precipices, smothering them in clouds of fine powder, and when it finally reached the valley it was partially turned to ice.

At the level which we had then attained the snow rested chiefly on a rock and gravel foundation, which was often exposed in the tracks made by the yaks. It only rested on ice close along the edge of the rocks, from which depended long icicles pointing straight down upon the surface of the glacier. On the top of the opposite or south wall, on the other hand, there was a thick sheet of pure blue ice, clothing the mountain as with a supple coat of mail and conforming to its every irregularity.

Though sorely against the grain, I now determined to turn back. We rapidly descended in our own footsteps and soon reached a more clement region, picking up the deserters and the yaks, which were still standing where we had left them, and reaching the camp at seven o'clock in the evening. There we found visitors awaiting us with gifts of provisions.

Apart from the splendid opportunity it afforded for taking our bearings, and apart from the observations I had made, this expedition convinced me, that the northern summit of the Mus-tagh-ata could hardly be reached in a single day's climb. It would be better, therefore, on a future occasion to allow two days, camping the first night at a considerable height, and continuing the next day with our yaks well rested and with only a light equipment. The Kirghiz and Islam Bai were very keen to make another attempt, so soon as a good opportunity presented itself.

But we had still three large glaciers to examine farther east, and therefore struck camp on August 8th, and moved to Terghen-bulak. Mollah Islam and I made a detour round the western foot of the mountain. I wanted to see the Yam-bulak glacier-stream at the spot where it received its contributaries. Where we crossed it, it was $33\frac{3}{4}$ feet broad, $13\frac{3}{4}$ inches deep (maximum), and had a velocity of $7\frac{1}{4}$ feet in the second, and a temperature of 42°3 Fahr. (5°7 C.). On both sides of it there were gigantic moraines of gneiss and crystalline schist, in pieces varying from 5000 cubic feet to small fragments, with binding material of glacial clay, though without any signs of stratification. Along the path of the stream, the soil was washed away from between the big blocks so that they encumbered its bed, causing waterfalls and cataracts. It was therefore no easy matter to get across the stream with the yaks, as the water was so muddy they could not see where to put their feet; and often I felt my animal disappearing, so to speak, from under me, when it stepped between two deceptive boulders, round which the current was foaming and eddying. It was a decided relief to find myself riding up the opposite bank. A magnificent view unfolded itself to the east, where the white glacier-tongue lay embedded between its gigantic moraines at the foot of the mountain.

We rode from the tongue of the glacier, up along the left lateral moraine, to the place where the ice issued from its rock-bound cradle. The marginal moraine consisted entirely of huge gneiss boulders, most of them measuring about 3500 cubic feet each; while the rock itself was a hard, dark crystalline schist, falling at an angle of twenty-one degrees towards the north-north-west. The moraine, then, received its material from higher regions. It was evident from other circumstances that the lower rocks could not contribute to its formation; for between them and it there were a *bergschrund* or fissure and a gravel-strewn declivity, which prevented the ice from coming into contact with the wall of rock.

It was no easy matter to make our way through this labyrinth of gneiss boulders. They were too big for the yaks to clamber over; hence there was nothing for it but to dismount, and let Mollah Islam go round with the animals, and meet me at the base of the moraine. Alone, and followed by my faithful Yolldash, I made my way as best I could, sometimes crawling over the rocks, sometimes balancing on them. They were separated from each other by dark, chilly fissures, in whose depths the water gurgled against the stones at the bottom. At one time I managed to toboggan down the side of a boulder so successfully that I jammed my foot in between it and another rock, and had to take off my boot to set myself at liberty. In other places I found it better to wade through the water, under, and between, the blocks; and it was with a feeling of intense relief that I at last succeeded in extricating myself from that dangerous and gloomy labyrinth, where I might easily have got lost if I had not had a compass. After many adventures I reached the slope at the foot of the moraine. Then looking back, to my dismay, I beheld Yolldash on a huge boulder, whining and howling dismally, and not able to move either backwards or forwards. Then he disappeared behind the boulder. I heard him splash into the water, and finally he emerged from *underneath* the moraine, evidently elated, though slightly lame of one paw. At the same time he was annoyed with me, for having decoyed him into such an awkward predicament.

After traversing a sloping piece of greensward, down which a fresh stream was flowing, we reached the tongue of the Chal-tumak glacier, which had the considerable inclination of 24°9. Its surface was black with gravel, through which solitary white pyramids stuck up; but the side of the glacier was polished like steel.

It was twilight when we reached the new camp, where everything was in order. Not far off lay the aghil (aul or tent-village) of Chal-tumak, consisting of four uys (tents). The chief, Togda Bai Beg, a handsome, refined-looking Tajik, came at once to pay his respects. He told me, that the village had altogether twenty-five inhabitants, and that one tent was inhabited by Tajiks (Aryans, speaking a Persian dialect), and the other three by Naiman Kirghiz. He said, that they lived in the neighbourhood the whole year round, but wandered from yeylau (summer grazing-ground) to yeylau, stopping one or two months at each place. In winter it was terribly cold, and there were heavy falls of snow, making it difficult for the sheep to find pasture. After a continuous snowfall, enormous avalanches were frequent, carrying down boulders and *débris* with them.

The kind old beg gave us a sheep and a bowl of yak's milk, and was only sorry, he said, that his great age prevented him from coming with us on our mountaineering trips. He told us the old story of the sheikh, who went up Mus-tagh-ata and saw a white-bearded man and a white camel, and brought down from the top an enormous iron pot, which is now kept at a masar (tomb) in the Shindeh valley. We talked for a long time, chiefly about my plans; and it was late in the evening before the old man went back to his lonely home among the moraines.

The air was milder than usual. The night was bright and still; and the snowfields gleamed silvery white in the moonlight. The moraines flung out their deep shadows, and underneath gaped the dark abyss of the valley through the weird stillness of the night. Every now and again the distant bleating of the beg's flocks, or the tinkle of running water, penetrated to our ears.

On August 9th we explored the left side of the Chaltumak glacier, riding up the moraine to a point on the flank of the mountain, which gave us a splendid view over the glacier. It was quite regular in shape, and was intersected by a double system of crevasses, one transverse, the other longitudinal. This resulted in a series of ice-pyramids, and gave the glacier a chequered appearance. The stones and fragments of rock which fell from the moraine into the crevasses caused the intersecting lines to look like black stripes.

At the place where we were standing, the gneiss cavities had been some time or other polished by the ice of a former branch of the ice-sheet. This ice-sheet still covers immense areas on the side of Mus-tagh-ata, wrapping the

TOGDA BAI BEG

body of the giant like a tattered mantle, hanging down the declivities in points and folds; while its edge is often broken off so abruptly that the beautiful, blue-green ice, seen underneath the white snow with which it is capped, produces quite a dazzling effect. It is of course only on the convex parts of the mountain that this glacial formation, which resembles the Norwegian glaciers, can be developed; for in the concave parts we found the usual Alpine glacial structure—a bowl-shaped *névé*-basin and a deep, narrow glacier-bed.

On the return journey we kept between the ice-pyramids and the lateral moraine, where a stream glided noiselessly along like oil flowing in a well-greased metal pipe. It had undermined the base of one of the pyramids so much that every minute it threatened to topple over.

Finally we paid a visit to Togda Bai Beg, who called together the elders of the village and offered us dastarkhan (refreshment). His aul lay on the bank of the glacier-stream, and was surrounded by pastures on which the camels, yaks, and horses of the aul were grazing, and where the women were at work milking the sheep. Several of these Tajik women were pretty, and looked happy and good-natured in their picturesque, but slovenly, dress. They seemed to have frequent errands to the tent, and generally took the opportunity to have a good look at the strangers.

The view to the east was one of the grandest I have ever seen. In front of us the colossal mountain mass, soaring up to a giddy height—to the ethereal workshops in which the eternal snow spins the delicate webs which it sends down the slopes of the mountain as offerings to the sun; where the winds gambol at their will; and where the stillness of death divides sovereignty with the bitter cold. Calmly and majestically the glacier moved from between its mountain portals like a king issuing from his royal hall; and the moraines towered above it like ramparts fencing round an impregnable castle. The turbid glacier-stream danced joyously down its stony bed, as glad as a schoolboy off for a holiday, happy at escaping from the thraldom of the ice, and at reaching warmer and more genial regions.

On August 10th we rode up beside the glacier-stream, on whose banks we were then encamped. It led to the right side of the neighbouring Terghen-bulak glacier, from which indeed it derived the greater part of its waters; but it also received several affluents from the ice-sheet. The erosive power of the stream is enormous, and its bed was filled with round, polished stones. At one o'clock it carried 210 cubic feet of water in the second.

The right lateral moraine was about 100 feet high, and hid the glacier, except for a few detached pyramids nearly fifty feet high. The yaks toiled on cautiously and with their accustomed phlegmatic unconcern up the deep gully between the moraines and an enormous gravel slope, which had accumulated at the foot of the perpendicular wall of rock to the north, and which was crowned by the massive ice-sheet. Its edge partly overhung, and was in part broken off; and from it the icicles hung down their dripping tips to a distance of more than 30 feet. From the sharp edge of the rock, immediately underneath the ice, the glacier water spouted forth in innumerable cascades, large and small—crystal-bright jets which fell to such a depth that they were shattered to pearl-seed or powdered into a mist of rainbow-coloured spray before they reached the bottom. The stronger gusts of wind dashed the spray against the rocks, down which the water then trickled, and finally found its way to the stream under and over the gravel slope in a thousand tiny rills and rivulets.

The Terghen-bulak was a triple glacier fed from three sides. The middle ice-stream was much larger than the other two, and occupied much the greater area. A smaller arm joined it from the right; and its bed was sunk deeper in the mountain, so that the surface of the main glacier was considerably higher than the surface of the branch. Between the two rose a huge shoulder of the mountain; and in the angle between the two ice-streams, below the outermost point of the rocky shoulder, there was a triangular hollow, forming, as it were, an eddy or backwater, such as may be seen at the bottom of the pier of a bridge in a river. On the left there was a broad, clean offshoot from the ice-sheet, but it was overpowered to such an extent by the bigger mass of the main glacier, that it was pressed in like a narrow wedge between it and the rocky mountain-arms.

The ice groaned and cracked; stones and boulders rattled down into the crevasses; and there were glacier-tables on their pedestals. From every direction came the sound of trickling, dropping water. The surface of the ice was soft and rotten. Everything in fact tended to denote, that this glacier also was in a condition of great activity.

As we were riding back down the mountain, we saw a couple of big grey wolves, which took to their heels among the moraines. The animals seemed to be very common in that region, and now and then were said to carry off a yak calf, so that Togda Bai Beg was right to guard his flocks with a pack of savage dogs.

The same evening that chieftain prepared a little makeshift yurt, and other necessaries, for a two days' ascent of Mus-tagh-ata, which we thought of trying again the next day, August 11th.

CHAPTER XXIX.

MY THIRD ATTEMPT TO ASCEND MUS-TAGH-ATA

WHEN we rose betimes the next morning, prepared to make a fresh attack upon the giant, the chill night air was sweeping down off the mountain, and the minimum thermometer showed a reading of 23°4 Fahr. (–4°8 C.). Along the banks of the stream, and between the stones in its bed, there were pieces of ice, against which the water lapped and gurgled. On the whole, however, the stream had dwindled to an insignificant rill, muddier than usual, probably because the clear, glacial water had frozen in the higher regions. The weather was particularly favourable for an ascent; not a cloud was to be seen, and the slight breeze there was soon dropped. We intended climbing to a height of 20,000 feet, spending the night there, and continuing as high as we could possibly get the following day. For this reason we took with us the little tent, four large bundles of teresken for fuel, alpenstocks, ropes, ice-axes, fur coats, and provisions—all carried by nine strong yaks.

"Bismillah!" (In God's name!) cried the half-dozen Mohammedans, when we were ready, and we started leisurely up the mountain. I intended to exert myself as little as possible, in order to save my strength for the following day, when the real climbing, with a light equipment, and only three men, would begin. My yak was therefore treated as a beast of burden from the very outset. A Kirghiz, riding or on foot, led him by his nose-rope the whole time, while another cudgelled him behind. For whenever the animal thought my plans were unduly ambitious, he stopped to cogitate, wondering what this perpetual scrambling was going to lead to. By this arrangement it was not even necessary for me to goad the yak, an occupation which in itself is very exhausting, and I could sit quietly with my hands in my pockets, only taking them out every now and again to look at the aneroids. The needles of these instruments had very little peace during the days we were vainly trying to scale the "Ice Mountains' Father."

Our little caravan struggled leisurely zigzag up the mountain-side, which terminated in a long level ridge on the left side of the Chal-tumak glacier. The yaks grunted and panted, and their blue tongues hung out of their mouths dripping.

The ridge was the same gravel-covered backbone we had reached on August 9th, and we took our first rest at the point where we halted then. Immediately south of this, the ice-mantle threw out a projection with steep walls, and at its base the fallen pieces melted together into a sheet of ice. By one o'clock we had reached the altitude of 17,000 feet above the level of the sea. Here the snow lay in scanty patches in the crevices; it was only in the larger depressions, and in the clefts at the edge of the gorge, that it was heaped up in any considerable quantity. It was soft, sticky snow, which melted in the sun, and the ground was consequently wet where it had lain. The naked ridge finally tapered off and disappeared under the ice-mantle. The latter was not broken off abruptly, but was quite thin at the edge, so that we had no difficulty in getting upon it, and was covered with a thin layer of snow, which the yaks occasionally slipped through. But we soon got on deeper snow; and then they went as steadily as they had gone before over the gravel and *débris*.

Suddenly we heard a deafening crash and roar from the right-hand rocky wall on the other side of the Chal-tumak glacier. It was an avalanche which had slipped from the ice-mantle. Large blocks of blue ice were hurled from the edge, clashing together, and crumbling into fine white powder as they struck against the outjutting rocks; then they fell like flour upon the surface of the main glacier.

The sound reverberated like thunder near at hand, the first echo being flung backwards and forwards many times between the rocky walls before it finally died away, and was succeeded by the usual silence. But a mist of powdered ice-needles hung a long time in front of the glacier. Meanwhile we had a splendid opportunity of observing how the glacier worked. The ice-mantle kept slipping, slipping, ponderous and massive, over the edge of the rocks. Again and again it broke off at the crevasses and ice-falls; great blocks of ice being precipitated into the depths below, and reaching the main glacier in powder as fine as flour. This nevertheless melted into its surface, and in that way built up a regenerated parasitic glacier.

From the same considerable altitude we also saw plainly how the Chal-tumak glacier was fed from every side by fractures from the ice-mantle.

Where the small patches of crystalline *débris* underlay the snow, the latter was longer in melting; but about midday the radiation increased to 112°8 Fahr. (44°9 C.), and the atmosphere was brilliantly clear and pure. The gravel was succeeded by a layer of snow, three to six inches thick, which prevented the yaks from slipping, although the angle was as much as twenty-four degrees.

Here we saw the tracks of four kiyick (wild goats). The animals fled up the mountain in the direction of two swellings of the ice; and in another place we found the skeleton of an animal of the same species lying among the snow.

The naked ice-mantle stretched up before us in all its dazzling whiteness. We knew of course quite well that it would bear us; all the same, we felt as if we were venturing out on thin ice when we stepped upon this unknown tract, never before trodden by the foot of man, and where perhaps the many dangers inseparable from a glacial landscape threatened us.

We soon found ourselves in a labyrinth of intersecting crevasses, which, however, were as a rule not more than a foot broad. We were obliged to steer a zigzag course, in order to evade them, since they generally widened out in both directions. Sometimes we crossed them on snow-bridges; in other places the yaks stepped across them without difficulty. The Kirghiz declared, that for safety's sake we had better follow the track of the kiyick; and we did so. The bridges along their track sometimes held; but as often as not the yaks went through, for although the snow had supported the light weight of the swift-footed wild goats, it was not strong enough to bear the solid burden of the yak.

Farther on we spent a whole hour in getting over a part of the ice which was terribly cut up by transverse crevasses, and where we had several nasty falls in consequence. As usual, we had the yaks to thank that matters went as well as they did. When a yak put his forelegs through the deceptive snow and fell into a hidden crevasse, he carefully lodged his muzzle on the other side, and so scrambled up again.

The ice was now covered with a layer of snow eight inches deep; but it soon increased to fifteen and twenty inches, so that the animals had hard work to shuffle and wade through the hindering drifts; on the other hand, the crevasses were less frequent. Then for a long time the "going" was better. The ice-mantle seemed to be evenly rounded off above us; but we hoped to find a passage between the lofty ice-swellings, with their blue glistening edges and snow-sheathed surfaces.

In several places the ice-mantle bulged up into bosses and hills, and we went from the one to the other. We were just on the comparatively level summit of one of these upswellings, when Mollah Islam's yak, which was being led by its owner at the head of the procession, suddenly disappeared, with the exception of its hind legs and horns, and the teresken faggots. These still remained visible above the snow. The animal had fallen into a crevasse a yard wide, which had been completely snowed over, and was suspended over a yawning abyss in the ice. There it lay grunting and puffing like a creature doomed; but by its immovability it showed that it fully realized the danger it was in. If it had moved ever so little, it would have been precipitated into the crevasse, which grew narrower as it descended.

A long delay ensued in consequence. The Kirghiz twisted ropes round the yak's body and horns, and made them fast to the other yaks. Then both animals and men hauled as hard as they could, and the heavy beast was successfully hoisted up. A little farther on we nearly had a repetition of the same performance; only the yak stopped in time to save himself. Next it was one of the men who went through, and remained hanging at his armpits. After that we thought it was about time to call a halt, and make a reconnaissance of the ice, which was crossed and re-crossed in every direction by pitfalls.

We found that the ice-cap on which we were standing was chequered throughout by crevasses running in all directions, intersecting each other, and cutting off our advance on every side. Then, to make matters worse, we discovered a crevasse nine to twelve feet broad, and eighteen feet deep, and at the bottom of it great masses of snow were piled up. We peeped cautiously over the edge, and saw that the chasm extended in both directions like an enormous trench. Northwards it ran as far as the trough of the Chal-tumak glacier, and south-westwards to the foot of one of the highest of the ice-swellings. To get over it, or round it, seemed equally impossible; so we stopped and held a council of war.

The layer of snow which sheathed the ice-mantle was ten inches thick, and stretched across the crevasses like a tarpaulin. It was only across the broader chasms that it was cracked or had fallen in. Where the yaks broke through, they left gaping holes, which on our first looking into them appeared to be pitch dark. But when our eyes became used to the darkness, we saw that it was only a blue glimmer, and that the bottom of the chasm was buried in snow. The icy walls were of the clearest blue, and the glacier-water trickling down them froze into rows of long icicles hanging down the abyss. The deepest of these crevasses was twenty-two feet three inches deep.

Evening was coming on, and I was again constrained to

THE TERGHEN-BULAK GLACIER

beat a retreat; for it would have been useless to wait till the next day, and then try to find another passage. It was plainly impossible to venture upon an ascent of Mus-tagh-ata from this side without special appliances, which were not at our disposal. Above us towered the loftiest summit of the mountain, and down its precipitous sides glided the eternal ice, streaming in part to the collecting-basin of the glacier; and where the declivities were convex and the ice-mantle was checked by the relief of the underlying ground, it built itself up into veritable terraces, walls, towers, and solid blocks of enormous dimensions. To get past these seemed, so far as we could judge from the spot where we stood, altogether beyond the reach of human power.

Our first two ascents up beside the right wall of the Yam-bulak glacier had taken us over incomparably more favourable ground; we determined to try that route once more before we finally abandoned the project as hopeless.

We had only reached an altitude of 18,500 feet, it is true; but as a set-off, the trip had been attended with important cartographical results. We had got a splendid insight into the disposition of the higher regions—the cylindrical shape of the mountain, and its covering of ice, which is so difficult of interpretation, and of the relation of the ice-mantle to the several glaciers. The latter, which are in reality colossal ice-streams, looked like insignificant white bands from that altitude, of no magnitude at all in comparison with the stupendous volume of the ice-mantle.

On Sunday, August 12th, we rested; and, as was my wont, I read the Bible lessons for the day during the quiet forenoon, and afterwards studied Heim's *Gletscherkunde*. The weather was anything but inviting for an excursion. The atmosphere was thick; it was blowing hard; and the mountains were wreathed in thick clouds. All my men were away on leave, having been invited to a festivity of some kind by Togda Bai Beg. Only Yolldash and I were at home, enjoying our rest, which never was more delightful than when the weather was bad, and the wind whistled and howled among the rocks outside. I never felt lonely amid those distant glaciers, where one day was, on the whole, so like another—why, I shall not say, as I might lay myself open to being thought sentimental; but anyhow I had not much time to think about it, having more than enough to do. The only thing which disturbed me was, that the summer was passing so quickly, that I did not see any possibility of being able to carry out the whole of my programme. The days were always too short. As soon as I got my clothes on in the morning, the first thing was to read the meteorological instruments, while Islam Bai prepared breakfast. Our fare never varied, and consisted of the following courses:—*chisslick* (mutton roasted over the fire on a spit), *ash* (rice pudding), and bread, which we sometimes procured from the Kirghiz and sometimes baked ourselves; and the whole was washed down with tea. I soon grew so tired of the chisslick that I could not bear the sight of it, and lived on rice and bread. And our fare was to be precisely the same for two years and a half, all the way to Peking. Occasionally I opened a tin of preserved food; but the supply was small, and the time long, and I had to be chary of these delicacies. Happily I never tired of rice and tea, and thrived on the simple diet. There was always plenty of yak's milk and cream for the tea; so that we had no need to economize in these products. I had brought a good supply of tobacco with me from Tashkend, chiefly consisting of pipe and cigarette tobacco, but also a few cigars; and I must confess that I felt very sorry for myself, if I had not a pipe in my mouth whilst we were about our glacier work.

When the weather compelled us to remain "indoors," I always had plenty of work to do, such as sketch-maps, section or profile drawings, notes, etc., to work out. The inside of the yurt was so comfortable, that it felt quite like home. In the middle of the "floor" there was a little fire, fed with teresken faggots and yak dung; otherwise the ground was covered with felt rugs. Immediately opposite the entrance was my bed. The packages, generally, were arranged round the sides, and there too were the tins and boxes of provisions, guns, saddles, instruments, etc. I had only two meals a day: breakfast was served again at supper-time. When I got into bed, I generally read, by the light of a dying candle, one of the Swedish newspapers of which I have already spoken. And then I turned over and slept like a log—no matter how boisterously the wind blew outside, or how desperately Yolldash howled at the wolves in the mountains—till Islam Bai woke me up in the morning.

CHAPTER XXX.

MOONLIGHT ON MUS-TAGH-ATA

I HOPE I am not tiring the reader with these, perhaps, rather monotonous descriptions of glaciers; but I have thought it proper to treat this subject somewhat exhaustively, as it is virgin soil, and every step I took was new. Only the Yam-bulak glacier had been visited before, viz. by Bogdanovitch, in 1889; but I made up my mind, I would not leave the mountain before I had mapped and examined them all. There are only two or three left, and those I will describe as briefly as possible.

We set apart August 13th for an expedition to the Chum-kar-kashka glacier, riding thither up the side of the enormous lateral and terminal moraines of the Terghen-bulak glacier, and over very rugged country, covered sometimes with gravel, sometimes with sparse vegetation. A swelling of the ground, starting from the vicinity of the former glacier, dipped down into the Sarik-kol valley, where it was continued in the pass of Ullug-rabat. This serves as an important watershed, in that the glacier-waters from the Chum-kar-kashka glacier flow to the left, to the Little Kara-kul, while the streams from the ice-mantle farther south drain into the little lake of Gallchötöck, and thence, southwards, to the Yarkand-daria. Beside the lake stood an aul of six yurts, subject to the begs of Tagharma.

This glacier resembled the Kamper-kishlak glacier, and, like it, trended towards the right. The right lateral moraine was of relatively small size; the left of tolerable dimensions. The tongue of the glacier was level and rounded, with no crevasses worth mentioning; the only fissures that seemed to be at all developed were those at

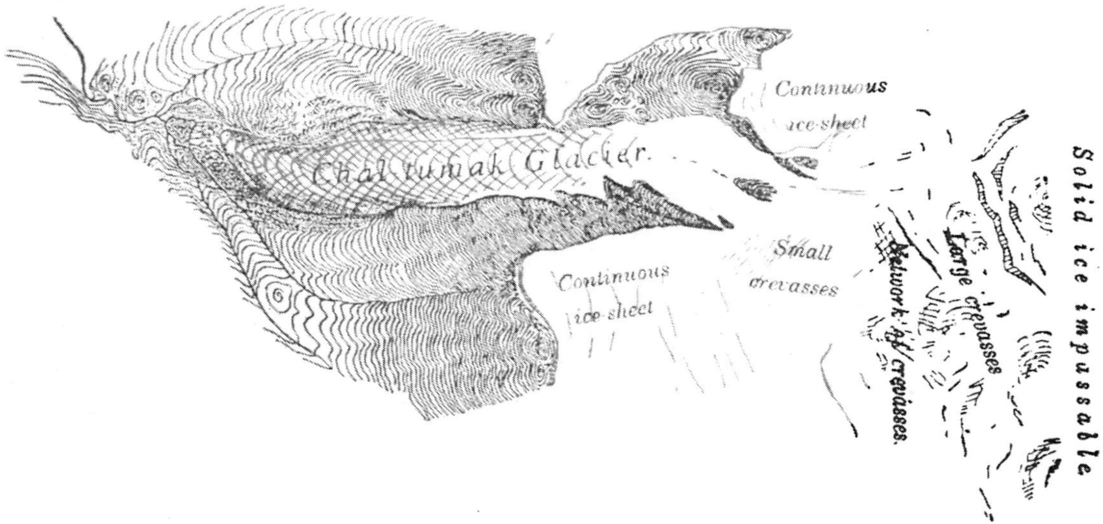

THE CHAL-TUMAK GLACIER

CHAL-TUMAK GLACIER, LOOKING NORTH

the sides. Towards them, and generally falling into them, ran a number of little streams of the clearest glacier-water. The largest was as much as 35½ inches broad and 9 deep, and had a temperature of 32° Fahr. (0°02 C.). The ice along its channel, in which the water ran noiselessly, was polished and gloriously blue. Otherwise the whole surface was excessively soft and rotten; all the stones had sunk deeply into it, making gaping holes. The surface of the ice resembled a maze of upstanding needles or leaves, and we were able to walk on it without slipping, as easily as on snow.

Getting on to the glacier was easy enough. But getting down again from the left side was a very different matter; for the glacier was very much swollen, and the side abrupt and steep, forming a couple of high steps down to *terra firma.* We found innumerable small pools on the ice, a yard in diameter and about eight inches deep; they were covered with a thin crust of ice even during the daytime, so that we got an occasional foot-bath. Here also we put in measuring-rods, to find out the rate at which the ice was moving.

On August 14th we rode up along the left lateral moraine of the Terghen-bulak glacier, and then out on to the moraine which is carried on the back of the glacier. This we afterwards followed down to its face. The two lateral moraines were very large; but only began in the lower part of the glacier's course, where they appeared on the surface of the ice like small black wedges. Gradually however they became broader and broader, and finally, at the lower end of the glacier-tongue, formed a stupendous mass of stones and *débris.*

The Terghen-bulak was hard at work. Rumbling and rattling sounds were heard continually. Large blocks of ice were precipitated with a deafening crash into the crevasses. New fissures appeared in all directions; and swift streams, abounding with water, flowed between the ice and the lateral moraine. The latter was 400 yards in breadth at the lower part of the glacier, and was at first wonderfully level, and easy to travel over. Afterwards it rose considerably above the surface of the ice: but as the stones lay in a single thin stratum, the ice projected through them in fine needles, "razor-backs," and pinnacles. This was due to the stones having gradually sunk into the ice, imparting to the surface a peculiar knotted and rugged appearance.

We managed to get entangled in a labyrinth of moraine-ridges, pyramids, and ice-clefts. After crossing the moraine, we went on over the middle of the glacier; and we had many adventures in the twilight, which quickly turned to darkness. The travelling was so bad that we preferred to walk, jumping over the crevasses and streams. The Kirghiz drove the yaks before them, and it was a pleasure to see with what agility the animals scrambled up icy slopes several feet in height, in which they were sometimes obliged to scrape out a step before they could get foothold. At last we reached the right lateral moraine. There we discovered several small glacier-lakes on the ice. Owing to the sluggish movement of the ice-masses they were always convex at their lower end. The two lateral moraines stretched a good way farther down than the middle of the glacier; for the ice they covered was sheltered from the sun, and consequently slower in melting.

Below the glacier-tongue we had to pass a succession of old terminal moraines, built up in front of it like ramparts, and broken through by the united stream. It was now become quite dark, and I was obliged to follow closely in the footsteps of one of the Kirghiz, in order to see where I was going. Another man goaded on the yaks; while a third was looking for one of the beasts, which had gone astray on its own account among the moraines, and was not recovered until the following day. After much trouble and many detours we managed to make our way back to camp without further adventure.

One of the points in my summer programme was to ride into the Pamirs; and as some of our stores showed signs of giving out, particularly the tea and sugar, I

THE TERGHEN-BULAK GLACIER, LOOKING SOUTH

I.-24

decided to combine this expedition with some "shopping" at Fort Pamir.

But, as a journey of this nature would probably occupy a whole month, and we could not be back at Mus-tagh-ata before the autumn, I wished, before starting, to try another ascent, divided, as I mentioned before, into two day's-marches.

Accordingly, on August 15th, we wended our way back along the well-known path to our old camp; and although it blew and hailed in the evening, we made everything ready for a last attempt the following day.

Fully equipped for a two day's-march, and accompanied by six Kirghiz, my faithful attendant Islam Bai, and ten yaks, I made a fourth attempt, on August 16th, to climb Mus-tagh-ata from the same point whence we had tried it previously on April 18th and August 6th.

After reaching the snow-line, we followed our old trail, which was, at any rate, a guarantee against accidents. The path could be seen quite plainly, winding zigzag up the mountain by the edge of the rocks which fenced in the glacier-gorge on the right. The snow, not being deep, had melted away in large round patches in our former footsteps, exposing the bare gravel underneath. Higher up every footmark was filled with bluish-green ice, and highest of all covered with a sprinkling of snow as thin as paper. In some places, indeed, the track was partly obliterated, though not so much but that we could see it; and naturally we followed it, as we knew by so doing we were safe from danger. It had actually never snowed here for ten days.

With Islam Bai and one of the Kirghiz I reached, at four o'clock, the point we had stopped at on the 6th. The other men followed more slowly, Yehim Bai riding at their head. As soon as we were all together again, we held a consultation, and decided to spend the night where we were, as there a few small islands of rock protruded through the sea of snow. The ten yaks were tied to loose boulders of schist, and the Kirghiz swept away the snow as well as they could from the sharp gravel beneath, and so cleared a place on which to put up the yurt. This was small, and very rough and ready, providing sleeping-room for three only. It had no *tunduk* or smoke-vent, as the poles met at the apex, and were simply thrust through a bundle of rope and rags to keep them in place. Although we tried to level the ground as much as possible with a spade, the yurt still stood on a slope; and we had therefore to anchor it with strong *arkhans* (camel's-hair ropes) to a couple of boulders. A slight breeze sprang up in the evening and blew for an hour, driving clouds of fine snow through the many cracks and crevices; so the Kirghiz banked up a wall of snow all round the tent on the outside.

At first everything went well. We made a big fire of teresken faggots and yak dung, which warmed us and thawed our stiffened joints; but unhappily the yurt was filled with suffocating smoke, which made our eyes smart, and only found its way out leisurely through the open entrance. The snow inside the tent melted, it is true; but when the fire slackened, it all turned into a mass of ice.

Meanwhile the Kirghiz began to complain, one after the other, of headache; and two of them were so bad, that they asked to be allowed to turn back, to which I consented the more readily as they were manifestly in no condition for further fatigue. As night approached, other symptoms developed, such as continual singing in the ears, slight deafness, a quickened pulse, and lower temperature than is normal, combined with persistent sleeplessness, probably the result of the headache, which towards morning became unendurable. Besides all this we suffered from slight attacks of breathlessness. The Mohammedans complained bitterly the whole night. Our furs were oppressively heavy. A recumbent position only increased the breathlessness; and I could plainly feel my heart beating violently. When the tea was ready, there was no demand for it. And as the shades of night came on, the depression of the Kirghiz grew very evident; for they were as little used as I to a night spent more than twenty thousand feet above the level of the sea.

STARTING TO ASCEND MUS-TAGH-ATA

A grander camping-ground, however, I have never pitched tent on than the snow-clad slopes of this one of the loftiest mountains in the world, at whose foot the glacier-tongues, streams, and lakes were already wrapped in darkness, and on the edge, too, of one of the most fantastic of glaciers—a few steps to the south and we should have fallen down an abyss twelve hundred feet deep on to blue ice that sparkled as bright as steel.

I had expected a picturesque sunset; but that evening it was nothing out of the common. The sun sank into

THE RIGHT LATERAL MORAINE OF THE YAM-BULAK GLACIER, LOOKING EAST-SOUTH-EAST

clouds illumined by a fiery yellow flare, which glowed for a long time after the sun had set, and threw up the mountains of the Pamirs in sharp relief. The whole Sarik-kol valley lay for some time in darkness, while the sun was still shedding its last rays over the top of Mus-tagh-ata. But soon even our camp was shrouded in cold, dark shades. The top of the mountain glittered for a moment like the ruddy crater of a volcano, and then the light of the day was swallowed up in endless space.

I stepped out to see the full moon rise, and watch it dim the stars, which only just before had glittered so brightly in the deep blue heavens. It was not far to the boundless realms of space; and the sovereign of the night rose with a splendour so dazzling that it was only by an effort of will that I was able to keep my eyes upon her. I seemed to be regarding a burnished silver shield suspended in the sunshine, or a gigantic electric lamp. Serenely yet majestically the moon sailed above the opposite wall of the glacier defile, with its grand, black, perpendicular rocks, the glacier itself being still in shadow in the depths below. Every now and again I heard the dull crack of a new crevasse forming, or the crash of an avalanche falling from the ice-mantle. The moon shed her silver light over our camping-ground in lavish measure, conjuring forth the most entrancing effects. The yaks were thrown up in dark, sharply-defined relief against the white snow, their heads drooping low, silent as the stones they were bound to; every now and then they ground their teeth against the fibrous pad of their upper jaw, or crunched the snow under their feet, as they changed position. The tent looked like some weird figure of a seated giant; the ring at the top of the poles being his head, and the frame hung with felt mats his body. The three Kirghiz who could not be accommodated inside the yurt made a fire between a couple of large rocks. When this died out they doubled themselves up in a kneeling posture with their heads on the ground, enveloped in their fur coats, and crowded together round the dying embers like bats in winter. From the yurt and the yaks long narrow shadows, intensely dark, streamed out across the north-west slope, in sharp contrast with the sparkling snowfields, on which myriads of small ice-crystals glittered like fire-flies. All round the tent, where the snow had been trampled down, the light and shade alternated in small patches. On the steep slopes in the north-west the beautiful curves and noble outlines of the vast snowfields, modelled by the capricious winds, were lit up with a magic glamour. But I looked in vain for the marvellous tints called forth on the snowfields by the sun. The only alternation was of black and white—the silver of the moon, the gloom of the shadows, at once barren and monotonous like those on the surface of the moon herself, but at the same time grand, enthralling.

Although the Sarik-kol valley was vividly illumined by the moonshine, it was not easy to recognize the landmarks in the prevailing grey of the gravel detritus. It was only with difficulty that I could distinguish the darker yeylaus

THE HIGHEST PART OF THE YAM-BULAK GLACIER

(summer camps) of Kamper-kishlak, Yam-bulak, and Su-bashi, their pasturages watered by the glacier-streams. The outline of Little Kara-kul lake was but slightly marked. The entire landscape, in this direction, right up to the crests of the mountains of the Pamirs, was an inextricable chaos, without any point to arrest the eye.

The scenery was most beautiful in the quarter of the moon. I stood as though chained to the spot in the crackling snow, and could do nothing but look and look, and admire. A magic scene so grand that neither pen nor brush could depict it adequately! The architecture of Nature was conceived here on a bold and masterful plan —the blue glacier sunk between its black walls of rock, sheathed in mail of ice and snow—the five-headed mountain giant towering above the low valleys of the earth. The rocky wall immediately in front of me lay in such deep shadow that I could barely distinguish where its transparent ice-mantle ended and the black mountain-wall began. To the left, and a few hundred yards above me, the outermost parts of the glacier were bathed in the moonlight. The dark crest in the south-east was alive with white-veiled figures, dancing a perilous elf-dance past the giddy precipices, across the icy surface of the glacier, away over the northern summit of the Ice Mountains' Father. These light clouds, dancing before the gentle southern breeze, formed in rapid succession concentric rings, haloes, and the like, in all the colours of the rainbow. It required no great stretch of fancy to transform the clouds into any conceivable shapes,—ghosts in while draperies chasing each other, dancing fairies, sportive ogres, a procession of the mountain king with his sons, the souls of the departed being led by their white-robed guardian-angels from earth to happier places. I seemed to see the white camel which brought the dervish down from Mus-tagh-ata, the forty horsemen who supported Khan Khoja against the Chinese, the blessed ones of Janaidar, the city of perfect happiness. In spite of the cold I remained standing in the snow fascinated, entranced, following with mingled wonder and surprise the hurrying train of the thousands of fantastic shapes.

A dead silence everywhere — not an echo from the opposite wall of rock. The attenuated air was inert; it needed an avalanche to make it vibrate. The breathing of the yaks was visible, but not audible. The animals stood silent and motionless, as if they too were under the witching spell of the night. The clouds flitted noiselessly by. The moon seemed to be gazing down fixedly upon the insignificant mortal who had had the audacity to defy one of the mountain giants of the world. A curious feeling of being at a vast distance from the earth took possession of me. It was difficult to realize, that the four continents lay actually below my feet; and that a girdle drawn round the earth at the level where I then stood would cut off only the tops of a very few mountains in Asia and South America. I realized more forcibly than ever man's littleness as compared with the inconceivable magnitude of creation. I seemed to be standing on the confines of space—cold, silent, boundless.

The inside of the tent showed the reverse of the medal. Islam Bai and Yehim Bai were sitting in their fur coats, as near to the dying embers as they could get, uttering never a word. We all froze, so that our teeth chattered; and to add to our discomfort, when we made up the fire, the tent became filled with stifling smoke. After the evening's observations had been taken, each man crept into his fur coat and blankets, the fire was allowed to die out, and the moon peeped inquisitively in through every slit and crevice of the tent.

The aneroid showed 14$\frac{1}{3}$ inches pressure, at a temperature of 25°5 Fahr. (–3°6 C.). Water boiled at 176°9 (80°5 C.); and the minimum temperature sank to 10°4 Fahr. (–12° C.).

It was a long, wearisome night, which seemed as if it would never end. No matter how closely we drew our knees up to our chins or crept together in our endeavour to keep warm, it was impossible for mere physical heat to do battle against the penetrating cold from outside; and we felt it the more in that the south-easterly wind increased hour by hour during the night. None of us could get a moment's sleep; at last, towards morning, I fell into a sort of doze, but was awakened by want of air. The men moaned and groaned as though they were being stretched on the rack; not so much on account of the cold, however, as from the constantly increasing headache.

At last the sun rose upon our misery; but the day that dawned was anything but favourable. A south-west wind, almost violent enough to be called a hurricane, swept along the sides of the mountain, smothering us in clouds of fine powdery snow. The three Kirghiz, having passed the night in the open air, were half dead with cold, and could scarcely drag themselves into the yurt, where a large fire was burning. We all felt ill and depressed. Nobody spoke; nobody would eat anything; and when the tea, which was not even properly hot, was ready, I was so exhausted I could hardly lift it to my lips. The yaks were still standing where we left them the previous even-

OUR CAMP NEAR YAM-BULAK-BASHI

ing, motionless as statues. The top of the mountain was shrouded in impenetrable clouds of blinding snow; and to have continued the ascent on such a day, and over ice probably seamed with crevasses, in the teeth of that terrible buran, finally perhaps to lose our bearings in those inhospitable regions, would have been to tempt providence and court certain destruction.

I at once realized the folly of setting the mountain at defiance. But as I wanted to see what sort of stuff my men were made of, I ordered them to prepare for a start. Not one of them uttered a word of grumbling. All rose at once, and began to strike camp; but they were manifestly greatly relieved when the order was countermanded.

One peep through the tent-opening made us glad to creep back again inside. There, at any rate, we had shelter from the wind—a wind which penetrated furs, felts, and felt boots. I earnestly hoped that by midday the gale would abate, and we might continue our work. But on the contrary the storm waxed more violent, and by twelve o'clock it was evident the day was lost. I therefore left the three Kirghiz behind to strike the tent and load the yaks, whilst I and Islam Bai and Yehim Bai, wrapping everything round us we could lay our hands on, mounted our animals, and down the snowdrifts we raced at a spanking pace. The yaks literally flung themselves headlong down the declivities, diving like otters through the snow, and in spite of their clumsy, heavy bodies never stumbling or slipping a step. To sit in the saddle was something like riding a high sea in a rocking, pitching skiff. Under such circumstances a man who was not sure of his seat was likely to have a pretty bad time of it. Often I was obliged to fling myself backwards, till my back touched the back of the yak, and I had constantly to adjust my balance to his unexpected, but agile and dexterous, movements.

How glorious it was, when we had left the clouds of blinding snow behind us up above, and saw our camping-ground far down below our feet, on a level with the top of the Finsteraarhorn!

We ate our dinner, of which we stood much in need, washing it down with steaming tea. Then, our vital energies restored, we were soon sleeping the sleep of the just, each in his corner. But the whole of the following day we felt like convalescents recovering from a long illness.

I had now attempted the ascent of Mus-tagh-ata four times, but each time without success. I do not say however that an ascent of the summit is an absolute impossibility. To reach it up the face by which we forced a passage on August 11th is impossible—impossible that is without extraordinary appliances, such as it would be absurd to think of using in such a place. But by the route we followed on April 18th, and again on August 6th and 16th, there were, as far as I could make out with my field-glass, no insurmountable physical obstacles in the way; and any climber possessed of sufficiently strong lungs ought to be able to work his way up to the northern summit. And although that is not the higher of the twin peaks, it is connected with its loftier brother by a slightly depressed *col.* Between and below the two extends the *névé* or *firn* of the great Yam-bulak glacier; but how far it admits of being traversed is another question. In all probability it is cut up with crevasses and covered with deep snow, so that it would require some days to effect a passage across. The barriers behind which the eternally Happy of the legendary city of Janaidar have entrenched themselves are indeed insurmountable!

Man's physical functions are influenced in no small degree by the rarefaction of the air; and in order to ascertain in what way this acted, I registered at different altitudes the temperature of the body and the pulse in myself (29 years old), in Islam Bai, a native of Osh in Fergana (43 years old), and in the Kipchak Kirghiz, Yehim Bai from Shugnan (40 years old).

The following table shows the results of my investigations:—

Date and Hours.		Temperature.		Pulse.	Altitude.
July 28, 10 p.m.	Myself .	96°8 Fahr.,	36° C.	98	13,450 ft.* (13,550 ft.)
	Islam .	97°5 "	36°4 "	92	
	Yehim .	96° "	35°6 "	66	
July 29, 10 p.m.	Myself .	95°9 "	35°5 "	88	14,440 ft. (14,100 ft.)
	Islam .	97°3 "	36°3 "	92	
	Yehim .	95°5 "	35°3 "	74	
August 5, 9 p.m.	Myself .	96°8 "	36° "	88	14,440 ft. (14,100 ft.)
	Islam .	97°5 "	36°4 "	90	
	Yehim .	97°9 "	36°6 "	84	

* The altitudes given in the paper I sent to the Royal Geographical Society are those repeated here in brackets. They are not quite accurate, as in Kashgar I had not the means of applying the necessary corrections to my calculations. The figures which are not in brackets give the corrected altitudes.

Date and Hours.		Temperature.		Pulse.	Altitude.
August 6, 12 noon.	Myself .	95°9 Fahr.,	35°5 C.	86	17,390 ft.
	Yehim .	96° „	35°6 „	82	(17,200 ft.)
August 11, 2 p.m.	Myself .	97°2 „	36°2 „	94	
	Islam .	96° „	35°6 „	86	18,700 ft.
	Yehim .	96°6 „	35°9 „	84	(18,600 ft.)
August 16, 8 p.m.	Myself .	95°6 „	35°3 „	106	
	Islam .	97°9 „	36°6 „	98	20,660 ft.
	Yehim .	97°9 „	36°6 „	116	(19,500 ft.)
August 17, 9 p.m.	Myself .	97° „	36°1 „	102	
	Islam .	97°9 „	36°6 „	82	14,440 ft.
	Yehim .	98° „	39°7 „	84	(14,100 ft.)

Although this table contains a number of exceptions, it would certainly seem to indicate that the temperature decreases, whilst the pulse quickens, according as the altitude increases. There would also appear to ensue a moment of sluggishness; for on descending from a considerable height the pulse continued for some time to beat more quickly than the normal rate. In my own case the temperature varied, as a rule, not much more than a degree, and my pulse remained fairly regular. This was probably due to the fact that I carefully avoided all unnecessary physical exertion, while my men, on the contrary, often walked. The greatest variation of the pulse was in the case of the Kirghiz, Yehim Bai. At 13,450 feet his pulse was 66, and at 20,660 feet it was 116; that is to say, it quickened at the rate of fifty beats in a little over 7200 feet. The irregularity in the figures of the table is no doubt attributable to several other causes, such as, for instance, greater or less physical exertion, greater or less susceptibility to the rarefaction of the air, accidental indisposition, and the like. Nevertheless I always made a point of taking these observations after a rest of suitable length, so as to eliminate the effects of breathlessness, violent perspiration, and undue accelera tion of the heart's action, as also to allow of recovery from the worst feelings of fatigue.

Our experience demonstrated, on the one hand, that it was impossible to reach the summit in one day, the horizontal distance of which from the western foot of the mountain is very considerable; and on the other hand, that it is not prudent to sleep at the height of 20,000 feet, because a night spent at such an altitude impairs the physical strength and induces a feeling of lassitude and depression. The best way to reach the top would, without doubt, be to wait for a clear, calm day in the beginning of July, to break up camp early from a depôt situated 15,000 feet up, and from there make the final ascent in a single day. Should any such attempt be made, the yaks ought to be taken as high as they can possibly be got, and when they cannot be got any further, the ascent should be continued on foot. Unfortunately I had no time to make a new attempt, partly on account of the advanced season of the year, partly on account of the stormy character of the autumn.

In any case the western foot of the mountain is the best point of departure for making the ascent, because it is at an altitude of from 12,000 to 13,000 feet to start with, and the slope on that side is less steep. From the east, south, and north the mountain is inaccessible.

A bold Alpine climber in good training, and accompanied by a couple of hardy and experienced Swiss guides, would probably reach a considerable height, and possibly the northern summit itself. But even a Swiss guide, however well trained, would find himself in quite an unknown world, for the summit of the Mus-tagh-ata is directly exposed to the full force of the sun's rays, and exceeds the highest mountain in Europe by fully 9000 feet.

Farewell then, Father of the Ice Mountains! Thou didst suffer me to kneel before thy snow-white footstool; but didst not permit me to behold thy august presence face to face and eye to eye. Farewell, thou mighty sovereign of the giants of the Pamirs, at once a corner-stone of the earth's loftiest mountain-range and the topmost pinnacle of the Roof of the World! At thy knees thy mighty children, the Kwen-lun, Kara-korum, Hindu-kush, and Tian-shan, kneel together hand in hand. Farewell again, thou beauty-spot on the venerable face of our Mother Earth, whose cheek is furrowed with such deep and unfathomable wrinkles around thee! In my memory I still hear the rippling of thy mountain-brooks, bringing strange messages from those sublime regions which no mortal foot hath ever trod. Like the holy Dalai-lama, thou permittest none but thy chosen children to approach the sacred precincts of thy temple. Shed then thy saving light as from a lofty beacon-tower across the desert ocean, which stretches to a boundless distance from thy eastern flank. Let the gleam of thy silver brow scatter the dust-haze of the desert hurricane—let the cool refreshing airs of thy palace of eternal snows be wafted towards the weary traveller toiling through the burning heats of sun and sand—let the life-giving streams, which flow from thy mighty heart, abound in strength for thousands of years to come, and for thousands of years to come still maintain their fight against the all-devouring, all-devastating desert sands! Amongst the lights of Asia thou art, and always wilt be, one of the brightest, as thou art amongst the mountains of the earth one of the noblest, one of the most sublime!

CHAPTER XXXI.

TO FORT PAMIR AND BACK

ON August 18th I paid a last visit to the Yam-bulak glacier, to take out the sticks which I put in on August 3rd for the purpose of measuring at what rate the glacier moved. The advance during the interval of fifteen days was scarcely perceptible. There was however a slight movement, most marked towards the median line of the glacier, where it amounted to close upon one foot a day. I made an interesting observation in the neighbourhood of the lateral moraine. The glacier there spread out, giving rise to a back current near the edge of the ice, resembling in its origin and effects the backwater at the side of a river, although the time required for the movement to become perceptible must, in comparison with its extent, be very long indeed. The ice, which might be expected to pile itself up above the eddy, is easily kept down by the agents of dissolution.

The appearance of the ice had very much changed in the interval. On the occasion of our first visit it was covered with snow and hail. Now, on the contrary, it was fully exposed, with edges as sharp as knives, while all the stones had sunk into deep holes; and the ice was, as a rule, slippery and dangerous to walk upon.

On our return we observed a phenomenon which we had not remarked before. The pool beside the right lateral moraine was situated in a fissure, caused by an earthquake, which stretched all the way from the tongue of the great Kamper-kishlak glacier to the immediate vicinity of the scene of our measurements. For the most part it was single, but occasionally double, resembling a trench or dyke, about sixteen feet deep and fifty to seventy feet across, with the bottom encumbered with gravel, sand, and earth, which had gradually fallen into it. Both edges were continuous and maintained the same uniform level. Now the moraine showed a decided subsidence at the point where the earthquake fissure penetrated beneath it. The Kirghiz told me, that the fissure was caused by a violent earthquake eighteen years ago (*i.e.* 1876), when Yakub Beg was still alive. It affected Tagharma, Tur-bulung, and the whole of the west side of the Mus-tagh-ata, but was not felt at either Su-bashi or Kara-tash-davan. The lateral moraine had thus undergone no change for fully eighteen years. The fact that the earthquake was not felt at Su-bashi, only two hours distant, shows that it was probably a tectonic or fundamental shock of purely local extent. How far it affected the glaciers, the Kirghiz were unable to tell me. On the surface of the glacier itself there was naturally no trace of any subsidence, since any rift that might be made would necessarily soon be filled up. It would, however, have furnished an ideal opportunity for the investigation of the thickness of the ice and its inner structure. Earthquakes are not relatively frequent in the vicinity of the Mus-tagh-ata; slight shocks only being felt from every third to every fifth year.

When I left Kashgar in June, it was my intention to remain only two months in the neighbourhood of the Mus-tagh-ata. But I had rather under-calculated the time I should require, so that, when the two months expired, only half my work was done, and I had no provisions left. I was compelled therefore to travel to Fort Pamir to procure a fresh supply. As, however, I knew that the Chinese were watching me, and almost looked upon me as a spy, and as I did not wish to fan their suspicions unnecessarily, I resolved to cross the frontier during the night through an unguarded pass, and return subsequently in the same manner, without their having any idea of the excursion. I only took with me two of the Kirghiz, and my ever faithful Islam Bai; the rest were dismissed.

AN OLD KIRGHIZ FROM SARIK-KOL

Then, with the assistance of Togdasin Beg, we spread abroad the report, that I had gone to Kara-korum, on the southern flank of the Mus-tagh-ata.

On the evening of August 19th I carried all my baggage and my scientific collections to the tent of one of my Kirghiz friends, old Yehim Bai, who hid them safely behind his carpets and felts. After our return from Fort Pamir we learned that the Chinese, who were greatly astonished at my disappearance, had instituted a search after me. Hereupon Yehim Bai thought it advisable to transfer my baggage to a safer hiding-place, and concealed it under an enormous boulder lying in front of the Kamper-kishlak glacier, at the same time taking the precaution to wrap the boxes in felts to protect them from the weather.

We made our preparations for the journey in Yehim Bai's tent. We had four capital horses. Having packed up carpets, felts, instruments, and other necessary equipments, and prepared provisions for three days, for we were going to ride through a wholly uninhabited district—a distance of about eighty miles—we sat a couple of hours round the fire, talking and drinking tea, and getting a good meal of the old, inevitable fare, mutton and yak's cream. But as soon as the moon broke through the driving clouds sufficiently to light up the silent country, we lashed the loads on the men's horses; and at eleven o'clock, of a windy night, rode, well wrapped in furs, in single file, down between the ancient moraines of the Mus-tagh-ata.

A ride of two or three hours brought us to the Sarik-kol valley; thence our path wound up the opposite side, and through the Mus-kurau glen to the pass of the same name, situated in the Sarik-kol chain, the boundary-mountains on the east side of the Pamir plateau. In this glen was the critical point of the journey, namely, a Chinese karaol (watch-house), or sentry aul (camp), placed there for the purpose of guarding the frontier next the Russian possessions in the Pamirs. We rode past it in deep silence and at a slow pace, so near indeed that the Kirghiz with their eagle eyes were able to see the tents. But none of the guard challenged us; the dogs even did not bark, although we had Yolldash with us. My men were terribly alarmed, and their spirits only revived after we left the aul behind us; for they knew that, if they were caught, two or three hundred lashes on the bare back certainly awaited them.

At four o'clock on the morning of August 20th we safely reached the Mus-kurau pass. There I took some scientific observations; and there too we were overtaken by a furious snowstorm. From that point the surface gradually inclined towards the west. We rode through the broad valley of Nagara-kum (the Drum-Sand), the bottom of which was covered with fine yellow drift-sand; while over the slopes on either side it assumed the form of well-shaped dunes. The sand was brought thither by the west and south-west winds, the winds which nearly always prevail in the Pamirs. But as they are unable to surmount the plateau-rim of the Sarik-kol Mountains, they drop their sand in the valley and heap it up along the foot of the mountains. As the tract is entirely destitute of water, it is uninhabited in summer; but the Kirghiz visit it during those winters in which there is a sufficient fall of snow to provide them with water. We only saw water at one spot, Sarik-bulak (the Yellow Spring), where a tiny spring bubbled up out of the ground, affording nourishment to verdure of a fairly good quality. In that place we rested from ten o'clock to one p.m.

Towards evening we emerged upon the broad plains of Kosh-aghil, plains as hard and as level as a pavement. The vegetation consisted of nothing but scattered teresken bushes, which in the gleam of the setting sun cast their shadows a long way across the ground. Our route led through the characteristic landscape of the Pamirs—broad, level, waterless valleys, bounded by low mountain-chains, rounded and greatly worn.

We reached the Murghab at dusk, now in the season of the summer floods swollen to a majestic river. We encamped on a little patch of meadow on the right bank, and spent the night in the open air.

One word more about my faithful Yolldash. He accompanied me again on this journey across the Pamirs. The hardest day's travel never drew from him so much as a growl. At night he kept the most vigilant watch over our camp, and was always in excellent spirits. Nor could he be counted among the cowardly ones of the earth. Whenever we approached an aul, off he would dash ahead like a flash of lightning, and pick a quarrel with the dogs of the place. Although he set on to right and left with a determination worthy of all praise, he was of course always beaten; yet he never displayed the slightest fear even when outnumbered by half a score.

Now however, having to foot it all the way to Fort Pamir, he galled his hind-paws. The men therefore made him a pair of skin boots, which gave him a ridiculous likeness to Puss in Boots. It was irresistibly comical to see the extravagant care with which he first made trial of his wonderful foot-gear. At the outset he only used his fore-legs, and dragged himself along in a highly ungraceful sitting posture; then he tried running on three legs, lifting each hind-leg in turn; but finally he found out that the boots were practical, and were meant to protect his paws from further hurt.

The following morning we crossed over to the other side of the Murghab, and continued down its left bank, *i.e.*, westwards. At length, after we had passed a succession of spurs which projected into the valley *en échelon*, like the side-scenes of a theatre, the valley suddenly opened out before us into the expansion through which it receives its tributary the Ak-baital, and in which Fort Pamir is situated. We rode hard all day. About five o'clock we perceived the light blue smoke slowly curling up against the darker background of the mountains; and an hour later rode into the courtyard of the fort.

All was silent and still; there were no officers about. But a Cossack sentry challenged "Who goes there?" I made myself at home in the solitary fortress, and soon discovered the reason of its being deserted. It appeared that a young lieutenant from St. Petersburg had been a guest at the fort since the previous day, and in his honour a picnic was being given by the officers in the neighbourhood. It was not long before the whole party returned, my old friend Captain Saitseff at their head. The younger officers who had been under him the previous winter were now in the field, engaged in active operations under General Yonnoff against the Afghans in Shugnan; and their places had been filled by others, who were to spend the winter at the fort under the command of Captain Skersky, an officer of the general staff.

Two other changes had been made since my former visit. The lonely fort, which one of my friends in Fergana called a paradise, because there were no women within its walls, was now honoured with the presence of the young wife of the new commandant, Madame Skersky. German by birth, and a lady of an exceptionally sweet and amiable disposition, she did the honours at table with exquisite charm. Tastes, as we know, differ; but in my opinion the fort was now infinitely more like paradise than it had been before. Threadbare tunics and dusty boots had given place to a more becoming exterior, whilst linen cuffs, blacking, and the little arts of the toilet-table afforded evidence of their existence: everything in fact bore witness to the ennobling presence of woman.

In addition the fort had also started a band of twelve men, which played during dinner every day outside the windows of the mess-room. The mess-room itself had been re-christened; it now bore the name of *vayenny sobranye* or "the military club," and its walls were papered with maps of the Pamirs and plans of the fort.

Fort Pamir is overlooked on the south by the latitudinal chain of mountains which divides the valley of the Murghab from the Alichur Pamirs, known as the Bazar-darah. Just at this point it makes a bend to the left, forcing the Murghab close in under the rocks, so that the river almost describes a semicircle, and in places sweeps along with great velocity.

The Cossacks had rigged up a boat, by stretching oiled canvas over a light frame-work; and with it they used to lay their nets and cross the river to the fishing-grounds under the opposite bank. One day Captain Saitseff and I tried our luck in this improvised craft. We embarked a good way up the river, each taking an oar; then we let the boat drift with the current round the elbow, taking care to steer clear of some treacherous sand-banks near the corner. In certain places, where the water was forced through deep narrow channels, the boat sped along at a giddy pace close to the cliffs. The panorama changed continually, and, owing to the numerous short twists and turns of the river, gave rise to the most curious optical illusions. Although the boat kept gliding onwards all the time, the horizon seemed to keep moving backwards and forwards, so that, whilst at one moment we had the opening of the Ak-baital valley on the one side of us and at another straight in front of us, at yet another time we had to look well about us before we could perceive it at all. One moment the fort was on our right, shortly afterwards it had moved over to the left; until we were perfectly bewildered. The lapping of the water against the banks was barely audible; for the main current glided like oil along its bed, and the boat was carried on like an unresisting nutshell by the irresistible flood. Once or twice the frail craft scraped against the stones at the bottom, but no harm came of it; and after an hour's exciting work we landed, as wet as a couple of water-spaniels, in still water, a good way down the river, at a spot where it again widened out for a short distance.

On the other side of Shah-jan (the King's Soul), the place where the first Russian fort was erected a few years ago, 2½ miles below the present fortress, the valley of the Murghab contracts; at the same time the river becomes narrower and deeper, and increases in velocity. At that point stood a Kirghiz aul of six uys (tents), and there was the last safe ford, a passage that is always used by those going to the western Pamirs.

When on August 27th I started for Yeshil-kul, I was escorted the whole of the first day's march (twenty-five miles) by Captain Saitseff and a young lieutenant. The Kirghiz misled us at Shah-jan, by advising us to cross the river 6½ miles further on, because, they said, the road on the right bank was the better, and the flood had gone down. When we arrived at the spot which they indicated as a safe ford, one of the Kirghiz was sent across first to show the way. But the river was four feet deep in the middle, and the man's horse lost its footing, and was carried down stream. Fortunately it managed to touch the bottom again, and so reached the other side, but its rider was dripping wet up to the waist. After one or two more Kirghiz had ridden over, Captain Saitseff set his horse at the stream, and reached the opposite side in safety, but so wet that he deemed it prudent to take off his boots, which were full of water, and to strip well-nigh to the skin, and spread out his clothes to dry on a hill-side facing the sun. As I had no inordinate desire for a bath, I waited until the three camels came up, which were carrying our baggage, and climbing on to the tallest of them, managed to reach the opposite bank without getting a stitch wet.

A KIRGHIZ GIRL

As soon as Captain Saitseff's clothes were dry, we continued our journey, reaching the entrance to the valley of Ak-alkhar at dusk. There we encamped in the shelter of a huge isolated rock that stuck up out of the ground. Captain Saitseff had brought a good dinner with him, including a couple of bottles of claret; and by the light of coloured Chinese lanterns and a blazing camp-fire, we made a right good feast. Speeches were made on various topics; songs were sung without end, but to very halting melodies, in fact the echoes of entire operas struck against the cliff walls, but, I must confess, in such inharmonious tones that, had an operatic singer heard us, he would have been tempted to use his legs rather than his voice. Happily our only audience were the Kirghiz, who stood round us in a ring, looking very much astonished, apparently under the impression that we had taken leave of our senses on the way. Midnight was approaching when our musical entertainment came to an end, and we were overcome by the sound sleep which was invariably ours.

The next day we halted at Ak-alkhar, for there Captain Saitseff had sowed some barley and wheat, turnips and radishes; and all had succeeded beyond expectation, although it was at an altitude of 11,000 feet. During the course of the day I mapped part of the river towards the west, and afterwards we spent another jolly evening together, parting early on the morning of the 29th, the Russians to return to Fort Pamir, and I and my men to continue our ride up the valley of Ak-alkhar.

In two day's-marches we crossed the Bazar-darah chain and discovered a new pass (15,970 feet), to which I gave the name of Saitseff. It was only of secondary importance, as it was difficult to cross, the incline being very steep and the declivities covered with fine schistose gravel, in which the horses had hard work to keep their footing. A barely visible path showed that the sole frequenters of this pass were kiyick, tekkes, and arkharis, that is to say, wild goats and wild sheep.

On the southern side of the pass the country dipped gradually down through the defile of Mus-yilga to the broad valley of Alichur, inhabited by the population of 120 Kirghiz uys (tents). This valley, in the longitude of Ak-alkhar, lay about 2000 feet higher than the valley of the Murghab. Two more days brought us to Sumeh, at the east end of the Yeshil-kul (the Green Lake); on the way we passed Ak-balik (the White Fish), or as the place is also called Balik-masar (the Shrine of the Fish). Several springs gushed out of the ground on the northern side of the valley, and converged upon a small pool about ten feet deep and twenty yards or so in diameter. The water was a deep blue colour, constantly varying its tints, but always crystal clear, and with a temperature of 39°2 Fahr. (4° C.). Up and down it swam a number of fat fish, about a foot long and with black backs. From the culinary point of view, they looked particularly tempting; we therefore made a long halt beside the pool for the purpose of catching some of them. We had neither rod nor tackle. Still what mattered that? With the help of some pack-thread, and the hook of a Swedish watch-chain, and a piece of mutton for a bait, we soon hauled up three "beauties." After we reached camp, the men fried them in yak butter for supper, and anticipated a splendid dish. But, alas! our hopes were dashed; the fish were uneatable, having a rank disagreeable flavour. Yolldash however relished them; though he apparently regretted his excesses later on, to judge by the dismal howling he kept up all night.

On the left bank of the Alichur river we rode past a simple grave, surrounded by a stone wall. It was the burial-place of seven Afghan soldiers, who fell two years previously in a skirmish with the Russians. Some rags of felt and the poles of the tent they had lived in still remained. We took some of the latter to make our fire of, in spite of Yehim Bai's protests, that it was sacrilege to plunder a grave.

The night of September 2nd we spent at the rabat (rest-house) of Sumeh, which consisted of three gumbez (hive-shaped towers), built by Abdullah Khan of Bokhara; and on the following morning we visited a hot sulphurous spring, which issued from the ground in the neighbourhood, with a temperature of 141°1 Fahr. (60°6 C.). In the same place we also inspected a cube-shaped Chinese *tamga-tash* (seal stone) or inscribed stone, showing that there was a time when the Chinese considered themselves masters of the Pamirs. On its upper face there was a hollow space, in which a stone tablet bearing an inscription was originally inserted; but it has been removed to St. Petersburg.

We then continued our way westwards along the northern shore of the Yeshil-kul, over the vast gravel slopes, which have rolled down from the disintegrated hills above, and stretch down to the lake at an angle of thirty-three degrees. At this point the Alichur valley became so contracted that the lake was barely two miles across, while its length was as much as fourteen. The lake was undoubtedly very deep, for the water was a greenish blue colour, and had a temperature of 64°4 Fahr. (18° C.), though it was not so limpid as the water of the Little Kara-kul. Its altitude was 12,460 feet.

Several side-valleys, with streams flowing through them, reached the lake along both shores. The largest was known as Chong-marjanay; and although its volume, at the time we saw it, was not more than 105 cubic feet in the second, it had nevertheless formed a delta that projected some distance into the lake.

We halted on a small spit of low-lying land, Kamper-chick, close by the side of the lake, spreading out our felt carpets on the ground in a thick clump of bushes, which were already dry and bare of leaves. Having made tea and eaten a very simple supper, I jotted down the experiences of the day in my diary by the light of an enormous fire, which lighted up the whole neighbourhood; then, having wrapped myself in my furs, I fell asleep to the monotonous murmur of the waves.

On September 3rd and 4th we explored the western end of the Yeshil-kul, a particularly interesting spot. The south shore was overhung by a branch of the vast range of mountains which divides the Yeshil-kul from the country of Shugnan, and which bears in that region the common name of Kara-korum (the Black Stony Tract). Its summit, near the western end of the lake, where the river Ghunt issued, was covered with snow; and we could even discern a rudimentary glacier, which in former times must have been very much larger, and together with its moraines must have completely shut in the valley in that quarter. The Yeshil-kul was thus formed in the same way as the Little Kara-kul. That is to say, it is the reservoir or collecting basin of the drainage of the Alichur valley, which afterwards passes out of it across, if I may so say, the moraine threshold; then, under the name of the Ghunt, it cuts its way through a narrow glen, steep and wild, and finally joins the river Pänj. The moraine was composed of huge blocks of granite, and was excessively difficult to get across. I was at first astonished

YESHIL-KUL, LOOKING SOUTH-EAST FROM ITS WESTERN END

to find that the river Ghunt, which has the name of being as large as the Murghab, was but an inconsiderable stream, with a volume of scarcely more than 280 cubic feet of water in the second. But the mystery was soon explained: the greater portion of the current found its way ***underneath*** the moraine, where it was plainly audible as it hurtled along.

We returned to Fort Pamir through the Alichur Pamirs and over the pass of Naisa-tash. There the report reached us, that Togdasin Beg had been punished with three hundred lashes on the bare back for not having informed Jan Darin, that I had crossed the frontier, and that the beg was lying half dead in his tent. As I was afraid that the Chinese might get hold of my possessions and the collections which I had left behind, we took cordial leave of the hospitable Russians and hurried back to the Mus-tagh-ata *viâ* the Sarik-kol pass (14,540 feet). Arriving there unobserved on September 16th, we were met by the information that after all the report was false. Togdasin Beg was safe and sound, and came to see me that very evening; nor had the Chinese discovered my possessions, although they ransacked everything belonging to the Kirghiz who had been in my employ. The things were still safe in their hiding-place under the rocks.

Whilst we were away winter had advanced with giant strides. The snows had crept further down the mountains, and the whole of the Sarik-kol chain was covered with a thin white veil. The streams had shrunk into rivulets, and Nature seemed to be fully prepared for her long winter sleep. The Mus-tagh-ata towered above us, icy-cold and uninviting, so that we had not the slightest wish to molest him further.

Instead of making any further attempt to storm the citadel of the Father of the Ice Mountains, we travelled southwards along the foot of the mountain, my object being to finish my cartographical work of the summer. On September 20th I made a fresh trip over the Chum-kar-kashka glacier in quest of the rods we put in on August 13th. The change in their situation indicated only the very slightest movement; in the middle of the glacier the greatest velocity amounted to slightly under 1¾ inches a day. This slow advance is probably characteristic of all the glaciers of the Mus-tagh-ata, and is consequent chiefly upon the long winter, the great amount of radiation, and the heavy evaporation. The movement due to gravity is to some extent neutralized, owing to the diminution in the mass and weight of the glacier through the agencies just mentioned.

The Chum-kar-kashka glacier is an important landmark. All its streams seek the Little Kara-kul and finally the Kashgar-daria; while the drainage of the region to the south of it flows into the Yarkand-daria. All the streams which we crossed in the further course of our journey had eroded fairly deep channels in the lower slopes of the mountain; the which slopes consisted of detritus and old moraines, rounded and levelled down, strewn with occasional blocks of gneiss, and sometimes embellished with tiny meadows. On our left the rocky mountain-walls dipped abruptly under the detritus slopes, and were crowned by several sharp crests. On the same side too the Kok-sel glacier issued from an enormous couloir. The moraine was of an extraordinary size, and was strewn with

ISLAM BAI AND TWO KIRGHIZ WITH THE PLANE-TABLE ON THE CHUM-KAR-KASHKA GLACIER

gigantic boulders of gneiss; whilst its stream was fed from several directions. We now found that the further we went in a westerly direction, the smaller were the glaciers and the larger the old moraines. This is no doubt due to the greater energy of the agents of dissolution on the southern than on the northern versant.

On September 21st we made a long circuit round the base of the mountain towards the east-south-east and east, as far as the glacier-stream of the Sar-aghil glaciers, and on the 22nd we passed the Shevär-aghil and Gherdumbeh glaciers. Both these were inaccessible, owing to the insurmountable moraine-walls which surrounded them; not even the yaks could climb them. The conformation of the mountain was in that quarter extremely rugged; in fact, it was a sheer wall, with craggy contours and irregular ridges and cols, and the glaciers were so short that they seldom emerged from between the arms of the mountain. Its lower slopes presented the characteristics of an ancient moraine-landscape, with *cirques*, ridges, erratic blocks, and pools; and further on they gradually merged into the plains of Tagharma. The next two

KARA-KORUM, ON THE SOUTH OF MUS-TAGH-ATA

fundamental rifts in the central mass of the mountain were called Kara-korum. They possessed no glaciers; but the ancient moraines at their base were deeply excavated by running water, and the entire region was strewn with gigantic fragments of a beautiful grey gneiss and smaller pieces of crystalline schist; among which a number of hares were hopping about.

Finally we branched off to the north-east, entering the glen of the Tegherman-su. There we halted by the side of the brook, in a pleasant camping-ground among the grass and bushes; and there we rested over September 23rd. The minimum thermometer gave a reading of 41° Fahr. (5° C.), showing that we had descended to lower regions. At 4 p.m. the temperature of the water in the brook was 46°9 Fahr. (8°3 C.), and it was pure and bright, and good to drink. The volume of the stream was 70 cubic feet in the second.

It had been my intention to make the entire circuit of the Mus-tagh-ata from the Tegherman-su in a north and north-westerly direction till I came to the Little Kara-kul. Unfortunately the Kirghiz declared this project to be impracticable, owing to the east side of the mountain being a labyrinth of precipitous and jagged crests, which it was impossible to surmount even on foot. In order to convince myself of this, I made a reconnaissance to the source of the brook, and found that the Kirghiz were quite right. There was nothing for it, therefore, but to go round the mountain by the old way, *viâ* Gedyäck and Ullug-rabat, and on September 30th, 1894, we reached our old haunts on the east shore of the Little Kara-kul.

CHAPTER XXXII.

BOATING ADVENTURES ON THE LITTLE KARA-KUL

THIS time we encamped beside the Little Kara-kul from the last day of September until October 9th, partly because we needed rest, and because it was unwise to pass directly from the higher-lying regions down into the warm valleys; and partly because I wished to take soundings of the lake, which would, I hoped, verify the observations I had made during our first visit in that region regarding the formation of the lake. Quite near our camp there was an aul of six yurts; and the first day after our arrival I consulted with its inhabitants, and with Togdasin Beg and some of my own men, as to the best way of taking the soundings. There were, of course, no boats. One of the Kirghiz had indeed *seen* a boat on the upper Amu-daria; the others had not the faintest idea what a boat was like, and could not even conceive how such a thing was made. Throughout the whole of the broad valley of Sarik-kol there were only six small birches, growing on the saint's grave of Kayindeh-masar; but to touch them would have been looked upon as sacrilege. Apart from those trees, there was not a bush within a hundred miles.

The only things to be found in our immediate neighbourhood were raw hides and *oks*, or the slightly bent poles which support the cupola-shaped felt-roof of the Kirghiz yurt. But how these materials could be turned into a boat the cleverest of the Kirghiz was unable to form a conjecture. I set to work and made a little model of a boat out of some oiled linen, with a mast, sail, rudder, and keel, and very well she sailed, greatly to the amazement of the Kirghiz. Togdasin Beg said bluntly, that a thing of that kind on a large scale would cost me my life, and I had better wait till the lake froze, which he thought would happen in about six weeks' time. The temperature at night had already fallen to 14° Fahr. (– 10° C.), and every morning the small lagoons on the lake shore were covered with a thin coating of ice, which, however, melted as the day advanced. The lake itself was too rough to allow of ice being formed. During the whole of the ten days we spent on its shores, full-fledged gales flew from the south with swift, strong wings, racing one another across the lake as if consumed with impatience to get to the Bulun-kul; just as though there were not a single molecule in the atmosphere, and the great Jan Darin, with the whole of his lanza (garrison), sat in the vacuum gasping for breath. But I was not dismayed. I had heard the sea-waves boil and break before then, and preferred braving vigorous Æolus to waiting till the ice formed.

I had the tent pitched barely two yards from the shore, so that I might lie and listen to the music of the waves; and the "dockyard," where the boat-building was to take place, was close beside the tent. Here we lay down the keel and lashed the tough ribs to it with ropes, and in less than a couple of hours the frame was ready; it was only six feet long and three feet broad. A horse which had been so considerate as to die the day before contributed his skin, and a sheep also gave us materials. Thus things were beginning to look more ship-shape. The finishing touches were added in the form of a mast and a sail of scarlet cotton stuff. To each side we fastened two inflated goat-skins, and another was lashed at the stern, which somehow pointed suspiciously downwards. Our oars were made out of oks split at one end, and a piece of goat-skin stretched across the fork. For our rudder we took a spade, pure and simple, and fastened it firmly to her stern.

It was a very queer craft which left the slip on October 3rd. Honestly speaking, she scarcely did credit to

Swedish boat-building, being entirely wanting in the noble lines and beautiful proportions for which our cutters are famous. On the contrary, she was everywhere as warped and angular as an empty sardine-box. As our brave craft, in which I was going to navigate the Kara-kul for a whole week, lay bobbing up and down near the shore on her inflated goat-skins, she put me strangely in mind of some unknown antediluvian creature hatching its eggs.

Togdasin Beg turned up early the next morning to inspect the monster. He pulled up at a respectful distance. His expression was indescribably comical, and seemed to say: "Why, you don't mean to tell me a *boat* looks like that? I never could have imagined such a thing!" Then, the next moment an ironical smile crossed his lips, and he seemed to be thinking to himself—"What a crazy-looking affair!" But he had the tact not to say anything, and I bit my lip to keep a straight countenance. Meanwhile I invited him to go for a sail later in the day. After some demur, he accepted the invitation. When it came to the point, he was far less afraid than his fellow-tribesmen.

On the day our boat was launched, the Kirghiz assembled from far and near; and there were even a score or so of women, with their big white turban-shaped head-dresses, peeping from behind a moraine-mound. I asked the old men, if they thought Jan Darin would be able to keep from laughing if we put him on board, and sent him out on the lake. The idea tickled them so, they were ready to split with laughter.

In a word, the whole thing was a sensational event, a very uncommon *tamashah* (spectacle); and reports of it spread like wildfire over the whole of the eastern Pamirs. On our way back to Kashgar we used to be asked at the Kirghiz auls where we halted for the night, even at great distances from the Little Kara-kul, if it were true, that a stranger with wings had flown up Mus-tagh-ata, and later had flitted backwards and forwards across the lake? Mollah Islam even went so far as to compose a song, which was afterwards sung of an evening to the music of a *gedyäck* (violin), and no doubt will be handed down to posterity in the form of a legend.

It really was a supreme moment in my existence, when the boat was launched. The Kirghiz followed its movements with bated breath, and were astounded at my temerity, when I stepped in and went for a short sail in her, for it was blowing hard. But the little craft, with her five goat-skin bags, rode the water gaily, and Togdasin Beg was so encouraged by the sight that on my next trial-trip he willingly accompanied me.

Never did bluer, purer, fresher waves rock a more ramshackle contrivance than ours: she seemed to feel about as much at home on the water as a hen or a cat. No pride at being the first to ride the waves of the Kara-kul; no exultation at being at such a sublime altitude above the level of the sea! Anxiously she swayed on the crisp curling waves; which seemed as if they took a malicious pleasure in playing with her fears. Oh what a boat that was! A perfect menagerie of a boat! Her carcass compounded of horse and sheep and goat; in character a mule; in her movements recalling the graceful gambolings of a cow. And yet she did full honour to her descent: for she was as obstinate as a mule, and when she dropped into the trough of the waves, she kicked and plunged like a mustang. Oh that Irish pig of a boat! She never understood when you called to her "Starboard" or "Larboard." "Right" and "left" were words that meant to her the exact opposite of what ordinary folk understand by them. To all the rules of navigation she was perfectly indifferent, and you might labour at her tiller like a galley-slave: she just deluged you with water and went her own way. No matter whether we wanted to go south or wanted to go north, she always imagined we had a head-wind to face; and if we tried to tack ever so little, she was bound to fall off, till she got wind and wave behind her. In a word, she was every bit as stubborn as a yak!

As the wind blew constantly from the south, every time

OUR MAKESHIFT BOAT ON THE LITTLE KARA-KUL

we wanted to use our precious boat, we had to tow her round to the south shore, and then let her drift with the wind across the lake, taking soundings as we went. This method was inaugurated on October 4th, when the boat was towed by a horse through the shallow water to the middle of the southern shore. Then I and one of the Kirghiz, Mohammed Turdu, got into her. There was not much wind; but it was cold, so that I was well wrapped up in my furs. Before we had got very far from the shore, one of those hurricane-like squalls from the south swept over the lake, ploughing up the water furiously before it. We lowered the sail and held fast to the sides; for the boat was plunging like a restive horse. Our situation was critical: the boat was drifting out to the middle of the lake, and it was a long way to either shore. I was steering, when all of a sudden she dipped astern, and a sea broke over us, half filling the boat and wetting us to the skin. The goat-skin bag which held up the stern had got adrift, and was floating off over the water on its own account. Every wave that reached us broke right over us, although I tried to take the sting out of them with the oar, while the Kirghiz Mohammed baled away for dear life.

Our position was really serious; particularly when both the starboard goat-skins began to collapse, the wind oozing out of them with a shrill hissing sound, and the boat took a list to starboard. The seas broke over us from all sides, leaping upon us like malevolent sea-trolls, with wild dishevelled hair.

Thus we drifted, tossing on the angry waves over unknown depths. I was afraid the other goat-skin bags would part company with us, or would lose their buoyancy before we reached the shore, and kept calculating whether or not I should be able to swim the intervening distance. Nor were my spirits raised by Mohammed Turdu becoming dismally sea-sick; he would assuredly have been as white as a sheet, had he not already been as sunburnt as any gipsy. He baled the whole time, and baled double measure: on the one side water and on the other——

Poor fellow! he had never been in a boat in his life before, and had never heard of sea-sickness. He fully believed his last hour had come.

The Kirghiz crowded the nearest shore on horseback and on foot, expecting every moment to see the boat go down. But happily we succeeded in keeping her afloat; and it was with a feeling of indescribable relief that we at last saw she was gliding over shallow water. Safe and sound, but wet through, we finally reached the shore, hurried to camp, and kindled a huge fire, at which we slowly dried our clothes.

Our first sounding expedition was thus a complete fiasco. The only discovery we made was that the drift-sand contributed, in as great a degree perhaps as the glacial mud, to the levelling up of the lake-basin; for, while the glacier-streams only develop energy during the summer, sandstorms are a common occurrence all the year round. In the night, however, the drift-sand which drops from the passing storms is blown away across the slippery surface of the ice. Several times on the lake we were enveloped in clouds of sand so thick that we could hardly make out the shore-line; and in the evening, after the storm had subsided, the water was still muddy. The everlasting mutton broth actually crunched between our teeth when we took it at supper.

The following day we accomplished three good lines of sounding without any further adventure; and on the 8th set out from the western end of the southern shore. We began work late in the day, so as to let the wind settle a little first, and drifted gently across the lake, dispensing with the sail so as not to disturb the accuracy of the soundings. Hour after hour passed; then dusk came on, and it was quite dark when we reached shallow water. We were only a couple of hundred yards from the northern shore, when suddenly a dead calm set in, and the next moment a violent gale from the north, which tossed the boat back into the lake, as though it had been a mere nutshell. We felt that now we had the whole lake before us, and the night. Row as we might,

MY HORSE-SKIN BOAT IN A HEAVY STORM ON THE LITTLE KARA-KUL

we could make no headway: the wind was too strong for us, and pitilessly drove us out to the very middle of the lake. It was pitch-dark, until the moon rose, and comforted us a little; while Islam Bai, who was uneasy at our non-appearance, made a large fire at the camp, which served us for a lighthouse. The north gale was, however, of short duration, and by dint of hard rowing we managed to reach camp about midnight.

One great advantage in navigating those waters was that we did not fear meeting other craft or being run down by careless roysterers returning home late of an evening. We were the unquestioned masters of the Little Kara-kul, and had plenty of sea-room to turn our boat in; for the lake was about two miles long, two miles broad at the south end, rather more than half a mile at the north end, and a mile in the middle.

I have made fun of our noble craft. Let me now say a word in its praise, as a sort of memorial on its grave. The completion of my soundings and the continuance of unfavourable weather put an end to our trips on the lake. I was sorry to have to take our pleasure yacht to pieces, and return the various materials to their respective purveyors, instead of sending it to the Ethnographical Museum at Stockholm; for beyond a doubt it would have been one of the stars of the collection. It had indeed served to show the Kirghiz what sort of thing a boat is; but it is doubtful whether it impressed them with any exaggerated admiration of Swedish navigation.

Meanwhile we had ascertained the bathymetrical or depth relations of the Kara-kul, having taken 103 soundings altogether. All these I marked on an enlarged map, on which I afterwards drew out the curves of depth. The maximum depth was 79 feet in the southern half of the lake; in the middle it varied between 50 and 70 feet. Along the whole of the southern shore, where the glacial streams entered the lake, there was a fairly steep deposit of mud; whereas on the north the moraine sank down to the lake level at a gentle inclination. At the north-west corner, where the Kara-kul stream issued from the lake, numerous small erratic blocks of gneiss projected above the surface of the water. Close to the south-eastern shore, under the steeper cliffs, the sounding-line touched bottom after uncoiling about 5 or 6 feet; whereas everywhere in the northern half of the lake it ran out to 1000 feet or more. Near the middle of the west shore there was a small island, Kindick-masàr, every spring the breeding-place of innumerable wild-geese. In the same quarter too we discovered two large shallow creeks, and some submarine dunes of drift-sand, formed in the shelter of certain projecting rocks.

With regard to the changes of colour in the lake, the deeper parts were a deep blue, the shallow parts light green, and the strips along which algæ grew dark violet.

The Kirghiz were very decided in their statements, that there were no fish in Little Kara-kul; and in point of fact I only found one, a small one, floating dead on the water. It was of the same species as those of which I collected specimens from the neighbouring Bassyk-kul, and was probably dropped in Little Kara-kul by a bird.

The water was fresh, and good to drink. During our stay the temperature near the shore varied between 53°6 Fahr. (12° C.) and 37°4 (3° C.), and in the middle of the lake, at the bottom, it was 46°4 Fahr. (8° C.).

In several places numerous small springs entered the lake; and in all such places there were open holes in the ice nearly the whole winter. Little Kara-kul freezes in the middle of November, and the ice begins to break up in the middle of April. The Kirghiz described the ice as resembling a sheet of looking-glass, so smooth that the wind sweeps away every particle of snow. They also told me, that they could see broad woods and pastures (algæ) at the bottom of the lake through the ice, and that on winter nights the images of the stars twinkled as brightly as the actual stars did in the sky above.

Now that we had work to do every day, our life passed as quietly and peacefully as it did during our former stay beside the lake. Sometimes, when the day's work was done, and it was blowing hard, I used to go and sit on a rock by the shore, and imagine that the waves which came rolling in to my feet were beating against the wooded isles of the Skärgård at home; and a thousand memories of my native land would crowd in upon my mind, lighting up as with torches the dark night of my loneliness. I imagined myself a pilgrim resting in one of the most beautiful of Nature's temples, at the threshold of which the snow-capped mountain-giants kept watch and ward. At their feet lay the lake wonderful, set like a jewel of the purest water, its bright placid surface making a glorious mirror for them to behold their own stern features in.

It would be unjust to call the Little Kara-kul a lifeless lake. In the course of my topographical labours I many a time disturbed thriving broods of wild-duck or wild-geese contentedly feeding among the rushes by the shore. On our approach they would fly out into the lake, with legs drooping and necks outstretched. At night too I often heard the wild-geese calling to their young, or heard their hoarse honking as they sailed away over the tent in large flocks. Occasionally there were gaps made in one or other of the broods; for we were not averse to vary the deadly monotony of our daily fare.

Most beautiful of all however were the atmospheric effects. With a master hand were painted the most enthralling and gorgeous pictures—scenes so utterly unlike each other that I sometimes fancied myself transported to two or three different parts of the world all within the space of a few minutes. For instance, the sun would rise in a sky of purest blue, the atmosphere being still and warm, Mus-tagh-ata standing out in clear and sharp-cut relief, with the most delicate details of its blue shimmering snowfields, and every varying tint of its rounded and precipitous altitudes, traced in lines of matchless beauty. The dark mountain-sides would be reflected in the ever-changing mirror of the lake, now a light lovely green, now a deep intense blue, while the hush of a perfect Sabbath day brooded over the whole scene. Then, all

KENG-SHEVÄR (THE PLACE WHERE THE IKE-BEL-SU ISSUES FROM THE MUS-TAGH RANGE) SHROUDED IN MIST

of a sudden, white clouds, immediately followed by dark ones, would rustle up over the northern horizon. The sky above the Pamirs would put on a steel-grey wintry aspect: in a moment the entire vault of heaven would be packed with clouds. The wind would whistle in sudden gusts, then would blow with unmitigated fury. The lake immediately under the shore became as green as the deep sea, but further out glowed a dusky violet. From end to end it would be streaked with running lines of white spray; while the waves dashed themselves with headlong violence against the shores, which they have been crumbling down and eating at for thousands of years. But within an hour the storm would be all gone. Then would come a shower of hail; and then a heavy downpour of rain. The wind would die away. The lake would lose its brightness, and become grey from the splashing of the raindrops.

But this spell of bad weather seldom lasted long, and left no traces behind it. Every afternoon, as regular as clockwork, the east wind came piping over the pass of Kara-tash and down the valley of the Ike-bel-su, wreathing the landscape in a misty haze. With the exception of our immediate surroundings, every object became lost to sight. The shore faded away in both directions. Right before me sky and water melted together. Not a glimpse of the mountains that overhung the lake met my searching eye. I could easily have imagined I was standing on the brink of the boundless ocean.

On one occasion the mist caught up the artist's brush, and used it with magnificent effects, or rather contrasts. We were returning from an expedition to the Ike-bel-su. Its valley was filled with murky mist, which surged up the lower slopes of the Mus-tagh range, darkening every hollow in their flanks. And so swiftly, so silently, did it boil up and up, that the mountains speedily vanished from sight, like the image on an unfixed photographic plate when exposed to the light. While the lower regions were thus enshrouded in thick gloom, the towering summits of the Mus-tagh-ata shone out brilliant and vivid, like electric lamps streaming across the billows of the onrolling mist. The sun sank behind the mountains; instantly it was twilight. Higher and higher crept the mist up the mountain-sides. The topmost peaks of the great mountain, and the snowfields glancing like silver mail on its shoulders, were bathed in a scarlet glow, shading away to a glorious fiery yellow. Less and less grew the sunlit altitudes. With ill-omened ease and haste the envious shadows mounted up the faces of the precipices. One moment the crowning summit glittered out over the deluge of mist; then paled—a pyramid faintly, indistinctly outlined against the dark background of the sky; then, at the end of a few swift-ebbing moments, it too was engulfed in the unfathomable ocean of mist.

And then came the beautiful pictures of the night. The mist vanished. The moon floated up above the mountain-tops, pale and cold, moving with frigid majesty through the dark blue sky, strewn with its glittering stars. The hollow flanks of the mountains were draped with long scarf-like shadows, showing all the blacker by reason of the rocky promontories being bathed in the silver moonlight. A silence as of the grave held the mountains awe-struck in its spell. I could hear my own heart beat.

It was not without regret that I left this glorious little Alpine lake, which I had come to look upon almost as my own possession, and on whose hospitable shores we had spent so many peaceful, refreshing, and profitable days. But all the same we left it on October 9th. A furious gale was blowing from the south. The waves sang their melancholy, but soothing, song, to which I never grew tired of listening—sang in honour of our departure. But the echoes soon died away in the distance, as we once more shaped our course upwards, towards the untrodden realms of the mighty glaciers.

MY CARAVAN ON THE MARCH

CHAPTER XXXIII.

LIFE AMONG THE KIRGHIZ

BEFORE we leave the highlands of the Pamirs, and return to Kashgar, I should like to say a few words about the Kirghiz, the people among whom I had now so long sojourned. I have already described their baigas or mounted games, and the important part they play in their otherwise monotonous life. The predominant interests of the Kirghiz are the care of their flocks, and the periodic migrations which depend upon them. They spend the summers on the yeylaus (summer pasture-grounds), on the higher slopes of the Mus-tagh-ata and the Pamir mountains; and in winter, when the cold and snow drive them down from the mountains, they seek the pastures (kishlaks) in the valleys. The members of the same aul are, as a rule, kinsmen, and always graze the same yeylaus and the same kishlaks. No other aul is permitted to encroach upon pastures thus appropriated without previous agreement.

When a child is born, the kinsmen come the day afterwards to offer their congratulations. A sheep is slaughtered and a feast held, and prayers are said. On the third day the child receives its name, which the mollah looks up in a book, every day having its own name, and by that the child is known. To this is added the word Ogli (son), together with the father's name; for example, Kencheh Sattovaldi Ogli.

When a young Kirghiz wishes to marry, his parents choose him a suitable wife, whom he is obliged to take; if, on the other hand, the bride-elect is not willing, the marriage may be abandoned, though the girl too is in most cases dependent on the will of her parents. If the youth has no parents, he chooses a bride for himself; but he must always pay *kalim* (dowry) to her parents. A rich Kirghiz pays as much as ten or twelve jambaus (one jambau equals £9 to £10); a poor one pays a couple of horses or yaks. The girl's parents therefore always endeavour to secure her a bai (rich man) for a husband; the young man's a plain and poor daughter-in-law, who will be content with a modest kalim. If the girl be young and pretty, a very large dowry is always asked.

Near the Mus-tagh-ata there lived in 1894 an unusually pretty Kirghiz girl, Nevra Khan, who had suitors from far and near; but her father asked such an unconscionably high kalim, that she had reached her twenty-fifth year without being married. A young Kirghiz, who was head over ears in love with her, begged me to "lend" him the sum demanded; and even the parents of the young people tried to get round me, though naturally without success.

After the contract is made, the betrothal may last an indefinite period; but as soon as the entire kalim is paid, the marriage takes place. A new yurt is pitched, and within it the wedding is celebrated in the presence of as many guests as like to come. Dastarkhan (refreshments) of mutton, rice, and tea are served; then the mollah reads out aloud the duties of the young couple towards each other. Baigas are held. Everybody wears their best khalat (coat). The bride is dressed in all her finery and ornaments. If the man belongs to another aul, the ceremony is performed at the girl's aul, whence the newly married couple are escorted to their future domicile by all the guests.

When a Kirghiz dies, the body is well washed, and dressed in clean white clothes; then, having been wrapped in linen and felts, it is carried with as little delay as possible to the grave. The ground is dug out to the depth of three feet, and at the bottom of the hole, but at the side, another horizontal trench is excavated, and in that the body is laid. Then the outer grave is filled

KIRGHIZ GIRL FROM TUR-BULUNG

up, and the place covered with a stone; or if the dead man were a bai, his grave is marked by a small dome standing on a rectangular base. For forty days after the interment the grave is visited by the mourners.

The household goods of a Kirghiz family are not many. When they flit, two or three yaks generally suffice to transport all their belongings. The yurt (uy) itself, with its wooden pole and thick felt covering, the saddles, horse-cloths, "bedclothes," and loose carpets are the most bulky. Next come the household utensils, among which the *kazan*, a large iron cooking-pot, is the most important; furthermore china basins (*chinneh* and *pialeh*), flat wooden dishes (*tabak*), iron or copper cans with handles and lids (*kungan* and *chugun*). A number of other things, such as a loom, a kneading-trough, a corn-sieve, hatchets, sacks for keeping corn and flour in, a cradle, a fiddle, and a guitar, an iron stand for the cooking-pot, pokers, etc., are never wanting in a well-appointed uy. Most of these articles are bought at Kashgar, Yanghi-hissar, or Yarkand, though there are native blacksmiths and carpenters in the Sarik-kol valley. The wood for their yurts is procured from the valleys on the east side of the Mus-tagh-ata, as no trees grow in the Sarik-kol valley.

In every tent there is always a place set apart, the *ash-khaneh* (larder), in which they keep milk and cream in many forms, as well as other kinds of food. The drink chiefly in favour is *ayran* (boiled milk diluted with water, and left to become sour), a particularly refreshing drink in the summer. *Kaimak* is yak's cream of the most delicious description, thick and sweet and yellow, with a flavour of almonds. Ordinary milk is called *sut*. All these various kinds of milk are kept in goat-skin bags.

The Kirghiz live chiefly on yak's milk and mutton. A sheep is slaughtered once or twice a week; and the inhabitants of the aul then enjoy a good square meal. They crowd into the tent, round the fire, where the meat is boiling in the kazan. The portions are distributed amongst those who are present. Then each pulls out his knife, and eats away till nothing is left but the bare bone;

and even that is cracked in order to extract the marrow, which is considered a great dainty. Both before and after the meal the hands are washed, and when it is finished, they are carried to the beard, whilst all cry together "*Allahu akhbar!* (God is great!)." The five daily prayers of Islam are said punctually by the oldest man of each aul.

In daily life the women drag the heavier load. They pitch and strike the tents, weave carpets and ribbons, wind ropes and yarn, milk the yak-cows and the goats, tend the sheep, the children, and the household. Their flocks are guarded by a number of savage sheep-dogs, which live on what is left over at meal-times.

The men may be said to do nothing. As a rule, they sit round the fire all day long, or at most drive the yaks to and from the higher pastures. But they often visit their neighbours to buy or sell, or barter their stock. In the winter they generally spend the whole day inside the yurt, sitting round the fire (which is fed with *tesek* or yak's dung) talking, while the storm howls outside and the snow swirls in dense clouds round the yurt.

Thus the Kirghiz passes his life, peacefully and monotonously, one year being exactly like another, with the same occupations, the same recurring migrations. As time passes, he grows older. He sees his children leave him and make new homes for themselves. His beard grows white; and finally he is carried to the nearest saint's grave, at the foot of the snow-covered mountains, among which he and his forefathers have struggled through an existence which, though scant of joys, has yet been free from serious cares.

For this reason, then, they looked upon my long sojourn among them as an interesting episode. They had never before had an opportunity to see a *Ferenghi* (European) at close quarters, or to observe him going about all his mysterious occupations. They could never understand, why I insisted upon visiting every single glacier, why I sketched everything, and actually went the length of hacking pieces of stone off the rocks and filling my boxes

GROUP OF KIRGHIZ WOMEN

with them; for to them they were as commonplace and uninteresting as possible.

Their knowledge of the outer world is very limited. They only know the district they live in, but that they do know extraordinarily well; as also the routes across the Pamirs, and to the principal towns in the west of East Turkestan. But anything beyond that is a sealed book. They have heard of Russia, England, China, Persia, Kanjut, Kashmir, Tibet, Hindustan, the Great Kara-kul, Lop-nor, and Peking. Their sole knowledge of the busy places of the world is derived from the towns in that part of Asia, or from itinerant merchants; but they seldom pay much heed to what they learn from these sources, for it is mostly matter that is foreign to their own concerns, and the echoes of the peacock "madding crowd" never reach them. To them the world is flat, and girdled by the sea; while the sun circles round it every day. Try how I would to make them comprehend the real facts, they were never able to grasp them; they only answered with imperturbable assurance, that at any rate the place in which they themselves lived stood still and never moved.

The old men often told me the story of their lives; and it was always interesting and instructive to listen to, not least for the sake of the language. Among the older Kirghiz, Beg Bulat, of Rang-kul, had had a varied and adventurous life. In the days of Yakub Beg he served for twelve years as a yuz-bashi (chief of a hundred men) in Tagharma. After the death of Yakub Beg, in 1877, the Chinese took Kashgar. Two years later Hakim Khan Tura marched with a thousand men from Margelan to Tash-kurgan, where he was joined by Beg Bulat and his brother, and five hundred Sarik-kol Kirghiz. For an entire week they besieged the Tajik population of Tash-kurgan, but were unable to conquer them. A large Chinese force then entered the mountains for the purpose of quelling the revolt; and the Kirghiz Abdurrahman Dacha was sent by Hakim to Tash-kurgan to make terms of peace, but was killed by the Tajiks. Hakim Khan Tura then led his force to Chakker-aghil, at the opening of the Ghez valley. Whilst waiting there, Kurushi Dacha, Beg Bulat's brother, learned that the Chinese intended to put to death all who had participated in the revolt, unless they gave up Hakim. Kurushi thereupon deserted his leader and went to the Little Kara-kul. He was then ordered by the Chinese to attack Hakim at Muji, and did so. Hakim fled across the Kizil-art pass, and many of his men fell. Beg Bulat continued to command the remnant of the Kirghiz forces. But they too were scattered, and Beg Bulat retired to Rang-kul; while his brother was taken prisoner by the Chinese and beheaded in Kashgar. Beg Bulat, fearing a similar fate, fled to Ak-baital; but was followed by fifty Chinese horsemen, who came up with him at that place, and captured him, and took him and his family through Kashgar to Turfan. There he lived in exile for nine years; but the beg of Turfan, who was a Mohammedan, let him be at large, and allowed him to engage in trade undisturbed. As he invariably conducted himself well, the Chinese authorities eventually not only permitted him to return to his own country, but, valuing his abilities, offered him the appointment of beg of the eastern Pamirs. But he refused it, saying that he would not serve a people who had killed his brother. After that the Russians entered the Pamirs. At the time of my visit old Beg Bulat was living at Rang-kul in poverty and obscurity.

Thus we used to talk, often till late in the night, while the blue flames played about the glowing embers of the camp-fire, dimly lighting the interior of the tent, so that the rugged features of the bearded men seated round on the carpets could hardly be distinguished. I do not know whether the Kirghiz parted from me with regret; for living amid a cold, niggardly, unyielding climate, the hearts that beat in their breasts are hard and unsympathetic, and unresponsive to the warmer feelings. Yet many a friendly "*Hosh!* (Farewell!)," "***Khoda yoll versun!*** (God prepare the way!)," and "*Allahu akhbar!* (God is great!)" followed me when I went away; and they stood

A YOUNG WIFE, OF THE KARA-TEIT TRIBE OF KIRGHIZ

a long time on the shore of Little Kara-kul watching my caravan with wondering eyes; and when I left their hospitable country for the last time, no doubt many of them thought within themselves: "Whence cometh he? and whither goeth he? and what wanted he here?"

CHAPTER XXXIV.

RETURN TO KASHGAR

ON October 9th we marched to the aul of Tuya-kuyruk (12,740 feet), and the next day continued up the valley of the Ike-bel-su, whose volume was now reduced to 70 or 80 cubic feet in the second, very different from the foaming river we saw during the summer. Upon reaching the enormous and imposing glacier of Kok-sel we struck off to the left, pursuing a zigzag course up the steep slopes on the right side of the valley, which consisted partly of solid gneiss and partly of fragments of rock fallen from the heights above. That evening we reached the aul of Tur-bulung, the inhabitants of which were on the point of changing their quarters to the Little Kara-kul; for the winters are extremely raw and severe at Tur-bulung, and snowstorms of daily occurrence. Wolves, foxes, and bears were common in the same locality.

The night we stopped at the aul, the night of the 11th October, there was an unusually high wind, and the Kirghiz continually lighted torches and held them up to the smoke-vent, crying "*Allahu akhbar!*" in order to ward off the wind. Every time an extra violent gust came, they all leapt up and laid hold of the tent, although it was already well secured with ropes and stones. All the same, we managed to make an excursion to the Kara-yilga, where the luxuriant pasture attracted numbers of wild goats and arkharis or wild sheep (*Ovis Poli*). Islam Bai shot one of the latter on a glacier; but unfortunately the animal fell down a crevasse and could not be got up again.

On the 12th we rode across the Merkeh-bel pass, of

evil repute. The incline from the west was not particularly steep; but the snow was nearly sixteen inches deep. It was a curious pass; the summit broad and dome-shaped, covered with a thin glacier tongue, over which we rode for a mile and a quarter. The adjacent mountains were relatively low; those to the right (the south) entirely sheathed in ice, those to the north being either bare crystalline rocks of a black colour or sprinkled with thin patches of snow. The east side however was inconceivably steep, consisting of a moraine littered with fairly large fragments of rock and layers of schist with sharp points and edges. There I found it advisable to walk, for the horses continually threatened to come down on their knees. Fortunately this time we had hired yaks to carry our baggage. By degrees the declivity became less steep, and we got down to the valley of Merkeh without further incident, and encamped in a solitary yurt at an altitude of 11,780 feet.

The following days we travelled at a good speed down towards the plains of East Turkestan. In the glens on the east side it was snowing steadily; and on October 13th there was a high wind into the bargain, so that we rode through driving snow the whole day. The stream that traversed the Merkeh valley, being augmented by a number of tributaries from a series of small side-glens, had excavated a deep channel through the conglomerate terraces, along which we were often obliged to ride.

The bottom of the stream was encumbered with large fragments of gneiss and clay-slate. At Sughet (9890 feet), which derives its name from the willows that grow there, the tents were deeply embedded in the snow; but the chief, Togda Mohammed Bai, had a friendly reception for us.

On October 14th we marched to Chatt, the camp of Mohammed Togda Beg, chief of the Eastern Kirghiz. On the way thither we passed the Kara-tash-yilga, traversed by the stream that comes down from the pass of Kara-tash. The following day's march took us over a secondary pass, Gedyäck-belez (13,040 feet), with a soft rounded summit, composed of slippery yellow clay or fine schistose gravel. Through the adjacent glens floated detached clouds of impenetrable mist.

Our camping-station for the night bore the curious name of Sarik-kiss (the Yellow Maiden).

After leaving, on the 16th, the entrance to the glen of Keng-kol on our right, we were once more in a well-known district, and that evening put up at Ighiz-yar, in the same caravanserai in which we had stayed before. I was very pleased to lay aside my cumbrous, heavy winter clothing, which the mild air now made superfluous. And how good were the fruit and the Kashgar bread and eggs which we had for dinner!

On October 19th I once more took possession of my room at the consulate at Kashgar, delighted to see the pile of newspapers and letters which had accumulated during the course of the summer.

I now settled down at the house of my old friend Consul-General Petrovsky, and was able to enjoy a period of much-needed rest. We spent the long autumn evenings, as before, by the fireside, discussing many an important Asiatic problem. I will not dwell upon my reminiscences of Kashgar, except a couple of incidents which I must mention. My first care was to arrange and label my geological specimens from the Mus-tagh-ata, and to develop the photographs I had taken. After that I wrote a few scientific papers on the work of the summer.

In the beginning of November a breath of air from Europe penetrated to our lonely colony in the far east. Mr. Kobeko, a privy councillor, who was making a tour of inspection through Russian Turkestan, arrived in Kashgar. He was a pleasant, refined, and well-read man, and during the week he stayed with us the days flew past more quickly than usual. I shall never forget the evening of November 6th, the anniversary of the day on which the great Gustavus Adolphus died. We were all sitting round the large drawing-room table, tea-glass in hand, talking politics, and discussing the future of East Turkestan, to the crackling of the fire and the singing of the samovar—when a breathless Cossack courier entered the room without knocking, and going up to Mr. Kobeko handed him a telegram from Gulja, the last station of the Russian telegraph system. It contained news of the death of the Emperor Alexander III. All present rose to their feet, and the Orthodox Russians made the sign of the cross. Deep sorrow was depicted on every countenance, and for a long time there was a dead silence in the room. It had only taken the short space of five days for the sad news to penetrate into the very heart of Asia.

The day after the arrival of the telegram the Dao Tai and Tsen Daloi came to offer their condolences to Consul Petrovsky. With their many-coloured ceremonial costumes, their gongs and drums, their parasols and standards, and with all their pomp and state, they presented a strange contrast to the silent sorrow of the Russians.

The result of the violent changes of climate that I had been exposed to was an attack of fever, which came on in the middle of November, and kept me a prisoner in bed for a month.

Another misfortune overtook me in the Russian bath, to which I went accompanied by two Cossacks and Islam Bai. The bath was heated and everything arranged; but after I had been in a considerable time, the Cossacks imagined that I ought to have had enough of it, and came to see what I was doing. On their entrance they found that I had fainted. Some pipe in the heating apparatus had sprung a leak, and the fumes nearly did for me. The men took me to my room at once, and I gradually came round; but for two days afterwards I had a splitting headache.

Then came Christmas. Christmas! what a host of memories, of regrets, of hopes lie in that one word! Yes, it was Christmas in Kashgar. The snow fell softly; but evaporated immediately in the arid atmosphere, so that it did not even make the ground white. There was a sound of bells in the streets and market-place; but they were caravan bells and rang all the year round. The stars shone brightly in the sky; but not with the same magic brilliance as those of our northern winter nights. A light twinkled here and there in the windows of the houses; but they were not Christmas candles swinging on the fir-branches, only lamps fed with Kanjut oil, as simple as in the time of Christ Himself.

Could there be a more suitable person to pay a visit to on this holy-tide than the Swedish missionary Mr. Högberg, who had come to Kashgar with his family during the summer? Mr. Macartney, the English agent, and Father Hendricks went with me, and we took a few small presents for Mr. Högberg's little girl. The time-worn lessons for the day were read, and the Christmas psalm was sung to an accompaniment on the harmonium. Then in the darkness of Christmas Eve Father Hendricks and I strolled round to Mr. Macartney's house, where mulled wine and Christmas cheer awaited us. But shortly before midnight Father Hendricks went away; nor could we persuade him to stay longer. He was going home to his lonely cabin in the Hindu caravanserai, and on the stroke of twelve would read the Christmas mass, alone, alone, always alone!

On January 5th, 1895, Mr. St. George Littledale, with his undaunted wife, and a relative Mr. Fletcher, arrived at Kashgar, and I spent many a pleasant hour in their company. Mr. Littledale was unusually genial, manly, and unassuming in character, and I esteemed it a great privilege thus to make the acquaintance of one of the most intrepid and able of living Asiatic travellers. He himself regarded his own travels with a critical eye, was always modest, and had no pretensions. He said, that he travelled simply for pleasure, for sport, and because the active, changing life was more to his taste than the gaieties of London. But with the journey he began in the year 1895 he has written his name indelibly in the annals of Asiatic exploration, by the side of those of his distinguished countrymen, Younghusband and Bower.

In the middle of January our English friends left Kashgar in four large arbas (carts) draped with carpets;

and an imposing sight they made as they drove out of Mr. Macartney's yard. They equipped their large caravan in Cherchen, and thence crossed Tibet from north to south.

At the same time we heard with dismay of Dutreuil de Rhins's sad end. He was attacked and murdered in the summer of the same year at Tam-buddha. The news was brought by four of his men, who had returned to Kashgar.

Then came the Russian Christmas, twelve days after ours, and the consulate became busy and animated again. Cossack waits woke me up with plaintive songs on Christmas morning, and in the consul's house there were great festivities.

It was a great pleasure to me, on my return to Kashgar, to meet a fellow-countryman in the person of the missionary, Mr. Högberg; who had come there with his wife and little girl, a Swedish lady missionary, and a converted Persian, one Mirza Joseph. In the first place, coming there at all with two ladies had been an imprudence; for the Mohammedans could not be brought to believe other than that Mr. Högberg had two wives. But when, later on, Mirza Joseph married the Swedish lady missionary, the prospects of the mission in that town were destroyed for many a year to come; for in the eyes of the people of Kashgar Mirza Joseph was still a Mohammedan, and such, according to the Koran, are forbidden to choose their wives from among an unbelieving people. I gladly pass over the construction put upon this marriage, and the unpleasantness it caused; but to many in Kashgar it afforded a painful illustration of the way in which missionary work is often mismanaged, and how lightly missionaries take the grave responsibilities which they have voluntarily incurred.

When Mr. Högberg found that it would be dangerous to begin an active propaganda at once, he wisely restricted his energies to the manufacture of various common household articles, such as the people of Kashgar would find useful, and such as they made themselves in a very primitive fashion. For instance, he constructed a capital machine for the treatment of raw silk, to say nothing of spinning-wheels, bellows, etc.—all extremely well made and a source of admiration and astonishment to the natives.

It was always a pleasure to meet him and his wife; for, like all the other missionaries with whom I have come in contact, they were kind and hospitable people, and looked at the future from the bright side. One cannot but respect people who labour for their faith in the light of honest conviction, despite the errors of judgment they may fall into.

ACROSS THE TAKLA-MAKAN DESERT

CHAPTER XXXV.

TO MARAL-BASHI

AT eleven o'clock on the morning of February 17th, 1895, I, together with Islam Bai, the missionary Johannes, and Hashim Akhun, set off to travel eastwards to Maral-bashi.

Our caravan consisted of two large arbas, or arabas, on high iron-rimmed wheels, each drawn by four horses. The straw roof of the first, in which I drove with Johannes, was lined on the inside with a kighiz (felt carpet), and the opening at the back was also closed with felts, to keep out the dust as much as possible. The bottom of the arba was covered with felts, cushions, and furs, to make a soft comfortable seat; but over the bad roads the vehicle jolted to such an extent that we might as well have been on a rough sea, and the noise it made was deafening. The owner of the vehicles accompanied us; and each team had its own driver, with a long whip, who sometimes walked by the side, sometimes sat on one of the shafts, and whistled. In the other arba were Islam and Hashim, together with all my baggage; and our two dogs, Yolldash and Hamrah, were tied under my cart. The two arbas creaked and groaned along the highway, by the side of the west wall of the town, till we came to Kum-därvaseh (the Sand Gate), whence it was nearly two hours to Yanghi-shahr, the Chinese quarter of Kashgar. There we had a ridiculous adventure.

A Chinese soldier rushed out on us, stopped the horses, and declared that Hamrah was his dog. A large crowd quickly gathered round the carts. I gave orders to drive on. But the man shouted and gesticulated, and finally threw himself on the ground under the wheels, declaring that the dog was his, and demanding that he should be given up to him. To pacify the fellow, I agreed that Hamrah should be let loose and kept back. If he then followed the Chinaman, the dog was his; but if he followed us, he was ours. No sooner was the dog untied than he set off as fast as his legs could carry him along the road, and disappeared in a cloud of dust. The valorous Chinaman looked very much crestfallen, and slunk away amid roars of laughter from the crowd.

The day was dull and cold and disagreeable; the sky gloomy; the air still, but filled with a thick dust-haze, which obscured the view. A dense cloud of dust, caused by the great amount of traffic which passed up and down, hung in the willows that lined the road.

At this season of the year the Kizil-su had hardly any current; what little there was was frozen under the double bridge. After passing it we turned to the east, and thus had the river on our left. It was nine o'clock at night when we reached the village of Yaman-yar (the Miserable Place), having driven the last two or three hours in pitch darkness. We ourselves turned in in a rest-house, but the two *arabakeshes* (arba drivers) slept each in his own vehicle, so as to protect my baggage against thieves.

On February 18th we drove through a number of small villages as far as Faizabad (the Abode of Blessedness), the chief town on the road between Maral-bashi and Kashgar. It happened to be bazaar-day, and the narrow streets were thronged with an unusually busy crowd, resplendent in colour. The inhabitants of the neighbouring villages resort to the place once a week to lay in a supply of provisions. On the way thither we met or overtook numbers of wayfarers, some on foot, some on horseback, conveying to market various kinds of country produce, such as sheep, goats, poultry, fruit, hay, fuel, wooden household utensils, etc. The long bazaar echoed with the shouting and din of the multitude, as they pushed their way up and down it, squabbling with the stall-keepers, whilst the vendors vociferously cried up their wares. Every now and again we met women in large round caps and white veils, Chinamen dressed from top to toe in blue, donkey-caravans slowly forcing their way through the throng. The place was as lively as an ant-heap.

At each end of the bazaar there was a gate, closed with wooden doors; but the town was unwalled. Counting the outlying farms, the place numbered between 700 to 800 houses or families. The greater part of the population were Sarts (Jagatai Turks); though Dungans were also numerous, and there were a few Chinese colonists. The town produced rice, cotton, wheat, and other cereals, melons, apples, pears, grapes, cucumbers, and various species of vegetables.

February 19th. After leaving Faizabad we entered a dead level plain, greyish-yellow, and of a monotonously barren appearance, covered with dry, finely powdered dust, which blew up at the slightest breath of wind. The dust penetrated everywhere, searching into our furs, into everything we had inside the cart, and collected in thick layers on the roof. We covered the cart with the tent-felts, to try and protect ourselves a little, letting the folds hang down in front as far as was possible without shutting out the view. The dust was so thick and deep that it was like driving over a vast feather-bed, and the wheels of the arbas were almost sucked down into it. Our progress, heavily laden as we were, was necessarily very slow. When walking, the whole foot sank into the dust at every step, and the track you left behind you was nothing more than a series of "caved in" dimples. The unfortunate horses strained at their traces with all their might, till the sweat ran down their sides; they too were smothered with dust, and were all of the same dirty grey colour. Three of them were harnessed side by side in front and pulled by means of long traces; the fourth was between the shafts. The shaft horse balanced the cart, which had to be properly packed, so as not to press upon him with too great a strain. If he stumbled, we might expect a shaking.

Shortly after noon we rested the horses for four hours at the caravanserai of Yanghi-abad (the New Town). In the courtyard there were a number of other arbas, loaded with fuel, from the nearest *yangal* (forest). Then we drove the whole night, from five in the evening to five next morning, through the pitchy darkness. The road was wretched in the extreme; the arbas lurched and swayed miserably. But, being softly bedded, we were soon rocked to sleep in our cushions, furs, and felts.

February 20th. During the night we managed to lose ourselves, for the arabakeshes seized the opportunity to take an occasional nap. After a good deal of hunting about, in the course of which we were overturned, we eventually got back into the right track. At the village of Kara-yulgun (the Black Tamarisk) we crossed the Kashgar-daria by a wooden bridge. Soon after that we passed through the village of Yaz-bulak (the Summer Spring), which derives its name from the fact, that in summer the river overflows its banks, and inundates large expanses of the low, flat country on each side of it. Even at that season of the year there were sheets of flood-water still remaining, although frozen over, and in them grew an abundance of kamish (reeds). During the warm season of the year the great road makes a considerable detour to avoid these inundated parts. About five o'clock we arrived at a place of this kind, where a frozen branch of the river stretched right across the road. We were going at full speed, till down went the leaders on the slippery ice. There was a tremendous crackling and splintering. The ice broke, and the wheels of the arba went through to the axle. There it stuck, as if fixed in a vice. All the horses were taken out and harnessed to the back of the vehicle; but it cost us an hour's hard tugging and hauling before we succeeded in righting the cart. After that we tried another place. My arba got over without mishap; but one wheel of the second cut like a sharp knife into the ice, making it hum and whine like a steam-saw. We were obliged to unload the baggage, and carry it across. As the

ONE OF MY ARBAS (CARTS) ON THE ROAD FROM KASHGAR TO MARAL-BASHI

weather was cold and disagreeable, Islam Bai made me a huge fire on the bank, while the others were working away to get the arba across. At half-past one in the morning we reached the village of Ördeklik (the Duck Village), and there baited a while.

February 21st. Just beyond the station we entered a thin poplar forest, which however gradually became thicker. The road was in some places rather deeply trenched in the loess, and often ran between low conical hills, crowned with tamarisk and other bushes. The courtyard of the rest-house of Tungan-masar (the Grave of the Dungan Saint) was surrounded by cart-sheds on piles, with a roof made of twigs and branches. The saint's grave was indicated merely by a pole hung with tughs or offerings of rags. We encamped for the night at Kara-kurchin, a good way from the river.

February 22nd. We drove the whole day through a forest, which was said to be the haunt of tigers, wolves, foxes, deer, antelopes, and hares. The station of Chyrgeh was rather more than four miles from the Kashgar-daria.

These station-houses, with their stacks of hay and fuel, their sheds and carts, were often very picturesque and full of life—cattle, sheep, cats, dogs, and poultry. Eggs, milk, and bread were obtainable everywhere. The traffic was mostly carried on by means of donkey-caravans, conveying cotton, tea, carpets, hides, etc. between Kashgar and Ak-su.

The distance between the two places is about 340 miles, and is divided into eighteen *örtäng*, *i.e.* stages, each a day's march for an arba or a caravan. The Chinese mails, on the other hand, are carried in three and a half days, especially if they contain documents of importance. At every station there is a Chinese post-superintendent and three Mohammedan assistants, one of whom acts as servant to the Chinese postmaster, while the other two carry the mails. The mail-bags are only taken to the next station, whence they are immediately conveyed another stage by another man on horseback. Every station keeps ten horses, and the mails are carried quickly and punctually. Since the Chinese Government, at the suggestion of the British Government, introduced telegraphic communication, the old postal service no longer possesses the importance it used to have, particularly between Kashgar and Ak-su, and from thence to Kara-shahr, Urumchi, Khami, Su-chow (Su-chau), and Liang-chow-fu. It was strange to see telegraph-posts so far in the interior of Asia. They were put up in as straight a line as possible and with scrupulous care. When the Chinese were working at them, they were accompanied by an army of Sarts, with arbas, who provided them with victuals and tools.

February 23rd. The forest ceased some distance before reaching Maral-bashi. From the point where it did cease the road was bad, and the country bare and uninteresting. We crossed the Kashgar-daria a second time, at a spot where it was dry, by a small wooden bridge, and drove past the Chinese fort of Maral-bashi, with its battlemented walls of kiln-made bricks and small towers at the corners. It was said to have a garrison of 300 men. The chief bazaar of the town, which ran from west to east, was very long, very straight, and very dirty, and was lined with the shops of the Chinese and Sarts. Off it opened the gates of the caravanserais. We were allowed a couple of rooms for ourselves and our paraphernalia in a miserable hovel.

February 24th. Maral-bashi, together with the neighbouring kishlaks, was said to amount to a thousand households. The town is also called Dolon, and in certain parts of East Turkestan, for instance in Yarkand, this name is the only one in use. The word *dolon* signifies "a wild wooded tract, without villages," and is used here in contrast with Kashgar and Ak-su. The inhabitants, who are proud of being called Dolons, have the same language, customs, and religion as the rest of the population of East Turkestan, but seem to be somewhat differentiated from them, in that they approach more nearly to the pure Uigur type.

I took a walk through the little town, which is not

of much importance, though, like Faizabad, it has two small gates, here also situated at each end of the bazaar, and called Kashgar-därvaseh and Ak-su-därvaseh (the Kashgar gate and the Ak-su gate). There were two principal mosques, called Dolon and Mussafir, with simple façades of grey clay, and wooden balconies inside the courtyard. The former was situated near the Ak-su-därvaseh, and outside of it there was a burial-ground (*gabristan*). Here we came upon the Kashgar-daria, containing a little water almost stagnant; and from it ran ariks (irrigation canals), which were used for driving mills situated near the banks.

We went to look at one of these mills; it was simply a thatched shed, resting on piles. The corn was ground in a corner of the shed, between horizontal mill-stones, brought from Kashgar at the cost of 100 tengeh (22*s.* 6*d.*) each. They can be used for about five years before being worn out. Just at that time maize (*konak*) and wheat (*bogdai*) were being ground. The miller's perquisite was one-sixteenth of the flour ground, and he could grind from 32 to 40 chärecks (= 16 jings or 24 lbs. avoir.) in a day. In another place rice was being husked. Raw rice before being husked (paddy) is called *shall;* whereas pure white rice, freed from its awns, is called *grytch.* The husking mill consisted of a water-wheel, running on a horizontal crank and driving a couple of wooden hammers, which fitted into two hollow slanting grooves, in which the raw rice or paddy was poured. The rice was freed from its husks and awns by repeated beatings of the hammers, the refuse being afterwards sifted away. Every sackful of rice was put three times through the mill. For this the miller got a tithe of the husked rice, and he could finish 15 chärecks in the day. As a chäreck of rice cost 4 tengeh in Maral-bashi, the man thus earned 6 tengeh (1*s.* 3*d.*) a day. Large quantities of rice, maize, and wheat are grown in the neighbourhood.

In the morning a Chinese official and four begs came to welcome me in the name of the amban (governor of the town). The begs were extremely civil and communicative, and considered that my plan of crossing the Takla-makan Desert was feasible. They told me, that there once existed a large town called Takla-makan in the desert midway between the Yarkand-daria and the Khotan-daria; but for ages it had been buried in the sand. The whole of the desert was now known by this name, although it was sometimes shortened to Takan. They reported further, that the interior of the desert was under the ban of *telesmat* (an Arabic word, meaning "witchcraft," "supernatural powers"); and that there were towers and walls and houses, and heaps of gold tacks and silver jambaus (tack and jambau being Chinese coins). If a man went there with a caravan and loaded his camels with gold, he would never get out of the desert again; but be kept there by the spirits. In that case there was only one way by which he could save his life, and that was by throwing away the treasure. The begs thought that, if I followed the Masar-tagh as far as I possibly could, and took a supply of water with me, it would be possible to cross the desert. But under no circumstances could horses cross it; they would certainly die.

CHAPTER XXXVI.

AN EXCURSION TO THE MASAR-TAGH

FEBRUARY 25th. From Maral-bashi I made an excursion to the Masar-tagh, a mountain-range a day's journey to the east of the town. Only one driver, Islam Bai, and Yolldash were of the party, and the lightly laden arba carried us swiftly along the road. After a couple of hours' driving the mountain became visible through the dust-haze, as a somewhat darker background, with a serrated crest. We turned off to the right from the high-road to Ak-su, and struck across a hard, barren steppe, with thinly scattered tussocks of grass. Then we passed between two spurs of the mountain. The one on the right, which was larger than the other, was a wild, rugged highland region, exhibiting proofs of severe weathering and of the erosive power of the wind. Its rock was a species of light-green crystalline schist. At the base of the mountains there was sufficient grass for a few small kishlaks (winter pasture).

Not far from the north-east foot of the mountain stood the Ullug-masar (the Great Tomb), surrounded by a grey wall of sun-dried bricks. The first place we entered was a large square courtyard, in which a ring of long sticks were thrust into the ground round a bush. Both sticks and bush were hung with flags and pennons, some white with red edges, others entirely red or blue, others again were three-tongued, with vandyked edges, and so on. Thence a door led into a *khanekah* or prayer-house, the floor of which was covered with carpets. At the far end there was an open woodwork screen, and behind it the tomb of the saint, marked by an ordinary tombstone, in a square dark room decorated with flags, tughs (rags), deers' antlers, and the horns of wild sheep. The shrine, together with its *gumbez* (dome), was built of kiln-burnt bricks, and was visited every Friday by pilgrims from the neighbourhood. In the outer court there was an *ashbaz-khaneh*, or kitchen, where they cook their food.

We took up our quarters in a hospitable house in the kishlak of Masar-alldi (In Front of the Saint's Tomb), and were at once visited by the dignitaries of the place. I got a good deal of valuable information out of them. For instance, they told me that in that part of its course the Yarkand-daria was divided into two arms, and went on to describe three very large lakes situated in the neighbourhood, which not only increased in size when the river was in flood, but also abounded in fish. I was especially interested to learn that the Masar-tagh continued in a south-easterly direction through the desert as far as the Khotan-daria; though the information seemed on the whole to be doubtful, as none of the men had themselves seen how far the mountains extended into the desert.

Some of them called the desert Dekken-dekka, because a thousand and one towns are said to be buried under its wastes of sand. Moreover vast stores of silver and gold might be found in them. It was possible to reach them with camels; and probably water would be found in the depressions.

February 26th. It was now my object to obtain a general idea of the Masar-tagh. Accordingly we took a guide, and drove along their eastern foot in the arba, having on our left a marsh, shut in by barren sand-hills. After a three hours' drive we reached the Kodai-daria (the Swan River), the northern branch of the Yarkand-daria, a good hundred and twenty yards broad, and covered with soft ice, which bore men on foot, but broke under the weight of the arba. The boat which the Dolons used when the river was high was frozen fast in the ice. In summer, when the river is in flood, enormous volumes of water flow through both branches, causing them to overflow and unite into a lake-like expansion, while at the same time considerable stretches of the woods on the right bank of the river become half inundated.

In the beginning of April a large number of Dolons resort thither with their flocks, and there spend half the year in the woods, dwelling in reed huts erected in situations where they are safe from inundation. These summer camps, some of which still remained *in situ*, are called *yeyliks*. Thus the Dolons may be said to be semi-nomads.

When I could get no farther with the arba, I mounted a horse, and taking one man with me, rode over the Masar-tagh by a very difficult pass, and then proceeded along the western foot of the mountain, till I came to the reedy Shor-kul (Salt Lake), which, however, contained perfectly fresh water and swarmed with wild geese. The mountain was built of a species of coarse-grained, eruptive rock, encumbered all along its base with fallen fragments of stone, which were polished and carved by the wind into grotesque, saucer-like hollows, overtopped by rounded masses poised on narrow stalks or pedestals. The Shor-kul, which lay parallel to the left bank of the Yarkand-daria, was a typical fluvial lagoon. It owed its origin to the gradual deposit of sediment in the bed of the river, lifting the current above its banks until it overflowed on to the lower-lying country on each side.

We returned to camp by way of the Ullug-masar. The Masar-tagh we found consists of crystalline schist, porphyry, and a species of rock resembling syenite. It stands like a ruin in the angle between the Kashgar-daria and the Yarkand-daria, and is itself looked upon as a masar or saint's tomb.

February 27th. We now returned, in a north-north-east direction, to the great Ak-su road, which we struck at Char-bagh (the Four Gardens). Once more we crossed the Kashgar-daria, or rather the numerous branches into which it was there divided, each spanned by a small wooden bridge. Soon after that the hill of Akhur-masar-tagh loomed out through the dust-laden atmosphere, one of its projecting spurs crowned with the masar Hazrett-Ali. There had been some wind in the morning from the east; but towards midday it came on to blow rather strongly, enveloping everything in an impenetrable dust-haze, while clouds of dust hung along the road in the track of our arbas. Every now and then we caught a glimpse of trees and bushes, of houses and villages, looking as though they were covered with dirty water. There were but few travellers on the road in such weather.

Mount Tumshuk, which sent out four spurs towards the north, now came into view. On its steep slopes, built up like the seats in an amphitheatre, but clinging to the naked rock like swallows' nests, were a number of ruined houses and walls, ascending as high as 60 to 80 feet above the level ground. Two different periods of architecture were plainly distinguishable. The houses of the older period were built of burnt bricks, while those of the later period were constructed of sun-dried clay. On the level ground, at the foot of the mountain, there were also a great many ruins. All these are the remains of an old city, which was no doubt protected by a citadel crowning the mountain behind. The region is now sterile and uninhabited; changes in the channel of the Kashgar-daria having in all probability led to the desertion of the town.

February 28th. One hour north-west of the station Tumshuk lay another collection of ruins known as Eski-shahr (the Old City). These too I visited. The best-preserved building was a square structure, each of its sides ten yards long, built true to the four cardinal points, and with a doorway to the east. It was constructed of hard burnt bricks, and had probably been a mosque. The corners in the interior were decorated with friezes in relief. The doorway too was embellished with ornamental brick-work, and perhaps in its day had been covered with tiles.

There was a hill in the vicinity, from which two parallel ridges projected towards the north-west; there we discovered the ruins of former stone walls. The style of architecture was Mohammedan; accordingly these archæological remains could not date back more than 1150 years.

The storm still continued. About midday the sun was darkened, as when a thunderstorm threatens; sand and dust whirled along the ground, and rose in spinning columns into the air. Thinking discretion the better part of valour, we hastened to return to the rest-house at Char-bagh, and a disagreeable drive it was. Every breath we inhaled was charged with choking dust; even the horses in front of the arba disappeared from view every now and then, so that, when we reached our destination, we were absolutely smothered with dust.

March 1st. The storm subsided, and we had good weather for the return journey to Maral-bashi, where to my delight I found letters awaiting me from home. The post-jighit (courier) who brought them was a capable fellow, an old Sart from Osh in Fergana, whom I had seen before on the Murghab. I took him for the time being into my service.

An old man of eighty, who heard that we were going to try and cross the Takla-makan Desert, came to my house, and told me, that in his youth he had known a man who, whilst going from Khotan to Ak-su, lost his way in the desert, and came to an ancient city, where he found innumerable pairs of Chinese shoes in the houses; but directly he touched them, they crumbled to dust. Another man started out into the desert from Aksak-maral, and by pure chance stumbled upon a town, amid the ruins of which he unearthed a quantity of gold and silver *jambaus* (Chinese coins). He filled his pockets with them, as well as a sack he had with him. As he was going off with his booty, a pack of wild cats rushed out upon him and frightened him so much that he threw everything away, and took to flight; when, some time afterwards, he plucked up courage to venture his luck a second time, he was unable to find the place again. The mysterious town was completely swallowed up in the sand.

A mollah from Khotan was more successful. He had fallen into debt, and went into the desert to die. But instead of dying, he discovered a treasure of gold and silver, and was now an exceedingly rich man. The number of those who had gone into the desert with the same design, and never returned, was legion. The old man solemnly assured me, that the evil spirits must be exorcised, before the hidden treasure could be sought for

A DERVISH FROM EAST TURKESTAN

with any likelihood of success. The spirits bewitch the unhappy beings who venture thither, so that they become confused and bewildered, and without knowing what they are doing they go round and round in a circle, retracing their own footsteps, and go and go until they fall down from sheer exhaustion, and die of thirst.

There is a tribe of ne'er-do-weels hanging about the places round the outskirts of the desert, who firmly believe that sooner or later they will discover the hidden treasures which lie buried among its sands. These gold-seekers are always looked at askance by their neighbours, and should be avoided. They will not work; but live on the hope of making their fortune at a single stroke. They are parasites, a burden upon their neighbours, who in their "spare time" occupy themselves with thieving and robbery. For needless to say, they never find any hidden treasure.

But whence do all these legends come? How explain all these confirmatory accounts of buried cities, and these varying traditions of the great city of former times, Takla-makan, which was swallowed up in the sand? Is it merely by accident that these legends fly from mouth to mouth in Khotan and Yarkand, Maral-bashi and Ak-su? Is it merely by accident that this ancient city is always known by the same name? Is it merely for the sake of making themselves interesting that the natives describe these deserted houses in detail, which they say they have seen, and where, they say, in former times there were great forests, the home of the musk-deer and other big game? No, it *cannot* be by chance; these legends *must* have a foundation and a cause. Deep under them there must verily be some reality for them to rest on; they ought not to be scorned, they ought not to be despised and neglected.

To these fabulous, these adventurous tales I gave the eager ear of a child. Every day added to the allurements of the perilous journey I contemplated. I was fascinated by all these romantic legends. I became blind to danger. I had fallen under the spell of the weird witchery of the desert. Even the sandstorms, those terrible scourges of Central Asia, which have their cradle in the heart of that sand-heated furnace—even they were in my eyes beautiful, even they enchanted me. Over there, on the verge of the horizon, were the noble, rounded forms of the sand-dunes, which I never grew tired of watching; and beyond them, amid the grave-like silence, stretched the unknown, enchanted land, of whose existence not even the oldest records make mention, the land that I was going to be the first to tread.

March 2nd. Having paid and settled up, we left Maral-bashi, and drove south-west towards the village of Khamal (the Wind), situated on the left bank of the Yarkand-daria. The road led across a slightly broken steppe country, with scanty herbage, tussocks of grass, and bushes. Khamal was inhabited by thirty families, who cultivated wheat and maize; their fields being irrigated by an *arik* (irrigation canal) led from the river. During the summer, when the river is in flood, it overflows and inundates wide tracts along the banks. The spring-floods, caused by the melting of the winter ice, likewise bring down considerable quantities of water, as we witnessed every day.

March 3rd. Through jungle and reeds, through poplar groves, across small belts of sand, and through marshes, where the ice was just on the point of breaking up, our creaking carts ploughed their way along the western bank of the Yarkand-daria. Wild boar abound in the jungle, and do much damage to the crops in the villages around. To prevent this the natives put up sheds here and there about the fields; and there they live and keep watch when harvest time is approaching.

The amban (Chinese governor) of Maral-bashi had given orders beforehand to the *on-bashis* (chiefs over ten men) of the various villages, that they should receive me in a fitting manner; and as a matter of fact his words were carried out to the letter. At every place we stopped at we found rooms ready prepared, and everything we needed in the way of food for ourselves and for our animals was provided for us.

Aksak-maral (the Lame Deer), where we made our next stop, consisted of thirty houses, most of them occupied by Dolons, who reared cattle and sheep, and grew wheat and maize. The winters there are cold, but the snowfall is inconsiderable. The springs are windy. The small amount of rain which falls generally comes in the autumn, often to the detriment of the crops.

During the night, when the air was still and cold, and the currents set up by the active radiation of the day-time ceased to rise, the atmosphere generally cleared. So it did to-day. During the morning and afternoon the sky was an ashen grey; but in the evening the moon and stars shone fairly bright in the zenith, although near the horizon they were swallowed up in the dust-haze. In the morning again the blue sky was only visible at the zenith, but gradually merged into grey towards the horizon.

March 4th. Our day's march took us across a very extensive marsh, through which the Chinese authorities had built a road some seven years previously. As it was built to withstand the encroachment of the floods, it was constructed of piles, stakes, fascines, and earth. It wound through the marsh like a narrow ribbon; and in certain places was carried over bridges, so as not to check the free flow of the water. In spite of this however the road is frequently inundated during the months of June, July, and August, compelling travellers to go all the way round by Kashgar. The marsh is in reality a low-lying lagoon, and is said to have existed from time immemorial. It is called Cheraylik-tograktasi-köll (the Fair Poplar Lake).

Ala-ayghir (the Dappled Mare) was the name of the next station, a kishlak of twenty-five Dolon families. The same conditions of life and climate obtained there as in the foregoing villages. There too east winds prevail during the spring. Between Maral-bashi and Yarkand there was Chinese postal communication, as well as in general a very lively traffic, carried on chiefly by means of arbas (carts) and donkey-caravans. Camels are very seldom used.

Ala-ayghir was situated rather more than half a mile from the Yarkand-daria; but when the river rises in the summer, the water reaches the village. Two years ago even the winter shore-line ran just below the village; but I was told that, more particularly during the last few years, the river has shown a tendency to shift its channel somewhat to the east.

March 5th. We drove ten hours to-day, often over heavy roads, soaked in water, so that the wheels of the arbas cut deeply into the sandy mud. We passed three villages; and at the fourth, Meynet, we turned in at an unusually comfortable caravanserai. On the wall was posted a large yellow placard, in Chinese and Turki characters, conveying the following paternal announcement: "Whereas I (the Emperor of China) have heard that certain begs have imposed unlawful taxes on my people, and have furthermore monopolized their rights of fishing, it is my will and desire that all such infringements be forthwith reported to the nearest Dao Tai, and if the latter will not listen to and remedy the same, the people shall address themselves direct to me.—Kwang Tsü." Poor Kwang Tsü! He has never even heard of the village of Meynet; and what cares he for the fishing in the Yarkand-daria? Meynet boasts of fifteen Dolon households. The belt of river-forest was at that point only a few miles broad, and soon thinned and died away in the desert. Wolves were common, and preyed upon the flocks. On the other hand, there have been no tigers for many years, except that a couple of years ago a single tiger showed himself at Ala-ayghir.

March 6th. The first few miles ran through luxuriant poplar woods, until we came to the river. It was there divided into two principal branches and many smaller ones, still sheeted with soft ice, except that there was a belt of open water close under the banks.

Our stopping-place for the day was Lailik (the Dirty Clayey Place), the last village in this direction subject to the amban of Maral-bashi. On the south it adjoined the Yarkand district. Its population consisted of fifteen Dolon families. Fishing was carried on in the river, the maximum height of which at the season of high flood was said to approximate the added statures of five men. The velocity of the current was pretty considerable, though not so swift as the pace of a mounted man. It takes a man on horseback four days to reach Maral-bashi, whereas the river wants as much as ten days to do the distance.

March 7th. Lailik was for some time our headquarters, as considerable preparations had to be made for our expedition across the desert. The most important difficulty was the procuring of camels. I had been rather misled by the merchants in Kashgar, who told me that Maral-bashi was the best place to get good camels. We hardly ever saw a camel there. I had no resource except to try and procure some from Kashgar. This mission I entrusted to Mohammed Yakub, who in any case had to go there to post letters and bring others back. A fairly good camel cost 500 tengeh (£5 15*s.*) in Yarkand; but in Kashgar only 400 (£4 12*s.*). Yakub took with him letters to Consul Petrovsky, and to the aksakal, asking them to assist him in the transactions, and within ten days he was to be back again, bringing with him eight fine camels and two men.

Our arabakeshes were now dismissed, being paid 200 tengeh (£2 6*s.*) for the journey from Maral-bashi. They thought of going to Yarkand to try to get work there, and meant to fill their two arbas with firewood from the last patch of forest along the road. A donkey-load of firewood was worth three tengeh (8*d.*) in Yarkand, and an arba would hold ten such loads, so that the men hoped to make an extra sixty tengeh (13*s.* 9*d.*) by the return journey.

Islam Bai was dispatched to Yarkand on horseback to buy several things that were required for our desert expedition, for example iron tanks for water, bread, rice, ropes, and a number of tools, such as spades and hatchets. I also instructed him to bring a supply of sesame oil (*yagh*), and the chaff from the crushed seeds of the same plant (*kynchyr*), etc. The oil was intended to feed the camels on in the desert. A *jing* (not quite one pint) of oil will sustain a camel for a month without other food; though it is always a great advantage to find supplies of herbage during the march, so that the animals may to some extent freshen up and recover from their exertions. In March and April they cannot well go longer than three days without water; but in the winter, and on level ground, they can last out six or seven days if necessary.

My party had vanished like chaff before the wind. The missionary Johannes was the only one now left.

March 8th. I walked through the young forest as far as the river in order to take some observations; and found a ferry-boat, which was punted across in seventy seconds, and which could carry seven horses, six donkeys, and twenty men at once.

The two banks were very dissimilar. The left bank was low, flat, and bare, with many sandbanks. The right bank was worn perpendicularly by the current, which ran immediately underneath it; and was luxuriantly wooded with poplars and tamarisks, whose roots stuck out of the fine alluvial soil of which it was composed. The river thus showed a marked tendency to press against the right bank, and eat it away. But the current meandered so much that in other places it was the left bank which was eroded, although on the whole to a much less extent than the right bank.

The forest on the right bank was six feet above the level of the stream; nevertheless it is overflowed in July. The breadth of the river was 200 feet, the maximum depth 6 feet 3 inches, velocity of the current 2 feet 8 inches in the second, and its volume 3060 cubic feet in the second; a volume which must be inconsiderable when compared with the masses of water which in the height of summer pour down towards Lop-nor. The temperature was 46°9 Fahr. (8°3 C.), and there was no ice anywhere. The water was however only transparent to a depth of barely two inches.

CHAPTER XXXVII.

THE SHRINE OF ORDAN PADSHAH

MARCH 9th. With the view of employing profitably the time while my men were away, I decided to visit the shrine of Ordan Padshah in the desert, two days' journey west of Lailik. I got hold of a man who knew the way; and at eight in the morning we were in the saddle, riding at a smart pace west-nor'-west, first through forest, which gradually passed over into brushwood, then across steppe-land, which in its turn gave place to the desert. The sand however was not deep, nor the sand-dunes high; but the latter had their steep slopes facing westwards, indicating the prevalence of easterly winds at that season of the year.

It was an interesting excursion; for the region had never before been visited by a European. After leaving the large village of Mogal (Mongol) on our right, we came to Terem, where the beg placed his house at my disposal. I required little room, however, for I had nothing with me beyond the barest necessaries, and only had two horses.

The villages of Terem and Mogal consisted of 200 households each, and were governed by a beg and eight on-bashis; though a Chinese tax-collector also lived there. The word Terem means a "cultivated place," and the inhabitants told me, that in point of fact Terem was in former times famous for its good harvests and abundant water-supply. People came thither from all parts to buy corn. The change which has taken place must unquestionably be attributed to the alteration in the course of the river. The place now gets its water-supply from the great irrigation canal of Khan-arik, which issues like a main artery from the Ghez-daria, and, passing through the villages of Tazgun and Khan-arik, stretches its last network of arterioles as far as Terem. But the supply is insufficient, irregular, and uncertain, and consequently the harvest often fails.

In the case of the Khan-arik there exist special regulations, made by the Chinese authorities, by which each village is only allowed the use of the water for a certain time. Terem had now been furnished with water for three months past; but in twelve days' time the supply would be cut off, and for four whole months not a drop would reach it from the irrigation system. The inhabitants would be obliged to content themselves with what their wells would yield. Late in the summer they would again have the use of the life-giving waters for the space of thirty-four days.

On March 10th we left Terem, and rode in a westerly direction through steppe, desert, and marsh. Here I made the important discovery of four ancient river-beds, now however dried up, but still very plainly marked, each from one hundred to a hundred and ten yards broad, and running towards the north-north-east. They could not possibly be anything but deserted channels of the Yarkand-daria. In Bai-khan-köll (the Rich Khan's Lake), a salt and shallow sheet of water, with marshy shores overgrown with kamish (reeds), we nearly stuck fast altogether. The lake is largest in winter, when it becomes frozen; but in summer the water evaporates almost entirely, despite the fact that the lake receives the overflow of the ariks of the Yanghi-hissar. In the district of Kizil-ji we crossed by a bridge another prolongation of the ariks of the Yanghi-hissar. In that neighbourhood there was a saint's tomb called Kizil-ji-khanem, an interesting fact, for the name occurs in the map of Edrisi, the famous Arab geographer of the twelfth century.

At the point where the desert proper began, and where the sand-dunes were about twenty-five feet high, stood the insignificant village of Lengher (the Rest-Station). There a dervish resides during the great annual religious festivals, to take charge of the pilgrims' horses, which are left to graze on the grass and kamish which abound in the neighbourhood. He also sells maize to the pilgrims, and supplies the shrine with fuel. Beyond this place the sand-dunes were fairly continuous; but as they ran south-south-west to north-north-east, and we were riding south-south-west, we were generally able to take advantage of the intervening hollows, where the soil was hard clay.

An hour's ride short of the shrine we caught up a party of forty-five pilgrims, men, women, and children, who were on their way thither from Lengher to pray at the tomb of the saint. Fifteen of the men carried tughs, *i.e.* long sticks with white and coloured pennons fluttering from the ends. At the head of the procession rode a flute-player, and on each side of him was a man banging away at a drum as hard as hands and arms could move. Every now and then the whole concourse shouted "Allah!" at the full pitch of their voices. When they drew near to the shrine, they greeted the sheikh who had charge of it with wild howls of "Allah! Allah!" while the standard-bearers performed a religious dance.

It was dusk when we reached the khanekah (prayer-house) adjoining the shrine, and standing in a village of twenty-five households. Most of the people only sojourn there for a short time; but four families remain the whole year round to take care of the saint's tomb. The principal sheikh, who also has control over the Hazrett Begim's tomb, was for the time being absent at Yanghi-hissar. He constantly travels backwards and forwards between the two shrines, spending some time at each, and for this reason has a wife at each. One of the resident custodians informed me, that every winter 10,000 to 12,000 pilgrims visit the shrine of Ordan Padshah; but in the summer there are usually not more than 5000, as at that season of the year the heat and scarcity of water render travelling irksome. The pilgrims who came from Lengher at the same time we did brought with them two sacks of maize as an offering, and placed them in a bronze vessel in the prayer-house. Then they made a thorough good meal off it, in which they were joined by the custodians of the shrine. The tribute was, however, a prayer for a fruitful year.

There were eight houses in the village, standing in two rows, with a street running east to west between them. To the north two or three more houses were half buried in the sand-dunes, which were threatening the village itself.

I was assigned an exceptionally comfortable room in the upper storey of the guest-house, with latticed windows, looking out upon the dreary desert on the south. In spite of the hideous din that was kept up in the street below all night long, by the pilgrims marching in procession backwards and forwards, playing flutes, singing, beating drums, and waving flags, I slept soundly till morning. When I awoke, I found a furious sandstorm blowing, and clouds of dust whirling in through the latticed window and dancing in giddy eddies round the room.

March 11th was devoted to making a nearer acquaintance with this curious place of pilgrimage, which has only been visited once before by a European, namely by Major Bellew in April 1874. He reached it from the west, I approached it from the east; our investigations therefore supplement each other.

In addition to the principal sheikh, the permanent *personnel* of the shrine consisted of an imam or reader of prayers, a *mutevelleh* or steward of the shrine properties, and twenty *supehs* or men-servants. All these are fed and maintained at the exclusive expense of the pilgrims. These, according to their circumstances, bring horses, sheep, cows, poultry, eggs, seed-corn, fruit, khalats (coats), and other useful articles. With the exception of the live stock, everything goes into the largest of the metal vessels set apart for receiving the pilgrims' offerings. Of these there were five, all built into a brick fireplace in the walls of the *kazan-khaneh* or "cauldron-house." The Altyn-dash or Gold Stone, as the largest of the five vessels is called, was about five feet in diameter, and

A SAINT'S SHRINE IN CENTRAL ASIA

The Atturlik Ata-masar at Tashkend

was made of bronze; it is said to date back eight hundred years, from the time of Ordan Padshah himself. Next came a handsome copper vessel, 3 feet 4 inches in diameter, a present to the shrine by Yakub Beg of Kashgar, who himself made three pilgrimages to the place. The other three were smaller and of various sizes. When there is a great influx of pilgrims, the custodians of the shrine make *ash* or pillau (mutton with rice and spices) in the biggest vessel for everybody at once. At other times the smaller vessels are used, according to the number of the pilgrims. The "cauldron-house" was built two years ago. The old one is now half buried in a sand-dune; which already threatens to enclose the new structure within the horns of its hollow crescent. The winds which determine the movement of the sand-dunes in this region blow from the north-west.

On the windward side of the nearest sand-dune was a half-buried grave-mound decorated with tughs. It contained the dust of Shah Yakub Sheikh, and was said to be 710 years old. According to the direction in which the dunes are at present moving, the tomb will soon be entirely exposed again. The maximum breadth of the sand-dune was nearly 400 feet, and its height about 16 feet, so that it overtopped the roofs of the houses. The little village stands in the clay hollow between the leeward side of this sand-dune and its nearest neighbour on the south-east, on a space some 170 yards broad. In violent storms the sand is blown right across from the one dune to the other.

The khanekah or prayer-house contained an oratory, and a balcony, with an eastern aspect, supported by sixteen pillars. Immediately north of the village the freshwater spring, Chevätt-khanem, bubbled up out of the ground, filling a round pool surrounded by a wooden railing. The water was tolerably clear, considering that the sand was only cleaned out once a year; but it issues so slowly, that it is insufficient on festival-days. On such occasions the pilgrims have to fall back upon another spring, Cheshmeh (a Persian word meaning "a spring"), which yields saltish water, and is ten minutes further away.

At a distance of twenty minutes towards the north-west stood the saint's masar or tomb, a truly extraordinary structure. It was composed of a sheaf of two or three thousand tughs, each with a pennon attached, stacked up in the shape of an Eiffel tower. Standing forty feet high, on the top of a sand-dune, it was visible to a great distance. An attempt has been made to render the dune stationary by planting sheaves of kamish (reeds) in the sand round the masar; and the expedient has been to some extent successful, for the portion of the sand-dune upon which the masar stands projects so far towards the north-west, *i.e.*, to windward, that it is now threatened by the dune which comes next on that side.

The sandstorm raged with undiminished violence, so that the hundreds and hundreds of pennons flapped and fluttered furiously, with an endless series of small reports. These tughs are brought there year after year by the pilgrims, so that the curious sheaf goes on increasing in size. To prevent the whole structure from being blown over, the sticks are secured at the top by a couple of square wooden cross-pieces. A number of smaller bundles of tughs form a fence, thirty yards square, all round the tomb.

The imam told me something of the story of Ordan Padshah. His real name was Sultan Ali Arslan Khan; and eight hundred years ago he was at enmity with the tribe of Togdarashid-Noktarashid, among whom he was endeavouring to propagate Islam. In the midst of the strife he was overtaken by a kara-buran, or black sandstorm, from Kharesm (Khiva), which buried him and the whole of his army. Hence to this day he plays an important part in the martyrology of East Turkestan.

In the afternoon we rode through the villages of Dost-bulak (the Friend's Spring), Khorasan, and Psänn due north to Achick (Bitter), the yuz-bashi of which received me in a friendly spirit, telling me a good deal about the climate and the roads in the vicinity.

March 12th. Having an eight hours' ride to Terem, we started early, and rode through a strong nor'-westerly gale. The district between the two places was chiefly of a marshy steppe-like character, with occasional thickets of tamarisk, thistles, and tussocks of grass; which, when they get thoroughly dry, are often uprooted, curled into balls by the wind, and so swept along the ground. The surface was covered with fine, loose dust, which was driven up like smoke before the gale. We often rode through swamps of stagnant arik-water, and were sometimes constrained to make detours to avoid the more sodden places. In so doing we managed to lose our way several times, but were put right by shepherds, who with the help of their dogs were guarding their flocks of goats and sheep.

Not a glint of the sun was discernible. The sky was a ruddy yellow, sometimes turning to murky grey. When we eventually reached Terem, by way of Kötteklik (the Dead Forest), both horses and riders were smothered in ash-grey dust.

March 13th. The gale still continued unabated. To-day, however, the wind veered round to the north and north-east. It was thus a three days' storm, what the natives call a *sarik-buran* (yellow storm), because it just tinges the sky yellow.

From Terem we rode south-east to the village of Terek-lengher (the Poplar Rest-house) on the Yarkand-daria. It was nine hours' smart riding through a country known by the name of *ala-kum*, *i.e.* alternating steppe and sandy desert. In the vicinity of the river we crossed a bridge spanning the Khandi-arik, an important irrigation canal, which takes its rise a day's journey above Yarkand, and supplies a great number of villages with water. Nine years ago it was repaired by command of the Chinese, a task which is said to have given employment to eleven thousand men. This vast undertaking seems to have been considerably simplified in the first instance by the utilization for long distances of a former bed of the Yarkand-daria. Between the canal and the river several former river levels were clearly distinguishable. The villagers declared that at one time the river flowed close past their village, although it was now situated two miles from it. They expressed themselves as well satisfied with this caprice of nature, for it had allowed them to extend their fields over the alluvial soil of the former river-bed.

March 14th. The wind subsided a little to-day, and shifted right round to the east. I noticed that the storms often began in the west, and later veered round by way of north to the east. We kept along the river in a north-easterly direction till we reached Lailik. For some distance the river bank was very much eroded, rising like a vertical wall to the height of thirteen feet, and disclosing a horizontal stratum of fine yellow soil, sand, and alluvium, riddled by numberless roots, which sometimes hung swaying over the water. The first half of the journey took us through a series of villages; then the country was barren, until we reached the woods near Lailik, where we arrived just after midday, and found everything in good order under Johannes' care.

CHAPTER XXXVIII.

ON THE THRESHOLD OF THE DESERT

MARCH 15th. This day marked the beginning of a long period of waiting, extremely trying to my patience. Day after day went by, but no camels arrived. I would gladly pass over these twenty-five days altogether, but find in my note-book certain incidents and facts that are not without interest. I made it my business to gather all the information I could about the desert that stretched to the east. For instance, to-day I heard of two men who a few years ago started from the village of Yantak, on the right bank of the Yarkand-daria, taking with them provisions for twelve days. After three days they reached a disused river-bed, deep and stony, with a wooden bridge across it, but so dilapidated that it would not bear them to walk on it. They thought at first of following up the course of the river; but as they found no water in that direction, they retraced their steps, and went down stream, and there discovered quantities of nephrite or jade. After another seven days they reached the mountain of Masar-tagh, where they found kamish and obtained water by digging.

Shahr-i-katak, as a rule curtailed to Ktak, is another legendary town which haunts the same part of the great Asiatic desert. Its reputed situation varies a good deal. At Lailik I was told it lay five potais (twelve and a half miles) west of the village, and that many years ago a man found the ruins there; but when it was searched for afterwards, it could not be found. The people say that none but Allah can lead a man thither. No matter how perseveringly he may search himself, he will never find the place unless God wills he should. I heard also that twelve men were just about to set out from Yarkand into the desert in quest of gold. They generally choose the spring for these expeditions, as they say that the sand-storms are then more likely to expose the gold. A month previously a man had gone into the desert, and had not returned. At Yarkand the people believe, that the traveller through the desert often hears voices calling him by name, but that if he follows them, he goes astray and dies of thirst. It is interesting to compare this with what Marco Polo has to say of the great Lop desert: "But there is a marvellous thing related of this desert, which is, that when travellers are on the move by night, and one of them chances to lag behind, or to fall asleep, or the like, when he tries to gain his company again, he will hear spirits talking, and will suppose them to be his comrades. Sometimes the spirits will call him by name, and thus shall a traveller ofttimes be led astray, so that he never finds his party. And in this way many have perished."*

To-day Islam Bai returned from Yarkand, bringing with him four *chelleks* (iron tanks) for water, six *tulums* (goat-skins for water), sesame oil and seed-husks for the camels, petroleum, bread, *talkan* (toasted flour), *gauman* (macaroni), honey, sacks, spades, whips, bridle-bits, bowls, cups, and divers other requisites.

March 18th. During these days I had frequent opportunity of observing how closely the radiation was dependent upon the amount of dust with which the atmosphere was charged. When the atmosphere was nearly clear, the radiation went up 114°8 Fahr. (46° C.); but after a violent buran it sank to 69°1 Fahr. (20°6 C.). This was on March 16th; after that the air gradually cleared, so that the radiation on March 17th went up to 81°7 Fahr. (27°6 C.), and the following day it was 97°9 Fahr. (36°6 C.) Concurrently with this the minimum temperature during the night sank after the buran had ceased, whilst the atmosphere gradually cleared. For

* From YULE'S *The Book of Ser Marco Polo*, I. p. 203 (1874).

example, before the buran the minimum thermometer read 21°2 Fahr. (– 6° C.); during the last day of the buran it rose to 31°3 Fahr. (– 0°4 C.), but again fell to 28°4 Fahr. (– 2° C.) and yesterday to 25°7 Fahr. (– 3°5 C.). In other words, the radiation increased in proportion as the dust dropped back to the earth and was blown away. In the same way the temperature of the air rose in the shade at midday in proportion as the atmosphere cleared; thus on March 16th, 17th, and 18th respectively I got readings of 41°7 Fahr. (5°·4 C.), 45°3 Fahr. (7°4 C.), and 51°8 Fahr. (11° C.) The quantity of dust with which the atmosphere was charged thus exercised considerable influence upon the readings of the meteorological instruments.

On March 19th we moved over to the large village of Merket, on the right bank of the Yarkand-daria, whence the caravan was to make its start for the desert. In the morning a number of the inhabitants of Merket came to escort us to their village. The beg, Mehemmed Niaz Beg, arrived with a present of chickens, eggs, and dastarkhan (light refreshments). He was a tall man, with a thin white beard, and looked energetic and severe. Transport horses were employed to carry over our baggage; and after the on-bashi of Lailik and his pretty wife, who had both been very kind and hospitable during my stay in their house, had been well rewarded with money and cloth, we marched down to the ferry, which conveyed us and our large caravan across in four trips. The ice had evidently ceased to melt farther to the south, for the river had fallen eleven inches since March 8th; and from this time onwards it would continue to sink, until the summer floods came down from the mountains.

After a quarter of an hour's ride in a south-easterly direction, we passed the village of Anghetlik, which received its irrigation water from an eastern branch of the Yarkand-daria. At the end of an hour we reached the village of Chamgurluk, and after another three-quarters of an hour were in Merket. The beg placed his own house at my disposal, and I was soon installed in a large and pleasant room, covered with carpets, and with niches in the walls.

Counting in the surrounding kishlaks (winter villages) Merket numbered a thousand dwellings, of which 250 were in the immediate vicinity of the bazaar. The village of Yantak, a short distance farther north, had 300 houses. Yantak, together with Anghetlik and Chamgurluk, constitute a *beklik* or *beglik* (administrative division under a beg); while Merket has its own beg. In the latter place dwelt two tax-collectors, two Chinese merchants, and four Hindu money-lenders from Shikarpur. It was a fruitful region, producing wheat, maize, barley, beans, turnips, cucumbers, melons, beetroot, grapes, apricots, peaches, mulberries, apples, pears, and cotton. In good years the crops are so plentiful that large quantities of seed-corn are exported to Kashgar and Yarkand; but in bad years the reverse is the case, and grain is imported from Yarkand.

Although Merket is so close to the banks of the Yarkand-daria, it does not derive its irrigation water from it, but from the Tisnab-daria, the river of Kargalik, which flows parallel with the Yarkand-daria. When the current is low, this river does not reach further than Yantak; but at other times it advances a considerable distance farther north, and forms two small lakes, which however are dry at all other seasons. Its right bank too is bordered by a belt of forest, but not more than twelve and a half miles broad at the outside. The winters are cold, though the fall of snow is small, and the snow melts directly; the summers on the contrary are hot. The rainfall is distributed equally over the whole of the warm season, and sometimes is so heavy that it destroys the flat roofs of the houses. North-easterly winds prevail; and the storms last from two to four days, loading the atmosphere with dust, and occasioning a "rain" of dust, which settles on the vegetation in the form of a thick greyish-yellow down.

Strange to say, Merket has never before been visited by any European. The name appears for the first time, though in the form Meket, in General Pievtsoff's account of his travels; but he could not visit it whilst the Yarkand-daria was in flood. The Chinese, however, have long known the place; it is mentioned under the name of Mai-ghe-teh in the *Si-yi-shuy-dao-tsi*, a work published in 1823. According to Chinese transcription, Yantak or Yantaklik becomes Yan-va-li-ke and Tisnab becomes Tin-tsa-bu. The author of the work in question states that this river unites with the Yarkand-daria; and that certainly would be the case if the water were not employed for irrigation,

ENTRANCE TO A BAZAAR IN A CENTRAL ASIAN VILLAGE

and did not become dissipated in the small lakes already mentioned. His description, however, may have been correct enough eighty years ago.

In Merket, too, there were some of the loafing gold-seekers I have mentioned. One man told me that, along with some companions, he had travelled for twenty days on foot through the desert, carrying with them supplies of food and water on donkeys. After going seven days east-north-east by the side of gigantic sand-dunes, they reached a long straggling mountain. They had occasionally seen a few tamarisks, and in some places had obtained water after digging. My informant, besides many others, was in the habit of going out every year into the desert to look for gold, but as yet had found nothing. They called the desert Takla-makan; and the general consensus of opinion was, that given strong camels we ought to be able to cross right over it to the Khotan-daria.

In the evening I held a levee. Niaz Beg and the on-bashi of Anghetlik, Togda Khodia, each presented me with a sheep; while the Hindus gave me a goodly supply of potatoes and butter, both exceedingly welcome. Afterwards we were entertained for a long time with the music of a *setar* (zither) and a *ghalin* (small harp), which, played in a slow time, sounded very well together, although the music was rather melancholy.

March 20th. Togda Khodia was a thorough gentleman. He often came to see me, and would sit talking in my room by the hour together. When I began to grow impatient at receiving no news of the camels, he always exhorted me to patience, saying with unruffled composure, and with a conviction which allowed of no demur, "*Kelladi! kelladi!*" (They will come! They will come!). But nothing was heard of them; and precious time was being wasted. I felt that we were heaping glowing coals on our heads; for spring was upon us, and during the hot season of the year the desert is simply a furnace.

Meanwhile Togda Khodia gave me much valuable information. To-day, for example, he told me that the inhabitants of Merket are Dolons, and that in their own opinion they are in no wise different from the people of Kashgar. They possess a few slight dialectical differences of speech, that is all. But Togda Khodia himself considered them very different from their neighbours. Their natures were hard and cold, and they were so unforgiving that trifling disputes would linger on for years.

The observances of Islam were jealously kept at Merket. On the last bazaar-day, in the middle of the fast, a man ate before the sun set. He was immediately seized, flogged, and with his hands tied behind his back was led in a rope through the bazaar, from every corner of which the following questions and answers were re-echoed as the offender passed.

"Did you eat?"

"Yes."

"Do you mean to do it again?"

"Never."

It is also customary to blacken the culprit's face before he makes his penitential promenade through the bazaar.

On March 21st I visited the bazaar. It was very spacious, and every trade and calling had a special alley allotted to it. Nevertheless there was no trading done except once a week, namely on the bazaar-day, when stalls and wares are brought out of the houses and arranged on platforms built in front of them. At the time of my visit there were a number of women sitting on the platforms sewing. The women were always unveiled, generally bare-headed, and wore their thick black hair in two long plaits. Sometimes, however, their heads were covered with a small round coif or calotte. A particularly popular occupation with them seemed to be the extermination of certain undesirable parasites, and it was a by no means rare thing to see one woman with her head resting in her neighbour's lap.

Immediately outside the village there was a sand-dune 25 to 30 feet in height, running south-south-west to north-north-east, as regularly constructed as though it had been built of set purpose. Its summit, which was crowned by the masar (tomb) of Chimdereh Khan, commanded a fine view over the village, with its flat-roofed houses surrounding small square courtyards.

At last, on March 22nd, Mohammed Yakub came back from Kashgar, bringing a bulky mail-bag, but no camels! I was thus left precisely where I had been at the beginning of the month. Now I fell back upon my excellent Islam Bai, and on the next day sent him off to Yarkand post haste with peremptory orders, not to come back again without camels. Happily I had my meteorological and astronomical observations, to say nothing of the letters I had just received, and of old Togda Khodia, to help me pass the time. I did not find Johannes the missionary much of a resource. He was one of those morbidly religious people, who imagine that true Christianity is incompatible with a sober joy in life, as well as with good spirits. This was no doubt partly due to his being a converted Mohammedan: such proselytes are often ten times worse than their teachers. However, he was good-natured and helpful, though he always seemed to be depressed and in dull spirits.

A few days afterwards I fell a victim to a very bad and painful sore-throat, known by the name of *gorkak*, very prevalent thereabouts. After I had tried the beg's prescription, which was to gargle my throat with warm milk, but to no purpose, he proposed that I should give the *peri-bakshis* or spirit-exorcisers a trial. I told him that I did not believe in such nonsense; but that the peri-bakshis were welcome all the same.

After dark, when there was no light in the room save what came from the glowing coals on the hearth, the peri-bakshis were introduced—three big, bearded men, in long white *chapans* (cloaks). Each carried a drum (*doff*) of extremely tightly-stretched calf-skin, and on these they proceeded to perform by tapping them with their fingers, beating them with the flat of the hand, and thumping them with their fists. The drums gave out such a volume of sound that it might have been heard at Lailik, six or seven miles off. The performers beat the instruments at an incredible speed, and all three in exactly the same time. After tapping the drums with their finger-tips for some time, all three would give a bang at one and the same moment, and then follow it up with half-a-dozen hollow whacks with their fists. Then the finger-tapping would begin again, and the whole process be repeated without a moment's cessation. Sometimes they sat still; sometimes they were so carried away by their peculiar music, that they got up and danced; and sometimes again they tossed their drums into the air and caught them with a bang. At every round, which lasted five minutes, the beating recurred in a certain order, which explained the fact that all three were able to keep time so well together. The full measure of rounds for putting evil spirits to flight is nine; and once the exorcisers have begun, it is impossible to stop them until the "full tale of bricks is told!"

The peri-bakshis are called in mostly at births and by sick women; for the women are much more superstitious than the men. The exorcisers enter the sick-room, and gaze attentively into the flame of the oil-lamp, where they say they can see that the woman is possessed of an evil spirit. Then the drums begin at once, while the invalid's friends and acquaintances gather inside and outside the room. But the performance does not end there. When the last thundering roll of the drum has died away, the assembly withdraws, and the peri-bakshi and the sick woman are left alone in the room together. In the middle of the floor the sorcerer drives a rod with great force, having a rope tied to the top of it, while its other end is fastened to the ceiling. The woman pulls and tugs at the rope until she succeeds in getting it loose, while the peri-bakshi bangs at his drum. The moment the rope breaks loose from the roof, the spirit departs out of the woman.

The hunting falcon too is credited with similar powers of exorcism, and is therefore called *ghush-bakshi* (the falcon exorciser). The peris or evil spirits are supposed to fear her greatly. During the pangs of childbirth, the woman sees evil spirits flitting about the room, though they are invisible to other people. The falcon, however, sees them, and is let loose in the room to chase them out. It is very evident that the falcon, the drums, and the rope and stick all tend to the same end—namely to distract the woman's attention to a certain extent, and so make her forget herself.

March 26th. Niaz Beg administered justice at his own house every day. His usual seat was beside one of the columns which supported the roof of the verandah, and so long as the proceedings lasted he assumed a very severe expression of countenance. On the platform by his side sat his *mirza* or secretary, who entered the proceedings in a protocol. Round about him stood his men and the officers of the law, and before him the culprit.

To-day there was a very curious case. A man had five wives. The fifth, a handsome, stalwart young woman, had run away to Kashgar with another man. The beg had given information to the authorities there, and they found the woman and sent her back to Merket, where she was now to answer for her transgressions. After she had been convicted of unfaithfulness, the beg gave her a slap on either cheek, and she began to weep. The only thing she had to say in her own defence was that life with the other four wives was altogether unbearable. She had a knife on her person, and when the beg asked her, what she was going to do with it, she answered, that she meant to kill herself, if she were compelled to return to her husband. Her punishment was, that for a time she should go and dwell with the mollahs, till she should be in a better frame of mind, and then should quietly return home to her husband.

After that another young woman was brought forward, her face bleeding and lacerated, and followed by her mother and her husband. She also had left her husband; but in this case the man had taken the law into his own hands, and had cruelly kicked and mishandled her. Several witnesses confirmed the statement, that he had made use of a razor; this however the defendant denied. To make him confess, the beg gave orders for his hands to be tied behind his back, and then had him strung up to the branch of a tree. He did not hang there long before the device produced the desired effect. The man was taken down, and forty strokes of the rod were administered on that part of the body which seems to have been providentially provided for castigation. Meanwhile he declared that his wife had beaten him on the back. Forthwith he was stripped; but as no marks were visible, a second whipping was the result.

In these distant regions the sense of justice is somewhat elastic. If the accused has a well-lined purse he gets off scot-free, and in any case the beg receives certain tengeh for his trouble. If the plaintiff is not satisfied with the verdict, he can appeal to a higher authority—the nearest Chinese mandarin—and to him the beg must answer in his turn. The Chinese administration is admirable. One prudent feature in it is that they allow the natives to retain the same system of local self-government which obtained in the time of Yakub Beg of Kashgar.

Cases of conjugal infidelity are not on the whole uncommon, nor are they punished with particular severity. As a rule, the woman has her face blacked, is placed backwards on a male ass, and with her hands tied behind her is taken through the streets and bazaar of the village. Monogamy is the rule; it is very seldom that a man has four or five wives. If a woman marries a Chinaman or a European, she is considered impure; and when she dies, is not interred in the general burial-ground of the place, because she has consorted with "one who eats swine's flesh," so that her body would pollute the graves of the Faithful.

With regard to *kalim*, or the dower of a bride, the customs of these people are much the same as those of the Kirghiz. The kalim is paid to the bride's parents, and varies according to the man's circumstances and means. A bai, or rich man, gives as much as two jambaus (£9 to £10 each). As a rule everything is paid in kind; but the bride's trousseau is compulsory kalim. A poor man offers merely a measure of food and clothes. The amount depends entirely upon the demands of the parents; but beauty and physical charms are of less importance than among the Kirghiz. If a young couple cannot obtain the consent of their parents, it is not unusual for them to run away. They generally come back, however, after a few months, and invite the old people to a feast, when all misunderstandings are cleared up.

On another occasion the beg gave judgment on two

men who had been gambling. One of them had a deep gash in his ear, and the whole of his face and chest were covered with blood. He had lost seven tengeh (1*s.* 6*d.*), and promised to procure the money in the bazaar. The winner however demanded his winnings on the spot, whereupon the loser drew his knife, and slashed himself on the ear, crying, "You shall have that instead of your money." The beg ordered the winner to be publicly whipped. The other man was to be whipped as soon as his hurt was cured. The winnings, needless to say, found their way into the beg's pocket.

CHAPTER XXXIX.

THE START FROM MERKET

ISLAM and Yakub came back on 8th April. After a great deal of haggling and trouble, they had succeeded in getting at Kargalik eight splendid male camels for a trifle over £6 10*s.* apiece. It had somehow got wind amongst the inhabitants, that we absolutely ***must*** have camels for our desert journey; and in consequence they put up their prices to double or three times what they usually were. A further difficulty arose out of the fact that the only animals which would serve our purpose must be such as were accustomed to the level plains, and to travelling in desert regions—animals which were used to moving over sand and could endure heat and other privations. These qualities were of much more consequence than the appearance of the beasts, and their condition of flesh.

During the morning we christened the camels, and measured their girths between the humps, with the view of ascertaining how they would compare in that respect at the end of the journey. Here are the names and measurements of the several animals:—

Ak-tuya (The White Camel)	8	years	old,	7ft. 9in.	in girth
Boghra (The Male)	4	„	„	7ft. 8½in.	„
Nähr (The Tall)	2	„	„	7ft. 4½in.	„
Babai (The Old)	15	„	„	7ft. 5½in.	„
Chong-kara (The Big Black)	3	„	„	7ft. 3½in.	„
Kityick-kara (The Little Black)	2	„	„	7ft. 3in.	„
Chong-sarik (the Big Yellow)	2	„	„	7ft. 6½in.	„
Kityick-sarik (The Little Yellow)	1½	„	„	7ft. 0in.	„

How little we foresaw that only one camel, namely Chong-kara, would survive the journey! Ak-tuya, a handsome white camel, which led the string, with a big copper bell provided with a heavy iron tongue, did get to the other side of the desert; but he died soon afterwards from the fatigues of the march. Boghra was an exceptionally well-proportioned animal, patient and good-tempered; I chose him to ride upon. Nähr was a vicious beast, always trying to bite and kick the moment anybody went near him. Babai, the oldest in the troop, and of a grey colour, was the first to succumb. The other three were young, lively things; having had a long rest, they were always ready to march, and took real pleasure in being on the move.

They chanced to be just "moulting" when they arrived. Every day big shaggy cots of their thick, warm winter hair fell off, so that they had a patched, shabby appearance so long as the process of shedding lasted. Each camel was provided with a good soft pack-saddle, stuffed with hay and straw. Islam brought also a whole armful of *arkhans* (ropes of camel's hair) to tie on the baggage with, and three large camel-bells.

The animals were tethered in a large courtyard immediately opposite Niaz Beg's house, and were given their fill of good hay, a luxury they enjoyed for the last time. It was very pleasant to stand and watch my own splendid camels crouched on the ground, eagerly munching the fragrant hay, and see how their big brown eyes shone with placid enjoyment. Our two dogs, Yolldash and Hamrah, were however of a different opinion. The former in particular could not tolerate the camels. He barked at them till he was hoarse; and was visibly well pleased with himself when he could get near enough to snatch a tuft of hair out of one or the other of them.

Islam Bai had further engaged two trustworthy men in Yarkand. One, Mohammed Shah, was a greybeard of fifty-five. He was accustomed to looking after camels, and was the only person who could go near the refractory Nähr without being bitten. Although he had left wife and children behind in Yarkand, the desert had no terrors for him. He was a capital fellow, as honest as the day.

I can see him now as plainly as though it were only yesterday we parted. His philosophic serenity never deserted him. When the clouds of misfortune gathered thick round our ill-fated caravan, his good humour never failed; there was always a smile on his face. Even when he lay in the delirium of death, a gleam of triumphant serenity shone in his eyes, and the light of an inward peace spread over his withered copper-brown countenance.

The second man, who was to help in the management of the camels, was Kasim Akhun, a native of Ak-su, but at that time an inhabitant of Yarkand, forty-eight years of age, unmarried, and a caravan-leader by profession. Of medium height and strongly built, with a black beard, he was of a serious disposition, and never laughed, though always friendly and pleasant; but he had very often to be reminded of his duties.

We wanted yet another man. Him Niaz Beg found for us in another Kasim Akhun from Yanghi-hissar. He was of the same age as Mohammed Shah, and every spring, for six years past, had gone a ten to fourteen days' journey into the desert in quest of gold, taking his food on the back of an ass, but not venturing further in than he was able to get water by digging. During our journey, in order to distinguish him from the other Kasim, we called him sometimes Yollchi (the pointer out of the road), sometimes Kumchi (the man of the desert). A few years previously he had flitted to Merket, and now left wife and grown-up children there behind him. His subsequent fate was in part of his own causing. He was brutal and of a violent temper; and the other men, whom he attempted to tyrannize over, soon came to hate him. He conceived that his experience of the desert warranted him in assuming a domineering tone; and he entertained an especial grudge against Islam Bai, because Islam was appointed karavan-bashi, or caravan-leader, and the other three men were bidden obey him. Some of the inhabitants of Merket warned us against this man, telling us that he had been more than once punished for theft; but the warning came too late. When I engaged him, I thought we had lighted upon a treasure-trove, for he was the only man in the place who knew anything of the desert.

Our menagerie of live-stock also embraced three sheep, which we intended to kill one after the other, half a score hens and a cock, which woke us up in the morning. These last travelled in a basket perched on the top of a camel's-load of baggage. The first few days the hens laid two or three eggs; but as soon as the water began to fail, they stopped laying. The cock was an eccentric animal; he entertained a rooted objection to riding on a camel's back. Every now and again he used to wriggle through the covering of the basket; and, after balancing himself awhile on his elevated perch, flew down to the ground with a noisy cackle. Every time we pitched camp, the poultry were let out for a run. They imparted a little life to the otherwise desolate surroundings; and a few handfuls of corn were thrown down amongst the sand, to keep them employed and in motion.

On April 9th we made our final preparations; we packed the two or three bags of bread which had been ordered beforehand, and filled the four iron tanks with fresh water from the river. They held 17½, 19, 19, and 27 gallons respectively; add to this 17½ gallons in a goat-skin, and we get a total of 100 gallons, amply sufficient for a 25 days' march. The tanks, which were oblong in shape, were specially made for conveying honey from India to Yarkand, being surrounded by a wooden grating to protect the thin iron plates against damage from knocks. Grass and reeds were packed in between the tank and the grating, to prevent the sun's rays from beating directly upon the iron.

A few words about the plan of my journey. Przhevalsky, and Carey and Dalgleish, were the first Europeans who ever saw (1885) the mountains of Masar-tagh on the left bank of the Khotan-daria. The first-mentioned wrote in this connection: "After three short day's-marches (from Tavek-kel) we arrived at that part of the Khotan-daria where the Masar-tagh chain overlooks its left bank. The eastern portion of the range does not exceed 1¼ miles in breadth, and rises to a height of some 500 feet above the surrounding country. It consists of two parallel ridges, strikingly dissimilar. The southern ridge is composed of red argillaceous slates, interspersed with numerous beds of gypsum. The other, or northern, ridge is a homogeneous mass of white alabaster. Flints are obtained from the Masar-tagh at a distance of sixteen miles from the Khotan-daria, and taken to Khotan to be sold. Beyond that point we lost sight of the mountains, which became blended with the sandy desert. But they bent round towards the north-west, and, increasing in height in the middle, stretched, the natives told me, as far as the fortified post of Maral-bashi on the river of Kashgar. Of vegetation there was not a trace. The slopes of the mountains were buried in drift-sand, half-way up from the foot."

Relying upon the data thus given him by the natives, Przhevalsky indicated on his map a chain of mountains stretching at an oblique angle across the desert. His mistake was natural enough; for he was told, that at Maral-bashi too there is a mountain known by the name of Masar-tagh; and what more natural than to suppose, that it was simply the continuation of the Masar-tagh of the Khotan-daria? Carey was more cautious. His map shows only so much of the range as he was able to see from the river.

I reasoned therefore that, if from Merket we steered our course eastwards, or rather towards the east-north-east, we were bound, sooner or later, to come in contact with the Masar-tagh; and, like the natives, I was convinced, that we should find a lee side to the range, where the drift-sand would not be blown together, but we should be able to make long, easy day's-marches on firm ground, and possibly might even discover springs and vegetation, and perchance light upon traces of an ancient civilization. On the maps which I had at hand the distance through the desert as the crow flies measured 180 miles; and if we did only twelve miles a day, the entire journey ought not to take us more than fifteen days. Our supply of water was therefore, by every calculation, more than sufficient. I was quite satisfied with my estimate, and thought we had an easy task before us. As an actual fact, the journey took twenty-six days, or nearly twice as long as I anticipated.

April 10th. Long before sunrise the courtyard was all alive. Our various boxes, bales, and other impedimenta were carried out and weighed, so that the camels' burdens might be suitably adjusted, and the several packages properly roped. These preliminaries over, they were placed along the ground two by two, at such distances apart that a camel could just get between them, and be made to kneel down whilst his load was fastened to his pack-saddle. After he got up on his feet, a big rope was lashed criss-cross right round the whole, and fastened to the horizontal bars in the framework of the pack-saddle. We took with us an extensive equipment, provisions for several months, particularly rice and bread, preserved foods, sugar, tea, vegetables, flour, and so forth. In addition, we had a large supply of winter clothing, felts, and carpets; for, after leaving the Khotan-daria, I intended making for Tibet. Then I had my scientific instruments, photographic apparatus, with close upon a thousand plates, some books, a year's issue of a Swedish journal, of which I purposed reading one number every evening, a cooking-stove with its appurtenances, metal utensils, crockery, three rifles, six revolvers, a supply of ammunition packed in two heavy boxes, together with a multitude of other things. Add to all this, water-supplies for twenty-five days, and it will be clear, that each camel had a pretty heavy load to carry.

Whilst the animals were being loaded, I measured my first base-line of 400 metres (close upon a quarter of a mile). Boghra walked it in five and a half minutes. This was a daily recurring task, for the contours of the ground varied a good deal; and the depth of the sand made a very appreciable difference in the time the camels took to do the same distance.

The 10th of April 1895 was a great day in the annals of Merket. The courtyard, every alley, every house-roof in the neighbourhood, was crowded with people, all anxious to see us off. "They will never come back again—never," we heard them cry one to another. "The camels are too heavily laden; they will never get through the deep sand." These croakings did not disturb me in the least. The ground burned under my feet to get off. And we had an antidote to their ill-omened prophecies in the action of the Hindus, who, just as I put my camel in motion, flung a few handfuls of *da-tien* (Chinese bronze money with a square hole in the middle) over my head, crying, "Good-luck go with you!"

The camels were tied together in two strings of four each. A piece of stick was thrust through the cartilage of the animal's nose. A rope, fastened to one end of the stick, was loosely knotted to the tail of the camel in front, in such wise that, if the second camel fell, the knot would come undone of itself.

The other end of the piece of stick terminated in a knob, which prevented it from slipping out of the animal's nose. The four young camels went in the first string. After them followed Boghra with me on his back; and behind him Babai, Ak-tuya, and Nähr. Mohammed Shah never left hold of Boghra's bridle; so that I had no need to trouble myself in the least about my camel, but gave my attention wholly and undivided to my compass and watch, by which I steered our course and measured the length of our day's march, and to the observation of the country we were travelling through. Islam Bai had shown much ingenuity in arranging my load for me. It consisted of the two boxes which held my most delicate instruments, and such things as I generally needed when we encamped for the night. On the top of the boxes, and between the camel's hump, he spread pelts, carpets, and cushions, so that with one leg on each side of the front hump, I rode as comfortably as though I were sitting in an easy-chair. When all was quite ready, I said good-bye to Niaz Beg, whom I rewarded handsomely, as well as to the missionary Johannes and Hashim. The former had already said at Lailik, that he did not really mean to go with me through Takla-makan. Now, when he saw the caravan ready to start, his courage completely failed him, and for the second time he deserted me in the moment when danger had really to be faced. I despised the fellow. Notwithstanding his pretended piety, he utterly lacked the courage which makes a man place all his reliance upon God. What a strange contrast to Islam Bai, the Mohammedan, the beau-ideal of a good and faithful servant, who throughout the days and months that followed never once hesitated to follow his master, no matter where I went, even when I rushed into dangers which prudence should properly have guarded me against!

Spring had come. Signs of the change manifested themselves more and more every day. The temperature rose slowly but steadily; the minimum remaining permanently above freezing-point. The sun began to have some power. The spring breezes murmured in our ears. The fields were being sown with corn, the rice-grounds put under water. The air was alive with the flittings and buzzings of flies and other insects. It was with this beautiful Asiatic spring-time all about us, the season of perennial hope, that we set out on our journey to the country where all things are gripped in the deathly embrace of a thousand years' torpor, where every sand-dune is a grave, a country whose climate is such that, compared with it, the sternest winter would be a smiling spring.

On through the narrow lanes of the town, crowded with people, strode the long string of camels, with a grave and majestic mien, holding their heads high. It was a solemn moment. Every spectator was impressed. A dead silence reigned throughout the crowd. When my mind goes back to that moment, I am involuntarily reminded of a funeral-procession. I can hear the dull monotonous clang of the caravan-bells still ringing in my ears. And of a truth their slow mournful cadences were the virtual passing-bell of most of us who set forth on that eventful day for the sand-wastes of the terrible desert. A sad and peaceful grave amid the eternal ocean of sand—such was to be their melancholy end!

The environs of the town were level, the town itself scattered about amongst the old *tograks* (poplars), fields, groves, orchards, and irrigation canals. For half an hour or so we marched on quietly through these pleasant surroundings; then all of a sudden there arose a fearful uproar. The two youngest camels, being full of spirit, broke loose from their halters, shook off their loads, and, frisky as two playful puppies, began to race round the fields, till the dust rose in clouds behind them. One had been loaded with a couple of water-tanks. Upon being thrown off, one tank sprang a leak, but luckily near the top corner, so that but little real damage was done. The runaways were soon caught, and their burdens lashed on again. After that each was led separately, for we had plenty of help, fully a hundred mounted men accompanying us to the outskirts of the village. An hour later two other camels broke loose. Several things were chafed and bruised, and the ammunition-box was trailed on the ground. Mohammed Shah said, that "camels always get refractory after a spell of rest. They wanted to stretch their limbs; but a few days' steady tramping would make them as quiet as lambs." After that, as a precaution, each camel was led by a single man.

But even then, as so often happens during the first day or two after starting on an expedition, we had several unforeseen hindrances to contend against. For example, the left-hand side of a camel's load would be heavier than that on the right-hand, and so had to be adjusted; or a bag of rice was on the point of slipping off, and had to be tied faster; and so on.

CHAPTER XL.

SKIRTING THE DESERT

THE second day's march passed off more quietly, and in a much more orderly manner. Profiting from our first day's experiences, we weighed and distributed the packages more successfully, and loaded our most precious possessions—first amongst them the water—on the quietest camels. I myself sat perched at a pretty good height above the ground, and had a splendid view in every direction. At first the motion made me feel somewhat giddy; but I soon became accustomed to the monotonous and unceasing jolting backwards and forwards, combined with the peculiar swaying motion from side to side, and suffered no ill effects from it whatever. But I can readily believe it would be very disagreeable to anybody subject to sea-sickness.

Having left behind us the last house and field belonging to Merket, we struck into a level steppe (*däsht*), where thickets and tangled bushes grew pretty well everywhere, and there were even clumps of poplars in a few places. The wind blew in gusts from the west-north-west, and greyish-yellow "sand-spouts" drifted eastwards at a great altitude, their upper ends slightly bent over in the direction of the wind. The surface of the ground was partly covered with fine, soft dust, partly with deposits of salt; but we soon passed into a region of nothing but sand, blown up into small low dunes or ridges. However, it proved to be only a narrow belt, for on the other side we once more came upon plenteous plant-life, chiefly kamish (reeds) and poplars; and there on the brink of the ravine we pitched our camp for the night.

Half an hour later the loads were all off the camels, and the animals themselves were tied together in a ring, to prevent them from lying down and getting stiff-legged. After standing a couple of hours, they were let loose to browse upon the thickets of reeds. Our camp, with its many packages and animals, made a very picturesque appearance; and it gave me a feeling of deep satisfaction to think, that all those things were mine. My tent, a neat Indian officer's tent, which Mr. Macartney had given me, was pitched underneath a poplar tree. Within it young Lieutenant Davison had died during his journey across the Pamirs to Kashgar. But it had been well disinfected, and I was not superstitious. The ground inside was covered with a variegated carpet, and all round its sides were ranged my boxes, instrument-cases, photographic camera, and my plain, simple bedstead. The other boxes and packages, together with the water-tanks, were left outside in the open air. My men kindled a fire, and crouched round it, to prepare dinner—rice pudding and eggs, for of these last we had brought a good supply. The sheep were turned out to graze, and the poultry made themselves quite at home amongst the scraps from the cooking-pot. The dogs, having swallowed the pieces of meat that were thrown to them, began to chase one another over the sand-dunes. In a word, we made quite a rural picture.

As soon as the camp was settled, my first care was to examine the ravine which had stopped us. It ran from north to south, and had undoubtedly been formed by a branch of the Tisnab-daria, but was now dry. It was 20 feet wide and 5 feet deep; and when I bade the men dig a hole in the bottom, the water began to trickle up as soon as they got 3 ft. 6 in. down. The temperature of the water was 49°8 Fahr. (9°9 C.), whilst that of the air at the same time, viz., two o'clock in the afternoon, was 76°6 Fahr. (24°8 C.). Although tasting bitter and nauseous, it was greedily drunk by both dogs and sheep. The camels were not allowed any water until nearly an hour before the start next morning.

From the very outset we were obliged to exercise the most rigid economy with our supplies of fresh water; and therefore used the water from the ravine for boiling our eggs in, for washing the dishes, and for personal ablutions. Mohammed Yakub, who had followed us all the way to camp, brought us the very welcome present of a couple of copper vessels filled with fresh river-water; so that every member of the caravan was able to quench his thirst to the full without our having to open the water-tanks.

It had been a warm day; but no sooner did the sun set than we felt it cool, and put on our extra coats. In the evening it was a dead calm. The tent flap was thrown back, but the flame from the candle never quivered. Our "Desert Man" gave us a taste of his knowledge. He advised us at first to keep for some days to the right bank of the Yarkand-daria, till we came to a mountain called Chackmak, and to a large lake, which was connected with a river that flowed to the north. To reach that place would take us eighteen days, and from there one day more would bring us to the Masar-tagh, the loftiest mountain in all that region. From the Masar-tagh to the Khotan-daria on the east was no great distance. North of Mount Chackmak there was a track which the gold-seekers were accustomed to use, and which led to a *yagatch-nishan* or sign-post. Beyond that mark the desert was known by the name of Kirk-kishlak or the Forty Towns, because of the numerous ruins of ancient cities which it contained.

April 11th. After a quiet and refreshing night's sleep I awoke before sunrise, and found the weather the reverse of agreeable. A violent nor'-easter whistled through the camp, and the air was thick with dust, so that, except in the immediate vicinity of the tent, the whole landscape was shrouded in a uniform grey haze.

Unloading the baggage and putting up the tent took next to no time at all; but to get everything loaded up again, and all started, required a good two hours, although that included the preparations for breakfast. The camels objected to be loaded; but afterwards, during the re-

SANDSTORM AT THE EDGE OF THE TAKLA-MAKAN DESERT

mainder of the march, behaved very well. All vegetation gradually ceased, and we lost ourselves in a labyrinth of sand-dunes, 15 to 20 feet high, and of irregular formation, though they had for the most part a north-south strike. We tried to skirt round them as much as possible; still there were a few difficult ridges which we were compelled to go over. On one or other of these the camels which carried the water fell; luckily it was only the forelegs which gave way in each case. But we could not get the animals up until after we had taken off their loads: and then we had to pack them on again. The camels were very clever at sliding down the sandy slopes, making use of their hind legs as a break in doing so. In the middle of the day we got entangled in sand-dunes so high that we were obliged to make a long detour to the north to get out of them. Yollchi asserted, that it was no use going east, for we should only be forced to turn back, there being nothing in that direction but *chong-kum* (big sand). Our route that day was a sinuous line along the edge of the "big sand." The dunes dropped again to only 10 feet in height, and occasionally we travelled over soft dust, with a tolerably level surface. And not a few times we rode into a kind of *cul-de-sac* between the horns of the crescent-shaped dunes, and were compelled to turn back. Every now and again we passed a few solitary poplars and shrivelled reeds, at which the camels snatched as they rolled on past them.

The nor'-easter blew all day long; the sky was clouded and grey; and it was raw and cold. We halted at dusk, after doing about 13¼ miles, pitched our camp on the top of a hard, level dune, where we had comfortably dry ground under our feet. Close by were some withered poplars, from which we obtained fuel for our fire, and clumps of reeds, which furnished fodder for the camels. These last were warm after their long tramp, and were led about for a time, to cool, to prevent them from taking cold.

We found a spot between two dunes where the sand was already damp. There we dug our well, and came upon water at a depth of 2½ feet: its temperature was 49°1 Fahr. (9°5 C.), and it had the same brackish flavour as the water in the ravine the day before.

April 12th. We travelled nearly fifteen miles, still along the edge of the great sandy desert, which sent out promontories to the north. Several of these we were obliged to cross over. In other respects barren desert alternated with narrow belts of steppe, upon which grew scanty tussocks of grass, withered and hard as glass, and which snapped off with a crackling sound at the least touch. The easiest ground to travel over was firm, level sand; but in several places the earth was covered with a coating of dust, in which every footmark of the flat-footed camels was sharply outlined. The dust was as soft as wool, and in two or three places so deep that the animals dropped in it up to the knees. Sometimes a thin crust of salt, which "crunched" under the camels' hoofs, was spread over the horizontal portions of the sand. Solemnly and slowly the ungainly beasts strode on one after the other, stretching down their long necks to pluck the tussocks of grass which grew within their reach, as though they had a premonition of the hard times in store for them.

At camp No. III. two of the men as usual dug a well; but could not get down lower than six feet. Still there was no water. We then left the well to itself for a couple of hours, and the water percolated through and gathered in a little pool at the bottom of the hole. The dogs and poultry were always deeply interested spectators of the digging. They knew perfectly well what it was for, and were always fearfully thirsty. So far all was going well: our precious stores were as yet untouched. The stock of camels' provender was likewise undiminished, the animals having to content themselves with kamish (reeds) and brackish water. The dogs were fed on bread, the poultry on corn and egg-shells. The first day the hens laid three eggs, the second day two, the third one. However, we had a good supply without that, packed away in chaff in a basket.

MARCHING IN A SANDSTORM

During the course of the day we came across the track of herds of antelopes going towards the south-east. Yollchi told us, there was a large lake in that direction called Yeshil-kul (the Green Lake). But neither he nor any other person known to him had ever seen it, he had only heard speak of it; so that the information must be accepted for what it is worth. He added, that it was fed by natural springs, for no stream ran into it. It is however remarkable, that the older maps show a lake of that name; but it is given a different situation, namely south-south-west from our camp No. III.

April 13th. By the morning there were seven inches of water in the bottom of the well. All day long, during a march of 12¾ miles, we travelled continuously amongst the sand-dunes. They were all crescent-shaped, with their convex side towards the east, and the horns or wings and the steeper face looking towards the west or south-west; proving that at that season of the year the prevailing winds blew from the east and north-east.

Poplar trees were common everywhere throughout the day's march. On some of them the leaf-buds were already beginning to burst; and the fresh green tufts made the camels' mouths water. In most cases the dunes seemed to shun the poplars, but formed a circular wall round them, leaving the trees in the middle of the hollow. There too, finding shelter from the wind, dried branches and withered leaves lay in little heaps.

It was a warm day. The dogs hunted vainly for water, eagerly running towards every little depression which looked at all like the places in which we dug our desert wells. For lack of better protection from the sun, they lay down in the shade of every poplar we passed, having first scratched away the top layer of hot sand, till they came to the stratum that still retained some of the coolness of the night.

Islam Bai rode on the first camel, which was also led by Yollchi, our guide. But as Islam commanded the better view, he often corrected Yollchi, and suggested taking other directions. That gave umbrage to the ill-natured "Desert

Man"; so that two or three times he flung down the rope, threw himself on the sand, and challenged Islam to guide the caravan himself. When we came to camp, a violent quarrel broke out between the two men. Yollchi came to my tent, and said that, if he was to be interfered with by Islam, he had better go back; and he also accused Islam of being close-fisted with the bread. He was considerably taken aback, when I quietly remarked, "Yes, he had better go back"; but added that, "before he did so, he must repay me the 100 tengeh (*22s. 6d.*), which he had received in advance as his first month's wages." That brought him to his senses, and in the most earnest tones he begged to be allowed to remain with me. I allowed him to do so; but on the distinct understanding, that henceforward he was to obey Islam. I had my misgivings however that, when we came to face the loneliness and monotony of life in the desert, the differences between the two men would break out again. But there were no more quarrels. Although Yollchi nourished a growing spite against Islam, he wisely held his tongue. He always kept himself to himself, never talked to the other men, and slept apart, a little distance from the rest; nor did he ever go near the camp-fire until after Islam and his comrades had gone to bed. Were they right, I wonder, in suggesting that Yollchi purposely led us in the wrong direction? If so, he paid the penalty; for he died of thirst in the desert.

At the depth of about 3¾ feet we came upon water, with a temperature of 50°7 Fahr. (10°4 C.). The dogs were so thirsty, that they tried to fling themselves into the hole, and we were obliged to tie them up to prevent them from doing so.

April 14th, Easter Day, we only travelled 11½ miles. In one place the dunes on their sheltered side were a steel-grey colour. Upon examination I found that they were coated with a thin crust of mica. I also made the discovery, that the green poplars only grew amongst the dunes. Where the dunes came to an end, there the poplars ceased also. Possibly the trees or their roots help in the formation of the dunes.

A HALT IN THE DESERT, TO WATER THE ANIMALS — NOON

We then came to a belt of desert, absolutely barren, the ground being a hard, level plain of a variety of brown colours, crossed by low dunes of yellow sand, that looked like logs of wood lying on the earth. Many small pebbles were scattered over the plain. During this day's march we came across the first traces of the wild camel; at least Yollchi said it was a wild camel, but I was not at all sure of it. Further on the camel-tracks became numerous. But, on the other side of the argument, it was not very likely that tame camels would have run away into the desert by themselves. We also observed the droppings and footmarks of horses; and Yollchi swore that the wild horse ranged that part of the desert. On the top of one of these dunes I halted a moment, in order to observe through my field-glass a troop of animals grazing on a bed of reeds a long way off towards the north. But before I could make out whether they were horses or antelopes, they disappeared, going off northwards. The dry grey clay was built up into small terraces and ridges, so strangely like the grey clay houses in the towns, that I could not rest until I went and examined them at close quarters.

That day the dogs were very restless, and several times went off a long way from the caravan. Once they were absent a quarter of an hour, and when they came back, they were wet underneath. Evidently they had discovered water somewhere. After going about 11½ miles we stumbled by chance upon a pool. I bade Kasim try what it tasted like. "Sweet as honey," he replied after swallowing a good mouthful. The consequence was, that we pitched the tent and made our camp by the side of the pool. Men, dogs, sheep, poultry,—all hastened to quench their thirst; and as the day had been hot, we were all properly thirsty. The water was as clear as crystal and perfectly sweet, and bubbled up out of a spring, afterwards running into a hollow of the ground some eighty or ninety yards long by about four wide; so that the water stood at about the same general level below the surface that it did in the wells we had dug. All the same, it was not more than four feet down. The temperature was 71°.4 Fahr.

(21°9 C.) at five o'clock in the afternoon; at the same hour the temperature of the air was 77°9 Fahr. (25°5 C.). Water-spiders and beetles were very numerous. The latter hummed about over the plain, and off went the hens in chase of them. The first of the sheep was slaughtered here with the usual ceremonies; and the dogs got a good meal out of the blood and offal. In a word, considering it was the desert, the place was quite idyllic. The sun disappeared from sight in the dust-haze, whilst still twenty degrees above the horizon; thereupon the heat decreased with marvellous rapidity. By nine o'clock at night the temperature of the spring water had fallen to 59°4 Fahr. (15°2 C.), proving that its temperature varied directly with the temperature of the air.

This pleasant camping-ground tempted us to give up a day to rest, which was equally welcome to us human beings as to the animals. We all enjoyed a good long sleep, and spent the next day in putting several things in order: the water-tanks were filled up, clothes were washed, saddles and straps mended. The day turned out hot, the sand becoming heated to 112°3 Fahr. (44°6 C.). But two or three whirlwinds came up out of the north-north-east, and cooled the air splendidly; whilst without any reproach of conscience we could drink as much water as ever we liked. As for the camels and dogs, they drank so much that you could actually see their skins swelling out. The rest also suited the hens: they managed to lay four eggs. During the night the dogs barked incessantly, and kept running back along the route by which we had come, and on which we had seen the tracks of the wild camels. No doubt the denizens of the desert were accustomed to frequent the springs during the night; but finding us in possession of the place they kept themselves at a safe distance for that night.

On April 16th we did 16¾ miles, through a country where sand-dunes fifteen or sixteen feet high alternated with steppes of withered reeds, which "crunched" under the camels' feet and sent up little clouds of dust when trodden upon. Tamarisks and poplars occurred in sporadic clumps. We passed two pools of water, like the one we left in the morning. All three lay along the same line, stretching east-north-east; in all probability they mark the course of a former affluent of the Yarkand-daria.

We put out further and further into the unknown ocean of sandy desert. Not a sign of life to be seen; not a sound to be heard, except the monotonous ding-dong of the bells tinkling in time to the soft tramping of the camels. Every now and again we made a short halt, whenever in fact we were at all uncertain of the course we ought to steer—opportunities which the men seized upon to eat their simple breakfast, consisting of a few handfuls of *talkan* (toasted flour) steeped in water, which they supped out of wooden bowls. The water in the tanks became tepid during the course of the day. For my own part, I always missed out breakfast, and contented myself with two meals a day.

April 17th. To-day there was a fresh westerly breeze; but the sky remained perfectly clear. On several occasions I noticed that the duststorms were only raised by the easterly and north-easterly winds; whilst no matter how strongly it blew from the west, the sky always remained pure and clear.

Before we had gone very far we perceived in the north a tolerably high mountain, like a cloud or slight thickening of the atmosphere fringing the horizon. Hour after hour we rode towards it; but the mountain grew no plainer to the eye, nor did we seem to approach any nearer to it. The dunes reached sixteen feet in height, and were often very difficult to get over. Between them the reed steppes became more frequent and the reeds ranker in growth. A few hares leapt out from amongst them as the caravan drew near. This day too we passed some small pools; but they were surrounded by saline incrustations, and the water in them was brackish. Away towards the east-north-east a former river had cut its sinuous way through the desert; the channel, which was half choked with sand, and contained only a few disconnected pools of water, was forty-five yards wide and six and a half feet deep. Another river-bed, quite dry, was twenty-two yards wide. In the north there were a few dark flocculent clouds, like smoke drifting up from the ground. Yollchi's explanation was as follows:—The mountains we saw were the south-eastern continuation of Masar-tagh, stretching down to the right or southern bank of the Yarkand-daria. The two dried up river-beds had been affluents of the Yarkand-daria, which used to receive a portion of their waters during the height of the summer. The clouds we saw in the north were columns of steam or evaporation from the Yarkand-daria, reflected against the pure blue sky. In all these explanations he was unquestionably right; at a later period I was able to test two or three of his statements, and found things to be exactly as he had said.

For a whole hour we travelled between two parallel ridges of sand, which stretched north by fifteen degrees east. The one on our right was more than thirty feet high, and both had rounded outlines. The level steppe between them was overgrown with exuberant thistles and poplars. We crossed the ridge on our right, and then passed along a second valley running parallel to the first. At the end of seventeen and a half miles we pitched camp No. VII. under the shade of a couple of leafy poplars. We had no need to dig for water; there were several indications that a lake or running stream could not be far off. North of us was a thick forest of poplars. Mosquitoes, flies, and moths were abundant. At night the last-mentioned fluttered round my candle in hundreds.

CHAPTER XLI.

AN EARTHLY PARADISE

APRIL 18th. The new day dawned with a fresh nor'-easter blowing. The tent threatened to go over, although we had anchored it during the night. The sky preserved its uniform grey tint, and the midday heat remained absent. We decided to march straight for the highest point of the mountains ahead, being persuaded we could reach it before evening. But it was not to be: we lost our way in the poplar wood, and the mountains disappeared from view in the dust-laden atmosphere.

The sand-dunes were all round us, branching away irregularly in every direction, and growing all over them was a large forest of poplars. The ground was littered with heaps of withered leaves, dried tree-trunks, branches, and sticks. Of the desert there was not a trace. In and out amongst the trees we wound a hundred, a thousand times; and it was as much as I could do to see for the branches I was riding under. We came to an extensive marsh, around which the poplars were already wearing their full mantles of spring-time greenery. To our amazement we perceived traces of human beings and of horses, as well as ashes and charred wood, showing that a fire had been lighted. It was clear, we had reached the districts to which the Dolons are accustomed to drive their flocks to graze in the spring, and from which the inhabitants of Maral-bashi fetch their fuel.

Our path was soon stopped by several long narrow creeks running out from the marsh. But we were obliged to cross them; so one of the men went into them barefooted and sounded their depth. The bottom consisted of hard clay, strong enough to bear the camels. Advancing a short distance further, we found the marsh terminated in a long lake extending towards the north. We skirted its eastern side, keeping along the flanks of the tolerably high sand-dunes which sloped down to the edge of the pure blue water. The forest was still dense, in many places so tangled with thickets that we were compelled to make detours so as to get out into more open ground. But, as I said, for the most part we kept close to the shore of the lake, getting many a picturesque glimpse of it through the trees. The fresh green of the leaves contrasted strikingly with the deep blue water, and both against the grey haze in the background.

The lake, which was nearly a couple of miles wide in its widest part, although it narrowed greatly towards its northern and southern extremities, has no doubt been formed by a branch of the Yarkand-daria, and fills during the season of the summer overflows. In the winter a large portion of the water remains, freezes, thaws again in the spring, and dwindles on till the summer brings it the usual increase. On the edge of the dunes I observed a higher shore-line, indicating that in the previous summer the level of the lake had been half a yard higher than it was at the time of our visit.

At length we left the lake on our left, and soon became lost in a tangle of reed-beds of unprecedented thickness and the height of a man. As the camels forced their way onwards amongst the dry, brittle reed-stalks, there was quite an orchestra of crackling, rustling sounds. Only we who were riding had a free outlook.

The reed-beds passed, we plunged into another forest, so thick that, after one or two narrow escapes of being swept off my camel by the branches, I was obliged to get down and go on foot. In a part of the forest where all the trees, although young, were dead, we literally stuck fast. The men were forced to get out their axes and hew a path. This occasioned a great loss of time; but after considerable labour we managed to struggle out once more on to the level steppe. There, on the summit of an isolated dune, whose horns pointed to the south and south-west, we pitched our camp.

With the idea of making our presence known, in case there was anybody in the vicinity who could give us a little topographical information, we set fire to a dry poplar thicket at the foot of the sand-dune. The flames shot out their ruddy reflection to a long distance; but never a human being showed himself. We were all tired after our toilsome day's march of sixteen miles, and went early to bed. The camels, however, were best off; every day they got full rations of both water and food.

April 19th. When the tent was struck, we found a scorpion under the carpet, an inch and a half long. Upon being disturbed, he made violent efforts to use his tail. We were all tired with our exertions of the day before, and it was after nine o'clock when we got started. The little mountain-chain towards which we were now steering our course loomed up on the east, and ran towards the south-east, where it became lower, and finally was lost in the haze. There was another mountain in the north. According to the itinerary I had mapped out for our journey, the latter ought to be the Masar-alldi. Between the two ranges winds the Yarkand-daria; but we were unable to see the river.

This day we covered only 7¾ miles; for, although our route lay across a steppe, the steppe was excessively cut up by ravines and marshes. But the mountain became gradually more and more distinct. Its weathered, rugged outlines were easy to make out. The sand-dunes climbed up its northern slopes to a pretty considerable height. Along their foot was a chain of small fresh-water lakes, separated from one another by low isthmuses. A channel entering into the largest of the group revealed the fact that they drew their supplies of water from the river. During the summer they no doubt shrink together and form only a single lake. Keeping between the lakes and the mountain, we steered at first towards the east; afterwards, in order to get round a spur of the range, we altered our course towards the north-east. We pitched our camp on the shore of the lake under the shade of some leafy poplars. The mountain appeared to stand quite alone, unconnected with any other and without continuation in any direction.

Our second sheep was killed, and the dogs, which for several days had been without meat, being fed on bread alone, were given a good meal. A hawk began to hover above the poultry, but was frightened off by a rifle-shot, which missed it.

April 20th. Our camp was so pleasantly situated that we could not resist the temptation to indulge ourselves with another day's rest. It turned out a broiling hot day, despite a fresh breeze from the north-east all night and all the morning. The radiation rose to 146°3 Fahr. (63°5 C.), and at two o'clock in the afternoon the sand was heated to 126°9 Fahr. (52°7 C.). We had an incessant craving for drink, and flew to water at least every half-hour. We had hard work to keep the water in the iron tanks even tolerably cool; but we did what we could by wrapping a damp cloth round them, and hanging them on a bough in the shade, where they could catch the breeze.

Islam Bai went out in quest of wild-geese. He shot a couple; but they fell into the lake and he was unable to get them. The other men spent the day sleeping. For my own part, I walked to the top of the nearest hill, and discovered a vein of porphyry piercing the same species of rocks that I had observed in the mountain system of the Masar-alldi. I had a magnificent view. In the west-south-west the two limpid sheets of water which we had passed the day before reflected their environing mountains, with their sand-coated sides, as in a mirror. Mount Masar-alldi lay north-west of us; and between it and our camp, and stretching round to the north-east, was a steppe of moist, luxuriant grass, thickly studded with glittering pools and marshes. In the east too I saw a mountain crest, and in the south a maze of small weathered peaks belonging to the same system which overhung our camp. The poplar groves and reed-beds on the north tinted the steppe green and gold; the mountains were softened into violet shades; the sheets of water glanced dark blue.

Whilst I sat admiring the scene from the top of the hill in the cool of the afternoon, the wind gradually died away, the sun set, steppe and lakes became enveloped in a light mist, stillness and peace reigned over the scene. The only sounds my ear could catch were the gentle hum of the mosquitoes and midges, the croaking of a frog or two in the marsh, the distant scream of a wild-goose, and every now and again the tinkle of the camels' bells amongst the reeds. It was a glorious spot. I enjoyed its soothing beauty to the full. How different from the days which followed! How often during the next two weeks did my mind fly back to that idyllic scene as to an earthly paradise!

But in those regions the twilight is very short, and I hastened to get back to camp. The men were already fast asleep, except Islam Bai, who was busy getting my dinner ready—mutton broth, fried potatoes, and tea. The thermometer read 68° Fahr. (20° C.); but during the night it fell to 50°7 Fahr. (10°4 C.), and I felt it actually cold. Near these lakes we again came upon traces of human beings. There were one or two deserted reed huts on the shore; and next day, 21st April, when we continued our journey between the lakes and the mountain, we came, on the other side of some high dunes, upon the wheel tracks of arbas (high wooden carts) going through a poplar wood. The discovery vastly surprised us all. My men at once set them down as marking the road which they had heard speak of as following the left bank of the Khotan-daria. But I surmised it was some hitherto unknown track, which skirted the base of the Masar-tagh as far as the stream just mentioned. To clear up the mystery, we resolved to follow the trail as far as it went, no matter where it led us to; but we had only advanced a little way, when the wheel-tracks disappeared, and the path came to an end. Shortly afterwards the poplar wood came to an end also.

After that we continued to move towards the south-east, keeping between the mountains which overhung our last camping-place and an isolated ridge which lay to the east. Our route lay across a hard level steppe, thinly overgrown with grass, where travelling was unusually easy. The camels marched in regular time, and their bells tinkled in strict accord with their paces. At the foot of the eastern ridge there was another lake; and to our amazement we perceived three horses grazing on its banks. It was now plain there were people in the neighbourhood. Who were they? How were we to find them? I told off two of my men to follow a fresh trail, which led between the sand-dunes and up the slopes of the mountain in the west. Ere long they returned, bringing with them a man from Maral-bashi, who occasionally came to that spot to fetch salt, of which, he said, there was a large deposit in the mountain. I saw some of what he had gathered: it appeared to be of excellent quality. He took it to Maral-bashi, where he said he made a first-rate price of it in the bazaars. When I asked him, in which direction the town lay, he pointed towards the north-west, and told me it was two short day's journey to it. The mountain we had seen in that quarter was, as we supposed, the system of the Masar-alldi. About the country to the south-east, and the distances to the Khotan-daria, he knew nothing; he was only able to add, that he had heard there was nothing but sand to the south, with not a single drop of water anywhere, and he knew that the desert was called Takla-makan.

We said adieu to the lonely salt-gatherer, and continued south-south-east across the hard, barren, trackless plain. As we advanced, the mountain on our right gradually decreased in height, until it merged in a sand-ridge, which eventually became lost in the desert. This mountain therefore had no continuation. We could only surmise, that it was the eastern range which was connected with the Masar-tagh that Przhevalsky marked on his map as terminating near the Khotan-daria.

The ground we were now travelling over consisted of

CAMP NO. IX., ON THE SHORE OF THE DESERT LAKE

hard, dry clay, cracked in thousands of directions, plainly proving that it was under water during the summer. We kept close to the shore of the lake all along, until it began to narrow, and we were compelled to make detours round the marshes which extended some distance from it. From the southern end of the lake several long narrow creeks stretched out like fingers into the gradually rising ground. It is worthy of remark, that all these desert lakes were situated at the foot of the mountains.

At length we reached the eastern shore of the lake by a long roundabout way, and there pitched our camp. Believing that this was the last place in which we were likely to obtain fresh water, we gave up the following day, 22nd April, to rest. The camels and sheep were given their last good meal off the reeds which grew beside the lake. I climbed to the top of the mountain, and therefrom gained a commanding view of the surrounding country. The mountain itself jutted out in a south-easterly direction like a cape into the desert ocean, and only showed one solitary peak of no great altitude. Except for the range on which I stood, there was not a glimpse of a hill to be seen. We had reached the south-eastern extremity of the Masar-tagh of Maral-bashi; consequently it had no connection with the Masar-tagh of the Khotan-daria. To the south-east, south, and south-west, as far as eye could reach, there was nothing but the dreary desert ocean! The horizon on that side was a straight line. When, during the days that followed, we went on and on towards the east-south-east and east without discerning a single trace of a mountain-chain, I could not help thinking, that the continuation of the Masar-tagh of Maral-bashi would crop out again further on in the desert, and that we had left it on our right; and yet again that was hardly likely.

Before the day came to an end, we took counsel together. Yollchi assured me, that the Khotan-daria was only four days distant to the east. The best Russian maps I had made the distance about 78 miles, and at the rate of about 12½ miles a day we should reach the river in six days; but at two day's-march from its bank we ought to be able to get water by digging, as we had done near the Yarkand-daria. However, I bade the men take sufficient water to last ten days, that is, to fill the tanks half full, so as not to overstrain the camels in the deep sand. With such a margin I felt perfectly safe against all risks; indeed there would be a sufficient supply to water the camels twice during the six days. Yollchi and Kasim were told off to fill the tanks. They were at it a long spell in the evening, and all the time I heard the precious fluid pouring into the iron vessels. All the loads were got ready that night, so that we might start early in the morning.

CHAPTER XLII.

IN THE BAN OF THE DESERT

APRIL 23rd. It proved to be a warm day; but the camels had profited from their rest, and we did seventeen miles before halting. At first our route lay across the thinly grassed dusty steppe, which stretched away south-eastwards from the lake, and was dotted all over with small mounds and terraces of clay, that bore a striking resemblance to houses. After we had gone about an hour and a half, the sand began to take the form of low furrowed ridges. Then ten minutes further on and we were in the midst of a regular chaos of sand-dunes, all linked together, running without break one into another. Their prevailing direction was from north-east to south-west, and their steeper faces all fronted towards the south, south-west, and west. They were 20 to 25 feet high, and often extremely difficult to get over. My men called them *yaman-kum* (hateful sand), *chong-kum* (big sand), and *ighiz-kum* (high sand); to their crests or summits they gave the name of *beles* (pass). Already we perceived several peculiar sand formations. When two systems of sea-waves clash together, they mount on the top of one another up to double their original height. In like manner some of these gigantic sand-waves were piled up in pyramidal masses over-topping the level of the rest. This was where two separate dunes were driven one across the other by the ever-varying winds.

Right across our path, running from north-north-east to south-south-west, was a ridge of gigantic dunes, exceeding in altitude all others we could see; they were probably formed over uneven ground. It was wonderful to see with what surety of foot the camels clambered up the steep inclines, which the men only climbed with the utmost exertion, slipping back at every step they took. The ridge rose to relatively but an inconsiderable height above the general level; all the same, it afforded a wide view. Why did I not pale with horror when my gaze swept eastwards over that unending ocean of fine yellow sand, and its gigantic billows peeping up one behind the other for miles upon miles? I can only suggest, it was because I believed that the star of my fortunes, which had always shone so clear above my head, would not become extinct now. On the contrary, to my eyes the desert ocean was invested with a fascinating beauty. Its silence, its unbroken stillness, exercised a magic charm over me. It was a grand, a majestic sight. The wizard power of the *desiderium incogniti* was drawing me on with an irresistible spell to enter the castle of the desert king, where I was to unseal the revelations of bygone centuries, and discover the buried treasures of old-world legend and story. My motto was "Win or lose." I knew nothing of hesitation, nothing of fear. "Onwards! Onwards!" whispered the desert wind. "Onwards! Onwards!" vibrated the camels' bells. A thousand times a thousand steps to reach my object; yet accursed be the first step I take backwards!

The dunes increased rapidly in height, the maximum being some 60 to 70 feet. It was terrible work getting over them. The camels slid cleverly down the steep slopes. Only one of them fell, one of the two that carried the water-tanks, and had to be unloaded and reloaded. Sometimes, when our path was stopped by abrupt declivities, we were obliged to stand still, whilst the men dug out and trampled down a path for the animals. By this the dunes had increased to a height of 80 to 100 feet. When I stood at the base of one of them, and looked up at the caravan creeping along its brink, I thought how little it looked. As far as possible we kept to the same curving line of summits, so as to escape going up and down more than we could help. As a consequence of this, our track was very

"THE DUNES INCREASED RAPIDLY IN HEIGHT'

zigzag. We took all the advantage we could of the softer, rounded summits, going from the one to the other; nevertheless we were very often obliged to go down a steep slope which we found it impossible to get round. When, after some little hesitation, the camels began to slide down the loose sand, every man's utmost watchfulness was needed, for the sand poured down after them in a torrent, covering them to the knees.

We missed the small patches of hard clay soil of which we had passed so many during the first few days of our desert journey. We were now entirely amongst the sand. The last of the tamarisks, which still defied the visitation of death, was left behind. There was not a blade, not a leaf, to be seen; nothing but sand, sand, sand—fine yellow sand—whole mountains of it, stretching over boundless spaces, as far as the eye, with the field-glass to help it, was able to reach. No bird gave animation to the expanses of the sky. All traces of gazelle and deer had long since ceased. Even the very last promontory of the Masar-tagh had vanished from sight in the dust-haze that obscured the atmosphere.

The poor dogs! How they suffered from the heat, in their thick hairy coats! Hamrah in particular whined and howled, and lagged behind time after time. We spent a whole hour vainly looking for a suitable camping-ground, and at last, about dusk, found a very small patch of hard clay, where the last two tamarisks grew. Both trees were instantly peeled by the camels. Other green food there was of course none. We gave the animals oil and sesamum husks. We set about digging a well; but, as the sand still remained dry at a depth of 2¼ feet, we abandoned the attempt. Then we missed Hamrah. We whistled; we shouted. The dog did not appear; nor did we ever see him again. Half-way from our last camp Mohammed Shah saw him scratch up the sand underneath one of the very last tamarisks we passed, and then lie down in it. The men believed the dog had died of sunstroke. With greater probability the sagacious animal had grown tired of running through the sand, had scented out, that there was nothing but the terrible desert before us, and wisely judged that evil was in store for him if he followed us. Having therefore turned the matter well over in his mind, he made his choice, and turned back to the last lake we had left; then, having drunk and cooled his coat with a good bath, he would no doubt make his way to Maral-bashi, although to get there he would have to swim over the Yarkand-daria. When I got back to Kashgar, I made inquiries after the dog; but I could learn nothing of him. Yolldash stuck to us faithfully; but poor beast! his fidelity cost him his life.

A strange and inexplicable feeling came over me, when I encamped for the first time in the dreariest desert there is on the face of the earth. The men spoke but little; not one of them laughed. An unwonted silence reigned around the little fire of tamarisk roots. We tethered the camels for the night close to our sleeping-place,[1] to prevent them from breaking loose and going back to the lake, where they had their last good browse. A deathlike silence held us all under its spell; even the camels' bells were frequently silent. The only sound to be heard was the heavy, long-drawn, measured breathing of the camels. Two or three stray moths fluttered around my candle inside the tent; but no doubt they had travelled with our caravan.

April 24th. I was awakened at half-past three in the morning by a hurricane-like wind from the west. Clouds of sand were swept into the tent. The storm whistled and rattled amongst the tent-ropes and tent-pegs, and the tent itself shook to such an extent that I expected every moment it would be blown away. The wind struck us from every quarter, for our camp was pitched in a sort of hollow, surrounded on all sides by dunes of drift-sand. There was one gigantic ridge on the north of us, another on the east, and yet another on the west, this last inclining one degree to the south. The surface of the dunes was corrugated all over, the lines of corrugation running from north to south. On the south there was a fourth dune, lying almost parallel to the third, and with an inclination of ten degrees towards the north. The steep faces of the sand-ridges in that part of the desert were turned towards the south and the west, the flatter, easier declivities towards the east and the north—an arrangement which was the exact contrary of what we should have preferred.

Notwithstanding the violent gale, the sky was perfectly clear. But then the wind came from the west; while it is only the easterly winds which bring the dust-storms. It turned out a hot day, although the air was somewhat cooled by the wind. Clouds and columns of sand whirled in a mad dance across the desert, so that every now and again we became entirely swallowed up in them. But, as they seldom exceeded a dozen feet in height, the zenith retained all the while its fresh blue colour, and the sun's rays beat down upon us with undiminished fierceness. The horizon was veiled in an unbroken yellowish-red haze. The fine drift-sand penetrated everywhere—into mouth, nose, ears; even our clothes became impregnated with it, so that we experienced a disagreeable grittiness of the skin, to which, however, we soon grew accustomed. The haze on the horizon was very embarrassing; for we often found it difficult to decide which way to go. It would have suited us very much better, had things been reversed — namely the zenith been clouded, but the horizon clear. Meanwhile the top of every dune afforded us an opportunity to observe how the drift-sand stood over like a plume or inverted tassel on the brink that faced the direction of the wind; how one moment the minute grains of sand were whirling round and round in a frenzied dance on the windward side of the dune, then the next moment quietly settled down on the lee side in fine crumpled folds, as though some mighty master-hand were weaving them together after a tastefully designed pattern. But when our heads rose up to the same level as the sandstorm, which came whistling between the summits of the dunes—the effect absolutely baffles description. We shut our eyes and mouth tight; we lowered our heads against the fierce blast, which shrieked and moaned about our ears. But, the whirlwind passed, we stood still and literally shook the dust off our clothes by the pound. I had brought with me a good stock of snow-spectacles, with a fine mesh-work of black wire across them ; these now proved invaluable, although the fine sand partly forced itself in between the tiny meshes.

There was however one advantage attending a westerly gale. It tended to level down the abrupt faces of the sand-dunes, and hurl them over on to the eastern sides. And yet what can one hurricane effect as against the labour of centuries?

My men set out in the morning full of hope that before evening we should reach a part of the desert where the dunes were lower, and where we should be able to find water, and maybe pasture for the camels, and fuel for a fire as well. But no such thing. The sand-hills grew higher and higher, and we drifted further and further into the unknown terrors of the desert. Only once during the day did the dunes become really lower, namely forty to fifty feet. In that solitary spot we caught a glimpse of a few patches of bare level soil, partly clay, partly sheeted with saline incrustations.

At first it had been my intention to keep steadily on towards the south-east, in order to find out how far it was before the Masar-tagh cropped up again out of the sand of the Takla-makan Desert. But we saw no glimpse of a mountain, and so gradually bent our course round to the east, under the belief that that was the shortest way to the Khotan-daria. Islam Bai was our pilot now, and excellently well he did the work. He went on a good distance ahead, picking out the easiest path, and holding the compass in his hand all the time. Down he went behind a dune, and became lost to sight; but he soon reappeared on the crest of the next ridge, then down again; and so it went on, time after time. The caravan followed slowly in his footsteps. Our line of march thus formed an undulating curve, winding across the troughs of the desert waves, and over the saddles of the dunes, *i.e.* the lower transverse ridges which connected the loftier crests, and

A DESERT SANDSTORM

thus afforded relatively easy passages from one depression to another. But when Islam stopped, and stepped aside up a pyramidal peak, and putting his hand to his brow, to shade his eyes, gazed fixedly eastwards, I confess I did not feel very comfortable. The action would bear only one interpretation: the road was growing still more difficult. Sometimes he came back quite discouraged, crying, "*Hetch yoll yock*" (Perfectly impassable), "*Her taraf yaman kum*" (Hateful sand everywhere), or simply "*Kum-tagh*" (Mountains of sand). When that happened, we were forced to make a wide detour to the north or south, so as to get past the hindrances which blocked the direct line of advance.

All the men walked, barefooted, the perspiration rolling off them, all alike silent, weary, and downcast at finding their hopes of easier sand so bitterly and so constantly deceived. Time after time they stopped to drink; but the water itself was hot, its temperature being 86° Fahr. (30° C.); for it was incessantly washed backwards and forwards against the heated sides of the iron tanks, which we were no longer able to shade with bundles of reeds, for the camels had eaten them all up to the last stalk. Anyway we all drank excessive quantities of water, in order to increase the transpiration, for the wind struck cool upon our skin.

The caravan crept slowly on at a snail's-pace. We always took a general look-round from the top of each outstanding eminence; but towards every point of the compass it was always the same monotonous, discouraging outlook—one sand-ridge peeping up behind another—a billowy ocean without a shore, actual mountain-chains of nothing but fine, yellow sand. The camels still continued to climb up and slide down the slopes with the same marvellous surety of foot; nevertheless we were often obliged to make a path for them. These difficult places, which the men called *davan-kum* (sand-pass), generally discouraged us all a little; but whenever we were favoured with a good piece of level ground (*darah*) between the dunes, we quickly recovered our spirits, and pushed on with fresh vigour, the men crying, "*Khoda kalesa*" (God grant it!), "*Inshallah*" (With God's will!), and "*Bismillah*" (In God's name!). But after advancing a little way, a fresh ridge would face us, and fresh crests tower up ahead as far as the eye could reach.

On the top of a commanding dune we made a long halt, for the purpose of reconnoitring, and of quenching our thirst. Occasionally poor Yolldash and the sheep, which were dying of thirst, were given their fill. Yolldash was wild the moment he heard the sound of water. Every time anybody went to the water-tank, he came running up, wagging his tail. The last survivor of the sheep followed us with the patience and fidelity of a dog. The men grew so fond of the creature, that they said, they would sooner perish of hunger than kill it.

But the camels were visibly tiring. Heavy falls grew more and more frequent. When they fell on a steep incline, they were unable to get up without help. One of the beasts, which came down near the summit of a ridge, we were obliged to free entirely from his burden, saddle and all; and then, all putting our shoulders to him, we rolled him seventy feet down the slope into a hollow between two sand-dunes. It was only then that he was able to recover his feet.

After going eight miles, we had had enough of it for that day; and camped on a small patch of bare ground, so hard that we did not even attempt to dig a well. Every trace of organic life had now absolutely ceased. No moths came fluttering round my candle at night. Not a single yellow leaf came dancing down the wind to break the dead uniformity. As soon as our duties were finished, we sat down and discussed the doings of the day, and what should be done on the morrow. It was truly touching to hear Islam Bai doing his best to keep up the courage of the others. He told them about our former journeys, about the masses of snow we encountered in the Alaï valley, "which were much worse than the sand," about the glaciers of Mus-tagh-ata, and our several ascents of the great mountain.

CHAPTER XLIII.

THE CAMELS BREAK DOWN

APRIL 25th. As a consequence of the limpid purity of the atmosphere, the minimum thermometer sank to an unusually low level, not more than a couple of degrees above freezing-point; and in the morning a nor'-wester was blowing and the air was again thick with dust. All day long therefore the temperature remained more than ordinarily low; we had no grounds for complaining of the heat, even at noon. Under the clear night sky radiation had been very active; then came the veil of dust, shielding the earth like an umbrella, so that the sun's rays were a long time in warming the ground. Meanwhile the air grew so thick, that we had difficulty in seeing beyond the next dune or so.

The terraced patches of clay and silt, which lay embedded between the sand-dunes, and on which we preferred if possible to encamp, were formations of a remarkable character. They consisted of a series of horizontal flakes of clay, brittle, friable, and saline, and crumbled to pieces at the least touch. The several flakes did not lie at the same level, but generally rose layer above layer like a series of steps. There was not a trace of sand in them, nor of vegetable matter either. They were pure alluvial clays; of that there could not exist a doubt. Probably they were the last surviving fragments of the bed of the great Central Asian Mediterranean, which has dried up in the course of countless centuries, and the different terraces possibly indicated different sea-levels. As a rule none of these patches of clay was bigger than the deck of a brig; and the sand-dunes in their restless onward movement keep pouring over them and covering them up.

When morning came, I made a most unwelcome discovery. I had noticed the day before how the water washed very noisily to and fro in the water-tanks, and I looked into them to ascertain the cause. They contained only *water enough to last two days!* I asked the men why they had not obeyed my instructions, and put in sufficient water to last ten days. They answered that Yollchi was responsible for the quantity of water brought. When I reproached Yollchi, he answered, "We might be perfectly easy; for it was merely a four days' journey from the last of the desert lakes to the place where we could get water by digging for it." This statement agreed with the maps I had. Consequently I relied upon the man, all the more since his information hitherto had invariably turned out to be correct. We were all without exception convinced, that we were every bit as near to water by going east as by going west; consequently nobody said a word about going back to the last of the desert lakes. And yet what suffering, what loss, what sorrow would have been spared both to ourselves and to others, who were anxious about our fate, if we had retraced our steps to that little desert lake! However we all agreed to watch over the water we had, and husband it like gold. Privately, I instructed Islam Bai not to let the two water-tanks out of his sight for a single moment. From that morning the camels never got a drop more water to drink.

Thanks to the dust-haze, the air remained beautifully cool. The crests of the dunes gleamed out of the gloom like fantastic ghosts, yellow dolphins with arched backs, mocking us for our audacity in daring to defy them. The thick atmosphere embarrassed us considerably in judging of distance and perspective. We were often brought up suddenly at the bottom of a dune, which, owing to its blurred outlines, we still imagined to be a good way ahead of us.

In front of us extended an endless world of ridges and

MARCHING ALONG THE EDGE OF A SAND-DUNE

hummocks of sand. The greater portion of the dunes stretched from north to south; but the highest ones extended from east to west. The horizontal terraces of clay, which were at least evidence that the ocean of sand was not quite without a bottom, and which buoyed us up with the hope that we should ultimately get beyond the sweep of its sand-waves, had now entirely ceased. Everything was completely buried under sand; the dunes were sand; every hollow between them was sand. It was plain we were entangled in the very worst part of all the desert; and I became painfully conscious of the seriousness of our position.

I travelled all that day on foot, partly to spare my excellent camel Boghra, partly to encourage my men. The camel Babai kept stopping every minute. Time after time the cord that he was led by broke, and his nose became sore and tender. At last he lay down on the sand, and refused to exert himself any further. We took off his load. Then he got up. We fastened his load on again as he stood. But he walked slower and slower, stopped oftener and oftener, and had to be led all the time by one of the men. Finally we relieved him of his burden and divided it amongst the other camels, and left him to make his way alone in the wake of the caravan. It was a terrible sight to see "the ship of the desert," man's only hope on that endless sea, become a wreck. We gazed and gazed impatiently eastwards, seeking some abatement of the difficulties of the road; but we gazed in vain. There was nothing but mountains of sand as far as the eye could pierce. All of a sudden a gadfly came buzzing amongst the camels. Instantly our hopes rose to fever point; we believed we were nearing "land." Yet in all probability it was merely a deceiver, which we had not observed before—a straggler which had quietly lain hidden in the hairy hide of one of the camels.

Babai delayed us continually; at last we decided to halt for an hour, so as to afford him an opportunity to rest. We gave him a few pints of water and a few handfuls of hay out of his own pack-saddle; he devoured them voraciously. When his saddle was taken off, we perceived he had an open sore on his back, where a rough piece of the saddle had chafed his unhealthy yellowish flesh. His legs trembled; his tongue was white. It was painful to see the poor creature. Leaving Mohammed Shah to look after him, the rest of us went on. For a long time we heard the sick animal crying after us.

The highest dunes now rose 150 to 200 feet above their bases. Further on again they sank to 100 to 120 feet.

"*Karga! karga!*" cried Islam Bai, as he pointed to a raven, which circled two or three times round the caravan, hopped about on the summit of a dune, and finally disappeared. This incident awakened universal joy. We looked upon it as an indication that the Khotan-daria was not far off. The raven was hardly likely to have sought the depths of the desert for the mere pleasure of the thing.

After we had gone 12½ miles, Chong-kara, the big black camel, refused to go farther. This obliged us to make camp No. XIII. We gave the camels what was left of Babai's saddle to eat; for we had a good reserve supply in the saddles of the other seven, which were all stuffed with hay and straw.

My dinners grew gradually simpler; till at last I was forced to content myself with tea, bread, and tinned foods. The men lived on tea, bread, and talkan (toasted flour). Our fuel had pretty well run out. The small supply we had started with was all done, and we had no resource left but to sacrifice some of the less valuable packing-cases. In the evening we again took counsel together. We considered that, at the most, we had only three days to the Khotan-daria, but hoped before then to come to a belt of poplars, where we should be able to obtain water by digging for it. A couple of gnats came and kept me company in the tent. The question was, had they travelled with us or had they been blown to that spot by the wind from some wood in the vicinity?

April 26th. At daybreak, whilst the men were occupied with getting the tent down, and preparing the caravan for a start, I set off alone, on foot, to try and find a passage eastwards. From that point I travelled on foot all the way to the Khotan-daria; consequently I was no longer able to calculate the distance from the camel's paces. Instead of that, I adopted the device of counting my own, an occupation which greatly interested me. Every hundred paces I went was so much space won towards "land": and with every thousand my hopes of safety rose a degree.

Meanwhile, with my compass in one hand and my field-glass in the other, I hastened eastwards, due eastwards; for there ran the river of safety. The camp, the camels were soon lost to sight behind the summits of the sand-hills. My only companion was a solitary fly, which I regarded with unusually friendly eyes. Otherwise I was alone, absolutely alone, in the midst of a death-like silence, with a sea of yellow sand-dunes before me, rolling away in fainter and fainter billows right away to the horizon. Deeper Sabbath peace never brooded over any graveyard than that which environed me. The only thing wanting to convert the simile into actual fact was the headstones to the graves.

I soon fancied the dunes were not so high as usual. I tried to maintain the same level as far as possible, by keeping to their crests and circling round the highest points. I knew the poor camels would have many a toilsome, many a weary step to take in my wake. A bewildering chaos of ridges, lying north-east to south-west, and east to west, were flung across one another in the strangest fashion. Our position was desperate. The dunes burst up to heights of 140 to 150 feet. As I looked down from the top of one of these giant waves, the depression at my feet, on the sheltered side of the dune, looked a long way below me, at a giddy depth. We were being slowly but surely killed by these terrible ridges of sand. They impeded our advance; yet over them we must. There was no help for it, no evading them. Over them we must—a funeral procession, marching to the doleful clang of the camels' bells.

The steeper faces were now turned towards the east and south-east. Evidently the north-west wind had prevailed in this quarter during the past few days. A good crisp breeze was cutting across from that direction even then. On its wings rode every now and again a few small tufts of some species of white vegetable down. Over one of the ridges rolled a handful of dry and withered thistles, closely matted together. Unfortunately these scant tokens of organic life were wafted thither by the north-west wind. In all probability they had travelled a route coincident or parallel with ours.

Noon came, and I was near fainting from fatigue and thirst. The sun glowed like a furnace above my head. I was dead beat: I *could* not go another step. Then my friend the fly swung round to the other side of me and buzzed such a lively tune, that he roused me up. "Just a little bit further," he buzzed in my ear. "Come, drag yourself on to the summit of the next dune. Tramp off another thousand paces, before you give in. You will be all the nearer to the Khotan-daria—all the nearer to the flood of fresh water which rolls down to Lop-nor—all the nearer to the dancing waves of the river which sing a song of life and spring, and of the spring of life." I tramped off the thousand paces. Then I dropped on the top of a dune, rolled over on my back, and pulled my white cap over my face. O burning sun! hasten, hasten westwards; melt the icefields of the Father of the Ice Mountains; give me but one cup of the cold crystal streams which pour from his steel-blue glaciers and foam down his mighty flanks!

I had walked eight miles. It was delightful to rest; and there was a stir of air on the dune top. I fell into a kind of torpor; I forgot the gravity of our situation. I dreamt I was lying on a patch of cool emerald-green grass, underneath a leafy silver poplar, and a gentle breeze was whispering through its trembling leaves. I heard the wavelets beating their melancholy cadences against the shore of a lake, which washed the very roots of the poplar. A bird was singing in the tree-top—singing a song of mystic meaning which I did not understand. A beautiful dream! How gladly would I have continued to steep my soul in its false illusions! But alas! alas! the hollow clang of the funereal bells again woke me up to the grim realities of that evil desert. I sat up. My head was heavy as lead; my eyes were blinded by the glittering reflections of the eternal yellow sand.

Up staggered the camels, their eyes dull and lustreless, like the dying gleams of the setting sun. It was a look of resignation, a look of indifference; all desire for food had gone out of it. Their breathing was laboured and slow; their breath more disagreeable than usual. There were only six of them, led by Islam Bai and Kasim. The other two men had remained behind with Babai and Chong-kara. Even at the beginning of the day Chong-kara's legs had failed him. "They would come on to camp," said Islam, "as quickly as they were able."

After that the desert showed us another of its features. Every now and again we stumbled into level pools of inconceivably fine dust, lying embedded between the dunes. We sank into them up to the knees, as though we trod on soft mud. Accordingly, after that we kept a vigilant look-out for these treacherous spots. In other places the sand was covered with a thin sprinkling of minute particles of flints with sharp edges. They appeared to exercise much the same sort of influence upon the sand-dunes that oil does upon the waves of the sea. Where they were present, the dunes were flattened down, rounded off, and lost their delicate rippled surface.

Between two of the sand-dunes we made a strangely unexpected discovery, namely a portion of the skeleton of a donkey, or, as the men asserted, of a wild horse. There was nothing but the leg bones, which were white as chalk, and so brittle that a mere touch caused them to crumble to pieces like ashes. The best-preserved parts were the hoofs. They were too large to be those of a donkey, too small to have belonged to a tame horse. What was the creature doing out here in the desert?

How long had the bones lain there? To these questions the obdurate desert sand returned no answer. For my part, I fail to see why those bones may not have lain where we found them for thousands of years. I ascertained subsequently from several instances, that the dry, fine desert sand unquestionably does possess the property of preserving organic matter for a very long period of time. Perhaps the skeleton had lain buried beneath the sand for centuries, and had only quite recently been exposed through the drifting away of the superincumbent dunes.

We were all completely done up through weariness and the cravings of thirst. We were unable to drag ourselves on more than another mile and a half, and then halted on a patch of hard, level clay. There too we lighted upon a number of curious objects, namely small, brittle, white snail-shells, tiny pebbles, which some time or other had been rolled and polished by water, amorphous pieces of flint, a fragment of a mussel-shell, and a large quantity of pipe-like formations of limestone, as though lime had been moulded round the stalks of reeds.

It was evening when Yollchi and Mohammed Shah struggled into camp, tired and thirsty, supporting their steps on their hand-staves. They came alone. The two camels refused to go any further, and so they had left them to their fate. As soon as it turned a little cooler I sent a man to fetch them. He found that they had picked up a bit, and towards midnight brought them in.

Our spirits all revived that evening. Looking to the east with my field-glass, I thought the dunes were much lower, 40 to 50 feet at the most. To-morrow we should be through the high sand-ridges, we should perhaps be able to encamp in the woods of the Khotan-daria! A glorious thought! It put life into us all.

From this point I did without the tent. It was necessary to husband our strength for more essential exertions. We all slept comrade-like under the open sky. Yollchi however held aloof from us, and never spoke unless he was spoken to first. There was a traitorous look in his eye;

we felt more comfortable when he was out of our sight. The word that was oftenest heard during the day was "*Yaman*" (Bad; things look bad). But after a while something of the grim humour of despair began to creep over us. We passed some flakes of stone. One of the men advised another to look for gold. But no matter how the day went, our spirits invariably rose as we drew near to the next camping-place. Besides, what was the use of worrying ourselves about the morrow; only let us rest after the toils and fatigues of *that* day, and recover from *its* deceptive hopes! After the heat of the day the coolness of the night was always welcome.

In the evening, about six o'clock, a bright idea occurred to me. Why not try to dig a well? Islam Bai and Kasim were instantly all eagerness. Whilst the former made haste to get my "dinner" ready, the latter set to work to dig. He rolled up his sleeves, spat in his hands, and laid hold upon the *ketmen*, a sharp-pointed Sart spade, the blade of which was put on at right angles to the shaft. The dry clay crackled, and Kasim sang as he dug. After the other two men came into camp, all three took their turns at digging. In answer to my question, whether there was water there, Yollchi smiled scornfully, and said, "Oh, yes, there was plenty of water, if we dug down thirty *gulatsh* (fathoms)!" Kasim got down about a yard. The clay was mixed with sand and it was *moist!* Yollchi was put to shame, and worked with double zeal. The hopes of all of us revived. I hurried through my simple meal, and with Islam hastened to the well. And at it we went, all five of us, as hard as we could work. The hole grew deeper. The man digging could not be seen from the level ground; nor was he able to throw the sand to the surface. A rope was tied to the handle of a bucket, and by that means the loose sand was drawn up to the top. A third man emptied the bucket. Gradually a circular mound rose round the opening, until I set to work and shovelled it away to make room. We began work at six o'clock. At that hour the temperature of the air was 83°5 Fahr. (28°6 C.); of the surface of the earth

80°2 Fahr. (26°8 C.). At a depth of 3½ feet the argillaceous sand showed 61°9 Fahr. (16°6 C.), and at five feet 54°3 Fahr. (12°4 C.).

The material we dug through was clayey sand of a greyish yellow colour, and contained in places reddish-brown husks, the relics of some species of decayed vegetation. Of stones there was not a trace.

It was pleasant and refreshing to lie on the cool sand. The water in the iron tanks was 84°9 Fahr. (29°4 C.). A tinful was embedded in the sand that was thrown out of the well, and it speedily became cool enough to quench our thirst.

Slowly and gradually the sand grew moister. It was evident there was water, although Yollchi believed it was a long way down to it. When we got down about 6½ feet, the sand was so moist that we could squeeze it into balls, and by so doing made our hands moist. And how pleasant it was to cool our heated cheeks against it. In this way a couple of hours passed. The men had grown tired. Their breasts and shoulders, which were bare, dripped with perspiration. They kept stopping to rest oftener and oftener, and every now and again swallowed a mouthful of water. Nor did our conscience reproach us for the extravagance; for were we not going to fill our empty tanks at the well we were digging?

In the meantime it had grown pitch dark, and the work went on by the light of a couple of candle-ends stuck in niches in the sides of the well. Their own instinct brought all the animals round the mouth of the hole. The camels, waiting impatiently, stretched their long necks over it and sniffed at the cool, wet sand. Yolldash came and squatted down on it, with his legs outstretched before him. Every now and then the hens too came and took a peep at what was going forward.

Inch after inch we forced our way down, working with the energy of despair for life—dear life. The hope of deliverance gave us new strength. We were resolved not to be beaten; we would dig on all the next day before we would give in. We *would* find water.

DIGGING THE DECEITFUL WELL

We were all standing in a ring round the gaping hole we had made in the ground, talking about it, and watching Kasim, who, half naked as he was, looked strange and eerie in the dimly lighted cavity at our feet, when all at once he stopped, letting the spade drop out of his hands. Then, with a half-smothered groan, he fell to the ground.

"What is the matter? what has happened?" we asked, one and all stupefied with amazement.

"*Kurruk kum!*" (The sand is *dry*!) came a voice as if from the grave.

A couple of spade-strokes convinced me that the man was right: the sand had become as dry as tinder. The deceptive moisture was possibly due to a fall of snow during the winter, or to a shower of rain. But we did not know that; and the sand-dunes do not betray their secrets. We got down as far as 10¼ feet; and there the temperature was 52°2 Fahr. (11°2 C.).

This unwelcome discovery made, we became instantly conscious of our weariness, and realized how much of our precious strength we had wasted during the three hours we had toiled in vain. We literally collapsed, became unnerved, lost all our energy. A deep and bitter gloom darkened every face. We shunned one another's glances. We staggered away each to his sleeping-place, seeking oblivion of our despair in a long and heavy sleep. Before I lay down, I had a private conversation with Islam Bai. We did not conceal our apprehensions from one another. We recognized the extreme gravity of our position, and pledged each other to keep up our own and the other men's courage to the utmost extremity. According to my maps, we could not be very far from the Khotan-daria; nevertheless it was as well to be prepared for the worst. Before lying down, I took the opportunity of the other men being asleep to examine the contents of the last of the tanks. It contained sufficient water to last one day. We should have to watch over it as if it were gold. In fact, if we could have bought one more day's supply of water with all the money we had, we should not have hesitated about it a moment. We resolved to measure out the last precious portions drop by drop. It *must* be made to last three days: that could be done, if we confined ourselves to two cups a day to each man. For three days the camels had not tasted a drop, nor did they get a drop more. Yolldash and the sheep got a bowlful each once a day, and on that they managed very well. Then we two also sought rest, leaving the patient, docile camels standing in a circle round the mocking well, waiting in vain for what they could not get.

CHAPTER XLIV.

NO WATER LEFT

AT sunrise of April 27th we did all we could do to preserve the camels' strength. We took out the hay stuffing of one of the saddles and gave it to them; they devoured it greedily. Then they looked about for water; but we could only moisten their lips. After the hay they got a sackful of old bread and some oil. To relieve their burdens a little we left behind us my tent-bed, a carpet, and several other articles of minor importance.

As soon as I had swallowed my tea, I hastened on in advance. I was consumed with impatience to get on, for the dunes were lower than usual, not more than thirty-five feet in height. All the same, I observed that the brown substratum, which every now and again peeped out from underneath the sand in the hollows between the dunes, was slightly uneven in contour; so that the lower elevation of the dunes may have been due to inequalities in the natural surface of the earth, and to the top of the higher parts being less deeply buried in sand. Consequently I did not deceive myself. An hour later I was again entangled in a maze of lofty sand-dunes, quite as difficult to cross and equally boundless as heretofore. The larger agglomerations of dunes stretched from east to west; whilst the secondary or transverse dunes lay from north to south or from north-east to south-west. The steep slopes were now turned towards the east and towards the south. But not a sign of life, not a single tamarisk to break the straight line of the horizon, nothing to indicate the approximate presence of "land." My senses reeled as I gazed across that desolate ocean of sand, in the depths of which we had hopelessly lost ourselves. Again and again, from the top of every sand-ridge I came to, I swept the horizon with my field-glass, hoping to discern in the east the dim dark line of the woods of the Khotan-daria. But all in vain.

Going down the side of one of the dunes, my eye fell upon a small object resembling a root. I stooped down to pick it up, when suddenly it darted away and disappeared in a little hole on the edge of the dune. It was a lizard, of the same yellow colour as the sand. How did the creature live? Did it eat nothing? Did it never want a drop of water to drink?

It turned out a splendid day. The sky was flecked with light feathery clouds; the heat was not at all oppressive; radiation was less active than usual. At the end of three and a half hours I was overtaken by the caravan; which continued to go well all day long. But when they came up, Mohammed Shah and the two sick camels were already missing. "They were coming on slowly after them," said the other men. High up in the sky we perceived two wild-geese, scudding away to the north-west. This again revived our hopes; for we conjectured that they came from the Khotan-daria, and were making for the little desert lake that lay at the foot of the mountains we had passed. And yet, after all, we were only trying to deceive ourselves; for wild-geese only fly at such a great height when they are migrating from place to place; and when they are doing that, what signifies to them the crossing of a desert some 200 miles broad?

I got up on Boghra's back for a while, and he received the accession to his burden without murmuring. As soon as I was mounted, I felt myself terribly tired; yet when I noticed how the animal's knees tottered at every step he took, I got down again and walked.

That day the sand-hills were the highest of any we had yet crossed — fully 200 feet high. The way I estimated their height was this. I stationed myself a little way off a dune along the top of which the caravan was moving. I knew by previous measurement the exact height of one of the camels. On a pencil I marked notches at equal distances apart, each space representing the height of the camel. Then, holding the pencil up to my eye, I measured how many notched spaces were required to cover the height of the dune; in other words, I measured how many camel's-heights it was. Apart from that my eye alone told me that the camel was an extremely small object as compared with the dune, which was more like a high hill. It will readily be understood that, over gigantic billows of sand like this we could not advance very rapidly. We were compelled to make many a detour, involving great loss of time, in order to avoid them; in fact, we were sometimes compelled to travel for a time in the exactly opposite direction from that in which we wanted to go.

Yolldash kept close to the water-tanks, in which he could hear the last few drops of the precious fluid splashing against the sides, and whined and howled every time he heard a splash. Whenever we stopped, uncertain which way to turn, he yelped, and sniffed at the tanks, and scratched in the sand, as if to remind us that we ought to dig a well, and to let us know that he wanted water. When I lay down to rest, the dog would come and crouch in front of me, and look me straight in the eyes, as if to ask me whether there really was no hope. I patted him, and spoke soothingly to him, and pointed towards the east, trying to make him understand that there was water there. At that he would prick his ears, jump up, and run in that direction; but he soon came back again downcast and disappointed.

After some trouble Islam Bai and I climbed to the top of a pyramidal dune, and took a long and searching reconnaissance of the country ahead through my field-glass. But there was no abatement of the billows of sand, no gap in the dunes towards which we could steer our course. Everywhere the same curdled sea of giant sand-waves. No matter which way we looked, we were surrounded by the same desolate, lifeless landscape. As the result of our deliberations we resolved to keep pushing on as long as the six camels were able to walk, and until a really serious crisis confronted us. That crisis occurred at six o'clock that same evening, on the slope of a dune looking towards the north, where we made camp No. XV., a camp shut in on every side by "ugly" country.

Shortly after reaching camp, we were joined by Mohammed Shah. He said, that even at the beginning of the day's march the camels refused to move, and he had therefore abandoned them to their fate. One of the two carried a couple of empty water-tanks; and the other had no load. If I had been there when they stopped, I should have had them shot; for the old man said, that at the most they could not last longer than two days. But he believed they might be saved, if we could find water before night. As it was, until then, they were abandoned for lost, and would have to wait in patience for a painful death. God grant it came speedily!

Mohammed Shah's report made an extremely painful impression upon me. I was to blame for the loss of the innocent lives. It was I who was answerable for every moment of agony, every pang of pain, which the men and animals of my caravan suffered. I was not present, it is true, when the first camels were delivered up to the power of the evil desert. But in imagination I saw the action vividly. It weighed upon my conscience like a nightmare, keeping me awake at night. I saw Babai lie down when Mohammed Shah left him. The other camel remained standing, although his legs trembled under him, and with expanded nostrils and shining eyes, followed the departing caravan with a wistful and reproachful look. But the caravan soon passed out of sight. Then I imagined him slowly turning his head towards his companion, and thereafter crouching down beside him. Then they both stretched out their necks along the sand, half closed their eyes, and lay motionless, breathing heavily through their expanded nostrils. Their weariness in-

THE FIRST TWO CAMELS ABANDONED IN A DYING STATE

creased; they rolled over on their sides with legs outstretched. Their blood coursed slower and slower, thicker and thicker, through their veins; the rigid torpors of death gradually stiffened their limbs. The pauses between their breathings became longer and longer, until at last the end came. In all probability Babai would die first, for he was the weaker. But how long did that death-struggle last? We shall never know. My blood curdled with horror, as the thought flashed across my mind, that perhaps they might live some days, and be buried alive by the sandstorms. Ah well! they are now sleeping their century-long sleep under the moving billows of the remorseless and interminable desert.

Later on in the afternoon we perceived that the western sky was full of thick steel-blue clouds, heavily charged with rain. They were the symbols of water and of life. *We* were surrounded by aridity and death. They widened out; they drove closer together. The sight of them fairly fascinated us. We could not take our eyes off them. Our hopes of rain grew stronger from moment to moment. We set out two of the empty water-tanks. We spread out the tent-covering on the ground, with one man at each corner, ready to hold it up. We waited and waited. But the clouds slowly drew over to the south, vouchsafing us not a drop.

Islam Bai baked bread for me for the last time. Mohammed Shah declared that we had fallen under the spell of *telesmat*, *i.e.* witchcraft, and should never find our way out of the desert. With superb calmness, as if stating a mere matter of course, Islam Bai remarked, that the camels would fall one after the other, and then it would be our turn. It was simply the inevitable course of events. I answered, I was convinced we should *not* die in the desert. Yollchi mocked at my compass—my *kebleh-nameh* (the shower of the direction to Mekka)—and swore it was it which was deceiving us, by leading us round in a circle. No matter how many days we travelled, he said, the result would be just the same. The best thing we could do was not to exert ourselves unnecessarily: we were bound to die of thirst at the end of a few days. I assured him, that the compass was a perfectly trustworthy guide, and had led us due east all the time; he had only to note the rise and setting of the sun to convince himself of the fact. His reply was that the dust-haze, together with telesmat (witchcraft), affected even the sun, so that it was no longer to be trusted to.

On April 28th we were awakened by an unusually violent hurricane of wind out of the north-north-east, which enveloped the camp in blinding clouds of sand. Up over the dunes dashed the whirling columns of sand, down they plunged on the lee side, and careered away one after the other in a frenzied dance. I tossed a handful of pieces of paper on the wind, and watched how they dropped to the ground directly they got to the sheltered side of the dunes, and there remained. The atmosphere was choked with dust and sand; it was so thick that we were unable to see the summits of even the nearest dunes. We could not possibly have steered our course by the sun that day. There was not the faintest glimmer of light in the sky to indicate his position. This was the worst storm we had experienced throughout the whole of our journey through the desert, one of those terrible kara-burans or "black storms," which convert day into night.

We slept the previous night under the open sky. The night being cool, I lay down wrapped in my furs, with a *bashlik* (hood) pulled round my head. In the morning, when I awoke, I was literally buried in sand. A thick sheet of fine yellow sand covered my neck and breast. Fine yellow sand had penetrated through every opening in my clothing. When I stood up, it slipped down inside my shirt next my skin; so that I had to take off my clothes and shake them. My furs were indistinguishable from the surface of the dune. Every object about the camp was in a precisely similar plight, half smothered in sand. It cost us a great deal of trouble to fish them all out with our hand-staves.

The going that day was fearful. We could not get a glimpse of our surroundings; we did not know which way

THE LAST FIVE CAMELS

to go. But the air was cool; and that and the gale made us forget the cravings of thirst.

That day I was unable of course to go on in advance; my footsteps would have been obliterated almost instantly. All we could do was to stick close together, men and animals in a clump. If you once get separated from your companions in such a storm as that, it is utterly impossible to make yourself heard by shouting, or even by rifle-shots. The deafening roar of the hurricane overpowers every other sound. If you do get separated from them, you are bound to wander astray, and so become irretrievably lost. All that I could see was the camel immediately in front of me. Everything else was swallowed up in the thick impenetrable haze. Nor can you hear anything except the peculiar whining and moaning, made by the millions upon millions of grains of sand as they whiz without cessation past your ears. Perhaps it was this eerie sound which worked upon the imagination of Marco Polo, and led him, when speaking of the Great Desert, to write thus:—"Even in the daytime one hears those spirits talk. And sometimes you shall hear the sound of a variety of musical instruments, and still more commonly the sound of drums. Hence in making this journey 't is customary for travellers to keep close together. All the animals too have bells at their necks, so that they cannot easily get astray. And at sleeping time a signal is put up to show the direction of the next march."*

We had a hard and trying march. Through the greater part of the middle of the day it was as dark as pitch; at other times we were environed by a dim, murky light, half yellow, half grey. Several times when the sand-blast met us full in the teeth, we were nearly suffocated. In fact, when the more violent gusts struck us, we crouched down with our faces on the ground, or pressed them against the sheltered side of a camel. Even the camels turned their backs to the wind, and stretched out their necks flat along the ground.

* From H. YULE'S, *The Book of Ser Marco Polo the Venetian.* London 1874-5, vol. i. p. 203.

The sand-hills grew no lower, but towered up in front of us as high as ever they did. No sooner had we surmounted one summit than we saw another looming out of the haze ahead of us. During the course of the day one of the younger camels gave up. It was easy to see the animals were exhausted. They staggered, their legs trembled, a dull, glassy look was in their eyes, their lower lip hung limply, their nostrils were expanded. We were in the act of laboriously surmounting the summit of a dune, where the storm seemed to rage with tenfold fury, when Yollchi, who was leading the dying camel last of all in the order of march, came hurrying forward alone. He was afraid to lose sight of us, lest he should not find us again. The camel had not been able to get over the last crest, he said; but had fallen close to the top, and rolled over on his side, and would not get up. I commanded the caravan to halt, and sent back two of the other men, to see if they could not somehow persuade the camel to rise and follow us. They disappeared in the dust-haze; but soon came back, saying that the trail was already obliterated, and they had not dared to go too far from the caravan.

Thus we lost our third camel, which, like the other two, was abandoned to a painful death in the desert. We gradually became hardened to these affecting losses. Our only concern now was to save our own lives. When people fall into such desperate straits as we were in, their feelings get blunted, and they grow indifferent to the sufferings of others. Every morning when we started, I used silently to question myself, Whose turn will it be next to start on the long, dark journey that hath no end?

At six o'clock in the evening we stopped, having travelled 12¾ miles during the day. After carefully considering our situation, we agreed to abandon everything that was not absolutely necessary. I and Islam Bai went through our stores *seriatim.* We unpacked the cases of sugar, flour, honey, rice, potatoes and other vegetables, macaroni, and two or three hundred tins of preserved foods. The greater part of these things, together with several furs and felts, cushions, books, a big bundle of journals, the cooking-stove, and petroleum-cask were stowed away in boxes, and covered up with carpets, and left in a hollow between two dunes. On the summit of the next dune, which was visible for a long distance, we planted a staff, and fastened to it a number of a Swedish journal, so as to make a flag. It was our intention, if we found water, to come back and fetch the things we left. Consequently, during the course of the evening we made a score of laths out of the lid of a packing-case, and tied a number of the same journal round each. These little flags we purposed to stick in the tops of the highest dunes we crossed during the succeeding days, so that, like buoys in an unfamiliar fairway, they might serve to guide us to camp No. XVII., where we left our stores.

I picked out all the tinned provisions which contained anything of a liquid nature, such as mushrooms, lobsters, and sardines. My men, having convinced themselves that the tins contained no pork or bacon, ate up their contents with great delight. What they did not eat were used next day. The remainder of the water, scarcely 3½ pints, was put into two *kungans* (iron pitchers). We took with us the last two tanks, in case we should discover water. The camels had another of the saddle stuffings; but they did not eat it with any appetite, for their throats were parched up. I had tea for the last time, and made a thorough good meal off moist tinned provisions.

April 29th. We started at daybreak with the five camels which still survived. Just as we were starting, Islam Bai came and with a heavy heart told me he had found one of the iron pitchers empty, and that he and the other men suspected Yollchi of having drunk the water, for they had heard him moving stealthily about and fumbling in the dark. However we had no proof that he was guilty; but our suspicions against him were strengthened, when he came creeping to my feet, complaining of pains in the breast and stomach. We believed it was all pretence. Nevertheless it was my duty to set an example to the rest, and keep up the other men's courage, so I gave him half of my allotted portion to drink. After that we lost sight of him; nor did he show himself again until the following morning.

We vainly scanned the horizon for "land." There was not a sign of a living creature to be seen. The desert ocean extended before us and around us to an infinite distance. The country decreased a little in elevation; but the relative dryness of the atmosphere remained unaltered. The ridges now stretched from north to south; their steep sides being again turned towards the west, which of course greatly added to the difficulties of our advance. Looking eastwards from the top of a high crest, we had before us an unending succession of steep banks of sand, which, by an optical illusion, looked like a series of easy steps. Westwards the eye glided across the long sloping windward faces of the dunes, so that towards that quarter the surface appeared almost level. The effect of this was to reduce us to despair. We fancied the dunes were growing higher and higher, and consequently the road more and more difficult with every step we took. Here, too, the sheltered sides of the dunes frequently showed a sprinkling of minute fragments of micaceous schist of a steel-grey colour.

This day our hopes were spurred by the discovery of the skeleton of a vole (gen. *Arvicola*), as well as of a hoary, withered poplar. And yet it was building upon an extremely slender foundation; for the vole's skeleton may have been carried to the spot where we found it by a bird, and the poplar was without a root. If only it had been rooted in the ground! That alone, for as little a thing as it was, would have kindled our hopes anew.

We travelled through that awful sand the whole day; consequently our pace was painfully slow. The camels' bells echoed at longer intervals apart; for the poor creatures were half dead with fatigue. All the same they still marched on with the same calm dignity and majestic gait which always distinguish them. Their excrement contained next to no straw, for they were living almost entirely upon their own flesh, and were growing fearfully thin. They presented a wretched appearance, every rib they had plainly showing through their hair. The three camels we had abandoned were no doubt by this time dead; in any case, it was too late to do anything to save them, even though we should come across water immediately.

It was a still, calm day, although the atmosphere was still saturated with dust. The men said, and with truth, that it was God's blessing the past few days had been cool, and we had not had the burning sun to contend against. Otherwise every camel we had would have given in, and we ourselves should be on our last legs.

I walked for twelve and a half hours without stopping; we covered altogether nearly seventeen miles before we encamped for the night. Eastwards there was not the slightest sign of an improvement in the surface of the country. The same billowy sea of sand stretched right away to the horizon; there was not a single object except sand upon which the eye could rest.

April 30th. The thermometer fell to a minimum of 41°2 Fahr. (5°1 C.), and even when morning came, it was decidedly cold. Clouds of fine dust still floated about in the atmosphere; but it cleared sufficiently to let us see the position of the sun, *i.e.*, a faint brightening that loomed through the haze. We gave the camels another saddle stuffing and all the bread we had, and so considered they would be able to last out another day. There were two tumblerfuls of water left in one of the pitchers. Whilst the men were engaged in loading up for the start, Islam Bai caught Yollchi, with his back to his comrades, and the pitcher at his mouth. There ensued an unpleasant and painful scene. Islam Bai and Kasim, boiling with rage, flung themselves upon Yollchi, hurled him to the ground, struck him in the face, kicked him, and would assuredly have killed him, had I not intervened with my authority, and compelled them to let him get up. He had drunk half of what there was, leaving about one-third of a pint.

At noon I proposed moistening each man's lips, and in the evening intended to divide what was left into five equal portions. I wondered how many days we should hold out after that. Mohammed Shah said, that once in Tibet, many years before, he had struggled on for thirteen days without water.

Again the funereal bells began their mournful ding-dong, ding-dong; the caravan got into motion for the east. At first the dunes were only twenty-five feet high; but we had not advanced far, before we were once more struggling through the mazes of *chong-kum* (big sand). A little wagtail circled round the caravan, twittering, and once more caused our rapidly expiring hopes to flicker up. Islam Bai was so encouraged by the incident, that he proposed to go on in advance with the iron pitchers and fetch water for us all. But I said "No." I needed him now more than ever; and we went on all together.

From the very start almost Yollchi was missing. The other men believed that he was unable to keep up with us any longer, but would die on our track. They were all embittered against the man. At the last lake we passed he swore, that we only needed to carry water sufficient for four days, and undertook within that space to bring us to a region where we could get water by digging for it. But the men believed that, from the very beginning, he had entertained a treacherous design against us, that he had of deliberate purpose led us into a part of the desert where we must inevitably perish of thirst, that he had stolen some of the water for his own secret use whilst he hastened, after the wreck of our caravan, to inhabited parts to fetch some other "gold seekers" of the same stamp as himself to come and plunder my goods. It was not easy to determine how much of truth there was in this theory; and the matter was never cleared up.

Every evening up to this point I had kept a fully detailed account of each day's incidents in my journal; and those accounts constitute the foundation of my description of that awful journey. The last lines I wrote in my book, which might have been the last I ever was to write at all, were penned on the afternoon of April 30th, and ran as follows:—

"Rested on a high dune, where the camels gave up. We scanned the eastern horizon with a field-glass—nothing but mountains of sand in every direction, not a blade of vegetation, not a sign of life. Nothing heard of Yollchi, either in the evening or during the night. My men maintained, he had gone back to the stores we left behind, intending to keep himself alive on the tinned provisions, whilst he fetched help to carry off the rest. Islam believed he was dead. There were still a few drops of water left for the morning, about a tumblerful in all. Half of this was used in moistening the men's lips. The little that remained was to be divided equally between us all in the evening. But when evening came we discovered that Kasim and Mohammed Shah, who led the caravan, had stolen every drop! We were all terribly weak, men as well as camels. God help us all!"

My account of what happened during the immediately succeeding days rests upon pencil notes scribbled on a sheet of folded paper. But besides recording the course of events, I never under any circumstances omitted to note the bearings of the compass, and to count the number of paces I took in each direction. When at last I found leisure to rest on the banks of the Khotan-daria, it was my first and principal concern, to write out my notes with complete fulness of detail, so long as the particulars were fresh in my memory.

CHAPTER XLV.

THE CAMP OF DEATH

MAY 1st. The night was cold; the thermometer fell to 35°9 Fahr. (2°2 C.), the lowest reading we had during the twenty-six days we were crossing the desert. But the atmosphere was pure, and the stars glittered with incomparable brilliancy. The morning dawned calm and gloriously bright—not a speck of cloud in the sky, not a breath of wind on the tops of the dunes. No sooner had the sun risen than it began to be warm.

The 1st of May! The day which in the northern land of my birth marks the beginning of spring. What a crowd of happy recollections, of joy, of pleasure, of cheerful gaiety, and above all what pleasant memories of the social cup and its pearly contents are there not associated with those poetic words—the 1st of May? I tried to persuade myself, that even in the barren deserts of the Far East the same day would also be a day of rejoicing. On the 1st of May a year ago I arrived at Kashgar, where I found both rest and comfort after the severe inflammation which attacked my eyes; and I hoped that this 1st of May would again mark a turning-point in our destinies—and it did!

Early in the morning Yollchi, whom we all looked upon as dead, once more put in an appearance in camp. He had recovered, and was so bold as to prophesy, that we should certainly discover water before the day was over. The other men refused to speak to him, but sat silent and downcast, drinking the last few drops that remained of the camels' rancid oil, which they had warmed, to some fragments of stale bread. All the previous day

I had not tasted a drop of water. But suffering the extreme tortures of thirst, I ventured to swallow about a tumblerful of the horrible and abominable concoction which the Chinese call brandy, stuff that we carried to burn in our Primus cooking-stove. It burned my throat like oil of vitriol. Yet what of that? It was at any rate liquid, and so calculated to maintain the moisture of my body. When Yolldash saw me drinking, he came running up, wagging his tail. But when I showed him it was not water, he slunk away downcast, and whining. Fortunately the men refused to touch the liquor. Afterwards I hurled the bottle with loathing into the side of a dune.

However in the meantime my strength left me, and as the caravan slowly struggled on, ever towards the east, my legs failed and refused to carry me further. In the still atmosphere the funereal camels' bells rang out clearer than ever before. We had left three graves behind us. How many more were we destined to leave by the side of our track? The funeral procession was rapidly approaching the churchyard.

Islam Bai went on first, compass in hand. The five camels were led by Mohammed Shah and Kasim. Yollchi followed close behind the last camel and urged on the string. Dead tired and tortured by a consuming thirst, I staggered on a long way behind in the rear of the caravan. Down they went out of sight behind each sand-hill in turn; then up they mounted again to the crest of the next after it. The echo of the camels' bells sounded fainter and fainter, and at longer and longer intervals, until at last they died away in the distance.

I dragged myself on a few steps further; then I fell again. I scrambled up, reeled on a short distance, and once more fell. This was repeated time after time. I could no longer hear the sound of the camels' bells.

A dead silence reigned all round me. But the caravan had left its trail behind. This I stuck to like grim death, all the time steadily counting my heavy, dragging footsteps. At length, from the summit of a dune, I once more caught a glimpse of the caravan. It had halted. The five camels were dead beat, and had thrown themselves down. Old Mohammed Shah lay flat on his face on the sand, mumbling prayers and crying to Allah for help. Kasim sat in such shade as he could find behind one of the camels, and gasped for breath. He told me, the old man was completely done up, and unable to go another step. All the way, ever since they started, he had been delirious, raving about water the whole time.

Islam Bai was a long way on ahead. We shouted to him to come back. He was now far the strongest of us all, and again proposed to hurry on on foot with the iron pitchers. He thought he could do thirty-five miles during the night. But when he saw the pitiable condition to which I was reduced, he abandoned the idea. After we had rested a while, Islam had another plan. He suggested we should seek a piece of firm ground, and use such strength as remained to us in digging a well. Meanwhile he undertook to lead the caravan. The white camel was freed of his load, consisting of the two ammunition-chests, two European saddles, and a carpet. These things we intended to leave behind. Then, with great difficulty, Islam helping me, I scrambled on the white camel's back. But the animal refused to get up. It now became clear to us all, that it was impossible to go on any longer groping our way in this fashion in the burning heat; especially as Mohammed Shah was perfectly delirious, laughing to himself, weeping, babbling, playing with the sand, and letting it run between his fingers. He was absolutely unable to go any further, and we could not of course abandon him.

We resolved therefore to remain where we were until the hottest part of the day was past; and then continue our journey in the cool of the evening and during the night. We let the camels remain where they had thrown themselves down, but took off their loads. Islam and Kasim once more put up the tent, so that we might get a little shade in the inside of it. They spread our last carpet and a couple of felts on the ground, and rolled up a sack to serve as a pillow. I then crept in, literally crept in, on my hands and knees, took off all my clothes, and lay down on the bed. Islam and Kasim followed my example, and so did Yolldash and the sheep; that is to say they too came inside the tent. Yollchi remained outside, keeping in the shade. Mohammed Shah still lay where he first fell. The poultry were the only creatures in the caravan which kept up their spirits. They sauntered about in the blazing sunshine, picking at the camels' pack-saddles and the provision bags. As yet it was only half-past nine. We had not covered more than three miles, and had an interminably long day before us. Nobody ever longed for sunset so earnestly as we did that 1st of May in the year 1895.

I was completely overcome by weariness, and scarce had strength to turn myself over in bed. At this time despair took possession of me—though never before, and never afterwards. All my past life flitted before my mind as in a dream. I thought I saw the earth, and all the noisy world of men and their doings; and they seemed to me to be at an immense distance from me, absolutely unattainable—I thought all this disappeared, and the gates of eternity stood ajar, and I felt as if in a few hours I should be standing on their threshold. I thought of my home in the Far North; and my soul was harrowed, when I pictured the uneasiness, the anxiety which would seize upon those who were near and dear to me when we never came back and nothing was heard of us. They would wait expectantly year after year, and they would wait in vain: no information would ever reach them. There would be nobody to tell the tidings of our fate. Mr. Petrovsky would of course send out messengers to inquire about us. They would go to Merket, and would there learn, that we left that place on April 10th, intending to steer our course due east. But by then our trail would be long obliterated in the sand; and it would be absolutely impossible to know in which direction we had gone. By the time a systematic and thoroughly exhaustive search could be set on foot, our bodies would probably have been buried several months under the unresting, devouring billows of sand.

After that an endless panorama of pictures from my former travels passed in succession before my mind's eye. I had travelled through all the Mohammedan countries of Asia for a whole year like a dervish, and now I had reached my last camping-ground. Fate said to me, "Thus far shalt thou go, but no farther." Here the strong pulses of my life were to cease. It was ten years ago when I first set out on my travels. I had admired the Palace of the Forty Columns at Ispahan. I had listened to the waves of the Saiendeh-rud beating against the pillars of Shah Abbas's marble bridges, and enjoyed the cool shades of Cyrus's mausoleum. In the temple halls of Xerxes and of Darius, and in the pillared arcades of Persepolis, I had learned to understand the truth of the poet's word:

> "Det härliga på jorden, förgänglig är dess lott."
> (To perish is the lot of all things here below!)

How beautiful it was to rest under the shade of the date-palms of Basrah! Would that the Tigris could offer me a few drops of its muddy water! What would I not have given the water-carrier of Bagdad for his skinful of the precious fluid, which he hawked about through her narrow streets and lanes, getting a few copper coins for an ass's load. I thought of my adventures in the land where the incidents of the *Thousand and One Nights* are every-day occurrences. Nine years previously I had left Bagdad with a caravan of Arabian merchants and Mecca pilgrims with fifty francs in my pocket, which I relied upon to take me to Teheran. But the slow rate of travel and the monotonous mode of life were too much for my patience. One dark night I ran away from the caravan, in company with an Arab to whom I gave the little money I had left.

Our horses were almost done up when we came within sight of Kermanshahan. I went to a rich Arab merchant living there, named Aga Mohammed Hassan. I remember how his eyes sparkled, when I told him I was a son of

THE CAMP OF DEATH

Charles XII.'s country. He wanted to keep me as his guest for half the year. I could only stay with him a few days; but during those few days I lived the life of Nur-ed-Din Ali in the *Thousand and One Nights.* Over against the house in which I lived there was an enchanting garden, full of sweet-scented roses and lilacs in full bloom. The paths were strewn with chips of marble, and in the middle of the garden there was a pure white marble basin filled with crystal water. From the centre of the basin a fountain shot up, a delicate rod of water, which broke at the top and fell back in a thousand drops, sparkling like a silver cobweb in the sunshine. And when at last I tore myself away from these fascinating delights, my generous host pressed into my hand a purse overflowing with silver coins.

I saw before me, every feature distinct, the noble and wise countenance of the unhappy Shah, Nasr-ed-Din, as he was when, his uniform blazing with jewels, he received King Oscar's embassy in the Imperial Palace at Teheran; and that carried my thoughts back to the Emaret Sepa Salar, where we lodged, and where of an evening we strolled underneath the spreading planes and cypresses.

All these scenes of the past flitted through my mind like a dream; but those adventures were as nothing in comparison with what we had just gone through.

Thus I lay all day long, wide awake, with my eyes open, staring at the white covering of the tent, without fixing my gaze upon any one definite object, but seeing everything in a blurred confused chaos. Once or twice only did my vision grow dim and faint, and my thoughts muddled; that was when I dropped off in a half slumber. In these few odd moments I imagined myself resting again on the green meadow-grass under the shade of the silver poplars. How bitter was the awakening to reality! When I came to myself, I fancied I was lying in my coffin. The funeral procession had reached the churchyard; the funeral bells had ceased their lugubrious tolling; the graves were almost ready; the next sandstorm would shovel them up level with sand. Who amongst us would be the first to die? Who would be the unhappy wretch that should die last—whose lungs would be filled with the pestilential stench from the corpses of his comrades? God grant, the end may come quickly—that I may not be over-long tortured with this fearful bodily torment—this fearful mental anguish!

The hours followed one after another as slowly as dying camels in a desert-wrecked caravan. I kept looking at my watch; every interval between looking seemed like an eternity. But stay—what was that? My body was bathed in a sudden coolness, so refreshing, so comforting! The tent-flap was rolled up. It was noon. Yes, a faint breeze was flitting across the overheated sand-dunes. But faint though it was, it was strong enough for my sensitive skin to feel it. It continued to grow stronger and stronger, until, about three o'clock, it became so fresh that I was obliged to draw a felt covering over me.

Shortly afterwards something happened which I can only look upon as a miracle. As the sun drew nearer and nearer to the horizon, so did my strength gradually return; and by the time he rested like a glowing cannon-ball on the tops of the dunes in the west, I was completely recovered. My body had regained all its former elasticity. I felt as if I could walk for days and days. I burned with impatience to be up and doing. I *would* not die. The thought of how the dear ones at home would miss me; the thought of how they would mourn for me; and how it would grieve them, if they were unable to send a wreath to be placed on my unknown grave—these were the thoughts that tormented me most. I resolved therefore during the immediately following days to strive my uttermost to keep going—going—going, to drag myself on, creep on all fours if I could not get on in any other way, but at all costs to keep struggling—struggling on towards the east, even though all my men—all my caravan should long have given up and died. The temptation to just lie there and wait—for oh how delicious it is to rest when you are dead tired! You quickly slumber off, and forget all your pains and anxieties in a long, heavy sleep, out of which you never wake again—this temptation I now put from me finally once and for all.

At sunset Islam Bai and Kasim both revived. I told them my resolve. They were both of the same mind as I was. Mohammed Shah still lay where he had fallen. Yollchi lay on his back in the shade of the tent. Both were delirious; neither answered when we spoke to them, but kept on muttering incoherently and confusedly to themselves. After twilight set in, Yollchi moved; and as his senses returned, the wild animal in him awoke. He crept up to where I was lying, shook his fist at me, and in a discordant, hollow, threatening voice, cried, "Water! water! Give us water, sir!" Then he began to weep, fell on his knees before me, and in a whining tone of entreaty begged me to give him a little water—just a few drops. What could I say to him? I reminded him, that he had stolen half of our last supply, that he had had more than the rest of us, and had been the last to get a good drink; consequently he ought to hold out the longest. Half choking with ill-suppressed sobs, he crept away.

Was there *no* means of imparting moisture to our bodies before we left this hateful spot—even though it were only a moistening of the lips and throat? We were all suffering incredible agonies of thirst, the men more than I. My eyes chanced to fall upon the cock that still remained alive. He was walking about amongst the camels with all the gravity of his kind. Why not tap and drink his blood? One of the men made an incision in the animal's neck. The blood trickled out slowly, and in small quantity. It was not enough; we wanted more. Yet another innocent life must be sacrificed. But the men hesitated a long time before they could bring themselves to slaughter our docile travelling-companion, the sheep, which had followed us through every danger with the fidelity of a dog. But I told them, it was to save our own lives, which might be prolonged a little if we drank the sheep's blood.

At length Islam, with an aching heart, led the poor creature a little to one side, turned its head towards Mecca, and, whilst Kasim tied a rope round its legs, drew his knife, and with one sweeping cut severed the arteries of the neck. The blood poured out in a thick reddish-brown stream, and was caught in a pail, where it almost immediately coagulated. It was still warm when we fell upon it with spoons and knife-blades. We tasted cautiously at first; it was repulsive. A sickening odour rose from the pail. I managed to get down a teaspoonful of the blood; but could not persuade myself to touch another drop. Even the men found it disagreeable, and offered it to Yolldash. Yolldash licked it, then went his way. We were sorry afterwards that we had killed our faithful friend to such little purpose; but it was then too late.

I understood now how thirst can make a man half insane. Islam and the other men gathered a saucepanful of the camel's urine. They poured it into an iron cup, and added vinegar and sugar; then, holding their noses, swallowed the abominable concoction. They offered the cup to me; but the mere smell nauseated me. All the others drank it except Kasim. And he was wise to abstain; for after a while the other three men were seized with violent and painful vomiting, which completely prostrated them.

Gaunt and wild-eyed, with the stamp of insanity upon him, Yollchi sat beside the tent, gnawing at the dripping sheep's lungs. His hands were bloody; his face was bloody; he was a horrible sight to look upon. I and Kasim were the only two who were fit for anything. Islam Bai pulled himself together a little, after getting rid of his nauseous draught. He and I, once more, for the last time, went through our baggage. We decided to abandon the greater part of it. I put together in a little heap such things as I considered were indispensably necessary, such as my drawings and route-plottings, specimens of rocks and of sand, maps, scientific instruments, pens, paper, the Bible and Swedish psalm-book, together with a number of other small articles. Islam Bai likewise picked out what he thought indispensable, such as provisions for three days (flour, tea, sugar, bread, and a couple of cases of preserved food). I proposed to leave behind all our Chinese silver money, half a camel load of it, amounting to nearly £280 in value. I hoped we should soon discover water; then we should be able to return and fetch what we were now putting aside. But Islam Bai would not hear of the money being left behind; and events proved that he was right. In addition to the things already mentioned, Islam found room for a couple of boxes of cigars and cigarettes, some cooking utensils, which we had brought on with us from camp No. XVII., all our weapons and a small supply of cartridges, candles, a lantern, bucket, spade, rope, and a number of similar objects.

Amongst the things left behind I may mention two heavy ammunition-chests, the tent, some felts, together with our last carpet, several cases filled with miscellaneous articles, cloth, caps, and khalats, which I had intended as presents for the native chiefs, several useful books of reference, both my photographic cameras, with over a thousand plates, of which a hundred or more had been used during our journey across the desert; further, some saddles, the medicine-chest, drawing materials, unused sketch-books, all my clothes, winter boots, winter caps, gloves, etc.

We packed up the things we were not taking with us in some eight packing-cases inside the tent, the tent-canvas being turned in underneath them, so that they might help to hold up the tent in stormy weather. We counted upon the white tent-canvas, which was visible a long way off, more especially as we pitched it on the top of a sand-hill, serving as a sign-post if we should come back in quest of the goods. I dressed myself entirely in white, from top to toe. If I was doomed to die in the sand, I wanted to be properly attired: I wanted my burial clothes to be both white and clean.

The things we deemed it indispensable to take with us were packed in five Sart *kurchins* or double wallets made of sailcloth. We stripped the camels of their pack-saddles, and put these on their backs instead. One camel carried the heavy things, such as the rifles, spades, and so forth, all wrapped up together in a *kighiz* or felt carpet.

Before starting, we opened a couple of boxes of preserved food; but although the contents were moist, we experienced the utmost difficulty in getting them down, our throats were so parched.

The camels had lain all day in precisely the same places where they fell in the morning. Their laboured breathing was the only sound that broke the deathly silence. The unhappy creatures were dying, but wore an air of indifference and resignation. Their big baggy throats were shrivelled up and of a whitish-blue colour. We had great difficulty in persuading them to get up.

CHAPTER XLVI.

THE CRISIS COMES

AT seven o'clock that evening the death-bells rang for the last time. In order to husband my strength, I rode the white camel, it being the freshest. Islam Bai, who had squandered his strength over the abominable draught he had swallowed, led the caravan at a miserably slow pace. Kasim followed in the rear, and kept urging the camels on. Thus we crawled away from the Camp of Death, steering east, ever east to where the Khotan-daria rolled on through its fresh green woods.

As we left the unhallowed spot, Yollchi crept inside the tent, and took possession of my bed, still gnawing away at the sheep's lungs, greedily—voraciously draining them of every drop of moisture. Old Mohammed Shah still lay in the same place where he fell. Before we left, I went to him, called him by his name, and placed my hand on his forehead. He glared at me, his eyes ashy-grey and wide open, and with a confused look in them; but an expression of unshaken calmness, of quiet rapture spread over his face, as though he expected the next moment to enter the pleasure-gardens of Paradise, and partake of its innumerable joys. Possibly for several days past he had seen floating before his dazed vision glimpses of Bihesht, about whose voluptuous delights he had read so many times in the Koran; and no doubt the thought of the joys to come comforted his spirit in the bitter agonies of shaking itself free from his body. No doubt he imagined his heavy life's work was done, and he had lain down to rest, and would never more toil and drudge in attending upon camels, never more wear out his old age in tramping with caravans from one city to another through the sand-wastes of East Turkestan. He looked terribly shrivelled up and wasted away, shrunk to a mummy-like old man. His copper-brown face was the only part of him that still wore any look of freshness. His breathing came very slowly and irregularly, and every now and again sighs mingled with the death ruckle which broke over his lips. Again I stroked his dry, wizened brow, placed his head in a more comfortable position, and said in as calm a tone as my emotion would allow me, that we were going to hurry on ahead, and should soon find water. We would fill the pitchers and hasten back to him. I bade him lie where he was till his strength returned; then he might come along our trail to meet us, so as to shorten the distance we should have to travel back. He tried to lift one hand, mumbling something, of which the only word I caught was "Allah." I understood only too well —and so perhaps did he—that we should never meet again. He had not many hours left to live. His eyes were dim and glazed; his slumber would pass gradually over into the deep sleep of death. He was entering upon his eternal rest, environed by the mighty silence, and by the ever-shifting sand-dunes moving on towards their mysterious goal.

With my heart bleeding and lacerated by self-reproaches at having this life upon my conscience, I dragged myself away from the dying man.

I also took farewell of Yollchi, and exhorted him to follow on along the trail of the caravan. That was the only way he could save his life. I did not upbraid him for leading us astray; nor did I reproach him with having deceived us, when he said he was well acquainted with the desert, and within four days would bring us to a place where we could get water by digging for it. What good would it have done, if I had rebuked him for putting only a four days' supply of water in the tanks instead of a ten days' supply? It would only have embittered the man's last moments; and I could not do that, I was so terribly sorry for him.

The last six hens made a tragi-comic picture, as, cackling contentedly to themselves, they feasted with every mark of satisfaction upon the carcass of the dead sheep. No doubt they had not yet missed the cock; but they would miss him afterwards.

Why did we not kill the poor things? Well, why did we not, with more reason, kill the two unhappy dying men, and so release them out of their misery? These are questions which cannot be answered at a distance. When death stands open-mouthed waiting for you, you grow less sensitive to other people's sufferings. We were all doomed. It was only a question of hours with us all; and it seemed the most natural thing in the world that the oldest and weakest should die first. And as each fresh member of the caravan collapsed and sank on the ground, it did not in the least surprise us: we merely asked ourselves, "Whose turn is it next?" To kill a human being, even though he is struggling in the agonies of death, is murder, and always must be. We did not abandon the camels without some slight hope of being able to return to them with water and save them yet. But the men could not possibly live so long. They were in fact virtually dead already. Otherwise, so long as there was the smallest chance of saving them, I should not—I could not, have left them behind. To have stayed beside them until the end came would have entailed the needless sacrifice of our own lives. We could do nothing to assuage their sufferings. For of water—the one thing they needed—the one thing that might possibly have saved their lives—we had none—absolutely not one drop. Nor could we have given them any comfort in the last dread moments: they were delirious—completely unconscious; their minds were dead already. But why did we not take them on with us? For the sufficient reason that it was physically impossible. They were much too far gone to walk; and the camels were much too weak to have carried them. Besides, even supposing the camels had been strong enough to carry them, to have taken dead men with us would, under the circumstances in which we were then situated, have been tantamount to an act of suicidal folly—an outrageous madness. Our own strength was seriously undermined. Our own lives depended upon a successful race against fast-ebbing energy and fast-running time; and we did not know how far we might have to go before we reached water—the precious life-restorer. We were stripping ourselves of everything except the barest indispensable necessaries, in order to husband our strength, to facilitate our progress, to economise time. To have burdened ourselves therefore with two helpless, hopeless sufferers, for whom we were utterly incapable of doing the least thing further, would only have been to imperil our own lives for absolutely no purpose. All the same, it wrung my heart to have to leave the unhappy men behind in the desert. My conscience was loud in its reproaches. I suffered intense agony of mind. Yet what could I do? The bitterness of that hour—it was more than I can describe: it is known to God alone!

As for the hens, I had a presentiment that they *ought* not to be killed, since they might be useful, if we did come back to fetch the tent. Besides, with the carcass of the sheep to feed upon, they would be able to preserve their lives for a long time. In this I was not wrong, as was proved in the end of May 1896, more than a year later. But I must not anticipate the natural course of events.

Meanwhile we marched on slowly, Yolldash still faithfully following us, although as lean as a skeleton. The camels' bells tolled a mournful peal for the dying veterans of the caravan. From the top of the first dune we surmounted, I turned and sent back a sigh over the Camp of Death, where my two attendants were breathing their last. The tent stood out like a sharply cut black triangle against the lighter-tinted western sky. Then I went down the dune, and it vanished from my sight. I experienced a feeling of relief, when it was no longer visible. I never looked back again.

Before us were the black night and the treacherous

ocean of sand. But I was buoyed up by an abounding energy and the joy of life. I *would not* die in the desert. I was too young. I had too much to lose. Life had still much to give me. Never before had I valued it as I did now. My travels in Asia should not end in that place. I must traverse the continent from side to side. There were numerous problems I wanted to solve before I reached my far-distant goal—Peking. Never before had I been so full of overflowing gladness, never before had my vital spirits been so buoyant with energy. I was determined I would get through, even though I should crawl it like a worm through the sand.

Our pace was slow, desperately slow. Nevertheless we kept scrambling over one high dune after another. At length another of the camels fell. He at once stretched out his legs and neck, prepared to die. We transferred his load to the back of Ak-tuya, the white camel, which seemed to be the strongest. We released the dying animal from the rope that bound him to the camel immediately in front of him, let him keep his ill-omened bell, and left him to his fate in the darkness of the night. With the other four camels we steered our way as well as we could see towards the next sand-dune.

The night was pitch dark. The stars twinkled brightly through the pure atmosphere; but their light was too faint to enable us to judge of the inequalities of the ground. We were stopped by every sand-dune we came to. For a few minutes, we had a level slope, which we got down easily enough; then all of a sudden a wall of sand would rise up immediately in front of us. The camels' strength was exhausted. Even the cool night air was incapable of revivifying them. They kept stopping incessantly. First one hung back, then another. Somehow the rope that bound them together would get loose, and one or two of the camels would lag behind, and we would go on some distance before we became aware of our loss. When we did perceive it, we had to halt, and turn back and fetch them.

Islam Bai was completely done up. He writhed in

continual pain, and was seized with repeated vomitings of an extremely violent and convulsive character; and, as his stomach was empty, they rapidly drained away what little strength he had left. Poor fellow! he suffered fearfully, writhed on the ground, and retched to such an extent that I thought he would bring up his very intestines.

Thus like worms we crawled along through the darkness. But I saw clearly, we could not go on in that way, stumbling blindly over the dunes in that happy-go-lucky fashion. I got down off my camel, lighted a lantern, and went on ahead to find out the easiest passages between the gigantic billows of the sandy ocean. I carried my compass in my hand, and steered due east. The lantern cast a faint glimmer along the steep dune-sides. But again and again I was obliged to stop and wait for the rest of the caravan. At about eleven o'clock I no longer heard the distant tinkle of the camel-bell—there was but one left now. The dense blackness of the night and a deathly silence environed me on every side. I put the lantern on the top of a dune, and lying down on the sand, tried to sleep. But not a wink could I get. I sat up and listened, holding my breath, hoping I might hear some faint far-off sound. I looked eagerly towards the east, to see if I could not catch a glimpse of a shepherd's fire, marking the forest beside the Khotan-daria. But no; there was no such beacon of hope. All was dark, silent as the grave. Nothing—nothing at all betrayed the least semblance of life. It was so still I could plainly hear my own heart beating.

At length I caught the sound of the last of the camels' bells. It sounded at longer and longer intervals; but it approached gradually nearer. When they reached the top of the dune on which I sat, Islam Bai staggered up to the lantern, fell heavily to the ground, and gasped out, that he could not take another step. His strength was totally exhausted.

Seeing that the last act of our tragic desert journey was now about to be played, and that all would soon be over,

ABANDONING THE WRECK OF OUR CARAVAN

I determined to give up *everything*, and hasten on eastwards as far as my strength would carry me. In a scarcely audible voice Islam whispered, that he could not go with me. He begged to be allowed to remain with the camels, and said he would die where he lay. I encouraged him, telling him, I was sure his strength would return after he had rested an hour or two in the cool night-air; and when it did, I solemnly *commanded* him to leave the camels and their loads—everything—and follow on in my footsteps. To this he made no answer, but lay on his back, with his mouth and eyes wide open. Then I bade him farewell, and left him, fully believing that he had but a short time to live.

Kasim was still fairly brisk. Like me, he had had the good sense to abstain from the abominable draught at the Camp of Death. The only things I took with me were the two chronometers, a bell, the compass, a penknife, a pencil, and a piece of paper, a box of matches, a pocket-handkerchief, a box of tinned lobsters, a round tin box full of chocolate, and, more by accident than by design, half a score of cigarettes. Kasim carried the spade, bucket, and rope, in case we should have to dig a well. Inside the bucket he put the sheep's fat tail, two or three pieces of bread, and a lump of coagulated sheep's blood. But in the hurry he forgot to take his cap, and when morning came, had to borrow my handkerchief, which he wound round his head, to protect himself against sunstroke.

But we were unable to derive much advantage from our wretched provisions, because our throats and their mucous membranes were parched up, as dry as the skin on our hands and faces, so that it was impossible to swallow. If we tried to get anything down, it stuck fast in our throats. We felt as if we were being suffocated and made haste to put it out. But a man who is tormented by the agonies of thirst gradually loses all sense of hunger. For the first few days the tortures of thirst are so poignant that you are on the brink of losing your senses. But when your skin ceases to perspire, or when your perspiration becomes imperceptible in consequence of the blood flowing continually thicker and slower through your veins, a rapidly increasing weakness takes possession of you, and quickly brings matters to a crisis.

It was exactly midnight when we abandoned the wreckage of our caravan, which only a few days before had made such a brave show. We were literally shipwrecked, and had to leave behind us our "ships of the desert," a prey to the merciless ocean of sand. We set out to seek the "coast"; but knew not how far we should have to travel over those rolling billows of sand before we reached it.

The four camels that now remained lay silent, resigned, patient as sacrificial lambs. They breathed heavily and with difficulty, and their long necks were stretched out flat on the surface of the dune. Islam Bai did not glance up when we left him; but Yolldash sent a wondering look after us. No doubt he believed, that we should soon come back again, perhaps with water; for the caravan was staying behind, and we never left it very far. I never saw the faithful creature again, and I missed him greatly.

I placed the lighted lantern close beside Islam, and left it there. For a little while it served us as a sort of lighthouse, telling us how far we were advancing away from it, and also guiding us in our course towards the east. But its pale rays speedily became lost behind the sand-dunes, and we were swallowed up in the night.

CHAPTER XLVII.

A DESPERATE MARCH

MAY 2nd. After leaving the death-doomed caravan behind, I felt I was freer to choose my own course. My only concern now was to keep pushing on, and to steer as straight a line as possible to the east, so as to shorten the road all I could. We marched on at a brisk pace for a good two hours without stopping; the sand continuing all the time every bit as high and heavy as it had been before. At the end of the two hours we both became so sleepy that we were forced to lie down for a while. But we were only lightly dressed. Kasim wore nothing except a simple jacket, his baggy trousers, and boots. I had on woollen underclothing, a thin suit of white cotton, a white Russian cap with a peak to it, and stiff leather top-boots. It was not long therefore before the chilly night-air woke us up. We walked on smartly till we got warm. Then the desire to sleep once more seized us, and this time with such overpowering force that we did sleep. At four o'clock the nipping air woke us up again, for it was just about dawn, and I felt chilled to the bone. We got up and walked on for five hours without stopping, that is till nine o'clock. Then, being tired, we gave ourselves an hour's rest.

Whilst we were resting, a crisp westerly breeze sprang up and cooled the air, so that we were able to go on a little way further. But by half-past eleven the heat grew so oppressive that everything turned black before our eyes, and we sank down on a dune utterly spent. There, on a steep slope facing north, where the sand was not yet heated by the sun, we rested the remainder of the day. Kasim dug out a hole immediately under the crest of the dune, going down till he came to the layers of sand that were still cool from the night-air. We took off every stitch of clothing and buried ourselves up to the neck in the sand. Then, putting up the spade, and hanging our clothes over it, we made a sort of screen to shelter our heads against the sun. And so we lay all day long, cool and comfortable; sometimes indeed we were actually cold. But the sand gradually grew warm from the heat of our bodies and from the sun-saturated atmosphere. Then we crept out of our hole, and Kasim dug a fresh one, heaping the cool sand all over me. How delicious it was! like a cold douche in the burning sunshine. We left nothing but our heads sticking out, and them we protected to some extent against sunstroke. One midge and two flies kept us company. But then they might have been blown by the wind from a great distance!

Thus we lay buried alive in the eternal sand, uttering never a word, and yet not being able to sleep. We did not move until six o'clock in the evening; then we got out of our sand-bath, dressed, and continued our journey at a slow and heavy pace, for in all probability the dry sand-bath had weakened us. Nevertheless we stuck to it doggedly, although we had innumerable stoppages, pushing on eastwards, ever eastwards, until one o'clock next morning. Then, thoroughly wearied out, we lay down and went to sleep on the top of a dune.

May 3rd. After a refreshing sleep we woke up at half-past four in the morning. We always travelled best just before sunrise, because, the air being then fresh, we were able to go long distances without stopping. That day our dying hopes once more revived, and our courage was rekindled. All of a sudden Kasim stopped short, gripped me by the shoulder, and with wildly staring eyes pointed towards the east, without uttering a word. I looked and looked in the direction towards which he pointed, but could see nothing unusual. But Kasim's eagle eye had discovered on the verge of the horizon the green foliage of a tamarisk—the beacon upon which all our hopes

THE FIRST TAMARISK

of safety were now concentrated. We steered our course straight for the solitary tree, taking the utmost precautions not to lose its bearings. Every time we dipped into the hollow between two sand-dunes we of course lost sight of it; but immediately we climbed the next dune, there it was still before us, and we were approaching nearer and nearer to it! At length we reached it. Our first act was to thank God for bringing us so far safe.

We revelled in the fresh greenness of the tree, and like animals chewed away at its sappy leaves. It was really alive. Its roots evidently went down to the water stratum; we were now within reasonable distance of open water. The tamarisk shot up from the top of a sand-dune, and there was not a yard of flat hard ground to be seen anywhere near it. A strange existence these tamarisks (*Tamarix elongata*) lead. Their branches and tough, elastic stems, seldom exceeding seven feet in height, are bathed in burning sunshine; while their roots penetrate to an almost incredible depth, and like syphons suck up nourishment from the subterranean supplies of moisture. In fact that solitary tree reminded me of a water-lily swimming as it were on the billowy surface of the desert ocean. Merely to look at the tamarisk was a pleasure, and to stretch our parched and weary limbs beneath its sparse shade for a little was rapture indeed. It was the olive-branch, telling us that there was an end to the sandy ocean after all—the outermost islet of the Skärgård* or skerry fence, proclaiming to the shipwrecked mariners the near proximity of the coast. I gathered a handful of leaves, which were not unlike the needles of the pine, and thoroughly enjoyed the sweet fresh scent they gave off. My hopes now rose higher than they were before, and with our courage renewed we again pushed on towards the east.

By this the dunes had decreased in height, reaching not much above thirty feet. In one of the hollows we came across two small, scanty patches of kamish or reeds (*Lasiagrostes splendens*); we plucked the wiry stalks and

* The belt of islands which fringes the eastern coast of Sweden.

chewed them. At half-past nine we came to another tamarisk, and saw several more farther on. But our energy was paralyzed by the intense heat, and we dropped exhausted in the shade of the bush; and as we had done the day before, dug a hole in the sand and buried ourselves in it naked.

For nine mortal hours we lay as if dead. Kasim hardly had strength enough to cover me with fresh sand. At seven o'clock we started again in the twilight, at first with tottering limbs. After walking for three hours, Kasim stopped short again, exclaiming "Tograk!" (poplar). I saw something dark looming up two or three dunes ahead; and sure enough he was right. It was three fine poplar trees, with their leaves full of sap. But the leaves were so bitter that we could not chew them: we rubbed our skin instead until it became moist.

We were so completely spent, that we lay for a couple of hours utterly incapable of making a closer examination of the locality. We began to dig a well close to the tree-roots. But we had to stop. We literally had not strength enough to do it: the spade kept turning in our hands and falling out of them. The sand was scarcely damp at all; the water was clearly a long way down. Nevertheless we hung about the place a little while, and tried to scratch the sand away with our hands; but we soon found we could not do much that way, and gave up the idea of digging a well.

Our next plan was to gather together in a heap all the dry branches we could find round about the poplars, and set fire to them, making a huge flaming bonfire, which flung its ruddy glare a long way across the dunes. Their tops, catching the murky gleam, looked like ghosts stalking out of the darkness. Our object in making the bonfire was, partly to give a signal to Islam Bai, supposing he was still alive, which however I very seriously doubted, and partly to give the alarm to anybody who might chance to be travelling from Khotan to Ak-su, by the road that runs down the left side of the Khotan-daria.

Our purpose being a good one, we kept up the fire with feverish energy for fully two hours. Then we left it to die out of its own accord. Kasim fried a slice of the sheep's tail, and after very great exertions managed to swallow it. I had but little better fortune with the lobsters. The rest of our "provisions" we left behind us, not wishing to burden ourselves unnecessarily. But I took the empty chocolate tin with me. I was going to drink the water of the Khotan-daria out of it! After that we had a good sleep beside the fire, which prevented us from feeling the chilliness of the night.

May 4th. We began to move at three o'clock in the morning, and at four o'clock made a start. Then, with our strength drooping at every step, and our legs tottering under us, and with innumerable halts, we stumbled on till nine o'clock. Then the desert ocean once more opened its ravenous jaws before us, and appeared to be waiting with malicious joy the fatal moment when it should devour us. After the three poplars, we saw no more; and the tamarisks were so few and far between, that we could scarcely see from one to the other. Our courage began to sink; we began to be afraid it was merely a depression we had passed, and that we should soon be engulfed again in the everlasting sea of sand. At nine o'clock we fell helpless at the foot of a tamarisk, and there we lay, exposed to the burning sun, for ten mortal hours.

Kasim was sinking fast. He was incapable of digging a hole in the sand to lie in; and, as he was also unable to cover me with cool sand, I suffered terribly from the heat. All day long we never spoke a word. Indeed, what was there we could talk about? Our thoughts were the same, our apprehensions the same. The fact is we really could not talk; we could only whisper or hiss out our words.

Where now were the sandstorms which a week ago interposed such a perfect screen between us and the sun? We looked in vain for the black cloud, which alone could shield us from the coppery glow. Sun and desert had conspired together for our destruction.

But even that long weary day had an end; the sun once more dipped down towards the west. By a desperate effort I roused myself, shook the sand off my body, which looked as if it were encased in tight-fitting parchment of a reddish-brown colour. I dressed myself, and called upon Kasim to come with me. He gasped in reply, that he was unable to go any further, and with a gesture of despair gave me to understand, that he considered all was lost.

I went on alone, alone with the night and the everlasting sand. It was still as the grave, and the shadows seemed to me to be darker than usual. Occasionally I rested on the dunes. Then it was I realized how lonely I was, alone with my conscience and the stars of heaven, which shone as brilliantly as electric lamps. They alone kept me company; they were the only things I saw and knew; and they inspired in me the conviction, that it was not the valley of the shadow of death I was walking through. The air was perfectly still, and cold; I could have heard the faintest sound a long way off. I placed my ear close down upon the sand, and listened; but I heard nothing except the ticking of the chronometers, and the faint and sluggish beating of my own heart. There was not a sound to indicate there was any other living creature throughout all the wide universe of space.

I lit my last cigarette. The others we had smoked the day before; and so long as they lasted, they had to some extent stilled the tortures of thirst. I generally smoked the first half, and gave the rest to Kasim. He puffed and sucked away at the paper mouthpiece for a long time, and declared it did him a world of good. But that last cigarette I finished myself, for I was absolutely alone.

May 5th. I dragged myself on and on until half-past twelve, when I sank down under a tamarisk. After trying in vain to kindle a fire, I dosed off.

But what was that? There was a rustling in the sand. I heard footsteps. I saw a human figure gliding past in the darkness. "Is that you, Kasim?" I asked. "Yes, sir," he answered. The coolness of the night had revived him, and he had followed in my footsteps. The meeting cheered us both, and we continued our way for a time in the pitch-dark night.

But our strength was rapidly deserting us, our legs tottered under us; we struggled hard against weariness, against the desire for sleep. The steep faces of the dunes now looked almost exclusively towards the east. I slid down them. I crept long distances on my hands and knees. We were growing indifferent; our spirits were flagging. Still we toiled on for life — bare life. Then imagine our surprise, our amazement, when on the long sloping surface of a dune we perceived human footsteps imprinted in the sand! Down we went on our knees and examined them. There was no doubt of it. They were the footprints of human beings. Somebody had travelled that way. Surely we could not be very far from the river now; for what could bring people out into the sandy waste? In an instant we were wide awake. But Kasim thought, that the trail looked wonderfully fresh. "Just so," I rejoined, "that is not at all strange. There has been no wind for several days. Perhaps our signal fire of the night before last has been seen by some shepherd in the forest beside the river, and he has come a little way into the desert to ascertain what was the cause of it."

We followed up the trail till we came to the top of a dune, where the sand was driven together in a hard compact mass, and the footprints could be more distinctly made out.

Kasim dropped on his knees; then cried in a scarcely audible voice, "They are our own footsteps!"

I stooped down and convinced myself that he was right. The footprints in the sand were plainly enough caused by our own boots, and at regular intervals beside them were the marks of the spade; for Kasim had used it as a staff to support himself by. It was a discouraging discovery. How long had we been going round and round in a circle? We comforted ourselves with the assurance, that it could not possibly have been very long. It was only during the last hour, that I had been so overcome with sleep that I forgot to look at the compass. But we had at any rate had enough of tramping for a while, and at half-past two in the morning lay down and slept beside the track.

We awoke at daybreak, and pushed on again. It was then ten minutes past four. Kasim was a fearful object to look at. His tongue was white, dry, and swollen, his lips bluish, his cheeks sunken, his eyes dull and glassy. He suffered from a convulsive hiccough, which shook him from top to toe; it was like the singultus or hiccough of death. He had hard work to stand up; but he did, and managed somehow to follow me.

Our throats were on fire with the hot dryness. We fancied we could hear our joints grating, and thought they would catch fire from the friction of walking. Our eyes were so dried up, that we were scarcely able to open and shut them.

When the sun rose, we turned our eager eyes towards the east. The horizon was sharp and distinct, and had a different outline from what we were accustomed to see. It was no longer denticulated as if formed of innumerable series of ridges of sand; it was a horizontal line, showing scarce perceptible inequalities. After going a little further, we perceived that the horizon was edged with a black border. What joy! What blessed fortune! It *was* the forest that lined the bank of the Khotan-daria. We *were* approaching it at last.

Shortly before five o'clock we came to a *darah* (strictly speaking, valley) or depression in the sand, and I soon arrived at the conclusion, that it was a former bed of the river. Numerous poplars grew in its lowest part. There must be water not very far below them. Once more we seized the spade; but we had not strength enough to dig. We were forced to struggle on again towards the east. We travelled at first across a belt of low, barren sand. But at half-past five we entered the thick, continuous forest. The trees were in full foliage, and their leafy crowns filled the forest beneath with gloomy shadows. After all we were not to lose our spring, the season dedicated to hope!

With my hand to my brow, I stood riveted to the spot by the marvellous sight. It cost me an effort to collect my senses. I was still half giddy, as if newly awakened from a hideous dream, or distressing nightmare. For weeks we had been dragging ourselves, slowly dying by inches, through the valley of the shadow of death, and now!—All around us, in whichever direction we turned our eyes, life and springtime, the singing of birds, the scent of the woods, green leaves in every variety of tint, refreshing shade, and over there, amongst the hoary patriarchs of the forest, innumerable spoor of wild animals—tigers, wolves, deer, foxes, antelopes, gazelles, hares. The air was alive with flies and midges; beetles went whizzing past us as swift as arrows, their wings humming like the notes of an organ; and the morning-songs of the birds trilled from every branch.

The wood grew denser and denser. At intervals the stems of the poplars were entwined with creepers; and our progress was often interrupted by impenetrable labyrinths of dead trees, branches, and brushwood, or equally often by dense thickets of thorny bushes.

At ten minutes past seven the forest grew thinner. We saw between the trees indistinct traces of both men and horses. But it was impossible to determine how old they were; for the forest protected them against the obliterating effects of the sandstorms. What joy! what bliss! I felt —I was sure, we were saved now.

I suggested that we should go straight through the forest, steering due east, for in that direction the river could not be very far away. But Kasim thought, that the trail, which undoubtedly marked a road of some kind, would gradually lead us to the river banks. And, as the trail was easy to follow, and kept all the time in the shade, I adopted Kasim's suggestion.

Weak and struggling, we followed the trail towards the south; but by nine o'clock we were completely done up by the tropical heat, and dropped on the ground in the shade of two or three poplars. With my naked hands I scratched out a hole between the roots, and lay there, tossing and turning all day long from the heat, without being able to sleep a wink. Kasim was stretched out on his back, muttering deliriously and moaning to himself; nor did he answer when I spoke to him, not even when I shook him.

The day seemed as if it would never end. My patience was tried to the uttermost; for I felt certain the river must be in our immediate vicinity, and I was dying to get to it.

It was seven o'clock before I was able to dress myself. I called upon Kasim to come with me to the water. But he was beaten at last. He shook his head, and with a gesture of despair, signed to me to go on alone, drink, and bring back water to him. Otherwise he would just die where he lay.

I took off the blade of the spade and hung it on a branch which stretched across the path, so that I might be able to find again the point where we entered the forest; for I now had hopes of being able to recover the baggage we had left behind: we had only to go due west from the place where we struck the forest and we should come to it. I considered that Islam and the other men were already dead. The spade-shaft I took with me. It would be a staff to help me along, and would also serve as a weapon if I wanted one.

I cut right across the forest, still directing my course to the east. It was anything but easy work. Two or three times I very nearly got stuck fast in the thorny bushes. I tore my clothes, and scratched my hands. I rested unceasingly on roots and fallen tree-trunks; I was fearfully tired. Twilight came on. It grew dark. It cost me almost inconceivable efforts to keep awake. Then all at once the forest came to an end, as abruptly as though it had been smitten by fire, and to the east stretched a dead level plain of hard, consolidated clay and sand. It lay five or six feet below the level of the forest, and showed not a single trace of a sand-dune. I recognized it at once; it could not possibly be anything but the bed of the Khotan-daria. And I soon had my

CRAWLING THROUGH THE FOREST IN SEARCH OF WATER

inference confirmed. I came across the trunks and branches of poplar trees, half buried in the ground; I noticed furrows and sharply broken edges a foot high or more, all evidently due to the action of a running stream. But the sand was as dry as the sand in the desert dunes. The river-bed was empty, waiting for the summer floods to come down from the mountains.

It was inconceivable that I should perish in the very bed of the river I had been so long and so desperately seeking; that I could not believe. I called to mind the tendency of the Yarkand-daria to shift its channel to the east, and recollected the ancient river-bed we had crossed in the forest. Very likely the Khotan-daria obeyed the same tendency. Very likely *its* current clung by preference to the eastern bank; I must therefore find it, if I would find the deepest places in the river-channel. I resolved to cross over to the other side before I gave up all hope.

I now changed my course to due south-east. Why so? Why did I not keep on towards the east, as I had always done hitherto? I do not know. Perhaps the moon bewitched me; for she showed her silver crescent in that quarter of the heavens and shed down a dim, pale blue illumination over the silent scene. Leaning on the spade-shaft, I plodded away at a steady pace in a straight line towards the south-east, as though I were being led by an unseen, but irresistible, hand. At intervals I was seized by a traitorous desire to sleep, and was obliged to stop and rest. My pulse was excessively weak; I could scarcely discern its beats. I had to steel myself by the strongest effort of will to prevent myself from dropping off to sleep. I was afraid that if I did go off, I should never waken again. I walked with my eyes riveted upon the moon, and kept expecting to see its silver belt glittering on the dark waters of the stream. But no such sight met my eyes. The whole of the east quarter was enshrouded in the cold night mist.

After going about a mile and a half, I was at length

able to distinguish the dark line of the forest on the right bank of the river. It gradually became more distinct as I advanced. There was a thicket of bushes and reeds; a poplar blown down by the wind lay across a deep hole in the river-bed. I was only a few yards from the bank when a wild-duck, alarmed by my approach, flew up and away as swift as an arrow. I heard a splash, and in the next moment I stood on the brink of a little pool filled with fresh, cool water—beautiful water!

CHAPTER XLVIII.

HUMAN BEINGS AT LAST

IT would be vain for me to try to describe the feelings which now overpowered me. They may be imagined; they cannot be described. Before drinking I counted my pulse: it was forty-nine. Then I took the tin box out of my pocket, filled it, and drank. How sweet that water tasted! Nobody can conceive it who has not been within an ace of dying of thirst. I lifted the tin to my lips, calmly, slowly, deliberately, and drank, drank, drank, time after time. How delicious! what exquisite pleasure! The noblest wine pressed out of the grape, the divinest nectar ever made, was never half so sweet. My hopes had not deceived me. The star of my fortunes shone as brightly as ever it did.

I do not think I at all exaggerate, if I say that during the first ten minutes I drank between five and six pints. The tin box held not quite an ordinary tumblerful, and I emptied it quite a score of times. At that moment it never entered my head that, after such a long fast, it might be dangerous to drink in such quantity. But I experienced not the slightest ill effects from it. On the contrary I felt how that cold, clear, delicious water infused new energy into me. Every blood-vessel and tissue of my body sucked up the life-giving liquid like a sponge. My pulse, which had been so feeble, now beat strong again. At the end of a few minutes it was already fifty-six. My blood, which had lately been so sluggish and so slow, that it was scarce able to creep through the capillaries, now coursed easily through every blood-vessel. My hands, which had been dry, parched, and as hard as wood, swelled out again. My skin, which had been like parchment, turned moist and elastic. And soon afterwards an active perspiration broke out upon my brow. In a word, I felt my whole body was imbibing fresh life and fresh strength. It was a solemn, an awe-inspiring moment.

Never did life seem to me richer, more beautiful, more valuable than it did that night in the bed of the Khotan-daria! The future smiled upon me from the midst of a magic sea of light. Life was worth living. The talk about life being a vale of misery seemed to me utter nonsense. An angel's hand had guided me through the darkness of the night to the little pool in the river-bed. I imagined I saw a heavenly being floating by my side, and thought I could hear the rustle of his wings. Never before, and never since, have I so vividly realized the sublime influence of the Eternal.

After drinking my fill, and making sure of my wonderful escape from a miserable death, and after the ecstasy had subsided which came upon me when I felt new life streaming through my veins, and as soon as my entire physical being had entered upon a more normal course, I drank several more tins of water. After that my thoughts began to flow back in ordinary channels, and I awoke to the realities of the moment, and became attentive to my immediate surroundings.

The pool was situated in the deepest part of the river-bed, near the eastern bank, and had been left behind by the preceding summer's flood. It lay therefore below the general level of the river-bed, so that I had been unable to observe it until I almost stumbled into it. Had I gone fifty paces farther to the right or fifty paces farther to the left, I should have missed it; and, as I learned afterwards, it was a long distance to the next pool both up and down the river. The merchants who are accustomed to travel every spring with their caravans between Khotan and Ak-su know where all these pools are, and always make them their camping-places for the night. Perhaps I should have lost my way,

THE AUTHOR CARRYING WATER IN HIS BOOTS, IN THE BED OF THE KHOTAN-DARIA

if I had not found the pool; perhaps my strength would not have held out until I reached the next.

The eastern bank of the river was fringed with the dry yellow reeds of the previous year, and the young, green spring sprouts were pushing themselves up between the tall close-set stalks of the old. Behind the reed-beds towered the forest, sombre and threatening, with the silver crescent of the moon hanging in the crown of a tall poplar. I sat beside the pool; and noticed that its bright surface, seen under the dark shadows of the forest, was black as ink. The pool was about twenty yards long.

Then I heard a rustling in the thicket close beside me, the sound of stealthy footsteps, and the crackling of the dry reeds as they were pushed aside. It might have been a tiger. But anyway I felt not a quiver of fear. I had just been granted a renewal of life. The mere thought of seeing a tiger's head, with its glittering eyes, peeping out of the reeds, had a sort of fascination for me. I would look into them fearlessly, and ask the beast how he durst think of taking my dearly bought life. But the intruder, whatever he was, withdrew. His footsteps died away in the reeds. Whether it was a tiger, or some other wild animal of the forest, which had come down to the pool to drink, it had at any rate deemed it prudent to remain at a distance so long as the place was haunted by a human being.

Then my thoughts flew back to Kasim, whom I left lying alone in the forest, fighting against death, unable to move a yard, still less drag himself a distance of three hours to the pool of water. He was in urgent need of immediate help. The chocolate tin was too small to carry water in: it would merely have wetted his lips. What was to be done? How was I to carry him a sufficient quantity of the life-giving elixir?

My boots! Of course; my Swedish waterproof boots. They were quite as good, quite as safe, as any other utensil. Plump they went into the pool. Then I threaded the spade-shaft through the straps, and carrying it like a yoke over my right shoulder, hastened back with a buoyant step along the track by which I came.

The boots were filled to the brim with the precious liquid that was going to give fresh life to Kasim. Some of it was spilled owing to the haste I was in; but not a drop came through the leather. Master Stjernström in Stockholm never made a pair of boots before which not only saved a man's life, but also travelled right across Asia and back again. In consequence of this my boots afterwards became in their way famous.

The moon still poured her soft mellow light along the river-bed, so that I had no difficulty in following my own footmarks through the sand. Besides, it was no longer heavy walking, my weariness had disappeared, and I almost flew towards the forest that lined the left bank. In the forest it was not so easy to get along. My socks were thin, and my feet were continually getting pricked by thorns and splinters. But a worse evil was a thick veil of cloud, caused no doubt by the rising mist, which came between the moon and me, so that the forest became pitch dark, and I lost the trail. I lighted matches, and vainly tried to rediscover it. I had recourse to my compass. I shouted "Kasim"; but my voice died away among the thousands of poplars without eliciting an answer. For a while I went on at haphazard, constantly shouting my attendant's name with all the strength of my lungs. But at last I grew tired of that aimless wandering; I was only getting lost deeper and deeper in the silent forest. I resolved therefore to stop and wait for daylight. I chose out an impenetrable thicket in which lumber, dead branches, and shrivelled tree-trunks lay heaped together in wild confusion, and set fire to them. In a trice the flames were leaping up fiercely; the dry branches crackled, spluttered, exploded. The draught from the bottom was so strong, that it whistled and sizzled, and a tall column of fire licked the trunks of the poplars standing near. It was as light as noontide: the forest, lately so black, was lit up with a reddish yellow glare. Kasim could hardly help seeing such a fire as that, or hearing its loud crackling, for he could not be any great distance away. Again I shouted out his name, and, with the light of the fire to help me, again looked for my trail; but I did not find it. I lay down flat on the sand, and watched the furious burning of the fire; and so watching fell asleep. For a couple of hours I slept calmly and well; having first taken the precaution to lie down in a spot where the fire could not reach me, yet near enough to be safe from tigers and other wild animals.

Day was breaking when I awoke. The fire had dwindled a good deal since its progress was checked by a fresh belt of live poplars, which it had only been able to blacken and scorch; and a heavy column of smoke hung over the forest. My boots, which were leaning against a tree-root, had not lost one drop of their precious contents; the earth underneath them was not even damp. I swallowed a mouthful of water, and set about looking for my trail of the night before, and now I quickly found it. When I came to Kasim, he was lying in the same position in which I left him. He glared at me with the wild, startled eyes of a faun; but upon recognizing me, made an effort, and crept a yard or two nearer, gasping out, "I am dying."

"Would you like some water?" I asked quite calmly. He merely shook his head, and collapsed again. He had no conception of what was in the boots. I placed one of the boots near him, and shook it, so that he might hear the splashing of the water. He started, uttered an inarticulate cry; and when I put the boot to his lips, he emptied it at one draught, without once stopping; and the next moment he emptied the second.

May 6th. Kasim went through the same series of changes that I had gone through the evening before. As soon as he recovered his reason, we took counsel together; and as the outcome of our deliberations, decided that our best plan was to go back to the pool, and take a good rest somewhere near it, and wash ourselves, a luxury we had not enjoyed for more than a week. But Kasim was still so weak that he was unable to keep up with me. He reeled about like a drunken man, and kept constantly sitting down. Seeing that he was on the right track for the pool, and that I could not do more for him than I had done already, I hurried on ahead. When I came to the pool, I drank and bathed; and then waited fully an hour. But Kasim did not come.

Hunger began to be importunate. It was of the first importance that I should find human beings as soon as I possibly could, both for the sake of food, and also to enlist their help to return into the desert to the assistance of Islam, and to fetch such of our goods as might be saved. In the meantime therefore I left Kasim to his fate, and hastened on at a rapid pace up the right bank, that is due south. My boots were still so wet that I was unable to get them on, and so went barefoot.

At nine o'clock there sprang up an extremely violent storm from the west, which drove clouds of sand and dust before it across the bed of the river, and darkened the sun, so that I had not the smallest occasion to complain of excessive heat. But the thick haze completely shut out every view of the surroundings, so that I could see neither the forest on my right nor that on my left. After going a stretch of about three hours, I was again tormented by thirst, for my mouth and throat were parched by the hot drift-sand and the buran (storm), and between them they nearly choked me. I turned aside into the forest and sought shelter in the undergrowth. I sat there a while, full of anxious thought. All at once it flashed across my mind, that it might be days to the next water-pool, and that it would be unwise to leave the one which I had in such a wonderful manner discovered. Moreover, I thought it would be an excellent thing to see Kasim again. I therefore turned back towards the north. But I had barely gone half-an-hour when I stumbled by chance upon a tiny pool, scarcely a yard across, and containing a little muddy water with a faintly saltish taste. I drank an enormous quantity of it. I was overcome with weariness; but did not know what was the wisest thing to do. There was water here, and I had no immediate

"WOULD YOU LIKE SOME WATER?" I ASKED

use of Kasim. On the other hand, I found I was unable to travel far towards the south. Perhaps it would be best to wait, and as soon as the storm ceased, by means of signal fires, warn any persons who might chance to be travelling the forest road that ran along the river-bank.

I therefore cast about for a dense thicket close to the pool, and well protected from the storm. Placing my boots and cap under my head for a pillow, I slept deeply and heavily—the first good sound sleep I had had since 1st May. When I awoke, it was already dark and the storm still roared through the forest. It was eight o'clock in the evening. After another good drink out of the pool, I made a big bonfire, and sat down beside it, and stared into the flames for a long time. But I was tormented by the pangs of hunger. With the view of cheating my stomach a little, I gathered some grass and shoots of reed, and a bunch of young frogs out of the pool. The frogs were refractory; so I gave them a nip at the back of the head and swallowed them whole. After "supper" I scraped together a big pile of dry branches to feed the fire with during the night.

If only I had had Yolldash with me to keep me company! Perhaps he was still alive, and had followed our trail to the river. I whistled as loudly as I could, whistled again and again. But no Yolldash came scampering up. Then I dropped off again.

May 7th. The storm had ceased, although the atmosphere was still heavily charged with dust. This "black buran" suggested a gloomy and depressing idea. It was the first since the caravan collapsed. It had come to cast the first shovelfuls of earth over my dead attendants and the camels, and it would blot out every trace of our trail through the sand; so that Islam Bai, supposing he still lived, would perhaps never be able to find us. But then again, he had a compass. And even supposing we did come across men, and supposing they were willing to go with us into the desert as far as the tent, we should now experience the utmost difficulty in finding it, seeing that we could no longer retrace our footsteps through the sand.

Then I thought of another thing. There was not a single trace of human beings in that immediate locality, not a sign of anybody having passed that way at all recently. Perhaps nobody travelled that way during the hot season? If I waited there for help, I might perchance die of hunger before help came. My last examination of Przhevalsky's map seemed to show that we should strike the river in the district called Buksem, about 25 Swedish, or 150 English, miles from the town of Khotan. If I went well, I ought to travel that distance in six days.

To decide was to act. At half-past four off I started. I followed the middle of the river-bed in as straight a line as I could; and as a consequence of the almost dead level, the channel was pretty nearly straight, and varied from half a mile to two miles in width. I took the precaution to fill my boots with water; but at the end of some hours my feet were so sore and blistered, that I was obliged to try and protect them by doubling my socks over them and by bandaging them in strips of my shirt.

After a while I came upon another small pool, containing fresh water. I emptied my boots of the brackish water I was carrying, and filled them with the sweet. After that I followed the left bank of the stream, and there to my great joy discovered a sheepfold constructed of branches of trees. But upon examining it, I saw it was a long time since it had been used. In the river-bed close beside it I perceived signs of a well having been dug.

Weariness and the heat of the day combined drove me, about half-past eleven, into the shelter of the forest. There I halted, gathered young reed-shoots and grass, cut them up fine, and mixed them with water in the chocolate tin. That was my breakfast.

After noon I went on again hour after hour, until I really could go no longer. It was eight o'clock when I stopped, and made my fire, and "camped."

May 8th. I started before daybreak, still keeping to the left bank, which ran towards the south-south-west. Strange I did not meet anybody! Perhaps the caravan-road lay deeper in the forest, so that I might easily pass people without seeing them. I thought I had better go and look; so I crossed through the forest, going due west. It was only about half a mile wide, and on the other side of it I came upon that terrible ocean of yellow sand, which I knew so well, and now fled from with horror. Another hour later, the sand-dunes, which stretched from north-north-west to south-south-east, came down in several places close to the brink of the river. Along the edge of the desert there were poplars growing singly and at wide intervals apart. Overcome by the heat, I threw myself down under the shade of one of them to rest. On my way to that point I had passed no less than eight small pools; in most of them however the water had a faint saltish taste.

After resting a couple of hours, I continued my solitary journey towards the south. If there was a caravan-road alongside the river, it was manifest it did not follow the left bank, for nobody would travel through the sand-dunes unless they were compelled to do so. I must cross over and see what promise there was in the forest on the right bank. At this place the river-bed was about a mile and a quarter wide. But I found no caravan-track in the forest on the right bank either. I therefore went back to the river-bed, and travelled close beside the bank and the edge of the forest. About 350 yards further on there were two small islands in the river, covered with bushes and poplars; and between the southern island and the river-bank I perceived, shortly before sunset, the fresh footmarks of two barefooted men, who had gone that way, but in the opposite direction, that is towards the north, driving four donkeys before them.

Footprints of human beings! A remarkable, an encouraging sight! I was not absolutely alone, then, in that inhospitable region. The footprints were so fresh that every detail of the men's feet was plainly marked in the sand. At the most they could not be more than a day old.

Strange I had not met them, seeing that we were travelling in opposite directions. But perhaps they rested during the day and only travelled at night? Where had they come from? Where were they going to? Where was their last camp? Was it in a dwelling-place of men, or was it merely by the side of a pool in the river? To follow them up would have served no purpose, for they had too long a start of me; I should never be able to catch them up. I had no alternative therefore but to follow the trail in the opposite direction. I observed the impressions of these human feet with the greatest interest and attention; and led on by them, I hurried along southwards, keeping close to the right bank of the Khotan-daria.

CHAPTER XLIX.

WITH THE SHEPHERDS OF THE KHOTAN-DARIA

TWILIGHT was beginning to spread its dusky wings over the silent scene, when, as I was passing a projecting headland, I thought I heard a wonderful sound. I stood stock-still; I held my breath and listened. But all was silent as before. I concluded, it must have been a thrush or some other bird which had several times startled me already, and made me stop and listen. But no; there it was again, an unmistakeable shout; and it was immediately followed by the lowing of a cow, a voice which in my ears was welcomer than the singing of a prima donna.

I hurriedly pulled on my wet boots, so as not to look like a madman, and with my heart in my mouth hurried in the direction from which the sounds proceeded. I pushed my way through thorny thickets, I jumped over fallen tree-trunks, I stumbled, I tripped again and again, I forced myself through dense beds of kamish, through heaps of crackling branches. The farther I went, the more distinctly I heard the voices of men talking, and the bleating of sheep, and through an opening in the forest I caught a glimpse of a flock of sheep grazing. A shepherd with a long staff in his hand was keeping watch over them; and when he perceived me, in my tattered clothes and blue spectacles, breaking out of the tangled thickets, he was not a little startled and amazed. Probably he took me for a goblin of the forest, or an evil spirit from the desert, who had lost his way and wandered thither by mistake. He stood as though rooted to the spot with terror, and could do nothing but stare at me open-mouthed. I greeted him with the usual "*Salaam aleikum!*" (Peace be with you!), and began to tell him in a few words how I came thither. But he turned abruptly on his heel, and disappeared into the nearest thicket, leaving his sheep to their fate.

After a while he came back in company with an older shepherd, who was more amenable to reason. I greeted him in the same way as I had done the first man, with "*Salaam aleikum!*" Then I told him the whole story of my journey across the desert. When I said, that I had eaten nothing for a week, and asked them for a piece of bread, they led me to a hut close by, constructed of branches, and scarcely five feet high. I sat down on a ragged felt carpet, and the younger shepherd brought out a wooden platter, with some freshly baked maize bread. I thanked them, then broke off a piece and began to eat; but I had not eaten above half-a-dozen mouthfuls when I turned suddenly faint. The shepherds gave me a pan of sheep's-milk, which tasted excellent. After that they went away, and left me for a little while alone, except that two big dogs stayed behind and barked at me unceasingly.

Soon after dark, the two men returned to the hut, accompanied by a third shepherd. Meanwhile the sheep had been driven into the sheepfold, to protect them from tigers and wolves during the night. I and the three shepherds slept under the open sky beside a big fire.

May 9th. At daybreak the shepherds went off with their flocks. Their hut stood on a little hill on the edge of the forest, and through the trees commanded a view of the Khotan-daria. A small creek came close up to the hut, and in it was a pool of fresh water. But in addition to that, the shepherds had digged a well in the bed of the river, so that they had a plentiful supply of good, clear water.

At noon the three men brought back their flocks, so that they might rest around the well during the hottest part of the day. This gave me an opportunity to become better acquainted with my hosts. Their names were Yussuf Bai, Togda Bai, and Pasi Akhun; and they were pasturing 170 sheep and goats, besides 60 cattle, belonging to a bai (rich man) in Khotan. Winter and summer alike they lay out in the woods with their flocks, and for their monotonous work were paid collectively only 20 tengeh* (or 9 shillings) a month, together with maize meal and bread. After their flocks had eaten up all the grass in one pasture-ground, they moved on to another; and in each fresh place they came to, they built a hut, unless there was one there already, left standing from the previous year. They had been only five days in the spot where I found them; and they were shortly going to a better place. The district as a whole was called Buksem (Close Tangled Wood).

The life these shepherds lead must be exceedingly lonely and devoid of pleasure, and one day remarkably like another; yet they looked both cheerful and contented. Togda Bai was married; but his wife lived in Khotan. When I asked him, why she did not accompany him into the forest, he told me that the Chinese, who sometimes travelled that way, would persist in molesting the native women, so that for this reason he preferred to be alone. Once or twice a year however he got leave to go into the town to see his wife. My arrival at their camp was clearly an important event in their monotonous life. All the same, they looked askance at me; it was evident they regarded me as a suspicious character. But their suspicion was to some extent disarmed by the fact that I was able to speak their own language, and readily conversed with them.

They lived almost exclusively upon maize bread, water, and tea, this last strongly flavoured with pepper. Twice a day they baked a large loaf, and divided it between them. They mixed the maize flour with water and salt, kneaded the dough and shaped it in a circular wooden vessel or dish, then spread it out in the form of a flat cake upon the glowing embers, and covered it up with hot ashes. In three-quarters of an hour it was cooked, and tasted exquisitely. I fairly revelled in it; and the shepherds were generous, despite the fact that they knew perfectly well, I had not a single tengeh to give them in return.

* A tengeh of Khotan is equivalent to two tengeh of Kashgar; and a tengeh of Kashgar is worth about 2¾*d.*

Their personal belongings were not many. They consisted, in the first place, of the clothes they wore, namely a *chapan* or outer coat, a *telpek* or sheepskin cap with the wool on the outside, a *belbagh* or girdle, in which they carried their utensils for making tea. Their lower extremities were swathed in long bandages, and their feet encased in pieces of sheepskin fastened on with cord. Besides their clothes, they possessed a large wooden platter (*kazang*), another of medium size (*ayag*), and a small one (*jam*), a gourd (*kapak*) for holding water, a large ladle or spoon (*chumuch*), roughly shaped out of the root of a poplar, a felt carpet (*kighiz*), and a three-stringed guitar (*jävab*). But by far the most important of their belongings was the axe (*balta*), a most useful implement, whether they wanted to make a hut, or cut firewood, or clear a path for their flocks through the thickets, or in the spring lop off the young shoots and branches of the trees to feed their sheep and goats on. Another indispensable instrument was the steel (*chakmak*) for striking fire; but once they have got a fire lighted, they take care not to let it go out until they move on to another place. Before driving their flocks into the forest to graze, they covered up the fire with ashes; and when they came back again in the evening, they opened out the ashes, placed a few dry sticks on the embers, and quickly fanned them into a flame. But they also used dried dung for fuel. They kept their maize meal in a sack, and placed it and all their other belongings on the roof of the hut, to keep them safe from the dogs.

There was first-rate pasturage, they told me, on both banks of the river, all the way to the town of Khotan, and it grew more plentiful as the town was approached, except that in the immediate environs there were no pastures; so that the bais who owned sheep kept them all the year round in the forests that fringe both banks of the Khotan-daria. In the seasons during which the river was dry, people always travelled along the bed of the stream, which was as hard and dry as a street; and only travelled by the forest paths when driven out of the river-bed by the water.

After the noontide heat was passed, the shepherds again went off into the woods with their sheep and goats and cattle, and I was left alone, though not for long. For a caravan of about a hundred donkeys, carrying rice from Khotan to Ak-su, went past the hut. The caravan leaders rode straight on without observing me; but Pasi Akhun had seen them, and told them of my adventures. As soon as they were gone by, I went into the hut to rest; but almost immediately, hearing the rattle of stirrups and the echo of voices, I hurried out again. It was three well-to-do merchants, each riding a capital horse, on their way from Ak-su to Khotan. They had left the former place eleven days before, and hoped to reach the latter in six days more.

They came riding through the forest at a smart trot, and bore straight down upon the shepherds' hut. They hastily dismounted, and advancing towards me, without hesitation, as though they knew I was there, and had come to seek me, they politely greeted me. I invited them to sit down. Then one of them, a well-dressed man with a black beard, told me some news which beyond measure delighted me. The day before, whilst riding along the left bank of the river, some twelve hours north of Buksem, they saw a man, more dead than alive, lying by the side of a white camel, which was grazing on the border of the forest. Like the good Samaritan, they stopped and asked him what was the matter. All he could answer was to gasp out "*Su! su!*" (Water! water!). One of the merchants immediately rode off to the nearest pool, and brought the man a *kungan* (iron pitcher) full of water. The sufferer, who, I soon understood, could be nobody but Islam Bai, drained the pitcher at a single draught. They gave him bread, and raisins, and nuts to eat. He revived, and told them how he came to be there in the pitiable condition in which they found him.

Islam then begged the three merchants to look for

me; although, he said, he did not know whether I was alive or dead, for he had lost my trail two days before. If they found me, he earnestly besought them to lend me one of their horses, so that I might ride to Khotan, and rest and recover from the journey. Thereupon they looked for me all along the road, until at length they found me in the hut; and they now offered me the use of one of their horses, that I might accompany them to Khotan. But I never hesitated a moment as to the course I ought to pursue. I decided to stay where I was until Islam Bai rejoined me. Seeing that he had succeeded in bringing one of the camels out to the river, probably he had saved a portion of my belongings. Possibly my diaries and maps relating to our desert journey were not lost. Possibly we might even be able to reorganize the remnants of my shattered caravan!

My hopes as to the future began to revive and shine out in rosy colours. During the morning I had been considering the effects of the shipwreck of my caravan, and what plans I should adopt for the future, so that my journey might yield the best results possible under the circumstances. I had almost made up my mind to accompany the first best merchant that went past to Khotan, and thence go on to Kashgar, whence I could send jighits to the first Russian telegraph station with despatches for Europe for a fresh stock of instruments and a fresh equipment, and with them, and what I could effect with the rest of the capital I had left behind in Kashgar, I might travel to Lop-nor, and thence return home through Siberia. But now that Islam Bai was alive, and had brought out one of the camels, I felt certain we might make an attempt to recover the tent, and the stores we had left in it; so that, instead of curtailing my plans for the future, I began to extend them.

I therefore let the three merchants go on their way, after they had given me a good supply of wheat bread, and lent me eighteen silver tengeh (about 8*s.*). We arranged to meet again in Khotan, and settle the accounts outstanding between us. The shepherds were now thoroughly satisfied of the truth of my story, and I dropped hints that their generous services to me should not go unrewarded.

May 10th. A strong north-easterly gale loaded the atmosphere with dust. I lay and slept inside the hut all day long. The tremendous physical exertions I had undergone during the last few days of that terrible desert journey now took their revenge upon me. I felt tired to death, like an invalid who is convalescent after a year's illness.

At sunset I was awakened by the screaming of a camel, and hurried out. There came Pasi Akhun, leading Ak-tuya, the white camel, with Islam Bai and Kasim following behind him. My excellent Islam flung himself with sobs of joy on the ground before me, and clasped my feet with his hands. I at once lifted him up and bade him calm his emotion. In his own mind he had as little expected to see me as I had expected to see him.

The white camel was laden with two *kurchins* (double wallets of canvas). One of them contained all my instruments (except those for measuring altitudes), my drawings, and itinerary notes, paper, pens, and such like; the other the Chinese silver money, the lantern, teapot, cigarettes, and several other things. Moreover Islam had saved the two Husqvarna rifles, and brought them wrapped up in a felt.

Islam ate a piece of bread, and rallied a bit, and then told me his story. For several hours after we left him on the night of May 2nd, he lay where he fell; but finally he managed to get up and follow our trail, though very slowly, for the four camels, which he brought along with him, resisted being urged along. Later on in the evening of May 3rd, he saw the big signal fire, which we made beside the three poplars; but it was a great way off. However it gave him fresh courage, for by it he knew, not only that we were alive, but that we had reached the outskirts of the forest, perhaps discovered water. He reached the three poplars on the morning of May 4th, and observed the marks of our abortive attempt to dig a well. But as the day was oppressively hot, he stayed several hours in the shade of the poplars. With his axe he blazed the bark of one of the trees, and sucked out of the wound fully a cupful of sap, which both quenched his thirst and strengthened him. There he left one camel-load of goods. On May 5th he continued to press on in our footsteps, and on the following day arrived at the first dry river-bed, where he again observed our unsuccessful attempt at a well. There he lost one of the camels, the one which had been freed from its load. The animal broke loose, and of its own accord went off towards the east. Up to that point Yolldash, although dying, had dragged himself along after the caravan; but from that time Islam never saw him again, and therefore concluded he must be dead. On May 7th my riding-camel Boghra fell, and about an hour later Nähr also. The latter carried all the instruments for measuring altitudes, cigars, tea, sugar, candles, and some macaroni. At last Islam succeeded in reaching the river with the white camel; but when he saw it was dry, he gave way to despair, and deliberately lay down to die, calmly and in peace. That was on the morning of May 8th; and as if by a miraculous interposition, at noon on that same day the three merchants came that way, saw him, and gave him bread and water, and he was saved. Shortly after that, he fell in with Kasim, who told him, that I had got on splendidly, but that he had not the slightest idea where I had gone to. Kasim was stupid enough to say, he believed I had gone to the north, towards Ak-su; but Islam was fortunately sharper-witted, and decided to look for me towards the south, in the direction of Khotan. Then he met Pasi Akhun, whom I had sent in quest of him, and now—there he was.

Thus, as will be seen, Islam Bai had acted like a hero; for whilst I and Kasim thought only of ourselves, he had done his utmost to save that portion of my belongings to which he knew I attached the greatest value. He had therefore gradually transferred them all to the back of the white camel, which still continued to be the strongest. Thanks to Islam, I was now in a position to carry out my journey as it was originally planned. Two and a half years later, after Islam Bai reached his native town of Osh in Fergana, King Oscar rewarded him with a gold medal.

That evening round a big fire near the shepherds' hut we celebrated our escape from the clutches of the desert in a "sumptuous" feast. After many "ifs" and "buts" Pasi Akhun allowed himself to be persuaded to sell us a sheep for thirty-two tengeh (about 15*s.*). It was at once slaughtered. I had a *chesslik* (steak) of kidneys, grilled over the glowing fire; whilst the men boiled some of the choicer parts in a pot. By this my pulse had risen to sixty. But it was only three days later, when I had properly rested and recovered, that it got up to eighty-two.

May 11th. The grass in that locality being all finished, the shepherds proposed to move to "other pastures green," about six miles down the river, and on the right bank. We loaded our belongings on Ak-tuya, and went with them. We pitched our camp on a little mound which stood beside the river, and was surrounded by thickets and kamish, and overhung by some ancient poplars. Between two of the poplars my attendants made me a forest hut; its frame consisting of branches, whilst the walls and roof were formed of boughs twisted and laced together. It afforded splendid protection against the sun, and was further sheltered by the adjacent trees. The ground inside was levelled and spread with felt carpets. The sailcloth knapsacks, which contained the pieces of Chinese silver money, were my pillow; a small wooden cigarette box served me for table. My instruments, map portfolios, drawing-books, and writing-materials lay in convenient disorder at the foot of one of the poplars. Considering our circumstances, I could not have wished things better. I was perfectly comfortable and cosy in my forest-hut, quite as comfortable as if I had been in my own study in Stockholm.

Islam and Kasim made themselves at home beside the usual fire, underneath a third poplar. The shepherds quartered themselves with their flocks in the reeds close by. Twice a day Pasi Akhun brought me a bowl of rich milk and a piece of maize bread, and I had sufficient tobacco to last a couple of weeks. The most consummate epicure never got richer enjoyment out of life than I did during the days that followed; and yet my lonely life in the forest bore not a little resemblance to the existence which Robinson Crusoe led on his island.

May 12th. Shortly after one o'clock we perceived a small caravan approaching our camp from the north. They were advancing along the bed of the river, but were still a long way off; and we impatiently awaited their arrival. Islam and Kasim hastened down to the river-side, so as to call to them and guide them to the hut. They turned out to be a party of four merchants, belonging to Khotan, who left the town of Kucha thirteen days earlier. They had gone thither some time before with a supply of grapes, which they sold, and with the money the grapes fetched they had bought ten horses, some donkeys, and a cow, and were now taking the animals to Khotan, where they expected to make a good price of them.

They told me, that at Sil, the place where the Yarkand-daria was joined by the Khotan-daria, the former river contained so much water, that it reached up to the waist of a man on horseback. All the way up there were small pools in the bed of the Khotan-daria, and failing them, it was always easy to get water by digging a well. The summer flood was expected in the beginning or middle of June; but it would not attain its maximum volume for from one to two months after that.

We pounced upon these four merchants like hawks, and in half an hour bought from them three first-rate horses for 750 tengeh (about £17 5*s.*), although they had only given 600 tengeh (about £13 15*s.*) for them in Kucha. Besides that we also bought three pack-saddles and bridles, a sack of maize for the horses, a bag of wheat-flour for ourselves, a pair of boots for Islam, who had gone barefoot ever since we left the Camp of Death, a pinch of tea, a ***kungan*** (iron pitcher), and two or three procelain cups—all for sixty-five tengeh (less than 30*s*.). This made us independent of help from Khotan; with the horses and the white camel we might now try to save the loads of the two camels which were the last to give up.

In the evening we had a visit from two young hunters. They were armed with long guns, which they supported on a rest when they fired them. They had only just come to the forests of Buksem in pursuit of deer; they wanted the antlers to sell to the Chinese, who gave a good price for them for medicinal purposes. As the young men were intimately acquainted with all that region, I instantly engaged them to accompany Islam and Kasim in quest of the Camp of Death.

CHAPTER L.

A RESCUE PARTY

MAY 13th. The four merchants continued their journey towards Khotan. The two young hunters went off amongst the underwoods; but after the lapse of an hour returned with a deer (*boghe* or *maral*) which they had shot the evening before. It was flayed and quartered, and Islam very soon had an excellent soup ready. The deer's flesh was both delicate and tasty.

One of the hunters, Kasim Akhun, told me that the sand in the desert, which stretched between the Khotan-daria and the Keriya-daria, was very high; but in crossing it you could get water by digging wells during the first few days.

The season was however already too far advanced, and I therefore gave up my original plan of crossing that portion of the desert as well.

During the course of the day the father of the two young hunters arrived. Ahmed Merghen ("Merghen" means "hunter") was a splendid type of the Central Asiatic, tall, slim, broad-shouldered, with a big nose and a pointed imperial. He was very friendly, and took a great interest in our adventures; and gave us valuable advice in our consultations for organizing a rescue party. Nobody could have been more willing than he was to make a trip into the desert. He was a godsend to us. He remembered having once lost his way whilst hunting, and then passed near the three poplars where I and Kasim had made our signal-fire.

The morning was spent in arranging the details of the rescue expedition, and at one o'clock the men set out from our camp in the forest. The expedition consisted of Islam Bai, Kasim, Ahmed Merghen, and one of his sons. They took with them the three horses and one camel, and by way of provisions, bread, flour, mutton, and three *kapaks* (gourds) and a *mesh* (goat-skin) filled with water. Just as they were on the point of starting, Ahmed advised me to move out to a little island in the bed of the river, for the place where my hut stood abounded in scorpions. He was right; for I afterwards saw several of these unpleasant creatures. Their trail in the sand bore a striking resemblance to a lace pattern. But I liked my forest hut so well, and was so cosily at home in it, and besides it would have been so much trouble to flit, that I preferred to stay where I was and defy the scorpions.

The rescue party left the camp at an hour which would allow them to reach that same evening the spot where I had hung up the spade for a sign-post. Ahmed went on foot with his gun over his shoulder; the other three men rode on horseback. It was a pleasure to see how easily my new friend the hunter, like a mighty Nimrod or man of the woods, made his way through the thick undergrowth, sweeping the bushes aside and moving amongst them with such a light step that he almost seemed to fly.

After they had gone, I was again alone with the three shepherds, and put on the armour of patience for perhaps a full week. The shepherds' camp lay a few hundred paces from my hut; but Pasi Akhun agreed to sleep near me, so as to keep up the fire during the night. He brought me bread and milk three times a day, and I could get plenty of water from a well in the bed of the river.

May 14th. When I awoke at five o'clock, the sky was dark with clouds, and there was a thick mist and a fine drizzling rain. Although the rain only lasted a very short space, and scarcely wetted the ground, it freshened the air —a rare and unexpected phenomenon! At seven I got up. But during the long solitary days I spent in that forest hut I was by no means idle. I elaborated the rough notes I had taken during the later stages of my desert journey.

and plotted some of my maps of the dunes. Betweenwhiles I lay down on my "bed" and read the Bible and the Swedish Psalm-book, in which I discovered many a masterpiece of Swedish poetry.

A big yellow scorpion came walking over my sleeping-carpet, and when I molested him to kill him, fought like a mad thing. It now struck me as little short of wonderful that, whilst wandering about the forest by myself, and sleeping and resting as I did at all hours amongst the undergrowth, I had never disturbed any of these venomous animals. Considering the feeble state I was in, a sting might have proved serious, for the scorpion's sting is not to be despised.

Half a score of merchants, with a caravan of forty donkeys, carrying raisins and *kishmish* (currants) to Ak-su, passed my hut, and stopped a moment to greet me. I bought a bag of raisins from them, and the shepherds got a treat.

These merchants told me that Masar-tagh consisted of two parallel ridges running towards the north-west, but that neither extended very far into the desert. The desert in the vicinity of the ridges was said to be extremely desolate and barren; high sand-dunes preponderated, and there were but few patches of bare, hard ground. The name was derived from a masar or saint's tomb, the position of which was indicated by *tughs*, or sticks with pieces of rag attached to them, stuck in the ground on a conspicuous spur of the dunes. The custodian of the shrine was a sheikh, who generally lived in Khotan, but spent a small part of the winter in the desert. He was rewarded for his services by the contributions, amounting to 200 tengeh (about £4 10*s.*) a year, of the owners of the sheep which grazed in that region.

The following days slipped past peacefully and quietly, and I gradually recovered from the almost superhuman exertions I had undergone in the desert. All the same, I had to summon up my patience; for it did get monotonous, sitting there alone day after day and night after night in my lonely hut in the midst of the forest. Yet

LANDSCAPE ON THE RIGHT BANK OF THE KHOTAN-DARIA

I had everything I wanted. I enjoyed the best of health, drank in the forest air, and listened with pleasure to the lisping murmurs of the north-easterly wind, as it dallied with the leaves of the poplars. The heat was never oppressive; for the atmosphere was generally impregnated with dust, and the thick forest shade kept it cool. It was as silent and peaceful around me as on an uninhabited island. The only break in the uniformity of the day was when Pasi Akhun brought me my "rations," or came to make up the fire. I used to get up at seven o'clock; but at that hour the flocks were already in the forest, grazing, and I found the bread and the milk-bowl standing by my side.

It was very strange that for three days I travelled along the river-bed without seeing a soul; whereas now caravans going between Khotan and Ak-su passed every day. As a rule each band of merchants came up out of the river to the hut, and gave me a friendly greeting. But unfortunately they never had any other wares except raisins, felt carpets, wool, cotton, and domestic animals. However it was always a pleasure to me to talk to them; and they gave me much valuable information about the trading relations of East Turkestan, and about the river Khotan, and the climate of the region generally.

The news of our journey, and wonderful escape, spread like wild-fire both up the river to Khotan and down it to Ak-su. A merchant from the former place told me, that we were the talk of the bazaars, and that our arrival was being awaited with great impatience. I was growing very anxious to reach Khotan, as I intended staying there some days to reorganize my caravan, so that I might make a start for Northern Tibet.

May 15th. Two or three merchants coming from the north reported to me, that they had met Islam's party. That was at the end of the second day after they started; and they intended resting one day, so as to replenish their supplies of water.

The next day brought the bai who owned the flocks which my friends the shepherds had charge of. He came to superintend the shearing of the sheep, a task which is done twice in the year, in spring and autumn. The wool sold in Khotan at five tengeh (*2s. 3d.*) for a *chäreck* (about 18 lbs. avoir.). When there is a good clip of wool, it takes ten to twelve sheep to give a chäreck; but at that season of the year the wool was thin, a good deal having been torn off by the thorny bushes of the underwoods, so that it would take fifteen to twenty sheep to yield a chäreck. The bai hoped to shear about thirty chäreck altogether; for he had another flock of 500 sheep some distance higher up the river.

At dusk on the 21st May Islam and the other men returned. The report they brought was not very satisfactory. They had travelled due west from the edge of the forest; but had not ventured to go as far as the place where we left the tent, because the days were getting hotter. The only things they brought back with them were those which we left behind under the three poplars, and which were of relatively little value. They had been guided thither by the dead body of the camel Boghra, for its pestilential stench was perceptible a long way off. But the most remarkable thing of all was, that they did not find the camel Nähr, who carried the three aneroids, the boiling-point thermometer, the field-glass, two revolvers, one of them a weapon of the pattern that is used by the officers of the Swedish army, fifty cartridges, 200 cigars, besides several other things. They easily discovered the place where Islam had left the animal; because he had tied his girdle to a tamarisk close by to serve as a sort of guide-post. The tamarisk was still there on the top of a sand-dune; but the girdle was gone. Instead of it the branches of the tree were tied together with a piece of white felt. Round about there were footprints of a man's boots, whereas Islam had been barefooted. The camel and his valuable load were gone. And not only could they not find the animal, they could not even find a trace of him.

The question was, who was this man who had taken away Islam's girdle and left the felt rag in its place? I asked Islam, whether he thought it could be Yollchi, who might have revived after we left the tent; but Islam pronounced that to be impossible, because he had never seen a glimpse of the man since he left the Camp of Death. Was it possible, it was either of the three merchants who had fetched Islam some water, and lent me eighteen tengeh? No; for they had travelled straight from Islam to Buksem, to look for me. Besides, how would they have been able to find the camel? We were completely at a loss; but were unable to do anything. If somebody had found Nähr alive, and had led him to the river, where he could get water and food, the finder, whoever he was, if he was an honest man, would have brought the animal to us. But if he had stolen the camel, together with his load, he must surely have left a trail of some kind behind him, and there were only two routes to choose between: either he must have gone northwards to Ak-su, or southwards to Khotan. But my shepherd friends always kept a sharp look-out upon the latter road, and they had seen no camel answering to our description of Nähr. There only remained therefore the route to Ak-su; and we gradually became convinced that the camel had been stolen, and his trail deliberately obliterated.

Ahmed Merghen then said, he had seen the trail of a camel in the forest, and had followed it. But it brought him to the young camel, which had broken loose at the three poplars and run away into the woods by himself without his load. He had evidently found water somewhere, and after his ten or twelve days' free grazing in the forest was in excellent condition. But he had become so shy, that he fled as though he had never seen a man before, and Ahmed had the greatest difficulty in catching him. I shall return to this point again later on, when I speak about the wild camel of Central Asia.

It may possibly occasion surprise, that I relate all this at such length and in such detail; but I do it for two reasons. In the first place, in consequence of my loss my plans were entirely upset, and altered; and in the second place, these events were followed a year later by a highly dramatic sequel.

My original plan of travelling into Northern Tibet was completely knocked on the head. I had lost my instruments for measuring altitudes, and my equipment was sadly crippled. The only course now open to me was to return to Kashgar, and re-equip and repair my losses. Although it was a longer road, I chose the route *viâ* Ak-su. And yet within less than a twelvemonth I could not resist travelling in Marco Polo's footsteps from Kashgar to Khotan. But before I give a brief account of our return to Kashgar, I should like to say a few words about those portions of the courses of the Yarkand-daria and the Khotan-daria which came under my own observation.

A comparison of these two rivers, which flow pretty nearly parallel to one another, and seek the same goal, shows that they are in more than one respect dissimilar. The Yarkand-daria is the most important river in East Turkestan. Its channel is plainly marked and deeply eroded; and it contains water all the year round. Indeed in the month of June its flood rises to portentous dimensions. Except when it is ice-bound in winter, the river can only be crossed by means of ferries. The Khotan-daria, on the other hand, remains dry during the greater part of the year; it is only in the height of the summer that its channel holds any quantity of water. But it is so broad and shallow, that the only place where a ferry can be used is at Khotan. The river flows through the worst section of the Takla-makan Desert, and has a far harder fight of it with the drift-sand than its sister stream to the west. Indeed the sand is seriously threatening to choke it up, and cut it off from the main river, the Yarkand-daria or Tarim, which it flows into—a fate which, as we shall see later on, has already overtaken the Keriya-daria.

Again, the belt of forest which accompanies the Yarkand-daria is frequently interrupted by steppes and marshes; whereas the Khotan-daria is accompanied by its forest-belts all the way to the confluence of the two streams, and the forest is thicker and altogether wilder than the forest of the Yarkand-daria. The sand-dunes nowhere approach near to the banks of the Yarkand-daria; but in the case of the Khotan-daria they stretch quite close up to the western forest-belt.

In one respect however the two streams agree. Both have shifted their channels towards the east, as is proved by the existence, in both cases alike, of former river-beds lying west of and parallel to their present courses, whereas there are no such disused channels to the east of them. It is also worthy of remark, that the caravan-roads which run alongside both rivers keep to the left bank; no doubt that is the safer side when the rivers are in flood. Moreover, almost all the towns along the middle course of the Yarkand-daria are situated on the left bank, and generally at some little distance from it. There are no towns along that part of the Khotan-daria which flows through the forest; the only inhabitants in those tracts being the nomad shepherds. The caravan-road down the Khotan-daria possesses only a local importance; but between Maral-bashi and Yarkand, that is along the middle portion of the Yarkand-daria, runs one of the chief commercial highways in the centre of Asia.

May 23rd. I was awakened at half-past three in the morning by a terrific buran (hurricane)—a perfect fury of a wind—from the west. It completely ruined my poor hut, and even threatened to tear up the trees by their roots. It roared and whistled through the tops of the poplars, which, being full of leaf, were bent over parallel with the earth, threatening every moment to snap in half. The branches, being dry, cracked and broke, and were flung to the ground. The reeds bowed in humiliation before the fierce tyranny of the storm. The entire forest roared and thundered, as though it were filled with the noise of many waterfalls. It was moreover choked with dense clouds of drift-sand, which was blown in almost solid masses across the level bed of the Khotan-daria. The hurricane only lasted half an hour, and was succeeded by the same perfect calm which had preceded it.

At half-past seven we were all ready to start from the camp where I had spent such a long time, although a time rich in pleasant memories. Indeed, my thoughts often fly back, and with both gratitude and sadness commingled, to the happy days I spent beside the Khotan-daria. It was there I got a new lease of life; it was there I shook off my feet the sand of that awful desert; it was there I once more saw human beings like-fashioned unto myself, men who received me with kindness, fed me, tended me. Finally, it was there I enjoyed a beneficial and much-needed rest in the delightfully cool air of the forest. I gave each of my shepherd friends thirty tengeh (13*s.* 9*d.*), and they were overjoyed. Then we went on our way, with the two camels and the three horses; and the last of the camels' bells once more echoed clear and sonorous, no longer sounding for a funeral, but ringing in a new life, with new hopes.

CHAPTER LI.

DOWN THE KHOTAN-DARIA

WE did not travel in one party, but divided. Islam Bai and the two hunters travelled by the caravan-road that traversed the forest on the left bank of the stream, in order to keep a look-out for the trail of the missing camel. Ahmed Merghen and I rode down the bed of the river, and Kasim followed us in charge of the two camels. But as we rode hard, we soon lost sight of him. In the afternoon we came to the little pool which had saved my life. There stood the reed thicket as before, and the poplars leaned over the water, which had dropped nearly five inches since May 6th. It retained the same shape however. There I rested a good hour, partly to wait for Kasim to come up, but more particularly that I might drink again of that splendid, that glorious life-giving water. Ahmed Merghen called the pool Khoda-verdi-köll, or the "God-given lake."

After a ride of ten hours we all met again in the part of the forest called Kuyundehlik (the Place of Hares). Several shepherds were encamped there looking after their flocks. Islam had not seen any signs of the camel in the forest. Even though there had been any trail, it would have been destroyed by the hurricane.

May 24th. We decided to rest a day, chiefly in order that some of the men might scour the forest, in that part from four to eight miles wide, with their dogs. Five shepherds, in charge of five hundred sheep and sixty cattle, had been four days at Kuyundehlik. It was only a short two hours' journey to the pool of God's gift. Had I gone north on May 6th, instead of going south, I should scarcely have fallen in with these men, for at that time they were encamped in another place; and it was several days from Kuyundehlik to the next shepherds' camp, near the confluence of the Khotan-daria with the Yarkand-daria.

A short distance below the camp of Kuyundehlik, the Khotan-daria divided into two arms. The arm on the west was narrow and winding, and hence was called the Inchicke-daria, as well as hidden in a thick wood; whilst the right-hand branch was broad, and entirely destitute of forest on its eastern bank. In the height of the summer both branches are filled with water. The latter washes the foot of a series of large sand-dunes known as Ak-kum (the White Sand). The shepherds asserted, that the Inchicke-daria was only formed about eight years previously. But the thick woods proved conclusively, that it was the older channel, and that the river was gradually abandoning it for its more easterly neighbour. The absence of forest on the right bank of the eastern branch proved also, that vegetation had not yet succeeded in maintaining its ground on that side against the persistent assaults of the drift-sand. When the Khotan-daria is in flood, caravans for Ak-su travel along the delta or island between the two branches, and consequently have to cross them by the fords. The distance between the fords is about two days' journey. During the dry portions of the year the pools in both the main branch and the Inchicke-daria occur near the right bank.

The district had a bad reputation for thieves and robbers, who make a practice of plundering small and weak caravans. But the new amban (Chinese governor) of Khotan had started a systematic war of extermination against the evil-doers; all whom he caught were summarily beheaded.

May 25th. My excellent friend Ahmed Merghen returned home to Tavek-kel near Khotan, but left his son Kasim with us. We rode down the winding bed of the Inchicke-daria, the banks of which were covered with young forest. Further back from the stream the trees were much older, and in many places stood so close together that it was not easy to pass between them. The tendency of the forests on both banks is to unite and form one continuous forest; and this will no doubt happen, as soon as the summer floods entirely desert this channel for the right-hand branch. In fact, the Inchicke-daria was only forty or forty-five yards wide as it was. After a long day's ride we stopped for the night beside a pool in the bed of the river, at a place called Bedelik-utak (the Clover-Field Lot).

May 26th. Kasim, Ahmed's son, refused to go with us further than one day's journey from Kuyundehlik; it was dangerous, both on account of robbers and of tigers, to spend the night alone in the forest. I, and my two men, Islam and Kasim, continued our journey therefore without a guide. As the river became more and more sinuous in its course, we resolved to strike further into the island, which consisted of prairies, interrupted by low dunes and small groves of forest-trees. But as the river-bed made the more convenient road to travel by, we soon went back to it. Both banks were planted with luxuriant woods, so that we often seemed to be journeying through a park, or rather a tunnel of foliage.

At length we reached the point where the Inchicke-daria rejoins the Khotan-daria. The forest opened out like a door, and before us was the level bed of the Khotan-daria, lying, in consequence of the more powerful erosive force of its larger volume of water, some five feet lower than the bed of the Inchicke-daria. We encamped a short distance below the confluence, in a tract called Bora-tyshkyn (Beaten down by the Storm). There was a little island in the river; but so infested with ticks and scorpions that we preferred to make our fire for the night in the bed of the river, at some distance from the bank.

May 27th. As is generally the case in that part of the world after a clear night and a west wind, followed by a calm day, it was pretty warm on the morrow, and the heat began to make itself felt early in the day. For instance, at seven o'clock in the morning the thermometer registered

76°8 Fahr. (24°9 C.). The hard, level river-bed ran almost directly due north, at the same time gradually narrowing to a general breadth of about half a mile, and winding in and out round projecting "buttresses" of forest. It will, of course, be readily understood that the high summer flood, being spread over the wide, shallow channel, is subject to active evaporation, so that the current necessarily diminishes in volume the further it advances towards the north.

Again the river divided into two branches—the Yanghi-daria (New River) on the left and the Kovneh-daria (Old River) on the right. We travelled down the former, and met a large donkey-caravan laden with groceries from Ak-su, from which place they started eight days before. The Kovneh-daria was shut in on both sides by sand-dunes exclusively. Despite its name, it is probably the newer channel, seeing that the forest-trees have not succeeded in establishing themselves along its banks. The result of my observations, upon the tendency of the Khotan-daria to shift its channel towards the east, goes to show that it does not do this regularly and conformably throughout the whole of its course, but does it piecemeal, a portion at a time. The river-bed gets choked up here and there with the alluvial detritus brought down by the current. In every place where this happens, the stream gradually rises above the general level of the adjacent land, and seeks a new passage towards the east.

In the evening we came upon a large pool, some 500 square yards in area, the largest I had hitherto seen. We made our fire on a hill overhanging the river, and from our camp obtained an extensive view of the surrounding country. In this place the current had delved a deep trench close under the right bank of the river, in which in the course of the next day's journey we found a string of small pools. Upon bathing in the large pool, I discovered that it was deep; for I was unable to reach the bottom.

May 28th. During the course of this day's march the river-bed gradually became wider. As a general rule, where the channel is broad and level, there are no pools, and the trenches made by the last season's floods are scarcely discernible; but where it is narrow, there exist numerous pools, and the trenches made by the current are plainly marked in serpentine curves. I also observed that the forest was appreciably thinner on the right bank than on the left; in fact, in many parts it ceased altogether, its place being taken by bare sand-dunes. Close under the western bank the river-bed itself was occasionally overgrown with grass; but that was never the case along the right-hand side of the river. Everything tended to show, that the current flows stronger on the right or eastern side than it does on the left or western. But in any case, the movement of the current towards the east takes place at such a slow rate, that the afforestation of its banks is enabled to keep pace with it. A few isolated poplars, like those near which we made our signal fire on May 3rd, still maintained a precarious existence on the west side of the stream; but they are doomed to perish.

At six o'clock we were still riding along the river-bed; Islam Bai had gone on in advance to seek out a convenient spot for camping on; when all at once the whole of the west became enshrouded in a dark yellowish-grey cloud. At first it looked like a low wall; then it rapidly mounted higher, till it reached half-way to the zenith; and then the next moment it was directly over our heads. The sun faded to a pale lemon disc; then totally vanished. A distant murmur arose along the border of the forest. It approached rapidly nearer. We heard the twigs and branches snapping off with a louder and louder echo. Towards the north-west the forest was enveloped in haze. Columns of sand and dust came spinning across the river-bed like theatrical wing-scenes moving on invisible rollers, alternately shooting on in advance of each other; and in a moment the forest was entirely blotted out. The first outfliers of the storm burst upon us; the black buran followed close at their heels, striking us with terrific violence, swallowing us up in its impenetrable clouds of dust. The sand was swept along in eddying sheets, which trailed along the ground, putting me in mind of comets' tails. Track, trenches, storm-driven boughs—nothing was to be seen. In such a storm as that your head goes round; you imagine the earth, the atmosphere, everything is in commotion; you are oppressed by a feeling of anxiety lest the next moment you yourself should be caught up in the frenzied embrace of the wind. It turned as dark as midnight, and for some time we durst not move a step from the spot where we stood. The instant the storm burst Islam was lost to sight; and it was only by the merest chance that we came together again. He just saw the dim outline of the caravan like some huge monster slowly crawling through the haze.

Seeing that the storm—one of the worst we had experienced—showed signs of lasting some time, we cautiously piloted our way to the river-bank, and sought shelter behind the thick brushwood in the heart of the forest. There we decided to encamp for the night. We afterwards dug a well in a depression of the river, and reached water after a few spades' depths. As soon as it grew dark (night), the men set fire to the undergrowth on the lee side of our camp. The flames, fanned by the gale, spread with portentous rapidity, giving rise to a magnificent, but wild, spectacle.

May 29th. The storm still continued. The air was so densely charged with dust, that we saw but little of our surroundings. Fortunately we were able to get along by keeping close to the left side of the river-bed, and in that way chanced to stumble on a sign-post, consisting of a pole with a horse's skull on the top, fixed in a poplar tree. Upon going up to examine it more closely, I discovered a path leading into the forest, a path which I took for granted went to Ak-su. We decided to follow it. It led us towards the north-west, along a plainly marked river-bed, now dry and in part sanded up, and shut in by sand-dunes, poplar holts, and bushes. In all probability it was a former arm of the delta of the Khotan-daria. At intervals, as the road crossed several belts of barren sand,

ATTACKED BY A SANDSTORM IN THE BED OF THE KHOTAN-DARIA

the caravan-leaders had erected poles and gallows-like arrangements to serve as sign-posts.

That afternoon we encamped near some shepherds from Ak-su, who were comfortably installed in the forest in huts made of stakes and reeds. At first they regarded us with some suspicion; but soon gained confidence, and offered us bread, milk, and eggs. They lived with their flocks in the woods all the year round.

The Yarkand-daria, which we now saw a short distance ahead of us, is generally ice-bound for about four months in the year. The shepherds said, they expected the summer floods in about three weeks, and would then be driven by the overflowing of the river higher up into the forests. Just at that time however the river was at its lowest level. The next day we crossed the stream at a well-known ford. Its breadth was eighty-five yards, its greatest depth 1½ feet, and its volume 265 cubic feet in the second.

On the other side of the river we continued on towards the north by a path which led to the town of Avvat (Abad), meaning "populous," through a district that was in very ill repute on account of highway robbers and stealers of live-stock. The road lay sometimes through tangled underwoods and thorny bushes, sometimes through kamish (reed)-beds and open steppes, sometimes past shepherds' camps and small villages, now close alongside the right bank of the Ak-su-daria, now at some distance from it.

May 31st. Towards evening we approached the bazaars of Avvat, a place of about a thousand houses, with a beg, a Chinese tax-collector, and a Hindu trader, Parman, who hospitably placed a comfortable serai (guest-house) at my disposal. All the same he was an arrant rogue. He lent money to the peasantry at usurious rates of interest, and whenever they were unable to pay what they owed him, took from them their wheat and maize and wool. The wool he sold in Ili (Kulja); the corn in the neighbouring towns and villages. He confessed to me, that he laid by 15,000 (Kashgar) tengeh (about £130) every year. The principal products of the district are rice, wheat, maize, and cotton. The little town stands on a branch of the Ak-su-daria, called the Kovneh-daria; it is crossed by a bridge which leads straight into the main street of the town.

June 1st. We rode the whole of the day through one continuous street, with canals on both sides of it, and shaded by avenues of trees, among which mulberries and willows predominated. The next day, at a place called Besh-arik-ustang (the Channel of the Five Branches), we came out upon the great highway which runs to Kashgar, and also crosses the Ak-su-daria to Yanghi-shahr (the New Town), a place enclosed within the walls of a Chinese fortress. Immediately we arrived, I sent a man with my passport and Chinese calling-card to the Dao Tai or chief officer of the district; but received back an indefinite sort of answer. Accordingly I did not take the trouble to call upon "his excellency," a man who was notorious for his arrogance and drunken habits.

June 3rd. We were now only a short distance from the Mohammedan town of Ak-su. Upon arriving there I was received with marked friendliness by Mohammed Emin, the aksakal (white-beard) or head of the West Turkestan merchants. He lodged me in his own good and comfortable house, sending the camels and horses to a neighbouring caravanserai.

June 4th. During the past three days the white camel had pined away, refusing to eat grass or anything except a few broken fragments of wheat-bread. On June 3rd he had walked the short distance from the New to the Old Town without stopping; but every time anybody went near him, he screamed out in a tone of suffering, as though he were afraid he was going to be hurt. At night he ate nothing; and next morning Kasim came with a concerned countenance to tell me that Ak-tuya was very ill. I hastened to the courtyard and found him lying on his side, with his legs doubled under him and his neck stretched out along the ground.

He was breathing heavily; and, after one or two long-drawn breaths, he died.

This was the camel on which Islam had saved my diaries, maps, instruments, and other things which I set the greatest store by. Naturally therefore I felt sorry to lose the poor beast, which had rendered me such a signal service. All the way down the Khotan-daria I went to him at every place where we encamped, and clapped him; but he always turned away his head and screamed, as though I were going to pull at his nose-rope. It seemed as though he knew I was the cause of the suffering he had endured. On the morning he died, the morning of the Feast of Mairam, it was still and quiet in the caravanserai courtyard. On that day no caravan came in, no caravan went out; ordinary work of every sort and kind was entirely suspended. Everybody was out of doors. The streets, the bazaars were gay with new khalats (coats) in the brightest and most variegated hues, new caps (calottes) in glowing colours, and snow-white turbans. Every person looked happy and contented. On this day the meanest servant is greeted with a "*Aid mubarek!*" (A happy holiday to you!) by his master; and from the windows of the minarets the muezzin's voice, uplifted in prayer and praise of the Almighty, sounds clearer and more musical than usual. What a contrast between the silent courtyard, where my dead camel lay, and this richly varied picture of life and happiness, every face beaming with delight, on this the greatest Mohammedan holiday of the year! As it happened, in the year of our visit to Ak-su, the Feast of Mairam fell on Whit-Tuesday. Mohammed Emin was going to sell the two camels for me on the following day. The money value of the dead animal was a mere trifle; besides, by this I had become accustomed to losing camels! But this poor beast had been the means of saving my sketches and diaries, and my purse for defraying the expenses of the summer; and I felt as if I had lost a faithful friend, a friend in whose fidelity I could trust implicitly, who had sacrificed his strength, and finally his life, to help me out of an awkward predicament.

His travelling-companion, the young camel, Chong-sarik, a giant of his kind, which Ahmed the Hunter had caught in the forest, left his manger and walked across to the white camel, and regarded him attentively with a look of wonderment. Then he quietly walked back to his manger, and with an unimpaired appetite went on munching the green sappy grass with which it was filled. He was the last of the eight. I had not the heart to sell him without knowing into whose hands he would fall. The custodian of the serai was of opinion, that he too would soon succumb to the hardships and privations he had undergone. Finally I gave him as a present to Mohammed Emin, on condition that he should be allowed to graze all summer on the fat meadows at the foot of the Tengri-khan.

CHAPTER LII.

FROM AK-SU TO KASHGAR

WE stayed three days in Ak-su, in order to organize a temporary caravan, for the return journey to Kashgar, the centre and base of my exploring journeys in Central Asia. Thus I had an opportunity, though it must be confessed a brief one, of seeing something of the town of the White Water (Ak-su), so called because of the abundance of clear, fresh water which pours through it from the eternal snowfields and glaciers. The town occupies a favourable position on the left bank of the Ak-su-daria. In summer enormous quantities of water roll down the river. In winter there is but a fraction of it left, and the little there is freezes. A short distance below the town the river divides into two branches, the Yanghi-daria and the Kovneh-daria; but they reunite before they join the main stream, the Yarkand-daria, or Tarim. Immediately on the east the town is overlooked by a terrace of conglomerate and loess strata, which rises to a perpendicular height of 150 or 160 feet, and has been carved out and shaped by the river floods. On all other sides the town is surrounded by numerous villages, fertile fields and meadows, splendid orchards, and brimming irrigation canals. Rice, wheat, maize, barley, cotton, opium, and a vast quantity of garden produce are grown with signal success. Ak-su, with its 15,000 inhabitants, is only half as big as Kashgar; nevertheless in respect of its agricultural products it ranks considerably higher. The keeping of sheep, which graze, as I have said, along the banks of the two large rivers, is likewise a flourishing industry.

Ak-su possesses a mixed population of divers races. Amongst others I noticed a great number of Chinese, a hundred or so of Andijanliks (people of Andijan) or merchants from Russian Turkestan, besides three Afghans, who have paid periodical visits to Ak-su for a space of over twenty years. Mohammed Emin, the aksakal or head of the Russian subjects trading to the town, was a Tashkendlik, *i.e.* a man of Tashkend, and had been domiciled in Ak-su for a dozen years. The Andijan merchants trade principally in wool, cotton, and hides. Of the last-named commodity some 30,000 are sent every year to Tashkend on the backs of camels, *viâ* the pass of Bedel, Kara-kol (Przhevalsk), Pishpek, and Aulieh-ata. The caravans only travel during the winter. All the hot months of the year the camels run at pasture on the grassy slopes of the mountains near the town. Moreover, all communications are greatly hampered during the summer by the high state of the water in the swollen rivers.

Of "lions" that would repay a visit there were scarce any. The chief mosque, which as usual was called the Mesjid-i-Juma or Friday Mosque, was not particularly remarkable, except that it occupied a picturesque situation on one side of a small open square, which communicated with the principal bazaar through a side-lane. The square, called Righistan, is the centre of the life of Ak-su. On market-days it is packed with people, and all sorts of commodities are offered for sale on a multitude of little stalls. Lumps of ice, collected in winter and preserved in subterranean cellars, are an important commodity during the hot season, and one that I personally enjoyed in liberal measure. In the principal bazaar there are two theological colleges, the Kok-madrasa (the Blue College) and the Ak-madrasa (the White College). Their façades are plain, with poor earthenware decorations, nor can their balconies or cloisters boast of any architectural merit. The mollahs or theological students live in cells, opening out upon the courtyard. Some of the students had previously studied five, and even ten, years at the theological

BAZAAR IN A CENTRAL ASIATIC TOWN

college of Mir-arab in Bokhara. The Chinese have two *lanzas* (a lanza consists of not quite one hundred men) at Yanghi-shahr. They maintain a larger garrison at Utch-turfan, which commands the Bedel pass over the Tian-shan Mountains into Russian Turkestan.

All over the Mohammedan world it is customary to celebrate the first few days of the Feast of Mairam by a great number of gala dinners, at which incredible quantities of *ash* (pillau or rice pudding) and *shorpa* (soup

SHOP IN A BAZAAR

made of green vegetables and macaroni) are consumed. Some of these feasts I shared in company with the aksakal Mohammed Emin. But the best entertainment of all was that to which the aksakal invited me, and at which I was the only guest. We rode out to his garden Sokha-bashi, situated about two miles from the bazaar. There a couple of gardeners live all the year round, and occupy themselves with the cultivation of grapes, apricots, melons, plums, cherries, and vegetables. We took our places underneath a leafy mulberry-tree, beside a canal filled with clear crystal water. A sheep was killed, and with his own hand the aksakal prepared an ash or pillau according to the most approved recipe of the culinary art. You take the best pieces of the meat, especially the breast and the kidneys, cut them up fine, fry them in butter in a pan over the fire, thereafter fill the pan with well-washed pure white rice, and add onions to flavour. This dish, when properly prepared, is excellent.

An aksakal is a sort of consular agent. The subjects of the Russian empire have their aksakal in each of the larger towns of East Turkestan. All these officers were

STREET IN A TOWN OF CENTRAL ASIA

subordinate to Consul-General Petrovsky in Kashgar. My friend Mohammed Emin, the aksakal in Ak-su, was one of the best Mohammedans I have met, a cheerful and worthy man of about sixty, with a white beard; he had an intimate knowledge of East Turkestan, and was able to give me much valuable information. Even before I reached the town, he had done me a service. He made inquiries on all the roads leading into Ak-su from the south after the thief who had, as we suspected, stolen the camel we lost; though without any result. Now he did me an even greater service. He declared his willingness to accompany me to Kashgar, a road he had travelled scores of times. I was very glad of this, for I knew he would be excellent company. He was quitting his post without permission; but for that I took it upon myself to answer to Mr. Petrovsky for him.

We had a journey of 270 miles before us to Kashgar; but we were in no hurry, and resolved to take things easy. By June 7th all was ready for a start. Mohammed Emin procured me some Sart *yakhtans* (boxes), and provided the needful provisions, such as sugar, tea, rice, vegetables, honey, and so forth. Mutton we should be able to buy everywhere along the road. I gave Islam Bai and Kasim a gratuity each for their faithful services, as well as dressed them out from top to toe in good new clothes. I had lost all my own clothes, and bought myself a costume which was half Chinese, half Sart. This was the only occasion during my travels that I deprived myself of the prestige and respect which the European dress always inspires.

We hired four horses from a karakesh (owner of caravan animals), paying fifty-five tengeh (12*s.* 6*d.*) for each horse all the way to Kashgar. We left Ak-su at five o'clock in the afternoon; but that day we only rode a couple of hours. Our first stop was at the caravanserai of Langar. We travelled that short stretch down a continuous avenue bordered with rice-fields under water, cultivated fields, gardens, and houses, and encamped on a piece of meadow in a fine grove of poplars. Ten years before that Mohammed Emin had rested in the same spot with Przhevalsky, who was then on his way home from his fourth journey. Afar off in the north through the light dust-haze we caught a glimpse of the glittering white peak of Tengri-khan, towering up to 24,000 feet; but it was soon enveloped in the shades of night, and so disappeared from our view.

On June 8th we crossed the Kum-daria (Sand River), the name generally given to the Ak-su in that part of its course. The river was split into a number of branches, and the crossing was beset with no particular difficulties. A few days after that the ferry would come into use; but five weeks later, when the river would be in full flood, even the ferry would be useless, and for some time all communication between the opposite banks would be interrupted. Every year an average of half-a-dozen men lose their lives through attempting to ride across the river when the current is too powerful.

On the other side of the river we met a caravan of some two hundred horses and oxen; each animal was dragging after it on the ground two long beams of poplar wood (*terek*). The aksakal told me, that a large dam or jetty was being built fifteen miles above the town, along the left bank of the Ak-su-daria, and that no less than three thousand men were engaged upon the work. The object of the dam, which is reconstructed every year, was to prevent the flood from doing injury to the terrace of conglomerate, and so eventually sweeping away both the Old and the New Town, and to force it over to the opposite or right bank. Thus the Ak-su-daria, which at that point flows south, also tends towards a more easterly course.

Four and a half hours later we rode across the Taushkan-daria (Hare River), the sister stream of the Ak-su-daria. It was much more difficult to cross, on account of the water flowing in a confined channel. We accordingly hired two *suchis* (water men), who, being naked, carefully led the horses across the stony river-bed.

June 9th. We reached the little town of Utch-turfan, which owes such importance as it possesses solely to its position as a sort of half-way house between Ak-su and the frontier of Asiatic Russia, and on the road by which the wool, cotton, felts, carpets, hides, etc. of East Turkestan are exported. There were some eighty prosperous Andijan (*i.e.* West Turkestan) traders established there, likewise under the authority of my friend Mohammed Emin. The town stands in the midst of fertile, well-cultivated fields, irrigated from the Taushkan-daria. In the far distance we saw the snow-white bastions of the great Tian-shan Mountains, and nearer at hand some ranges of low hills. The Chinese amban (governor) of Utch-turfan, Tso Daloi, received me with great politeness and invited me to dine with him. He was formerly stationed in Tarbagatai in Dzungaria, where he had come a good deal into contact with the Russians.

After resting a day, we left Utch-turfan on June 11th, escorted by the entire colony of Andijan merchants wearing their best khalats (coats). Our gaily-dressed cavalcade excited not a little attention in every place we passed through. But at Sughetlik (Willow Village), where we were again offered tea and refreshments, our friends turned back. We went on to Ott-bashi (the Beginning of the Pasture-Grounds) and encamped there in a park.

CROWD AT THE ENTRANCE OF A BAZAAR

The next day we reached the kishlak or winter-village of Bash-akhma (the River Source), and made our camp in a large Kirghiz aul consisting of nineteen uy (tents). The Kirghiz generally spend their summer there as well, for they are half agriculturists, growing wheat, barley, and opium, although they continue to live in their kara-uy (black tents). A few of them, however, have taken to clay cabins. They only sow the ground every other year, letting it rest and recover during the intervening years; hence it would be more strictly correct to call them agriculturists every second year. They possess also flocks of sheep and goats. The Kirghiz who devote themselves entirely to the keeping of live-stock, spend the summer in the mountains, and only come down into the valley of the Taushkan-daria for the winter. There are seven septs or families represented in the district; but all obey one *bi* or chieftain.

But I will curtail my account of this journey by hurrying over the next eight days. We travelled up the valley of the Taushkan-daria, crossed the ranges of low hills which shut in the valley on the south, and then continued in a south-westerly direction over the steppes and desert, until on the afternoon of June 21st we reached Kashgar—the westernmost town of China. The people we came in contact with were Kirghiz and Jagatai Turks. After the scorching heat of the Desert of Takla-makan, I thoroughly enjoyed the fresh mountain air. As it was the rainy period, it was still further cooled by the rains, which often fell in copious quantities, and by storms which drove up and down the valley from the east and from the west, as though they were being discharged through a rifle barrel. We passed the towns and auls of Utch-musduk (the Three Glaciers), Sum-tash, Kizil-eshmeh (the Red Springs), Kustcheh (the Autumn Place), Jai-teve (the Grave Hill), Sogun-karaol, Kalta-yeylak (the Little Summer Pasture-Ground), and Besh-kerem (the Five Fortresses).

In Kashgar I stayed barely three weeks, and busy weeks they were, as I worked hard at equipping and fitting out another caravan. My old friend Mr. Petrovsky, who during my absence had been advanced to the dignity of Consul-General, and in addition, shortly after that was, for his invaluable services to me, honoured by King Oscar with the star of a knight-commander of the Vasa order, welcomed me with much gladness and emotion, and did all in his power to help me with the preparations for my next expedition. As soon as he learned of our unlucky desert journey from the aksakal of Khotan, he had gone to the Dao Tai, and given him to understand that, unless he promptly made inquiries after my lost camel in both Khotan and Ak-su, he would hear of the matter from the Tsung-li-yamen in Peking. The Dao Tai did his duty;

and our astonishment may be imagined when, one day, whilst we were dining with him, he placed upon the table my Swedish officer's revolver. It had been among the things in the load which Nähr, the lost camel, carried. The weapon had been given by an unknown horseman to a peasant in the village of Tavek-kel. The search after the thief was renewed with redoubled zeal; but the Chinese mandarins never succeeded in getting any clue to the guilty

PART OF KUM-DÄRVASEH, ONE OF THE GATES OF KASHGAR

party. I gave myself but little further trouble about the matter, being entirely taken up with fresh plans and projects for the immediate future.

The very next day after my arrival at Kashgar I despatched a courier to Osh, with several letters and despatches, amongst others one for my teacher and friend, Baron von Richthofen in Berlin, asking him to send me a new and complete set of meteorological instruments—aneroids, boiling-point thermometers, etc. I telegraphed to Tashkend for clothes, provisions, and tobacco; and obtained a supply of cartridges and powder from the Cossack guard in Kashgar. The things which I had ordered from Europe could not arrive for three months. I could not possibly spend all that time in inaction; especially as the heat of the summer made me long for the fresh cool air of the mountains. The only thing that detained me in Kashgar was the non-arrival of my letters from Sweden. During my absence Consul-General Petrovsky had sent them to Keriya beyond Khotan, and they had not yet come back again. But here the Dao Tai came to my assistance, and did me the very great service of sending express couriers all the way to Keriya to fetch them. The men—for there was a fresh courier and fresh horses for each stage of the journey—took twelve days to go there and back; and, as the distance was 870 miles, they rode at the rate of about seventy-two miles a day.

In a couple of weeks I had completed my preparations for a fresh start. The kindness and self-sacrificing help I received from Mr. Petrovsky, Mr. Macartney, and the Swedish missionary, Mr. Högberg, were of such a character as I shall never forget. They all three vied with one another in their efforts to assist me. The first and the second lent me some aneroids and hypsometers; my countryman lent me several things of practical value. A tailor in the town made me some clothes of Chinese cloth, and sewed me furs together, and a tent. I bought horses, saddles, and stores of provisions in the bazaars. When we started again, on July 10th, I could scarcely believe that, only two months earlier, I had suffered a loss which at the time seemed as though it would utterly wreck all my plans.

But whither should we turn our footsteps now? To go to the north, and explore the Tian-shan Mountains, would have been going over ground that is already tolerably well known. The time was too short to admit of my going so far south as the Kwen-lun Mountains. To the west was the high plateau of the Pamirs, which

COURTYARD OF A MOSQUE IN CENTRAL ASIA

A GROUP OF KIRGHIZ AND A CHINAMAN

I had already crossed in several directions. Despite this, I determined once more to visit that region, and spend the hot months amongst the mountain giants on the Roof of the World, in continuing the investigations which I began the previous summer.

THROUGH ASIA

THROUGH ASIA

BY

SVEN HEDIN

WITH NEARLY THREE HUNDRED ILLUSTRATIONS FROM SKETCHES AND PHOTOGRAPHS BY THE AUTHOR

VOL. II

GYAN

Published by

Gyan Publishing House
5, Ansari Road
Daryaganj, New Delhi-110002
Phone: 011-47034999, 9811692060
E-mail: books@gyanbooks.com

Distribution Network
gyanbooks.com
India, USA, Canada, UK, Australia, France

ISBN : 978-81-212-1489-6 (Set)
ISBN : 978-81-212-2902-9 (HB)
First Published, 1898

2nd Impression 2021

Printed at: Gyan Press, Delhi.

Through Asia, Vol. II
Author: Sven Hedin

THROUGH ASIA

BY

SVEN HEDIN

WITH NEARLY THREE HUNDRED ILLUSTRATIONS FROM SKETCHES AND PHOTOGRAPHS BY THE AUTHOR

VOL. II.

METHUEN & CO.
36 ESSEX STREET, W.C.
LONDON
1898

Islam Bai.

TO

HIS ROYAL HIGHNESS

THE PRINCE OF WALES

THIS RECORD OF

NEARLY FOUR YEARS' TRAVELS

IS

BY HIS PERMISSION

RESPECTFULLY AND GRATEFULLY

DEDICATED

CONTENTS

A SUMMER-TRIP TO THE SOUTHERN PAMIRS

ACROSS THE DESERT OF GOBI TO LOP-NOR

THROUGH NORTHERN TIBET AND TSAIDAM

FROM TSAIDAM TO PEKING

LIST OF ILLUSTRATIONS

A SUMMER TRIP TO THE SOUTHERN PAMIRS

II.—I

1898

DR. SVEN HEDIN

CHAPTER LIII.

OVER THE ULLUG-ART PASS

ON July 10th, 1895, I left Kashgar with Islam Bai, two servants, and six horses, and did a short stage to the village of Tokkuz-ak (the Nine Whites). My other man, Kasim, remained behind in Kashgar as watchman of the courtyard of the consulate. One of the six horses, a little piebald stallion, was one of those I bought at the forest-hut, beside the Khotan-daria. It was a splendid animal, always full of go, and yet as tame as a lamb. For my own use I bought a big, but excellent, riding-horse, and rode him over the mountains and through the deserts of Central Asia for more than a year. Horses are cheap in Kashgar. The five I bought there cost altogether only 124 roubles, or between £12 and £13.

The next day, July 11th, we continued our journey towards the south-west, to the town of Upal (2000 houses), which is also a fortress manned by two hundred men, and the place of residence of two mandarins of inferior rank. It poured and pelted with rain the whole day long, so that the ground, which was a reddish yellow loess, was greasy and slippery. Thoroughly wet to the skin, we took up our quarters in a house near the bazaar, and made a big fire at which to dry our wet clothes. The gardens, and rice and other fields, were irrigated by water drawn from a little stream, which flowed through the town after racing down the valley of Ullug-art on the west, and which was partly maintained from fresh springs. The current has scooped out for itself a deep and tolerably broad trench through the loess deposits. But in the town its banks were not so precipitous; they rose gradually by a series of terraces, leaving room close down by the water's edge for the houses, which were built of sun-dried clay and covered in with flat wooden roofs. The opposite banks were connected by a wooden bridge.

A short time after we arrived at Upal, I witnessed an occurrence which I had never witnessed before, but which takes place every year in these regions. After a heavy, continuous rain the water which drains off the adjacent mountain-sides gathers into a *sil* (sudden flood or inundation), which in a few hours completely fills the river-bed, and may work very great destruction. In these sudden floods we see the agent which in the course of time has eroded the clay terraces so deeply.

About seven o'clock we heard a distant booming. It came rapidly nearer, at the same time increasing to a deafening roar. Down came the flood, a stupendous mass of water, rushing on with inconceivable violence, seething, foaming, and swiftly filling the river to the brim. The inhabitants ran down to the river-bank, uttering cries of alarm and gesticulating wildly. I and Islam Bai took our station on a protected roof. The next moment the avenues of willows and poplars, which lined both banks of the river, were covered by the flood. The ground seemed to shake under the impact of such a mass of unrestrained water. Clots of dirty foam tossed about on the tumbling waves. The spray smoked along the flood like a moving shower of mist. Tree-trunks, any amount of loose branches, haycocks, and other movable objects danced along the tossing current, drove against the banks, swung free, got caught in an eddy and plunged down out of sight, rolled up to the surface again, and once more became the sport of the irresistible flood. The bridge was broken down at the first onrush, and swept away, swaying from side to side, whilst its timbers creaked and groaned as it rolled over and over in the water.

The flood bore towards the right bank, and inundated

the principal street of the town. It poured into the lower-lying houses, and kept on rising and rising. The people who lived next the river came rushing out of their dwellings, shouting excitedly and dragging their household possessions after them, and sought safety upon the higher terraces. Some, bolder of heart, began to "cradge" or throw up temporary ridges of clay, to keep the water from entering their houses, and so washing away or destroying their property. In a couple of

A SHOP IN A BAZAAR

minutes the whole of the lower portion of the bazaar was muddy water. The air trembled with the awe-inspiring roar of the torrent. Women were wading up to the waist in water, carrying little children in their arms. Every house-roof was crowded with people. Those who had nothing to lose were able to give themselves up without qualm of conscience to the enjoyment of what was truly a magnificent spectacle. Fortunately the house in which we were lodged was a long way from the river, and never for a moment came in jeopardy.

As soon as everything was carried away to places of safety that could be so carried, the general attention was directed to the melon-gardens, on the slopes going down to the river. The gardens were trenched all over, and the water ran up the trenches with great speed. All the men of the town rushed off to the melon-gardens, caught up big armfuls of melons—ripe or not was all one—and ran with them to the foot of the terraces, where they threw the melons up to other men, who piled them up in heaps. In spite of that however a large portion of the crop was washed away by the flood. Meanwhile fifteen houses had entirely disappeared.

But no doubt the inhabitants of the place would profit from the disaster? Not in the least. The same thing happens every year. For no sooner is the flood past and gone than the people set to work and build up their houses on the very same sites where they stood before. The flood had already begun to subside by nine o'clock, and it fell so rapidly that by the forenoon of the next day, July 12th, the river had dropped back to its normal condition and was little more than a rivulet trickling along the bottom of its deeply eroded channel. Communication had been re-established between the opposite banks; but the scene presented was one of havoc and desolation. As a matter of precaution we stayed in Upal the rest of the day.

In the latitude in which we then were four passes led over the Mus-tagh or Kashgar Mountains, the eastern border-range of the Pamirs, namely Ayag-art (the Foot Pass), and Kazig-art (named from a Kirghiz sept?), which we had already left on our right as we journeyed to Upal; Buru-köss-davan (Wolf's Eye Pass), which was on the left of the road we had come; and lastly, Ullug-art (the Great Pass), the pass we chose. The last two are drained through the same glen, which issues upon the plains at a place called Orugumah, where the Chinese maintain a Kirghiz karaol (post of observation). The Kirghiz in that district belong to the Tavur sept. The most difficult of the four passes is Buru-köss; it is only used when the other three are snowed up. Ullug-art also is dangerous, and is not used unless the Ghez-daria is in flood and impassable. Under the most favourable circumstances it is only practicable during two months in the year, from the middle of June to the middle of August. And throughout the entire twelvemonth enormous masses of snow lie heaped up in the pass.

Upon leaving Upal we crossed a desolate steppe country, which rose by a slow and gradual incline towards

A MERCHANT OF EAST TURKESTAN

the entrance of the glen that gave access to the pass. But although the steppe was barren, it was trenched by several deep and wide ravines, the bottoms of which were green with fertile meadows, where sheep were grazing in large numbers. Having traversed the steppe, we rode in between the grandiose columns of black and grey clay-slate which mark the entrance to the glen. The ordinary poplar was common up to the end of our first day's journey, though we only saw one solitary willow; but after that tree vegetation ceased. The features of the glen were sharply marked; a little brook of crystal water ran down it in a bed eroded out of thick deposits of conglomerate. A short distance up, the glen was joined on the right by a little side-glen called Yamen-sara (the Paltry House).

On the afternoon of July 14th the atmosphere suddenly darkened in the higher regions of the mountains above us. It began to thunder and lighten, and the west wind drove the big dark clouds before it like sheep down the glen; and we were soon journeying through a pelting rain, which was both raw and cold. We put on our furs, and pushed on despite the rain. The path grew steeper and steeper the nearer we approached to the aul of Ullug-art. We could see it ahead of us, crowning a lofty conglomerate terrace high up on the right-hand side, and commanding an extensive bird's-eye view of the glen. The brook, now greatly swollen after the rain, raced down the glen, tinkling a metallic song. In the afternoon it came on to snow fast, and the ground was soon covered. The big feathery flakes drifted softly, softly down, like a flock of birds hovering on wing before settling; and great sullen clouds, heavy with snow, brooded over the mountains and the glen. I could easily have imagined it was the depth of winter, not the middle of July, the warmest month of the year. It was the general opinion of the Kirghiz that after this snowfall the pass would be impassable for three days, and if the storm continued it would possibly be closed altogether for that year. For it was no unusual thing for horses to be lost on the Ullug-art pass even in fine weather.

There was nothing for it, therefore, but to wait patiently until the weather improved; and fortunately we were well situated for waiting. The aul contained two first-class uy (tents), one occupied by Kipchak Kirghiz, the other by Naiman Kirghiz. There was plenty of pasture close by for our horses; and we bought a sheep from our hosts. The people, as well as the occupiers of another aul, lying still higher up the glen, only spend the summers in these elevated regions. In the winter they go down to the plains at the entrance of the glen.

A KIRGHIZ GIRL

We had decided to abandon the idea of crossing the Ullug-art, and on July 16th were just going to start for the Ayag pass, whither the Kirghiz undertook to guide us by a short cut, for they considered that pass would be much the easier of the two, when a man came down from the upper aul, and warned us not to venture by the Ayag-art. The pass itself was practicable enough, he said, but the river Markan-su, on the other side of it, would be impassable, especially if the weather was fine, and so we should be obliged to come all the way back again. He would answer for it, that we could get over the Ullug-art, and if I would give him 150 tengeh (£1 14*s.* 4*d.*), he and ten other men would carry all our baggage over on their backs. This would have to be done in any case, because, owing to the excessive steepness of the path, it was as much as the horses could do to climb up and down free of loads. Accordingly we went up to the higher aul, consisting of six yurts of Kipchak Kirghiz. It was scarcely an hour's ride. There we spent the night.

At half-past five on the morning of July 17th the weather was clear and calm, although a few light cloud skirmishers hovered above the pass. The day before had been sunny, and the snow on the eastern versant of the pass had melted considerably. An hour later we started, accompanied by the ten Kirghiz, who on their own account took with them two horses, provisions, and an axe. The path went up a steep, narrow gorge, close beside a torrent which murmured amongst the smooth, polished fragments of gneiss and clay-slate. On both sides the gorge was shut in by perpendicular conglomerate strata, which terminated in rounded dome-shaped hills, clad with green meadows. Herds of camels and flocks of sheep dotted the pastures, which were kept moist by the melting of the snows above them. Still higher up, the sky-line was broken by fantastically shaped peaks of bare rock and snow-clad ridges. At nine o'clock the gorge and pass were enveloped in thick clouds, and again it began to snow, and snowed on all the rest of the day. In a word, the weather could not have been worse; and our Kirghiz shook their heads ominously.

On our left I observed two small glacier tongues, with transverse terraces or shelves, and two terminal moraines. From them issued a couple of rivulets, which went to feed the brook that flowed down the glen. The summits on our right hand, which were freely exposed to the southern passages of the sun, possessed nothing more than the rudiments of glaciers. The glen grew so narrow, that we had to ride in the brook. The path was terribly steep. Every minute the horses kept stopping to catch their breath. At last we reached the foot of the actual pass. Then zigzagging backwards and forwards, backwards and forwards, we struggled up to the top. The snow was fully a foot deep, completely hiding the loose *débris* underneath, so that the horses frequently stumbled. The last portion of the ascent was a fearfully stiff piece of work. All our baggage had to be carried by the Kirghiz, who took turn about in getting up the heavy packages. Each box required two men; one carried the box on his back, whilst the other supported it and pushed it up from behind. The horses were led up one by one.

I reached the culminating point of the pass at eleven o'clock, and found there the masar (tomb) of Hazrett Ullug-art, consisting of a little heap of stones with staves stuck in them, to which pieces of rag were tied. The Kirghiz look upon the saint in the same way that their fellows do upon the guardian saint of Kizil-art, as lord over the pass and the weather, as meting out good fortune or ill to the traveller; his name is therefore constantly upon their lips, especially in all difficult places and all critical moments.

Whilst the Kirghiz were struggling with the packing-cases, and examining the descent on the west side of the pass, which occupied them a good hour and a half, I took observations on the top of the pass. The altitude by hypsometer was 16,890 feet, and the thermometer registered 31° Fahr. (−0°6 C.).

The ascent had been a tough piece of work; but it was nothing as compared with the descent. At first there was a scarcely noticeable incline; but it terminated in a formidable precipice, from which rocks of fantastic shape jutted out through snow. Down between these cliffy projections we had literally to slide and clamber on our hands and feet, now with our faces to the rock, now with our backs to it. The snow was two feet deep, and the Kirghiz were obliged to hew steps in it with the axe, before they could get the horses down. Then each horse was cleverly piloted down by two men, one leading the animal, the other holding on by its tail, so as to act as a sort of brake if the horse should lose its foothold. They managed to get them all safely down the first and most

THE PASS OF ULLUG-ART

difficult part of the precipitous slope, then it was the boxes' turn. A long rope was tied round each, and, two men holding the rope, the box was let slide gently down the face of the precipice by its own weight. Then came a talus slope at an angle of thirty-five and a half degrees, littered with loose *débris*. Down this the horses were left to make their way by themselves. My piebald stallion from the Khotan-daria stumbled, rolled some thousand feet down into an abyss, broke his spine, and died on the spot. Ullug-art is a perilous pass, the worst I have ever crossed in any part of Asia.

The weather was abominable. The wind, from the south-west, drove the snow about us in blinding clouds. It was only by snatches, when the snowstorm momentarily lifted, that I was able to get a glimpse of the magnificent panorama which lay spread out far down below our feet. On the left I got a bird's-eye view of a stupendous glacier, its surface shrouded in snow. Near its right-hand or upper edge there was a triangular moraine lake, fed by a stream which issued between two black, rugged cliffs from a secondary glacier above. The whole of the slope between the base of the secondary glacier and the moraine lake was strewn with pebbly *débris*, which, in consequence of the heavy rain and snowfall of the last few days, had become unsafe; in fact, the upper layer had already slipped, completely blotting out the track. For across that treacherous slope lay our path. Time after time whilst crossing it we slipped, and had great difficulty in avoiding a fall into the moraine lake some 160 feet below. It was a highly dangerous place, especially so if some of the large blocks of stone, which lay higher up, had started rolling down upon us. Here again therefore we unloaded the horses, and the Kirghiz carried their loads for about half a mile.

The gigantic glacier of Üllug-art overhung the upper end of the glen, presenting a slightly convex front between its enclosing cliffs. Our path ran down the slope between the ice and the right-hand side of the glen. We came to a second lake, immediately underneath the vertical glacier wall, which was reflected on its surface as on a piece of transparent glass. Several icebergs were floating on the lake, and its water kept changing from one shade of light green to another. The surface of the glacier inclined at a general angle of four degrees. Both the upper side-moraine, which we had already passed, and the terminal moraine were clearly distinguishable. A little further on we came to a third lake, the largest of the three, and some two miles wide. At that point we were again overtaken by a thick, blinding snowstorm, so that we could scarcely see where we were going to. This lasted an hour, until we were clear of the steep slopes. Then it cleared; although the snowstorm continued to rage in the higher regions of the mountains.

After that we made rapid progress down the glen on the western side of the Ullug-art; the glen growing wider at every mile, and the snow on the mountains around us diminishing at the same time in quantity. At length, after fourteen hours in the saddle, we halted between two conglomerate hills, near the junction of the glen with the broad, deep valley of Sarik-kol. Where we camped there was not a blade of grass; and we only got water by melting snow from a drift which lay in a sheltered crevice. We were now left to our own devices; for as soon as the Kirghiz had got us safely across the dangerous places, they went back over the pass.

A KIRGHIZ AUL, OR TENT-VILLAGE

The next day, July 18th, we rode as far as the yeylau (summer camp) of Muji, consisting of sixty yurts, inhabited by Naiman Kirghiz. They spend the summer there, grazing their sheep, goats, yaks, horses, and camels. On the 20th we reached the aul of Chakker-aghil, with six yurts, and there we rested beside a little lake of the same name a couple of days, a period which I utilized in making observations. The name Chakker-aghil (the Shouting Tent-Village) probably owes its derivation to the fact, that the auls thereabouts stand so closely together that you can shout from the one to the other. The water in the little lake was the same colour as the water of Kara-kul, a beautiful blue-green. It was in part bordered by detritus and sand, in part by reeds and seaweed (algæ), and on the west by rich meadows and marshes. The lake lay, as it were, wedged in the throat of the valley of Kamelah, and gathered into itself all the drainage-water of the valley.

I pass over our itinerary of the next few days, only mentioning, that the route took us through Bulun-kul, Kara-kul, Su-bashi, and Gedyäck—all of them districts that I had already visited. It was not until the 26th that I broke new ground, in that we crossed over the river basin of Tagharma, a stream which effects a confluence with the Kara-su, the river that drains the southern versant of Mus-tagh-ata. The conjoint stream then forces its way through the mountains in a narrow gorge called Tenghi. We travelled through the defile; which was only short. Further on the united Tagharma-Kara-su, known however by the latter name, Kara-su, poured itself into the Taghdumbash-daria, a stream which with almost incredible energy has cleft its way through the massive meridional mountain-chains that form, so to speak, the projecting rim of the Pamir plateau. That transverse valley, known as Shindeh-yilga, is, as might be supposed, close, confined, and wildly picturesque. The flood occupies it entirely, so that it is only in cold winters, when the river is ice-bound, that it is possible to reach Yarkand by that route.

Previous to the confluence of the rivers, we had been going down the stream. After the confluence we left the defile of Shindeh-yilga on the left, and ascended the upper part of the Taghdumbash-daria, the track leading towards the south on the west side of the upper stream. The road was level and firm, and frequently led across rich grassy meadows. Ahead of us we could see the fortress of Tash-kurgan, the goal of that day's march. After passing through the villages of Chushman (45 houses) and Tisnab (200 houses), we entered the lower valley of the Taghdumbash. It was broad and open, and wore a prosperous look, with its cultivated fields and pasture-grounds, on which innumerable herds of sheep, goats, and horned cattle were industriously grazing. On our right was a high platform of conglomerate formation, and on the top of it stood the town and fortress walls of Tash-kurgan (the Stone Fortress). The situation of the place put me forcibly in mind of Fort Pamir. The latter, like Tash-kurgan, stands on a conglomerate terrace, in a wide valley, and with a large river flowing past it; and it also commands an equally extensive view of its own neighbourhood.

Here an extremely joyful surprise awaited me. I fell in with my friend Mr. Macartney, who had been suddenly ordered to report himself to the head of the English Commission, appointed to act with a Russian Commission

KIRGHIZ AUL NEAR MUS-TAGH-ATA

of military officers for the delimitation of the frontier-line of the two empires on the southern Pamirs. I pitched my tent beside his, and we spent a right pleasant afternoon together.

On July 27th, along with Mr. Macartney, I paid a visit to the village of Tash-kurgan. Both village and fortress presented a melancholy appearance. The whole neighbourhood had been violently shaken by earthquakes lasting from July 5th to July 20th, and every house in the place was utterly ruined; the few which still stood had gaping cracks in the walls, reaching from roof to foundations. But then they were constructed of materials little calculated to withstand earthquake shocks, namely rubble and coggles, plastered with clay. There were also several cracks in the earth, stretching from south-south-

II.—2

west to north-north-east. The inhabitants, as well as the Chinese garrison, were living partly in yurts, partly in temporary tents. During the time the seismic disturbances lasted, some eighty distinct shocks were counted.

The most violent was the first; it was the shock which destroyed the town. The last happened this morning at ten minutes past eight o'clock. I was sleeping on the ground, as I always did, and distinctly felt the impact at right angles to the longitudinal axis of the valley, in other words it moved along an east-west line. The shock awakened in the mind an unpleasant sensation of anxiety. The earth seemed to heave and undulate. A detonation like a distant peal of thunder was plainly distinguishable. But everything was over in about a couple of seconds.

After looking at the damage done by the earthquake, I paid my respects to the commandant, Mi Darin, and two or three other mandarins, all of whom received me with great politeness. They had equipped their yurt with a table, chairs, and opium couches, and offered me all sorts of nice things. I took two or three whiffs at an opium-pipe, but failed to detect wherein lies its fascination.

* * * * *

In the early part of this work I have dwelt with considerable detail upon different parts of the Pamirs. The length to which this book is growing precludes me from describing this present expedition with anything approaching the same circumstantial minuteness. Perhaps I may be permitted on another occasion to relate the results of my 1895 journey in the southern regions of the Pamirs. I have still a long distance to travel before I reach Peking. If the reader has the patience to follow me, I hope to take him over the old caravan-road to Khotan, which Marco Polo travelled over so many generations ago. We shall then once more cross the great sandy desert, and discover cities buried in the sand, and evidences of an ancient and extinct Buddhist culture. We shall pay a visit to the desolate home of the wild camel, and discover the relic of the Lop-nor of the Chinese cartographers. Thence we shall make a forced march of some hundreds of miles back to Khotan. After that we shall cross the highlands and plateaus of Northern Tibet to the lake-basins of Tsaidam and make the acquaintance of Mongols, Tanguts, and Tibetans; then proceed through Kan-su, Ala-shan, Ordos, and Northern China; and finally, after travelling for three and a half years, reach the goal I had all along in view—namely Peking.

With all these vast vistas before me, I feel I must quicken my pace. But I cannot pass on without pausing for a little to describe one very important episode of my 1895 journey over the Pamirs. But it must have a chapter or two to itself.

CHAPTER LIV.

WITH THE ANGLO-RUSSIAN BOUNDARY COMMISSION

MR. MACARTNEY was on his way to Victoria Lake (Zor-kul), to join the Boundary Commission, and tried to persuade me to go with him. But as I was desirous of visiting the sources of the Yarkand-daria, I was obliged to decline his invitation. Nevertheless we travelled some days in company, separating on July 30th at Khojet-bai, as we then believed for ever; for Mr. Macartney was under orders to return to India with the Boundary Commission. Hence his road lay towards the west, up the valley of the Taghdumbash-daria; mine towards the south, up the valley of the Khunser-ab.

Two days more brought me to the northern foot of the Hindu-kush Mountains. There I stayed twelve days, making short excursions, exploring the valleys of the more important head-streams of the Khunser-ab, and climbing the pass of Khunser-ab (15,780 feet), whence I looked down upon the valley of Kanjut. From the summit of the pass to the highest village in Kanjut was only two day's-journey. There I observed that the streams from one of the glaciers on the pass flowed partly towards the Indian Ocean, and partly towards the Yarkand-daria and Lop-nor.

From the same place I endeavoured, but endeavoured in vain, to find a practicable path to the upper Yarkand-daria, over the passes of Uprang, Kara-su, and Ilik-su. The upper part of the Yarkand-daria is likewise known as the Serafshan or Raskan-daria. In every quarter I inquired, I was given the self-same answer: I could readily enough reach the river in the course of a few days, but there was no place where it could be crossed during the summer. The deep narrow gorge of the Ilik-su had in places been so terribly convulsed by the recent violent earthquakes that it was impossible for any animal, even for yaks, to traverse it: it was only practicable to men on foot. Thus I had got myself into a sort of mountain *cul-de-sac*. The only accessible districts which I had not yet explored were towards the west. Hence I resolved to seek those portions of the Pamirs which lay around the sources of the Amu-daria.

PART OF THE HINDU-KUSH, NEAR UPRANG

Accordingly we rode up over Taghdumbash-Pamir (the Mountain's Head or Roof of the World), and on 15th August surmounted the pass of Wakjir (16,190 feet), an important hydrographical centre. For from it rivers flow in three different directions—the Pänj, also called the Wakhan-daria, a head-stream of the Amu-daria, goes towards the west; the Taghdumbash-daria flows east; and on the other side of the Hindu-kush several feeders of the Indus descend towards the south.

On August 17th we reached Chakmakden-kul (the Lake of the Fire-steel), in which the Ak-su or Murghab has its origin.

Knowing that the Anglo-Russian Boundary Commission were working at Mehman-yolli (the Guest Road), a small transverse valley situated only a day's journey towards the north-east, I could not resist the temptation to pay them a visit. But I did not like to come down suddenly and without warning upon the Commissioners whilst in the midst of their delicate labour of defining the boundary from Victoria Lake to the Chinese frontier; so I wrote to the head of each Commission, asking if they had any objection to receiving visitors. My jighit (courier) brought back a cordial and pressing invitation from both chiefs. Accordingly on the evening of the 19th I pitched my tent at Mehman-yolli, on neutral ground between the Russian camp and the English camp.

I was already acquainted with the head of the Russian Commission; it was General Pavalo-Shveikovsky, governor of Fergana, my friend and benefactor. I held myself bound therefore to pay my respects to him first. But I could not get to his quarters without passing through the English camp. Mr. Macartney caught sight of me as I was on my way, and eagerly intercepted me with an invitation to dine with General Gerard, head of the English Commission.

There I was then, in a pretty dilemma. The only way out of it, the only way to preserve my neutrality, that I could see, was to plead my old acquaintance with General Pavalo-Shveikovsky, and to emphasize the unsuitability of my attire.

General Pavalo-Shveikovsky welcomed me with open arms. We sat talking until a late hour of the night; and notwithstanding my energetic protests and my hints of wishing to keep to neutral territory, he ordered an excellent yurt to be got ready for me at once, with a bed in it, a luxury which I had almost forgotten the enjoyment of.

The following morning I paid a visit to General Gerard, and met with a similar kind and friendly reception from him. I was immediately introduced to the several members of the English Commission. The second officer in command was Colonel Holdich, a recipient of the large gold medal of the Royal Geographical Society for his admirable trigonometrical and astronomical work in the frontier districts of India. The rest of the staff included Colonel Wahab, the topographer; Captain McSwiney, who spoke Russian fluently; Dr. Alcock, director of the Imperial Museum at Calcutta, and professor of the Calcutta University; and my friend Mr. Macartney, agent for Chinese affairs in Kashgar. In addition

END OF A GLACIER AT UPRANG

there were three pundits, or educated Hindus, for the topographical field-work.

Amongst the Russian staff I found several acquaintances from West Turkestan—Colonel Salessky, the astronomer; Captain Skersky, the new commandant of Fort Pamir; and the famous topographer Bendersky, who has travelled in every part of Western Asia, and who was one of the Russian embassy which visited Kabul in the time of Emir Shir Ali Khan. General Pavalo-Shveikovsky's principal assistants were however Mr. Panafidin, formerly

Russian consul in Bagdad, where he and I had several mutual friends and acquaintances, and Colonel Galkin, who had travelled in East Turkestan and Ili. Finally, I may mention Dr. Wellmann and four younger officers.

The Russian escort consisted of some forty Cossacks, with a military band of eighteen performers, besides a crowd of native jighits and caravan grooms. The English train consisted of about two hundred Indian soldiers, Hindus, Afridis, and Kanjutis.

It would manifestly be out of place for me to say a word touching the momentous labours of the Boundary Commission. Besides, they did not directly concern me. I will merely observe that, considering the opposing interests which the two camps represented, it was astonishing upon what a friendly and confidential footing they were. Both sides were animated by a frank and cheerful spirit. Englishmen and Russians were like comrades together. Had I not known the fact beforehand, I should never for one moment have dreamed that they were rivals, engaged in delimitating and fixing a common frontier-line. For of course, it was the object of the Russians to draw the line as far to the south as they could possibly force it; whereas the Englishmen wanted it as far north as it could be got.

The Russian officers' mess was located in a large, tastefully decorated yurt; the Englishmen had theirs in an immense, yet elegant, tent. Invitations to dinner from the one party or the other were an almost everyday occurrence. As for me, I spent one day in the English camp and the next in the Russian, and so on alternately; and was on very good terms with everybody in both camps. Most of the officers, Russian and English, spoke French; and if I may be permitted to say so, the gentlemen selected to serve on this important and delicate mission were a credit to the two Governments which appointed them. As for me, after my two years of lonely wandering through the desert regions of Central Asia, it was almost like a rising from the dead, to associate with such notable men, men distinguished alike for their knowledge, their scientific attainments, their high general culture.

Shortly after my arrival amongst them, General Pavalo-Shveikovsky gave a grand evening entertainment. At nine o'clock the Englishmen came over wearing their handsome, yet serviceable, full-dress uniforms. In front of each of the Russian yurts was stationed a guard of Cossacks, holding lighted torches, which shed a wild and tremulous flood of light across the bank of the Ak-su.

CHAKMAKDEN-KUL, LOOKING WEST

The guests assembled in the large reception yurt of white felt. The interior was draped with Oriental cloth and variegated carpets from Kashgar. The table glittered with bottles and decanters of European wines and liqueurs; whilst dotted about amongst them were dishes of solid silver, heaped with grapes, apples, and duchesse pears from the governor's own garden in Margelan. We took our seats in light and comfortable tent-chairs, lined with rugs and so forth. Whilst some of the company played cards, the majority kept up an animated conversation in different languages. Meanwhile the military band went through a long programme of Russian melodies, well-known marches, and "God Save the Queen"; and heard under such circumstances, at such a lofty altitude on the Roof of the World, the music was especially charming. After supper, the Russian general accompanied his guests by torchlight to their own quarters.

The 29th and 30th August were proclaimed holidays; and the officers got up a *tamashah* (spectacle, *i.e.* sports) for the entertainment of the men of their escorts and the Kirghiz of the neighbourhood. The first item on the programme was a shooting competition at 250 paces. In this some of the officers took part; and the first prize was carried off by Colonel Wahab, upon whom after that I bestowed the title of Champion of the Roof of the World. The scene around the firing-point was gay in the extreme, owing to the variety and magnificence of the various uniforms. The 1st Lancers, Hyderabad Contingent, made unquestionably the bravest show. Their uniform was a light brown, decorated with gold braid, yellow leather bandolier and sword-belt, tight-fitting breeches, and a tall, gold-embroidered turban, with blue points hanging loosely down. The uniform of the 20th Punjab Infantry was very similar, except that the turban was adorned with a black bushy plume, and had a gold-embroidered, upstanding centre-piece. The Afridis, natives of the districts around Peshawar, were tall handsome fellows, with a martial bearing. A vendetta of a more than usually stringent character obtains amongst their tribes. A murder is sometimes avenged, not only upon the nearest blood-relatives of the delinquent, but also upon his distant kin.

Amongst the onlookers I observed Gulam Moheddin Khan, the Afghan Boundary Commissioner, accompanied by his suite. The Emir Abdurrahman Khan's representative, whom I was nearly forgetting, wore a uniform that was resplendent with gold-lace and ornaments.

At the end of the shooting competition, the two generals distributed the prizes, consisting of a silver cup, cases containing knife, fork, and spoon, khalats, Asiatic cloth, and money (roubles and rupees). Hereupon General Pavalo-Shveikovsky invited us all, including the Afghan Commissioner, to a splendid *déjeuner*. Champagne flowed like water, and healths were drunk to all the world, even to the Crustaceans of the Indian Ocean, the special favourites of Dr. Alcock.

After *déjeuner* we went out to witness the second half of the programme, which was of a more lively and varied

GROUP OF KIRGHIZ FROM THE EASTERN PAMIRS

character. It began with a tug-of-war, a team of Cossacks being pitted against a team of Afridis, and then a team of Kirghiz against a team of Kanjutis. In each case the first-named won; although the struggle between the Kirghiz and Kanjutis was both tough and long. The excitement amongst the onlookers grew intense; even some of the officers were infected by it, as well as myself, though I of course preserved a strict neutrality. After that came foot-races, partly on the flat, partly in sacks, in which the winners hopped or rather turned summersaults over the tape at the winning-post. There were also three-legged races. The Kanjutis gave us a sword-dance, with mimic fights, and combats with the naked sword, a spectacle which put me in mind of similar games practised by the Chinese. At intervals the English offered various refreshments, amongst the beverages being punch.

The 30th August was Derby Day on the Pamirs. Some three hundred horsemen assembled on a piece of level ground at Kizil-rabat near by. The course was a trifle under a mile. The Cossacks, being matched against the Indian cavalrymen, easily beat them, with a good two minutes to spare. But Her Majesty's soldiers had their revenge in the next event, lemon-slicing; although potatoes perforce did duty instead of lemons. The next contest, tilting at the ring, was opened by General Gerard himself. He carried off two out of the three rings, and proved to be the victor.

Then came a comic interlude, namely, races between camels and yaks. The camels, unaccustomed to the rules of sport, burst away in a wild gallop, and screaming lustily dashed in amongst the spectators, creating a mild panic. The yaks on the contrary took matters with imperturbable placidity; the spirit of emulation could not be driven into them by any provocation. Two remained stock-still, notwithstanding that the cudgels of the Kirghiz played a lively tune upon their ribs. One turned to the rightabout and marched off in the opposite direction. Some progressed sideways at a jog-trot. Only two went straight down the course, walking with their accustomed grave philosophic calm.

The last event was not pleasant to watch, and must have been still more unpleasant to take part in. Two bands of Kirghiz horsemen, twenty in each, took up positions facing one another at 250 paces apart. At a pre-arranged signal they dashed towards each other at full gallop. Some few came through the shock unmoved; but the greater part went headlong to the ground, men and horses rolling over one another in indescribable confusion. Yet strange to say, only one horse suffered any injury. It took all day till twilight to get through the whole of the programme; and just as the gay throng of riders started for their respective camps, the race-course was swept by an icy buran.

The combined camp of the Commissioners made a striking picture. It stood on a patch of level ground, at the foot of a conglomerate terrace, on the left bank of the Ak-su or Murghab. The Russians were quartered in a dozen large, handsome Kirghiz yurts; the Englishmen and Indian soldiers in some fifty or sixty white army tents. Round about the outskirts of the camp were the yurts of the Afghans, Kirghiz, Wakhanlik (men of Wakhan), and karakeshes (caravan attendants) of different nationalities. The camp thus presented a kind of epitome of various types of Oriental life, side by side with the highest civilization of the West. A painter would have found never-ending subjects for his brush. The pencil of a dilettante like myself was kept hard at work all day long, for unfortunately I had lost my photographic apparatus in the desert.

Both the Russian and the English generals were perfect patterns and ensamples to their officers and men. Both had gone through many a stiff brush with the enemy. General Pavalo-Shveikovsky had an inexhaustible fund of stories and anecdotes from the Russo-Turkish war of 1877–78. General Gerard was famous throughout all India as one of the most daring spirits that ever tracked a tiger. With his own hand he had accounted for no fewer than 216 of the kings of the jungle, a number which, considering the relative scarcity of tigers now in India, must be accounted worthy of the most passionate lover of the chase. To General Gerard the tracking of a tiger was what the coursing of a hare is to ordinary sportsmen, a mere harmless pastime, combining exercise with pleasure; all the same, he had had many adventures and hairbreadth escapes, which it was very interesting to listen to.

CHAPTER LV.

FESTIVITIES ON THE ROOF OF THE WORLD

EVERY evening at eight o'clock the Cossacks had religious service. Then there echoed through the thin mountain-air the moving melodies of the solemn *malitva* (chant) and the Russian national hymn. Huge fires blazed all round the camp, both close in and at a distance, for the various Asiatic races to cook their suppers at; but all fires were extinguished long before the lights were out in the officers' quarters. The moon gleamed out at intervals between the rapidly scudding clouds, and lit up the broad, open valley of the Ak-su. A chain of mountains, the Emperor Nicholas II.'s Range, the highest summit of which is Salisbury Peak, shut in the valley on the north; another range, the Mus-tagh chain, bordered it on the south. The effect was enchanting in the extreme when a cloud came between the moon and the camp, so that the tents were in the shade, whilst the eternal snowfields of the distant mountains glittered as though silvered over.

These desolate plateaus, uninhabited save by a few half-civilized nomad Kirghiz, had never witnessed such a gathering as that which I have just described, and are hardly likely to witness anything similar to it again. I imagined the shy tekkes (wild goats) and wild sheep (*Ovis Poli*) gazing in stupefied amazement from their lofty pasture-grounds beside the glaciers over the bustling scenes below, rudely violating the century-long peace and tranquillity of the Ak-su valley. Where the frontier-line between the possessions of England and the possessions of Russia should fall was to them a matter of perfect unconcern. The jarring interests of men never invade the solitude of their sublime abodes. They are the subjects of none; they share their empire with the eternal snows alone.

Meanwhile the days flew past like hours, and I was amazed when September came, and I still found myself amongst that bright circle of officers of the two most powerful nations of the world. Several times I spoke of breaking camp for the little-known mountainous regions which tower up like fierce, snow-crowned giants around the head-waters of the Yarkand-daria. But every time I sounded that note, both of the generous generals, whose personal friend I am proud to say I gradually became, urged that I should remain a few days longer.

But finding nothing else would do, and as there were important matters calling me back to Kashgar, I determined to try a little *ruse de guerre.* One fine day I bade Islam Bai have the caravan all ready for a start, and went to General Pavalo-Shveikovsky to take my leave of him, telling him my caravan was ready and waiting for me. With a twinkle of mystery in his eye, the general answered that, if I would wait just one day longer, I should witness a remarkable event. Thus my little plot was nipped in the bud. I stayed on, not one day longer, but several.

The remarkable event, which, rightly enough, did happen on the following day, was the arrival of a telegram sent by Lord Salisbury to the telegraph-station which lay nearest the northern frontier of India, conveying the important announcement, that the British Government accepted the frontier which the Russians proposed to them.

This intelligence occasioned the greatest rejoicing in both camps. At every step I met happy, contented faces. The younger officers even danced for joy. During the following days the frontier pillars Nos. IX. to XII. were erected, thus finishing the labours of the Commission. They had defined and marked the frontier between England's and Russia's possessions on the Pamirs, and had nothing more to do except to strike camp and return home.

Stay, I am wrong, there was still one thing to be done. The two Commissions had been at work together some three months in all. It was inconceivable that they should separate, perhaps never to meet again, without dining together in each camp in turn. To these high and solemn functions I, although strictly maintaining my neutrality, was cordially invited; and as public dinners are something of a rarity in exploration journeys in Central Asia, I did not scruple to sacrifice two more days to the pleasure of taking part in them.

The dinner in the Russian camp took place on September 11th. General Gerard and I were given the places of honour on the right and left respectively of our host. My more than plain travelling-suit, which was moreover woefully threadbare, and which had never at any time been guilty of possessing such superfluities as collar and cuffs, presented a glaring contrast to the full-dress uniforms of all the generals, colonels, captains, and diplomatic agents—laces of the general staff, scarlet facings, gold braids, orders and medals for valour from the campaign in Turkestan, the Russo-Turkish War, Burma, Chitral, Afghanistan. But then, when I left Kashgar, I had not the remotest idea that that summer excursion was to bring me into contact with such distinguished company, and therefore had brought no suitable clothes with me. However, I kept up my courage; and the warriors flattered me by saying that my journey across the desert was a stiffer piece of work than many a hard campaign.

And then the surprises that were in store for us, real paradoxes of circumstance, when you call to mind that all this happened at the foot of the Hindu-kush in the centre of Asia! The *sakuska*, or ante-table of Russian usage, consisted of caviar, preserved meats, Swiss cheese, *pâté-de-fois-gras*, and almost every conceivable delicacy, whilst for dinner we were served, amongst other courses, with crayfish soup, lobster mayonnaise, asparagus, and so forth. The only thing which failed to make a due impression upon me was the *glacés:* I had been completely spoiled for *glacés* by the glaciers on the Roof of the World.

The wines were not from Turkestan, but from the choice vintages of France. What! Champagne on the Pamirs? Yes, even so. The first time it was handed round, our host asked for silence, and then proposed a conjoint toast to Queen Victoria and the Emperor Nicholas II. The next toast was drunk in honour of Abdurrahman Khan, Emir of Afghanistan, who was represented at the table by his general Gulam Moheddin Khan and a *mufti* (Mohammedan doctor of laws). With the third toast was coupled the name of Oscar, king of Sweden and Norway, who also had one subject present at the banquet. At midnight the official part of the proceedings came to an end, with the Englishmen chairing their host. Their arms were strong, and so it was "up to the roof on the Roof of the World." Then, whilst the spirit of festivity was still in the ascendant, we had several humorous speeches and songs, each and every one followed by a rousing cheer, and last of all, sung with tremendous dash and "go," the stirring English refrain, "For he's a jolly good fellow, which nobody can deny."

The next day General Gerard gave an equally excellent banquet, over which the same spirit of jollification reigned, and at which there was an equally long series of toasts. With a happy inspiration Captain McSwiney proposed a toast to the Ladies, and somebody suggested the extraordinary idea, that I was a fit and proper person to reply on the ladies' behalf. Being a devoted admirer of the sex, I was of course proud to speak for them. After various more or less apposite remarks, I came to my peroration, which ran to this effect: that if the ladies in the distant lands of Russia and England were as hospitable and as cultivated as their husbands and lovers, whose acquaintance I had had the pleasure of making, they must assuredly be no ordinary ladies, but angels from heaven, and their society an earthly paradise.

At the close of dinner yet another surprise awaited us. Immediately outside the bounds of the camp a huge pile of faggots and other inflammable materials had been built up; —curiously enough, the fuel had all been fetched for the purpose from Kanjut on the other side of the Hindu-kush. As soon as dinner was over, the bonfire was lighted; and its leaping flames lit up with weird effect the barren steppe and white tents which dotted it. Then representatives of the different races comprised in the English escort came forward one after the other and gave an exhibition of their several national dances. Amongst these perhaps the most striking was a sword-dance, which produced a somewhat startling effect in the red light of the bonfire. We watched the spectacle from a semicircle of camp-chairs, whilst turbaned servants handed round punch and other refreshments.

Early on the morning of September 13th we were all photographed together in one big group by the Indian pundits. After that came the hand-shaking and the "good-byes." The Englishmen went off towards the south, intending to travel to Kashmir and India *viâ* the Darkot pass; whilst the Russians turned their steps towards the north. General Gerard, who was going to England across Russia, accompanied his Russian colleague. Lieutenant Miles, who was stationed in Gilgit, was likewise given permission to go with the Russian Commissioners as far as Fort Pamir. That day we only travelled 14½ miles, as far as the Kirghiz aul of Ak-tash. Here we pitched our tents, and spent another right pleasant afternoon together.

General Pavalo-Shveikovsky pressed me to accompany him all the way to Margelan. But that I could not do; it would have taken me too far away from the scene of my labours. Not that it would not have been especially interesting to travel for a whole month across the Pamirs under such unique circumstances, as well as to witness the great reception which I knew awaited the English general in Margelan. He was to be met outside the town by a bevy of maidens, clad in white, who would scatter flowers under his horse's hoofs, and was to be fêted, and honoured with a military concert and display of fireworks. But I withstood the temptation, steeled by the thought that I had not come to Asia for the sake of pleasure; besides, I already knew the route to be travelled over.

General Gerard also had his temptation for me. He cordially invited me to go with Colonel Holdich and the rest of the English Boundary Commissioners to India. Which drew me with the strongest fascination—that distant land of fable and mystic dream, or the society of Colonel Holdich, I cannot say; but this I can say, I have seldom met a nobler-minded, pleasanter gentleman than Colonel Holdich, and I left him with the desire strong in my heart that we might soon meet again.

But my sense of duty got the upper hand at last. My road lay towards the east. There was still much exploring work to be done in the deserts around Lop-nor and in Northern Tibet. Moreover there was another powerful attraction in Kashgar, namely the post from Sweden, which should be in again by this. I therefore on 14th September bade farewell to the two generals and other officers, and watched them trot out of sight; then, accompanied by my own attendants, I turned my face towards the silent, solitary mountains which border the Pamir plateaus on the east.

The doings of the Anglo-Russian Boundary Commission belong henceforth to history; their labours fill a permanent niche in the story of the political relations of England and Russia in Central Asia. The territories of the two great powers on the Pamirs now touch one another; there are no ownerless districts, no buffer zone, between them to afford a handle for political intrigues. Kirghiz and Afghans are not now allowed to cross the new frontier-line unless they are provided with a proper pass.

Will that be the last boundary commission appointed by England and Russia in Asia? It might well be supposed so; and yet—the destiny of Persia is not yet decided. Besides, who knows what the future shall bring forth? Be that however as it may, it is certain that the members of the Boundary Commission of 1895 carried away home with them many a pleasant memory of their stay on the cold, inhospitable plateaus; the which plateaus no doubt, had they possessed the capability, would have been amazed at finding themselves the object of so much interest.

I am very proud of having been so fortunate as to have witnessed such a signal episode in the political history of Central Asia, and that not only because of the importance of the event itself, but also because of the real pleasure vouchsafed me in making the acquaintance of such an excellent set of officers and gentlemen.

CHAPTER LVI.

OVER THE MOUNTAINS TO THE YARKAND-DARIA

FROM Ak-tash we travelled eastwards, and the same day crossed the Sarik-kol range by the pass of Lakshak (15,240 feet high), and encamped on the other side at Keng-shevär, a place garrisoned by eight Tajiks and two Chinese. As far as a point a little beyond our camp the rocks bordering the route had been black clay-slates; but after that they consisted of a number of varieties of gneiss, some of them exceedingly beautiful in appearance. Consonant with the change in the rock formation, a marked change took place also in the landscape. The very name of the district we had just quitted, Kara-korumning-bashi (the Head of the Black, Stony Country), indicated a different region. The track we were following, which wound for the most part amongst gigantic fragments of rock which had crashed down from the mountains above, led north-eastwards through the deep transverse gorge of Shindeh, which cut through the eastern declivity of the Sarik-kol range. Beyond Yarutteck (the Boot Terrace), a small side-glen on the left, the cliffs frowned upon each other at close quarters, there being nothing more than a narrow chasm between their perpendicular walls. The gorge was almost entirely obstructed by huge blocks of gneiss, whose sharp angles and fresh, clean-looking fractures revealed that they had been hurled down during the recent earthquake shocks. It was anything but pleasant travelling. We frequently rode under ponderous arches of overhanging rock, full of cracks and crevices, which threatened every moment to come crashing down upon our heads. Time after time we crossed the little mountain-stream, whose blue, limpid water gurgled along between the boulders of gneiss. At length we came to the end of the gneiss. It was succeeded by granite. The gorge of Shindeh opened out like a trumpet upon the broad trough-like valley of Taghdumbash. The mountain-stream was divided into several branches, so that its water might be led off to irrigate the cultivated fields. We again pitched our tent a short distance from the fortress of Tash-kurgan.

We had now crossed the first of the great meridional mountain-ranges, which like bastions fence in the Pamir plateaus on the east. On September 16th we crossed the second by the pass of Särghak. We had considerable difficulty in procuring a guide. The Tajiks excused themselves on the plea, that they must look after their fields; but the truth was they dreaded the wrath of Mi Darin, if it should become known that they had guided a European through such a strategically important pass. At last we discovered a man who agreed to go with us on foot; but before we reached the summit of the pass he lagged behind, and we never saw anything more of him.

We crossed over the valley of Taghdumbash between the scattered fields and houses. The river possessed only one-third the volume it had when I measured it some six weeks earlier, and the water had become perfectly clear. On the east side of the valley we struck into a narrow gorge, which rose steeply, and was dry along the bottom. The predominating rock throughout the whole of that day's journey was micaceous schist. We climbed up the mountain-side along a steep, narrow ribbon of a path, which was exceedingly trying to both men and horses. In some places the rocks were so smooth we were obliged to roughen them with the pick-axe to enable the horses to get a proper foothold. Upon reaching the top of the spur—an undulating series of rounded eminences—we saw the valley of Taghdumbash, with its winding river and its green and yellow fields, far, far below our feet. Once more the landscape underwent a complete change. All

MI DARIN, THE COMMANDANT OF TASH-KURGAN

round us the predominating feature was low hills, with easy slopes, covered with hard silt, sand, and gravel *débris*, partly the results of weathering of the clay-slate, which in this part of the range cropped out but seldom. These undulating hilly uplands were intersected by several zigzag cañon-like ravines. Not a drop of water was to be seen; though there were plenty of dry watercourses, showing where the rains ran down. Our road was not difficult, but went up and down, up and down as though it never meant to end; and we crossed several secondary passes

A TAJIK TENT IN THE TAGHDUMBASH PAMIRS

before we attained the culminating point of the range (13,230 feet).

From that spot I obtained a broad general view of the surrounding regions. The range on which we stood was continued towards the south in several great snow-covered mountains, then curved round by the south-east towards Tibet, and finally became merged in the Kwen-lun mountain-system. Northwards the range we had just climbed stretched to Mus-tagh-ata, and thus formed a direct continuation of the Mus-tagh or Kashgar range. Deep down on the east lay the glen of the Utcheh, which flows into the Taghdumbash-daria.

Our road ran down into that glen, sometimes winding amongst the fantastic spurs and buttresses of the eastern slopes of the range, sometimes running steeply down an eroded ravine, and occasionally crossing a minor pass or saddle. The last part of the descent, just before we reached the glen, was inconceivably steep. We encamped in the little village of Beldir, which consisted of a single household. Its *yuz-bashi* (chief) was however chieftain over some fifty households, scattered throughout the glen. They were Tajiks, graziers and agriculturists, and spent the summers in the upper part of the glen, but for the winter moved lower down nearer the confluence of the Utcheh, a fair-sized stream, with the Taghdumbash-daria. After the confluence the river turned sharply to the east, and flowed directly into the Yarkand-daria. Close beside the confluence stood the large village of Beldir, which gives a second name, the Beldir-daria, to the Utcheh. The transverse defile by which the Taghdumbash breaks through the range is, as I have already said, called Shindeh. It is impassable because of the perpendicular cliffs which hem it in. Thus Beldir lies, as it were, at the end of a mountain *cul-de-sac*.

September 17th. We ascended the glen towards the south-east. It was sometimes squeezed between the conglomerate cliffs, then widened out considerably, so as to make room for patches of cultivated ground, upon which wheat, barley, and clover were grown, and finally opened out into a spacious cauldron-shaped valley, with an almost level floor and shut in on all sides by mountains.

This expansion of the glen, called Täng-ab (Persian, Narrow Water), was planted with several small villages, all inhabited by Tajiks. But the great altitude of the region, and its harsh climate, compel the people to adopt a mode of life which in some respects resembles that of the Kirghiz. Most of them own large flocks of sheep, goats, and yaks, besides numerous horses and donkeys. Some dwell in yurts and tents; some—more especially those who live by agriculture—dwell in houses constructed of sun-dried clay and stones, and covered in with flat wooden roofs. As the Tajiks themselves are Aryans, and speak Persian, so their houses are very similar to the Persian houses, even possessing in some cases a *bala-khaneh* or "upper house," reached by a flight of stairs.

September 18th. We continued our road along the

broad expansion of the valley till we came to the point where it bifurcated into the two secondary valleys of Lengher and Shuydun. A road through the former led to the large Tajik village of Marian, and thence to the Raskan-daria (*i.e.* the upper Yarkand-daria). Through the latter ran the road we took. Crossing the luxuriant pastures, we reached at length a rabat (rest-house or inn) at the foot of the Kandahar pass, and there we spent the night.

The next morning we awoke to a perfect winter scene. During the night it had snowed heavily, and the ground was covered a couple of inches deep. From the rabat the path ascended the mountain-side pretty steeply; but the snow levelled up the spaces between the stones and made it easier going. The summit or ridge of the pass (16,610 feet altitude) was as sharp as a knife; for the broken edges of the green clay-slates jutted out almost vertically. The descent on the other side was very difficult, so difficult in fact that the horses would scarcely have been able to get down loaded. But, having been warned of this beforehand, we had hired a party of Tajiks with three yaks, and with their help we got the boxes safely down. At the outset the path went straight down between nasty projecting buttresses of rock; down these we simply slid long distances over the deep snow. But lower down the descent was less precipitous. The quantity of snow on the ground was everywhere much less than on the western versant of the pass. The sky, which was clear in the morning to start with, clouded over again, and it snowed hard all the way to the little rabat of Kotchkor-Beg-Bai, in the bottom of the confined valley of Kandahar. Two or three Tajik families dwelt in the neighbourhood.

During the summer and autumn the flocks graze on both sides of the pass; but for the winter they move down to the district of Tong, whither we now directed our steps. In winter too the pass of Kandahar is generally preferred, if only it is at all practicable. As a rule, it is deeply buried in snow, and the Tajiks trample down a path by driving yaks on before them. If the pass is absolutely impassable, there is no other way of reaching Tash-kurgan except by going right round through Yarkand and Tagharma.

The snow continued to fall in big feathery flakes all the evening, and drifted together in loose snowdrifts. The air was cold, moist, and raw, and the darkness a darkness that could almost be felt. Our Tajik neighbours made first-class wheat bread, and some of the young girls came to my tent unveiled and offered me a few pieces. I accepted it, and rewarded them with some strips of cloth from Kashgar.

September 20th. When we awoke in the morning it was still snowing, and it snowed right on till eleven o'clock in the morning. The weight of the snow pressed so heavily upon my tent that the men frequently had to sweep it off, till I became literally encompassed by walls of snow. When we started again, we were joined by two young women, riding yaks. They were going a short distance down the glen to fetch fuel. They were uncommonly pretty and merry, and, their hair being black, and their eyebrows conspicuously marked, they put me in mind of gipsy lasses. They helped us with our caravan-animals, as though it were a perfectly natural thing to do; and their silvery voices, as they cried to them and urged them on, echoed musically against the steep mountain-walls. Their clothes hung about them in scanty rags; it made me shiver to see the thickly falling snow melting on their coppery brown bare necks and bosoms.

A short distance below our camp the glen contracted into a defile, which, owing to the fallen stones and huge fragments of rock, and the torrents of clear cool water which brawled amongst them, made the road both narrow and difficult. We repeatedly crossed and re-crossed the stream, in many places not without imminent risk of a bath. But just as often the path skirted the edge of the conglomerate terraces, the clay matrix of which had become softened by the melting snow, so that the ground threatened to slip away from under our feet.

Eventually the glen widened out every now and again, making room for groups of birches. At one of these places, called Tersek, our guide said, there were no trees lower down, and if we wanted fuel for a night-fire, we must stay where we were. The tent was therefore pitched underneath some fine hanging birches, whose foliage had already turned yellow. It was a particularly nice place for a night's camping; the only drawbacks were the gloomy, frowning sky and the thick veils of mist which wreathed the summit of the mountains. The two young women and our guide gathered up their bundles of fuel, loaded it on the backs of the yaks, and returned to their lonely cabins up the glen.

September 21st. We still continued our descent, the path being excessively steep, stony, and uncomfortable. Shortly after leaving our night's quarters we came upon a gigantic fragment of granite, bearing a curious resemblance to a colossal mushroom or petrified poplar. It had tumbled down from the mountain above and stood in the middle of the glen, which was for the most part shut in by mountains that turned their transversely fractured faces towards it. Clumps of birches, wild briars, and junipers were dotted about here and there.

CHAPTER LVII.

DOWN THE YARKAND-DARIA AND TO KASHGAR

WE made our next camp in the village of Lengher, amongst fields of wheat, barley, and clover. The population were Tajiks; but curiously enough, most of the geographical names in that district were Jagatai (Turki). The pass of Arpa-tallak, which we were to cross in a day or two, serves as a religious boundary between a predominatingly Sunnite population on the east and a predominatingly Shiite population on the west of it. Both sects however live on the best of terms with one another; there is nothing of the enmity between them which keeps the (Sunnite) Turks and the (Shiite) Persians at such deadly variance. They intermarry with one another; and are in constant communication backwards and forwards. The only tribute they pay to the Chinese is certain quantities of fuel and forage; but when Yakub Beg was master of Kashgar, the fiscal imposts laid upon them were almost oppressive. Nevertheless they are said to have preferred his rule to that of the Chinese; he was a Mohammedan like themselves, and he was their own *padshah* (king).

The rainy season in this valley coincides with the summer, and the quantity of rain that falls is often so plenteous that the river cannot be forded.

The recent earthquakes had brought most of the houses to the ground. One man who lay ill in bed died of terror; another, who was riding along the glen, was crushed by a fragment of rock which crashed down the mountain-side upon him. The glen was both wild and picturesque, the mountain scenery being on an imposing scale; consequently the people who inhabit it were frank, cheerful, and liberal-minded.

September 22nd. We rode through a string of eight villages, each consisting of several houses, with court-yards, surrounded by cultivated fields and gardens, in which walnuts, apricots, peaches, apples, melons, and other fruits were grown. After the barren mountain regions which we had left behind us, it was pleasant to catch the scent of freshly cut corn. We saw neither yaks nor camels in that district, only cattle, donkeys, horses, sheep, and goats.

The prettiest village was Tong, its luxuriant orchards and picturesque houses contrasting agreeably with the naked mountain-walls of the background behind it. The chief of the village, Hassan Beg, was a typical old man; he reminded me of a worn-out professor, being extra-ordinarily absent-minded, and yet constantly talking away in half-tones to himself. At Kandalaksh, a village a short distance lower down, we put up at the *min-bashi's* (chief-tain of a thousand men), and established ourselves on his balcony, where all the dignitaries of the place came to pay us their respects.

Tong lies only a mile or a little more from the Yarkand-daria. The river is known there simply as Daria (the River), or also as Tongning-dariasi (the Tong River). The names Raskan and Serafshan are only applied to the upper portion of the stream. In summer the river is so swollen that it cannot be crossed by any means whatever. Hence the inhabitants only travel to Yarkand in the autumn and winter. The journey takes a man on horse-back about three days. Traders from Yarkand visit the valley with clothes, sugar, tea, and other commodities. Hassan Beg and the villagers thought we might possibly get across the river; but the old man begged me to remain with him that night, so that everything might be prepared for ferrying us across in the morning.

September 23rd. When we came down to the river, I was astonished to find that the side-valley of Tong was broader than the principal valley upon which it debouched.

The enormous volumes of water which pour off the mountains towards that quarter have cleft their way irresistibly through the massive mountain-chains, and present views of signal grandeur both up and down the defile by which they break their way through. From the marks on the cliff-side I observed that the river was at that time 11½ feet lower than its highest level during the summer. All the same, a hollow roar echoed against the mountain-walls as the flood, still of considerable volume, rolled its greenish muddy waters along its deeply eroded channel.

The river stopped our way. We must get across it somehow. On the river bank we found half-a-dozen *suchis* (water men) waiting for us, in wide swimming-drawers, each man having a *tulum* (inflated goat-skin) tied round his chest. They had lashed together a *sal* (ferry-boat), which looked anything but trustworthy, seeing that it consisted of an ordinary stretcher supported by a dozen *tulums*. The horses were unloaded. Some of the provision-boxes were placed on the "ferry-boat." One of our horses was yoked to it. Then one of the suchis led him carefully down the polished rounded stones immediately under the bank, whilst his comrades balanced the boat. The horse soon lost his foothold, and disappeared, all except his head. The suchi then threw his right arm round the animal's neck, whilst with his left arm he swam and steered. The whole party were speedily caught in the current, and went swirling down at a giddy pace, the suchis swimming with all their might. The right bank immediately opposite to us presented a face of vertical cliffs. Towards these the swimmers pressed with desperate energy, striving to make a little sheltered bay immediately below them, in which an eddy circled over a shallow sandy bottom. At that spot the ferrymen cautiously landed their charges. Half a mile below the ferry the river made a bend, and the current swept over towards the left bank, forming a series of boiling rapids. Hence the anxiety of the suchis to get across the river before they were caught in and drawn down by the suction of the cascade; for once in the rapids, it would

CROSSING THE RASKAN-DARIA

II.—4

be impossible to escape being dashed to pieces amongst the rocks and crags.

After the baggage was all taken over, in four separate journeys, it came to my turn. I had waited impatiently, with something of the same feeling a youth has who wants to bathe and yet cannot swim. The raft oscillated unceasingly on its inflated skins; and every moment threatened to capsize, especially when it got amongst the tossing eddies, but that the suchis were on the alert and maintained its balance. I preferred to dispense with the horse, and bade four of the men take hold of the four corners of the "ferry-boat." The next moment we were in the grip of the torrent, and away went the raft like a mad thing. I was not accustomed to that mode of travelling, and everything seemed to be turned the contrary way on. The opposite cliffs seemed to be racing *up* the stream, and the perspective appeared to be constantly changing, like the views you get from the windows of an express train. Plying their arms and legs with well-practised skill, the swimming ferrymen forced the raft out of the sweep of the current, and at length we made the comparatively smooth water of the bay, and landed.

On the return journey, back to the left bank, the "ferry-boat" was driven some distance down the stream, and had to be dragged back to the point of embarkation by a horse. The other horses that still remained were swum across, each with a suchi to help him. Islam Bai preferred to cross in the same way; but he turned giddy and confused, lost his bearings, spun round two or three times in the middle of the river, and forgot which way he was going; and very nearly drowned his horse through forcing his head down too low in the water. He drifted down the river, and I was on tenter-hooks lest he should be swept amongst the rapids. But luckily he managed to reach the bank. I was thankful to have all the caravan, horse and man, safe and sound on the right bank of the Yarkand-daria! I paid the suchi one hundred tengeh (22*s.* 6*d.*), besides a present of a cap and a knife to their leader; and they were more than satisfied.

The river usually freezes towards the end of December; and in those places in which the current is not too strong, the ice is wont to be thick. It is then possible to ride along the ice up the valley to the village of Kichick-tong and the side-valley of Chepp, which leads to the pass of Korum-art (the Stone Pass), in the mountain-chain that overlooks the river on the right. The summer flood begins in the end of May and lasts three months.

Having safely crossed the Yarkand-daria, we reloaded and continued our journey down the stream by its right bank. But we had not advanced far before the road appeared to be blocked by a projecting spur, which shot perpendicularly down to the water's edge. But the Tajiks have hewn out a ledge or sort of cornice-path round the face of the spur—a work which probably dates from a remote antiquity; but the outside edge had crumbled away, so that the path sloped towards the abyss, at the bottom of which the river foamed. The path had been mended with stakes and branches and slabs of rock; but the boxes with which the horses were laden constantly scraped against the rocky wall. Besides, in some places the path was so narrow that the horses were quite unable to get along with their loads. One of them only escaped going over by the merest shave; he stumbled in one of the narrowest parts, and would unfailingly have been precipitated into the river, had not Islam Bai flung himself upon him in the very nick of time and so preserved his balance, while the rest of us hastily freed him from his boxes. After that I had all the baggage carried over the dangerous places.

We halted at Kurruk-lengher (the Dry Rest-house), situated in the entrance of the valley of the same name. It was a charming village, being encircled on all sides by gigantic cliff-walls, whilst itself embowered in parks and groves of leafy trees, amongst which the poplar, with its tall straight stem and spreading crown of foliage, was the most conspicuous. The gardens and fields were dependent for water upon the rainfall in the mountains around; so that the crops were not seldom a failure.

September 24th. We rode up the glen of Arpa-tallak, and in a violent hailstorm pitched our camp in a field near the village of Sughetlik (Willow Village), and on the following day crossed the pass of Arpa-tallak (12,590 feet). The path wound zigzag up the declivity, which was pretty steep and diversified by gently rounded knolls overgrown with grass. Patches of snow still lay on the slopes facing north; everywhere else the ground was sopping wet from rain and snow. The horses constantly slipped and slid on the slippery clay, so that we had anything but a pleasant ride, especially as there was a deep precipice on one side of us.

From the summit of the pass I perceived, to the west, the range which we crossed by means of the Kandahar pass. Eastwards was a panorama of mountain-crests, which died away into a yellowish haze in the far, far distance, where the desolate desert plains of East Turkestan began. On the east side of the range we were crossing there was no snow. Every village we passed after that was inhabited by Jagatai Turks; so that the Arpa-tallak pass forms a religious, as well as a climatic and ethnographic boundary. The track led east-north-east as far as the village of Unkurluk (the Ravines), where the people were engaged in thrashing their harvest. It was a very simple operation. The corn was spread out on the ground, and ten oxen, harnessed abreast, went round and round a pole in the middle, and so trod out the grain. Maize, wheat, and barley are the crops principally grown; and the fields are only sown every other year.

September 26th. We rested in the well-cultivated, well-inhabited district of Utch-beldir. The next day we emerged from the mountain labyrinth, and at the village of Kusherab once more crossed the Yarkand-daria, which was 85 yards wide, and had a maximum depth of 10¼ feet. The current did not flow at the rate of more than 1½ feet in the second, so that we had no difficulty in crossing by a large ferry, which took the whole caravan over in a single trip, and that without our having to unload the horses. We encamped in the village of Kachung, a place of 200 households. There, in addition to the ordinary cereals, rice was grown.

The next day's journey took us through the village of Yar-arik, which is supplied with water from a large canal, fed by the river, and thence north-eastwards to the village of Lengher. On our right stretched the boundless plains and the desert; on our left were the outermost ramifications of the mountains, dimly outlined in the dust-laden atmosphere. It was a landscape which reminded me of the sea at home, as soon as you have left the outermost rocks of the Skärgård.

In our last day's march we passed through the villages of Kok-rabat, Kizil, Yanghi-hissar, and Yappchan, and on 3rd October once more reached Kashgar, where I was welcomed by Consul-General Petrovsky with the same hospitable friendship as before.

Down in the plains it was still warm and close, and the sudden change of temperature laid me low with a violent fever, from which I did not recover until the middle of November.

The losses I had sustained during that unlucky desert journey were now replaced. I found awaiting me from Fuess in Berlin a case containing a set of first-class aneroids, hypsometers, psychrometers, and thermometers, all in excellent order, thanks to the care with which they had been packed in Berlin, and afterwards looked after by the Swedish consul in Batum. Besides, three loads of supplies had arrived from Tashkend, embracing several needful things, such as clothes, tinned foods, tobacco, etc.; so that I was quite as well equipped as when I first started my series of Central Asian explorations.

ACROSS THE DESERT OF GOBI TO LOP-NOR

CHAPTER LVIII.

FROM KASHGAR TO KARGALIK

AS soon as I had recovered from the attack of fever, and could get my new caravan properly organized, I left Kashgar for the last time. My departure made some stir. The great Shang Dao Tai himself in august person came, with every circumstance of pomp and parade, followed by his train of Chinese friends and servants, to pay me a farewell visit. My caravan of nine horses and three men, under command of my trusty Islam Bai, started on the morning of December 14th, 1895. I myself, accompanied by two servants, followed them at noon on the same day. It was precisely five years before, to the very day, that I first set eyes on Kashgar, the last outpost of European civilization in the centre of Asia.

There was quite a crowd assembled in the courtyard of the consulate to see me off—Consul-General Petrovsky and his hospitable wife, the Polish missionary Adam Ignatieff, fifty mounted Cossacks and their two officers, and lastly all the native secretaries, interpreters, and servants. After a last farewell to my host and hostess, in whose hospitable house I had spent so many happy and instructive hours, I vaulted into the saddle, and we set off at a gentle trot through the bazaars, followed by the Russian officers and their Cossacks, and the old Pole. The soldiers sang as they trotted along, and their cheerful voices echoed loudly through the narrow, confined bazaars. At the Swedish mission-house we stopped a moment, whilst I said good-bye to Mrs. Högberg and her children. Her husband joined my *cortège* on horseback. When, shortly afterwards, our good friend the Russo-Chinese interpreter Yan Daloi caught us up in his blue cart, it can be imagined what a gay, though mixed, procession it was which filed along the broad highway to Yanghi-shahr, enveloped in clouds of dust. At Yanghi-shahr farewells were said. When I cried with a loud voice, "Good-bye, Cossacks"; they all answered in unison, "God grant you a safe journey, sir!"

After that I was alone amongst pure Asiatics, my right-hand man being Islam Bai. And yet, as soon as the Cossacks' songs had died away in the distance, and the battlemented walls of Kashgar had disappeared below the horizon, I drew a sigh of relief at the thought that now I was on my way home. Nor was my jubilation greatly damped by the recollection that I still had to cross one-half the continent of Asia, and travel nine or ten thousand miles, before I could hope to set foot upon the quays of Stockholm.

I caught up my caravan in Kizil. Instead of keeping to the principal highway which led to that place, a road I already knew, I chose the desert road, so as to get a glimpse of the saints' tombs — Ordan-Padshah and Hazrett-Begim.

I allowed twenty-three days for the journey of 320 miles to Khotan. That gave me both time and opportunity to pick up an intimate knowledge of the road, which is not only a highly important highway, but in many respects one of the most interesting roads in Central Asia. But the length to which this book has already run prevents me from describing it in detail. Still the many fresh observations and discoveries I made, and the detailed diary I kept, will not have been wasted, for I hope to deal with the subject again on some subsequent occasion. My journeys in Central Asia have proved so rich in experiences, that a single book cannot suffice to record them all. Moreover, a large portion of my material is of such a character that it must be sifted and arranged, before being published, and some of it will involve a considerable amount of historical research; and all that is work which takes time.

The route to Khotan has been travelled over either wholly or in part by several European travellers, amongst whom the best known have been Johnson, Schlagintweit, Shaw, Forsyth's expedition, Grombtchevsky, Pievtsoff, Dutreuil de Rhins, Littledale, though these are by no means all. But I do not think I shall be too assuming, if I claim that I have gathered a more copious stock of information about the road, and the places I passed through, as well as about the branch-roads which strike off from it. All this would require a small volume to

A DERVISH TELLING STORIES

itself, so that I must refrain from dwelling upon it, but must hasten on to describe the districts in which I had no forerunners. I will confine myself therefore to a few incidents of the journey.

On 20th December we rode through the double gates of Yanghi-shahr, the Chinese quarter of Yarkand, and shortly after that through the Altyn-därvaseh (the Golden Gate) of Kovneh-shahr (the Old Town), or the Mohammedan quarter of the same city. The two quarters lie within half a mile of one another, connected by the great highway from Kashgar to Khotan. The space between the gates forms one long, broad bazaar, covered in with wooden roofs, and late of an evening is the scene of a lively traffic by the light of flaming oil lamps. In fact the road resembles an interminable tunnel, lined on both sides with stalls and stands; and the crowds, the shouting and noise, as well as the long strings of camels slowly piloting their way through the throng, announced that we had entered the precincts of a big city. As a matter of fact, Yarkand, with its dependent villages, possesses a population of 150,000, and is thus the largest city in East Turkestan.

To reach the house which the aksakal of the Andijanliks had prepared for us, we had to thread our way through a perfect labyrinth of crooked streets and lanes of the Mohammedan quarter.

We stayed two days in Yarkand, partly to give the horses a rest, partly that I might see something of the town and its environs. Accompanied by the aksakal, I rode over to call on the amban. His yamen or official dwelling was a much more imposing edifice than that of his colleague in Kashgar, being approached by not less than three lofty and picturesque gates, ornamented with sculpture and variegated colours. In the courtyard we found a great number of native suitors and litigants assembled, desirous of putting their cases before the amban, and getting the decisions of Chinese law upon their several complaints. There were men from the adjacent villages, complaining of a deficiency of water in their irrigation-canals; servants complaining that their masters had not paid them their wages in full; thieves awaiting a magisterial inquiry, and their consequent punishment.

The amban, Pan Darin, was a big, fat old gentleman, with a grey goatee beard. He received me with a polite and friendly smile, and graciously inquired after my plans. In the evening he sent me presents of forage, maize, and wood for burning; the next day, when he returned my visit, I presented him with a revolver. In my round through the city I saw the principal madrasas and mosques. The largest was the Kok-madrasa (the Blue College); its *pishtak* or arched façade was decorated with blue and green tiles, which however were not to be compared to the simplest specimens of the same kind of ornamentation in Bokhara. Its courtyard contained the tombs of several saints—*e.g.* Makhtum Assam, Shah Abbas Khojam, Khoja Danyar, Khoja Khutbuddin Khojam, Khoja Aberdullah Khojam, Khoja Burhan-ed-

STREET IN A CENTRAL ASIAN TOWN

din Khojam, and several others. The remaining madrasas were still smaller, and possessed not one trace of architectural interest—the Ak (the White), Yeshil (the Green), Khalik, Kasim Akhun, and Bedawlet madrasas. The last mentioned, which was built by Yakub Beg, boasted of thirty-six columns (*sutun*) and a verandah (*ayvan*).

The Nevrus-dung (New Year's Hill) on the north-east of Yarkand offered a bird's-eye view of the city. The hill was crowned by a minaret, consisting of nothing more than a roof supported on two or three wooden pillars; from it is caught the first glimpse of the new moon, which releases the faithful Mohammedan from the enforced fast of Ramadan. The hill stands just inside the city walls, which are thin, and crenelated, but in bad repair. They are built of sun-dried bricks, and undulate, with many bends, up and down the terraces which overlook the ancient bed of the river, but at the same time form a rough circle. Looking across the city from the top of the hill, you see an intricate mosaic of square and oblong house-roofs, with scarcely distinguishable narrow lanes winding between them. The only relief for the eye is afforded by the bazaars, gardens, and a few isolated willows. On the outside the walls are surrounded by a perfect labyrinth of cultivated fields, ravines, and irrigation-canals; whilst towards the north-east the most conspicuous feature is the Yarkand-daria, creeping its sinuous course across the desert on the way to its far distant outfall into Lop-nor.

Although the city gets its drinking-water from the river, the largest in Central Asia; yet, by reason of pernicious management, the water is actually little better than poison. It is conducted from the river by means of canals, and is stored up in reservoirs inside the city. There it stands and stagnates, and becomes gradually polluted by every sort of refuse and impurity. These reservoirs or *hauz* are in fact nothing more nor less than centres of infection, and nurseries for the propagation of bacteria. The people bathe in them; they wash their clothes in them, and abominably dirty some of them are; they wash their dishes in them; they toss into them the scraps that are left over from their meals; they leave them unfenced and unprotected against all sorts of nuisances; and yet this is the stuff they drink. To crown all, the reservoirs are only replenished when the malodorous mud at the bottom begins to be exposed.

One consequence of this gross neglect is an affliction called *boghak*, which attacks an extraordinarily large percentage of the inhabitants of Yarkand. A sort of tumour shows itself on the front of the throat, generally upon

"Adam's apple." In the most favourable cases it is as large as a man's closed fist, and in every case gives its unhappy bearer a strangely unnatural, and even repulsive, appearance. It is certainly no exaggeration to say, that 75 per cent. of the settled population of the city are afflicted in a more or less degree with this tumorous growth. In most instances it remains until death. If therefore in any other town throughout Central Asia a man is seen walking the streets with a *boghak*, he may

BAZAARS

confidently be pronounced an inhabitant of Yarkand; and contrariwise, if you observe a man in the bazaars of Yarkand, whose throat is free from the disfiguring tumour, you may fairly presume he is a stranger from Kashgar, Khotan, or some other town of East Turkestan. The people make no attempt to combat the affliction; although in some few cases, probably in consequence of change of residence, the growth is said to disappear of itself. The Hindus are reputed to be acquainted with a remedy against the disease; but as both they and the Andijanliks (people from West Turkestan) only drink well-water, they do not suffer from the disfiguring tumour.

The following legend is current with regard to this disease. When Saleh Peygambär was travelling through Yarkand, certain thieves stole his camel, and cut its throat, and left the carcass lying on the bank of the Yarkand-daria. Then the holy man solemnly cursed the entire neighbourhood, swearing that the inhabitants should be tormented with *boghak* to the very end of time. Ever since then the river water has been polluted by the dead body of the camel.

There is a colony of some forty Andijan (West Turkestan) merchants in the city, who import cloth, caps, khalats, sugar, matches, and so forth, and export wool, felt carpets, and other native commodities. They make large profits, and dwell together in a fine serai or guest-house, which was built twenty-six years ago. But neither the people of Yarkand nor the Chinese give them a good word. It is easy to tell them on the street, by reason of their neat attire, and their dignified bearing; and their houses are distinguishable by their cleanly rooms and well-kept courtyards. The Afghans and Hindu merchants likewise have their own separate serais.

The city is divided into twenty-four *mähällähs* or quarters, each governed by a *yuz-bashi* (chief of a hundred men), who has two or three *on-bashis* (chief of ten men) under him, and sometimes more. Besides these officials, there are a great number of begs, whose duty it is to maintain order in and around Yarkand.

On December 23rd we were ferried across the Yarkand-daria. Although it was the middle of winter, the river had a volume of 3280 cubic feet in the second, or a decrease of 2120 cubic feet in the second as compared with the measurement I made at Kusherab in the end of September. The entire district as far as Posgam was watered by irrigation-canals branching off from the right bank. Beyond Posgam the fields were irrigated from the Tisnab.

Travelling through continuously well-inhabited, well-

LI DARIN, THE AMBAN (GOVERNOR) OF KARGALIK

cultivated districts, and a long string of villages (all of which I entered on my map), we reached the town of Kargalik on Christmas Eve; but there was neither snow nor fir to recall the significance of the day. The people however showed us all the good-will that we are wont to associate with the holy season. We put up at the house of a merchant from Kokand in Fergana, and in the evening he entertained me to a first-rate dastarkhan, embracing apples, pears, raisins, almonds, and divers kinds of sweetmeats, presented on a dozen dishes. It was like a Christmas table, except that everything was placed on the floor. A little later on the ten begs of the town came in Chinese holiday attire and pigtails to bid me

II.—5

welcome to Kargalik; and lastly I received from the amban (Chinese governor), Li Darin, a number of useful presents, such as sheep, rice, wheat, maize meal, fuel, and forage for my horses. As soon as my guests were gone, and my journal for the day had been written up, I hurried into bed, to drown the memories of the day in the oblivion of sleep, for they crowded in upon my mind with especial importunity in that I was alone.

The amban of Yarkand was politeness itself; but he was easily outdone by his colleague of Kargalik. In fact, the attentions of the latter were tiresome. Before I had an opportunity to pay my respects to him, he called upon me, on Christmas Day morning, before I was awake; and when I returned his visit, and was riding across the yamen courtyard, I was received with a salute of three guns. The honour nearly cost me a summersault, for my horse was not accustomed to such demonstrative welcomes. The amban was an agreeable little old man of some fifty years of age, and of gentlemanly manners, with a small, grey, well-cared-for moustache, and big round spectacles. He invited me to stay to dinner with him. After dinner I sketched him; then to my astonishment in tripped his dainty young wife, on her tiny goat's-feet (scarcely two inches long), and in her turn begged me to make a sketch of her; she wanted to send her likeness to her parents in Peking. I was of course only too happy to comply with such a flattering request.

CHAPTER LIX.

ALONGSIDE THE DESERT TO KHOTAN

I LEFT Kargalik the next day; and the amban's courtesy went the length of sending a beg to act as my escort, and relieve me of all trouble during the journey. The town possessed five gates, the same number as Yarkand; and as we passed out of the eastern gate, the cannon again boomed forth a farewell salute. It did not take us long to get past the last village and reach the sterile plains. Hitherto the road had been plainly marked like a bright strip through the fields; henceforward there was no road. The track of each caravan is blotted out by the next storm that comes. The Chinese have therefore erected guide-posts all along that part of the route which crosses the desert. They stand at intervals of about a hundred yards, so that you can generally see six or seven at any one time. Whilst a sand-buran is blowing they are of little use; but directly the storm has ceased, they render excellent service, indeed they are then indispensable. It is said that some travellers, who have been so unfortunate as to miss their way, have never been heard of again. The custom of erecting these poles reminded me of Marco Polo's words—"And at sleeping-time a signal is put up to show the direction of the next march."

The road ran over a flat, barren plain all the way from the oasis of Besh-arik (the Five Canals) to the caravanserai of Kosh-lengher (Two Stations). The serai and willows of the latter place were visible a long way off; and in consequence of a mirage appeared to be lifted up a little above the dark line of the horizon. The serai was a first-class building, erected in the beginning of Yakub Beg's rule, of grey-green bricks, and enclosing a square courtyard paved with large paving-tiles. The four sides contained ten guest-rooms for travellers, all of them paved with stone; whilst the daylight found admittance through an aperture in the vaulted roof. Alongside this splendidly solid brick structure—a remarkable contrast to the clay hovels in which we were accustomed to put up—were several outhouses and stables, built of ordinary clay, and covered in with timber roofs. Immediately on the south-east of the station there was a large *köll* (reservoir) surrounded by rows of fine willows. There water is collected off the mountains and stored up against the hot season, when everything is parched up.

From Kosh-lengher it is reckoned one and a half day's journey to the beginning of the desert proper, which is known under the names of Takla-makan, Jallat-kum, and Adam-öllturgan-kum, or the Sand that Slayeth Men.

This region is characterized by a strictly continental climate, that is, the winters are harsh and the summers oppressively hot. The burans begin to blow towards the end of March, and continue till the close of summer. It is estimated, that there are on an average fifteen "black burans" every year. They almost always occur in the afternoon, scarcely ever in the morning or during the night. As a rule, they only last about an hour, and are rather more frequent from the west than from the east. Their violence is almost inconceivable; they drive across the open, level plains with a force that is absolutely irresistible. Sheep grazing around the villages are sometimes swept bodily away, or get separated from the rest of the flock in the dust-haze. This has given rise to certain peculiar local enactments: for instance, if a sheep goes astray from the flock when the weather is still and fine, then the shepherd is responsible, and must make good the loss to the owner of the sheep; but if a sheep gets lost during a storm, then no man is responsible. If straying sheep do damage to a man's field or crop, and the mischief is done in fine weather, the owner of

THE VILLAGE OF GUMA

the sheep must recompense the injured party; but not if the mischief is done during a buran or under cover of the haze of a dust-storm.

The custodian of the serai told me, that ravens and other birds are often blown by unusually violent burans all the way from Kargalik to Guma, or from Guma to Kargalik, and not seldom are dashed against larger fixed objects and killed. The following legend illustrates the effect which these wind-storms produce upon the native imagination. Many hundred years ago a holy man dug a well near the station of Chullak, which is now completely filled up again with sand. When the holy man got down about eighty fathoms, the earth opened underneath him and vomited forth a terrific wind, which swept the holy man right up to heaven, and since that time all the winds and storms have come out of that well. Another apothegm is more rational, in that it is based upon actual observation. For instance, it is said, that if the last buran came from Kargalik, then the next will come from Guma; but that it is either the same buran going back again, or else one that is hurrying to find the first.

Our next day's journey took us to Chullak-lengher (the Cripple's Serai), so named from the fact, that a long time ago an old woman who had no feet used to sit by the wayside in that place begging. The caravanserai was like that at Kosh-lengher, and had a reservoir some 95 yards square, and, when full, 24 feet deep in the middle. When I saw it, there were only about nine feet of water in it, and it was protected against contamination by a glittering covering of ice. The serai was built on a hill, and commanded a sheer unbounded view towards the east. The plains stretched away like narrow ribbons one behind the other, fainter and fainter, until they melted into the horizon. Earth and sky did not meet in a sharply defined line, but blended together in a yellow haze.

The entire distance between Kashgar and Khotan has been divided by the Chinese into *potai* (2½-mile distances), like the road between Kashgar and Ak-su. Hence the

Mohammedans also measure distances by potai, not as in other districts by *tash* (stone), *yoll* (road), and *chakerem* (shout-distances). The potai are indicated by flattened pyramids of clay, eighteen or twenty feet in height, and there are on an average ten such intervals or "miles" between every two stations. But no two potai are the same length. I measured some of them, and got the following results:—4068½, 4032½, 3830 yards respectively. What method of measurement the Chinese followed when they erected these "mile-stones" I do not know; anyway it cannot have been a very accurate method. At the rate

A POTAI OR "MILE-STONE" ON THE ROAD TO KHOTAN

we usually marched, it took us three-quarters of an hour to traverse a potai.

Our next station was the pleasant little town of Guma, an oasis in the desert well supplied with water. The route between Chullak-lengher and Guma ran across dreary steppes and barren plains. The 29th December we spent at Guma, and the following day went on to the village of Muji. Thence, on the last day of the year, we made a flying excursion in quest of a *kovneh-shahr* (ancient city), which I had been told was to be found in that neighbourhood.

We reached the ruins, which were scarcely a potai distant north-east of the caravanserai, across a barren steppe. They consisted principally of a number of tombs ranged along a series of clay terraces. We opened up two or three of them. They were backed on the outside

A SHRINE IN GUMA

with planks and posts; but the interior was choked with dust and sand, from amongst which we unearthed a few bleached bones and skulls. The shape of the latter, as well as the position of the tombs with respect to Mecca (their *kebleh*), proved them to have belonged to Jagatai Turks. Some of the skeletons were wrapped in rags; but they crumbled to pieces the instant they were touched. My examination of the site led me to the conclusion, that the place had been used as a burial-ground at no very distant date, probably not more than two or three hundred years back. Judging from the traces of houses and walls in the immediate vicinity, I concluded that the former inhabitants had been driven by the encroaching sand to migrate further to the south. Retreats of this sort, men flying before the persistent invasions of the desert sand, must have been going on for thousands of years; and there can be little doubt, that there are many strange things buried under the sand of the Takla-makan Desert.

That this region was once the seat of a very ancient civilization is indicated, amongst other things, by the innumerable quantity of fragments of clay-vessels and burnt bricks which lie scattered along both sides of the great caravan-route, and which the native inhabitants allege have come from an ancient city to which they give the name of Nasar. Occasionally too old coins are found, and rings, and articles in bronze, and a multitude of fragments of glass. Some of these last, of a light blue and green colour, I brought away with me.

The sight of these innumerable shards and fragments of glass lying scattered about the surface of the ground produced at first a curious effect upon my mind; for, when we dug down underneath them, we found nothing but sand and dust. No doubt their presence is to be accounted for by the action of the wind, which blows away the sand and dust, but leaves these objects behind, partly because of their shape, partly because they have a greater specific weight. For thousands of years the wind has gone on scouring away the superficial layers of the desert, and all the time these fragments of glass and earthenware have no doubt kept gradually sinking lower and lower, until finally they have come down to their present level. Unresting, slowly but ever surely, the implacable wind excavates and levels up the dreary expanses. The aboriginal inhabitants themselves have observed, that the erosive action of the wind is incomparably greater than that of water.

The different varieties of shards or crocks pointed to the following types of vessel—spherical bowls with two handles, some placed horizontally, some vertically; round pitchers with a somewhat enlarged neck; egg-shaped jars with a long, narrow neck; thick cups of blue burnt clay, as hard as a stone. Some of the fragments of bricks were enamelled in light green. The pieces of glass appeared to have belonged to small bottles and dishes, and to lotus leaves used for decorative purposes.

On 1st January 1896 we rode as far as Sang-uya, a little village of 150 houses. Steppe and desert alternated all the way, and the villages were in reality so many oases. In some places the road ran so close to the desert that it was easy to make out the sand-dunes. The mighty mountain masses of the Kwen-lun on the south could only be seen when the atmosphere was clear. At Muji, where they were known as the Dua-tagh, we were able to distinguish them, looming up in the far, far distance like a faint blue wall; but at Sang-uya we were unable to perceive them at all. During the hot season, when the burans rage, and the atmosphere is thickly impregnated with dust, the traveller may journey from one end of the road to the other, without the least inkling that one of the greatest mountain ranges on the face of the earth rears itself up immediately to the south of him. That Marco Polo never mentions a syllable about the range need therefore occasion no surprise.

The oasis of Sang-uya is very fertile, and produces wheat, maize, barley, melons and water-melons, grapes, apricots, peaches, apples, mulberries, cotton, onions, and other vegetables. The yield is amply sufficient for the needs of the place; indeed there is not seldom a surplus for export to the other villages in the neighbourhood.

STREET AND IRRIGATION CANAL IN GUMA

January 2nd. There was a tolerably fresh breeze all day from the east-north-east, and the dust trailed off in a thick cloud behind the caravan. Nevertheless the atmosphere remained very clear, and the Dua-tagh or Kwen-lun Mountains were plainly visible capped with snow. Immediately on the other side of Sang-uya we again entered upon a desolate waste—a level steppe, with a few scattered tamarisks, poplars, and reed-beds.

Half-way to Pialma, where we intended to stop the night, we passed a little lengher (rest-house), where in

CROWD IN MUJI

return for a small gratuity an old man furnishes wayfarers with water, drawn up in a bucket from a well 150 feet deep. Pialma was said to have 200 houses and about one thousand inhabitants.

On the following day we travelled through the same sort of dreary country as far as the solitary Ak-lengher (the White Rest-House or Serai), situated five or six miles ($2\frac{1}{2}$ potais) from the edge of the desert. It was only very seldom that we met other travellers; and those we did meet were generally either small parties of merchants from Khotan, encumbered with no more baggage than they could conveniently carry on their riding-horses, or peasants travelling from one oasis to another, sometimes driving in front of them a few donkeys laden with seed or vegetables.

Like all the oases along this route, Ak-lengher was situated by the side of a watercourse going from the south to the north; but it very seldom contains water, only in fact after heavy and continuous rains in the mountains. The oasis depends for its supply upon a well sunk 126 feet down through the clay. This formation, yellowish-brown in colour, contains sprinklings of rounded, polished stones, not exceeding two inches in diameter, and consisting partly of hard, fine-grained, blue-black slate crossed by delicate white veins, and partly of red and greenish-grey granite. The well is cleaned out two or three times a year; for lumps of clay fall in from the sides and stop the inflow of the water. A man is let down with a rope tied round his body, the other end of which is drawn across a horizontal roller resting on two short posts at the top. The mud and sludge are sent up in a wooden bucket, and emptied out all round the well mouth. The top of the well is protected against the sandstorms by a wooden roof, provided with a hatch or flap. At half-past three in the afternoon the temperature of the water at the bottom of the well was 55° Fahr. (12°79° C.), whilst the temperature of the air was 37°2 Fahr. (2°9 C.) at 4.30 p.m. The water was saline, with a bitter flavour, and undrinkable except with tea and sugar. In this connection I may mention that the well at Kizil (between Yanghi-hissar and Yarkand) was 119 feet deep, and that its water was sweet, with a constant temperature of 59°9 Fahr. (15°5 C.). The inhabitants however, misled by the alternations of the temperature of the air, asserted that in summer the water is cold, but in winter warm.

January 6th. After riding about 4½ miles (nearly two potais) we came to a belt of sand-dunes, high and continuous, in the middle of which there was a ridge of clay, with some poplars growing on it, and poles with tughs (offerings of rags) set up to indicate that there was a masar (saint's tomb) close by.

At the eastern end of the ridge were some wooden houses, the largest of them having a projecting roof supported on pillars. The masar, one of the most attractive I have seen anywhere, was called Imam Khakir, after the saint who lies buried within it; though the name Kum-rabat-pashahim (My King's Serai in the Sand), or simply Käptär-masar (the Pigeon Masar) is more commonly employed. For the peculiar feature about this holy tomb was that it afforded shelter and food to several thousand beautiful pigeons, of every possible variety of colour—yellow, white, brown, green, speckled, and so on. The rooms inside the serai were provided with an earthen floor, raised benches, and enclosures and perches in the walls; and these apartments the traveller shares with the pigeons, some of which are, maybe, sitting on their eggs or brooding their young, whilst others fly in and out of the narrow door-openings or window apertures. Outside, on the ridge of the roof, on the rafters, on the eaves, everywhere, they sit in close, serried rows, like beads on a rosary. In every direction you hear their cheerful cooings. The gentle birds betray not the slightest alarm at the presence of the strangers who share the house-room with them.

Fragments of skin were hung from poles fixed to the gables of some of the houses, to scare away the birds of prey. The *lengherchi* or "custodian of the serai" assured me, that if a hawk or other bird of prey dared to molest one of these sacred pigeons, it would instantly fall down dead. He had recently seen an instance of it himself. A hawk seized a pigeon; but was forced by some unseen power to drop its prey, and then the next instant the marauder fell dead.

It is an ancient custom, that travellers who journey past the tomb, bring with them a supply of maize, however little, to give to the pigeons; a gift which is likewise regarded as an offering made to the shrine of the saint.

The corn is stored up, so that the pigeons are always fed regularly: for the tomb stands in the midst of a perfectly sterile region, where not a blade of anything grows, nor do the pigeons ever fly away from the place. We brought a bag of maize for them from Pialma. The men put the bag down in the courtyard. I took a porcelain bowl and scattered the corn all over the ground, as far as I could fling it. What a flapping of wings, what a whistling of the air, what joyful cooings! The courtyard seemed to be alive with pigeons; they settled down like a veritable cloud. Some of them even came and perched on my shoulder and on my head; others went and helped themselves at the bag and out of the bowl. I was obliged to stand perfectly still, lest I should trample on them. They did not betray the smallest trace of fear.

I stayed there an hour enjoying the unusual and charming spectacle. Then, having drunk from the adjacent well, which came to within 6½ feet of the surface, whilst its water had a temperature of 35°9 Fahr. (2°2 C.), we continued our journey towards the well-cultivated and thickly inhabited tract of Sävvah; a place that with its dependent villages is administered by a min-bashi (chief of a thousand men) and eleven yuz-bashis (chiefs of one hundred men). That night we slept in the village of Milleh, the yuz-bashi of which exercised authority over 260 families.

On January 5th there only remained one day's journey to Khotan. The road improved as we drew nearer to the town. We travelled along a magnificent avenue of poplars, fifty feet broad, which ran through a bright and varied landscape of villages, cultivated fields, and irrigation canals. We passed through numerous large villages, *e.g.* Kum-arik, Sheidan, Gulbagh, Ak-serai, Chinakla (which possessed a masar shaded by a poplar 280 years old), Supa, Shuma, Borasan, Besin, and Tosanla. Then we came to the gate of Yanghi-shahr (the New Town), and immediately afterwards entered the principal bazaar of Khotan. Early in the morning of the same day the amban sent his interpreter, together with the aksakal of the West Turkestan merchants, to meet me. These officials conducted us to a large good-looking house, situated in a quiet and peaceful part of the city. It was the most comfortable house I had yet seen in East Turkestan; its walls were of wood, and were perforated with picturesque openings, and had a tastefully decorated roof.

CHAPTER LX.

CITY AND OASIS OF KHOTAN

KHOTAN is a city of extreme antiquity. The beginnings of its history are lost amid the dim obscurities of a remote and legendary past. Some of the principal notices of a more strictly historical character are cited in Chapter Sixty-two. Hence, after merely mentioning that the name was first made known in Europe through the travels of Marco Polo, the Venetian, I pass on to say a few words about its condition and products in modern times, *i.e.* at the epoch of my visit.

For generations, nay, I might say for many centuries, Khotan was especially famous as the place whence nephrite or jade was obtained. It occurred partly in the solid rock in the valleys of the rivers Kara-kash and Yurun-kash, partly in polished pieces out of the bed of the Yurun-kash. Jade (in Chinese *yü-tien*, in Jagatai Turki *kash-tash*) is in China esteemed amongst the greatest of rarities, and is used in the manufacture of small fancy boxes, bottles, cups, mouthpieces for pipes, bracelets, etc. One of the gates of Peking was called the Jade gate, because this precious mineral was brought into the city through it.

At the present time Khotan is an insignificant town, containing within its walls scarcely more than 5000 Mohammedans and 500 Chinese. Apart from jade, its most important products are silks, white felt carpets, hides, grapes, rice and other cereals, vegetables, apples, melons, cotton, etc.; its silk carpets are remarkable for their beauty and fineness. The Chinese place them on the table on occasions of ceremony; in West Turkestan they are hung on the wall.

Khotan is really the name of the entire oasis, embracing some three hundred villages. The town itself is however generally called Ilchi; the oasis contains also two other towns, namely Kara-kash and Yurun-kash. The trade with China is carried on partly along the Khotan-daria, through Ak-su and Turfan, partly by way of Yarkand and Maral-bashi; on the other hand, scarcely any of it passes Lop-nor. Trade with Russia goes by way of Kashgar; the Anglo-Indian trade by way of Leh in Ladak. In the bazaar of Khotan there are merchants from all parts of Asia—Chinese, Afghans, Hindus, West Turkestanis, and even Nogai Tatars from Orenburg.

I stayed nine days in Khotan. The amban, Liu Darin, showed me genuine hospitality; and every time I rode in or out of his yamen (official residence) honoured me with a salute of three guns. The very day of my arrival we exchanged the usual visits of ceremony and gave one another presents. I went to see him many times afterwards, and soon discovered, that even according to European ideas he was a man of honour, generous, upright, and just; and a real tie of friendship grew up between us. He was a man of seventy or so, tall, with strongly marked features, small intelligent eyes, and thin white moustache, and a very meagre pigtail. Of all the Asiatics with whom I came in contact on this present journey, Liu Darin is the one I like best to remember, and whom it would give me greatest pleasure to see again.

On this occasion, as well as when I got back to Khotan the second time, Liu Darin often invited me to his house. There, in company with the chief mandarins of the town, I dined on delicacies which would have delighted even a European gourmand. Among the dishes which were never absent at his big dinners was soup made of the edible swallows' nests, which is remarkable for its aromatic flavour. I always looked forward to Liu Darin's good dinners as a change in my homely and monotonous bill of fare—rice, mutton, and bread. They were something very different from the appallingly high ducks and ham steeped in molasses, to which our friend the Dao Tai of Kashgar treated us, no doubt with the very thrifty idea that, "as they never eat anything, it doesn't much matter what we put before them." But at Liu Darin's I ate like a Chinaman, and felt well after it; which is more than I can say of the Dao Tai's dinners.

Of the present Ilchi there is not much to be said. It is a place of no interest, a mere labyrinth of poor, insignificant houses, with narrow streets and alleys between them, such as I had seen in Yarkand. There were seven madrasas (theological colleges), twenty mosques, and a number of masars (saints' tombs) belonging to the orthodox Mohammedans. Of the masars, the chief was the Altyn Busrugvar masar. There are saints' tombs of the same name in Yarkand, Ak-su, and Turfan. All are said to have been erected to the memory of the sons of Khoja Isaki Väli, whose own tomb is at Chira, and one of the most venerated in the country. Pilgrims always go there before visiting Imam Jafer Sadik's tomb, in the sandy desert near where the Niya-daria loses itself in the sand. The Mesjid-i-Jami or principal mosque had a really beautiful colonnade, and the Hazrett-i-Sultan, like most of the religious monuments thereabouts, was built by the great Yakub Beg.

As in all Mohammedan towns, the bazaar was the centre and main artery of the life of the place. Off its streets branched a number of incredibly narrow, crooked, dirty lanes; but at intervals there were open squares, with tanks or ponds shaded by trees. In the middle of the town, close by the bazaar, there was a so-called *kovneh-sefit-potai* (old clay pyramid), with ruined tower and walls, a surviving relic of Haji Padshah's *ordu* or castle. This point overlooked the town, giving a good bird's-eye view of its square roofs and courtyards, as well as of the fields outside the walls. As they were at that season under water, and were separated from one another by ramparts of earth, they looked like the brightly polished squares of a chess-board.

THE RIGHISTAN, OR MARKET-PLACE, OF KHOTAN

The distant horizon was closed by a dark line of avenues and gardens belonging to the neighbouring villages.

There were two bazaar-days a week, when the country-folk came in with their produce for sale. The women also took part in the trafficking, and even when sitting in the bazaars were always unveiled. But they might just as well have kept their veils before their faces; for they were indescribably ugly and dirty, and covered with vermin, after which I often saw them unblushingly making chase. As a rule veiled women were an exception. The moral standard of the place was deplorably low, and infectious diseases very common.

Some forty odd West Turkestan merchants lived in Khotan and exported wool, carpets, felts, etc., and imported, as also did the Afghans, woven materials and a variety of colonial produce. Tobacco and opium are cultivated in pretty large quantities. The cultivation of silk too has reached a high level. The produce is sent partly to India and West Turkestan, and is partly worked up on the spot for further manufacture into carpets. Hides and sheep's wool are also important articles of export, and are for the most part sent to West Turkestan, by way of Kashgar and Narinsk.

An old Tatar, Mohammed Rafikoff, from Orenburg, who had lived ten years in Khotan, having built himself a comfortable house close beside the bazaar, owned a factory for tanning and for cleansing wool. It consisted of an enormous magazine tent and a small temporary house built in the Russian style, both standing beside the Yurun-kash. The old man told me, that he pulled the whole thing down every February, to make the people of Khotan believe that he was about to give up business and return home; with the result that they hastened to sell their skins as quickly as possible and at low prices. But when May came, he built the factory up again; and he had gone on doing this for ten years. When I expressed my astonishment, that the people of Khotan had not yet discovered the trick, he answered, that they were too stupid and too indifferent.

On January 11th I made an excursion to the village of Kalta-kumat (Short Sand), situated 2½ potais (6¼ miles) north-east of the town. To reach it I had to ford the river Yurun-kash and pass through the town of the same name, which is only a quarter of an hour from Ilchi. On the other side of Tam-aghil (the Stone Village) the desert began, with occasional sand-dunes and ravines left behind by the stream. After that the ground became excessively stony, and I soon perceived we were riding along an old river-bed. It could not have been made by any other stream than the Yurun-kash, which some time or other must have flowed there, and in opposition to the general tendency of the rivers in those regions, has since shifted its course to the west.

This disused river-bed is one of the places that yield the largest supplies of jade. Everywhere the ground was cut up by trenches six or seven feet deep, a few feet broad, and at most thirty feet long, although varying somewhat as regards size according to the amount of work done in them. The material which is thrown up out of the trenches consists of round polished stones, sand, and clay. It is among these stones that the jade is found. Very often a couple of months or more will pass without anything being discovered; then all of a sudden, in the course of a few days, the digger becomes relatively rich, or at any rate does a very good stroke of business. The prices of jade vary very much, according to the colour of the stone, and its purity and freedom from flaws. Yellow or white pieces, with reddish-brown marks, are considered rare; also a roughness on the surface called *gush* (flesh) increases the value. The plain green jade, on the other hand, does not fetch much. Two beautiful pieces were offered me for 100 and 140 *sähr* (£9 and £12 10*s*.) respectively; but the low state of my funds did not permit me to purchase them.

A little village of wooden and clay huts has grown up on the spot, and is supplied with water by a special arik. The ground is divided into clearly marked lots, so that each mining claim has its owner; thus obviating disputes

CHINESE SILVER AND BRONZE COINS, NEW AND OLD

Two-thirds of natural size

when a good find is made. Most of the miners are Chinese; though the Mohammedans also try their luck occasionally. Order is maintained by a beg.

My stay in Khotan was pleasant in every way. That I obtained no news of the camel that was lost in the desert did not disturb me much, as I had everything I needed in the way of equipment. My boxes were packed, and kept in a large room, in which a bright fire burned continually; and my men were lodged in rooms just outside. I brought with me from Kashgar a certain Mirza Iskender in the capacity of secretary. With his help I collected, translated, and noted down during the journey the names of every place and every geographical feature, not only along our immediate route, but also as far away from it as my various informants' knowledge extended, or I myself could glean *data*. Between Kashgar and Khotan I thus marked on my map over five hundred names, of which only a few of the most important were known to previous travellers. At Khotan we drew up a systematic map of the three hundred villages of the oasis, and of their situation with regard to the innumerable irrigation-canals, which are led from the Kara-kash and the Yurun-kash, and point northwards like fingers.

This is a matter which is wont to be neglected by travellers pushing on in forced marches, but is a study destitute neither of interest nor of importance. In the first place, it affords excellent linguistic practice. Eight hundred names, each consisting as a rule of a noun with its qualifying word, for instance, Kara-kash (Black Jade), furnishes a very extensive vocabulary; furthermore, the place-names are always characteristic, in that they give some idea of the products or the position of the place; finally, among eight hundred such names there are not improbably a few which by their mere sound involuntarily carry the mind back to a long-forgotten epoch, and thus point the way to important historical discoveries or questions.

In connection with this I must just say a word or two about the importance of asking questions. Personal observation must of course always rank first. But if a traveller passes through a place in the summer, he can have no idea as to its snowfall in the winter, and if he happens to be there on a clear day, he cannot know without asking whether rain is frequent. I always asked the same questions in the same order, namely—the population of the place, its products, saints' tombs, mosques, legends, whether spring or autumn sowing was customary, or both, whether the same ground was used twice in the same year for different kinds of cereals, or whether the ground produced only one crop in the season, or even in every second year; about trade and intercommunication, roads, the distances to the desert and to the mountains, the origin and volume of the water in the rivers, the time when they usually froze and when the ice began to melt, the system of irrigation and the local regulations connected with it, the wells, prevailing winds, frequency of burans, rainfall, snowfall, etc.

One question paved the way for another, and the whole thing took me from two to three hours; after that everything was carefully written down. Wherever there were human beings to question, I never turned in before midnight, hours after my men were snoring soundly. The answer I got to a particular question was sometimes the cause of my entirely abandoning an already conceived plan. For instance, I should never have risked crossing the desert a second time, had I not received information which made a successful issue of the enterprise almost a dead certainty. But as I have already observed, space forbids my recapitulating more of the great mass of material I collected in this way.

The nine days we spent in Khotan passed rapidly in work of this kind, and in preparations for my impending journey through the desert.

CHAPTER LXI.

BORASAN AND ITS ARCHÆOLOGICAL REMAINS

ON January 9th, 1896, I made an excursion to the village of Borasan, about three miles west of Khotan, one of the most important sites in Central Asia for the discovery of remarkable antiquities. The surface of the earth consists there of yellow loess-clay, as geologists call the loose soil which the wind has drifted up, in layers twenty-five feet thick, on the top of the hard stony conglomerate strata which form its basis. Through this soft upper material a stream, partly fed by springs, has cut its way down to the underlying conglomerate, having carved out a deep trench or cañon, with vertical, broken walls. In spring and summer, when the snows melt on the northern versant of the Kwen-lun Mountains, the stream swells to the dimensions of a river, and undermining the loess terraces, washes them away. In the autumn, after the summer floods are over, numerous relics of ancient industry, witnessing to a high degree of artistic skill, are found in those places where the torrent has swept away the crumbling loess. Small articles in terra-cotta, bronze images of Buddha, engraved gems, coins, and so forth—these are the objects which come to light. To the inhabitants of Khotan these things, unless they are made of gold or silver, are valueless, and they give them to their children to play with. But to the archæologist they possess an extraordinarily high value; for they exhibit proofs that the ancient arts of India, as refined by the influence of Greece, penetrated even to the very heart of Asia.

As I have just said, it was in the beginning of January when I visited Borasan. The stream was at that time nothing more than a paltry rivulet, the springs by which it is fed being then congealed by the winter frost. That season's harvest of antiquities had been already gathered in by the inhabitants of Khotan; for they never fail to make their annual search for gold and other treasures. Thus I found but few terra-cotta objects myself. The collection which I brought home with me, numbering 523 items, exclusive of coins and old MSS., was acquired partly by purchase in Khotan, partly through employing natives to search for me during the time I was making my expedition to Lop-nor. My attention was first drawn to these antiquities through seeing them in the house of Mr. Petrovsky in Kashgar. He had obtained a good many of them from West Turkestan merchants who were travelling through the city. But he too had also employed intelligent natives to collect for him; and in this way was become the owner of a very valuable collection of Borasan antiquities, which has been shortly described by Mr. Kiseritsky in the *Journal* of the Imperial Russian Archæological Society.* The terra-cotta objects are executed with a high degree of artistic skill in fine plastic clay, and have been burnt under an intense heat, a fact evidenced by their being frequently of a brick-red colour and by their extraordinary hardness.

Broadly speaking, they may be divided into two groups —(i.) those which have been fashioned under a naturalistic or purely imitative impulse; and (ii.) such as are the products of a more highly developed or inventive artistic sense.

The first class, of which a specimen is depicted on p. 761, seldom tell us much, nor do they throw any real light upon the period at which they were made. We

* The observations which I here venture to offer upon this subject must be regarded as being of a preliminary and tentative character. I propose to leave the detailed description of my collection to a competent specialist. This present chapter is based upon Mr. Kiseritsky's paper, which deals with precisely similar objects, derived from precisely the same site, and upon the lucid and able work of Grünwedel, entitled *Buddhistische Kunst in Indien*. In the next few pages I draw so frequently upon both these sources, that I mention them here once for all, and with full acknowledgments.

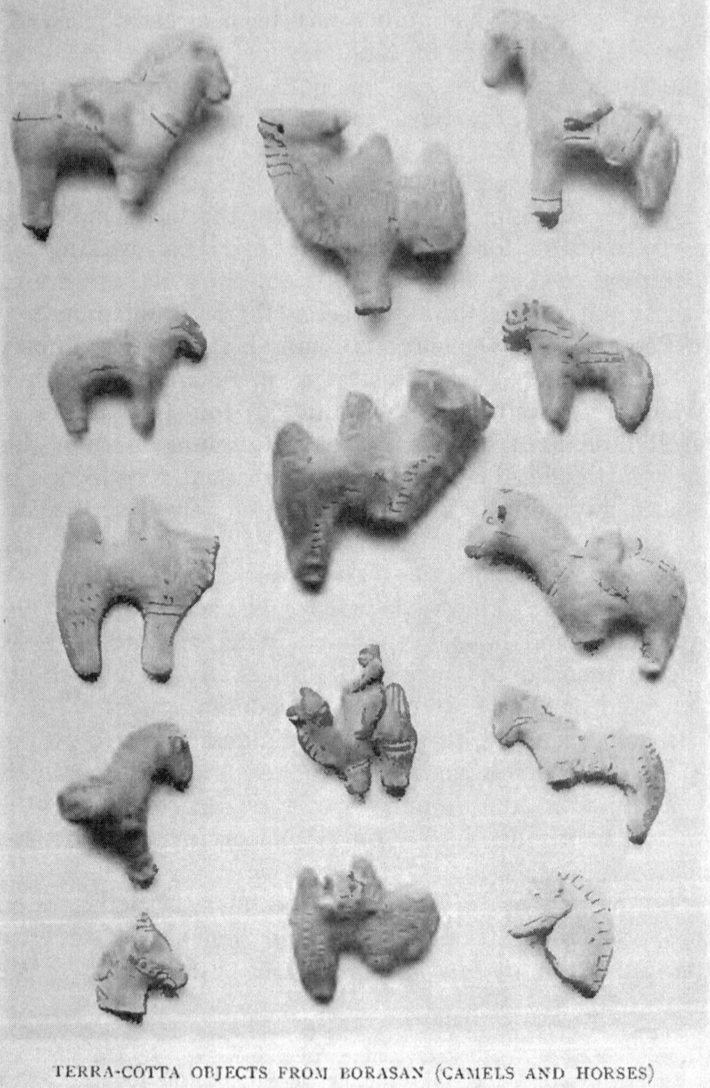

TERRA-COTTA OBJECTS FROM BORASAN (CAMELS AND HORSES)
30/77 of natural size

II.—7

TERRA-COTTA HEADS FROM BORASAN

11/27 of natural size

do learn from them however, that the people who anciently dwelt in Borasan, like their successors the modern inhabitants of Khotan, used the Bactrian or two-humped camel, as well as the horse, both for riding and as a beast of burden. The dromedary was equally unknown to them as to the present population of Khotan. The proper home of the latter is Persia: it is there that its geographical range touches the geographical range of the Bactrian camel. The camels in the illustration which carry neither rider nor burden, and are unprovided with reins, can hardly be meant to represent wild camels; for I have reason to believe that the wild camel, which now exists in the deserts to the north of Khotan, is the descendant of tame camels which lapsed into the wild state at a date subsequent to the flourishing period of Borasan art. On the other hand, a Chinese chronicle states, that in the year 746 A.D., *i.e.* in the time of the Thang dynasty, ambassadors came from Khotan to the Emperor of China, bringing amongst other gifts "a wild camel, which was as fleet of foot as the wind."

Nevertheless the naturalistic group is not altogether without importance. Certain of its characteristic objects tell us whence the men came who made them. This applies more particularly to the representations of human beings and apes. At the foot of the illustration on p. 764 we see the head of an ape, which has plainly served as the neck of a pitcher or jar, and resembles the ape *Macacus rhesus*, which ranges over India up to the southern base of the Himalayas. My collection contains about forty images of apes, many of them represented as playing the guitar. But these are exceeded in interest by the heads of human beings, which from certain indications (which it would take too long to particularize here) are easily distinguishable from the heads of Buddha. The greater portion of them, which are about two inches high, have belonged to statuettes, and exhibit the characteristic features of women, the manner of wearing the hair being displayed with extreme minuteness of detail. A single glance is enough to show that the type of feature is Indian. Here are the same almond-shaped eyes, the same dignified curve of the eyebrow, the same full cheeks, slightly arched nose, barely perceptible projecting chin, and frequently too the same manner of doing up the hair, as are exhibited in the representations of women on the reliefs of Barahat and Sanchi (Bhopal), and on the cliffs of Amaravati, in India. The last-named are assigned to the period of Asoka, king of Behar, or the period when in matters of art India stood under the influence of Persian models, that is to say the beginning of the third century B.C.

The characteristic head of a man, about 4½ inches high, in the middle of the picture, with its long, narrow, well-ordered beard, the straight eyes, both in one line, and the big Roman nose, points to a very different type from the Indian; in fact, it bears a striking likeness to the portraits of the great kings of the Achæmenian dynasty of Persia depicted on the ruins of Persepolis. But the long ears and the stigma or mark on the forehead have nothing in common with these unambiguous Persian traits, but are peculiar to Indian artistic ideals. The so-called *ûrna*, represented in so many images of Buddha by a gem between the eyes, owes its origin, according to Grünwedel, to the erroneous idea, that people whose eyebrows meet so as to form a single straight line are exceptionally talented. It is reasonable to suppose that the figure in the picture was intended to represent a Persian king or hero, and was painted by an Indian artist; or else that it was intended to represent a great personage of Borasan, and was executed by an artist who worked under the dominance of Persian ideas.

It is a fact, that during the Achæmenian period Persian artistic ideals did exercise a great influence upon Indian architecture and sculpture; although it is equally the fact, that the Indian artists preferred to adapt their Persian models to their own iconographic ideas, or in other words localized them and acclimatized them. At what date the political connection between Persia and India began, we do not know with any degree of certainty, any more than we know at what date it terminated. But what we do know with absolute certainty, seeing that we are told it by the cuneiform inscriptions of Bisutun (or Behistun) in Western Persia—inscriptions written in three languages, Persian, Medo-Scythian, and Babylonian, and interpreted by Brugsch—from these we know that Darius, son of Hystaspes the Achæmenian, who reigned from 521 to 485 B.C., counted amongst the thirty-two satrapies of his empire the two tributary peoples of the Hindhu, who dwelt along the river Indus, and the Gandhara, an Aryan tribe located south of the Cabul river. In the beginning of his reign the great king (Darius) was mainly occupied with the suppression of numerous rebellious vassals; but, that task accomplished, he set himself, according to Herodotus, "to explore vast regions in Asia." One of the exploring parties sent out by him, under command of Skylax of Karyanda, a town of Caria, sailed from Peukelaotis in the land of the Pactyans (Pakhtu, Afghans) down the Indus, then round Arabia and up the Red Sea to the Gulf of Suez.

Herodotus tells us, that the Sacæ or Scythians, as well as the Caspii, paid a yearly tribute of 250 silver talents to the Great King. The Sacæ (Saki) dwelt in the region now known as Kashgaria; in that region there are numerous geographical names still extant witnessing to their presence there in ancient times, such as Saki, Soku-tash, Tokkusak, and others. By what route the taste for Persian standards of art reached Borasan it is difficult to say; nor is that a matter of vital importance. There can in any case be little doubt, that that part of Central Asia was in direct communication with Gandhara (Gandara), as also that from the remotest antiquity there was a trade-route connecting Merv *viâ* Kara-teghin with Khotan, the capital of the Seres.

My collection contains also numerous representations of lions' heads; and they, like several of the ape pictures, exhibit a strong tendency towards anthropomorphism. Their shapes seem to indicate that they were employed to decorate jars; hence they occupy an intermediate position between the purely naturalistic or imitative group and the higher inventive groups. The two large heads (p. 769) belong distinctly to the latter group. In this type of figure Kiseritsky recognizes reproductions of the mythical national hero of Babylon, Izdubar (or Gizdhubar); on the other hand, it is difficult to shut one's eyes to the striking resemblance they bear to the ancient Greek satyrs.

Among the products of the higher inventive art the griffins (see p. 772) occupy a position of especial interest. They may be regarded as the successors, or developments, of the ancient *motif* of Garuda, or the fantastic winged bird which is so familiar in the ancient native art of India; it is the creature upon which the Indian deity Vishnu loves to ride. But they likewise possess unmistakeable kinship with the eagle-clawed griffin of Greek mythology, as it was depicted about the third century B.C.

Twenty-two years ago the German scholar Curtius, after careful study of such materials as were then available, arrived at the conclusion, that Greek art made its influence felt in India in the third century B.C.; and, in his opinion, the occasion which led to its introduction across the Indus was the victorious campaign of Alexander the Great, followed by the founding of the Hellenic kingdoms on both sides of the Indus after the death of Alexander, *i.e.* in the period of the Hellenic Diadochi.

Grünwedel distinguishes two periods of Indian art in antiquity—(1) The older, which shows the predominance of Persian ideals, dates from the time of Asoka, or the third century B.C.; to this period belong the artistic finds of the famous sites of Barahat, Sanchi, and Amaravati, together with several others. (2) The second period is that which he calls the period of the Gandhara monasteries, or the Græco-Buddhistic period. Between these two Vincent Smith interpolates the Indo-Hellenic school.

It is very probable that the terra-cotta objects which are found at Borasan date from the time when Alexander's successors were founding their kingdoms on the northern frontiers of India. The neighbourhood of Peshawar seems to have been the centre from which the ideas of

TERRA-COTTA LIONS' HEADS FROM BORASAN

23/57 of natural size

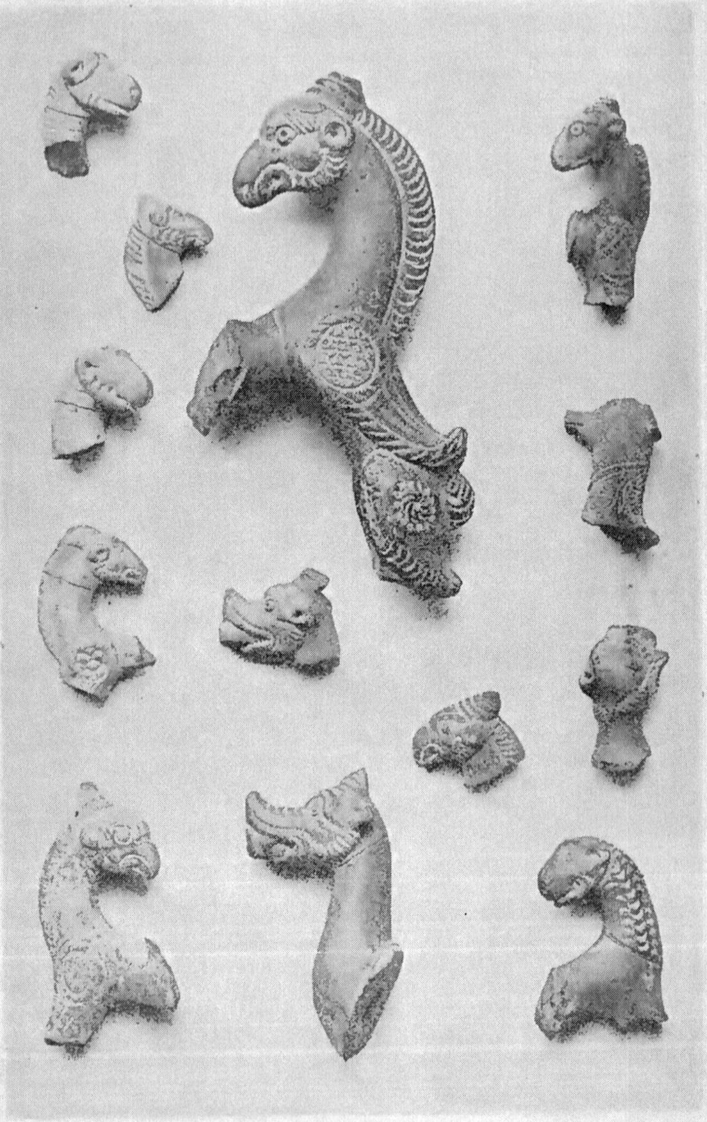

GRIFFINS FROM BORASAN

6/15 of natural size

Greek art became widely disseminated, even reaching, as we have seen, as far as Khotan.

In Khotan I had the good fortune to procure a number of images of Buddha, cast in bronze and copper, and likewise unearthed at Borasan. These, there can be no doubt, belong to a later age, after the influence of Greek artistic standards was completely swamped by purely native ideals. I am inclined to assign these bronzes to

BRONZE BODHISATVAS FROM BORASAN
One-half of natural size

the fourth or fifth century of our present era. They exhibit the same characteristic attributes as quite modern representations of the god.

The illustration on this page depicts a bronze image of Buddha of a different type, but likewise brought to light at Borasan. It is a product of pure Indian art of an antique period. An especial interest attaches to this shield-shaped object. At the first glance the bronze would seem to consist of seven distinct images of Buddha, one at the top and three at each side. In the ancient as well as in the modern religious art of India it is a quite common design to represent Gautama Buddha surrounded by seven *bodhisatvas.* The bronze we are now considering might be interpreted as such a design, the figure at the top being Buddha, with six, not seven, bodhisatvas at his side. But Gautama is always represented on a larger scale than his attendant incarnations, and in the bronze all six figures are the same size, and larger than the seventh. Hence the subject of the bronze must belong to another category.

"A being," writes Grünwedel, "whose special *satva*, or attribute, is *bodhi*, or the gift of recognition, gives utterance, in the presence of a Buddha, and whilst in the act of doing some pious deed, to the desire that in a later re-incarnation he may be a Buddha. According to the teaching of Buddhism, Gautama Siddhartha (the Buddha) himself gave utterance to a desire of this nature in the presence of a former Buddha, and was preceded by six such Buddhas, each of whom in his own time was the Light of the World and the all-embracing Predicate of Perfect Truth (Dharma). The good deeds which Buddha performs cause him at each fresh re-incarnation to make a continual higher advance, through successive grades, towards absolute perfection, until finally in the heaven at Tusita he resolves to assume a fresh incarnation in human shape, so as to show sinners the way of salvation, and at last enter himself into the bliss of Nirvana."

The bodhisatva of the present generations is Maitrêya, or Maidari, to give him the name by which he is known to the Mongols; I visited his great temple at Urga on my way home in the year 1897.

Thus we see that Gautama had six predecessors or bodhisatvas, and will be succeeded by yet another, who will be the last this present world will have. Now the seven figures on the bronze shield represent the six bodhisatvas who preceded Gautama, and the one that is still to come, namely Maidari; but Gautama Siddhartha himself is wanting. That however is easily accounted for. Though Gautama himself is absent, the aureole or rayed circle, which like a nimbus or cloud of glory surrounds his head, is clearly visible. The figure of Buddha himself, which was cast in a separate piece, has simply been broken off (p. 773). When complete it almost certainly had the same appearance and shape as the image of Buddha depicted on the left in the illustration below. The aureole, or wheel with spokes, "of which none is the last," played an important part in the religious symbolism of the Aryas of the *Veda;* indeed it was regarded by the Buddhists as a typical symbol of the Vedic religion in general. In the *Rig-Veda* the

BRONZE BUDDHAS FROM BORASAN
One-half of natural size

wheel is frequently employed as a metaphor for poetic similes. For instance, "Sakra, the God of Thunder, with the lightning in his hand, rules all men, even as the rim of the wheel holds the ends of the spokes in its grasp" (Grünwedel).

Of the three illustrations shown above, the middle one represents a Buddha with a lotus leaf for a background and the stalk of the lotus flower under his feet. In all probability the picture exhibited several similar leaves and stalks. If that were so, we should have a representation of a bodhisatva, a variation of the subject depicted on the shield.

CHAPTER LXII.

HISTORY OF KHOTAN

KHOTAN, close to which these antiquities were discovered, is, as I have already said, a very ancient town. The Sanscrit name for it is Kustana; the word is not identical, as many believe, with the Mongol *khoten* = "a town." In the second century B.C. the Chinese called it Yü-thien. In his *Histoire de la Ville de Khotan*, Abel Rémusat published translations of several important passages relating to the place from the Chinese chronicle *Taï-thsing-i-tung-tshi*. From these passages we learn that the Emperor Wu-ti of the Han dynasty, who reigned from 140 to 87 B.C., was the first Chinese monarch who sent emissaries to Khotan. Under the Emperor Ming-ti, in the year 73 A.D., the town was conquered by the Chinese; and since then, except for longer or shorter periods, it has been more or less closely dependent upon the Chinese empire, perhaps at no time more closely than at the present day.

The chronicle already quoted contains, under the dynasties Tsin, Liang, Wei, Chow, Suy, and Thang, *i.e.* for about two centuries onward from the year 397, several interesting notices of Khotan and its inhabitants. "It is a rich, populous, and flourishing kingdom." "They are greatly devoted to the religion of Buddha." "The women share in the feasts and gatherings at which strangers are present. They wear their hair in plaits, and ride camels and horses in the same fashion as men." "All the inhabitants of that region have deep-sunk eyes and big noses." "By character the people are gentle and considerate of others; but they are also crafty, flattering, and merry, as well as ceremonious in their manners. When they meet they greet one another by touching the ground with one knee. They use seals of jade (nephrite); and when any of them receives a letter, he touches his brow with it before opening it. They divert themselves, dance, and sing; but are also well skilled in the laws and in justice, and in the observances of their creed." "They burn their dead, and afterwards gather the bones together, bury them, and above the grave build a 'chapel' to Feo-tho (*i.e.* Buddha)." Very probably these "chapels" contained bronze images of Buddha like those shown on pp. 773 and 775.

What is of special interest to us is the undoubted fact, that their industrial arts had reached a high degree of development. One of the numerous embassies which were sent from Khotan to the Emperor of China carried with it, amongst other gifts, a number of glass vases. In several parts of East Turkestan, and not at Khotan only, I discovered numerous fragments of glass, which plainly belonged to small plates, mugs, cups, and ornaments of lotus flowers. But at the present time the art of making glass is entirely unknown in East Turkestan. The chronicler further tells us, that the Khotanese were skilful fabricators of copper tankards, and of textiles. Moreover they all used seals; of such I found about a score at Khotan.

According to the Chinese chronicle already quoted, about the year 400 A.D. Shi Fa Hian went to Khotan in order "to seek after the prescriptions of the law," and described a religious festival, which he calls, "the carrying round of the gods." "On the first day of the fourth month," thus runs the Chinese traveller's account, "the town was put through a great cleansing. The streets, market, and driving-ways were sprinkled with water. The gate of the town was hung with carpets and perfumed draperies, and a great number of ornaments. The king and queen, and the ladies of the court, came and took their seats under the awning (or baldachin) outside the gate. Kiu Ma Ti, the chief lama of the temple,

II.–8

walked in front of the image of Buddha; but when it arrived within three or four *li* (about one mile) of the town, they got ready a four-wheeled carriage, thirty feet high, and fashioned like the ordinary travelling carriages. This was decorated with divers kinds of valuable ornaments, ribbons, and banners, and upon it the image of Buddha was placed, between two images of Pho-sa, and surrounded by other images of the gods, all hung round about with a quantity of ornaments of gold, and silver, and marble. When the image came within a hundred paces of the gate of the town, the king took off his tiara, and put on a fresh robe, and walked out of the gate and went barefoot to the image of Buddha, bearing perfumes and flowers in his hands. As soon as he came near to the carriage, he cast himself down on the ground, and laid the perfumes and flowers at the feet of the god. As the carriage containing the image of Buddha passed in through the gate of the town, the queen and her ladies, who were waiting in the pavilion outside the gate, flung flowers over the god and over the carriage. There were as many carriages as there were temples, one for each, and fourteen in all. One day was set apart for each procession, in such wise that the first procession took place on the first day of the fourth month, and the last on the fourteenth day of the same month. When the carrying round of the images of the gods was finished, the king and the queen returned to their palace.

"At the distance of seven or eight *li* (about two miles) west of the town, there was a monastery called the new royal temple. They had been at work upon it for the space of eighty years, and three kings had taken care for the building of it. Its height was maybe about 250 feet. It was adorned with paintings and inscriptions engraved upon metal, and covered with gold and silver, and embellished with divers kinds of precious ornaments. Its highest part went up into a tower. They have likewise built a temple to Buddha, the beams of which were ornamented with the most precious carvings in wood. The columns, the gates, the windows and their openings,

GEMS FROM BORASAN
A little larger than natural size

were all covered with plates of gold. Separate rooms have been built for the priests, and they were extraordinarily beautiful and well decorated."

Thus we learn from the Chinese chronicle that about the year 400 Khotan was a city of some magnificence, and the seat of a vigorous and flourishing cult of Buddha.

In another place the same chronicler tells us that there were many temples and towers round about the town, and a large crowd of temple servants of both sexes. The great quantity of images of Buddha which have been unearthed from the loess terraces of Borasan, some of which I discovered myself, bear witness to the credibility of the Chinese traveller. Even at the time of his visit Borasan, the Birasana of Indian writers, had beyond question been for centuries a focus of Buddhism, and a centre of pilgrimage in great favour with the faithful. And the same deductions may be drawn from the terra-cotta images, which are at least seven hundred years older; in fact they date back to a time before there was any connection between China and Khotan.

But since the fifth century the town seems to have gradually declined in importance. The chronicles speak indeed of the embassies which the kings of Khotan sent to the Emperors of China; but nothing more is said about magnificent festivals.

We also possess a legend about an image of Buddha, dating from the year 632, and which at that time existed in the town of Pi-ma, west of Khotan (possibly to be identified with the existing Pialma). The image in question was twenty feet high, and was carved out of sandal-wood. It possessed certain wonderful properties, amongst others that of continuously emitting a bright light. In former times it was taken to the town of Ho-lao-lo-kia, whose wealthy inhabitants gave themselves up to luxurious living, and neglected their gods. Then there came a *rahan* or learned man, seeking to worship the image. But the inhabitants of the place grew wroth with the rahan, and buried him up to the lips in sand. But a pious man, who venerated the image of Buddha, conveyed food to him in secret. When the rahan went his ways, he said to the pious man who had saved his life, "Within seven days there shall come a rain of sand and earth, and it shall wholly bury this city, so that every man within it shall die, save thou only." Thereupon the rahan disappeared, and the pious man went and warned his kinsmen; but they all laughed him to scorn. Then he went and hid himself in a cave; and on the seventh day after midnight there fell a rain of sand, which buried the whole city. After that the pious man crept out of the cave, and went to Pi-ma; but he was hardly come there, when the image of Buddha transported itself thither after him.

As an instructive parallel to the legends which are in circulation at the present day about the buried cities of the Takla-makan Desert, I will cite a passage descriptive of the unhappy city of Ho-lao-lo-kia. "It is now nothing more than an extensive mound of sand. Several princes from other lands have often desired to dig out the site, and carry off the precious treasures and other objects which lie buried there. But every time they try to dig the sand away, a violent wind arises, setting up whirlwinds of smoke and a thick mist, which sweep away the path, and lead the workmen astray into the desert."

A man in Khotan told me that once he found a buried city in the desert, and in the houses there were dead bodies of people in positions which seemed to prove that they had been overtaken by death suddenly, being embedded in the sand in the same manner as the inhabitants of Pompeii were smothered in ashes. Strangely enough, the belief is generally current in all that region, that the city was sanded up by a single sudden catastrophe—a sort of revolutionary natural occurrence.

Now these legends and chronicle stories are not mere dreams or creations of fancy. They rest upon an actual substratum of truth; for in the Takla-makan Desert (as I shall presently relate) I shortly afterwards discovered two ancient Buddhist cities buried in the sand. But in their case the process of sanding up must have gone on for thousands of years.

Further, there exist also, from the same year 632, accounts which state that the inhabitants of Khotan possessed chronicles, and that their writing, laws, and literature were derived from India. This statement is interesting in the light of the MSS. which I discovered, and which are probably not of Indian origin.

The same Chinese traveller whom I have just quoted, Shi Fa Hian, also journeyed, in the seventh year of the

COPPER VASE FOUND AT WASH-SHAHRI
53/135 of natural size

reign of the Emperor Thaï Tsung of the Thang dynasty, from Khotan to Lop-nor. Speaking of this journey, he states that travellers going that way pass through the town of Ni-yang (*i.e.* Niya), so as to avoid going astray in the marsh; Ni-yang marking in that direction the limits of the country of Kiu-sa-tan-na, Khio-tan, or Kho-tan. This is the first time the name Khotan occurs in the Chinese chronicle. But the remarkable fact is, that the Chinese traveller knew Niya, a town which is not even mentioned by Marco Polo six hundred years later. And yet at the present day, six hundred years after Marco Polo, the Chinese traveller's description of Niya and its situation agrees in all particulars with the actual state of things, as I myself was able to verify. On the other hand, Marco Polo's Pein, which ought to be in the same region, cannot be identified.

Further on the Chinese traveller writes, "If you go east therefrom (*i.e.* from Niya), you enter the vast expanse of flying sand, so called because the sand is constantly moving, and because, when it is driven by the wind, it forms waves and hills. In that sand the traveller's track becomes blotted out, so that many go astray, and, lost amid those boundless expanses, where nothing meets the eye that can guide them, they perish of weariness; and this we know from the heaps of bones which you see in several places. In that sand there is neither water nor green growing thing; but a hot wind often rises, which takes away the breath of both man and beast, and not seldom is the cause of sickness. You hear almost always shrill whistlings or loud shouts; and when you try to discover whence they come, you are terrified to find there is nothing that has occasioned them. It often happens that men then get lost, for that place is the abode of evil spirits. After a thousand *li* you come to the ancient kingdom of Tu-ho-lo. It is a long time since that country was changed into the desert. All its towns lie in ruins and are overgrown with wild plants."

Marco Polo's description of the desert of Lop is so like that of the Chinese traveller, that one is almost tempted to think that he borrowed from it certain of his impressions. It is however extremely interesting to learn that, so far back as 1250 years ago, the country to the east of Niya was quite as much of a desert as it is now. As for the ancient kingdom of Tu-ho-lo, and its buried cities, I will merely state that, according to the Chinese rules of transliteration, Tu-ho-lo is the same word as Tukhari (or Tokhari), and that Tukhari was used to indicate the people who in the year 157 B.C. dwelt at Bulunghir-gol, but subsequently migrated to West Turkestan, where the existing name of Tokharistan perpetuates their memory. Further, the word Tu-ho-lo is the same word as Takla; and there can be hardly a doubt, that the towns which I discovered, and which the indigenous inhabitants call, as indeed they call the entire desert, Takla-makan, were inhabited by this people. Finally, the little village of Tokhla near Khotan, the place in which the inhabitants of the buried cities found refuge from the invading sand, also keeps alive the name, if not the memory, of that once powerful people, a race who, according to Klaproth and Vivien de S. Martin, were of Tibetan origin.

To return to the Chinese chronicle *Taï-thsing-i-tung-tshi.* After the year 632 it makes no further mention of the worship of Buddha at Khotan. It does however contain other notices of Khotan. For instance, in the year 964 it is said that the people of Khotan venerated the spirits; and in the years 1094–97 that the inhabitants of Khotan, Arabians, Romans, and other people, regularly sent tribute to the Emperor of China. The Arabians had conquered the town many years before that. The Arab chieftain Kuteybeh Ibn Muslim took Kokand in West Turkestan in the year 712; and then passed on and conquered the whole of East Turkestan, and thence spread abroad the faith of Islam. Chronicles, called *teskereh,* which narrate these events, are preserved at the tombs of the holy *imams.* I was fortunate enough to acquire one of these teskereh from the tomb of Imam Jafer Sadik, north of Niya. But it cost the Arabs a contest of twenty-five years' duration to overcome the people of the oasis of Khotan and force them to embrace the new faith. Possibly the magnificent temple, described by the Chinese traveller in the year 400, was then levelled with the ground, for the Mohammedans abhor the temples of idols. And anything they spared would most certainly have perished when the oasis was devastated, and the city captured, by the Mongol hordes under Jenghiz Khan in the year 1220.

However that may have been, it is incontestable that at the present day Khotan does not possess a single relic of ancient architecture, nor does it appear that any survived even in the time of Marco Polo. He passed through the town in the year 1274, and merely states that, "the people are subject to the Great Kaan (*i.e.* Kublai Khan, the first Mongol Emperor of China), and are all worshippers of Mahommet. There are numerous towns and villages in the country; but Cotan the capital is the most noble of all, and gives its name to the kingdom. Everything is to be had there in plenty, including abundance of cotton (with flax, hemp, wheat, wine, and the like). The people have vineyards and gardens and estates. They live by commerce and manufactures, and are no soldiers."*

This brief account of the famous merchant of Venice holds good even at the present day, with the one ex-

MEDALS FOUND AT KHOTAN

29/23 of natural size

ception that the present lord over Khotan is the Chinese (Manchu) Emperor Kwang Tsü.

Marco Polo tells us, that in Kashgar and Yarkand he encountered Christians of the Nestorian and Jacobite sects, "both of whom had their own churches"; but he is silent as to the existence of such Christians in Khotan. Now amongst the objects which I found at Khotan was the extremely interesting ancient medal depicted above; it proves that in former times Christian missionaries did find their way as far as Khotan. In all probability it was the badge of some Roman Catholic monastic order. On the obverse there is a figure of a monk crowned

* YULE, *The Book of Ser Marco Polo, the Venetian*, Book first, chap. xxxvi.

by the nimbus, worshipping a crucifix, and surrounded by the words **S. ANDREA AVELIN.**; on the reverse is the figure of a woman, St. Irene, also crowned by the nimbus and holding a palm or laurel leaf in her hand. With the saints' names to help us, it ought not to be difficult to determine the age of the medal. Nor is this the only Christian emblem I discovered in Khotan. I also brought home a miniature seraph or angel in gold, a copper cross, and several Byzantine gold coins.

God grant that the time may come when within those very ancient walls, which have witnessed the successive supremacy of the three predominant religions of the world, the Cross shall supplant the Crescent, even as Gautama's temple was formerly levelled with the ground before the green banner of the Prophet!

CHAPTER LXIII.

THE BURIED CITY OF TAKLA-MAKAN

ON January 14th, 1896, I left Khotan with a small picked caravan, consisting of four men and three splendid male camels; I also took with me two donkeys, to try what their staying powers would be like in a forced desert march. The men were Islam Bai and Kerim Jan from Osh, and the two hunters, Ahmed Merghen and Kasim Akhun, who helped us last year after our shipwreck in the desert of Takla-makan. Bitter experience had taught me, that for a journey through the great desert we ought to be as lightly equipped as possible, and therefore on this occasion I only took such things as were absolutely and indispensably necessary, the result being light burdens for the three magnificent camels. If this time we should be compelled to abandon the caravan, the loss would be the less serious.

I left my heavy baggage, and the greater part of my Chinese silver, at the aksakal's house in Khotan; hence sooner or later I should be obliged to return thither. We took provisions for fifty days; but we were absent four and a half months, and consequently during the greater part of the time had to make the best of what the country afforded. My first plan was to explore Przhevalsky's Masar-tagh, and afterwards proceed eastwards through the desert to the Keriya-daria, with the object of visiting on the way the ruins of an ancient town which I had heard spoken of in Khotan. The return journey was to be made southwards, up the bed of the Keriya-daria, and through the town of Keriya, back to Khotan. How this modest plan grew and developed into a formidable enterprise, resulting in extremely important and unexpected discoveries, the reader will learn in the following chapters.

Unfortunately I omitted to take my Chinese passport with me, and in consequence came pretty near finding myself in a fix; but this also ended well. According to my original plan I never dreamed of coming into contact with Chinese mandarins.

My instruments and other things required one box, the kitchen appurtenances another; and to these must be added several *kurchins* (double wallets of canvas), containing flour, bread, rice, dried vegetables, macaroni, sugar, tea, candles, lanterns, a kettle and saucepan, and divers other articles and provisions. Lastly we took furs and a large goat-skin sleeping-bag for my own use, some felt carpets, two hatchets, two spades, one *ketmen* (a Sart spade or hoe), and arms and ammunition. Tents and beds came under the head of luxuries. Throughout the whole of this journey I slept, like my men, on the bare ground, wrapped in furs, notwithstanding that it was the depth of winter and the temperature went down as low as −7·6 Fahr. (−22° C.). But then we were able to procure an abundance of fuel, and spring was coming on.

My new friend Liu Darin thought three camels were too few, and at his own expense desired to strengthen the caravan with two more, and two or three additional men. There was nothing I dreaded more than a cumbrous and heavy equipment; but I had the greatest possible difficulty to persuade him to abandon his purpose. When we rode out of the town through the Ak-su-därvaseh (the Ak-su gate), nothing would do but he must hasten on in advance as far as the village of Hazrett-i-Sultan, where he ordered a large red tent to be pitched, quite open on the side next the road, but provided with an awning upheld by poles; while its interior was furnished, in the Chinese manner, with chairs and a table upholstered in red cloth. Here, under the gaze of an enormous crowd of people, we conversed for a while, and smoked and drank tea, before parting. Then I mounted my splendid riding-camel, and to the jangling of the animals' bells, set off towards the north, following the left bank of the Yurun-kash. For four days we travelled through a barren region and scattered woods as far as Islamabad, the last inhabited village; there we crossed the river on the strong ice.

In the neighbouring village of Tavek-kel, on the right bank of the river, we gave the camels a day's rest, and made our final preparations before striking into the desert. To the east stretched the barren sand in a belt half as broad as the portion we crossed the previous year between the last lake at the foot of the Masar-tagh and the Khotan-daria. It was a much less dangerous journey; for we knew that the sand was not so deep, that we could always get water by digging down to it, and that we

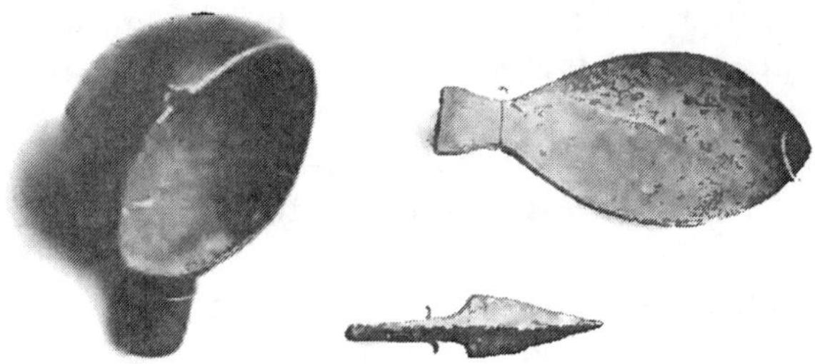

OLD COPPER SPOONS AND IRON ARROW-HEAD FROM TAVEK-KEL
Two-thirds of natural size

should find plenty of tamarisks and poplars. We engaged two guides in the village, who had several times visited the buried city in search of gold and other valuables, and who for fair remuneration promised to conduct us thither.

On January 19th we left the river and steered due east between the sand-dunes; which for the first few days were comparatively low—not more than six feet or so in height—and there was still a scanty herbage. On the third day the dunes increased to fifteen and thirty feet high, and formed a network running east and west, north and south, with their steep sides to the west, south, and south-west, and with pyramidal dunes piled up at the points of intersection.

As a rule our marches only lasted five or six hours a

day, as we were anxious not to overwork the animals. Every time we encamped, the same routine had to be gone through. Two of the men set to work without loss of time to dig a well; two of the others dug up tamarisk roots for the fire; whilst Islam prepared my dinner, and Kerim Jan busied himself with the camels and their pack-saddles. My work was to sit down on my carpet, with my furs and felt boots on, and write down my notes, sketch and measure the sand-dunes, their angles of inclination, their height, their direction, and the like. That done, I went to the well, which by that time was generally nearly ready. The first few days we found drinkable water at depths of 7 ft. 10 in., 6 ft., and 5 ft. 6 in., with a temperature varying between 48°2 and 53°6 Fahr. (9° and 12° C.). The ground was frozen to a depth of 8½ inches. In the third well the water was as fresh as river water. Strange to say, we found both here and near the Yarkand-daria and the Ughen-daria that the nearer the well was to the river, the salter its water.

We soon learned to know whether it was worth while digging or not. Wherever a live tamarisk (*yulgun*) or poplar (*tograk*) grew, or the ground consisted of sand moist near the surface, there was pretty certain to be fresh water at a depth of about six or seven feet. It was only at such places that we encamped. Each day, when our march was drawing to a close, I sent a man on in advance to choose out the most suitable spot to encamp in.

Meanwhile as we advanced the sand-dunes grew higher, and also became more barren. On January 22nd the dunes were forty feet in height. Here again we encountered the same curious accumulations of sand that we found in the western part of the Takla-makan Desert, that is to say huge massings of the sand-dunes in a north-south direction, parallel to the two rivers, Khotan-daria and Keriya-daria. In the depressions between them we generally found tamarisks, likewise stretching in narrow belts from north to south, and indicating the places where the water came nearest to the surface. These so-called *davans*, or "passes," can hardly be distinguished, except by changes in the perspective. As we mounted the imperceptible incline on the west side of a davan or accumulation of sand-dunes, the eastern horizon appeared to be quite near, and we could only count about a score or so of sand-dunes ahead of us. But when we reached the top of the pass, we were able to see over a vast expanse of the desert ocean, and could count the sand-dunes by the hundred. At the top of every pass therefore we made a short halt, to see which direction offered the best chance of easy progress. If from that position we were able to observe a tamarisk, we steered straight for it. Again and again it would be lost to sight behind the sand-dunes; but just as often would re-appear. Even when it seemed to be quite close to us, we invariably had a long tramp before we reached it.

On January 23rd the dunes rose up to nearly fifty feet. In a depression we nevertheless found two poplars with parched and cracked trunks, but the branches still alive and ready to burst into leaf. But that consummation was not vouchsafed to them; the camels and donkeys ate them up greedily. For the animals this journey was a regular banting cure; for, as it happened, it was the camels' rutting season, when they have less appetite, but are all the more inclined to fight. After the first few days, however they, became tame and docile.

By noon we reached a depression running from north to south and abounding in *köttek*, *i.e.* dead forest. Short tree stems and stumps, grey and brittle as glass, branches twisted like corkscrews from the drought, and sun-bleached roots were all that remained of the former forest. Beyond doubt a river ran there some time or other, and it could be none other than the Keriya-daria; for, as we have already seen, the East Turkestan rivers invariably incline to shift their channels towards the east. A few of the poplars were still alive, the last survivors of a dying race, the last outposts on the edge of the murderous sands, left behind and forgotten, as it were, when the forests which accompany the rivers followed the Keriya-daria in its movement towards the east.

For us however this strip of dead forest possessed great significance. My guides knew that the ancient city in the sand, which they called Takla-makan, was situated near its eastern border. As they said, judging from the features of the country thereabouts, that we ought to be near it, and as we had already come across some fragments of pottery, we decided to halt and dig for water; and came upon it at a depth of 6 ft. 7 in. I then sent the two guides to try and find the ruins. Meanwhile the other men took one of the camels, and fetched a big load of wood from the dead forest; and that evening and that night we made two glorious fires. And we had much need of them, for the temperature generally fell at night to somewhere between 5° above and 4° below zero Fahr. (– 15° and – 20° C.).

On January 24th we left the camp to take care of itself, while, with the men travelling as usual on foot, and carrying spades and hatchets in their hands, I rode my camel bareback to the ruins, which were now in our immediate vicinity.

None of the other ruined sites I visited in East Turkestan in the least resembled the curious remains we were now about to explore. As a rule the survivals of ancient towns in that region consist of walls and towers of sun-dried, or at least burnt, clay. In Takla-makan however all the houses were built of wood (poplar); not a single trace of a stone or clay house was discernible. They were also constructed in quite a different way. Although the ground plan in many respects resembled that of the modern houses, most of them were built in the shape of a small square or oblong within a larger one, and divided into several small rooms. The only portions that survived were posts six to ten feet high and pointed at the top, worn away by wind and sand, cracked and hard, but nevertheless as brittle as glass, breaking readily when struck.

There were hundreds of these ruined houses; but I

was unable to make out the ground-plan of the city, nor could I trace the streets, bazaars, and squares, because the whole of the site, which occupies an extensive area, from two to two and a half miles in diameter, was buried under high sand-dunes. The only houses which were visible above the all-engulfing ocean of sand were those that were built upon original rising ground, or now stand in the depressions between the sand-dunes.

Excavating in dry sand is desperate work; as fast as you dig it out, it runs in again and fills up the hole. Each sand-dune must be entirely removed before it will give up the secrets that lie hidden beneath it; and that is a task beyond human power—nothing except a buran can do that. All the same I succeeded in making a sufficient number of discoveries to derive an idea of the general character of the ancient city.

In one of the buildings, which the men called Budkhaneh (the Temple of Buddha), the walls were still extant to the height of about three feet. They consisted of kamish (reed) stalks tightly bound together in small hard bundles and fastened to stakes, and were plastered with a coating of clay mixed with chaff, making a tough, solid, and durable building material. The walls, which were quite thin, were plastered outside as well as inside, and were decorated with a number of paintings, executed in a masterly manner. They represented female figures, somewhat airily clad, kneeling with their hands folded as in prayer. Their hair was twisted in a black knot on the top of the head, and the eyebrows were traced in a *continuous* line, with a mark above the root of the nose, after the fashion customary among the Hindus of the present day. We also found pictures of men with black beards and moustaches, in whom the Aryan type was clearly distinguishable at the first glance; they were dressed in the same manner as the modern Persians. Besides these, there were figures of dogs and horses, and boats rocking on the waves—a strangely impressive picture in the heart of the arid desert—ornaments, running borders of ovals, each en-

THE FIRST ANCIENT CITY DISCOVERED IN THE DESERT EAST OF THE KERIYA-DARIA

closing the figure of a seated woman with a rosary in her hands, and above all lotus flowers in profusion. See the two accompanying plates.

To have carried away the wall, just as it was, was of course utterly out of the question. It will last well enough; but the plaster and the paintings peeled off at the least touch. I therefore copied the latter, taking the dimensions and noting down the colours. In digging on the outside of the wall we discovered a piece of paper, written in what were to me undecipherable characters, although many of them were quite well preserved. Near the same spot we also discovered a life-sized human foot modelled in gypsum. Like the paintings, it was executed with unusual refinement of taste, and had plainly belonged to an idol, an image of Buddha. The men's supposition, that we were in an old Buddhist temple, was not improbable. The commanding position of the ruin on elevated ground and the praying figures alike supported their view.

As there was nothing more to be found there, we attacked another building. The outer surface of its walls was destroyed, and only a few of the posts still remained; but these were sufficient to show, from the square holes and marks near the top, that the house had consisted of two stories, or like the Persian houses, and like many of the dwellings in Khotan, Kargalik, and Yarkand, was provided with a *bala-khaneh* (upper house).

In that place the sand was quite shallow, and by pure chance the men's spades unearthed a number of gypsum figures in relief, each from four to eight inches high, and flat at the back, showing that they had served as wall-decorations. They represented images of Buddha seated, against a background of lotus-leaves, or a wreath of flames; women standing, with one hand outstretched and the other laid over the breast, dressed in long, voluminous mantles, with hanging sleeves and open at the neck so as to show a necklace. The faces were nearly round; and the hair was gathered up in a knot on the top of the head. The ears were very long, with hanging lobes, as in Buddhist images of idols at the present day. The eyes were almond-shaped and oblique; and at the back of the head was a ring resembling a halo. Other figures represented women with bared breasts, holding a bow-shaped garland over their heads. Then there were friezes of divers kinds, fragments of pillars, beadings, and flowers—all in plaster. Of each of these I took a selection; some of them are shown on page 799.

In some of the other houses we also made discoveries, though of less importance. Thus we found a long piece of carved wooden cornice, the pattern of which I copied, a silkworm chrysalis, the axle of a wheel, which appeared to have belonged to a spinning-wheel or some implement of that kind, fragments and handles of earthenware pitchers, a well-preserved single helix or wooden screw, and a millstone of porphyry more than six feet in diameter. which was of course at one time driven by running water.

Among the sand-dunes there were several traces of gardens. Truncated stems of the ordinary poplars still stood in rows, marking the direction of ancient avenues. Nor were indications wanting that here apricot and plum-trees had formerly lived and thrived.

The walls of this God-accursed city, this second Sodom in the desert, had thus in ancient times been washed by a powerful stream—the Keriya-daria; and its houses and temples been watered by numerous artificial canals. Close to the city, and along the banks of the river, luxuriant woods tossed their quivering leaves in the breeze, as they still do beside the existing Keriya-daria; and in the hot summer days the leafy apricot-trees gave cool shade to the inhabitants. The streams were powerful enough to make millstones revolve. Silk was cultivated, and horticulture and the industries flourished. The people who dwelt there manifestly knew how to decorate their homes with good taste and a sense of artistic fitness.

At what period was this mysterious city inhabited? When did its last crop of russet apricots ripen in the sun?

PLASTER IMAGES OF BUDDHA

FROM THE FIRST ANCIENT CITY WEST OF THE KERIYA-DARIA

17/44 of natural size

MURAL PAINTING FROM THE FIRST ANCIENT TOWN IN THE DESERT EAST OF THE KERIYA DARIA

When did the sour green leaves of its poplars yellow for their last fall? When was the trickling hum of its mill-wheels silenced for ever? When did its despairing people finally abandon their dwellings to the ravenous maw of the desert king? Who were the people who lived here? What was the tongue they spoke? Whence came the unknown inhabitants of this Tadmor in the wilderness? How long did their city flourish, and whither did they go, when they saw that within its walls they could no longer have a safe abiding-place?

These are questions which I cannot definitely answer now. I can only refer to what I have said above in the chapter on the History of Khotan; reserving a full discussion of the many difficult and interesting questions arising out of my discoveries there for some future occasion.

This city of Takla-makan, for that is the name my guides gave to it—we will retain the name, for it is instinct with a wealth of mysterious secrets, of puzzling problems, which it is reserved for future inquiry to solve—this city, of whose existence no European had hitherto any inkling, was one of the most unexpected discoveries that I made throughout the whole of my travels in Asia. Who could have imagined, that in the interior of the dread Desert of Gobi, and precisely in that part of it which in dreariness and desolation exceeds all other deserts on the face of the earth, actual cities slumbered under the sand, cities wind-driven for thousands of years, the ruined survivals of a once flourishing civilization? And yet there stood I amid the wreck and devastation of an ancient people, within whose dwellings none had ever entered save the sandstorm in its days of maddest revelry; there stood I like the prince in the enchanted wood, having awakened to new life the city which had slumbered for a thousand years, or at any rate rescued the memory of its existence from oblivion.

However these questions may be finally answered, one thing comes out as unquestionably true. Such highly developed artistic feeling as is evinced in the pictures

I have described, never existed among the Turki races who now inhabit East Turkestan. There cannot be a doubt that the city was of Buddhist origin. We may therefore conclude *a priori*, and without fear of contradiction, that the city is older than the Arab invasion led by Kuteybeh Ibn Muslim in the beginning of the eighth century. Most of the saints' tombs which from time to time I have had occasion to mention are memorials of that proselytising campaign. I have already quoted the Chinese traveller, Shi Fa Hian, who in the seventh century A.D. visited the Tukhari (Tokhala, Takla, Takla-makan?), who dwelt east of the Khotan-daria, south of the Tarim, and south-west of Lop-nor. If along with this historical testimony we consider the inferences that may be drawn from the archæological data I collected, and from the observations I made regarding the rate at which the sand-dunes move, we may form an approximate calculation of the time which the sand has taken to travel from the city south-west to the region in which the last sand-dunes are now met with along the northern foot of the Kwen-lun Mountains.

Neither the fact, that the wooden cornice with its carvings was in a state of excellent preservation, nor the fact that the camels and donkeys consumed with relish the kamish (reeds) of which the walls were constructed, will warrant the conclusion, that the city belongs to a comparatively recent epoch. The slow rate at which the sand-dunes move militates effectually against any such supposition as that. Moreover, as I have already mentioned, the fine, dry desert sand possesses a certain power of conserving organic matter.

In the region of the buried city the prevailing winds come from the north-east and east, and are particularly violent in April and May. It is in these months that the greater number of the kara-burans or "black sandstorms" occur, which carry on their wings such vast quantities of sand and dust as to make day as black as night. In March and June come the *sarik-burans* or "yellow sandstorms," which, although less violent, nevertheless possess an enormous carrying capacity. During the other months of the year the wind blows less frequently and with greater variableness. On January 25th, with a tolerably strong south-west wind, I found that the crest of a sand-dune travelled $4\frac{1}{2}$ inches to the north-east in the space of forty-five minutes. The wind changed in the night, and the top of the dune then returned to the south-west, travelling $35\frac{3}{4}$ inches in nine hours. Assuming that in every year there are on an average twenty-four days in which the wind blows with hurricane violence towards the south-west, and that on each such day it blows almost uninterruptedly, so that a sand-dune will travel six to seven feet, it would travel altogether about 160 feet in the course of the year, and would therefore require a thousand years to reach the point at which the desert sand has now arrived in its journey towards the south. At the same time, it must be borne in mind that I have assumed the greatest possible number of burans in the year, and hence have obtained a minimum estimate for the age of the city. Then again the sand-dunes do not move directly south, but to the south-west, a circumstance which increases the probable age to some 1500 years. Finally we have to take into account the less violent wind which blows in the opposite direction; which probably adds yet another five hundred years to the age of the city. But I shall be able to return to this subject at greater length, and with exacter data, after I have worked out the meteorological observations which I brought home with me. We may further pretty confidently assert, that the inhabitants of the town were Buddhists and of Aryan race. Perhaps it is they who have given rise to the many legends about the people Tokta-rashid Nokta-rashid, against whom Sultan Arslan (Ordan Padshah) is said to have fought. It may be that this city flourished at the same period as Borasan.

At this point I may perhaps conveniently interpolate a few facts about the individual sand-dunes. The base is originally half-moon shaped, with the convex side gently sloping to the windward, and a concave steep side to leeward. At each end in the direction of the wind the dune sends out a horn or wing, which gradually tapers off, becoming lower and more pointed by degrees. When the dunes run into one another continuously, their original form is departed from; they merge into each other, and coalesce with their neighbours. In spite of that however they always preserve the same structural formation. Daily and hourly during a long desert march you cannot detect any deviation in this respect. On the sheltered side their angle of inclination is always thirty-three degrees, and from this they vary very little indeed. On the windward side, on the contrary, they incline at all angles from twenty degrees to one; sometimes they are even vertical, or overhang the foot, sloping as much as ten degrees *inside* the top outer edge. If you disturb the sand at the base of the dune, on the leeward side, fresh sand trickles down from the top, and a groove gradually shows itself running all the way up from the bottom. This marks the line at which the sand is packed closest, owing to its being exposed to the greatest wind-pressure. Hence, as soon as the groove has worked its way to the summit of the dune, it is easy to discern a double inner structure—namely, two series of strata, one parallel to the windward side, the other to the leeward. This structure, which corresponds to the lines of cleavage in a crystal, runs right through the dune from top to bottom. The fine delicate rippling of the surface is merely secondary and superficial, quite independent of the inner structure. It travels at much greater speed than the sand-dune itself. With a moderately strong wind, it will move 9½ inches in the hour. These ripplings owe their formation to the drift-sand, which, swept along by the wind, impinges upon the summit of the dune, and trickles down on the leeward side, where the sand is always loosest, since it settles through its own inherent weight, and is not consolidated by the pressure of the wind. It is impossible for camels to climb up the leeward side of a dune. When such an obstacle confronts you, you have no choice but to go round it. In the level spaces between the dunes the sand is also loose, so that the camels sink in to a depth of seven or eight inches. We always aimed therefore to keep as much as possible along the crests of the dunes; there the animals only sank in half an inch or less.

The davans previously mentioned consist of innumerable sand-dunes heaped together one on the top of the other, and appear to stretch across the entire breadth of the desert. Each davan, with its accompanying depression, has a breadth of about a mile and a quarter. A section of the whole in profile would give an undulating, denticulated line, the denticulations being the sand-dunes and the undulations the greater upswellings of the surface. The latter are probably due to the original contours of the desert, such as they existed prior to the irruption of the sand. In this part of the desert the great upswellings run north and south. Hence it is not improbable, that they have been determined by the courses of ancient rivers, or that the sand has accumulated along the strips of land that were never inundated by the rivers when they changed their beds.

CHAPTER LXIV.

A CURIOUS SHEPHERD RACE

OUR guides, being now superfluous, were sent back. They returned over our trail, resting at the wells we had dug. I continued my journey with the four men who started with me from Khotan.

On January 25th we crossed eight davans, running to eighty feet or more in height; though towards evening, when we halted, we found water at a depth of six feet.

The next day the sand was heavier, as we worked our way across eight davans. Beyond the eighth we came upon a number of tamarisks and dying kamish (reeds) in a depression, and were tempted to make a halt, although we had not gone far. To the east there was a huge davan, looking through the haze like a distant mountain. We held a council of war; it was decided to see first what lay beyond the formidable davan. It was as much as 130 feet high, and was the biggest we had so far encountered. At sight of it the men became very much depressed. The camels tramped along at a slow, sluggish gait, but the donkeys lagged a long way in the rear.

At last we reached the top. But to our amazement, there no longer was any davan! Still, we could not see far ahead, for the atmosphere was laden with dust from the last storm. Shortly afterwards we observed the track of a fox, and found a dead wild-duck. Tamarisks and other desert plants were more numerous. To our unspeakable delight, the sand-dunes became lower and lower. We saw the footprints of men and of horses. We emerged into the open, where the tall bare poplars faced us in serried lines of forest. We discovered a deserted hut, merely a roof resting on its uprights. That night we encamped on the banks of the Keriya-daria.

Thus we had successfully crossed the strip of desert and reached the river, whose luxuriant vegetation was a delightful sight to eyes which for a full week had rested upon nothing but yellow, yellow sand. At the spot where we halted for the night, the river was 105 feet broad, and covered with a substantial sheet of ice, through which we hacked a hole, that proved more prolific than the wells we had lately dug in the desert. The camels were given their fill of the icy cold river-water. We killed our last sheep, built up an enormous log-fire, and were all in the best of spirits, despite the fact that the dust-laden atmosphere obscured the view and shut out the stars above our heads. The hut had evidently been visited the day before, judging from the remains of a camp-fire, and the fresh tracks, which the wind had not yet obliterated. But we saw nobody.

On the following day, January 27th, we directed our course northwards, keeping along the left bank of the Keriya-daria. Our chief concern now was to find some-one who could give us information about the river. It had never before been visited by a European, and its course north of the town of Keriya was merely marked on our maps with a dotted line. But not a soul was visible. We plodded on hour after hour, sometimes through thick poplar woods, sometimes through thickets and fallen branches, and dense beds of yellow, withered kamish; sometimes making detours among the sand-dunes, wherever they approached so close to the river-bank as to completely supplant the forest.

The glittering river of ice wound away to the north with innumerable sharp turns, sometimes spreading out into lake-like expansions, so that the opposite bank became lost to sight in the haze. We frequently crossed forest-paths, which disappeared again in the undergrowth, and saw innumerable spoor of wild boar, hares, foxes, roe-deer, red-deer, and the tracks of tame sheep, and sometimes even the imprint of a human foot; but the forest was as silent as the grave—not a sound did we hear. All the sheep-tracks and footpaths of the shepherds went towards the south. We began to be afraid it was the time of year when the shepherds drive their flocks nearer to Keriya, and that we should not meet any of them.

When the day, and with it our march, was nearing its close, we passed, a short distance from the river, a bed of reeds surrounded on all sides by primeval forest. There we were agreeably surprised to hear the bleating of sheep. A large flock was grazing peacefully among the tall kamish. There must be people somewhere in the vicinity. We shouted; we whistled. There was no answer; nobody appeared.

I sent all four men into the forest, each in a different direction, whilst I stayed behind with the camels. At the end of a good half-hour Ahmed Merghen came back accompanied by a shepherd and his wife, who, terrified by our appearance, had fled and hidden themselves in the underwood. They were soon reassured however, and showed us the way to their *sattma* (reed hut), which was not very far away. There we spent the night. The poor shepherd was cross-questioned unmercifully. In fact, I thoroughly turned him inside out, exhausting the whole of his not very extensive stock of knowledge about the things of yesterday and to-day, and storing them all up in the pages of my diary.

"What is your name?" I asked; and was told in answer: "Hussein and Hassan."

When I remarked that the double name seemed rather unusual, the man explained, that Hassan was really the name of his twin brother who lived at Keriya, but that he himself always used both names, as they were twins. Hussein then told me, that to the north, as far as the river reached, were shepherds, camped with flocks and herds, but at long intervals apart, and they belonged to rich bais in Keriya.

The separate flocks ranged between three hundred and two thousand sheep. To each shepherd is assigned a particular district, beyond which he has no right to trespass, and in which he lives the whole year through, wandering from one woodland tract to another, and stopping ten or twenty days at a time at each *aghil* (sheepfold), according as the pasture holds out. For instance, our friend Hussein (and Hassan) had the run of thirty aghils situated within two day's-journey of one another. The owner of his flock lived in Keriya; and every spring and autumn came to shear the sheep and count them, as well as to bring maize-flour and other necessaries to the shepherds. Hussein himself only went to town every other year. From Kotchkar-aghil (the ram-fold), the point where we struck the river, Keriya was distant only four day's-journey. Farther down the river there were shepherds who had only been to Keriya once in their lifetime; nay, we actually met a man, thirty-five years old, who had never been there, and could not conceive what a town or bazaar was like. Most of them however do visit the town from time to time.

The forests of the Keriya-daria below the town were inhabited by about a hundred and fifty people, constituting a community apart, cut off from all communication with the outer world, far from all roads, inaccessible to every authority, surrounded on all sides by the grim silence of the desert.

The shepherds never see a human being, except their nearest neighbours, and the bais journeying to their aghils lower down the river. They are therefore half wild and excessively shy, born and bred as they are in the depths of the primeval forest. The only things they know anything about are the watching and keeping of their sheep, how to shear them, how to drive them to the pastures, how to cut down young trees and branches for them, milk them, and in due season separate the lambs from their mothers. They also make maize-bread, build their sattmas or reed huts, dig wells when the river gives out, or when they are at a distance from it, and other simple occupations of the kind. The *ketmen* (a Sart spade with the blade fixed at right angles to the shaft) and the *balta* (axe) are their most important tools. In fact they always carry the latter on their backs, pushed through their girdles.

It had surprised me to find that the shepherds of the Khotan-daria lived alone, leaving their wives and children

II.—10

at Khotan; and I thought to myself, that were I a shepherd and married, I should take good care to have my wife with me out there in the woods. But the Khotan-daria is, we learned, a thoroughfare, though not a very frequented one, which the Chinese sometimes use, and the shepherds were afraid of the licence with which the Chinese sometimes treat the native women.

It is otherwise beside the Keriya-daria. There there was no road, and the shepherds had their families with them. Hussein and his better half, who was childless, in their loneliness reminded me somewhat of Adam and Eve, except that they were clothed from head to foot in sheepskins.

With regard to the river, Hussein told me, that shortly above Keriya it is distributed through numerous ariks (irrigation-canals) to the fields in the district, so that the river almost disappears. It is no doubt partly for this reason that none of the travellers who have been to Keriya—Przhevalsky, Pievtsoff, Grombtchevsky, Dutreuil de Rhins, Littledale—have thought it worth while to explore the river. With the exception of Pievtsoff, they have all delineated its course on their maps far too short.

Below the town were many copious wells, formed by the overflow from the ariks. These again serve to feed the river anew. For this reason the natives say, that the river gets larger the farther it goes, although it might be expected that the reverse would be the case; but the assertion is of course only partially correct. In June and July, when the ice and snow melt on the mountains of Tibet, the flood comes down and fills the river to the brink; but it is never so swollen but that it can be forded in several places. The flood which goes past the irrigation-canals is called *ak-su*, or "white water," because it comes from the melting snows; in contradistinction to *kara-su* or "black water," which comes from natural springs. The water sinks rapidly in the autumn, and by the end of November freezes in large detached sheets, which become piled up one above the other, so that the river looks larger than it really is.

At the time of our visit, the river was in this, its

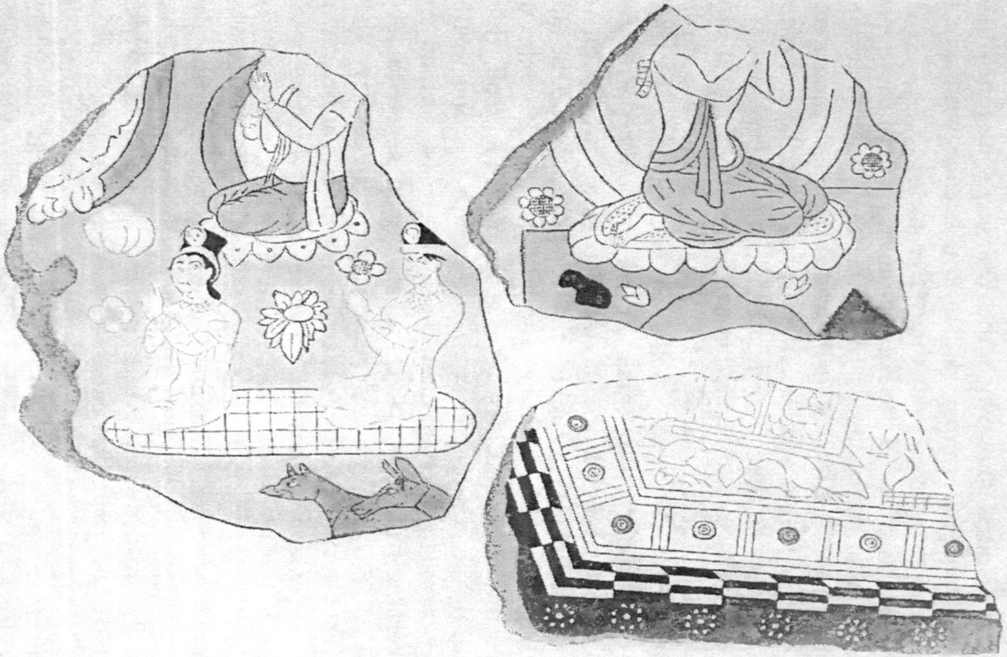

MURAL PAINTING FROM THE FIRST ANCIENT TOWN EAST OF THE KERIYA-DARIA

winter stage. It was expected that, if the atmosphere remained clear and still, the ice would break up in twenty days' time; otherwise it would be longer. When the thaw sets in, it causes a spring-flood of considerable volume. After that the bed is dry for a couple of months, and the shepherds are obliged to dig for water for themselves and their flocks. To be brief, the Keriya-daria exhibits precisely the same characteristics as its neighbour, the Khotan-daria, though in volume and length it is far inferior.

Hussein afterwards went on his way to the south and we to the north, marching along a dry channel which the river abandoned fifteen years ago, in favour of a new bed which it ploughed through the sand two miles to the east. This it now follows for a day's journey and a half; although it again exhibits a tendency to trend to the east. The belt of forest and reed-beds still remains beside the abandoned channel, living on its soakage water. But the time will come when the roots will fail to reach down far enough; then the sand will get the upper hand, and the forest will die down, forming strips of *köttek* (dead forest), like those we observed near the ancient buried city. Meanwhile new woods will grow up beside the newly-made channel.

On the evening of January 28th we met near *Kurruk-akhin* (the Dry Bed) three more shepherds, with a flock of 400 sheep. These men enjoyed the right of killing twenty sheep a year for their own sustenance; to which were added as extras all those that were mutilated by wolves or wild-boar, or those which broke their legs, or in any other way became disabled. Fifteen a year was the average number they counted upon getting in this way. Allowing for this, it required three years for a flock of 400 sheep to increase to 550; but, as the bai's forest pasturage was not able to support more than 400 sheep, sixty or seventy were sold off every year in Keriya. These and the two shearings of wool in the year constituted the bai's profits from his flock. In Keriya a first-class sheep cost about three-and-sixpence, and even a fairly good one could be bought for a little over a shilling.

CHAPTER LXV.

DOWN THE KERIYA-DARIA

AFTER a day's rest we pushed on again, still in a northerly direction. We now always took a man with us, to guide us through the woods. We often rode through primeval forest, in which the trees were large and stood close together, and where the camels had great difficulty in making their way through the underwood; whilst I had to keep a sharp look-out to avoid being swept off my camel by the hanging branches. On January 30th we passed the point where the new river-bed again re-united with the old. There the river reached the noble breadth of a hundred and ten yards. The ice was fourteen inches thick; in some places as bright as a looking-glass, in others thinly sprinkled with dust.

For the space of ten days the atmosphere remained charged with fine dust, which, lifted by the wind in the early part of the year, floats about in the air a long time before settling back to the earth again. Every year at this season the atmosphere becomes dust-clouded in this way—a very unwelcome visitation to the shepherds; for it is so fine that it feathers every blade of grass as with a light down, causing the sheep to have strangles. It settles on everything, colouring the yellow sand-dunes white, so that tracks made across them appear as dark lines, even at a great distance.

On February 1st the river began to show a more marked tendency to trend to the north-east. I had already conceived the idea of crossing the whole of that part of the Desert of Gobi from south to north, and trying to reach the Tarim river. It was therefore rather disturbing to

SHEPHERD FAMILY AT TONKUZ-BASSTE (KERIYA-DARIA)

observe this deviation of the stream to the right, for it might possibly become more pronounced the further we went. The river might even turn eventually and flow parallel with the Tarim, making direct for Lop-nor, which of course it could never reach! Each day the problem became more exciting. Would the expedition succeed, or should we be compelled to retrace our steps the way we had come?

Yugan-kum, the district we reached that day, answered well to its name of the "Mighty Sand"; for the river was overhung by high barren sand-dunes, which presented an almost perpendicular face to its channel. On the south however they were bordered by a steppe, where we again found shepherds. One of them accompanied us as far as the wooded tract called Tonkuz-basste (the Hanging Wild-boar). There two shepherd families were living like savages, camping in the open air round a fire. They were surrounded by a number of small children, whose only garment was an open fur coat. They were in charge of three hundred sheep grazing near by; but had also other live-stock, namely a cock, three hens, a pigeon, and a couple of dogs. Their household utensils, consisting of wooden dishes for baking, milking, and meals, were strewn about the ground. They kept their drinking-water in skins and wooden tubs, the latter hollowed out of the stems of poplars, and their flour in bags. I also observed a few *kungans* (copper cans), knives, a pair of scissors, wooden spoons, a *dutara* (two-stringed musical instrument), felt carpets, a cooking-pot, a horsehair sieve for sifting flour, and a few articles of clothing. Two of the men wore the most extraordinary foot-gear I had hitherto seen, namely, the foot of a wild camel, with its hoofs and everything complete. The shepherds and their families were easily tamed, and even submitted to being sketched.

Two of these shepherds told me that, a day's journey to the north-west, there was another ruined town buried in the sand. They called it Kara-dung (the Black Hill), because the tamarisks which grew on the sand-dunes close by looked black in contrast with the yellow sand.

February 2nd and 3rd were sacrificed to a visit to the place. On the way thither we made an interesting discovery—namely, that we were riding in the dry bed of a river, which ended among the sand-dunes in the vicinity of a little pool of salt water, called Sisma-köll.* Here again the river had deviated to a more easterly course; but at one time it manifestly flowed close past the ruins of the town.

This town was built on a smaller scale than the other, but its buildings belonged to the same epoch. I found the same style of paintings on the plaster, though in less good preservation, the same style of architecture, and the same building materials. One structure, quadrilateral in shape, with its opposite sides 279 and 249 feet long respectively, resembled a caravanserai; it was built round a courtyard, in the middle of which was a smaller square house. In another house the beams of the substructure were extraordinarily well-preserved. I did not make any discovery of unusual interest; but studied the manner in which the houses were constructed, the beams joined together, and the fireplaces arranged. I found however the axle of an arba (cart), showing there had once been roads there that could be driven on; and there were a vast number of shards from earthenware vessels.

These ruins are known to the shepherds and hunters of the Khotan-daria. My man Kasim, the hunter, had been there once before: it took him five days' travelling from the Khotan-daria. But curiously enough, none of these men had ever thought of extending their journey one day further to the east, where they would have found water in abundance, people who spoke their own language, sheep, bread, and everything they needed. As they only took, on a donkey, bread and water sufficient to last ten days, they had consequently only been able to stay one day among the ruins, where they spent the time, as usual, in searching for treasure. Both the forest-dwellers beside

* "Köll" is the same word as "kul" and means "lake."

the Khotan-daria and those beside the Keriya-daria were thus in the habit of visiting the place occasionally; yet they had never met each other! For this reason the former did not know of the existence of the Keriya-daria; neither had the latter ever heard of the Khotan-daria. Both alike called the place by the same name, and for the same reason, the contrast between the black patches of tamarisks and the yellow sand, a proof that geographical

SUBSTRUCTURE OF A HOUSE

In the second ancient town of the desert west of the Keriya-daria

nomenclature even in that remote and isolated region is not meaningless.

Having examined the ruins of Kara-dung, we returned to the Keriya-daria, and continued our journey. As we advanced, the river became more irregular, and shed off, as it were, a number of side-arms, which formed marshes. Near Tonkuz-basste it divided into two branches, which lower down, towards the north, gradually diverged. The shepherds told me, that seven or eight years ago the current flowed almost entirely through the right or eastern branch, but subsequently returned to the left branch, in which it was flowing at the time of my visit. This year however the winter water had begun to creep back into the eastern arm; and they expected the summer floods would follow it. The two channels thus alternate with each other. Every year the sediment which the stream brings down settles a hand's-breadth thick at the bottom, thus raising the bed, and driving the water to seek a lower level in the other channel. At the extremity of the eastern branch, which was accompanied all the way by woods, there were several small salt lakes, situated four day's-journeys from the forest region of Katak.

I call attention to this alternation in the river's bed, because it may serve to illustrate the ease with which streams change their channels in this level country. We were destined to find the same conditions at Lop-nor, only that in the case of the Keriya-daria it is a river which shifts its bed, whereas at Lop-nor it is a lake which changes its situation.

On February 4th we were the guests of the shepherds who live in the woods of Arka-chatt (the Further Island—or strip of land between two river-beds). The next day the physical conditions of the country assumed a very different aspect. On both sides the river sent off innumerable branches, which, generally mere ribbons of ice, sometimes cut off entirely from the main stream, wound away into the woods and disappeared. The belt of woodland as well as the reed-beds became gradually broader, so that we seemed to be marching across a sort of tropical delta. So far as the eye could reach, there was not a sand-dune to be seen. How far would these, for us, so favourable conditions continue towards the north? Were these woods connected with the forests of the Tarim? These questions were continually in my mind. Every day we came across shepherds, who did not know how far the river went. On the evening of the 5th we encamped at Chugutmek with four shepherds, who were in charge of 800 sheep and six cows.

At Sarik-keshmeh, a place we reached on February 6th,

the river was still 260 feet broad, and looked as if it would continue another 500 miles. It is worthy of note, that the powerful current of the Khotan-daria, which in summer conveys such large quantities of water right through the Takla-makan Desert, to pour them into the Yarkand-daria (which unites with the Ak-su-daria to form the Tarim), dies away during the winter to a narrow ice-bound ribbon, which fails to reach as far as Buksem, the point where I struck the river last year after that terrible march across the desert. This is due to the fact that the Khotan-daria is fed exclusively by the melting snows and glaciers of northern Tibet; whereas in both autumn and winter the much smaller Keriya-daria receives important additions from springs.

Nevertheless our river, which had hitherto been such a splendid guide to us through the desert, did come to an end, worsted in its fateful struggle with the desert sand. For upon reaching the woods of Katak on February 7th we learned that the river only continued another day's journey and a half to the north; beyond that stretched in every direction the eternal sand.

At Katak we halted a day, with a forest-man Mohammed Bai, a comical old fellow, who had spent his whole life in the woods, and did not know whether the country belonged to Yakub Beg or to the Chinese. These people never pay any taxes, and therefore never come into contact with the Chinese authorities. Probably the Chinese have no idea, that the woods of the Keriya-daria are inhabited. Otherwise these natives would assuredly be taxed like all the rest.

The water which was then flowing past Katak was said to be only ten days old. It flowed underneath the ice as through a pipe, and froze on piece by piece, so that the ice stretched like a long tentacle towards the north.

I was astonished to hear that three years previously a tiger had come up from the river to the sattmas (shepherds' reed huts) at Katak, and carried off a cow. Mohammed Bai and his shepherds brought back the

MOHAMMED BAI

remains to their camp-fire, in order to save the hide, and then went off and drove their sheep into the folds. In the meantime the tiger re-appeared and resumed his meal, although the cow was lying close to the fire. When he went away, the shepherds saw by his trail that he had gone down stream, *i.e.* northwards; but after a few days he came back and struck across the desert towards the east. It is very seldom tigers are seen in those parts.

This was very encouraging news; for I thought that possibly the tiger might have come from Shah-yar on the Tarim, for in the woods there tigers are common. But the old man was doubtful about it; and told us that to the north the sand was high, and that, even if there did exist a river called the Yarkand-daria or Tarim, it would certainly take us two or three months to reach it.

MOHAMMED BAI'S REED HUT (SATTMA)

During the thirty-five years he could look back through, the current of the Keriya-daria had certainly never diminished; but he had remarked that the sand had increased, and encroached more and more upon the woods. According to Mohammed Bai, the desert on the north reached to the end of the world, and it took about three months to get there.

Although quite cut off from the outer world, with his wife, his sons, and their children, Mohammed Bai was a Mohammedan, and punctually said his prayers; for, "if I did not," he explained, "the wolves and wild-boar would soon annihilate my flocks."

These forest-men pray daily to Hazrett-i-Musa (Moses), who is said to have been a shepherd himself, and is their patron saint. On the other hand, they do not know the names of the months or days of the week. But their mother-tongue they have not lost—for your native language follows you like the influenza to the uttermost ends of the earth. It sounded pretty much the same from their lips as it did anywhere else in the country; slight dialectic variations and a greater paucity of diction being the only differences observable.

When I asked these people whether they did not esteem themselves lucky to be left in such absolute freedom, and, above all, at having no dealings with the Chinese officials, they answered, that they thought the wolves and wild-boar were just as great enemies as the Chinese.

On February 9th we pushed on northwards again. The river, which had been nearly 280 feet broad near Katak—this however at a lake-like expansion—now shrank to fifty feet, and wound through the impenetrable forest in a hesitating manner and by a series of sharp turns. That evening we again encamped in the wilderness, for we had left the last of the shepherds' huts behind us. At that point the river had dwindled down to little more than a brook some fifteen feet across, with a volume of not more than thirty-five cubic feet of water in the second.

After our last guide left us the day before to return to his own place, we had followed the rapidly failing stream, sometimes through tamarisk thickets so dense that we were forced to cut our way through them with our hatchets, sometimes through small kamish-beds or across sand-dunes sparsely overgrown with vegetation.

It saddened me when we at length reached the point where the stream died away in the sand, under a sheet of soft ice; the river finally giving up its desperate struggle against the desert. All the same, the dry bed served us yet one day longer. It was narrow and deep, being generally reached by the summer floods, and its banks were occupied by primeval forest, so thick that nothing short of fire could effectually clear it. At intervals there were tunnels through the thickets, along which the wild-boar penetrate to the river for the purpose of uprooting the reeds that grow in its bed. The landscape reminded me in some respects of the creeks winding among the dark date-palms at Basra (Bussorah) on the Shatt-el-Arab.

On the evening of February 10th we encamped in the river-bed, and digging for water, found it at a depth of six feet. There for the last time we heard the wind rustling in the leaves of the poplars which were still left hanging sere and yellow from the previous autumn. On every side the eternal sand loured upon us. Once more we were about to confront its awful powers of destruction.

CHAPTER LXVI.

WHERE THE WILD CAMEL LIVES

IN my castle-building moments I had often conceived the wish to see a wild camel and possess its skin; but never, even in my wildest dreams, did I imagine I should make such close and intimate acquaintance with that remarkable animal as now proved to be the case. Although I had seen a stuffed specimen in the Academy of Sciences at St. Petersburg, brought home by Przhevalsky, and knew that Littledale and Pievtsoff and his officers had shot them, I could never help thinking of the animal with some degree of scepticism, and always imagined it enveloped in a sort of mystic glamour.

Lest, after this solemn exordium, the reader should be deluded into thinking I am a mighty Nimrod of the gun, I must hasten to explain that I have never shot a wild camel in my life. In the first place, I am no sportsman —a fact to which I owe the advantage of having had time for many a scientific observation that otherwise would not have been made. Secondly, I am short-sighted, which entails the great disadvantage, that the quarry is out of range before I have got a glimpse of it; and thirdly, even though I had been a sportsman, I should assuredly have hesitated to send a ball into such a noble creature as the wild camel. Then I always have the feeling that there is nothing very clever about taking a life which you have not the power to give back again; and failing that power, it appears to me questionable how far a man has the right to kill unnecessarily.

As, however, we were now approaching the special haunt of the wild camel, namely, the most inaccessible parts of the Desert of Gobi, I naturally was anxious not to lose the opportunity of getting a skin, which I hoped would eventually reach Stockholm. My own shortcomings as a sportsman were more than counterbalanced by Islam Bai and the two men from the Khotan-daria, who were all keen hunters, and were consumed with desire, not only to see this animal of which they had merely heard speak, but also to assail it in its desert home. In fact, the wild camel was our chief topic of conversation all through the forests of the Keriya-daria.

My wise friend, Ahmed the Hunter, declared positively: "They are descended from the tame camels kept by the dwellers in the ancient towns"; and let Przhevalsky think what he may, I have a suspicion that Ahmed is right. If I may judge from the collection of terracotta camels, which I discovered at Borasan, and which are probably two thousand years old, the camel was even then regarded as the chief domestic animal of the country; and what is more reasonable to suppose than that the buried towns in the Takla-makan Desert maintained communication with China and India by means of them? When the sand advanced, smothering the vegetation and filling up the channels, these ships of the desert no doubt found opportunity to free themselves from the tyrannical yoke of man. In their freedom they have increased to such an extent, that they are now found in numbers both in this and in other parts of the Desert of Gobi. The supposition is perhaps bold, but to me it seems probable, that if we could trace the wild camel's pedigree, we should only have to go back a hundred generations or so in order to reach the tame camel. And for this belief I will now adduce a few reasons.

Przhevalsky met with the wild camel in the Altyntagh and near Lop-nor; and from the observations he made, concluded that "all the present wild camels are strictly descended from wild ancestors; but they have presumably some time or another been crossed with tame camels, which have escaped from captivity. The latter—if indeed they were capable of reproduction—

must have left an offspring which in the succeeding generations has become more closely identical with the wild type." Dr. E. Hahn has also expressed a similar opinion in his book, *Die Hausthiere* (Our Domestic Animals).

Now this supposition naturally applies only to the camels which Przhevalsky himself encountered. He cannot possibly refer to the camels in the neighbourhood of the lower Keriya-daria, for the sufficient reason, that he had no idea of their existence. He circumscribed the distribution of the wild camel in the following manner: "It is the unanimous opinion of the inhabitants of the Lop-nor region, that the real home of the wild camel is the desert of Kum-tagh, east of Lop-nor. It is also found along the lower Tarim and in the Kurruk-tagh. Along the Cherchen-daria it is rare; still further west, towards Khotan, it is not found at all."

Dr. Hahn writes: "The deserts of Central Asia may be regarded as the home of the wild camel. All desert animals are widely distributed. It is therefore fair to assume, that the wild camel at one time inhabited the whole of the vast desert which stretches from the western borders of Further India and North Persia up to Mongolia. Where, and when, and by what race, the camel was first tamed is absolutely unknown. Probably it was by nomad desert tribes, who occasionally perhaps tilled the soil in the oases, but for the most part lived by hunting."

Although Przhevalsky's description of the wild camel agrees on the whole with the appearance of the camels that frequent the desert north of the Keriya-daria, the latter cannot be unconditionally relegated to the same category, seeing that they apparently inhabit a limited region, and that there is no connection between them and the camels of Lop-nor. What is true in the one case is not necessarily true in the other. Around Lop-nor wild blood may predominate; north of the Keriya-daria tame blood predominates. In any case the difference between the tame and the wild camel is, from a zoological point of view, almost negligible. Here again I may quote Dr. Hahn: "The wild camel differs from the tame camel merely through the absence of fat under the humps, which is thus a characteristic of the domestic animal." For my own part, I found that the three wild camels we shot had quite respectable stores of fat under their humps, though not indeed in quite such large quantities as in the tame camel.

The first time we heard the wild camel of the Keriya-daria mentioned was at Tonkuz-basste on February 1st. The shepherds thereabouts had not, indeed, seen them

HEAD OF A WILD CAMEL.

themselves; but they had sometimes observed their tracks in the sand, which approached the edge of the forest. After that not a day passed without something being added to our knowledge of their characteristics. Many of the shepherds further down the river had actually seen them, either singly or in herds of five or six. They told me they resembled their tame kindred to a hair, were of the same size, moved in the same way, and exhibited the same habits. The rutting-season too was the same, namely, January and February; and even the impressions of their feet in the sand were precisely alike.

I was told, that the wild camel was excessively shy,

and that as soon as he observed he was being followed, he fled like the wind, and did not stop for two or three days. He had a positive terror of the smoke of a camp-fire; and the shepherds declared that no sooner did he scent burning wood than he went off altogether, and kept away a long time. Once, a long time ago, somebody brought a couple of tame camels down the river, but

HEAD OF A TAME CAMEL

even after they were freed from their pack-saddles, the wild camels avoided them like the pest, apparently considering them enemies quite as dangerous as tigers and wolves. The shepherds declared further, that the wild camel notices at once the peg and cord in the tame camel's nostril, with which he is disciplined, and immediately scents his congener's burden, whether flour or meal or sheep's-wool, or whatever it may be, and notices that its humps are flattened and its hair chafed by the pack-saddle.

Although I am not a zoologist, I will nevertheless venture the supposition (which, however, I was in a position to modify later on) that these very qualities are simply traits of atavism, proofs that the wild camel was at one time tame: and that the generation which now wanders so freely among the sand-hills of the Desert of Gobi still retains an unconscious, instinctive terror of everything that recalls the slavery of their forefathers—the time when they stood bound by the camp-fire, when the tyrant man bored a hole through their nostrils with an awl, and when their humps were pressed and their hair chafed by his cruel burdens.

Mohammed Bai, the last shepherd we met near the river, who had spent all his life in the desert and forest, was as familiar with the habits of the wild camel as he was with those of his sheep. In fact, the ten or twelve persons of his little aghil lived chiefly on the flesh of the wild camel during the winter months. He had shot three that year, in spite of a wretched gun, which would not kill at more than fifty paces, so that he was obliged to conceal himself in the eye of the wind and patiently wait until a camel came within range. For the moment the wild camel scents danger he sets off as hard as he can gallop and does not stop for one or two days. The previous year the old man contrived to capture a young one, not more than a week old. The whole of the spring and summer it grazed with the sheep, and became quite as accustomed to people as any tame camel. Then it unfortunately died.

It might perhaps be inferred, that the ease with which the wild camel becomes used to men is but another trait of atavism, were it not for the contrary fact, that the tame camel quite as readily forgets that it has been the slave of man. When my caravan came to grief in the Takla-makan Desert the previous year one of the camels succeeded in reaching the Khotan-daria alone, and ranged the forest for several days uncontrolled. When Ahmed the Hunter found him, the animal was half wild and fled in terror at his approach. As a rule, however, the tame camel is a cantankerous and unamiable beast at the best. He never becomes so domesticated as the horse. If you attempt to pat him, you run the risk of being kicked, and if you stroke his face, he utters a discontented scream and emits a foul-smelling mucus. The camel I rode during this expedition was an exception to this rule: he and I were on the most cordial and confidential terms. But, then, he had found out that I never did him any harm or touched the rope in his nostril.

I was further told that the wild camel lives in the deepest part of the desert, and knows the depressions in which a few poplars and tamarisks grow sporadically. In summer the river flood travels a considerable distance beyond the last human dwelling; and so tempts the wild camel to come down to drink in herds and get a good meal of kamish. In winter, according to Mohammed Bai, he does not drink at all.

He avoids the forest, and never enters the jungle-like undergrowth, for there his view would be restricted and in case of a surprise he could not get away with sufficient rapidity. He loves rather the open wastes of the desert. If the tame camel is the ship of the desert, then assuredly the wild camel is the Flying Dutchman, who sails and sails and never founders, not even in those terrible places where the tame camel suffers shipwreck.

On February 9th we had our first intimation of his presence, in that we found a tuft of hair on a bush. The next day in the dry summer bed of the river we came across numerous fresh tracks and droppings. Our hunters were more excited than ever, made long detours on the outskirts of the desert, but returned with nothing, except that they had seen a herd of seven head disappear into the desert.

The following legend regarding the origin of the wild camel is current among the shepherds of the Keriya-daria. God sent a *peresh* (spirit) from heaven to earth, and there he was changed to a *divaneh* (dervish), and was bidden go to Hazrett Ibraham (the Patriarch Abraham), and ask that he would give him, a poor man, animals from his flocks and herds. For twenty days Abraham gave the dervish a thousand animals daily, the first day sheep, the second day goats, then yaks, horses, camels, and so forth. Then God asked the dervish, if Abraham had fulfilled his request; and the dervish answered, that Abraham had given him all that he possessed, so that he was now a poor man. Then God ordered the dervish to give all the animals back to Abraham; but the latter hesitated to take them, saying that what he had once given he would not take back. The dervish carried Abraham's answer to God; and God commanded all the animals to be homeless, and to wander about the earth without an owner, and any man that was so minded might freely take them and kill them. Then the sheep became arkharis (wild sheep), the goats tekkes, kiyik, and maral; the yaks fled to the mountains and became wild yaks; the horses were changed to khulans (wild asses); and the camels sought refuge in the desert.

On February 11th we marched through a Transitional region, in which the river-beds became less distinct, the forest gradually ceased, the tamarisks grew rarer, and the sand higher, although as yet it did not cause us any difficulty. Every now and again we sighted a solitary poplar growing along the line of the river-bed, now however choked with sand, while between them stood rows of dead tree-trunks as brittle as glass.

Over country of this description we pushed on all day. The tracks of the wild camel were now so common that we no longer paid any attention to them. In the afternoon we reached a tract where the old bed of the river was more easily distinguishable and the tamarisks more abundant than in other places.

Kasim, who always went on ahead with his gun over his shoulder, looking for the best road, stopped all of a sudden, as though he had been struck by lightning, and crouching down like a cat, signed to us to stop. Then he crept in among the tamarisks with the noiseless stealth of a panther. We at once became aware of a herd of wild camel two hundred paces away.

I always had my field-glass ready to hand, and was therefore able to follow the hunt that ensued from beginning to end. Kasim was armed with his primitive flint-lock, Islam Bai, who followed after him, had the Russian Berdan rifle. When Kasim fired, the camels started, gazed a few seconds attentively in the direction from which the danger threatened, then turned right round and went off towards the north at a trot. They did not however travel very fast; possibly they had not recovered from their surprise, or did not quite understand what it was all about. The camel at which Kasim shot went off at a slow, heavy, clumsy trot. We ran after the animal and came up with him the moment after he fell. He was still alive; but a knife-thrust in the neck put an end to his sufferings.

That evening the camp was all excitement, bustle, and talk. We had almost given up hope of even seeing a wild camel, and yet there one lay—I had almost said as large as life—before us.

I of course examined the creature from top to toe. It proved to be a twelve-year-old male, about the same size as our tame camels. The hair was short, except on the under side of the throat, the neck, the top of the head, the humps, and the outer sides of the upper part of the forelegs, so that in comparison with our domestic camels, he looked rather bare. He measured 10 ft. 10 in. in length from the under-lip along the belly to the root of the tail; was 7 feet in girth between the humps; the soles of the fore-feet were 8¼ inches broad and 8½ inches long, and their pads were coarser and less worn than those of the domestic camel. The hoofs too were longer and more claw-like, so that they left a plainer impression in the sand than those of the tame camel. The upper lip was a little less indented and shorter; the under lip did not hang; the eye was wilder. The humps were smaller, more regularly shaped, and more erect. The humps of the tame camel on the other hand, in consequence of the work he does, and of his larger secretion of fat, hang over a good deal. The colour was brown, slightly tinged with red, a little lighter than the tame camel; the hair was remarkably fine, and soft, and free from flaws.

But there was no time to be lost. The sun had set and the evening was growing chilly: at 9 p.m. we had 16°9 Fahr. (– 8°4 C.). "We must save the skin," I said; but Islam remarked that it was a camel-load in itself, and that just now we must keep the animals as lightly laden as possible, partly because we had the desert before us, and partly because we had to carry water. There was a moment's pause of doubt, which was cut short by Kasim, who had shot the camel, roundly declaring, that the skin should go with us even if he had to carry it himself.

The work was now redistributed. Islam and Ahmed skinned the camel; Kasim found out the most likely place to set to work to dig a well; while Kerim Jan looked after the camp generally and tended the camels, which were kept tied up that night in case they might take a fancy to go off and join their wild kindred. Meanwhile I got my own supper ready; and, as usual, wrote down my notes, and worked out the day's route.

Late in the evening we all assembled round the fire. The camel's skin was so heavy that it took three men all their time to drag it to camp; the head and feet, it is true, were not yet cut off. The men still had several hours' work beside the fire, before the skin was all off, and ready to be spread out on the ground and strewn with warm sand. The latter process was repeated several times during the night; the sand absorbed the moisture, so that the skin decreased very considerably in weight.

The well-digging, on the contrary, came to a less satisfactory conclusion. Kasim dug away indefatigably; but at the depth of 10 ft. 6 in. the sand was still relatively dry, so that the task was given up.

We therefore made up our minds to stay where we were the whole of the following day; for we had learnt by dear-bought experience, that it is fatal to venture far into the sandy desert without water. We resolved we would not advance more than one day beyond our last well. When we could no longer find water we would retrace our steps; although there is nothing I dislike so much as returning over the road I have gone.

All search the next morning, the 12th February, for a more promising spot for a well was fruitless. Kasim therefore set to work again courageously upon the old one, and at the depth of 13 ft. 8 in. actually succeeded in getting water. Its temperature was 56°7 Fahr. (13°7 C.), although the surface of the ground was slightly frozen. We let down a roughly made ladder to the bottom of the well, and with a bucket hauled up the water, which trickled very slowly out of a stratum of sand between two strata of clay. First of all the camels and donkeys were allowed to drink their fill; then, during the course of the day, four goat-skins were filled; so that we were able to strike camp again on the 13th with a clear conscience. The camel-skin, after its treatment with warm sand, was sufficiently light for a donkey to carry, although I must admit he always lagged sadly behind.

CHAPTER LXVII.

WHERE IS THE TARIM?

THROUGH dead woods and past solitary dying poplars we made our way northwards, over the rudimentary sand-dunes. For another half-day's march, we were able to distinguish plainly the old river-bed, although the water no longer reached it. The sand-dunes, however, increased in height from twelve feet to twenty, and then to twenty-five. Vegetation became sparser; while both east and west the barren sand-hills, rising up like mountain-ridges, approached quite near to the desiccated river-bed.

Immediately after we quitted the river-bed, we saw on our left a herd of six wild camels quietly grazing and resting—a big male, two young ones, and three females. Strange to say, they allowed us to approach within two hundred yards, so that I was in a position to get a good look at them, and observe all their movements, particularly as the sun was high and the atmosphere clear. The big male camel was lying down quietly beside a poplar, and the others stood and gazed at us with fixed attention and wonderment, but without showing any inclination to flight.

As we were travelling at a slow rate, Islam Bai was enabled to creep round them to within fifty paces. But the animals soon perceived there was danger in the air. The big male got up, and the herd moved slowly off towards the north-west, thus crossing our route and passing the tamarisk behind which Islam was lying in ambush. Islam fired, and the male camel, after going three paces, fell; when we came up with him a few minutes later he was quite dead. The ball had entered the neck, making a wound so small that we had some difficulty in discovering it, for the flow of blood remained in the hair.

He was a magnificent specimen. But the desert was spying upon us; we durst not tarry, even to save a second wild camel's skin. The men however cut the fat out of the humps; it proved a welcome addition to our rice-pudding (pillau). We also took a good supply of the hair, for twisting into ropes, for we needed some.

The humps on this camel were much more developed. The anterior hump rested on seven spinous processes of the dorsal vertebræ; the posterior hump on six. The seven processes were very prominent; whereas the six scarcely projected at all above the general level of the spinal cord. Between these apophyses, or spinous processes, stretched the tough yellow tendons; and as the fat was merely kept in place at the top by connective tissue, it was easy to cut it out. The carcass was allowed to remain where it was, as Ahmed said, a choice dastarkhan (tit-bit) for the wolves and foxes. The first camel that we shot and skinned became as hard as a lump of ice during the night; and no doubt the live ones would fight shy of the places where their dead relatives lay for a long time to come.

We had not gone far before we surprised a second herd of five wild camels, one male, two females, and two young ones; these also were incautious. After moving about fifty paces or so away, they stopped and waited until we were quite near; then they shambled a few yards further. This manœuvre was repeated three times. Islam shot a she-camel before I had time to stop him. The ball struck her in the joint of the right foreleg, and she immediately fell, dropping into the posture in which camels usually rest—that is, on the callosities at the knees and breast. She turned her head to the left, opened her mouth, thrust her lips into the sand, and screamed wildly with pain. Although she never looked up at us, I fancied I read in her dying glance an expression of hatred and terror of her ancestors' tyrants, who had now come, as it were, to punish the camels for fleeing from captivity. Just as the knife was about to put an end to her torture she died. I was ashamed at being the cause of this innocent and undoubtedly happy life being taken, and forbade any more shooting.

Our experience of the wild camel's shyness did not altogether bear out what the shepherds told us. We saw no indications of either caution or swiftness, but were easily able to get within short range. Moreover, we found that they were very easy to kill, falling at the first ball, no matter where it hit them, whether in the back, neck, or leg. That they were so little on their guard, as well as lean, was no doubt due to the fact of its being their rutting-season.

It was both interesting and amusing to watch our three tame he-camels. They got wind of the wild ones long before we saw them; and often long before we perceived any herd, they would gurgle, and lash their backs with their tails, while the foam dropped in flakes from their lips. When they saw the dying she-camel, they were half frantic, and had to be tethered; they ground their teeth and foamed at the mouth, and their eyes, at other times so placid, rolled with frenetic excitement.

During the next few days we saw several herds, and sometimes solitary individuals, in fact, we became so used to them that at last we ceased to pay them any particular attention. They. were generally browsing on the dry poplar leaves and tamarisks; and when they turned to flee, it was always in the direction of the high sand-hills. They moved along the tops of the sand-hills with amazing ease; though their gait was every whit as shambling as that of the tame camels, and they dragged their long ungainly legs after them in every bit as ungraceful a manner. But while the humps of the tame camel wobble and shake like lumps of jelly when the animal puts on any pace, those of the wild camel remained motionless and firmly erect. Their scream had the same mournful, melancholy note as the cry of our camels.

Meanwhile we lighted upon an unexpectedly happy solution of the water difficulty; on the evening of February 13th we only dug five feet and came upon clear fresh water, with a temperature of 42°1 Fahr. (5°6 C.).

On February 14th we accomplished a long march, although the sand was somewhat higher, and living tamarisks and poplars scarcer; but there were plenty of dead woods all day. Sometimes the hard white stumps were set as close as gravestones in a cemetery, and we were obliged to thread our way slowly between them. When the camels' loads scraped against them, they cracked with a noise like splintering glass. The steep sides of the sand-dunes faced the south-west. Our range of vision was curtailed on all sides by high menacing davans, to which we took care to give a wide berth. Every living poplar bore unequivocal traces of the visits of the wild camel. The bark and branches were eaten off as high up as the animal could reach. The reason we were still marching in the old river-bed was partly because of the impediments caused by the dead forest, and partly because certain ridges and ledges of clay, which at one time evidently bounded the river-bed, encumbered the spaces between the sand-dunes. The further we advanced towards the north the more the original irregularities of the surface were levelled down by the drift-sand, so that sometimes we were uncertain as to where the bed of the river was. A camel-track which we followed for a long distance led us astray, in that it took us too far to the west. At our next camping-place, the twenty-fourth since we left Tavek-kel, we found water at a depth of 5 ft. 5 in.; it was quite as good as river water, and its temperature was 44°1 Fahr. (6°7 C.). By chance we also discovered, at a depth of eight and a half inches from the top of a sand-dune, a layer of snow more than three-quarters of an inch thick; it was covered over with sand and lay parallel to the surface of the dune. This showed that it sometimes snows in those regions; also that it blows in the winter, for the sand-dune had increased nine inches in height since the snow fell. This was the only time I saw snow in the Takla-makan Desert.

On February 15th we lost our way among the sand-dunes, which sometimes rose to close upon 100 feet in height. The lee side of the dunes faced south-west, and the relation of the height to the distance between the crests of two adjacent dunes varied on an average in the proportion of 1 to 12·8. Poplars and tamarisks were very rare all day long; but towards evening we came across another strip of vegetation. From the spot where we encamped we counted forty-two live poplars. Only one camel-track was visible, and that an old one; but tracks of hares and birds were not uncommon. Not far off some hunter from the Keriya-daria had put up several poles as a sort of signal or mark, probably to indicate that that was the limit of their range towards the north. Our well that evening was 6 ft. 3½ in. deep and its temperature 45°5 Fahr. (7°51 C.). The ground was frozen to a depth of five and a half inches; the water-carrying stratum of sand rested on impervious clay.

February 16th. We continued our slow march towards the north. Every day I anxiously reckoned the distance we had travelled, and every evening counted the probable distance that still separated us from the Tarim. We were very anxious to reach it and say adieu to the perilous desert. During the forenoon the sand was less high than the day before, and we scanned the northern horizon impatiently for the first glimpse of the forest-belt of the Tarim. An oasis of some seventy vigorous poplars tempted us to halt. But Ahmed the Hunter discovered the track of a panther, and assured me that those animals seldom travel more than a day's journey from water. We therefore went on again; for it was quite evident the animal had not come from the south, from the Keriya-daria.

After that the sand-dunes rose again to fifty feet; the region assumed its usual sterile and desolate appearance. We only twice saw signs of the wild camel. When the light began to fail, we took up our temporary abode round an isolated poplar, which the camels soon stripped of its bark. All through this part of our journey through the desert the donkeys lived chiefly on the dung of the wild camel. It was too late to dig a well; but we still had some water left in our goat-skins. Having found some fuel, we sat round the fire talking, with a blue-black sky full of glittering stars above our heads.

The men were in splendid spirits, looking forward with hope to the morrow. Kerim Jan looked after our five animals. Ahmed and Kasim collected a heap of dry roots and branches. Islam crouched over the cooking-pot, with a long spoon stirring the contents—rice-pudding with onions, raisins, and carrots, all boiling together in the fat from the wild camel's humps. I myself lay on my stomach on my carpet, pipe in mouth, writing up my diary by the light of the fire. Round about us the sand-dunes arched their backs in weird silence. The poplars looked lonely and disconsolate in the gleam of the fire-flames. The stars seemed to fix us with their bright and penetrating glance, as if wondering whether we were some of the dwellers of the towns of ancient days mysteriously quickened into life again. And indeed who knows how many graves of the dead that have slumbered for thousands of years we trampled on in the countless footsteps we took over that eerie sand? Everything was so silent and still. It would have been altogether uncanny, but for the fierce crackling of the dry firewood. In that wonderful country I felt like a king. Mine was the march of a conqueror. I had subdued the land. It was mine, it belonged to me. I was the first European who trod that unknown, long-forgotten region. It was a grand thought that came to me by my own fireside. I dozed off, and slept immoderately well.

February 17th. The landscape still continued the same. The sand was high and heavy; davans appeared again both in the east and the west. One or two poplars were always in sight; although they were generally an hour's distance apart. The lines which went from the one to the other still stretched north and south, parallel with the Khotan-daria and the Keriya-daria, not with the Tarim; and no other sign indicated the proximity of this river. Upon reaching a couple of poplars, where the ground promised water, we halted. Water we must have, for we had come to the end of our own supply yesterday. We found it at 5 ft. 4 in., and with a temperature of 41°7 Fahr. (5°4 C.).

February 18th. The water took so long to run out that we were only able to fill one *tulum* (goat-skin) before we started in the morning. The ground became heavier and heavier. One davan was a good 130 feet high; however we slowly worked our way over the piled up sand-dunes till we at length reached the culminating point; whence the northern horizon was barely visible at an immeasurable distance. The sand was everywhere absolutely barren, and resembled the western part of the Takla-makan Desert. That day we were all unusually silent. Ahmed the Hunter only laughed once; that was when I pointed down into a yawning circular chasm between the wings of two sand-dunes, and asked him, if he would not like to slide down into the pit and fetch up a little water. Islam and I had been in worse case; and our spirits had their effect upon the others, who were beginning to feel very downhearted. We rested at a suitable place and dug a well. At five feet deep the sand was moist, but not moist enough to promise water; so we gave up the well. The water-supply in the goat-skin did for the evening and morning. The camels were hungry; we gave them their pack-saddles to eat. Twice during the day's march we crossed the track of a fox leading first a little way into the desert, and then returning and going due north, and this served to keep up our spirits. What in the world was the fox doing there? Looking for hares? Probably. But it ought to have been able to find them nearer home. We also saw a raven flying in the same direction. Ahmed thought he had been to have a look at the two dead camels we had shot, and was now hastening to the Tarim to fetch his kindred to share in the feast. Perhaps he was; all the same, the wind during the past few days had been in the north!

Ah well! Our water was at an end, and the well was dry. Was there a similar terrible desert before us, and a similar ghastly fate awaiting us, as in the western Takla-makan? No; this time we would be wiser. We held a council of war, and resolved to risk one more day's march to the north. The fox could not have come so very far from the Tarim; yet the fox is a wily animal, a dangerous guide, and we made up our minds to be on our guard against him.

If we did not find water on the morrow, we were to return to the well we dug at camp No. XXVII.

CHAPTER LXVIII.

THROUGH THE FORESTS OF THE TARIM

FEBRUARY 19th. After travelling a couple of hours through the high sand, we once more perceived signs of vegetation towards the north, namely the desert bush saksaul (*Anabasis Ammodendron*), which in the Turki dialect of Kashgar is called *sak-sak*, and in that of Khotan *köuruk*. The saksaul appeared to be supplanting the tamarisk, for the latter was conspicuously absent. We again observed signs of the wild camel, hare, fox, and lizard. The ground between some of the dunes consisted of what the men called *shor*, *i.e.* damp clay coated with saline incrustations. Every now and again we came across the yellow, wind-driven flags and sheaths of kamish (reeds). The Tarim could not be very far away.

The dunes were 25 to 30 feet high. From the top of a davan or pass I at length saw a small patch of kamish, and there we rested, so as to give the camels a meal. Before morning they had cleared the entire patch. A well we dug yielded water (40°3 Fahr. or 4°6 C.) at a depth of five feet; but it was salt and bitter, so that even the animals refused to drink it.

Ahmed was at last easy in his mind: for he had made the same observation I had, namely that the water in the desert wells always turns salt when you are approaching a river. At any rate, it was a good omen on my birthday; for we had now a sure indication that we were nearing the Tarim. In the evening we filled several vessels with water drawn from the well, and when the morning came melted the ice which formed on them during the night, and in that way got rid of a good deal of the saline impregnations. All the same it required an effort of will to get a few mouthfuls down, even in the form of tea.

February 20th. The fox did not mislead us more than one day. Before the morning was over, the dunes had sunk first to 16 feet, then to 6 or 7 feet, in height, whilst at the same time they were less closely packed together, and at length occurred only intermittently. Tamarisks and poplars began to appear singly and in scattered clumps; and at last we saw in the far-off distance the thin dark line of the forests of the Tarim. What a glorious sight! All danger was now over. Then the usual indications began to show themselves—*chiggeh* (rushes), the spoor of wild-boar, the track of a horseman, presumably a hunter who had recently crossed our line of march, then the footprints of a barefooted man, in all probability a shepherd. But the most remarkable of all the signs we observed were the fresh prints of the wild camels' cushioned feet. Perhaps however the wild camel haunts the narrow strip of country south of the Tarim? I do not know.

The ground was now level and open, and vegetation became more plentiful, whilst at the same time the sand-dunes gradually decreased in number. We crossed over a dry river-bed, which went from the west to the east, no doubt a side-arm of the Tarim when the river is in flood. There was still a small frozen pool in the bottom, and down to it ran a recently trampled path. We ought to have encamped there; but we did not. We pushed on further, for we were under the impression that another hour, or at the most two, would bring us to the river. The forest grew thicker, but was varied at intervals by open glades. One thing astonished us greatly: all the tracks of wild animals went east and west, and so too did a furrowed road made by the wheels of an *arba* (cart). Hour after hour we kept plodding on towards the north. But silence reigned supreme; there was not a token of life. It grew dusk; we still kept toiling on. It grew dark. We searched in vain for the river; and at last, at a late hour of the night, we fairly stuck fast in a dense thicket. Wearied out, we encamped in an abandoned sheepfold, and used up its posts and rails for our fire. It was the second night we were without water, and we were tormented with thirst. The men hunted about all over the thicket, but without success; and had to give it up and wait until the morning.

February 21st. The Tarim seemed to flee before us. All day long we sought for water. But though we discovered innumerable signs of men and horses going in every direction, yet of water we found not a trace. The road still led partly through the primeval forest, in which the trees stood so thick together that I had to use a stick to ward off the branches and prevent them from striking me in the face; and partly through luxuriant kamish steppes; and partly again across barren sand, with scattered tussocks of grass and desert plants. The desire for water was so painful that two or three times we attempted to dig a well, but it was only labour wasted.

In one place we came across three sattmas (reed huts), with bundles of reeds stacked up on their roofs. We also observed tracks of men and cattle, which could not be more than a day old. A patch of cultivated ground, and a post and threshing-floor, were further evidence of the proximity of human beings. We shouted. No answer came. The forest was intersected by several dried-up watercourses; but not one of them contained even the tiniest pool. We got deeper and deeper entangled in the interminable forest.

All at once Islam Bai, who was in advance, shouted back "*Su! su!*" (Water! water!). And rightly enough, there was a large pool in the bottom of a deep winding watercourse; but it was coated with thick ice. The caravan quickened its pace. The men hastened to get out their axes and spades; and in a couple of minutes they had hewn a hole and were down flat on their stomachs drinking.

We at once pitched our tent in a grove of grand old poplars. Putting all their strength together, the men dragged forward two or three dry tree-trunks, and when night came made a couple of huge bonfires, which lighted up the forest to a great distance. Once more we were getting on well; but we were even in better form when we heard a dog barking in the distance. Ahmed and Kasim hurried off in the direction from which the sound came, and after being a good long time absent came back accompanied by three men, whom I questioned and cross-questioned. Amongst other things, they told me that the first river-bed we crossed the day before was called the Achick-daria (the Salt River), and that the forest tract we were then in was known as Kara-dash (the Black Pool). There were several shepherds in the neighbourhood, in charge of some 4000 sheep belonging to bais in Shah-yar.

The following day we continued our journey towards the north-east with a guide, and at Teress crossed the Yarkand-daria (Tarim), which was 170 yards wide. Although the ice was tolerably strong, it bent and cracked under the weight of the camels. The animals were themselves afraid of getting a bath, and were therefore led across one at a time. All the same, they instinctively straddled wide, so as to spread their weight over as wide a surface as possible, and kept their heads close down to the ice, so as not to hurt themselves if their feet did go through. In the village of Chimen we once more enjoyed the luxury of a roof over our heads, although the most primitive imaginable.

Here I paid Ahmed and Kasim for the services they had rendered me; for they were leaving us to return up the Khotan-daria to Tavek-kel. I had taken a liking to these excellent forest-men, and was really sorry to part from them. But they were anxious to get back home in time for the spring sowings; they were also growing more and more uneasy every day as the distance increased from the districts they were acquainted with. I gave them not only the money we had agreed upon, but also the donkeys, and provisions to last them all the way to Tavek-kel. They undertook to carry the skin of the wild camel to Khotan, and they executed the commission like honest fellows. My chief consolation at parting from them was, that I now really needed other guides, men who were familiar with the forests of the Tarim and the intricate river-channels of the Tarim system.

On 23rd February we rode into Shah-yar, having been forty-one days in crossing the desert of the Takla-makan, a journey in which we had made many unexpected discoveries. I had mapped the Keriya-daria in detail, had proved beyond question the existence of the wild camel in the desert north of that river, had discovered a race of shepherds living in a semi-savage condition, and, most important of all, had discovered two ancient cities. My first journey across the Takla-makan had been disastrous; the second proved a series of triumphs. On the first journey I sought for ruins of an ancient civilization, and sought in vain; the second journey clearly demonstrated that the thousand and one legends of hidden treasures and cities buried in the sand were not altogether old wives' tales.

Whilst in Shah-yar a bright idea occurred to me. Instead of going back by the Khotan-daria, part of which I had already travelled down, why not strike direct for the Lop-nor, and get my boating trip on it, one of the principal objects of my journey, done with once for all? Instantly certain objections presented themselves. Before leaving Khotan I had not had the remotest idea of taking such a roundabout route of some 1500 miles. I had only come equipped for an expedition of fifty days. The worst of it was I had not brought a single map of the Lop-nor with me; and I had left my general Chinese passport behind me in Khotan. The amban of that place had, it is true, given me a local passport, valid for the province of Khotan. But I considered it as so much worthless paper, for we were only going to travel through the desert; and yet, as events subsequently proved, it was really invaluable. Besides, though this was of little moment as compared with the above-mentioned objections, we had only our winter clothes and felt boots with us, and my sketch-books, note-books, steel pens, tea, and tobacco were rapidly running to an end. But necessity knows no law. I had Przhevalsky's map of the Lop-nor by heart; and moreover I intended to make a thorough topographical examination of the entire neighbourhood. As for the want of a passport, I must endeavour to keep out of the way of any Chinese mandarins who would be likely to ask me for my credentials. The clothing difficulty could be easily overcome: we could make light summer suits for ourselves in Korla. In the same town we bought skin boots in the bazaar. I got some paper, though of wretched quality, in Shah-yar; nevertheless it did not impair the accuracy of my sketches. *Kok-chai* or green tea was to be had everywhere; and if the worst came to the worst, I could make shift with smoking Chinese tobacco in a nargileh or water-pipe, although the Chinese mix with the "weed" an evil-smelling oil and clay dust from a certain hill in China, under the idea that they thereby add piquancy to the "smoke." Islam Bai managed to procure fresh supplies of wheat, rice, bread, eggs, and sugar. The camels' pack-saddles were mended. Then, after a two-days' rest in Shah-yar, we were fit and ready for a new venture.

But first a few words about Shah-yar. The little town derives its water-supply from the Tian-shan Mountains. A short distance north of it the river Musart-daria (the River of the Ice-Pass), which flows to the south-east, divides into two branches; one of them enters the lake of Päsning-köll (the Lake in the Depression), whilst the other passes within a short distance of the town, and contributes its water through several ariks (irrigation-canals). At the bifurcation there is a dam, which holds up the water in the lake during the summer and thus tends to prevent inundations; but when the water is low, the dam is left open, and the water then serves the town, its villages, and cultivated fields. Shah-yar (the King's Terrace) is ruled over by a beg, two min-bashis, and several yuz-bashis. The first mentioned, Temir Beg (the Iron Chieftain), was displeased because I had not a passport; he tried to prevent me from advancing further, and forbade his people to show me the road. But we outwitted him. There is a wonderful magic in Chinese silver! In the environs of the town are cultivated rice, wheat, maize, barley, apricots, peaches, grapes, apples, pears, melons, cotton, and some silk. The products of greatest commercial importance are however sheep, hides, and wool, which are exported to Ak-su. Ten Chinese merchants and five from West Turkestan traded in the bazaar; also merchants from Kashgar, Ak-su, and Khotan. The only buildings in any way distinguished from the everlasting low clay houses were a *khanekah* (prayer-house), two madrasas, and a few caravanserais.

I need not dwell at length upon our journeying through the forest of Tarim, but will confine myself to one or two episodes, which to some extent illustrate the character of the region. I and the four men, with the three camels, left Shah-yar on February 26th. After passing the cultivated fields of the town, we travelled across boundless steppes, grazed by multitudinous flocks and herds. At first our course was to the south-east; and eventually we approached the Tarim. At the place where we struck it, the river was called the Ughen-daria. From that point we steered due east for several days, keeping between the Ughen-daria and the Inchickeh-daria.

February 27th. We were sometimes journeying through the forest, sometimes across the open steppe, dotted with shepherds' camps. We encamped in a sattma in the wooded district of Yollbars-bashi (the Place where Tigers Begin to Show themselves). A shepherd told me, that the Achick-daria was in that region called the Arka-daria (the Further River), that it only flows in the summer, and then several days' journey to the east disappears in the sand. South of that river, he said, the wild camel was not at all rare, and a long way in the desert there were ruins of a town which nobody had ever seen, but which everybody had heard speak of. Its name was Shahr-i-Köttek, *i.e.* the Town in the Dead Forest, or else Shahr-i-Katak—a place which likewise haunts the desert between the Yarkand-daria and the Kashgar-daria.

The same shepherd also gave me information about the

main stream of the Tarim. He said that in June its flood is truly enormous. It then rises every day for twenty days, until it is 300 fathoms (or 600 yards) wide, and as deep as a poplar is high, *i.e.* about 50 feet. It remains in flood about a month; then begins to subside, at first slowly, then faster and faster, until in the end of November the frost comes and sets its congealing hand upon it. The river, which always freezes from the bottom upwards, and thaws the reverse way on, from the top downwards, remains frozen for three and a half months. Ten days later on the shepherd expected the ice would be so soft and brashy that it would be impossible to cross the river on foot. The current is lowest in the beginning of May.

February 28th. Every day after leaving the Achick-daria we saw vast numbers of wild-geese; but at the place where we encamped to-day, a deserted sattma in a glade of the forest known as Tuppe-teshdi, they were more numerous than usual. Every three or four minutes a flock of from thirty to fifty went sailing past, all going due east, no doubt making for Lop-nor. Occasionally a group of four or five came lagging behind the main body. So long as the sun was up, they flew so high that they looked no bigger than little black dots against the sky; but immediately the sun set they came down to within sixty or seventy feet of the earth, and seemed to skim the tops of the poplars. Then we often heard a faint gabbling, as though they were taking counsel together as to which would be the most suitable resting-place for the night. Some flocks however still kept up at a considerable height during the night; probably they had not made such a long day's journey as those which flew lower, and which evidently meant to settle.

Marvellous creatures those wild-geese! They knew the geography of the region as well as if they enjoyed the advantage of using the very best maps and instruments. They always flew in a long string one behind the other; and each flock pursued exactly the same line of flight, over the very same poplars, and towards precisely the same point of the compass. Directly we heard them in the distance, we knew over which tree the first in the string would become visible. Their instinct of locality is amazing. But no doubt they have innumerable "sign-posts" all along the road. They always come down nearer the earth long before they settle; as though they knew the next resting-place was not far off. Once every year they make the extraordinary journey all the way from India to Siberia, and once a year back again, a journey which it would take a human being a couple of years to perform, at the cost of no small amount of trouble. It would be an interesting study for an ornithologist to trace out the flight-routes of the wild-geese and other migratory birds across the Asiatic continent; a map depicting their lines of flight would be invested with no ordinary value. Along the Tarim basin they almost certainly follow the course of the river. Lop-nor is with equal certainty an important rendezvous. Several flight-routes also intersect there; and there the wild-geese, like the wild-duck and several *Grallatores* (waders), stay some time. But how do they get over the lofty mountains, across the stupendous plateau of Tibet? In the parts of Tibet which I afterwards travelled through, I only observed wild-geese two or three times. On the other hand, the Sarik-kol valley, and Lakes Rang-kul and Chackmakden-kul, seem to mark an important migratory route. Another well-known flight-route is said to coincide with the meridian of Kucha as far as the Tarim, and thence down the river to Lop-nor.

The region through which we were then travelling was known by the general name of Ughen; but each sattma, together with the portion of the forest and pasturage which belonged to it, had a separate name. As a rule, the houses were constructed of clay, with a flat boarden roof; but in addition many of the people possessed light, airy summer-houses, with a projecting roof supported by pillars. On the whole, however, the shepherds of the Tarim led the same sort of nomadic life as the shepherds of the Khotan-daria and the Keriya-daria. But they were by no means so peaceful and good-natured: they often viewed us with jealous mistrust, and every homestead was guarded by half-a-dozen ferocious dogs.

With each day we advanced, we gained a better insight into the complicated river-system, and understood its character better. The main stream does not confine itself to one channel; but in its sinuous course through the forest often divides and re-unites. At Dung-sattma the Yarkand-daria (Tarim) was likewise known as the Yumulag-daria (the Round River), and its left-hand or northern branch as the Ughen-daria. But in different parts of the forest the river nomenclature is extremely confused, and it is scarcely possible to give a clear account of it without the aid of my detailed itinerary map. I shall have occasion to return to this interesting hydrographical problem later on.

It was not an easy matter to make progress through the dense forest, nor even across the open champaign, for there the reeds stood ten feet high; but luckily we had a trustworthy guide in Islam Akhun from Shah-yar.

On March 2nd we encamped on the bank of the Ughen-daria, at a spot where the stream was quite narrow; and on the following afternoon beside the clear blue waters of the Inchickeh-daria (the Narrow River), which flowed with a scarce discernible movement at the bottom of a deep and confined channel.

March 5th. We halted for the day in the forest-tract of Chong-tokai (the Big Forest), in order to give the camels a rest: and there we bought a sheep, and I took an astronomical observation. At that place the Inchickeh-daria was called the Chayan, and was twenty-six feet wide and five feet deep.

On March 6th we directed our march towards the north-east, accompanied by shepherds of Chong-tokai. The forest grew thinner and thinner, and soon became confined to a few scattered tamarisks and saksaul bushes, the latter growing on small conical mounds held together by the roots of the plant. The country grew more desolate; small sand-dunes appeared at intervals; and before we halted for the night we found ourselves in the middle of a barren sandy desert. This detached piece of desert, which extends to the neighbourhood of the Koncheh-daria, contracting however to the south of Kucha, enjoys no special name, but is generally called simply Kum (Sand Desert) or Chöl (the Desolate Plain). Here too there were rumours of ancient cities; but the reports were as usual vague. All I was able to discover were the blade of a flint knife and some fragments of vessels of burnt clay. Carrying with us a *tulum* (inflated goat-skin) full of water, we encamped in a very ancient dried-up river-bed, overhung by dunes twenty to twenty-five feet high. This channel made numerous abrupt turns, whilst preserving a general easterly direction. It had formerly served as an outlet for one or other of the streams which we had now left behind us; thus furnishing another proof of the great changes to which the drainage channels in those level regions are subjected.

The following day we traversed what remained of the desert, and once more entered the dense poplar forest. There by means of a bridge we crossed the Char-chak, an arm of the river, some thirty feet broad and ten feet deep. The bridge was constructed of elastic planks, and was ten feet above the surface of the water. The two bigger camels walked across with their usual calm confidence; but the youngest, which very often made a fuss, could not be induced either by fair means or by foul to set foot on the bridge. He stood like a log, utterly heedless alike of the rope in his nose and of the thick sticks which played upon his ribs. We were obliged to go another way round, and crossed the river at Uiyup-serker; there the refractory beast took a less precarious bridge in a couple of awkward bounds.

CHAPTER LXIX.

AT KORLA AND KARA-SHAHR

AT length on March 10th we rode into the streets of Korla. Our three camels, which were accustomed to the quietude and peace of the desert, grew restive at the noise and hubbub in the narrow streets. A troop of boys followed close at our heels, making any amount of fun of me; and I have little doubt I made a comical enough figure perched up on the top of my tall camel. In the bazaar I found some merchants from Russian Turkestan; and their aksakal (or agent), Kul Mohammed from Margelan, received me with flattering politeness. He placed two large rooms in the caravanserai at my disposal, and I shared them with a countless swarm of rats, which jumped and pattered about on the floor round my bed all night long.

The Chinese do not consider Korla of sufficient importance to have an amban all to itself: it is administratively dependent upon Kara-shahr, and has a garrison of only one lanza, subject to the authority of Li Daloi. Nay, worse than that, the new telegraph line from Peking to Kashgar *viâ* Lan-chow, Urumchi, Kara-shahr, and Ak-su, does not touch Korla. And yet the town stands on the great commercial and caravan highway between Peking and Western Asia; hence many wealthy and distinguished Chinese pass through it. But to me the most interesting feature about the place was, that it was situated on a river, the Koncheh-daria or Korla-daria, which flows *out* of the Bagrash-köll (Baghrach-köll), the largest lake in Central Asia, in comparison with which Lop nor is a paltry marsh.

On March 11th I measured the volume of the Koncheh-daria: it was 2530 cubit feet in the second. In the town the river was spanned by a wooden bridge, and I was astonished to observe, that it almost rested upon the surface of the stream; and yet it was the season of spring, when the rivers of East Turkestan are without exception at their lowest level, some of them indeed, like the Khotan-daria, quite dried up. No doubt the Korla-daria was governed by the same laws; that is to say, it attained its maximum volume in the summer. But if so, the bridge must infallibly be swept away like a chip, and all traffic along the great highway would be suspended. That was inconceivable. I was however given to understand, that the river has a constant level; it is always at the same height, never varying more than two fingers' breadth.

Moreover, as in contradistinction to every other river in the country, its water was as clear as crystal, a glorious blue, it became pretty evident to me, that the river must be in intimate and even peculiar dependence upon the Bagrash-köll. Putting aside the insignificant rivulets, which enjoy a merely temporary existence after a shower, the lake of Bagrash-köll is only fed by one stream; but then that is a stream of extraordinary volume, the principal artery of the Yulduz valley, called by the Mongols Khaidik-gol or Hädick-gol, and by the Mohammedans of Central Asia Kara-shahr-dariasi. This river does partake of the same character as the other streams of East Turkestan. During the summer its volume is enormous, and its water turbid, in consequence of the amount of sand it holds in suspension; in autumn and spring it is of a medium size; and in winter it approaches its minimum, being covered, like the lake into which it flows, by a thick sheet of ice.

This hydrographical problem had for me such an attraction that I was obliged to run up to Kara-shahr, which stands on the left bank of the Hädick-gol; nor was I in any way deterred by the fact, that the town was the seat of a powerful amban (Chinese governor), and that I had no passport.

I went thither on March 12th, taking only Kul Mohammed with me, and leaving Islam Bai and Kerim Jan behind in Korla, to look after the camels and baggage. It was a ride of thirty-six miles, and we did it in six hours; arriving just as the ice was breaking up, and the Mongols, or, as the Central Asian Mohammedans call them, Kalmucks (Kalmak), were getting out their punts to ferry travellers and caravans across the river. Thus I had an excellent opportunity to measure the volume of the river, which I did on March 14th, and found it was 1890 cubic feet in the second, that is to say, during those days there flowed every second 640 cubic feet more water *out* of the lake than flowed *into* it.

The marks of the highest level reached by the river during the previous summer were still visible. The ferrymen gave me general data bearing upon the seasonal changes of level that the river undergoes. Thus I was able to make an approximate calculation of the relative inflow and outflow during the year; and I got as my result, that the enormous quantity of 70,650 million cubic feet more flow into the lake than out of it. Nor indeed is this so very astounding, when you bear in mind, that Lop-nor, which at the very least receives as much as the Bagrash-köll, does not lose a single drop through any outflow, or by any other means except evaporation, and that an enormous quantity soaks into the ground. But then in that region, where the relative moisture of the air is so very insignificant, it is evaporation which plays the principal part in maintaining the balance between precipitation and drainage.

What is stranger, however, is that in winter the lake discharges a larger quantity than it receives. The explanation would seem to be this. The large basin enclosed between the Tian-shan Mountains and the Kurruk-tagh, a basin which it takes a mounted man three days to ride through from end to end and one day to cross, acts as a distributor or regulator of the water, much in the same way as the second ball in a scent-spray.

Finally, I may mention that the water which flows into

the lake is muddy, cold, and perfectly fresh; whereas the water which flows out is clear as crystal, is some degrees warmer, and has a *soupçon* of salt in it, all phenomena so simple as to stand in no need of explanation.

The large lake of Issyk-kul in Semiryechensk presents a problem which has been a standing puzzle to geologists, hydrographers, and travellers. The river Chu, a stream of some magnitude, flows across the perfectly level plain to within a couple of miles or so of the west end of the lake; but instead of entering the lake, as would naturally be expected, it flows on towards the north-west and pierces the great mountain-range of Ala-tau. Nor does it in any way add to the volume of the lake, except occasionally during periods of very unusual flood, and then it does sometimes send off a small side-branch. Various complex theories, partly geological, partly hydrographical, have been invented to account for this. I too have hit upon a theory, which enjoys the advantage of being at any rate simple. The relation of the Chu to the Issyk-kul is exactly paralleled by the relation of the Hädick-gol and the Koncheh-daria to the Bagrash-köll.

The distance between the point where the delta of the Hädick-gol enters the lake and the point at which the Koncheh-daria runs out of it is only 15 or 16 miles. Between the two points the lake is shallow and overgrown with luxuriant reeds; whereas its middle and eastern parts are deep and free from vegetation. Moreover the Hädick-gol sends off a long delta-arm towards the Koncheh-daria. On the way to Kara-shahr we passed, at the distance of about an hour and a half, a dry channel, which branched off from the Hädick-gol and joined the Koncheh-daria. I inquired into its character, and was told, that every fifth or eighth year the Hädick-gol overflows its banks, and a portion of its flood-water makes its way along that dry channel direct to the Koncheh-daria without passing through Bagrash-köll. The contour of the ground, I may remark, is almost perfectly level, and its elevation above the surface of the lake trifling.

Assume now, that the overflow occurs fifteen times in

the course of a century. Then, in the next following century it may possibly happen thirty times. And so it will go on, increasing in frequency in proportion as the Hädick-gol pushes out its delta further and further into the lake, until eventually the river will raise a barrier to its own further advance, and instead of flowing into the lake will pour the greater portion of its torrent along what is now an intermittent watercourse, partly choked with sand and soil. When that result is brought about, the river will no longer flow in its old bed, but will flow past the lake at a few miles' distance. Thus we have precisely the same peculiar conditions as those which obtain at Issyk-kul, namely a lake embedded between the lofty crests of the Tian-shan Mountains, with a large river flowing past its western extremity, so near as almost to touch it, yet without contributing to it one gallon of water. The lake would then decrease in area, whilst the salinity of its water would increase, precisely as is the case with the Issyk-kul.

Kara-shahr (the Black Town) fully deserves its name; for it is without comparison the dirtiest town in all Central Asia. It stands on the left bank of the river, on a level, barren plain, totally destitute of any feature of interest. Nevertheless it is a large town, very much larger than Korla, consisting of a countless number of miserable hovels, courtyards, bazaars, and Mongol tents, surrounded by a wall, and is the chief commercial emporium in that part of Chinese Turkestan.

Politeness dictated that I should make a call upon the amban of the place, Hwen Darin. Accordingly, with my local passport in my pocket, I went alone and unsuspecting to his yamen (official residence). He was a little old man, some sixty years of age, with a white beard, who received me smilingly, and with especial friendliness and politeness, and offered me tea, pastry, and an opium-pipe. Through the mouth of a Turki interpreter, I told him what had brought me there; and when I went on to express my regret, that I had not brought a more authoritative passport with me, he replied, with all the studied courtesy of a Frenchman, "You are our friend and guest. You do not need any passport. You yourself are a sufficient passport." I suppose Hwen Darin did not think I looked likely to imperil the peace of the country. Indeed he ordered another passport to be made out for me, valid for his own province. Then, at the end of about an hour, I said my adieus and left him; and in all probability we shall never meet again. But I shall always keep a warm place in my memory for the good old man: I can see him at this instant as distinctly as the hour we separated.

I will relate one other incident of my excursion into that neighbourhood. On March 15th, well satisfied with my little flying trip to Kara-shahr, I went back to Korla. As soon as I arrived, Islam Bai came and told me that, two days previously, as he was sitting beside a stall in the bazaar, talking to an Andijan (West Turkestan) merchant, five Chinese soldiers rode past. Their leader carried on a pole an emblem of the power and sovereignty of Kwang Tsü, Emperor of China. Now it is customary, when the said symbol is borne through the bazaar, or wheresoever else it may be, for everybody to rise to their feet, and for every rider to dismount, and all pay obeisance to it as to a Gessler's hat.

Islam Bai, being a Russian subject, did not consider —and quite rightly too—that he was under any obligation to pay homage to Chinese sovereignty, and consequently sat still. Thereupon the Chinese soldiers halted, dismounted, seized him, pulled off his chapan (cloak), and whilst four of them held him with his arms outstretched, the fifth scourged him till the blood ran down his back.

I instantly sat down and wrote the following letter to Li Daloi, the commander of the soldiers, partly to procure satisfaction for my faithful attendant, partly to uphold the prestige of the European:—

"During my absence your soldiers have beaten my servant, a Russian subject. If you can show me any treaty agreement between Russia and China which empowers Chinese soldiers to do such a thing, I will let the matter drop. If not, I demand the arrest of the delinquents and their punishment in the public square of this town. If you fail to comply with this demand, I shall return to Kara-shahr, and telegraph a report of the occurrence, not only to the Russian consul in Urumchi, but also to Fu Tai (the governor-general of East Turkestan, who also dwelt in Urumchi)."

This peremptory letter produced an instantaneous effect. Li Daloi came to me, and with a tearful voice humbly promised that my demands should be complied with. Then he went away; but soon came back again to report that the guilty parties could not be discovered, and nobody knew anything about the affair. Islam showed his back, and said, that the soldier who whipped him had a deep scar on his left cheek.

I therefore demanded, that the entire lanza who constituted the garrison should be paraded in the courtyard of the Andijan merchants' serai, where we were staying.

The soldiers passed one by one before Islam.

"This is the man," cried Islam, as the man with the scar went past him, and he seized him by the collar and dragged him before Li Daloi. The latter at once asserted his authority, and promptly issued his commands for the delinquent to be punished. Then ensued a scene which the good folk of Korla are not likely to forget in a hurry, for they crowded into the courtyard and even filled the roofs of the adjacent houses.

The soldier was stretched flat on the ground; two of his comrades held his arms, two others held his feet, and a fifth exposed the nether portion of his person, and he was thoroughly punished in the same way in which he had unjustly assaulted Islam Bai. When I considered he had had enough, I bade them stop, saying the one thrashing counterbalanced the other.

All the same this occurrence was neither pleasant nor agreeable. I prefer to travel peaceably and quietly through the land, but I could not pass over such gross ill-treatment of one of my followers. Nor need the sensitive fear that the Chinese soldier was any the worse either in body or soul. As for his soul, let us hope, he was a trifle repentant after he had digested his punishment, and his body would not suffer, if only he abstained from riding hard for a week or two.

When, later in the day, I went to Li Daloi to thank him for so promptly and satisfactorily meeting me in this matter, I perceived I was the object of a good deal of special attention in the town. The people in the streets made way for me. The street urchins no longer dared to laugh at me. All the time however I had been thinking of something which fortunately never once entered Li Daloi's head. Had he only been sharp enough, he would have met my demand with the counter-demand to see my passport, and to be furnished with evidence that Islam Bai really was a Russian subject. If he had done that, what could I have answered? It would then have been my turn to be deferential and courteous. But lucky for me, it never occurred to Li Daloi to ask for the passport.

The Mohammedan portion of the town was governed by three begs, one of whom, a white-bearded old man, had forty years before served under Vali Khan Tura, who murdered Adolf Schlagintweit, and the old man had also been in favour with Yakub Beg. Kul Mohammed, the aksakal of the Andijanliks (West Turkestan merchants), had been settled in Korla for many years; he was living there in 1877, when Yakub Beg died in the town. Yakub was waiting there with 6000 men for a favourable opportunity to attack the Chinese. Kul Mohammed gave a different version of the murder from the usually received account. The conqueror was going that afternoon to take tea with his confidential supporter, the influential Niaz Hakim Beg of Khotan. This was the man who at his prince's command built the before-mentioned caravanserais of Kosh-lengher and Chullak-lengher, on the road between Yarkand and Khotan. Niaz Beg, who had quarrelled with his master, mixed poison in Yakub's tea, and the poisoned cup speedily did its fatal work.

Korla and the fifty-five villages dependent upon it,

produce wool, sheepskins, fox-skins, cotton, silk, and rice, all of which are exported to Ak-su and Dural. Other productions of the same district are wheat, maize, barley, pomegranates, and a quantity of other fruits. A sweet yellow pear, called *näsbet*, which melts on the tongue, is famous throughout the whole of East Turkestan. The wheat is sown in March, and is ripe four months later; but in those villages which suffer from a deficiency of water, the wheat is sown in the autumn. Rice is sown in April, and the harvest takes place two months afterwards.

Korla ranks in the matter of size with Maral-bashi, Yanghi-hissar, Guma, and Shah-yar. Its bazaar was nothing out of the ordinary; but the town occupied a splendid situation beside the crystal stream, whose little eddies circled round and round underneath its small bridges. Building-sites within the town being rather restricted, many of the houses have been built on piles at the margin of the river. Several of them were quite picturesque, and through chinks in the floor you could see the blue-green current gliding along like oil underneath. The temperature was only 41° Fahr. (5° C.), nevertheless a dozen urchins were swimming and splashing about in it, and letting themselves be carried down by the current. I was told that every man in Korla can swim, and during the hot season they cool themselves every day in the fresh cool river.

CHAPTER LXX.

THE LOP-NOR PROBLEM

IN Korla we augmented the caravan by two fresh horses, replenished our commissariat-boxes, and engaged two excellent guides, who led us to Tikkenlik, a small village situated on the lower Koncheh-daria, at the point of confluence of two branches or bifurcating arms from the Tarim. From Korla to that village there were three routes. One followed the Koncheh-daria, the second skirted the mountains Kurruk-tagh (the Dry Mountains), and the third traversed the stony, sandy desert between the mountains and the river. The first was already sufficiently well known. Of the others I chose the third, and in the course of the journey discovered two ancient Chinese fortresses, and a long string of potais ("mile-posts"), that is, lofty pyramids of wood and clay, measuring the distance of the road in Chinese *li* (li = 485 yards).

This latter discovery was one of unusual interest. It demonstrated that in former times an important highway ran between Korla and—well, what place? The highway, which bore to the south-east, ends at the present time in a sandy desert. Now in this same latitude of 40° 30′ N. the Chinese maps placed the ancient Lop-nor; and, as I shall have occasion to show further on in my account of this very interesting journey, the Chinese maps were right.

The ancient highway I have just mentioned led therefore, there can be little doubt, to the former Lop-nor, and was abandoned after the lake became dried up in consequence of occurrences which I shall point out lower down. But that this highway formed an important link

CROSSING THE KONCHEH-DARIA

of communication is proved by these very potais, for the Chinese do not take the trouble to erect such conveniences, even at the present day, except along the most important caravan-routes.

Przhevalsky was the first European who visited Lop-nor. He however found the lake a full degree farther to the south than it was shown on the Chinese maps; moreover, he announced that its water was fresh, not salt.* In consequence of this, he became involved in a controversy with the German geographer, Baron von Richthofen—a controversy which has been awaiting a definite solution ever since Przhevalsky's death. Baron von Richthofen wrote a paper in the *Verhandlungen* (Proceedings) of the Geographical Society of Berlin, in which with singular acumen he demonstrated that a desert lake, such as Lop-nor, which possesses no outflow to the sea, must indisputably and of necessity contain salt water. Now, seeing that the basin discovered by Przhevalsky contained fresh water, and in view of the further fact, that the Chinese topographers never enter any geographical feature upon their maps unless they have themselves actually seen it, and yet they had a Lop-nor a full degree north of the position in which Przhevalsky placed the lake which he discovered, Von Richthofen suggested that Przhevalsky's lake must be a modern formation, which has come into existence since the Chinese mapped their Lop-nor.

Przhevalsky travelled to his Lop-nor by the great highway which runs between the Konchch-daria and the Tarim, and could not therefore possibly ascertain whether farther to the east there was or was not a lake, or the desiccated basin of a lake, because that question could only be answered by travelling on the east side of the Koncheh-daria; for there ought to be on that side a branch flowing from the Koncheh-daria into the old Lop-nor of the Chinese maps. In the controversy which raged between the two great authorities, both parties were right, as I shall show in what follows.

Since Przhevalsky first discovered his Lop-nor, it has

* See Introduction, pp. 15–18.

been visited by the following Europeans:—Carey and Dalgleish, Prince Henry of Orleans and Bonvalot, Pievtsoff and his two officers, and the geologist Bogdanovitch, and lastly by Littledale and his wife. But all these travelled by precisely the same route as the great Russian explorer, and therefore none of them, with the exception of Pievtsoff, has been able to add anything material to the masterly and conscientious description of the region which Przhevalsky gave in his account of his first journey (1876–77) to (his) Lop-nor, and which he supplemented himself after his second journey thither in the spring of 1885.

If therefore I was to be in a position to determine the controversy between Przhevalsky and Von Richthofen, as indeed I hoped to be able to do, I must above all things avoid travelling to the lake by the same route that my predecessors had trod, and instead of that must make it my special object to visit the spot in which the Chinese geographers placed their Lop-nor, and in which, according to Von Richthofen, it ought to be situated.

Full of high spirits and hopes of success, I left the village of Tikkenlik on March 31st, and journeyed exactly due east. My companions were Islam Bai, Kerim Jan, and two men who had an intimate knowledge of the country, and who told me, even before we left Tikkenlik, that a considerable distance to the east there was a long chain of lakes. At the very outset of the expedition we discovered, that the Koncheh-daria emptied itself north of Tikkenlik into a marshy lake called Maltak-köll. But on the other side of the lake it flowed out again, and added its waters to the waters of the two branches of the Tarim before mentioned, and known as Kok-ala. After the confluence the united stream, under the name of the Kunchekkish-Tarim (the Eastern River), flowed partly into the lake Chivillik-köll, and thence back again into the Tarim, and partly direct to the Tarim, which it reached at the ferry of Arghan (Przhevalsky's Ayrilghan), after losing a large proportion of its current by evaporation on the way.

CROSSING A BRANCH OF THE KONCHEH-DARIA COMING FROM MALTAK-KÖLL

The remaining portion of the Koncheh-daria flows east-south-east under the name of the Ilek (the River). We travelled along the left bank of this stream for three days, and then on April 4th, to my great satisfaction, I found that, as the Chinese represented, and as Von Richthofen believed, it does fall into a long, narrow lake, so long that for three days more we were able to travel along its eastern shore. The lake is however now almost completely overgrown with kamish (reeds), although a few years ago the Lop-men, or native inhabitants of the region, used to fish there. These people have different names for different parts of the lake, and usually divide it into four basins, Avullu-köll, Kara-köll, Tayek-köll, and Arka-köll. But in reality there is only one lake, almost divided in two or three places by out-jutting peninsulas.

The lake, like the Lop-nor of the Chinese maps, was situated approximately in 40° 30′ N. lat. The Chinese geographers of the present day still call the region between Tikkenlik and Arghan by the name of Lop-nor, a name which is absolutely unknown in the neighbourhood of the lake discovered by Przhevalsky. That lake embraces two basins, known as Kara-buran and Kara-koshun. The name Lop is given by the Lop-men and all the inhabitants of East Turkestan—in so far as they know anything about it at all—to the entire region which stretches all the way from the confluence of the Ughen-daria and the Tarim to Charkhlik.

In one respect there was a discrepancy. The lake which I discovered stretched from north to south, whereas the Lop-nor of the Chinese maps stretched from east to west. But for this divergence, at first sight so surprising, there is a perfectly natural explanation. In the first place, it must be steadily borne in mind, that the whole of the Lop region lies at almost the same horizontal level, so that even a slight change of relative *niveau* is capable of affecting more or less seriously the entire hydrographical disposition of the locality. Now there are two agencies constantly operating to bring about changes of this nature—namely, the prevailing winds and the sedimentary deposits of the river Tarim itself. The prevailing winds in the Lop region blow from the east and east-north-east, and sand-storms from the same quarters are common in March, April, and May. So long as we remained in the neighbourhood of the quadruple lake the atmosphere was calm, but no sooner did we leave it than a buran came on, and continued, with the exception of a lull of a couple of days, all the time we were travelling in that neighbourhood.

The power and force of these constantly recurring storms is almost inconceivable: they literally drive back the water of the lake and heap it up along the western shore. Then comes the drift-sand of the desert and fills up the gap left in the east. Nor was evidence wanting that this lake-complex formerly extended farther towards the east than it does at present. All along its eastern side there was a chain of small salt lagoons, marshes, and pools, which had been cut off from the lake by the encroachments of the sand in quite recent times. Closely parallel with them there was also a narrow belt of forest, for the most part poplars and tamarisks. Three stages of development were plainly distinguishable—far out in the desert, on the east, was a dead forest (köttek); then amongst the sand-dunes which approached nearest to the east shore of the lake fine living trees; and lastly, on the actual shore of the lake, young and tender saplings, the beginnings of a forest. Now trees cannot live without water. Hence the inference is unmistakeable, that the lake has moved westwards, and that the forest has followed the lake. The dead poplar trees which now stand far to the east, out in the midst of a dreary waste of sand-dunes, must formerly have stood on the shore of the lake, and drawn their nourishment from its waters.

There can hardly be a doubt that this long quadruple lake is all that remains of the old Lop-nor. The Ilek, which enters at its northern extremity, issues again at its southern extremity, that is from Arka-köll (the Farther Lake), and winds southwards with the most capricious meanderings, leaving about three miles to the east the ruins of the old Chinese fortress of Merdek-shahr. Then

A REFRACTORY CAMEL, CROSSING THE KONCHEH-DARIA

the river once more forms a long chain of small lakes, and finally rejoins the Tarim at Shirghch-chappgan. The largest lakes in this string are called Sadak-köll and Niaz-köll, being named after a couple of Lop-men, whose cabins stand on their shores.

Now it is only nine years ago when these lakes were last filled with water by the Ilek. Previous to that they were nothing but desert; although even then the present lake-basins and the river-bed were in existence, the deepest places in the latter making salt-water pools, at which the wild camels came down to drink. When Przhevalsky returned home after his second journey (1885) to Lop-nor, he disputed the existence of any lake to the east of the Tarim. As it happened, he was right, for the dry lake-basins and river-bed were not filled with water until three years later. On the other hand, Von Richthofen was equally right, when he postulated the existence of a lake in this very quarter — a lake which indeed actually existed, though in a condition of temporary desiccation.

The southern Lop-nor—I will retain the name, for it has become established on the best European maps—the southern Lop-nor, at the date of Przhevalsky's visits, was a lake of considerable size, so large that from the village of Abdal he was able to make a boat-journey of several days' duration on its waters eastwards to the fishing-station of Kara-koshun. Eleven and a half years later I attempted the very same boat-journey from Abdal, but could only advance for two short days, and then with great difficulty, because of the reeds. The fishing-station of Kara-koshun was entirely abandoned, the lake in its vicinity having become quite overgrown.

At the date of Przhevalsky's visits, Kara-buran, the other basin of the southern Lop-nor, was a large open lake more like a sea than a lake, for a man standing on the one shore was not able to see across it to the other. The name (the Black Storm) indicates sufficiently, that it lies in a region which is peculiarly exposed to the ravages of the terrific sandstorms. At the time I visited it, there was only an insignificant residuum of the former sea-like lake left close under the western shore; it had become choked with the sedimentary deposits of the Tarim to such an extent that even the shallow dug-outs (canoes) of the native fishermen would not float on its waters. In summer that fragmentary residuum is completely cut off from the Tarim and the Cherchen-daria, and in consequence the water quickly turns salt, and by the end of the summer has all evaporated. The site of the lake then becomes overgrown with luxuriant grass, and affords rich pasturage for the sheep and cattle of the people of Charkhlik. When in the end of April we journeyed from Abdal to Charkhlik, we travelled over a long stretch of alluvial ground, which, when Przhevalsky visited that region, was covered by the water of the lake Kara-buran.

In a word, the Tarim contributes to the southern Lop-nor an incomparably smaller quantity of water now than it did at the time of Przhevalsky's visits. Even Prince Henry of Orleans observed the same thing, although he visited the lake only four years later than the Russian explorer. Thus the lake is at present undergoing a process of shrinkage.

From Chegghelik-uy, where the river deflects to the east-north-east, its volume decreases with amazing rapidity, principally in consequence of the numerous small shallow lakes along its banks. These are in part natural, in part artificial, made by the fishermen of the region. But in either case the water which overflows into them is left to evaporate. Thus they maintain a continual drain upon the river. The subjoined table of measurements will corroborate what I have just said. I may remark that the distance between Chegghelik-uy and Kum-chappgan amounts to barely forty miles.

	Breadth of stream.	Maximum depth.	Velocity in the second.	Volume in the second.
Chegghelik-uy	50 yards	14 feet	1·7 feet	2530 cubic feet.
Abdal	49 „	20 „	1·2 „	2145 „
Kum-chappgan	33 „	22¼ „	·98 „	1775 „

These measurements were made between April 18th and April 23rd.

At Kum-chappgan the river splits up and becomes lost in a multitude of lakes and marshes, the largest of which, namely those in the middle, contain perfectly fresh water; whilst in the lagoons all round the outsides the water is salt. The table above shows, that the breadth, the velocity of the current, and its volume all decrease as the river advances to the east; whilst the depth increases.

We have thus found that the quadruple Lop-nor of the Chinese has become refilled with water during the last nine years, whereas during the last twelve years the southern Lop-nor has dwindled to a series of shallow marshes. Is not the conclusion, therefore, not merely justified, but even forced upon us, that the two lake-systems are mutually related in an extraordinarily close and intimate way; or in other words, as the northern Lop-nor increases, the southern Lop-nor decreases, and *vice-versâ*.

I cannot refrain from pointing to one or two other features which support the theory, that the lakes discovered by Przhevalsky are, geologically speaking, of quite recent origin.

Each of the streams of East Turkestan which unite to form the Tarim is accompanied by belts of poplar forest along its banks. Even the Keriya-daria, which is now cut off from the Tarim system and becomes lost in the sand, is no exception to the rule. In places it possessed a poplar forest so thick as to be quite impenetrable. The forest generally begins at the point where the several rivers debouch upon the plains, and consequently on the border of the same climatic region. Now rivers count amongst the safest and most reliable means of transport in the geographical distribution of vegetable species. Hence it would be only reasonable to suppose, that in the district in which the tributaries of the Tarim converge, the poplar forest would be more abundant than anywhere else. Now, as a matter of fact, at the point of present convergence the forest suddenly ceases altogether. The last specimens of *Populus diversifolia* which I saw at Chegghelik-uy were not more than thirty years old. The banks of both lakes, Kara-buran and Kara-koshun, were totally destitute of every trace of forest, old or new. They were both entirely surrounded by the barren desert. Close to and around the northern Lop-nor, on the contrary, I found both dead and living forest.

The explanation of this unequal distribution of forest is not far to seek: the southern Lop-nor is of such recent formation that the forest has not yet had time to reach its shores.

These arguments are based upon facts of pure physical geography. There are also others of a historical character. I have already mentioned more than once, that the Chinese cartographers entered upon their maps a large lake, surrounded by several smaller ones, in 40° 30′ N. lat.

Six hundred and twenty-five years ago Marco Polo visited the "town of Lop." Its ruins, which have now almost entirely disappeared, probably lie immediately south of the lake Kara-buran. If there had been any lake in that neighbourhood at the time of his visit, the great Venetian traveller could hardly have avoided taking some notice of it. True, he does not mention Yarkand, or Khotan, or the Cherchen-daria, a stream which he actually crossed over. All the same, it is a fact which deserves mention, that Marco Polo does not say a word about the existence of a lake occupying the position of Przhevalsky's Lop-nor; but he does give a detailed description of the Lop desert—"which is so large that the traveller needeth a full year to cross from the one side of it to the other."

The old chieftain of Abdal, Kunchekkan Beg, a friend of Przhevalsky, and also my especial friend, is eighty years old. Both his father, Jehan Beg, and his grandfather, Numet Beg (the dignity of beg being hereditary in the family), lived to be ninety years of age. Kunchekkan Beg told me, that his grandfather lived beside a large lake north of the existing Lop-nor of Przhevalsky, and that, where the latter now is, there was at that time nothing but the sandy desert. The first formation

LOP-MEN ON THE TARIM, NEAR KUM-CHAPPGAN

of the southern Lop-nor dates from the year when Numet Beg was twenty-five years old, in consequence of the Tarim seeking a new channel for itself, and the lake beside which he dwelt, and in which his forefathers had fished, dried up. It was he (Numet Beg) who founded Abdal, and there his descendants still live. According to my calculation all that happened about 175 years ago, or say about the year 1720.

In the winter of 1893–94 the Lop region was visited by P. K. Kozloff, who had previously taken part in the journeys of Przhevalsky and Pievtsoff. He travelled from Tikkenlik along the left bank of the Kunchekkish-Tarim, and discovered the lake Chivillik-köll, which I only saw at a distance. From Arghan he made an excursion to the lake of Sogot, which probably is the same as my Arka-köll. Thence he travelled by the ordinary road to Abdal, and afterwards turned towards the north-east along the southern shore of Kara-koshun.

I first learned of a *tura* ("gentleman," *i.e.* European) having been in the neighbourhood at Tikkenlik, and inquired, as accurately as was possible through the natives, which way he had gone, so that I might not unnecessarily visit the same places as he. One of the most interesting discoveries made by Kozloff was that of an ancient river-bed, which the natives called Kum-daria (the Sand River). It struck off from the Koncheh-daria a short distance north of Tikkenlik, and went due east, skirting the southern foot of the Kurruk-tagh.

Kozloff's explorations and my own have rounded off Przhevalsky's, and materially added to our knowledge of the entire Lop region. We now possess a detailed, accurate map of it. But the dispute regarding the Lop-nor is not by any means settled yet. Kozloff has written an article, *Lop-nor, with Especial Reference to Sven Hedin's Lecture before the Imperial Russian Geographical Society on* 15 (27)*th October* 1897, in which he attempts to controvert Baron von Richthofen's views and mine with regard to the position of the old Chinese Lop-nor. Immediately I returned to Khotan, I sent Von Richthofen an account of the discoveries I had made, and it was printed in the *Zeitschrift der Gesellschaft für Erdkunde zu Berlin*, vol. xxxi., 1896, pp. 295–361. My paper was accompanied by a note from the pen of Baron von Richthofen, in which, after a brief *résumé* of the earlier phase of the Lop-nor controversy, he went on to say, "Several travellers have, it is true, followed the course of the Tarim, but they have all trodden in the footsteps of Przhevalsky. It was for that reason Dr. Sven Hedin undertook to solve the problem. The fact of his choosing a more easterly route from north to south proves that he had a just appreciation of the question at issue. His observations, and the conclusions he has drawn from them, have enabled him to confirm the accuracy of my deductions in the *Verhandlungen* (Proceedings) of the Geographical Society of Berlin in the year 1878 (*vide* pp. 121–144)."

Kozloff analyzes the various accounts of the Lop-nor district — Przhevalsky's, Von Richthofen's, Pievtsoff's, Bogdanovitch's, his own, and mine, and arrives at the following result:—"The only conclusion I can draw from the above-quoted discussion is this—that Kara-koshun kul is not only the Lop-nor of my revered teacher N. M. Przhevalsky, but also the real historical ancient Lop-nor of the Chinese geographers. As it is now, so it has been during the last thousand years, and so it will continue to be." This result is all the more surprising, because on the very same page, only a few lines earlier, he writes thus, "I am entirely of Sven Hedin's opinion, that the ancestors of the present inhabitants of Lop-nor formerly dwelt beside a lake which lay to the north of Lop-nor. It was the lake Utchu-kul, regarding which Pievtsoff has left us an account." These statements imply a direct contradiction: they prove that the lake has not remained in its existing condition "during the last thousand years." But the uncritical character of this talk about the thousand unchangeable years is best demonstrated by Kozloff's own map. He there shows the "ancient bed (Kum-daria) of the Koncheh-daria" south of Kurruk-tagh, the "dry river-bed (Köttek-Tarim)"

6½ miles west of the meridional course of the Tarim, the "ancient river-bed of the Cherchen-daria" twelve miles north of the point where the Cherchen-daria empties itself into the Kara-buran, and the "dry river-bed of Shirgheh-chappgan" eight miles north of Abdal. I also discovered other ancient river-beds at Kum-chekkeh and Merdek-shahr. But the four I have cited from Kozloff are sufficient to show that, far from being permanent in its position, the lake of Lop-nor, together with the rivers which flow into it, is, on the contrary, subject to greater changes than perhaps any other lake of the same size on the face of the earth.

The problem is extremely interesting and fascinating from the scientific point of view; but the length and purpose of this present book warn me that I must refrain from entering upon it here. I intend to discuss the question thoroughly in a subsequent work. In the meantime my able and enthusiastic fellow-traveller, Lieutenant Kozloff, has thrown down the gauge of battle. It will give me great pleasure to take it up. That will be the second phase of the Lop-nor controversy. We possess all the materials for a solution. It only remains to prove which of the two groups of lakes, the northern or the southern, that which I discovered, or that which Przhevalsky discovered, is the older; whichever is the older must undoubtedly be identified with the Lop-nor of the Chinese maps. Which of the two parties is right is a matter of little real moment in itself. I trust that national prepossessions will have no weight in determining a question of fact. The essential thing to do is to unravel the truth; and in so far as it contributes to that end a controversy is always advantageous.

Thus we have learnt, on the banks of the "moving" lake, that the gigantic river-system which drains the vast central basin of the interior of Asia—embracing the Kizil-su, which flows down from the eternal snows of the Terek-davan; the Raskan-daria, which is fed by the glaciers of the eastern Pamirs, the Hindu-kush, and north-western Tibet, and whose current, running with a volume of 5330 cubic feet in the second, we only crossed at the risk of our lives in September 1895; the Khotan-daria, which traverses the Takla-makan Desert from end to end, cleaving its way with irresistible impetus through the sand-dunes; the Ak-su and the Taushkan-daria, which at the same period of the previous year we were only able to cross on horseback with the assistance of ten *suchis* or water men; the Cherchen-daria, which carries a portion of the rainfall of Northern Tibet down to the plains, and in summer grows so powerful that for a time it stops the road between Khotan and Lop-nor; and finally the Koncheh-daria, which, summer and winter, day and night, alike, has a steady flow of 2490 cubic feet in the second—we have, I say, learned that all these great streams are not strong enough to maintain a permanent lake in the heart of the limitless Desert of Gobi.

At Chegghelik-uy, in April, we found that the conjoint stream possessed precisely the same quantity of water that its tributary, the Koncheh-daria, had alone at Korla. Where does the rest go to? Well, a large portion of the water of the Koncheh-daria enters the northern group of lakes, and there evaporates; the desert sand, like a sponge, drinks up another portion; and the thirsty atmosphere, whose relative moisture in those regions is merely trifling, also absorbs enormous quantities. All these agencies drain away the volume of the stream. No wonder then that the small amount which survives the desperate struggle to cling to the surface of the earth is subject to such severe fluctuations both in respect of situation and of quantity.

The fishing-station of Kum-chappgan marks, as it were, the entrance to the tomb of the Tarim. There the terrible Desert of Gobi, whose murderous propensities the human will and the giant strength of water alike are powerless to subdue, proclaims, in the name of Him who governs every change that ensues on the face of the earth, "Hitherto shalt thou come, but no further; and here shall thy proud waves be stayed."

CHAPTER LXXI.

A BOAT EXCURSION ON THE NORTHERN LOP-NOR

IN the previous chapter I have offered a brief outline of the Lop-nor problem and controversy, and of the new points of view which my discoveries led me to take up. It now remains that I say a few words about our further journeyings in that region.

On April 4th we discovered that part of the northern Lop-nor which the Lop-men call Avullu-köll, and then for three days travelled along its eastern shore. The whole way we had extraordinary difficulties to encounter, chiefly owing to the fact that the sand-dunes, thirty to fifty feet in height, plunged straight down into the lake at an angle of thirty-three degrees. At intervals the sand drew back a space; and there a poplar forest grew. Wherever the dunes dropped to a lower elevation, the poplars were replaced by tamarisks, each rising from the top of a huge mound formed by the roots of the tree itself. So closely did these tamarisk mounds stand together in some places that we had to thread our way through a veritable labyrinth of them, so that it was often preferable to make a detour into the sandy desert to avoid them.

The lakes of the northern Lop-nor were so overgrown with reeds (as we afterwards found that Kara-koshun was also), that we were unable to see the open water in the middle, except from the top of the highest dunes near their shores. Two or three times, in places where the water was shallow, or there was none at all, we tried to force our way through the reeds, although they were twice as tall as the camels, and grew as close as those which the native inhabitants of the region bound together to make the walls of their cabins. One of the guides went on first to examine the nature of the ground; then followed the camels, trampling the reeds down with their feet, and breaking and thrusting them aside with their heavy, ungainly bodies. As I followed the guides, I seemed to be travelling through a dark tunnel, and was very glad to get out again, and have an uninterrupted view of the road before me.

The camels were so exhausted by the unfavourable country that we were obliged to give them a day's rest.

April 6th. As usual we encamped in the open air, on a high sand-dune, under the shade of a group of ancient poplars, which had just put on their brightest mantles of spring greenery. From our camp we commanded a wide view across the Kara-köll, and far away in the west saw the thick belts of reeds which encircle Chivillik-köll. The heat was already oppressive—at one p.m. 91°6 Fahr. (33°1 C.) in the shade—and the atmosphere was absolutely still, a rare thing at that time of the year.

During these still, calm days we were greatly tormented by gnats. All the way we rode we were accompanied by a pillar of a cloud of those pestilent insects. Their sole object in life seemed to be to torment human beings, and try their patience to the uttermost. But after the sun set, and we encamped for the night, they were worse than ever. Millions upon millions of them hummed around us, as eager and voracious as though we were come there solely to give them a treat for supper! How is it possible to write when a thousand gnats are fighting for the joy of stinging your hand, and that in defiance of the piece of cloth you flap in your other hand? Or where is the pleasure, with the thermometer standing where I have just stated, in surrounding your camp with a ring-wall of fire, and almost suffocating yourself with smoke?

When we came to the basin of Kara-köll, we hit upon a crafty device for retaliating upon the gnats. At sunset

THE REEDS OF KARA-KÖLL ON FIRE

we set fire to the dry reeds of the previous year. The flames spread across the lake with the rapidity of a prairie fire, and the smoke hovered like a light veil over the neighbourhood of our camp. I lay awake half the night, enjoying the glorious vigour of the flames, and rejoicing in the vengeful thought, that countless hosts of gnats were being wafted like chaff to the ends of the world on the drifting soot. At other times I had been obliged to protect my poor skin at night by a weapon of defence that was not at all nice; namely smearing my hands and face with nicotine. And I had to smoke really very hard, so as not to run short of the essential juice! I brought with me from Khotan sufficient tobacco to last, as I calculated, fifty days; but that had all vanished long ago in smoke. I bought a supply of Chinese tobacco in Shah-yar, but that was only for use in case of urgent necessity. I further supplemented my store at Korla, by investing a threepenny piece in a barrel of the bitter, sour native tobacco, compared with which the aroma of the strongest "twist" is as pure Havana.

Speaking of setting fire to the reeds, my guide told me, that on one occasion when somebody set fire to the reeds of Kara-köll in stormy weather, the fire burnt on for three summers and three winters. That is of course an uncommonly fine mare's-nest, and the Asiatics do know how to manufacture the article, and even go the length of believing implicitly in the products of their own facile skill; still, even when allowance is made for that, it is perfectly clear that, once a fire has seized upon the dry reeds, it goes on burning for an extraordinary length of time. The old chief of Abdal, Kunchekkan Beg, was pleased to believe that, if the reeds of the southern Lop-nor were to be set on fire, they would burn for at least a week. In consequence of the strong draught sweeping through the dry reed-stalks close to the surface of the water, the flames rage and roar as though they were fanned by a gigantic pair of bellows. The reeds crackle and burst, and burn down to the water's edge, whilst showers of sparks and long spiral clouds of smoke float away through the air.

When on 9th April we encamped at Kum-chekkeh we had not seen a human being for seven days. There we found, dwelling on the bank of the river Ilek, three fishermen's families, who only a short time before had flitted thither from the vicinity of the northern Lop-nor. At that point the river, after filtering through the reed-beds in the lakes, was bright as silver, and of a lovely dark blue. Thence it flowed south in a deeply eroded channel; and at the distance of two long day's-marches rejoined the river Tarim, forming another chain of small lakes on the way.

From Kum-chekkeh I sent my caravan on in charge of Islam Bai to the confluence of the two streams, whilst I myself, with two men to row me, made an excursion by canoe to the extreme end of the southern Lop-nor, that is, of Kara-koshun. The excursion took eight days, rest-days not included. It was a splendid trip. No craft ever bore a more grateful passenger. After the heavy, hot, toilsome marching through the everlasting sand, the quietude, the rest, the ease were perfectly delicious—indescribable!

The dwellers around the old as well as the new Lop-nor call themselves Loplik, *i.e.* Lop-men, and their canoes or dug-outs *kemi*, a word which signifies "boat," "ferry," or any sort of swimming apparatus. The canoes vary of course very much in size. The largest I saw was over 26 feet long, and 2½ feet broad. The one I travelled in was about 20 feet long, but barely more than 1½ feet across. Three men, working hard, can hew a canoe out of a poplar in five days, the tree being, of course, sound at heart and free from cracks. The people never use sails, but always row, using an oar with a thin, broad blade. They call their oar, which they ply with great strength and dexterity, *gedyäck*, the same word that is employed to designate a musical instrument which resembles a guitar in shape. Out on the open lake the rowers generally knelt; but in the thick reeds they stood up, so as to see better, and faced the way they were going, and so punted the canoe along. As a rule there are two oarsmen to each

THE AUTHOR IN A CANOE ON THE KARA-KOSHUN

canoe, and the last of the two usually stands, so as to see over the head of the man in front of him.

I took advantage of a rest-day to make several trial-trips on the lake, so as to ascertain my oarsmen's average rate of speed, in other words, to obtain a unit of time and distance by which to measure the length of the journey before me. We started on April 11th, one rower in the bow, the other in the stern, and I in the middle, sitting as comfortably as in an easy-chair on a pile of felts and cushions, with my itinerary note-book, compass, and pen in hand, the other instruments, knotted sounding-line, tape-measure, and provisions for two or three days being stowed away in every nook and corner that was free. I had a pleasant companion in my Chinese dog Yolldash the Third. When we left Korla he was a little yellow puppy, and as he was not strong enough to run beside the caravan in its long journey through the sand, I had him packed into a basket, and let him ride on one of the camels.

The first day's riding made him "sea-sick"; but he soon became accustomed to the motion. When he grew tired of running, he would simply lie down beside a tuft of grass, and wait till one of the men went back and fetched him, and put him in his basket. Throughout the rest of my journeying in Asia, this little dog never quitted my side; he was my intimate companion in every day's march and every adventure. He accompanied me in the canoe, and quickly showed his satisfaction at such a comfortable mode of progression. He was with me throughout the long journey back to Khotan, in my travels through Tibet, through Tsaidam, through China, Mongolia, and Siberia. Yolldash accomplished the greater portion of all that long journey on his own feet, and when we at last reached St. Petersburg was in first-rate condition. Unfortunately dogs are not allowed to be taken into Sweden from Russia; consequently, on the very threshold of home, I was forced to part from my faithful fellow-traveller. I left him in the best of hands however, with Mr. Backlund, councillor of state, in Pulkova. There his Asiatic manners, being somewhat uncultivated, were quickly dressed out of him, and he is now waiting with impatience to start on a fresh journey to the great deserts of Central Asia.

All being in readiness, the oars dipped in the water, and the canoe glided with the supple ease of an eel over the dark blue meandering river.

But by this the atmosphere had lost its stillness and calm. During the previous night a hard "black buran" had sprung up from the east, and the sky was now black with it. The majestic old poplars humbly bent before the fury of its wrath. So long as we were on the river, there was no danger, for it flowed at the bottom of a deep narrow channel, protected by belts of reeds; and then again, the teeth of the storm were broken by the forest which grew along the river-bank. But this only lasted for a couple of hours or so. After that we were on the open lake the whole way. The two oarsmen were afraid of this part of the journey, and it required all my powers of persuasion to induce them to believe there was no danger; for we could all three of us swim, and Yolldash as well. To me the buran was rather welcome than otherwise; for that day at one p.m. the thermometer only registered 69°2 Fahr. (20°7 C.). The storm sang its shrill monotonous song in the leafy crowns of the poplars, a song that never wearied, a song that continually gave the key to new fantasies of day-dreaming.

And so we hastened along the dark pathway of the water, I idly watching the capricious play and interplay of the dimpling eddies as the swift canoe glided on past them. The narrow belts of reeds hedged in the river on either hand, and made me imagine we were gliding down a deserted Venetian canal.

Every now and again we stopped, that I might measure the depth of the river. Once the oarsmen stopped of their own accord, and said, that "just there" there used to be a permanent salt pool in the river-bed at the time both river and lakes were dry. I sounded, and found the depth was thirty-one feet, truly an extraordinary depth for a river with a volume of only 810 cubic feet in the

A LITTLE LOP-BOY FROM SADAK-KÖLL

second. One of my boatmen, the hunter Kurban, who had been ranging that country for fifty years, and knew it both when it was nothing but desert, and subsequently after the water returned nine years ago—Kurban told me, that Przhevalsky sent him and two or three other willing fellows from Abdal to procure him the skin of a wild camel. They shot a camel, and were handsomely rewarded for the skin with money, knives, and other things. But since the water came back, and people followed it to live there, the wild animals had entirely disappeared, having no doubt taken refuge in the desert farther to the east.

We came out upon the first of the lakes. The storm-lashed waves were boiling westwards, their crests tipped with plumes of foam. There was risk in venturing out upon them with the unsteady canoe; besides, the lakes were extremely shallow, and if the canoe were to strike against the sandy bottom, it would be certain to capsize, both wind and waves being on the larboard. We therefore hugged the eastern shore as closely as we possibly could, availing ourselves of the shelter of the high sand-dunes.

At length we happily reached a village without a name at the nearer extremity of Sadak-köll, a place where several families dwelt in reed huts. These people received me with the most natural hospitality, cooked the fish they had just drawn out of the lake, and gave me in addition wild-ducks' eggs, and the young, tender shoots of kamish (reeds), and bread; and as I consumed my simple, but very tasty, supper, I was the admired centre of a ring of laughing, chattering Lopliks (Lop-men) of both sexes and every age—indeed the young women were not in the least ashamed to let me see their fresh-coloured, though far from beautiful, features.

I afterwards discovered the cause of this unusual absence of shame and timidity. The good people had never before seen a European, although they had heard speak of the Chong-tura (Great Man), *i.e.*, Przhevalsky, who had visited their fellow-tribesmen farther to the south, with twenty Cossacks armed to the teeth, and long strings of camels, and a multitude of strange things. I therefore was a puzzle to them; for I was come quite alone, without followers, without a caravan, in a canoe, accompanied by two of their own people, speaking their own language, eating the food they ate, and almost as poor as themselves. Their preconceived idea of a European was thus sadly upset. The difference between a European and a Lop-man was really not so very great after all. On April 12th the storm was so bad that we could not go out. But the next day it abated a little, and we again embarked in the canoe. When their craft are not in use, the Lop-men draw them up on land, and pour water over them at intervals to prevent them from cracking. Even then a canoe seldom lasts more than ten years.

We started before sunrise, and had a glorious journey, partly over the open lake, partly through the reed-beds. The greatest depths in the latter portions of the lake were 11½ and 15½ feet. But at noon the storm freshened up to its previous unbridled fury, so that the rest of our day's journey was not without peril. The lakes were connected together by narrow straits or sounds; and the entrances to these we could only make by crossing wide open bays. How the men found their way was a perfect marvel to me. The shores of the lakes were extremely irregular, by reason of the great number of creeks, peninsulas, and islands which diversified them; and the entrances to the sounds were not perceptible until we were actually in them. To add to the difficulty of finding the way, the loose sand was blown in clouds off the tops of the sand-dunes on the east side of the lakes, shrouding the shores in a dense haze, and covering the lakes with a yellow veil of dust. The water was in a state of violent commotion. The waves seethed round the canoe, and the spray flew in gusty splashes from the summit of every wave, soaking us to the skin. We had to keep a very sharp look-out. We even went so far as to take off some superfluous clothing, that we might swim the more easily, if it should be needful to do so. In fact, we actually had to balance the canoes with our bodies and arms, and exercise the utmost vigilance lest we ran aground upon a treacherous sandbank.

Luckily we had no mishap. We threaded one sound after the other. Only once did we lay to under the shelter of a small sandy holm for about an hour, and that was in the middle of the large lake of Niaz-köll. After that the lakes were smaller in size, and finally we entered the river Ilek, and rowed along its smooth surface until we came to the village of Shirgheh-chappgan (Shirgheh's Canal), Shirgheh being the name of a Lop-man. Some half-a-dozen families lived in the village; and there I found my caravan, and Islam Bai and the other men grown rather uneasy at my prolonged absence.

CHAPTER LXXII.

ALONG PRZHEVALSKY'S LOP-NOR BY BOAT

AFTER I had rested a couple of days, the caravan continued its march by land towards Chegghelik-uy on the Tarim, whilst I proceeded thither by boat. The Chong-tarim (Great Tarim) curved backwards and forwards in the most capricious fashion, frequently describing an almost complete circle, so that we really steered all round the compass. Being now in the open, and unsheltered against the fury of the hurricane, my boatmen took the precaution to fasten two canoes side by side, holding them together by means of two poles lashed to the bulwarks and leaving about a foot's space between the two craft. This double canoe (*kosh-kemi*) was manned by four boatmen; and yet so furious was the storm, that their strength was put to the severest proof, although in the reaches in which the noses of the canoes were turned towards the west, they were caught by the wind and driven along at a perfectly giddy pace.

The forests gradually thinned away, until they ceased altogether, and the barren desert lined both banks of the river, the eastern as well as the western.

Chegghelik-uy is a typical Asiatic fishing-station—a row of yellow reed cabins along the river-bank, a score of canoes drawn up on land immediately in front of them, nets hung out to dry on long poles, and an all-pervading odour of rancid fish. Eight families are permanently settled in the place all the year round; but in winter they are joined by fifteen other families, who go down to Charkhlik in the spring, sow their crops, wait till they are ripe, and harvest them, and then return to Cheg-

A LOP-MAN IN HIS CANOE

ghelik-uy. Thus they are semi-nomadic in their mode of life.

The caravan went on further to Abdal by land, whilst I still continued the journey by water, across the scanty surviving portions of what twelve years ago was the broad lake of Kara-buran.

The storm had at length paused to take breath; but instead of it we had rain all day long (April 18th). During the heaviest downpour we took shelter for a couple of hours in the little village of Tokkuz-attam (the Nine Fathers), a place entirely surrounded by water. The lakes were throughout very shallow, owing to the thick deposits of fluvial sediment and sand; indeed there were long stretches where the water was scarce four inches deep, so that the boatmen had to get out and wade, and drag the canoe after them as though it were a hand-sledge.

We spent the night in the village of Chai, and next day rowed all the way to Abdal, a distance of thirty-seven miles (though only twenty-five miles as the crow flies). It was splendid travelling, for the weather was fine. The further the Tarim flowed to the east, the deeper and narrower it grew, whilst its banks became more and more desolate, till at last not a vestige of vegetation was to be seen.

When we drew near to Abdal it was evening, and the entire population of the place were out on the river-bank to welcome us. Seeing amongst them a little old patriarch of a man, I cried, pointing to him, although I had never seen him in my life before, "That's Kunchekkan Beg!" Whereat they were not a little astonished. But after the portrait of the old man given by Przhevalsky in his account of his fourth journey, it was not difficult to recognize him. On his part the aged chief welcomed me as though I were an old acquaintance, and led me to a clean "parlour" in his reed cabin.

Kunchekkan Beg was a fine old fellow. He talked away all the time without once waiting to be prompted, and gave me a store of valuable information. Przhevalsky had made him a present of his own photograph, as well as photographs of several scenes taken in the neighbourhood of the lakes, fish-nets, a cooking-pan, and various other useful articles. The old man preserved all his treasures in a sand-dune a little to the north of Abdal, so as to safeguard them from accidents by fire and the attacks of Dungan robbers. I tried to explain to him what our boats were like in Sweden, and how we manage our oars. The old man clapped his hands together, and

KUNCHEKKAN BEG, OF ABDAL

cried in a tone of great cocksureness, "Oh, I knew all about that long ago. The Chong-tura (*i.e.*, Przhevalsky) told me all that. I know exactly what things look like where you come from. I am almost as good a 'Russian' as you are."

On April 21st we went a trip along the river to the large village of Kum-chappgan, and the old chief, Kunchekkan Beg (the Chief of the Rising Sun), plied one of the oars with as much power and accuracy as he no doubt did sixty years before.

THE DAUGHTER-IN-LAW OF KUNCHEKKAN BEG

II.-16

I was told in Abdal that the river was in no sense navigable beyond Kum-chappgan, for at that place it split into a number of small arms and became lost in a multitude of lakes and marshes. Przhevalsky had rowed all the way to Kara-koshun along a chain of lakes. But these were now all overgrown with reeds, and the people who at the time of his visit dwelt on the shores of Kara-koshun had left it ten years ago. But at Kum-chappgan I found two men, who undertook to row me for two days towards the east-north-east, that is, as far as it was possible to get with a canoe. I was particularly anxious to have my map of these lakes as complete as possible, so I determined to make the journey; but had first to go back to Abdal, for we had brought no provisions with us.

I travelled back, not by the Tarim, but by the lakes of Abdal, which run parallel and close to its right bank, for they belong in reality to the class of side or riparian lagoons, which drain off the water of the river. Owing to the vast amount of sediment which the stream deposits in the course of the year, the river-bed has become raised above the level of the land immediately adjoining it on either side, and thus flows as it were in a raised channel. The water frequently takes advantage of weak spots in its enclosing banks, and bursts through, and floods the low-lying tracts in the vicinity. Besides, the Lop-men purposely make breaches in the river-banks, so as to let the water out to form artificial lakes. Then in the spring, when the river falls to its lowest level, they stop up the gaps, and after the water in the artificial lakes has sufficiently evaporated, they catch the fish which have swum out through the breaches. During the winter the people live upon dried fish and bread. But the inhabitants of Kum-chekkeh were genuine ichthyophagi or fish-eaters, for they lived entirely upon fish all the year round: the only additions to their diet being the eggs of wild-duck, the young shoots of reeds, and salt. According to Pievtsoff, the southern Lop-nor contains two species of mountain barbels (*Schizostorax Biddulphi* and *Sch.*

argentatus), one of loach (*Nemachilus yarkandensis*), one of carp (*Diptychus gymnogaster*), and the pike-like *Aspiorrhynchus Przhevalskii.*

We started for the trip on April 22nd in three canoes. In one were myself and three boatmen; in another Islam Bai, with the provisions, and two boatmen; and in the third, a tiny cockleshell of a thing, the old and experienced Tuzun, who was to go on first and pioneer the way through the reeds.

The weather was splendid. We did not stop at Kum-chappgan,

BOYS FROM KUM-CHAPPGAN, LOP-NOR

but pushed on down the largest arm of the river, the one on the left, and were soon lost among the tall reeds. Were it not for the narrow channels which the Lop-men keep open through them, these forests of reeds would be absolutely impassable; and even the channels (*chappgans*) they do keep open would grow over in one year if the young sprouting reeds were not pulled up by the roots every spring. As a rule a chappgan is about a yard wide, and is lined on both sides by reeds as hard and impassable as boarden walls, and not less than fifteen or sixteen feet high. In several places they were tied together in standing sheaves, or bent back over, so as not to fall forward and choke up the lode or channel.

The primary object of these chappgans, which intersect one another in a labyrinthine maze in every direction, and in which a stranger alone would infallibly be lost, is not however solely to serve as waterways. They are used principally for catching fish. We rowed over hundreds and hundreds of nets, and in the clear transparent water I could see countless shoals of fish swimming along underneath us. We caught a few as we went along and cooked them. Each family has its own chappgans, in which they alone are entitled to set their nets.

How the men found their way through such a confusing labyrinth I was puzzled to understand. Every now and again the channel we were in would open out into a small round basin fenced in on all sides by reeds; and from it would radiate half-a-dozen other basins, all exactly alike. As soon as the canoe put her nose into one of these lagoons, the boatmen dipped in their oars and made her skim across the open pool like a wild-duck, so that the water hissed off her bow, and I could not help fancying that in a minute or so we should dash our heads against a wooden wall. But no: with a swish and a crackle, the reeds bent apart to right and to left like curtains, and we glided into the next narrow tunnel-like chappgan.

Thus we raced merrily on the whole day long. At intervals I got a clear glimpse or two of the slowly dwindling Tarim. Some of the lakes we rowed across were sheets of considerable size; in one of them, Yok-kanak-köll, I sounded the greatest depth of any measurement I took in the southern Lop-nor, namely, fourteen feet. Thus the lakes are very shallow; in fact they were more like marshes than lakes.

In the afternoon we shot out into the largest of the lakes, Kanat-baglagan-köll (the Lake of the Tied Wing), probably so called from the fact that some time or other a wild-duck's wing was tied to the reeds to serve as a sign-post. We had the greatest difficulty in the world to wriggle across to the northern side; but as the shore consisted of moist mud impregnated with sand, I preferred to sleep in the canoe.

The next day we rowed on further across the large lake. Once when we stopped to take a sounding, Yolldash, thinking it was too warm in the canoe, made a dash over the side; but after a good long swim, he came to the conclusion that it was too far to land, and so climbed back on board. The tiny pioneer canoe led the way; then followed the provision boat; and last of all the one in which I sat. I ate my simple breakfast of wild-ducks' eggs and bread on the lake. Islam Bai handed the dishes to me by putting them in a wooden bowl, and setting it afloat on the water (which was perfectly smooth), and I caught it up as we darted past.

A belt of gigantic reeds, each fully 25 feet in height, and measuring 2¼ inches in circumference at the surface of the water, stretched diagonally across the lake. As the Lop-men seldom ventured so far as the point we had then reached, the chappgans were grown up again. The tiny pioneer canoe managed to get through pretty easily; but the two bigger, heavier boats had to work their way through inch by inch. The boatmen laid aside their oars and forced the boat on with their arms, using the reeds as a fulcrum. We were completely shut in on all sides. Not a drop of water was visible; it was entirely hidden by the reeds and the boat. Into that dark, close, warm tunnel not a gleam of sunshine penetrated. I drew a sigh of intense relief when we at length emerged from the watery defile and debouched upon the last open lake, with its surface crumpled by the breeze.

At noon we reached the very extremity of the open lakes; beyond that it was absolutely impossible to get through the reeds, either by canoe in the summer or on the ice in the winter. They stood as tightly packed together as the palings in a wooden palisade. In some places they were indeed so densely matted together, and so strong, that we actually walked along the top of the tangled mat they made, without for a single instant being reminded, that there was ten feet of water immediately under our feet.

BOATING AMONG THE REEDS OF THE SOUTHERN LOP-NOR

Before turning back, we forced our way once more to the northern shore of the lake. There, from the top of a characteristic tamarisk root-mound, I obtained a wide view in every direction. To the east there was not so much as a square yard of open water; nothing but a veritable forest of reeds of the rankest growth. In the opposite direction, towards the west, the narrow waterway by which we had come looked like a coil of blue ribbon winding through the yellow reeds. And an equally vivid contrast was afforded by the small green patches of young spring shoots scattered thinly amongst the serried reed-beds.

We returned to Abdal by the same way we had travelled out. The route having been already plotted, I had nothing to do except to lean back on my felts and cushions, and listen to the gulping of the water against the sides of the canoe, as well as watch the fascinating interplay of colour in the transparent water. Over the deeper parts of the lake it was ultramarine blue; but over the shallower parts it gleamed, in consequence of the reflection from the yellow reeds, like jelly made of Rhenish wine.

When we came out upon the Tarim (*the* River) immediately east of Kum-chappgan, the current was stronger against us, and we went slower than on the outward journey. On the way out, the canoes had been swept along this part of the river at a tremendous pace, and all the men had to do was to dip their oars in lightly every now and again to guide their slight, elastic craft. Now however, on the way back, they were forced to ply their oars with a resolute will.

I was anxious to gain time, and so kept the men hard at it as long as daylight lasted, and even a good way on into the night; nor did they murmur, for I promised to reward them well. The moon came out and illumined the narrow waterway as with the penetrating rays of a lighthouse. The night was still and mild. Nothing disturbed the brooding silence save the rhythmical swing of the oars and the occasional splash of a fish leaping to the surface of the river. It was a fascinating night, one I shall not readily forget.

CHAPTER LXXIII.

THE RETURN TO KHOTAN

THE first four months of the year we were continuously travelling towards the east, and putting an ever greater distance between ourselves and our new base of operations in Khotan. By the time we reached the goal of our journey, the farthest of the lakes of Lop-nor, we were fully six hundred miles from the place where I had left nearly all my baggage, and such of my money as I did not absolutely need. But the long journey had not been fruitless. I had achieved the objects I set out to accomplish; I had examined the ancient cities of the desert, had traced the course of the Keriya-daria as far as it goes, had crossed the Desert of Gobi, unravelled the complicated river-system of the Tarim, studied the problem of Bagrash-köll, and explored the neighbourhood of Lop-nor.

Our hard, forced march across the desert had tried us all severely. The summer with its oppressive heat was coming on, not at all a pleasant outlook for us, seeing that we had only our winter equipment of clothing with us; and we were all longing to get back to Khotan to rest. If only we could have flown there, we should certainly have done it; because, since the journeys of Przhevalsky, Pievtsoff, Dutreuil de Rhins, and the Littledales, both routes along the northern foot of the Kwen-lun Mountains are sufficiently well known; besides which, they have little of interest to offer. But not possessing the wings of the wild-duck, we had no other alternative but to ride. Hence, after a hearty farewell of the "classic" old chieftain, Kunchekkan Beg, we left Abdal, with our three camels and two horses, on 25th April.

I was right glad to have my face turned towards the west; for after I reached Khotan, there would only remain one part, the last, of my great scheme unaccomplished, namely, the exploration of Northern Tibet. Moreover I was eager to get to Khotan for another reason. In Kara-shahr I heard from Consul-General Petrovsky, that he had sent on to Khotan a big packet of letters for me from Sweden. What had been happening at home during all my long absence? That packet of letters drew me westwards with the force of a powerful magnet. When therefore the pertinacious storm from the east again began to blow just as we left Abdal, driving clouds of dust and sand before it, it seemed to me as if Heaven itself were minded to help us.

As I have before mentioned, these desert-storms are both grandiose and awe-inspiring. Along that portion of its course in which the Tarim, in ordinary circumstances, flows towards the east, the surface current, under the impact of the wind then blowing, flowed in the exactly opposite direction. For instance, whilst at Abdal the level sank sixteen to twenty inches, in the Kara-buran, to the west, it rose eight to twelve inches. Thus the lake expanded to an appreciable extent. When you are riding before such a storm, you have some difficulty in keeping your seat. Every moment you feel as if you would be lifted bodily out of the saddle. The horses stagger as though they were drunk, and the camels straddle wide so as not to lose their equilibrium.

Although the lake of Kara-buran had thus widened its borders, we nevertheless rode across it, that is to say, those portions of it which have dried up since the date of Przhevalsky's visit. After that we came to the lower course of the brook of Charkhlik, which would empty itself into the lake but that shortly before reaching it it disappears in low-lying ground. This brook also felt the effects of the storm; it too turned back in its course for a space, flooding the lower grounds on both sides to a great distance and blotting out the track. For the most part we rode at haphazard, through six or eight inches of water; and for as far as we could see, there was nothing but a boundless expanse of water, literally rent to tatters by the wind. The spray was dashed about our ears, the water was bodily driven up into the air, shivered into myriads of drops, and flung down again with a furious hissing and splashing. We could not however see very far; the atmosphere was so thickly laden with dust, that it was actually darkened. During the three days and three nights that this "black buran" raged without a moment's cessation, the temperature never rose above 59° Fahr. (15° C.) and 64°4 Fahr. (18° C.), and accordingly we felt it decidedly cool.

By the time we reached Charkhlik, a little "town" of about one hundred families, the storm had subsided and the weather was calm. But, on the other hand, our camp was in commotion. For the first thing, we were going to part with our three camels, which ever since we left Khotan had rendered us invaluable service. For months they had tramped with the endurance of Stoics through the terrible desert sand, had stalked with majestic gravity through the primeval forests of the Tarim, had forded rivers and morasses without showing any sign of fear, never complaining, seldom occasioning difficulties, but often quickening our courage by their imperturbable. calmness. But we had used their strength to the uttermost. They too urgently needed rest. To have taken them with us all the way to Khotan would have been cruel; for in Central Asia, camels do no work in the summer, but enjoy the privilege of grazing on the mountain pastures.

It was hardest to part with my riding-camel, a splendid male ten years old. The camel, as I remarked when speaking of the wild species, does not love men, and never becomes as tame as the horse; but with this particular animal I had always been on the very best of terms. Whenever the man approached him, whose duty it was to lead him by the rope through his nostrils, he screamed angrily, and snorted; but after he found out that I never touched the rope, he gave me a very different reception He allowed me to pat his nose, and stroke his face, without manifesting the least resentment. Every morning I used to give him two large cakes of maize-bread, and at last he grew so accustomed to be fed in that way, that at the stroke of the hour he used to come forward to my tent and remind me of it. Sometimes he even woke me up by giving me a regular poke with his nose.

Now however we were to part from our three veterans, who had for so long a time faced wind and weather together with us. I sold them to a merchant from West Turkestan for about one-half of what I gave for them. In

VILLAGE NEAR KHOTAN

A Bazaar-day

their place I bought four horses. When the purchaser led the camels away, I felt quite lonely. The courtyard looked empty and deserted. Luckily I still had Yolldash, who faithfully kept his place at my side in the hovel in which I was lodged. One day, when I sat writing on a felt carpet, the dog suddenly jumped up, and began growling and barking, with his nose close to the ground. At first I paid no heed; but he came quite close to me, and plainly showed that he was very uneasy. I then looked about for the cause, and discovered quite close to my foot a yellowish-green, ugly-looking scorpion, two inches long, striking out at the dog with his poisonous tail. But the dog's instinct warned him against seizing the creature in his mouth. I instantly killed the scorpion; and rewarded Yolldash with a large piece of meat, and patted him and caressed him, and gave him to understand that he was a "good fellow."

Charkhlik was ruled by a Chinese amban, Li Darin. When the Dungan revolt, which broke out in December 1894, spread to Si-ning-fu, and there assumed disquieting proportions, the Chinese stationed in the town a garrison of 265 men, armed with discarded English rifles of the period of the Crimean War. Agreeably to the prescribed custom and etiquette, immediately after my arrival I sent a messenger to Li Darin, bearing my Chinese visiting-card and the local passport which Hwen Darin gave me in Kara-shahr, and at the same time inquired, when I might have the honour of waiting upon him personally. In reply, Li Darin sent his interpreter to say, that before he could receive me, he must first see a larger passport, valid for the district over which he ruled. I bade the interpreter, a Mohammedan beg, and a very decent fellow, explain that I had left my "great passports" from Peking and Kashgar behind me in Khotan, because, when I set out on my journey, I had not intended to travel so far, and that it would be best for me to call upon the amban and fully explain matters to him myself.

The answer which came back was, that a man who travelled without a passport must be treated as a suspicious individual, that the amban would not receive me, that the southern route to Khotan was closed against me, but that, seeing I had the "little passport," I might, as a favour, return to Kara-shahr, and then go back to Khotan the same way I had come.

Truly a bright look-out! Three and a half months through the desert by a road I had already explored, and that in the height of summer; whereas by the southern route, *viâ* Cherchen, I could reach Khotan in a single month! I instructed the interpreter to tell his master, that I despised him, and that notwithstanding, and in defiance of him, I intended the very next day to set out for Cherchen.

I got back the laconic answer, "Go; but if you do, I shall arrest you, and send you back to Kara-shahr under an escort of ten soldiers." It was no use talking any more; I must act. I quickly made up my mind what I should do. I would start the next morning, as I had announced, for Cherchen. Li Darin should then arrest me and send me back to Kara-shahr. Thence I would go on to Urumchi and enlist the help of the Russian consul, to procure me not only a free passage to Cherchen and Khotan, but also a well-merited reprimand to Li Darin, as well as compensation for the loss I should sustain through the delay. I therefore made an arrangement with the merchant who bought my camels, to take charge of my baggage and the horses. I decided to take Islam Bai with me, and we packed a few necessaries in the straps at the back of our saddles.

At first I was seriously annoyed at having been so splendidly caught; for it was of course not to be thought of that I should use force or have recourse to craft against a rude and arrogant mandarin with 265 soldiers at his back. But before the day was over I viewed the journey to Urumchi, a distance of over four hundred miles, in quite a different light. I should travel along new roads and through interesting regions, and should see the Chinese capital of Central Asia, with its crowd of distinguished mandarins, and its little Russian colony. In the end my mind was quite set upon the journey; the only thing that drew me in the opposite direction was my letters in Khotan.

However my star was more powerful than that of Li Darin, amban of Charkhlik. Late that same evening there came to my quarters a mandarin of some fifty years of age, with delicate and distinguished features. He introduced himself as Shi Darin, commandant of the garrison. He told me he had received orders to arrest me next day, and was come to apologize for Li Darin's stupid conduct;

and he said he would try to talk the amban back to reason. After that the conversation passed over to other topics. Shi Darin was deeply interested in my travels, and asked me hosts of questions. When I told him about my disastrous journey across the Takla-makan Desert, he exclaimed loudly, and was ready to throw himself on my neck. "Oh, and so that was *you!* I was in Khotan at the time; nothing else was talked about but your unfortunate journey. Ling Darin told me about you, and we both hoped to have met you in Khotan."

The said Ling Darin was no less a person than Paul Splingaert, a Belgian, who had spent some thirty years of his life in China, and who for four years acted as interpreter to Baron von Richthofen in his travels through that country. He was now an influential mandarin in Su-chow, having become virtually a Chinaman, and married a Chinese wife; by her he had eleven children, of whom several were then being educated in a Roman Catholic mission-school at Shanghai.

Splingaert and Shi Darin had been sent by the governor-general at Urumchi to make a journey of inspection through East Turkestan, more particularly to inquire into the existence of gold in the mountains on the southern borders of the country. Thus they were staying in Khotan at the same time that I was wandering about the forests of Buksem. When they reached Kashgar, I had just started for the Pamirs; and when I returned to Kashgar in the autumn, they had already left. I had a great wish to meet Splingaert; as I was the bearer of greetings to him from Baron von Richthofen. But we did not meet until a year later, when I found him at the Russian embassy in Peking. He was then on the point of settling in Tien-tsin, having been appointed to an important position there through the recommendation of Li Hung Shang.

Having thus found out one another's mutual acquaintances, I and Shi Darin became real good friends, as though we had known one another for years. He remained half the night with me, shared my supper, smoked, talked. I showed him my route-maps and sketches, and put before him all the pros and cons of the Lop-nor problem. In this last he was especially interested, for he said he knew of his own knowledge, that the lake had formerly occupied a different situation.

Instead of going to Urumchi, we stayed all the next day in Charkhlik, and I made my return visit to Shi Darin. He received me with bright friendliness, and showed me the route-maps he had himself plotted of the mountain-roads south of Charkhlik and Cherchen, and I confess I was astonished at his work. Had the names not been written in Chinese characters, nobody could have told that the maps were not made by a European. The mountains were shown with the orthodox gradings of modern geographers. Then he showed me his English compasses, diopters, measuring-scales, and so forth. After that he took me all over the "fortress," and showed me his stores of ammunition and firearms, and proved himself to be entirely devoid of prejudice. In a word, he was not at all an ordinary Chinaman, but more like a European than a son of the Middle Kingdom. He had been stationed in Kulja for several years, and there been brought into contact with the Russians; and the consequence was, that not only was he an admirer of Western civilization, but he even condemned Chinese civilization. And his acquaintance with Splingaert, and association with him in their long journey, had strengthened his prepossessions in favour of Europeans. Whilst we were at dinner, I thought it would be a favourable opportunity to inquire what he was going to do with regard to arresting me. He replied, that he had spent all the morning, trying to instil a little reason into Li Darin: but that Li Darin had stubbornly persisted that, so long as the Dungans remained in revolt, his instructions were to stop everybody seeking to travel to Khotan *viâ* Cherchen. To this Shi Darin said that he replied, I was not a Dungan, but a peaceful European. The amban retorted, he did not know exactly who I was; I had no passport.

"Well, then, I suppose I must prepare to go to Urumchi?" said I.

II.–17

"To Urumchi! Are you mad?" cried Shi Darin, exploding with laughter. "No. Go on to Cherchen, as though nothing were the matter. I will be answerable for the consequences. The amban has issued the order for your arrest; but I am commandant of the garrison, not he, and I do not intend to supply a single soldier for any such purpose. And if Li Darin attempts to arrest you with the help of the native begs, I will send an escort of soldiers to protect you."

Could a greater *volta face* of Fortune be imagined? I was to be protected by the very soldiers whom Li Darin had threatened should arrest me! But then, conflicts of this kind between the civil and the military Chinese authorities in the towns of Central Asia are by no means rare occurrences. I observed the same thing in both Kashgar and Khotan.

The next morning we were all ready for starting again. And as though Shi Darin had not already sufficiently shown his good offices towards me, he now sent me a large supply of sugar and tobacco, the very things I wanted. In return I made him a present of some maps which I could do without, and of several small things. Once more therefore we were bound for the west. Our camels were browsing on the green leaves of the trees in a park on the outskirts of the town. As we rode past, we sent them a melancholy farewell; but they never for an instant stopped their busy feeding, nor deigned to waste a single glance upon us.

I must however hasten rapidly over the 560 miles which still separated us from Khotan. I would gladly linger over the details of the journey; but this book is still growing, and I hope moreover to return again to this region, in which I gathered a rich harvest of observations, in a subsequent work.

On the way to Cherchen we visited the ruins of Wash-shahri; and there I bought from a native an antique copper can.* Then we came to the Cherchen-daria, and so through its scanty woods to the town of Cherchen.

* See the illustration, p. 783.

From that place there are two routes to Khotan. By the northern road, through the desert, the route Marco Polo seems to have chosen, Khotan can be reached in ten days; but as it is almost entirely unpopulated, and at that season of the year the water in the wells was salt, and the gnats an intolerable plague, we preferred the southern route, which skirts the Kwen-lun Mountains, and is on an average 3000 or 4000 feet higher than the other route. By that road the air was fresh, the climate altogether delightful, and the scenery richly varied. The districts we travelled through were inhabited by a Turki stem or tribe called Taghliks (Mountaineers), whose livelihood is derived from the keeping of domestic animals, and also, though to a much smaller extent, from agriculture. This road took us four days longer than the northern road; but that was comparatively speaking a trifle.

Our first stage was to the gold-mines of Kopa. Here the native inhabitants seek their fortune in a very primitive fashion. The auriferous rock lies at a maximum depth of 300 feet. To get down to it, the miners dig a shaft (*kan*), and at the bottom of the shaft excavate narrow tunnels, like mole-runs, in a direction parallel to an old river-bed. This however would deserve a chapter to itself; and I must hasten on further across the Kirk-sai (Forty River-beds), through whose deep channels the mountain water, that comes from the melting snows, travels on its way to the glowing furnace of the Gobi or Takla-makan. Thence we rode across Sourgak, where also gold occurs, and so down into the lowlands and the desert, finding an excellent stopping-place in the little oasis of Yaz-yulgun (the Summer Tamarisk). In Keriya I was warmly welcomed by my Kashgar friend, Tsen Daloi, who had recently been appointed amban of the town.

We reached Khotan on May 27th, strong and well, but tired, and with the liveliest anticipations of the rest we were about to enjoy.

CHAPTER LXXIV.

THE SEQUEL OF MY DESERT JOURNEY

IT will be remembered how, during our disastrous journey through the desert of Takla-makan in April and May 1895, we had been obliged to leave behind the travelling-tent, and nearly all our baggage, to the value of about £275; and also two men who lay dying of thirst. In Kashgar the widows of these two men came to me, weeping and begging me to give them back their husbands. I consoled them as well as I could, and gave them what money I was able to afford. After that I was so occupied with the preparations for my journey to the Pamirs, that the occurrences of the desert faded from my recollection. I soon forgot the privations I had endured and the loss I had suffered; but the memory of my marvellous escape and rescue was constantly in my mind, steeling me with confidence in moments of danger.

When the Swedish army officer's revolver, which had been left on the verge of the desert amongst the baggage of the camel Nähr, turned up so unexpectedly at Kashgar in the summer of 1895, our suspicions were certainly aroused. But Consul-General Petrovsky and the Dao Tai sent instructions to Khotan for fresh inquiries to be made; but they led to nothing. I myself reached Khotan early in January 1896, and when I went away, I was fully convinced that the tent, baggage, and two dead men were long ago buried in the sand, where they would remain for a multitude of years. Imagine therefore my surprise when, the very day I got back to Khotan, Liu Darin sent to my house the greater part of my lost belongings, which I had not seen for more than a year.

But I must confess it was not with feelings of unmixed pleasure that I received them back again; for the recovery brought to light the fact that we had fallen amongst thieves and traitors. And then began the unfolding of a criminal romance which was as disagreeable to me as it was complicated in itself, to say nothing of the loss of time occasioned by the unravelling of it all. I will however tell the story succinctly, partly because it illustrates the character of the Mohammedan population, as well as the Chinese methods of administering justice.

Seyd Akhram Bai, aksakal of the West Turkestan merchants in Khotan, received the Swedish revolver from Yussuf, the merchant who gave water to Islam Bai when he lay dying of thirst. Yussuf no doubt meant it as a bribe to secure the aksakal's good-will and silence. But the aksakal had been already forewarned by Mr. Petrovsky, and so escaped falling into the trap. He subjected Yussuf to sharp examination; and Yussuf finally confessed, that he had received the revolver from Togda Beg, chief of Tavek-kel. The aksakal gave the weapon to Liu Darin, and the latter sent it to the Dao Tai, who sent it to me. Yussuf, finding that the matter awakened a certain amount of interest, thought it prudent to retire to Urumchi. Meanwhile the aksakal, hearing nothing more of the merchant, sent a spy to Tavek-kel, to keep an eye upon Togda Beg and his house.

Clad in rags, the spy went to Tavek-kel, and played his part so well, that Togda Beg took him into his service, and put him in charge of a flock of sheep. The man roamed about the neighbourhood, performing his duty to the complete satisfaction of his new master. His wages were very small; but one day when he went to the beg's house to receive the little that was due to him, he made an important discovery. As soon as the beg caught sight of him in the doorway, he jumped up and prevented him from going in. But the man had already seen sufficient: he saw how the beg, together with our three hunters of the Khotan-daria, namely, Ahmed Merghen, Kasim Akhun, and Togda Shah, as well as

Yakub Shah, the man who guided us to the first of the ancient cities in the desert, were sitting crouching round some boxes; and several articles, which could only belong to a European, had been taken out of them and lay scattered over the carpet. The spy kept his own counsel, received his wages, and walked slowly away; but as soon as he was well out of sight, he caught the first horse he saw, jumped on his back, and galloped off to Khotan, to report to the aksakal what he had seen. The aksakal at once carried the report to Liu Darin, and Liu Darin sent two officers of the law, with a party of soldiers, to Tavek-kel, to search the beg's house and take possession of the stolen property.

In the meantime the beg had speedily missed his new shepherd, and as a horse was also gone, he instantly guessed that something was wrong, and sent men on horseback as hard as they could gallop after the fugitive. But the spy had got too long a start; besides, he knew that his own life depended upon his getting to Khotan first. The beg was now in an awkward predicament: but he saved himself with the craft of a diplomatist: he hurriedly squeezed the things back into the boxes, and took them to Khotan, arriving there in company with the men Liu Darin had sent, and handed everything over to him (the amban), saying that they had only been found two or three days before. The hunters also went to Khotan at the same time, and all the conspirators put up at the same caravanserai. But there too the aksakal had a spy in his service. Next day this spy came and reported that during the night the beg had instructed the hunters what they were to say when Liu Darin questioned them about the affair; for there could be no doubt, he would very soon hold a formal inquiry as to where and when and how they found the things.

But first the aksakal had the hunters before him—the very men, be it remembered, who had gone with Islam Bai to look for the tent after our shipwreck in the desert, but without success. They told him, that in the course of the winter they had gone back to the three poplars, and from

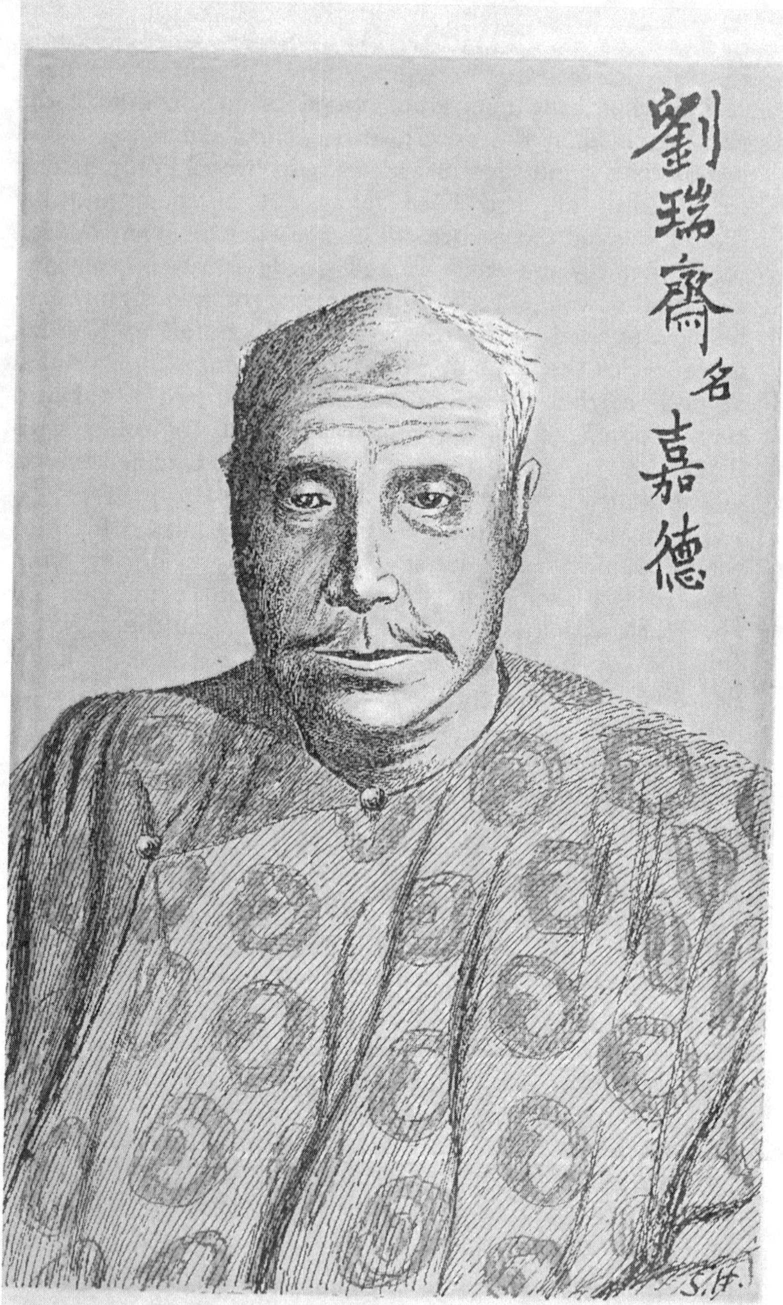

LIU DARIN, AMBAN OF KHOTAN

that point had followed up the trail of a fox, which ran due west into the desert. They followed it for some days, and at last came to a place where the animal had stopped and scratched in the sand. The sand there was as white as chalk; they discovered that the colouring was caused by flour. After that they dug down, and at last came upon the tent, so completely buried in the sand that the tops of the tent-poles were a foot below the surface. Then they fished up the different articles one after the other, and loaded them on donkeys' backs, and carried them to the river.

This was a most interesting story. It proved that the sand-dunes round the tent had increased more than six feet in height; although the increase might in great part be due to local irregularities, caused by the heaping up of the sand on the sheltered side of the tent. In the summer of 1895 there had clearly been heavy gales of wind; but the winter had been as usual calm and quiet, so that the fox's trail had not been blotted out, and was easy to trace. No doubt the foxes had scented the hens and the cases of provisions we left behind, and had gone across the desert in search of them. The hunters found the skeleton of one of the hens on a sand-dune a long way from the camp; but they saw nothing of the two dead men. Possibly they both crept on a little farther on the night of 1st May.

The aksakal quickly formed his own conclusions as to the truth of this story. Why did they not take the things straight to the amban, Liu Darin, instead of waiting until the spy found them out? Well, Togda Beg, who had formerly been a yuz-bashi (captain) in the great Yakub Beg's army, and was known to be a hard and unscrupulous man, and hated accordingly—he had got wind of the "find," and persuaded the hunters, who were good-hearted, harmless men, to keep the affair quiet, and then gradually sell some of the things, keeping those they could make use of themselves. Hence I only recovered some of my property, principally such articles as the natives could find no use for, such as a portion of my instruments, the plane-table and stand, the medicine-chest, my ulster, cigars, the petroleum cooking-stove, and the two photographic cameras. Unfortunately these last were of very little service afterwards; for the inhabitants of Tavek-kel had appropriated the plates and used them for glazing the grated window-openings of their houses. I was therefore still restricted, as regards the future, to my pen and pencil; hence it is only the earlier portion of this book which is illustrated from photographs.

The hunters fell in with Togda Beg's proposal, and had already disposed of articles to the value of £110. Ahmed Merghen and Kasim Akhun, who had accompanied me down the Keriya-daria, had kept their own counsel throughout the whole of the journey. But I suspect their consciences pricked them; for, whenever our unfortunate desert journey was talked about, they always used to say, that the things I had abandoned were certain to be found again, and that they would look for them as they went home from Chimen, as though they were seeking to cover their retreat. I also understood now, why Togda Beg lodged me in an ordinary house when I visited Tavek-kel, and did not offer me the hospitality of his own. The stolen articles were concealed there in carpets and felts, and possibly something might have been discovered.

The amban, Liu Darin, also held an inquiry, in the course of which he elicited, that the locks of my boxes had been forcibly broken open. (I left them locked and put the key under one of the boxes that unlucky 1st May, 1895.) He asked how the men had dared to do such a thing, and whether they did not know that both the Chinese law and the Mohammedan *shcriet* (theological law) forbade them to lay hands upon another person's property. They replied, the boxes were so heavy, that they were obliged to break them open, in order to carry the contents piecemeal.

All this had taken place two or three months before I got back to Khotan. The hunters had been put to torture to make them confess; after that they were beaten and cast into prison. But the cunning beg was still at large.

After my return to Khotan the case was taken up again. The aksakal had a spy in the amban's *yamen* (official residence), and it was his business to report what took place there. But we were satisfied, Liu Darin would do what was right in the matter, and would not let himself be bribed. The thieves' destinies were in my hand. Chinese processes of torture often make men cripples, and the suspense in which the poor fellows were being kept, whilst awaiting their doom, must have been terrible. It was of course my intention from the beginning to let them off with a good fright. I did not wish them to be harshly treated; for had not the All-Merciful stretched out His hand to me when my life was in jeopardy?

Liu Darin put on the mantle of a judge, and asserted his authority with dignity and effect. He demanded a list of the articles I had lost, together with their several values; and armed with it, he himself, in his own august person, travelled all the way to Tavek-kel, and pursued his investigations all over again. After that the case was continued in Khotan. The evidence was very conflicting. Liu Darin wanted therefore to have recourse to the rack and the grill; which I opposed with all the energy I was master of. Then he must at least use the rod; and all through the inquiry both rod and executioners were present ready to hand. But when I declared that, if they were employed, I must withdraw, for according to the custom of my country it was wrong to ill-use even a criminal, Liu Darin gave way, and respected my scruples.

The hunters all agreed in maintaining that they had given the whole of the property to Togda Beg, and that if any things were wanting he was the only person who could tell where they had gone to. On the other hand, Togda Beg swore, that the hunters had stolen the missing articles. Liu Darin's Solomon-like judgment was therefore this: "One of the two parties is lying, but the inquiry has not established which party it is. I therefore condemn both parties to pay back to our guest within two days the value of the articles which have gone amissing, that is five thousand tengeh (nearly £120)."

Immediately, and in the presence of the culprits, I observed, that the amban's decision was perfectly sound and just; but that I would not take money from the thieves, however guilty they were.

To this Liu Darin replied, with firm decision, that, even though the money were a matter of indifference to me, it was a matter of the greatest importance to the Chinese themselves, to teach their subjects, that they could not plunder a European guest with impunity, otherwise the same thing would happen again the next time a traveller came that way.

However I did not consider it satisfactorily proved that the camel which had been left near the river had also been plundered. Moreover the hunters asserted, that some of the things had been left behind in the place where they found the tent. For these reasons I managed to get the fine reduced to a thousand tengeh (£22 10*s.*). If I gained nothing else, I gained at least the respect of the culprits themselves.

The quick sense of justice and the resolute energy which Liu Darin showed in protecting the interests of a European are very unusual qualities in a Chinese mandarin. But I have already observed, that Liu Sui Tsai, to give him his full name, was an exceptionally capable man; and this was proved yet again in another instance. The annual tribute which the oasis of Khotan pays collectively to the Chinese imperial exchequer amounts to about 3000 *jambaus* (£33,000). At Khotan, as indeed in most of the towns of East Turkestan, the governor is changed every three years; but even in that period he generally finds time to "scrape together" a few thousands, for a large portion of the taxes that are levied sticks in his own pocket. Liu Darin had been governor of Khotan three years; but every year he had sent the whole of the tribute without deduction to Peking. His rare integrity had excited considerable attention at Urumchi, and he had just been promoted to be amban of Yarkand, and was to leave

A BAZAAR-STREET IN KHOTAN

for his new sphere of labour the same day I quitted Khotan.

We had a thoroughly pleasant time of it in Khotan. At the command of Liu Darin, the wealthiest man in the place, Alim Akhun, placed his fine summer residence at my disposal; and everything was ready for me when I arrived on the 27th May. I was led through a gate, then across two or three courtyards, and finally into a large garden surrounded by a high square wall. A pavement of stone slabs led to a rectangular brick house, standing on a stone terrace in the middle of the garden. The interior contained only one large apartment, with fifteen windows, the wooden gratings of which opened like jalousies. The terrace was surrounded by a moat, filled with water and crossed by four small bridges. The house had been built for Yakub Beg, the famous ruler of Kashgar, and was surrounded by willows so full of leaf and so closely planted, that not a ray of sunshine was able to pierce through to banish the cool, delicious shade. The temperature in the open rose to 100°.4 Fahr. (38° C.): under the trees it was eighteen degrees Fahr. lower. The water rippled along the moat; the wind whispered in the tops of the trees. Although storms of dust were prevalent at that season, none invaded the peace of the garden.

The house had only one door. A wooden platform about a yard high ran all round the other three sides, leaving the middle of the stone floor free. I furnished the platform with packing-cases and carpets, and in one corner set up my bed. There I sat cross-legged, with a box for a table, and worked until far on in the night. The place was not unlike a student's room, except that the large quantity of travelling paraphernalia gave it an unusually picturesque appearance.

The kitchen was situated in a little clay house near the entrance-gate to the garden, and to secure me in some degree from interruption, Islam Bai rigged up a temporary bell between the two houses. I only had two meals a day. Islam came and announced, "*Ash tayer, tura*" (The rice pudding is ready, sir), then spread a cloth on the platform at my side, and arranged the dishes. Pudding with onions and mutton, soup with vegetables and marrow, fresh bread, sour milk, tea with sugar and cream, eggs, cucumbers, melons, grapes, and apricots—why, I lived in clover, like a prince! Chinese mandarins came to pay me visits. Native traders came bringing antiquities and articles in jade to sell. My only companion was Yolldash. The Mohammedans bestowed upon him the title of Yolldash Akhun or Mr. Travelling-Companion. He kept watch over my house, and by the wagging of his tail manifested his interest when Islam came with the dinner-tray.

How I did enjoy my rest in that beautiful garden! It was so still, so peaceful. Not a sound of the noisy bazaar penetrated thither, not a whiff of the unwholesome atmosphere of the streets. No doubt it was the great contrast with the desert that made the place so delightful; and I enjoyed it none the less that my letters from home contained nothing but good news. After dinner I strolled awhile about the garden, drinking in the scent of the ripening mulberries and peaches, of swelling roses and tulips, the last having a shade of green. There was also a roe-deer, with a blue ribbon and bells round its neck, which sometimes came with short nimble jumps and wanted to play with me. In a word, it was the most delightful place a man could dream about, a perfect paradise in fact, only—there was no Eve.

In the stable stood my fifteen new horses. My riding-horse of the summer of 1895 was the only old one, but it had been left behind in Khotan when I set out for Lop-nor. It was now getting a good rest against the hard work in store for it. Liu Darin sent me an abundant supply of maize and green fodder. I protested that, if he would do so, I should be obliged to start again all the sooner; but he paid no heed to my protests. On the contrary, he begged me to stay; he assured me it was the way every true Chinaman would treat his guest. Nor was that all; when I made my next start, he gave me provisions for a month for every man and animal in the caravan. In fact, I cannot reckon up all the proofs of kindness and friendship which that excellent mandarin lavished upon me. There is however one thing I must mention. He procured me a Chinese interpreter, Fong Shi, a pleasant and agreeable young Chinaman, who wrote his mother-tongue with ease and spoke Jagatai Turki fluently, and—did not smoke opium. He left his wife and child behind him in Khotan, Liu Darin making himself answerable for their maintenance. But I also paid Fong Shi three months' salary in advance, and that money he gave to his wife. Whenever I could find leisure, he was to give me lessons in Chinese, and we began at once, even before we left Khotan.

When evening came, Islam let down the blinds before the windows and lighted a couple of stearine candles; and then I sat down and worked on steadily till two o'clock in the morning. One dark and stormy night I was awakened by Yolldash barking like a crazed thing at one of the windows. But owing to the melancholy moaning of the wind in the trees I was unable to hear anything unusual. I crept to the bell. The wire was cut; though I never knew whether it was broken by the storm or done on purpose. I went out upon the terrace; the dog, quivering with rage, instantly jumped down into the bushes. I saw a couple of dark figures stealing away towards the garden-wall. I hastened to Islam, who had the firearms, and woke him up. He took a rifle and fired two or three shots at random. The next morning we found a ladder propped against the wall. The thieves, for such the intruders were, had left it behind them in their hurried flight. After that I always kept a loaded revolver by my side. We also stationed two night-watchmen in the garden; and, as the custom is in protecting the bazaars against thieves at night, they sounded three strokes upon a drum every minute. Henceforward I was not disturbed.

But the time flew rapidly. I could not afford to sacrifice more than one month to rest, and soon longed to be up and moving again. By the end of June everything was ready for another start. Islam Bai, in whom I reposed the most absolute confidence, had engaged a fresh set of attendants, and bought fresh supplies. A tent-maker in the bazaar made me a big new tent for my men's accommodation. I intended to use the same tent which I had left behind me in the desert, and now so strangely recovered from the sand of the Takla-makan.

The men who were to go with me celebrated their departure by a feast on the last afternoon. Coloured Chinese lanterns were hung all round one of the small courtyards. They had a full band of flute-players and drummers; and a couple of dancers, one disguised as a woman, gave exhibitions of their skill, anything but an edifying performance; whilst the Mohammedans sat round in a circle, and applauded and enjoyed themselves. Then tea and rice-pudding were handed round; and so the festivities were kept up until the early hours of the morning.

THROUGH NORTHERN TIBET AND TSAIDAM

CHAPTER LXXV.

OVER THE KWEN-LUN PASSES

ON June 29th we were all up at sunrise. My peaceful house in the garden was cleared out. The horses with the pack-saddles were brought in, and loaded with packing-cases and boxes. Some of them, in consequence of the long rest, had become restive and shy, and throughout the first day had to be led separately.

Whilst the men were getting the caravan arranged for the start, I went to pay my farewell visit to Liu Darin, and presented him with a gold watch, which I bought from a wealthy merchant from Ladak. To the military commandant of the town, who had presented me with a very good carpet for my tent, I gave a revolver, together with our surplus ammunition. Alim Akhun got a bell and a khalat. In fact, I overlooked nobody who had been in any way helpful to me. The Tatar merchant, Rafikoff, undertook to send home my archæological collections, the wild camel's skin, and a number of carpets I bought in Khotan; and thanks to his care and the kindly offices of Mr. Petrovsky, everything reached Stockholm not a bit the worse for the journey.

It was ten o'clock before everything was ready, and the long caravan, consisting of twenty horses and thirty donkeys, led by a troop of men on foot and on horseback, got into motion for the east. Yes, we were at last bound for the Far East!

It took us barely an hour to reach the left bank of the Yurun-kash, which had now a very different appearance from what it had a month earlier. Then it consisted of a single channel, which we rode through without any difficulty whatever. Now it was divided into four arms, the biggest current being in the channel nearest the right bank. The river was in fact in its summer flood, and the torrent raced down so violently that the ground shook under our feet. I had measured its volume the day before, and found it amounted to 12,700 cubic feet in the second; but fortunately the stream had fallen fourteen inches during the night. In spite of that, we were obliged to requisition the services of a score of water men (suchis). First they took over the horses with the provisions, the tent, and the heavier baggage. Alongside the fourth and most difficult arm stretched a low gravelly island, and there the ferrymen used a long, narrow, but very clumsy boat, in shape like a heavy oblong box. In this primitive craft I, Yolldash, and the more perishable boxes were ferried over. Yolldash was anything but comfortable at crossing in such a "wobbly" affair. The water was fearfully muddy, and its temperature 57°9 Fahr. (14°4 C.).

Beyond the Yurun-kash the road ran through an unbroken succession of villages, all embowered in luxuriant summer greenery, and across a countless number of irrigation-canals, each full to the brink. This network of channels despoiled the river of no small portion of its water.

We spent the first night in a first-rate house at Sampulla; and on the next day, June 30th, passed through the last villages on the south-eastern margin of the oasis of Khotan. The last irrigation-canal stopped at Kutaz-lengher (the Station of the Yak), and then all vegetation ceased with extraordinary suddenness, as sharply as though it had been scalded off with boiling water. Beyond the dividing-line there was not a green blade to be seen. Before us stretched the absolutely sterile *sai*, a sort of Transitional region between the desert and the mountains, with which we had already made acquaintance at Kopa and Sourgak. The surface was hard and yellow, and had a very gentle inclination upwards. Between the belt of sai, which is properly a gravelly talus at the foot of the mountains, and the sandy desert ran the narrow belt of detached oases, with the caravan-road. The sai was seamed by numerous small torrents, deeply eroded, which poured off the northern versant of the Kwen-lun Mountains. The largest of those we crossed were the Ullug-sai, Keriya-daria, Niya-daria, Tollan-khoja, Bostan-tograk, Mölldya, and Kara-muran. At the points where these several streams burst from the mountains, there were a number of small villages, around which barley is grown, and in that, and in the breeding of sheep and cattle, the inhabitants find their chief means of

THE CHAPP OR RAVINE OF TOLLAN-KHOJA

subsistence. Hence in East Turkestan three varieties of oasis may be distinguished:—(i.) those along the courses of the rivers; (ii.) those which are situated at the edge of the desert and are watered by artificial irrigation-channels —to these all the towns belong; and (iii.) those which lie at the points where the mountain torrents break out of the mountains, and where there is generally a plentiful supply of grass.

At Kutaz-lengher we made a short halt to water the animals; and there the aksakal of Khotan, Iskender, and the rest of the horsemen who had accompanied us, turned back home. The aksakal took my last letters, and after that I was cut off from all communication with Europe. I should hear nothing more from home until I reached Peking in the Far East.

The next few days we rode along the foot of the mountains, through a country that was beautifully fresh and green, and through the villages of Hasha, Chakkar, and Nura, and so arrived at Dört Imam Sebulla, near Pulur. It had originally been my intention to strike up into the Tibetan plateau from this last-mentioned place; but that I found to be impossible, because the narrow, difficult mountain-path was completely blocked by the unusual quantity of water in the Keriya-daria. We had therefore no other choice but to go back to the great caravan-road. We reached it at the town of Keriya, and stayed there four days; and there we crossed the river.

Thence it took us three days, by way of Oy-tograk and Ovraz, to reach Niya, a little town of 500 *uylik* (houses), with a beg, two yuz-bashis, and four on-bashis (chief over ten men). The oasis is supplied with water from the Ullug-sai or Niya-daria; but in case the river dries up, there are reservoirs to fall back upon. They are, however, quickly exhausted, and for the greater part of the year the people are dependent upon wells, which are thirty to forty feet deep and contain good, fresh water. The oasis is not therefore suited for agriculture, and the gardens do not look so flourishing as in the other oases.

Niya derives such importance as it possesses solely from the fact, that two days' journey to the north, at the point where the river loses itself in the sand, is the tomb of the saint, Imam Jafer Sadik, which every year, especially in the latter part of the summer and autumn, is visited by from 3000 to 4000 pilgrims. And as at Ordan Padshah, it is upon their gifts *in natura*, and the money they give, that the five sheikhs and temple servants subsist. In this way the shrine has become possessed of about 4000 sheep, which graze in the forests of the Niya-daria. The river, after forming a small lake which supplies the place with water, loses itself in the sand a short distance north of the tomb.

At Niya, which we left on July 18th, we once more turned towards the foot of the mountains, and after passing through Chicheghan-lengher and Yulgun-bulak came to the river Tollan-khoja, which has cut a deep channel through the conglomerate strata. On the way we had an awkward misadventure. Islam Bai saw a troop of antelopes grazing a short distance ahead. He rode on in advance, dismounted, tethered his horse, and stalked them through a ravine. The shot (unfortunately it missed) frightened the horses, which were now going by themselves, without being led. Off they started in a wild race for the steppe, an undulating plain dotted with tussocks of grass. Luckily the horse which carried my instrument-cases was prevented from joining in the mad gallop, for it was always led by one of the men. As for the others, they disappeared in a cloud of dust, and only came to a stop when their loads slipped off their backs and got about their feet, preventing them from moving. Some of the boxes were broken; one that contained cooking-utensils was smashed to atoms, and its contents scattered all over the steppe, several china cups being shivered to fragments.

When we got into the neighbourhood of Kara-sai, we heard for the first time of a pass over the Kwen-lun Mountains which was said to lie south of Dalai-kurgan, about one day's journey south-east of Kopa. I decided to go back to Kopa, to pick up more definite information, as well as to procure guides. I also wanted some camels for the journey through Northern Tibet. I heard there were several, grazing in charge of their drivers, on the upper yeylaus (summer pasture-grounds) of the river Mölldya; and therefore sent on one of the trustiest of my men, Parpi Bai, to go and bring some for me to look at. Parpi Bai performed his errand capitally. When on July 28th we halted to rest at Mölldya, he met us with thirteen good camels, and brought their owners with him too. I had previously despatched a courier to the beg of Kopa, Togda Mohammed Beg; and he now rode up and helped me in the bargaining, by keeping down the

TOGDA MOHAMMED BEG, OF KOPA

price to a reasonable figure. For 1275 tengeh (£30) I bought six male camels of the variety which are accustomed to travel in mountainous districts, and which had had a thorough summer's rest.

Leaving Kopa on July 30th, we directed our march towards the east-south-east, and crossed over a series of ravines, called *chapps*, deeply excavated in the conglomerates, but dry, except after rain. At the Mitt, an affluent of the Kara-muran, the landscape became picturesque. The river emerged from between the granite cliffs through a gateway less than fifty yards wide. But immediately after it emerged, it spread itself out in a broad channel which it had carved through the conglomerates, and was joined from the right by the Yakka-chapp, at that season a mere dry ravine with a stony bottom. Like those of the Mitt, its sides were almost vertical, and flung back the rattle of the caravan with a sharp echo. By means of this ravine we ascended to a series of loess hills, soft in outline and overgrown with grass. Then the track swung off to the south-east, towards the entrance of a transverse valley, traversed by a little brook on its way down to the plain. The district was called Dalai-kurgan, and was inhabited by eighteen families of Taghliks (Mountaineers), who owned amongst them some 6000 sheep. They lived in small huts partly excavated out of the loess terraces. We encamped on the left bank of the stream, in the entrance to the valley, and let all our animals run free on the luxuriant grass.

Immediately south of us towered up the mighty mountain chain which the Chinese call Kwen-lun (Kuen-lun); the Taghliks however had no general name for it. The secondary range, which was pierced by the Dalai-kurgan stream, was called the Tokkuz-davan (the Nine Passes) east of the Kara-muran; though at Dalai-kurgan itself that name was not in use. The Taghliks maintained there was only one pass giving access to the high plateau of Tibet, namely the pass of Chokkalik; but they would not undertake to say that we could get through with our camels. I decided therefore to reconnoitre the pass before sending on the whole of the caravan.

Accordingly on August 1st, accompanied by Fong Shi, Islam Akhun, Roslakh, and two Taghliks, I rode up the valley of the Dalai-kurgan to the pass of the same name (14,330 feet in altitude), and on the following day pushed on eastwards to the principal pass (16,180 feet). Thence I obtained a magnificent view of the ocean of tumbling mountain-peaks. The ascent was certainly steep; still we thought the camels could manage it. But the descent on the other side was very much worse, owing to the sharp jagged rocks which protruded through the almost precipitous gravelly slope. After carefully considering the matter in counsel together, we decided to make the attempt. The baggage could be lowered down the gravel slope; the horses and donkeys would be able to take care of themselves; and if the camels could not manage it, we could roll them up in felt carpets and so haul them down. Having come to this decision, we returned to Dalai-kurgan over the pass of Sarik-kol (13,720 feet), arriving there on the evening of August 3rd.

The caravan was given another day's rest, and then the long string of animals started for the aghil of Sarik-kol (the Village of the Yellow Valley), and there they got their last bite of fresh sappy grass.

On August 6th the caravan, divided into several separate groups, each in charge of a specially appointed leader, and the whole making an imposing appearance, wound slowly up the glen towards the pass of Sarik-kol. The pasturage continued to diminish in extent as we climbed higher; what there was clung for the most part to the banks of the little stream. The bed of the torrent wound mostly through soft earth, but sometimes through conglomerate strata, and its bottom was littered with pieces of bright grey and green granite. In the highest part of the glen the naked granite rocks hung right over the stream, although in places they were still crowned with patches of grass. Meanwhile the glen gradually contracted, and grew steeper and steeper. Slowly, painfully, the animals clambered up the gravelly talus, which choked the trumpet-shaped gap cut through the crest of the range, and over which the beds of the torrents radiated like the ribs of a fan upon the head of the glen below. The camels toiled cautiously up the loose gravel slope. Every minute one or other of the horses or donkeys fell, and lost ground whilst they were being unloaded and loaded again; then they would push on at a quicker pace in the endeavour to catch up with the caravan. I usually rode in the rear, so as to have an eye upon them all; and it was with a feeling of

OUR CAMP IN THE SARIK-KOL VALLEY, LOOKING SOUTH

real relief that I saw the last of the animals disappear behind the summit of the pass.

The southern side of the pass was much less steep, and led down into a wide glen with plenty of loose soil, but rather scanty yeylaks (pasture). On both sides it was shut in by imposing mountain-spurs, like those which overhung the Sarik-kol on the north. In consequence of the inconsiderable fall and the relatively feeble erosive power of the water, the solid rock was not eaten away, although the crest of the main range presented very fantastic outlines.

We kept beside the rivulet which babbled down the middle of the glen until we reached the broad main valley of Lama-chimin, and were just turning to the left, *i.e.* eastwards, towards the pass of Chokkalik, when the aksakal, or chief, of the Taghliks, who was to guide us over it, blurted out that there was a more convenient pass called Yappkaklik in the upper valley of the Mitt. When therefore he told me that Chokkalik was the only pass across the range, he told me a deliberate lie. The fact was, he was afraid to show us a hitherto unknown path into Tibet, through fear of the Chinese. But, having brought us so far on the road, he plucked up courage a little, and gave me fuller and more definite information. I reprimanded him smartly for having deceived me and taken us under false pretences all the way over the passes of Dalai-kurgan, Chokkalik, and Sarik-kol. All the same, I was not sorry to have had the opportunity of making a reconnaissance of the district.

We therefore turned and directed our course south-west, and then due south, crossed the brook that came down from the pass of Chokkalik, left the lower extremity of the glen of Dalai-kurgan on the right, and so threaded the transverse glen of Mitt, considerably further to the west. This glen too was pretty wide, and so level that to us, accustomed as we were to the steep slopes, it appeared to incline towards the south; but the course of the torrent, flowing in the opposite direction, convinced us that we were the victims of an ocular delusion. The stream issued from between two lofty granite spurs which formed a sort of gateway, and meandered in a broad, shallow, silent current across an almost absolutely level plain. Its bed was lined with soft mud, into which the horses sank over the fetlocks; there was not a pebble or a splinter of stone to be seen in it. At intervals the stream spread out into lake-like expansions, and the shore-lines showed that when in full flood it very nearly stretched from one side of the glen to the other. There were several very sharp turns in its course, and in places it was divided by low islands of mud. Its volume was augmented by rivulets from two or three springs, situated at the foot of the mountains on the left, and the water in them was perfectly clear and fresh, although there were thin white lines along their edges, indicative of saline evaporations.

We pitched our camp at the foot of a conglomerate terrace on the right bank of the stream, commanding a magnificent view to the south. The valley continued to widen out, and finally ended in an extensive plain, upon which several side-glens debouched, and which was crossed by the river Mitt, split into a great number of arms, many of them containing water. In the far, far distance, still to the south, I perceived a line of snowy peaks, imperfectly distinguishable through the hazy atmosphere, peeping up over the tops of the intervening ranges, which abutted upon the plain *en échelon*.

Our camp was the scene of much life and bustle, notwithstanding that there was but a scanty supply of pasturage, and that much poorer in quality than it was at Lama-chimin. In the middle of the camp were the two white tents, with the provision-bags, boxes, saddles, and other *impedimenta* piled up between them. The horses were coupled two and two together to prevent them from straying too far away, but the donkeys and camels were allowed to run freely at large, and tugged greedily at the grass.

CHAPTER LXXVI.

MY CARAVAN: ITS SEVERAL MEMBERS

THIS was the first camp in an entirely uninhabited region. Our faces were now set towards unknown, uninhabited Tibet, and two months were to clapse before we again came into contact with human beings. In a word, we burnt our ships behind us, and had the comfortable feeling of being safe beyond the reach of all the mandarins of China. But for the future we should have to make longer and quicker marches, and only stop in places where there was grass. But in this regard the Taghliks gave us only the poorest Job's comfort, for with one voice they declared that the country to the south was everywhere absolutely barren. This agreed fully with the experience of the Pievtsoff expedition farther to the east, so that I was fully prepared to see the caravan animals gradually become exhausted and perish on the way. But I saw no danger as regarded ourselves; for, supposing things came to the very worst, I hoped we should be able on foot to reach inhabited regions either on the south or on the north.

But beyond that camp the Taghliks were not accustomed to go; and as they had no geographical names for the tracts in front of us, I was obliged to enter the various geographical features on my map under purely conventional signs, such as numerals and the letters of the alphabet. It is very curious that several names in that particular district point to a Mongol source of nomenclature, *e.g.* Kalmak-chapp (the Mongol Ravine), Kalmak-utturgan (where Mongols Have Dwelt), Kara-muran (the Black Water), Dalai-kurgan (the Fortress of Dalai), and Lama-chimin (the Lama's Grazing-grounds).

Here then our valuable animals enjoyed their last good meal of sweet, fresh grass in peace and quietness, all unconscious of the fate that was in store for them. Ere two months were gone most of them lay dead on the barren plateau of Northern Tibet; and yet, when we started, we had by no means a niggardly cavalcade. We brought with us to the foot of the mountains no less than seventeen horses, twelve donkeys, and six camels, besides a number of other animals hired for a short period. At Sarik-kol we added four other horses and seventeen donkeys to the troop, the donkeys being laden with sacks of maize intended as fodder for all the animals of the caravan. Thus we had fifty-six beasts in all, and when I add that, by the time we reached the border-ridge of Tsaidam, we had only three camels, three horses, and one donkey left, and that all seven were worn to skin and bone, and barely able to crawl, or in other words that we lost 90 per cent. of our caravan, you will be able to form some idea of the terrible hardships the poor animals had to undergo. Their loss was no real hindrance to us, for we lost them gradually and proportionally with the decrease in their loads (provisions); but it was very painful to witness the poor brutes' sufferings.

In the aul of Sarik-kol we bought a dozen sheep and two goats, intending to slaughter them one after the other as we went along. I wished to take a score of sheep: but my men assured me, that at the enormous altitudes at which we should be travelling the stomach lost all desire for meat food, and would tolerate nothing but rice. All the same I found that the sheep we did take with us were in brisk demand, and only lasted through half the journey. After the last was killed, we had to content ourselves with the meat of the wild yak.

Lastly, I must not forget to mention as belonging to our travelling menagerie three magnificent dogs—my faithful Yolldash from Korla, who always slept by my side and guarded the tent with such zeal that he would allow nobody to come inside except Islam Bai. Then we had Yollbars (the Tiger), from Kara-sai, a big, yellow, shaggy brute, and a black and white dog, Buru (the Wolf), from Dalai-kurgan. These two attached themselves to the men's tent, where they made a fearful rumpus at night, and sometimes barked at the caravan animals if they strayed too far from camp. Whilst on the march all three dogs scampered about the caravan, chasing and playing with one another; but the moment they caught sight of any game in the mountains, off they would race, and would remain a long time absent from the caravan. They were always vivacious and wide awake, enlivening both the monotony of our marches and our otherwise silent camps. In fact, they bore the journey across the plateaus best of all the animals in the caravan. They did not appear to suffer in the slightest degree from the extreme rarity of the atmosphere. And they always got plenty to eat; for there were the offals of the slaughtered sheep, and of the yaks and wild asses we shot, and in default of anything better, the horses, camels, and donkeys which fell exhausted by the wayside. In the latter part of the journey one and often more animals gave up and died at every camp.

I had eight attendants, each with his own appropriate duties to perform, namely, Islam Bai, caravan-bashi (leader), Fong Shi, Chinese interpreter, Parpi Bai from Osh, Islam Akhun from Keriya, Hamdan Bai from Cherchen, Ahmed Akhun, who was half a Chinaman, Roslakh from Kara-sai, and Kurban Akhun from Dalai-kurgan. From this last-mentioned place we hired seventeen Taghliks, under the command of their aksakal (chief), to help us over the most difficult of the passes, and it was arranged that at the end of a fortnight or so they were to return home. The two Taghliks who went with me to make the reconnaissance ran away after our return to camp, fearing they would be punished for having led me to a difficult pass when there was an easier one nearer. They slunk away immediately their aksakal made up his mind to show me the way to the pass of Yappkaklik, but we did not miss them until we encamped for the night. They did indeed escape well-deserved punishment, but they also lost payment for the horses which I hired of them for making the reconnaissance journey.

We had a splendid ride all day, and in spite of the great altitude it was so warm in the sun that I wore only a light summer jacket. But no sooner did the mountains in the west cut off the sun's rays than we at once began to feel the chilly coolness of the evening, and I donned my ulster and winter cap. At nine o'clock in the evening the thermometer registered 41°4 Fahr. (5°2 C.).

From the other tent came the noise of the men jesting and talking, until the ash (pudding) came in, then the din was deafening. My Turkestan attendants considered themselves too good to eat with the temporarily engaged Taghliks; besides, they placed but little confidence in them, and in so doing they were right. The Taghliks therefore were not allowed inside the tent, but had to eat their meals in the open air. During the meal my men discussed the prospects of the journey, and in these discussions Parpi Bai was looked upon as our chief authority, for he had travelled across Tibet several times before. He was with Carey, and his murdered companion Dalgleish, with Bonvalot and Prince Henry of Orleans, with Dutreuil de Rhins, who was likewise murdered, and with Grenard; he had also taken part in some Russian expedition, though he could not tell me which it was. To have lighted upon him was therefore a godsend, for nobody knew the Tibetan plateau better than he did. It is true, evil tongues calumniated him, saying that he had a wife in more than one of the towns of East Turkestan, and that he deserted them in turn as soon as he grew tired of them. Islam Bai considered that the fact of Parpi Bai having been a follower of two Europeans who were murdered was not a good omen. However, all the time he was with me, the man did his duty in an exemplary manner, was always polite and dignified, and enjoyed great influence amongst the other men, not only on the ground of his experience, but also on account of his age: for he was close upon sixty, and the oldest man in the company. He told me how Bonvalot's caravan-animals gave up and died one after the other: and how Dutreuil de Rhins's caravan was decimated, and finally, after the attack at Tam Buddha, completely disorganized and scattered. These tales caused the other men to take alarm, and they began to think they might consider themselves lucky if they got through the perilous journey with their lives.

The spot beside the Mitt where we encamped was called by the Taghliks Laika or "the Clayey," and rightly so, for the river had there laid down wide-spreading deposits of soft miry clay. The Mountaineers were familiar with the country for about one day's journey beyond that point, and gave me the names of a few of the more conspicuous geographical features, but farther than that they do not venture towards the south. They told me that the transverse gorge, in which the Mitt pierces through the range which we crossed by the pass of Sarik-kol, is very deep and narrow, and quite impassable at all seasons of the year. It is, they said, choked with huge fragments of rock, which have crashed down the precipitous mountain-walls that shut it in, and amongst them the river foams violently along, almost filling the space from side to side. Farther to the west there was another pass, Pelazlik, which led to the upper Kok-muran, and to a district abundantly supplied with yeylaks, hence for that reason called Chimlik.

Higher up the valley of the Mitt there were *kans* or gold-mines, which however do not go deeper than the stature of a man. At that time there were gold-prospectors from Keriya working there. Fortune had not favoured them at Kopa, and ten days before they had moved on to the Mitt valley in the hope of better luck. They proposed to remain there a month longer. These prospectors visit the Mitt valley every year, but cannot work more than about six weeks in all, partly because they are unable to carry provisions with them to last a longer time, and partly because the ground begins to freeze early in September, and remains frozen right away till the beginning of the following June. The gold is obtained by washing in a rocker: but the yield does not seem to be very satisfactory, for the output only averaged about two tengeh (11*d.*) a day for each man. As there was not a blade of grass in the neighbourhood of the "mines," they sent their donkeys to Lama-chimin to graze, leaving the animals to look after themselves whilst they searched for gold.

The summer precipitation falls for the most part in solid form; in winter the quantity of snow is so great that both valley and pass are completely closed. At the time of our visit the weather was cool, so that the volume of the Mitt was not more than 140 cubic feet in the second. Lower down the stream was joined by several tributaries; and after a quiet sunny day it swells to a very considerable stream.

We had not been accustomed to the cold nights, and felt the first frost (minimum 27·1 Fahr. or −2·7 C.) that came very severely; but no sooner did the sun rise next morning than it was speedily warm again.

On the following morning we discovered that two other men had run away; and I had to find fault with the aksakal again for not keeping his men better under control. There were still thirteen Taghliks left, and they would be sufficient. The reason I wanted so many men was, that the caravan marched in five separate sections.

The camels, which travel at a slow pace, started first under the leadership of Hamdan Bai, and accompanied by two or three Taghliks. After them followed the horse caravan, carrying my personal belongings, such as the tent, kitchen utensils, etc.; this section was in charge of Islam Bai, Parpi Bai, and some of the other Turkestan men. They got over the ground quickest, and so soon took the lead. It was their duty to pick out a convenient place for camping in. The donkeys, which were entrusted to the rest of the men, started at the same time as the horses, but they were soon left behind by the latter, and generally came in at the same time as the camels. The sheep and goats made another caravan. I, Fong Shi, and one of the Taghliks, who knew something of the country a couple of days' journey ahead, brought up the rear; for I was incessantly occupied all day long in noting the contours of the ground on my map, in making geological and hypsometrical observations, sketching, and so forth. Going last, we came into camp some hours after the horse-caravan, and found the tent already erected and dinner bubbling and steaming in the cooking-pots over a fire made between two stones. It was splendid after the long, tiring ride to go straight into my tent, the floor spread with the costly carpet which I received as a gift from the commandant of Khotan just as I was leaving the town. Along one side of the tent stood my bed, made of furs, felts, and two or three cushions; on the other side my boxes, ranged in order. The moment the two tents came in sight. Yolldash, who always kept close at my horse's heels during the march, used to scamper off in advance and lie down on my bed. When I drew up to the camp, the cunning rascal came and stood in the tent opening, cheerfully wagging his tail, as if to welcome me, and impress upon me the fact that *he* was the real master of the house. But after that he had to content himself with the mandarin's carpet; for I took possession of the soft bed, and at once set about working out the notes I had made during the march, sketching in the itinerary of the day, entering the meteorological observations, labelling specimens, and so on.

Fong Shi promised excellently well, and I valued his companionship highly, for in respect of intellectual attainments a cultivated Chinaman is a long way the superior of a Mohammedan mollah. In my spare hours, and often indeed whilst on horseback, we pegged away at lessons in Chinese, conversing as much as my limited vocabulary would allow. The only drawback to having Fong Shi with me was, that the Mohammedans were jealous of him being so much in my company and sitting in my tent whilst giving me a lesson. They called him jestingly *kilyick-tura* or the Little Master, and made a fuss that, being faithful Mohammedans, they were asked to dress food for a heathen Chinese. Two or three times I was obliged to intervene to preserve peace between the parties.

CHAPTER LXXVII.

WE ENTER UNINHABITED REGIONS

AUGUST 7th. We had a long and difficult day's journey. At first we kept along the terrace between the river and the foot of the mountains, in which granite was now succeeded by dark clay-slates. Then we descended a steep hillside to the Kizil-su (the Red Water), which issued from a broad valley on the left. Leaving the broad open valley of the Mitt on the right, we struck up through the valley of Yappkaklik, which was also broad, and rose with a gentle ascent between the massive mountain-spurs which enclosed it. This valley too was joined by several side-glens. The first we passed was a so-called *bikar-yilga* or *cul-de-sac*, which was said to terminate in a wall of inaccessible *ak-chakkil-tagh*, or "white wild cliffs." The second led to a gold *kan* (mine), where the men had been so successful in their search for the precious metal, that they had obtained sufficient for the season, and were already on their way home.

The valley gradually curved round towards the east. Far away in the south was a perfect chaos of mighty mountain-peaks and snow-clad summits. The sai (the word *sai* means also a river-bed filled with stones) of Yappkaklik was traversed by a turbid stream, which gathered up numerous little brooks and torrents from the side-glens as it passed. It was itself very broad and shallow, and generally occupied at least one-half of the bottom of the valley, which consisted of soft humus, with a scanty growth of vegetation. The clay-slate cropped out only at the top of the enclosing mountains, and at their base, where the river when in flood had washed away the superincumbent soil. On the whole the mountains showed tolerably rounded outlines, and were covered with strata of soft earth and detritus.

As we advanced, the valley gradually contracted, and its surface became more broken and encumbered with gravel. The ascent to the pass of Yappkaklik grew steeper and steeper; nevertheless all the animals, including the camels, acquitted themselves wonderfully well. We fully expected to have to carry their loads up the last and steepest portion of the ascent, but happily none of them needed help even there.

I myself, with my two followers, reached the summit of the pass an hour before the camels and donkeys. Looking back we saw them far down below like little black dots struggling up and up. Towards the west the eye ranged over an unlimited sea of mountain-peaks and crests; whilst to the east also the view of the complex mountain landscape was almost equally grand. The valley on the other side of the pass, which stretched towards the east, was so choked with mud and gravel that it looked like a piece of blue-grey ribbon flung down across the yellow-grey mountains. The pass itself formed a moderately sharp crest, thickly strewn with disintegrated rocks and fragments of black clay-slate. In this respect it resembled the pass of Chokkalik, but was incomparably the easier. For the slopes were less steep, and the altitude lower, not exceeding 15,680 feet. We had splendid weather; the thermometer showed 57°6 Fahr. (14°2 C.).

The descent into the valley on the east was not difficult, although we passed several very narrow places in its upper part. But it soon widened out, and further down a little rivulet trickled along the middle of it.

On the terraced bank of the stream we came upon a grand specimen of the *khulan* (wild ass). Upon being surprised by the dogs, the animal fled down the valley with the speed of the wind, but kept stopping to look at us from a distance. We afterwards learned, that the men in charge of the horse-caravan, which preceded us, had seen a troop of about a score of khulans when they passed the same place. Islam Bai sent a shot after them; but one of the animals was cut off from the rest of the troop, and followed on behind the caravan.

The soft ground of the west side of the valley was grooved by a number of chapps or ravines. The east side was shut in by a mountain-spur of more solid consistency. This we crossed at its lower extremity by the little secondary pass of Kum-boyan (the Sand Pass), on the top of which was a cairn of stones built by the Taghliks. On the south of Kum-boyan we first passed the end of a side-glen, and then reached the upper valley of the Kara-muran, which flowed in a broad sai towards the north-west, and further down received from the east the stream that came from the Chokkalik-davan (pass).

A three-legged dog, which came with the Taghliks, was unable to go further than the foot of Kum-boyan, and as we rode away from him, his melancholy howls echoed with anything but a cheerful sound against the bare rocky walls.

It was quite dark when we reached the tent, which Islam Bai had pitched beneath a precipitous rock close beside the Kara-muran, now shrunk to an insignificant stream. There was not a blade of grass to give the animals; we had to feed them with maize and barley. The steep cliff was lit up by the ruddy reflection of the brightly blazing fires, the fuel being hard, namely dry *yappkak* plants collected during the march. All the men (except myself) had a headache and were drowsy after their long ride. Islam Bai and Fong Shi suffered terribly from mountain-sickness and were obliged to turn in at once. It was midnight before I had finished my day's work; the plotting of the day's march occupied five pages.

The night was perfectly still, but cold (minimum temperature 36°3 Fahr. or 2°4 C.); although not cold enough to pierce through our furs and felts.

Early in the morning a violent gale set in from the west, which, owing to the conformation of the rocks in the neighbourhood of our camp, developed locally into a cyclone. In an instant down went my tent flat with the ground. Fortunately my instruments were all packed up, so that none of them were injured.

I settled with five of the Taghliks, including the lying aksakal, and they returned home on foot, very glad at not being obliged to go further. We still had eight Mountaineers left with us.

The Taghliks called the neighbourhood where we encamped Bulak-bashi (the Head of the Spring). This was the last name I entered on the way to unknown Tibet, and indeed the last Turki place-name I wrote down during my Asiatic journey. In my journal I have called that place camp No. I.; and the place where we encamped beside the source of the Kara-muran on August 8th, camp No. II.

A small brook, one of the head-streams of the Kara-muran, flowed past the camp at Bulak-bashi; but after we advanced a little way up the valley it became dry. When the stream is low, the water evidently trickles along underneath the gravel, and bursts forth into daylight lower down. In contrast to the sharply accentuated transverse glens through which we had hitherto been travelling, the valley of the Kara-muran expanded towards its upper extremity; the surrounding mountains decreased in relative altitude, but still formed continuous chains of massive proportions, which stretched out their spurs into the valley. The stream was bordered on each bank by a conglomerate terrace, which diminished in elevation in proportion as we ascended. The sai was barren nearly all the way. The only vegetation was yappkak; and their thinly scattered tufts only grew in those spots which the water could reach. The roots were hard and tough. The floor of the valley was covered with fine compact gravel, easy to travel over. There was not the smallest vestige of a path, nor any evidence of human beings having been there before us. The last indication of the presence of our fellow-men was the cairn of stones on the pass of Kum-boyan.

After a while the conglomerate terraces came to an end altogether, and the sai was furrowed by a great number of small dry, shallow watercourses, all about the same size. I concluded that, when the spring floods come down, the valley is filled from side to side with a broad but shallow stream.

In proportion as the valley expanded, the view in advance widened out more and more. We were travelling through a Transitional region, like those I have already described as existing in the Pamirs—that is to say, a region representing the intermediate stage between a Peripheral region and a Highland Plateau region. Even in its upper part the valley was joined by several small subsidiary glens, and over the head of them, on our right, we caught every now and again glimpses of a mighty mountain-chain, its summits covered with snow. It was Arka-tagh or the Further Mountains—further as compared with the Altun-tagh or Astun-tagh (generally, but incorrectly, known as the Altyn-tagh), on the south of Lop-nor.

The landscape was monotonous in the extreme, a uniform grey, and absolutely barren, not a vestige of life, not a trace of even a khulan (wild ass). But then there was not a blade of vegetation anywhere. I saw no living creature, except a light-green lizard, which scuttled in amongst the gravel.

About ten o'clock in the morning a little snow fell; but the westerly gale continued to blow in fierce gusts all day long, driving clouds of dust and sand along the bed of the stream. Fortunately for us we had the wind right behind us. The drift-sand accumulated in sheltered corners behind the projecting crags, settling itself in the form of rudimentary dunes, though sometimes it amounted to nothing more than a mere yellow sprinkling of the ground.

In those high altitudes the abrasive power of the wind plays a very important part. The west wind, which is said to be the prevailing wind, sweeps away all the finer materials, leaving the gravel behind and exposed; until that in its turn becomes disintegrated and is swept away. The surface of the mountains was everywhere weathered and porous. It was evident there was an enormous difference between the temperature of the day and the temperature of the night; and this is the most destructive of all the disintegrating agencies. Next after it ranks the wind, which carries away all the finer particles of detritus. Precipitation occupies here the third place; it only falls during two months in the year—and not even then with absolute regularity—and falls in the form of rain.

This type of valley is characteristic. A transverse profile would give a straight base-line (the sai), with the mountains shooting vertically down upon it from both sides, without any talus at their feet.

The higher we ascended, the finer the gravel, until eventually its place was taken by coarse sand. The buran (storm) enveloped every feature of the landscape in its yellow haze. The horses speedily disappeared from sight. Even the camels and donkeys outpaced us that day, and their trail was already half obliterated as we rode along it. In the upper part of the valley we again turned towards the south. Immediately beside us the rock was black clay-slate; but right ahead were two isolated towering masses of red sandstone, forming a gigantic gateway, and towards them we steered our course. They marked the termination of the valley of Kara-muran. Beyond them lay a country of highly diversified features, much levelled down by denudation, a country corresponding to the trough-shaped catchment-basins in the mountain-chains of the Peripheral regions, only that this was shallow and of more than average width. The river did not originate in any definite head-stream, but was formed by a number of small rivulets or furrows (then dry), which converged from every direction upon the chief catchment-basin of the valley. The ground at the foot of the western mountains, that is on our right, was littered with huge fragments of rock fallen from the summits above, and strangely split and fractured, forming a series of crenelations. Seen from a distance, they looked like big red cubes, but when we came nearer they assumed the dimensions of houses of colossal size.

South of the twin mountains of red sandstone we rode across a boundless arena-like plain, covered with sand, which was rippled on the surface, though without any

ONE OF OUR TAGHLIKS

apparent tendency to form dunes. The plain was surrounded by circles of low hills and peaks still lower, the latter so irregularly disposed that I was unable to distinguish any continuous chain running in any definite direction. They were, there could be no doubt, the survivors of former mountain-chains, the portions which have resisted the tooth of denudation longest.

The gale still continued, and about four o'clock developed into a snow-buran. Our backs were lashed by the fine-grained snow, and the clouds raged off to the east, blotting out every feature of the landscape, so that we had some difficulty in keeping in the track of the caravan. But the ground had been warmed by the sun during the day, and the snow quickly melted. At length however we caught a glimpse of the white tents through the driving snow. The caravan had halted at the foot of a small isolated sandstone hill, where there was a tiny spring, which supplied us with water. A little scanty yappkak grew in the neighbourhood, and with that the animals had to be content. Otherwise it was a barren and desolate region, and the men's spirits fell, so much so that in the evening there was a lively dispute amongst our Taghliks as to which of them should go with us all the way until we again came to inhabited districts. They all wanted to go back; those inhospitable regions had no attraction whatever for them.

August 9th. As usual the night was still; the minimum temperature was 19°4 Fahr. (– 7° C.). In the morning my ink was frozen to a lump of ice. Although it was only the beginning of August, yet we were in the middle of winter!

My friend Fong Shi was in a very queer way. He complained of splitting headache and sleeplessness, and was unable to retain on his stomach what he ate. At his urgent entreaty I agreed that, if he was not better today, he should go back.

Nobody ran away during the night, so that the caravan was able to start again in the accustomed order of march. The sheep and two goats, which were driven by a man specially appointed for the purpose, travelled well. The goats were very useful in several ways. They always went at the head of the flock, and so incited the slower-footed sheep to keep up with them; and every morning they gave me a cup of milk to my tea. The increasing cold made a change necessary in the arrangement of my tent. The small projection which I dubbed the boudoir was taken in, so that we could draw the side opposite the opening closer together, and so retain the heat more effectually. The ends of the tent-covering, which hung down all round, were folded in underneath the carpets and kept in place by the packing-cases, thus shutting out all draughts, whilst the tent stood as firm as a rock even in a stiff gale.

We were now travelling east-south-east across the slightly undulating plain. So far as we could see, the solid rock nowhere cropped out, though there were several low hills of gravel and sand. Immediately in front of us was an insignificant crest, on the left a spur of the Astun (Altyn)-tagh, and on the right another low range. The surface was so soft and loose that the horses sank in over the fetlocks, and so level that, had it not been for the small dry rain-channels, it would have been difficult to tell in which direction it sloped. To make it worse for the animals, it was damp from the snow. Then on the east came a series of level tablelands, backed by mountain-ridges in the far distance.

The watercourses all inclined towards the west, until we came to a little lake about two hundred yards in diameter, probably one of the sources of the Kara-muran, though for the time being it was cut off from all connection with it. But the water-marks on its shore seemed to indicate that, when the rains come, it rises, and then sends off a current towards the west-north-west. The water was slightly saline, and the basin into which it was gathered had a white ring round it, about two feet above its then existing level.

From that point we deviated towards the south-east, and struck up a small transverse glen that pierced the range on our right. There the black clay-slate once more predominated. Nevertheless the naked rocks were very rarely visible. All the hills were smothered under loose *débris*, sometimes yellow sand, sometimes pulverised red sandstone, and sometimes again fine black powdered clay-slate, looking in the distance like coal-dust or soot. We crossed over quite a number of minor ramifications of the mountains, as well as the barren sais between them. These last now inclined towards the north-east, and belonged to the river system of the Cherchen-daria; but they were all dry, and the men were afraid we should not find water that afternoon.

We soon ascertained that the sais converged upon one main glen, dry however like the rest, which stretched towards the east. Seeing that the Arka-tagh was immediately to the south of us, and that the route we were following led us over one mountain-spur after another, we concluded it would be wiser to alter our course for the south, and endeavour to cross the Arka-tagh, so as to get upon the Tibetan plateau with as little delay as possible. We had gone but a short distance in the new direction when we discovered a small spring, and there, to make sure of water, we decided to halt. Camp No. III. was totally devoid of life, save for an occasional abstemious yappkak, and at their tassel-like tufts the hungry animals snatched ravenously. The water trickled out of the spring drop-wise, and a few yards lower down disappeared in the sand. But the men dug a trench, and when sufficient water had collected, brought up the animals to drink one after the other in their proper turns. That day we travelled thirteen miles; on the two preceding days the distances were sixteen and a half and eighteen miles respectively.

August 10th. My journal for this day begins thus:—"Fong Shi still in a condition of high fever, with pulse at 120 and an excruciating headache." Indeed he looked as though death had laid his grisly hand upon him, and declared that the further he went the worse he got. I resolved therefore to dismiss him. Islam Bai too was afraid the man would die if we took him any further, or his illness might compel us to make a long halt, which in that barren desert might prove disastrous. So long as he was well, Fong Shi was a first-rate companion; but to have to listen to his constant complaints, as I had during the last few days, was very wearisome. But if we let him go back, how should we manage when we came to China? It was not an inviting prospect to have to travel through China without an interpreter. Luckily I had profited so well from Fong Shi's lessons, that I already knew the most important vocables, and the rest I could no doubt learn later on if it were really necessary.

The engagement of Fong Shi had turned out a big mistake. He had already drawn three months' salary in advance; and now I had to pay for his return, by giving him a horse and provisions for the journey. Further than that, I gave him a supply of quinine capsules and a fur coat, and sent Roslakh with him to act as his escort, and help him if he should fall ill on the road. Upon reaching Dalai-kurgan he intended to rest for a while. He was however grateful and touched when we parted. Thus the young Chinaman's proud dream of one day riding through the gates of Peking and beholding the palace (yamen) of his fabulously mighty emperor, as well as of perhaps securing, through my recommendation, a lucrative post, and finally, though by no means last in his estimation, of exchanging the Turki wife he had left behind in Khotan for a Chinese bride—this proud dream was pricked at the foot of Arka-tagh. Sadly and silently he stood alone in the desert, gazing after us, as we continued our way towards the far distant goal of his youthful ambition.

During the night it snowed smartly, and the ground was still damp when we marched down the little glen in which we had encamped. It was now arranged, that the horse-caravan, which moved the quickest, should determine the direction of our marches. I ordered Islam Bai to keep on as straight as circumstances would allow for the south, our object being to cross over the Arka-tagh; beyond that he was left free to choose his own course. But that was principally dependent upon the contour of the ground: he was obliged to choose the road that presented fewest hindrances to the advance of our caravan animals. I never had any occasion to find fault with his selection of the road; for he had a keen, sharp eye, and was a good judge of how much the camels could do.

The glen gradually widened, and at the same time opened out upon an undulating tableland. At its lower extremity there was, on the left, a particularly picturesque piece of mountain scenery—an agglomeration of regularly formed truncated cones, with grooved sides. The cones themselves consisted partly of red sandstone, partly of a species of conglomerate, extraordinarily hard and of a brick-red colour, resembling breccia. Their apexes were formed by a horizontal layer of coal-black tuff, having the same level throughout. The tuff-caps protected the

ARKA-TAGH, SEEN FROM THE TIBETAN PLATEAU (SOUTH)

underlying stone from disintegration, and had been the means of preserving the isolated beacon-like pyramids, so that they commanded the whole of the tableland, being visible to a great distance. The earth around their bases was strewn with fragments of tuff of different sizes, looking like black spots on a red background; and as we advanced further, we observed fragments of the same rock, but less black in colour, scattered a long distance over the red sand. The tuff, which was inclining to violet, contained an abundance of vesicles, was almost as porous as a sponge, and rang sharply when struck with the hammer. Several hours later we could still see the fiery red gleam of the curious mountain-cones, with their raven-black caps.

On the south side of the Arka-tagh we encountered several similar groups of isolated table-mountains.

CHAPTER LXXVIII.

AMONGST THE SPURS OF THE ARKA-TAGH

ALONG the foot of these mountains was a dry sai, running towards the east; it was of large size, but probably only carried water after heavy downfalls of rain or snow. On the south-east it was bordered by a ridge in the shape of a spoon turned alternately up and down—a type of surface-contour which we often met with afterwards. Beyond the ridge came a small depression, the bottom of which was white with salt, although now dry. These temporary salt-pans likewise belonged to the typical characteristics of the region.

Often however the ground was perfectly level, so that we journeyed across a veritable plateau. The view in every direction was unlimited, the horizon in the far, far distance being bounded by relatively low hills; but there was nowhere a glimpse of either snowy peak or glacier.

The atmosphere was pure, so that we were able to see the horse-caravan like little black dots a long, long distance in advance. I used them as fixed-points for drawing three-mile base-lines for my route-determinations. The only vegetable growth that bid defiance to the niggardly soil was yappkak. There were however numerous indications that *boghe* (antelopes) visited that region, at any rate occasionally. Islam Bai made many attempts to stalk these swift-footed animals, but never once succeeded in catching them napping.

The sky was for the most part thickly veiled with clouds, white and beautiful, and so soft and plastically formed that they looked like living creatures, as they sailed slowly and silently past us, close down near to the earth, but permitting occasional glimpses of the pure blue firmament to peep through. Upon climbing a small mountain-ridge, we perceived a lake in the west-south-west ensconced between two low ridges. The lake itself was too much out of our direct line of march to be worth a visit; but we crossed over the gully which formed its eastward continuation. At this place the red species of conglomerate before mentioned, with granite, and after the granite green slates, occurred in strata disposed almost vertically. They did not however project more than a foot or so above the broken surface of the detritus with which the ground was strewn, but were visible from a great distance, framing in the landscape with red and black lines.

Then we rode up another watercourse, still moist from the last fall of snow, and came out upon yet another ridge, higher and broader than the last. From its slightly rounded summit a view as welcome as it was unexpected burst upon our sight. Before us lay a gentle hollow, green with yeylaks (pasture), thin of course, but all the same extremely welcome to our beasts, which had tasted no green fodder for four days. The horses in particular looked pined, and neighed continuously for grass. Emin Mirza, a capable Taghlik, who since the departure of Fong Shi acted as my secretary, pointed out with well-grounded surprise, that the caravan was going on past the hollow. There was, it is true, a little pool close by, but its water was salt, and Islam was principally concerned to find fresh water, the chief necessary of life. The grass was so thin and short and fine, that it would only have mocked the animals' patience to let them graze there. That the place was known to the boghe (antelopes) was evident from their numerous spoor. The voles too lived upon the roots of the grass. We saw their runs, but none of the animals themselves. On our right there was another low ridge, and in one of its gullies a thicker growth of grass; it had however been cropped close by the denizens of the desert. But moss thrived in the moisture which oozed out of a spring, beside which the tent was already pitched. That day we travelled fifteen miles.

During the day there had been a fresh breeze from the north-west. I could not have done without a suit of warm clothing in my saddle-straps, for the weather was extremely fickle and changeable. So long as it was still and clear, it was hot enough in the heat of the sun to broil you; but the very next moment, if a cloud happened to obscure the sun, or a violent gust of wind swept down upon you, you shivered and flew to your furs.

Next morning three men were ill, and begged that we would rest there a day, at camp No. IV. I agreed to their request all the more willingly in that the six days' continuous hard travelling had exhausted all the caravan animals; and as we had plenty of both water and grass, it was a very suitable spot to stay in. The only thing of which there was a short supply was fuel. The tufts of yappkak grew isolated and at wide intervals apart; but the men went out and gathered all they could find in the vicinity. It snowed all night and all the next morning, so that the ground was white; but immediately the sun rose, the snow began to melt, and it melted with marvellous rapidity, owing to the dryness of the atmosphere. The snow was hard and granular, and rattled vivaciously upon the tent felts.

The rest did us all good. Peace and silence reigned all round the camp; and the animals strayed to a great distance in their search for more nourishing grass.

During the course of the day the sick list grew longer. Most of the men complained of headache. Even Islam Bai kept his bed and gave vent to melancholy plaints; and as he was caravan-bashi or baz (caravan-leader), this cast down the spirits of the other men. The weather was not very encouraging. The sky was thick with clouds, and dark and gloomy. Snow fell with but short intermission throughout the day, so that the ground was white; and after three o'clock it froze. Add to this that a full-blooded west wind was racing past, and it will be evident that there was no temptation to open-air exploration. I preferred to sit still in my tent, wrapped in my furs, and busy myself with back work or reading.

We slaughtered a sheep, and although there were so many of us, the meat went a very long way, for mountain-sickness takes the appetite. I myself had lost all relish for mutton; the meat never became properly tender, no matter how long it was boiled. Even the rice-pudding (pillau) was not palatable: the grains of the rice refused to soften and swell. Thus there was nothing for us but the everlasting thin mutton broth, with tea and bread as hard as a stone. Our fare was the same at every meal, twice a day, and at last I became so tired of it, that the approach of meal-times made me almost shudder; and I only recovered my usual equanimity when I had got the meal done with and my pipe lighted. Otherwise I was getting on capitally, scarcely knew that I was at an altitude of 16,300 feet above the level of the sea. The only things which made me aware of the fact were shortness of breath and quickened beating of the heart when I walked or underwent physical exertion. At night I was so muffled up in furs and felts that I often woke up gasping for breath and with a disagreeable feeling of anxiety weighing upon me; but the headache from which I suffered the first day or two had entirely disappeared.

About sunset the weather improved. The thick black clouds drifted away to the east, revealing the intense blue sky above our heads. In the west there was a ruddy glow like the reflection of a distant prairie fire, and the flanks of the mountains nearest us were illumined with vivid reds. But to the north the mountains were still enshrouded in thick clouds, from which magnificent lightnings flashed all the evening.

On the morning of August 12th the gully beside which our camp was pitched was filled with a torrent of muddy water—yesterday's snow melted. But it was only the lower portion that was thawed by the sun; the upper portion was still frozen. During the day's march we passed several brooks of clear water.

The gully led up to a small secondary pass through one of the ramifying arms of the Arka-tagh. The prevailing rock was a fine-grained red clay-slate. The yeylaks became fewer and poorer in quality; nevertheless there were still plenty of antelopes and hares, and occasionally we observed the droppings of khulans (wild asses).

The pass crossed, we entered a glen of strongly marked contours, about two and a half miles broad, which curved round from the west-south-west towards the east. Its bottom was much diversified and destitute of water, nor was there a vestige of grass. At that point there did not appear to be any suitable pass for crossing over the Arka-tagh. We therefore turned and followed the glen towards the east, for in that direction the country was open. The mountain-spurs fell away on both sides; but in the background there rose a lofty chain of the grandest dimensions, glittering from top to bottom in the silver mail of its snows. Indeed they were so brilliantly bright that at first we took them for white clouds on the horizon. It was the continuation of Arka-tagh. As I have just said, we were marching towards the east, so that we had the Arka-tagh partly on our right, partly in front of us. Thus the range makes a slight curve to the east-north-east.

Farther, leaving the glen on our left, we began to ascend the lower slopes of the Arka-tagh, crossing over innumerable ravines, most of them with a little water in the bottom. Towards the north the country was quite open, an extensive undulating tableland, with not so much as a hill to restrict the view, but bounded in the extreme distance by a lofty chain overtopped by several snowy peaks. That was the southern aspect of Tokkuz-davan.

In the Arka-tagh we had constantly in view a stupendous double-peaked mountain. Hour after hour we rode towards it, without seeming to get a bit nearer. Our next concern was to find a suitable camping-ground with pasturage; we were in no anxiety about water that day. We pitched the tents, after a march of eighteen miles, by the side of a large brook, where the grass was pretty fair. The caravan animals still stood it very well; but the men, especially Islam Bai, were only in a poor way.

We were compelled to spend August 13th and 14th at camp No. V., and for a distressing reason. At first the men tried to make out that the animals needed rest; but on the morning of the 13th Islam Bai was reported to me as being seriously ill. The poor fellow had been distressed at the idea of my losing so much as a single day on his account, and for that reason bade the other men throw the blame upon the beasts. He was in a high fever, with high pulse, palpitation of the heart, and headache; but he did not believe it was mountain-sickness, for he coughed up blood, and was so weak that he could not lift his hand to his mouth.

In my journal are these words: "Islam begged the other men to try and persuade me to go on again in the morning, and leave him behind with two of the Taghliks, who also were unwell. He proposed to hand over the boxes and keys, as well as the control of the provisions and ammunition, to Parpi Bai. If he got better, he would try to work his way back over the Tokkuz-davan to Cherchen, and thence home *viâ* Kashgar. I gave him quinine and morphia and applied a mustard plaster, to draw the blood away from his head. After that he slept several hours. I am very uneasy about the poor fellow. His case does not look very hopeful; he has never been ill before. It would be terrible to lose him. I should then be lonely indeed. He has been with me from the very beginning, has shared all dangers and privations with me, has always borne the burden and heat of the day, and been a real help to me. It always fell to him to see after the preparation and equipment of the caravan; and it was he who engaged trustworthy men to help, who bought the provisions and took charge of them, and generally kept a prudent and provident eye upon everything. Islam was worth any ten other men; in short his loss would be irreparable. Yet there he lies, like a broken-down old man, moaning as if on the point of death. It would be hard for him to be taken away now, on our last journey — the seventh we have taken together — after sacrificing his home in Osh for three long years in order to accompany me.

"I am encountering difficulties in my attempt to penetrate into Northern Tibet. Our camp is like a hospital; it is impossible to travel with a troop of invalids. Under such circumstances a man is tied hand and foot. He has no alternative but to leave the incapable behind, after first seeing that they shall be properly protected and cared for, or else—abandon the journey. This last alternative is one of which I have a horror. I would rather perish than turn back. I *must* explore those unknown highland regions which stretch away south from the Arka-tagh. How delightful it is up here in the bright, fresh mountain air, amongst these constantly changing scenes, as compared with the monotonous deserts, with their grey skies, their close sultry atmosphere, their scorpions, ticks, and gnats, and dearth of water! I revel in the thought that I have left those inhospitable tracts behind me. But my men are afraid of the silent mountains; they long to get back to the lowlands.

"Besides being unfortunate in itself, Islam Bai's illness is attended with another mischievous effect. When the other men see that their caravan-bashi (leader) is broken down, they lose heart and their spirits fail, and they begin to think we have death in the camp.

"My confidence however in some degree keeps up their courage. They are pleased when I visit the invalids, and they like to come to me to talk over our plans for the future. Nevertheless they do not talk much; their cheerful songs are silent."

Apart from this, the days we rested there were uneventful. At noon the brook swelled considerably, and turned a brick-red colour; but towards evening it sank again, at the same time clearing back to its pristine purity. The atmosphere was inconceivably pure and transparent, so that the contours and every detail of even the furthest distant mountains stood out sharply. I sent out pioneers towards the south-east. They reported the existence of a deep valley traversed by a stream, which Hamdan Bai thought might be the Pattkaklik (the Muddy), a tributary of the Cherchen-daria; and he believed it was by its upper extremity that Littledale reached the pass by which he crossed the Arka-tagh. Hamdan Bai ought to know, for he was one of Littledale's company; it subsequently proved however that he was wrong in his surmise.

Parpi Bai believed we should come to plenty of grass in a fortnight. The miserable stuff at Camp No. V. was so bitter, that the horses would never have eaten it, had they not been driven to it by hunger. There were no traces of even khulans: it was evident they knew of other and better pasture-grounds.

Under these circumstances Parpi Bai voted for making a move as soon as possible; for if we stayed there any longer, the horses would fall ill. Two of them were looking queer already; they would not eat, but lay quiet in one place all day long. The others however, as well as the donkeys and camels, were in good condition, considering the hard marches we had made. We still had corn sufficient to last them thirty days, and provisions for ourselves for two months and a half.

In the evening I gave Islam Bai half a grain of morphia. He again got a good sleep, and next morning felt very much better. He succeeded in swallowing a little bread and tea, got up, and walked about a short time wrapped in furs. He hoped he should be able to follow us next day. The weather was disagreeable. Between twelve and four o'clock it hailed, and after that we had a smart shower of rain. Whilst it was hailing the temperature (four o'clock) was 60°8 Fahr. (16° C.); but the rain brought it down to 48°2 Fahr. (9° C.) in the course of a few minutes. The absolute altitude was 16,300 feet.

Every evening just about sunset I had the pleasure of seeing the camels come forward to the tent, slowly, with rocking humps, solemn as judges, to get their daily measure of maize, which was poured out on a piece of sailcloth spread on the ground. Then they knelt down round it and ate up the corn ravenously; but their meagre diet did not make them ill-tempered.

CHAPTER LXXIX.

SEARCHING FOR A PASS

AUGUST 15th. Happily Islam Bai was so much better that we were able to start at the usual time; though one of the sick horses died, and was left behind as a memorial of our visit. It was the first that perished, and alas! was to be followed by too many of the others.

The sky was flecked with fleecy clouds, which brushed against the tops of the mountains, imparting a flattened appearance to the landscape. The "roof seemed to be so low" in the east that you felt as though you could not walk upright under the clouds.

We continued to follow the broad and regular longitudinal valley which ran along the northern foot of the Arka-tagh. It was almost level, or had at any rate an almost imperceptible slope. The white double peak gleamed like a beacon at its eastern extremity. The Arka-tagh on our right was hidden by its own outlying ranges. On our left too there was now a lofty chain, though free from snow. The longitudinal valley was crossed by a deeply incised transverse gorge, filled with conglomerates, through which a mountain-brook had carved a deep channel, now containing a little water. Its sides were a reddish colour, from a brick-red, slaty species of rock, but its bottom was tightly packed with fine gravel of green crystalline slates, granite, and porphyry, probably rocks which prevail in the higher regions of the Arka-tagh. This gigantic trough, which caught up several little streams on its way across the longitudinal valley, cut through the mountain-chain on the north (which now completely hid the Tokkuz-davan) by an extremely narrow portal, and on the other side probably bent away towards the north-east.

The longitudinal valley became narrower and steeper. We travelled along the left bank of the stream, and had to cross over a long series of *chapps* (ravines). The largest of them, thirty to thirty-five feet deep, with perpendicular sides in many places, contained a little water; and there was a scanty supply of grass in the immediate neighbourhood. It was therefore a lucky accident that, just when we reached the spot, the weather forced us to stop and encamp, notwithstanding we had done only a very short day's march (ten miles).

About noon thick clouds gathered in the west and raced at a terrific pace towards the east; and yet close down upon the earth the wind blew towards the north-east. They speedily encircled us, and closed in upon us. In the east alone there was a patch of glorious blue, but it was rapidly dwindling. On every other side we were hemmed in by dark threatening clouds of a steel-blue colour. Then we heard a faint soughing and moaning behind us. The sound approached nearer, waxed louder. The wind began to blow furiously from the west; and down upon us burst a hailstorm of unparalleled violence, pelting the earth and the mountain-sides till they appeared to smoke again. All at once we were enshrouded in gloom. The thunder crashed deafeningly, and, as it seemed, immediately above our heads; but there was not a single flash of lightning. The landscape was blotted out by the thick driving hail; we could see nothing but the white line of hailstones along the ground close at our feet. They were no bigger than grains of maize, but the wind drove them with such force that I distinctly felt them through my fur coat and cap. Under this undeserved punishment the horses became restive. We were obliged to stand still for a quarter of an hour or so just where we were; it was impossible to see where we were going. There we sat in our saddles, with our backs turned towards the wind, and our cloaks drawn up over our ears, whilst the hail rattled about us. In two or three minutes the country, lately so smiling, sunny, and peaceful, had put on the garb of the Polar Regions: the earth was as white as chalk.

For fully an hour we were unable to proceed; but as soon as the worst of the squall was past, we dismounted and made haste to get up the tents. The hail continued a full hour longer, and lay an inch thick on the ground. It all disappeared however before the evening; for, as usual, the hail was followed by pouring rain. We managed therefore to get thoroughly wet through before the tents were up. The poor beasts had to stand out in the freezing cold. But the camels did not mind it in the least; they set to work upon the grass.

On 16th August we started early. It was windy and cold, and the sky was covered with clouds. About seven o'clock they broke up and scattered; but not for long, for they soon began to pack together again. It was not at all easy to tell where they came from. At first you would observe nothing more than a mere wisp of a cloud; which would grow bigger and bigger with extraordinary rapidity, and finally invade every inch of the sky.

The preceding evening I sent some of the men up the ravine beside which we encamped. They came back and reported, that at its upper extremity it was steep and narrow, and choked with stones. We thought it best therefore to continue along the latitudinal valley. We therefore crossed over the ravine, though not without much difficulty, and advanced over hummocky ground and past a little lake of about 270 yards in diameter. It contained clear, fresh water; and on its surface were about a dozen wild-geese, resting in their long autumn flight to India.

We now began to be conscious of the fact that we were ascending. Yeylaks occurred, but in thinner and thinner patches. The valley was entirely shut in by the lofty mountain-ranges on both sides. The rainfall off their flanks and from out their side-glens was gathered into a stream, which lower down united with that beside which we had pitched camp No. VI. We were at length approaching the upper extremity of the longitudinal valley. Its culmination was marked by a small depression, dry however; and on the other side the water flowed towards the north-east. We turned off towards the east-south-east up a side-glen, which, like the latitudinal valley, was shut in between two big spurs, and, again like it, was traversed by a little brook, which ran so close to the cliffs on the right that it had exposed the green clay-slates.

But all this while we were simply marching at random; we did not know how far this side-glen would allow us to advance. It gradually inclined however to the south-east, skirting a huge mountain peak on the right. When we reached the foot of the mountain, we were again overtaken by a heavy hailstorm, followed by rain and snow, but not so bad as to prevent us from continuing. We now came to expect this sort of weather about one hour after noon, no matter how bright the morning might have been.

In the thick of the storm we approached another tolerably level watershed, which, like the former one, sent off its precipitation to both the east and the west. I now began to understand more definitely, that in the region through which we were travelling, the Arka-tagh system consisted of a number of parallel ranges, strangely ill-provided with transverse valleys. The latitudinal valleys between the ranges we were able to traverse without any difficulty. The side-glens only permitted us to creep the merest trifle further towards the south.

After journeying eastwards for about an hour, we struck up one of these side-glens; but it soon became very steep. The ground in the entrance of the glen showed a curious formation: it consisted of fine detritus, intersected by a number of tiny rivulets which led nowhere, and was consequently so soft that the animals sank in it over their hoofs, and this tried them a good deal.

Meanwhile we plodded on up the glen, which rapidly contracted; and at its upper extremity mounted a steep pass, which we hoped was situated in the main chain of the Arka-tagh. It cost us a good deal of hard labour to get the horses up. Yet no sooner had we accomplished that than we were enveloped in clouds, and assailed by a gale of snow and hail. and wrapped in an impenetrable mist. We were unable to see which way to go, and yet I was reluctant to lose the opportunity which the pass afforded of obtaining a general view of the complicated and bewildering mountain region in which we were entangled. After a short consultation, we decided to rest where we were, on the top of the pass, which attained an altitude of 17,235 feet. That day we had travelled 16½ miles.

The camp was hastily arranged. It was raw and cold, and very disagreeable. The least exertion brought on palpitation of the heart and shortness of breath. The wind cut through everything, and the hail swept through the pass with merciless violence. There was no grass, not a particle of anything to make a fire of, and the water had to be fetched from a crevice in the rocks a long way down the pass. But about five o'clock it cleared up sufficiently to let us see, away in the south and south-west, a sharp snowy crest of some reddish rock; but there did not appear to be any practicable pass over it. The pass upon which we were encamped only led over another spur of the Arka-tagh. We had therefore climbed it to no purpose. Immediately south of it however was a deep and precipitous ravine, the gathering trench of rivulets that poured down from an inextricable labyrinth of mountain-chains and peaks, and their connecting ridges. Towards the east however we believed we could distinguish a slight notch in the Arka-tagh, and there was a latitudinal valley running straight in that direction. All around us was a perfect chaos of mountains, some raven black, others brick-red or green, the highest of all white with snow. Relatively they were of no great elevation: we seemed to be at the same altitude as most of them.

But the vast ocean of mountains was soon wreathed in thick clouds and a driving snowstorm. Away they flew in a mad race over the mountain-tops—those dense heavy masses of cloud, trailing the fringes of their snowy draperies along the rugged earth, and leaving ribbons of white snow behind them. The thunder crashed so that our ears tingled; the heaviest peals made the ground tremble, and the clouds were slashed by flashes of vivid lightning. Our position on the summit of the pass was not free from anxiety. I had the tent put up in such a position that the crest of the range was thirty feet or so higher than the tops of the tent-poles.

That evening we had to wait a long time for the camels and donkeys; in fact, I sent two or three of the men back to look for them. They came up at dusk; their drivers had experienced considerable trouble in getting them up the pass. My supper was more meagre than usual. We boiled the water for tea with one of the packing-cases, which we could manage to do without. We took counsel with the Taghliks, and decided to continue in the same direction, down the steep eastern side of the pass. To attempt to travel southwards was a sheer impossibility.

The moon shone with dazzling brilliancy and was encircled by a magnificently beautiful halo—a disc of vivid yellow edged with violet. But the queen of the night soon withdrew behind the clouds, and the winds roared through the pass from every point of the compass. The night however was still, but cold (minimum temperature, 22°3 Fahr. or −5°4 C.), so cold that I could not get warm until I crept into my nest of furs.

In the morning there was nothing to make a fire of; so I had to content myself with cocoa made with half-melted ice. It would have been a splendid drink in the hot desert, but up amongst the chilly mountains it was rather too cool. The camel and donkey caravans started very early in the morning, and we found out that they had gone down the same way we came up the afternoon before. Leaving Islam Bai, the caravan-leader, to see that the camels and donkeys recovered the right road, I and Emin Mirza went on down in the direction I had ordered the night before. After an hour's ride we came upon the trail of the donkeys and sheep. They had merely gone another way round the mountain upon which we spent the night. The camels however had been taken in a wrong direction; but we hoped their drivers would soon find out their mistake and come in search of us.

We therefore continued along the latitudinal valley we had travelled up the day before, that is, still towards the east. Hitherto we had observed certain characteristics common to all these latitudinal valleys of the Arka-tagh. They all received their greatest number of tributaries, as well as their largest, from the south, and their smallest, if any at all, from the north. Moreover the streams which coursed down them leaned strongly towards the low mountain-chain which shut them in on the north; and its slopes were in every case steeper than those of the chain which fenced the valleys on the south. On the other hand, the latter were richer in detritus; the bare rock being frequently exposed on the flanks of the northern range.

After going about eight and a half miles, we perceived our donkeys grazing in the distance, on a high terrace which overhung the left bank of the crystal brook we were following. There, amid a scene of extraordinary beauty, we pitched our tents, a process which demanded every man we had, for there was a fierce nor'-wester raging. The passable grass, coming after the enforced fast of the preceding day, rendered a rest imperative for the animals. When, late in the day, Hamdan Bai came in with the camels, he recognized the locality. Only the year before Littledale had encamped barely ten minutes to the north. He had travelled from East Turkestan, and halted there for a few days in order to search for a more westerly pass over the Arka-tagh. But his search had been as unsuccessful as ours. He then tried the valley which opened out on the east, and found there an easy pass, which led to a small lake on the south of the Arka-tagh. We proposed to profit from Littledale's discovery, for Hamdan Bai undertook to guide us to the pass by which the English traveller crossed the range.

The 18th August was consequently given up to rest. I went no further than Littledale's camp. There were still signs of a fire having been made between some soot-grimed stones, and the ground in the vicinity bore numerous traces of his caravan animals, so that we now had plenty of fuel. It was even possible to discern a sort of pathway which the animals had trodden, and by the side of the brook was an old shirt that somebody had flung away. At this spot the streams which drained both the eastern and the western portions of the latitudinal valley united, and pierced the northern range by

SCENE OF LITTLEDALE'S CAMP,

NOT FAR FROM MY CAMP NO. VIII. IN NORTHERN TIBET

a picturesque gorge. The neighbourhood was a vast quarry of black clay-slate. Weathered on the surface, it split into thin laminæ, and alternated with hard crystalline schists; both varieties of rock being very much folded. At noon the confluent stream had a volume of 210 cubic feet in the second; the water was as bright as glass and babbled along with a cheerful noise, tumbling over or foaming round the water-worn stones in its bed. Our camp was pitched in a sharp loop of the winding stream, and as it were upon a sort of little peninsula, skirted by the brook which drained the western part of the latitudinal valley. The volume of water was lowest in the morning, and increased as the day wore on, so that it reached its maximum in the evening. But during the night it sank again, and became edged with a thin fringe of ice.

The cold made itself felt immediately the sun set, the thermometer falling to five or six degrees above freezing-point. But it was the everlasting wind that was so tiring, and that made the tent cold, because it did not subside until after darkness set in. The nights were always calm and bright. Owing to the active radiation, the uppermost layer of the earth invariably froze; but just as invariably it thawed again immediately the sun rose in the morning.

That night the minimum temperature was 12°2 Fahr. (−11° C.). The altitude above sea-level was 16,675 feet.

CHAPTER LXXX.

THE DECEITFUL TAGHLIKS

THAT evening we made an arrangement with the Taghliks. Three of them, after being paid for the time they had served, were to return home by the same route we had come. Two of the others were to go with us over the Arka-tagh and were then to be dismissed, whilst the rest were to accompany us, like my other attendants from East and West Turkestan, until we again reached inhabited regions, wherever that might be.

The last section of the Taghliks, namely those who were to go with us right through, begged me to advance them the half of their wages. I saw no reason why I should not grant their request, and I paid them. Some of the men from East Turkestan, whose families lived in Keriya and Khotan, sent some considerable portions of their wages by the three Taghliks who were going back, and who agreed to give, before they started the next morning, written acknowledgments of the moneys they had received, as well as pledges that they would deliver them to the proper parties.

This business satisfactorily settled, we all went to bed. The Taghliks slept, as they usually did, in the open air, protected by a rampart of maize sacks, saddles, and other *impedimenta* of travel.

Imagine therefore my men's surprise when they awoke at five o'clock on the morning of August 19th and found that every Taghlik, except my secretary Emin Mirza, had disappeared. Islam Bai woke me at once and told me what had happened. We held a council of war. My men had slept like logs all night, and had heard no suspicious sounds. They believed the Taghliks ran away about midnight, no doubt hoping that the long start would secure them against pursuit. Besides, they knew that in a region so ill provided with grass as that we were travelling through, every day was precious. When we examined our stores, we discovered that ten donkeys, two horses, and a goodly supply of bread, flour, and maize were missing. The worst feature was, that the Taghliks had drawn half their wages in advance, and had taken the money of the other men as well, without leaving any written acknowledgments. It was evident the flight had been planned beforehand, and they had deliberately set themselves to get as much money into their possession as possible. But we were all amazed, that they had been able to get away without making any noise. One of the men recollected hearing the dogs bark furiously about midnight, but he thought at the time, that they were barking at the camels, which were accustomed to stray away from the camp, flitting about like shadows in the darkness.

But we were not going to be cheated so easily. We examined the ground in the neighbourhood of the camp, to find out which way the thieves had gone. It seemed they had departed in ones and twos in different directions, and made for a common rendezvous at the foot of the mountains on the north, so as to mislead us at the outset if we attempted to pursue after them. Two or three of them walked; a couple rode the horses; the rest were mounted on donkeys. But seeing that several of the donkeys were pretty well done up, the runaways would scarcely be able to march very fast. I therefore ordered, that they should be instantly pursued, and at all costs, by fair means or by foul, should be brought back to camp No. VIII. They had deceived us so shamefully, that they deserved punishment. Parpi Bai, who was a capital fellow, took command of the pursuing division, which consisted of Hamdan Bai and Islam of Keriya. Armed with rifles and revolvers, and mounted on the freshest horses we had, they followed the trail over the pass in the northern mountains, and rapidly disappeared from sight. If the runaways refused to come with them, my men were instructed to fire off half-a-dozen shots, but were not on any account to injure any of the Taghliks.

We who remained behind in camp had nothing to do but wait patiently till the men came back. The day passed. The night passed. No sign of the pursuers' return. I began to fear they had taken the wrong road, in which case the second error would be worse than the first. But at last, at five o'clock on the next afternoon, they turned up, their horses dead beat, with the following tale :—

At a brisk trot they followed up the trail all day and all the next evening. Their horses were tolerably fresh, and had no loads to carry except their riders. They passed our last two camps, Nos. VII. and VI., and a little way beyond the second perceived, about midnight, a fire burning in the distance. They rode towards it. It had been made, as they expected, by our runaways. The two horses and the donkeys were grazing close by. Five of the Taghliks sat round the fire, warming themselves. The others had already gone to bed. The entire company, men as well as animals, were dead tired after their long forced march. But they had enjoyed the advantages of a rest before starting, and of a downward road after they did start. Hence they had pushed on without stopping; but as most of them walked, they were bound to be overtaken by our mounted men.

Parpi Bai and his two companions galloped up to the fire. The Taghliks leapt to their feet, and fled in different directions. But Parpi Bai went after them and fired his rifle in the air, shouting to them to stop instantly, or he would shoot them down. Thereupon they flung themselves prone on the ground, crying for mercy, and crept back to the fire. Parpi Bai bound them—every man and took away all the money they had about them. Then, after two or three hours' sleep, he and his two companions started back early in the morning, bringing the Taghliks with them, except the three whom I had dismissed and given permission to return. The leader of the gang, a fellow about forty years of age, who had plotted the flight, was made to walk the whole way to camp, with his hands tied behind his back.

It was ten o'clock at night when the runaways, guarded by Islam of Keriya, arrived in camp, and my property was restored to me. But that did not give me back the two valuable days we had lost, and which we could ill afford to lose. The leader of the Taghliks was brought forward to my tent, and the other culprits were made to stand in a semicircle behind him. I charged him with being a thief, and told him that, if he had fallen into the hands of a Chinese amban under circumstances similar to those in which he then stood, things would go queer with him. To teach him that neither he nor any other man could treat a European in the shameful way he had done, I adjudged that he should receive a dozen strokes of the rod, but not severe strokes, although my other men were urgent that he should get a good sound drubbing. Moreover I condemned the thieves to atone for their treacherous conduct by work, to be bound every night until we felt we could trust them, to pay Parpi, Hamdan, and Islam the three days' wages they had lost, to accompany us as far as I thought fit to take them, and when I at length dismissed them, the payment they were to receive should depend entirely upon my good will, and upon how they had behaved themselves in the interval.

It was a picturesque scene, that night court among the desolate mountains. The men stood silently round the tent-opening, wearing their furs, under the faint light of the moon and the gleam of my candle. It was no pleasure to me to be obliged to punish them. But they fully deserved punishment, and that it did them good was proved by their subsequent conduct, which was irreproachable.

Both animals and men, that had taken part in the flight and pursuit, were of course completely exhausted by their forced marches, so that we were compelled to sacrifice yet

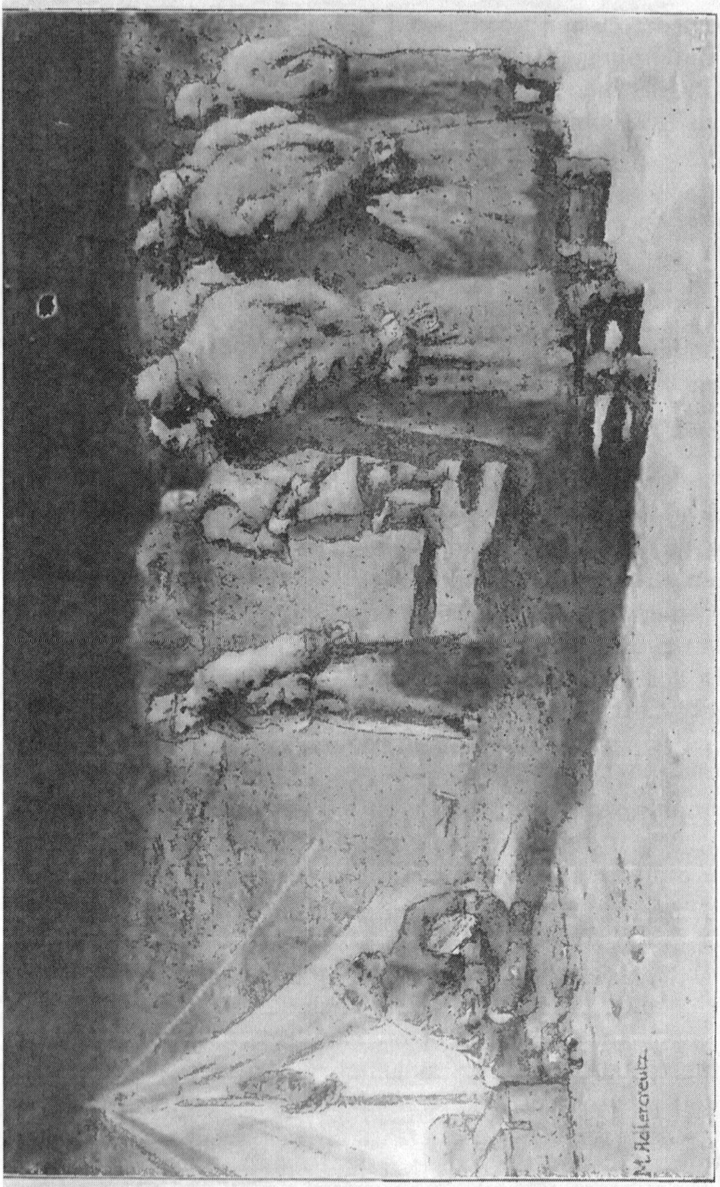

TRIAL OF THE TAGHLIK RUNAWAYS

another day—the third in all—at camp No. VIII. The weather still continued wintry. After midday it snowed from time to time, and after three o'clock a violent buran bore down upon us out of the north-west. It blew my tent over, but the tackle creaked and strained some time before it gave way, so that I was prepared for the upset, and no injury was done to anything inside. At eight o'clock it came on to hail, the hailstones rattling loudly upon the tent-covering. Then it was still again. By night the whole country was white with snow, except in the bottom of the brook, where the stream wound in a black sinuous line. The buran continued all night, and the tent bent to such a degree under the weight of the snow that several times I was forced to get up and shake it off. In that way the snow became packed up like a wall all round the tent, thus making it warmer and keeping out the draught. The snowstorm did not stop until well on in the afternoon of August 22nd, and until then we were unable to move.

That day we made an extremely short march, not more than two and a quarter miles, the reason being that there was said to be no grass farther on. We merely travelled up the left side of the valley before mentioned, which opened out from the east, and which, like the western latitudinal valley, was hemmed in by branch ranges of the Arka-tagh of a very considerable magnitude, till we reached the spot where Littledale's caravan had encamped. and there we pitched our tent. We were greatly indebted to him, for we found such a large quantity of dry dung from his animals that we had fuel and to spare. It is curious how well animals' dung keeps in those regions. for that which we gathered had lain more than a year. At first indeed we thought it was left by khulans, for some of those animals had visited the spot quite recently. The truth seems to be, that in those high altitudes it never rains, the downfall always assuming the form of snow or hail, otherwise the dung would soon become pulverized, then dry, and finally be blown away by the wind.

To-day again it began to hail about one o'clock. The wind was our most insufferable enemy. Every day, day after day, it visited us, bringing the hail in its train, and almost always at the same time, and it continued until evening, sometimes indeed all night long. It chilled the atmosphere and penetrated into the tent, making the candle flicker and flare, no matter how closely I drew the felts. And then my bed got so chilled, that when I crept in, it was like putting my feet into half-thawed ice, and there I lay, shivering and shaking, with chattering teeth until I got warm.

August 23rd. I was awakened early in the morning by a violent fall of snow. Winter was upon us again. The horses' backs were white, and as they stood tossing their empty nose-bags, they looked both wearied and disgusted. I called the men up, and they made haste to get the caravan ready for a start, for I expected we should have a long, hard day of it: we hoped to cross over the Arka-tagh by the pass which Littledale discovered, and which Hamdan Bai had undertaken to guide us to.

The long string of caravan animals filed slowly off up the valley, which soon contracted, whilst the bordering mountains decreased in relative altitude, and at the same time assumed rounder forms. The rocks were only exposed in the ravine which the river had eroded. Everywhere else the surface was covered with soil. The stream was in some places broad and shallow, and increased in velocity the higher we ascended. The water, as bright and clear as crystal, tumbled merrily along among the fine gravel with which its channel was strewn. The rocks were composed of a hard crystalline slate of a dark green colour. Then we came to an expansion of the valley, the gathering-basin of the river, in which it received a great number of small tributaries from the mountain-slopes around.

After being compelled to wait a considerable time by a blinding snowstorm, we went on again towards the south-east, up a strongly accentuated valley through which flowed one of the largest affluents of the river. This fresh valley bifurcated in two several places. At the first bifurcation we came upon a relic of Littledale's expedition, namely the carcass of a donkey shrivelled up like a mummy and in no degree decomposed. It was evident that neither wolf nor bird of prey had scented the carrion. Thus far then we had, rightly enough, followed Littledale's route from our camp No. VIII.

Now at length we perceived before us, in the east-south-east, the pass we had been so long seeking in the crest of the Arka-tagh. But when I and Emin Mirza reached the summit of a secondary pass, lying north of the principal pass, we were amazed to see that the trail of the horse-caravan (which according to the usual order of our march led the way) branched off down a side-glen leading to the left, that is towards the north. Hamdan Bai, who was now acting as our guide, had plainly taken a wrong turn. But it was no use to shout to him, he could not hear us, being too far in advance.

After I had taken the usual observations (18,300 feet), there was nothing for it but to follow in Hamdan's track, for the day was wearing on, and I did not care about sleeping out without my tent and my tea. We soon perceived that the glen, into which they had turned aside, curved round towards the west, so that the horses had gone very much astray, and before I and Emin Mirza had advanced very far we met them coming back, and Hamdan Bai, our guide, marching along at their head, looking very crest-fallen at his inconceivable stupidity. He had kept forging on ahead without thinking, until he crossed his own track, which he made earlier in that same day, and thus actually described a complete circle, and to crown all even climbed a pass, all to no purpose. Hamdan persisted, that just about that point Littledale had really made a short detour to the north, and he expected the valley would now soon bend round towards the east and the south. I never saw such rank stupidity and utter lack of the sense of locality! I took my gentleman smartly to task, and the others too for having followed him so blindly like a flock of silly sheep.

Having advanced some distance farther we encamped, after a march of 13½ miles, in the entrance to a side-glen, although there was not a mouthful of herbage to be found, except a species of moss with tiny red flowers growing between the stones.

Contrary to expectation, it was a beautiful evening. The atmosphere was absolutely pure, and the snow, and the white clouds above it, gleamed dazzlingly white under the full moon. It was dark when the camels came in, gliding up to the camp like silent though majestic shadows. As soon as their loads were taken off their backs, the poor beasts began eagerly looking about for grass. The horses and donkeys were tethered, for we did not let them feed until they had rested a couple of hours. Except the cooks, the men too used to rest as soon as they had erected the tent. Then for one or two hours peace and silence reigned in the camp. I seized the opportunity to take an observation of the moon, by no means an easy task, for it was terribly cold (24°8 Fahr. or $-4°$ C. at nine o'clock). The finely graduated circles in the prismatic circle clouded as often as I attempted to read them; and in such a highly rarefied atmosphere it is impossible to hold your breath, even for two or three seconds together.

When the time came at which the horses and donkeys were usually fed, they began to whinny and paw the ground with impatience, and when the nose-bags were slung round their necks, I liked to hear them crunching and grinding the hard maize between their strong teeth. Their meal ended, they were let run loose for the night, but were collected together early the next morning.

It was so silent, so still in those lofty solitudes, we felt as though we were visitors on some strange planet. The vast spaces of the sky gloomed upon us dusky blue from over the snowy summits of Arka-tagh. It was a world in which all things were motionless, rigid, eternally fixed, save for the twinkling of the stars, the slow and solemn procession of the clouds, the sparkling of the snow crystals. The only sound that reached the ear was the metallic, but musical, plash of the water as it struck against the icy mail of the river below. The nights were sublime; in beauty they easily surpassed the days. A thousand pities no other living creature but ourselves was able to sleep under their fascinating protection! And yet the river slept, for the frost seized it in his embrace and converted it into ice, and its babble gradually died away in slumber; and so it slept until the sun rose the next morning and warmed it to life again, reminding it that for Nature's children there is no rest: they must ever be spending their energy without cessation in shaping and re-shaping the crust of the patient earth.

CHAPTER LXXXI.

OVER THE ARKA-TAGH AT LAST

THUS it was not until August 24th, that we had the satisfaction of crossing the Arka-tagh. As soon as Hamdan Bai convinced himself and us, that the little glen really did lead to the summit of the range, we once more effected a start. The winding stream trickled along underneath its icy crust; the snow was hard and compact. The same slaty rocks as hitherto still predominated, but cropped out almost vertically. The approach to the pass was not particularly steep, and upon reaching the top we were at length gratified with the view towards the south which we had so longed to behold. But it was not Littledale's pass. The pass by which he crossed the range was situated a few miles farther to the east. This Hamdan Bai was able to confirm by sufficient proof: Littledale's men built a cairn of stones on the summit of the pass they crossed by, but there was no cairn on that by which we crossed. Probably the range can be surmounted in several places in the neighbourhood, possibly at the head of each glen, for the pass by which we reached the other side was very little lower than the crest of the range itself. Although the snow lay in thin patches in the glens on both sides, there was none in the pass itself, and yet the absolute altitude was very considerable, amounting to 18,180 feet.

From the south-east right round to the south-west we had an uninterrupted view of almost boundless extent, only intercepted on the east and west by outliers of the main range. The southern face of the Arka-tagh was much steeper than the northern. We descended through a winding glen shut in on both sides by subsidiary chains, which projected at right angles from the sides of the pass. Both chains were shorter than the corresponding spurs on the north, their altitudes decreasing rather abruptly, until they merged in an undulating level, and finally in an extensive tableland. As I gazed southwards across that vast high plain, I observed here and there what looked like minor irregularities of the surface, intermingled with low hills, but in reality they were disconnected portions of surviving mountain-chains. The southern horizon was edged as far as I could see both east and west by an imposing range of dark blue mountains, which however, owing to the contrast with the broad plain, appeared to be relatively low. Towards the south-east and south-west the range was overtopped by peaks and crests covered with perpetual snow. To the south-south-west and nearer there was a small lake, apparently the gathering-basin for the drainage waters of the greater portion of the region which lay spread out before us. We had thus reached the first basin on the Tibetan plateau not provided with an outflow.

After a good rest on the summit of the pass, we went on down its southern side. I was very pleased to know that at last I had left behind me East Turkestan, and the regions which drain into Lop-nor. We had crossed the Kwen-lun Mountains, the Arka-tagh, and the basin which stretches between them, and were now treading the plateau of Northern Tibet, the vastest upswelling on the face of the earth. To the east every inch of the ground was unknown territory, except along the route which had been followed by Bonvalot and Prince Henry of Orleans, and that by which Dutreuil de Rhins and Grenard had travelled. In fact the latter must have been near where we approached the Tibetan plateau; but we did not observe anything which enabled us to identify it. Littledale's route we had already left behind us. But we were still a long way from the most westerly region that drains into the Pacific Ocean, and for a considerable time to come we should be travelling in parts which do not contribute one drop of water to any of the great oceans of the earth.

We descended, then, beside the stream in the glen on the south. The weather being splendidly fine, every mountain-slope was streaked with foaming rivulets from the rapidly melting snows. At the lower end of the glen we emerged from the mountains. Then, leaving the glen brook on our right, as well as a small solitary, detached portion of the range, the last outlier of the Arka-tagh, we directed our march towards the south-east, having on our left the southern spurs of the Arka-tagh. Here we obtained a splendid view of a vast stretch of the mighty range bathed in brilliant sunshine. It consisted of an aggregation of peaks, most of them rounded at the top. But there was one crest especially conspicuous; it was jagged and pinnacled, and there were numerous clusters of black rocks projecting through its covering of snow. This was the twin peak we had seen between camps No. IV. and V. When I first perceived it, it loomed up on the far distant horizon; now happily it was behind us.

The surface was everywhere covered with fine sand and dust, soft and moist, and consequently very tiring to the caravan animals. The next stream we came to was joined by numerous tributaries, and gradually bent round south and south-east towards the small lake I have already mentioned, thus describing a semicircle round a hill that rose isolated from the tableland. At its foot on the south-west we discovered to our surprise some herbage, which our animals did not refuse after their enforced abstinence of the previous day. One of the camels and one of the horses were pretty spent, and one of the donkeys had given in on the pass.

I climbed the little hill on foot, and from its top obtained some splendid views. I observed what appeared to be several small glaciers stretching south from the region of perpetual snow on the summit of Arka-tagh. Looking towards the east, Arka-tagh faded away on the farthest horizon on my left, whilst on my right was the

THE ARKA-TAGH WHERE WE CROSSED IT, SEEN FROM OUR FIRST CAMP TO THE SOUTH OF IT

mountain-range I had before noticed in the south. It was, we afterwards discovered, a continuation of the Koko shili Mountains. Between the two ranges extended the broad tableland already mentioned, its eastern horizon forming a perfectly straight line, scarcely perceptible at its southern extremity. Towards the west too both ranges stretched as far as the eye could see, but the country between them was more diversified.

The little hill on which I stood was very interesting. The bare rock, the usual dark green slates, cropped out on its north-eastern and eastern flanks at an angle of 16° to the north-north-west. But its summit was apparently capped by a horizontal layer of blue-black tuff, some sixteen feet thick, with numerous round and elliptical vesicles, partly filled with a white mineral substance. The tuff itself was a good deal weathered, and numerous sharp angular pieces lay scattered about on its surface. I also observed several other isolated hills similarly capped with tuff farther to the south.

As I walked back to my tent, Yolldash at my heels, the sun was already setting in a sky as pure and blue as turquoise, save that a few snow-white fleecy clouds (cirri-cumuli) floated along in isolated groups. But hardly had the upper edge of the sun disappeared below the horizon, when its place in the west was taken by a black, threatening mass of cloud. Close down upon the earth the atmosphere was perfectly calm, but in the higher regions it was blowing hard, as we saw from the dark steel-grey clouds, whose edges were tinted various shades of blood red, vivid yellow, and violet by the setting sun. Some portions of the clouds were entirely black; others reluctantly allowed the sheaf of the sun's rays to penetrate through them. It was a sublime, and yet a fantastic, an awe-inspiring spectacle. I could not tear my eyes away from it. Then came the first puffs of wind, ruffling the calmness of the atmosphere, at first feeble and in intermittent gusts, but soon more violently as well as more frequently. The squall swooped down upon the camp. The wind blew with indescribable fury. The men ran to the tent-ropes, and held on like grim death, else the tent would have gone over. Down swished the hail, so fiercely that it actually whistled past our ears. The horses and other animals were alarmed and stopped grazing, and in five minutes—the squall was past, driving east at a terrific pace. No fresh clouds appeared in the west. The atmosphere again became still and calm, and a splendid, bright starry evening followed. But it was not destined to last, for all the early part of the night everything was shrouded in a thick mist, so thick that we could not even see the little hill at the foot of which we were encamped.

During the squall, and frequently afterwards too, it seemed to me that the clouds swept along in actual contact with the surface of the earth. When the black storms drove past with their hanging fringes of cloud, the glittering white snowfields on the mountain-sides became dark and gloomy; but in the morning, when the air was again clear and bright, the eternal snows dazzled us with, if it were possible, an even more glorious brilliancy.

August 25th. We travelled towards the south-east, and for more than three hours across an almost level plain. The little brook flowing towards the south-west proved however that it was not absolutely horizontal, but that there was a slight fall towards the small lake into which it emptied. On the way we crossed three glacial streams, but none of them powerful enough to excavate a definite channel for itself. They were each split into a great number of rivulets, which united and divided again and again in a highly capricious manner. The ground beside each rivulet was sopping wet, so that the horses sank in over the fetlocks, and every time they lifted their feet the action was accompanied by the "skwulsh" of watery suction.

The next brook we crossed flowed towards the east, so that we had passed over a watershed without observing it. Here and there we perceived small patches of yeylak (grassy herbage), with abundant droppings of khulans (wild asses) and antelopes near them. About two miles off on the left we passed another small round rocky protuberance, standing quite isolated, and capped with tuff. Then we became aware of a little lake, not more than a mile and a quarter long, but very irregular in outline, having a number of long narrow creeks running out in every direction. This, the second depression destitute of an outlet, was the gathering-basin of all the streams in the immediate vicinity. From this I was led to infer, and as it subsequently proved to infer rightly, that the whole of the vast plain, which stretched between the Arka-tagh and the continuation of the Koko-shili Mountains, consisted of a series of similar small self-contained lake-basins, unprovided with any outflow to the ocean.

We continued to advance in the same direction until stopped by a long narrow gully, and to get round it we were forced to make a detour to the south, crossing on the way a brook which poured a large quantity of water into the gully. The surface now became more broken, a series of softly rounded hills, troublesome to cross, stretching away towards the north-east. We could still see the glaciers of the Arka-tagh gleaming behind us and on our left; we seemed to increase the distance between ourselves and them only very, very slowly. The mountain-range on the south had now vanished from sight, except when we were on the tops of the hills. The brooks flowed in divers directions, as though they were unable to make up their minds which way to go. There was very little rock visible, beyond black lines of slate where the laminæ peeped up vertically out of the ground like grave-stones. To our agreeable surprise several times during the course of the day's march we passed patches of scanty herbage, the thin kind of grass which the Taghliks call *sarik* or *yeylak-sarik* (yellow grass).

Then we went over some hills, and crossed a brook flowing towards another lake in the east-north-east, and so came to a spacious valley with a river running down it. Here we saw grazing the first wild yak we met with. The river formed a remarkably sharp loop to the east, south, and south-west, round a hill which had much steeper slopes than any of the hills we had previously encountered. Upon reaching its summit, we were uncertain which way to go, for on every side we were hemmed in by extremely broken country—a perfect labyrinth of hills, with brooks winding amongst them in every direction without any apparent order, except that they all joined a deep stream, with green transparent water, and a volume of 175 cubic feet in the second, flowing towards the south-west.

After the almost monotonous regularity of the rivers of East Turkestan, all of which flow towards one common centre—Lop-nor, it was an unfamiliar and even strange experience to witness this irregularity of direction and this diversity of slope. One hour of our march the brooks would flow towards the east, the next towards the west, or south, or north. Even yet we could not gather where the last stream really meant to go to. However, we still continued to push on steadily to the south-east, ascending a steep glen or gully, on whose grass-grown sides there were such enormous quantities of yak and wild ass dung that it would have served us with fuel for several years. Nor were there wanting plenty of fresh spoor of the animals themselves.

At length we reached the pass at the head of the glen, and lo! a magnificent picture spread out at our feet. On the farther side the pass plunged down steeply to an exceptionally large lake, extending from east to west. Its water was a beautiful light green colour, but over the shallow parts yellow. And now the difficulty of deciding which way to go was seriously increased, for at its eastern end the lake was overhung by almost perpendicular mountains; while in the west, but at some distance from it, were a series of low fenny marshes, and from the south we were cut off by the lake itself.

After weighing the matter for a while, we decided to halt and make a reconnaissance of the surrounding country. The caravan piloted its way carefully down the steep slopes to the northern shore of the lake, and there the men pitched the tents in a tolerably sheltered spot between two hills. For it was blowing hard from the south-east, a fact of which I became painfully cognizant as I stood on the crest of the pass to sketch and make my observations. I could see to an immense distance. In the south-east was a snow-covered mountain. South of the lake the country was less broken, but there were three other lakes with wet and marshy ground between them. I therefore sent Islam Bai along the lake shore, to find out whether the caravan would be able to advance eastwards. He brought back word, that there was an easy road.

We had barely got comfortably settled down in our tents, when the usual westerly storm came on, this time succeeded by a downpour of rain. Hitherto we had not suffered from want of water, a thing we had anxiously feared before we started. But there was an abundance of water everywhere, nor was grass so scarce as the Taghliks tried to make us believe, no doubt with the view of deterring us from the journey. There was relatively good pasturage around the large lake we had just come upon. The men therefore begged for a day's rest, especially as some of the horses and donkeys were very much done up. The sick camel had not been able to get more than half way of our last day's march, and had been left beside a pool of fresh water. Hamdan Bai, who was in charge of the camels, believed that the sick one was suffering from fever, for he was seized with fits of violent shaking, and coughed a good deal, and for four days had not eaten a mouthful of maize. Whilst we rested, two of the men went back to see how he was faring.

The mountains echoed with the rolling thunder, and the storm-clouds drove eastward as usual.

The day's rest was welcome to both men and animals, for the rarefied atmosphere, to which we only gradually became accustomed, was very trying to our strength. The sick camel was brought into camp No. XII. during the course of the morning, and was able to eat some maize.

Parpi Bai maintained very confidently, that the lake we had reached was not the same lake which Dutreuil de Rhins's caravan passed; but although I knew the

French traveller's route only very imperfectly, I thought it must be the same. The boiling-point of the thermometer gave its altitude as 16,165 feet above sea-level.

In the afternoon the weather was abominable, and prevented me from carrying out the excursion I had planned —namely to the mouth of the stream which entered the western extremity of the lake. It hailed and poured with rain all the afternoon, the landscape being enshrouded in a sort of autumn mist, so that we saw nothing of the large lake beside which we were encamped. Probably the heaviest downfalls occur in this region in the autumn. In the evening the rain ceased, the mist dispersed, the atmosphere became clear and transparent; and the lake glistened like a mirror, reflecting the most beautiful interplay of colour, whilst the Southern Mountains soared upwards like a steel-blue wall.

The treacherous Taghliks, who ran away from camp No. VIII., were bound every night, and made to sleep under a thick felt rug which was spread over the maize sacks, for we should not have been surprised if at any time they had attempted to give us the slip again. Their leader now earnestly begged to be allowed to return home, and as we no longer needed him, his request was granted. I was afraid he would not be able to travel all the long distance by himself; but he told me he intended to make his way to some gold-prospectors he knew of working on the northern flanks of the Arka-tagh. I gave him some money, and a sufficient supply of bread and flour to last him a fortnight, and moreover presented him with a donkey to carry his stores, and with this he was very well satisfied. The rest of the Taghliks preferred to go with us right through to Tsaidam, whence they proposed to return home over the Chimen-tagh or over Bokalik. As during the past few days their conduct had been quite exemplary, they were freed from their bonds at night, and for the future were allowed to sleep in peace.

On August 27th, when we started to continue our journey along the northern shore of the lake, the solitary Taghlik took his leave of us, and turned back along our

A PART OF THE EASTERN ARKA-TAGH, SEEN FROM THE SOUTH

trail, driving his donkey on before him. I was really sorry for the poor fellow at having to travel all that long way by himself, but he was only too glad to get away from us. He had plotted to cheat us, but had fallen into his own trap: it had not been quite so easy to deceive us and rob us as he had imagined.

The sick camel was now mending nicely, and got through the day's march very creditably.

The ground was very favourable for the animals, for we kept close to the lake side, and so escaped the eternal up-and-down hill, which was so exceedingly tiring. The green slaty rocks fell tolerably steeply towards the lake, but at their foot, and between them and the water, was a gravel slope, stretching a considerable distance into the lake. The strip of shore varied in breadth, though in general it was narrow. The ground was hard and very little cut up by rivulets. The water of the lake was perfectly clear, but salt, and at noon had a temperature of 41° Fahr. (5° C.). A narrow fringe of white scum, mingled with brown decayed *algæ*, rocked on the waves as they beat upon the shore. The only living creatures we observed were wagtails and flies. East and west there were magnificent views—the winding shore of the lake, with its mountain offsets, showing a fascinating interplay of colour effects, the slightly crumpled surface of the lake, and arching all in a sky of the purest blue.

This lake, like all those which we encountered later, was long and narrow, a form evidently due to the latitudinal mountain-ranges on the north and south. The farther we advanced towards the east, the more indented and irregular was the outline of its shore. In places we came across small lagoons, and round them the ground was soft and muddy. Shortly before reaching the end of the lake, which terminated in a creek, we had to climb over another cluster of low hills. Then we came to the yellowish-red stream, which flowed into the creek at the end of the lake, through a delta with innumerable small arms and several large ones.

The stream was bordered on the left (as we rode

towards the south-east) by hills of red loess, gently rounded, but sterile. The ground however soon became so soft that the animals were scarcely able to plough their way along with their burdens; we therefore turned up a side-glen to avoid it. The glen led us to a watershed, on the other side of which the drainage channels all flowed towards the east. There we were overtaken by the usual afternoon storm, which lasted an hour.

All day long we had on our left, that is to the north, the spurs of the Arka-tagh, each spur being entirely free from snow. But from camp No. XIII., which we made on the sheltered side of a low hill, we beheld a glittering white double peak soaring above the tops of every other mountain.

The region we were now travelling through swarmed with khulans (wild asses), but they kept at such a distance from us that all attempts to get a shot at them were unavailing. Yolldash however was of a different opinion. He galloped after them, and derived a never-ending delight from putting them to flight. He repeated the manœuvre time after time, and after every chase came back to the caravan, panting and puffing, and with his tongue hanging out. It was comical to watch him when he caught sight of a fresh troop of khulans. He pricked his ears, his eyes sparkled, and for a while he squatted down on his haunches and gazed at them fixedly, without moving, then he slowly stalked them for a while, and finally set off as hard as he could race, like an arrow from a bow. But no sooner did the shy animals catch sight of the dog than off they went with the speed of the wind, and in a few moments left their pursuer far behind them. Nor did Yolldash learn wisdom from experience. At the sight of the next troop off he went again, and so tired himself out to no purpose.

When we drew near to the place where we intended to encamp for the night, I missed the dog. I thought that, as he was tired, he had perhaps joined the camel-caravan; but the camel-caravan came in without him. The last time any of the men saw him, he disappeared at the heels of a troop of khulans behind the hills on the right of our line of march. I was afraid he had continued his pursuit too far, and lost the trail of the caravan, and so had gone quite astray. I sent a man back to the place where the dog was seen last; it was where we left a donkey that was completely exhausted. But the man came back without having seen any trace of the dog, and he left the donkey behind dying. A couple of horses, which had also given up, were on the other hand brought into camp. The camels stood the fatigues of the journey best.

Once more it was evening. I had my tea, and bread and rice pudding, and then smoked a pipe or two, whilst I worked out the notes I took on the road during the day. When I lay down to sleep, I felt quite lonely without Yolldash, for he was my best companion, and ate and slept at my side. But at three o'clock in the morning I was awakened by something pushing against my bed. There was "his lordship," wagging his tail and licking my face, literally beside himself with joy. The poor beast had been on foot all the afternoon and night seeking us; he was actually too tired to eat, but with a sigh of intense relief curled himself up at once in his usual sleeping-place.

August 28th. The ground was quite level, and with the exception of the two sick horses, all the animals marched well. The Southern Mountain Range was now clearly distinguishable; its snowfields were at a less altitude than those of the Arka-tagh. This day we crossed another low pass. The watershed we passed over the day before must therefore have been of secondary importance only, especially as the intricately winding stream, which we had followed most of the day, curved round it on the north. Now however the drainage channels all flowed definitely towards the east, converging upon a tiny freshwater lake. East of the pass stretched a broad shallow valley, to all appearance quite level; but it had a slope, as was proved by a deep dry watercourse.

There was an abundance of grass everywhere in that region, and consequently great numbers of khulans. One solitary khulan, a beautiful animal, striped with brown and greyish-yellow, kept ahead of the caravan for close upon two hours, but always at a long distance from us. Sometimes he trotted, sometimes he galloped, with his little tail sticking straight out behind him, but always with his head proudly arched, the incarnation of vigilant energy. Ever and anon he stopped and turned round and gazed at us, and uttered a curious sound, something between the horse's whinny and the donkey's bray. But no sooner did we approach nearer than off he went again, and so on time after time, as though he wanted to show us the way. Then Yollbars, our other big shaggy dog, set off after him. Strange to say, the khulan was not in the least alarmed, but stopped as soon as he saw the dog. At this Yollbars was taken suddenly aback, and stood stock still. That seemed to divert the khulan. He plucked up courage and charged straight down upon the dog. It was now Yollbars' turn to flee, and back he came galloping to the caravan with his tail between his legs.

The ground still continued extraordinarily level. True, we had numbers of low hills on both sides of us, but they were either ramifications of the mountains behind or stood singly isolated. The usual hailstorm came on at half-past one—came as unfailingly every day about the same time as though its onset were regulated by clockwork.

At length we turned off towards the south-east, enticed by some green hills a little way off. There we found another small lake, into which various tiny brooks emptied themselves. We halted on its southern shore after a march of 16½ miles.

The water in the lake was slightly saline, but had a very disagreeable flavour, so that we were unable to drink it. Islam Bai tried to stalk a khulan, but was unsuccessful. The evening was clear and still, not a sound reached our lonely camp. We were alone in the boundless wilds of Tibet.

CHAPTER LXXXII.

THE WILD ASS

AUGUST 29th. Crossing over the hills which bordered the east side of the lake, and then a brook of clear bright water, we approached a broad trough-like valley paved with hard gravel, so that it was easy travelling for the animals. The lake was thus on our left. The stream which flowed into it formed an extensive delta at its western end. After that the lake was hidden behind a low, softly rounded ridge; and on our right we had another similar ridge, beyond which the great snowy peaks of the Southern Mountains glittered in the distance.

In the depression between the ridges, in which there were thin patches of grass, we surprised a khulan. As usual he ran on a short distance ahead of the caravan, pursued by the dogs, but took no further notice of them. Every time he stopped, he viewed the caravan with close attention and great wonder, pricked his ears, expanded his nostrils, and arched his head high. Islam Bai managed to get within range of him, by creeping down a ravine between two hills. He fired two shots at the wild ass; but the animal moved off a few paces none the worse for them. He merely sniffed the wind, and gazed at us with continued curiosity and wonder.

At the third shot he turned and trotted slowly off towards the east, but went rather lame. When we came up to his trail, we saw it was sprinkled with blood. The wild ass was evidently wounded. That being so, we must have the skin at all costs. We now took the khulan for our guide; but he led us further to the north than we wished to go. He was hit in the right hind-leg.

which he trailed uselessly behind him. But he had a good start of us.

Islam Bai and Parpi Bai went after him as fast as their horses were able to get over the ground; whilst I and Emin Mirza followed at our usual pace. Meanwhile the khulan had stopped to rest, and when we came up to the spot where he rested, we discovered a large pool of blood. He could not hold out long now; all the same he led us a chase of two full hours. At length he conceived the unfortunate idea of quitting the easy valley and trying to climb the flanks of the hills on the left.

At this point we passed another small salt lake on our right, and upon reaching the top of the ridge beheld again the eastern end of the large lake whose southern shore we had followed. Then, crossing over more gentle hills, where the ground was soft and tiring, we approached a small pass, which descended on the north-east pretty steeply to a perfectly level sai (a slope at the foot of a mountain). The stream, which coursed along the sai towards the lake, was split into several arms.

In the middle of the wet sandy belt between two branches of the river the khulan at last fell. Islam Bai and Parpi were by this close upon him; they instantly jumped off their horses and bound his forelegs. And there the creature lay still alive in the most natural position, and regarded us without any perceptible sign of fear. Every now and again however he endeavoured to get up, and struggled on a step or two, but soon fell again. He was wounded in the right hind-leg above the heel, and a portion of the bone showed in the wound, which was very bloody. The khulan was a splendid specimen of his race, a male in fine condition, evidently the sentry of the troop of five which we saw a little way back. His curiosity and desire to protect his companions had led him a little too far, and so into danger. His teeth indicated that he was about nine years old.

On the whole the wild ass bears the closest resemblance to the mule: in other words, he comes intermediate between the horse and the ass, but is nearer to the latter than to the former. The ears are longer than the horse's, but shorter than the ass's. The tail resembles that of an ass, and only has hair at its lower end. The mane too, which is black and thin, is like that of the ass, in that it is short (about four inches long), and stands stiff and upright. It is continued along the spine in a black line, and finally terminates in the tail. On the back the animal is a reddish-brown colour, which gradually passes over into white down the ribs and sides; underneath it is white. The nose is grey; the ears dark, but white on the inside; the legs gradually shade off to white down by the hoofs. The hoofs are strong, though not quite hard, and are

A WOUNDED KHULAN (WILD ASS)

as large as the horse's. The eyes are brown, with a big black pupil, of the same shape and appearance as in the horse and domestic ass. The chest is broad and strongly developed, so as to accommodate a pair of powerful lungs. The neck too is massive and muscular. But the muscles of the hind legs are especially thick and sinewy, well adapted for developing great speed. The nostrils are very much larger than the horse's. When the wounded khulan sniffed after his companions and snorted, and also when he uttered his harsh scream or neigh, his nostrils expanded into two large apertures, surrounded by taut sinewy muscles, and projected almost straight out before him. In short, the wild ass's nostrils are constructed on a similar scale to his lungs, the whole respiratory apparatus being specially adapted for the highly rarefied atmosphere he lives in. The Persians therefore in slitting up the nostrils of their tame asses, when they are going to employ them for transport purposes in mountainous regions, really obey a law of nature. Experience has taught them that the animals can then breathe more easily.

Our khulan had, if I may be allowed the expression, a more pronounced Roman nose than the tame ass; that is to say, the profile of his face curved more sharply outwards. The expression of the eyes, which were well protected by eyebrows and eyelashes, was gentle and peaceful. In length, from the edge of his upper lip along his spine to the root of his tail, he measured 7 ft. 7 in. His girth just behind the forelegs was 4 ft. 10 in., and in front of them 5 ft. 3 in. Round the neck immediately behind the ears he measured 31½ inches, immediately in front of them 35 inches. Round the head over the eyes he measured 33¾ inches, and round his nose 18½ inches; whilst the space between the crown of the head and the edge of the upper lip was 25½ inches.

Whilst I was measuring and sketching him, he lay perfectly still and quiet, and did not appear to feel any pain from his wound, in which the blood had already coagulated, and he was so destitute of fear that he let me stroke him over the nose without resenting it. When I had done with the beautiful creature, he was given his quietus with a well-directed thrust of a knife. Then the men set to work to flay him, taking very special pains not to injure the skin, which was afterwards spread out on the ground to dry. The best portions of the flesh were taken care of; the rest was left where it was, whilst the dogs feasted on the scraps and offal.

Camp XV., which we reached at the end of fifteen and a half miles, was pitched at the foot of a hill. As the men had worked hard to capture the khulan and get me his skin, and as our animals were a good deal spent, the next day was given up to rest, and as it happened, it was a Sunday.

The westerly storm! No, it did not forget us—nothing of the kind. At half-past one down it swooped with the same unerring certainty it had displayed on each of the days preceding, and in its wake followed a blinding snow-storm. After it had passed, it turned out a splendid afternoon; the sunset was magnificent, the hills and mountains in the west being outlined like inky black silhouettes, whilst in the east they were bathed in vivid reds and yellows.

The next day, August 30th, every man made the most of the opportunity to sleep all he could, whilst the caravan animals roamed over the hills plucking the grass. I made an excursion to the lake that lay to the west of the camp.

A GULL (HANGHEITT) FROM NORTH TIBET

The chief drainage artery of the locality poured its water into a small lagoon, whence it made its way into the lake by a number of small channels. The water, although perfectly clear, was so salt that it stuck to my fingers. Near the shore there were a quantity of white gulls (the men called them *hangheitt*), diving under the waves as they curled towards them. The ground was covered with fine gravel and coarse sand, derived from the same green slates which were everywhere so prevalent. Six or seven feet above the existing level of the lake I observed another shore-line, but could not make out whether it was due to a higher level during the inflow of the summer floods or whether it was simply caused by the beating of the waves. Now that I commanded a full view of the lake I perceived that the waves could be both high and strong; for they came rolling up from the west tipped with spray, and beat upon the shore with the harmonious regularity of a ring of bells. At three o'clock in the afternoon the temperature of the water was 55°9 Fahr. (13°3 C.) as compared with 52°3 Fahr. (11°3 C.) for the air. The surface of the lake, which lay between the arms of the two ridges, had approximately the same altitude as camp No. XV., or 16,195 feet above the level of the sea. For the sake of clearness, I decided to number these several lakes; this one of which I have just been speaking was therefore No. 5.*

August 31st. Immediately to the east of the camp we discovered a tiny freshwater lake, fed by a glacial torrent from the Arka-tagh. After passing a low range of dark mountains on our left, we turned off towards the east-south-east across a rolling grassy country. Then we entered another latitudinal valley, poorly supplied with water, but tolerably well grassed; and there we observed numbers of khulans, antelopes, and hares. Beyond the 8th lake we crossed another magnificent watershed, on the other (east) side of which all the watercourses drained into lake No. 9. This was an isolated central basin, for it was encompassed by the large lakes into which the Arka-tagh and the great Southern Mountains poured their melting snows. This day we could not see the Arka-tagh: it was hidden behind its own outlying chains. But the snowy peaks of its counterpart frequently glittered down upon us; for we advanced at such a slow rate that we seemed to get no nearer to it. To lake No. 10 it sent down a river of some magnitude. A short distance beyond this last we encamped beside a spring, having done 18½ miles between camp No. XV. and camp No. XVI.

East-south-east of the camp we had a grand peak, covered with vast expanses of snow, among them some small glacier formations; we also caught glimpses of a number of peaks towering up in the west.

* Many of these small lakes are not shown on the map, printed at the end of this volume.

Thanks to the level ground we were travelling over, and to the grass, though this was somewhat scanty it is true, the caravan animals still held out capitally, although we had already lost several of the donkeys.

September 1st. At first our road lay across a low level ridge, with a hard surface, which would have been first-rate for the animals, had it not been that it was honeycombed like a rabbit-warren by a small rodent (*teshikan*). We saw some of the creatures bobbing into their holes with a little squeak; but the holes caused the horses to stumble incessantly.

SUNSET AT CAMP NO. XV.

On my map I distinguished the high, dominating peaks which overlooked our line of march from both sides by letters of the alphabet, and determined their position by a series of bearings taken from various points. To-day right underneath one of these peaks the green slates came to an abrupt termination. Then for some distance the surface was strewn with pieces of tuff, about two cubic feet big, of the same kind as that we met with before; the ground between was barren. In the distance we frequently saw herds of five or six *yurgheh* (antelopes) —an animal with a long, narrow, lyre-shaped horn, and called by the Tibetans *orongo.* Although Islam tried his hardest, he never succeeded in getting within range of them. They gazed at us attentively, then with quick, elastic leaps disappeared behind the desolate hills.

Beyond the snowy mountain-peak we again found fine, close-growing herbage; and the ground was actually spotted brown with the droppings of the wild yak, so abundant were they. The men always had two or three

THE GREAT SALT LAKE OF CAMP NO. XV.

View from its Eastern Shore

empty sacks hanging at the camels' harness during the march; and as they went along, they filled them with that splendid fuel. Thanks to the favourable country, we accomplished not less than 20½ miles before we halted at camp No. XVII.

September 2nd. We skirted pretty near to the Southern Mountains, and discovered two or three new lakes. Although the ground was strewn with fragments of green slate and black tuff, the bare rock was not visible. Animal life was represented by antelopes, a fox, swallows, and larks. But our most interesting discovery this day was, that human beings had once been there before us. At one point there was a well-defined gap in the Southern Range, and through it appeared very conspicuously a rounded mountain-top capped with snow; and on the left of the mountain there was plainly distinguishable an easy pass leading over the range. As soon as we came opposite that strongly marked feature, Parpi Bai rode up to me, and said that he recognized the locality again. "That was the pass by which the caravan of 'Bovolo Tura' (M. Bonvalot) and Prince Henry of Orleans had crossed the range."

Further on, we went down into yet another broad, shallow valley, in which were a couple of small lakes and some marshes. According to my reckoning, we could not now be very far from the route followed by the celebrated French travellers. And as I had Bonvalot's map in my pocket, I thought I ought to be able to identify the more prominent geographical features. I could now understand why at this point the red line indicating M. Bonvalot's route made a bend on the map. Bonvalot's map was not however sufficiently detailed; still there can be little doubt that his Dôme du Sature answers to my Mount D., and his Volcanoes des Ruysbruk are simply the black tuff hills, fragments of which were visible on every side of us. The marshes and lakes which I have mentioned are named by him "*fondrières et lacs gêlés*" (morasses and frozen lakes).

Seeing that the camel-caravan had taken quite a wrong direction, namely towards the north-east, I sent Parpi Bai after them, to turn them back towards the south, the direction in which the horse-caravan had gone. In the broad valley we were travelling down one of the men, made a discovery which proved conclusively that our route and that of Bonvalot and Prince Henry of Orleans intersected just at that point. He found camel droppings, old and discoloured, and two or three pieces of white felt carpet (*kighiz*), such as is put on camels' backs to protect them against the chafing of the packing-cases. We showed them to Parpi Bai. He pronounced them to be pieces of Charkhlik kighiz; and added, that the French travellers had as an actual fact bought a supply in that place. He recollected also, that just before they climbed the pass they did encamp in the place where the man found the pieces. This was for me an exceptionally happy find, since it enabled me to fix precisely where my route intersected that of the French explorers.

VIEW, LOOKING WEST, FROM CAMP NO. XVIII

We pitched camp No. XVIII. beside lake No. 14, after a march of $17\frac{1}{2}$ miles; the camp stood at an altitude of 16,750 feet. East-south-east there rose a cluster of pyramidal peaks and glaciers, which the men were afraid would prevent us from advancing. Our poor animals were getting in a bad way. Already one horse had been abandoned, and two others were so done up that they travelled with the donkeys, and without their loads. Indeed one of them was left behind in camp No. XVIII.

The evening passed and the night came, and nothing was seen of Parpi Bai. We began to be anxious about the camel-caravan. I saw that we must make up our minds to sacrifice the 3rd September as a rest-day. The missing caravan turned up during the course of the next morning. They had been obliged to leave a horse and a donkey on the road. One of the goats too was upon his last legs, and was killed. The camels and other animals were still in pretty good condition, and were turned loose to graze.

Early in the morning Islam Bai caught sight of a yak cow, with two calves at her heels, grazing on the other side of the lake. Taking a rifle, he set out on horseback to try and get a shot at her. He came back at noon, and with some degree of elation told us, that he had "potted" the yak with a couple of balls, one of which penetrated under the spine. Leaving his horse tethered at some distance, he stole upon his prey on foot. The inexperienced calves were wholly unconscious of danger, and their dam, running to warn them, fell an easy victim; but directly she fell, the young ones fled behind the nearest hills.

CHAPTER LXXXIII.

HUNTING THE WILD YAK

EARLY in the afternoon I started for the dead yak, intending to measure and sketch the animal. But she was already inflated with gas, and as hard as a drum, whilst a liquid mingled with blood trickled noisily out of her mouth. From the inner corner of her upper lip to the root of her tail she measured 8 feet. The length of the head, from the base of the horn to the upper lip, was 22½ inches; the circumference of the muzzle 17½ inches; above the eyes 29½ inches; round the neck behind the ears 28 inches. Her height at the shoulder was 4 ft. 6 in.; at the loins (her legs being stretched straight out) 4 ft. 5 in. The tail, including the tuft at the end, measured 31½ inches in length; whilst the length of the horns on the outside was 17 inches, and on the inside 15¾ inches, and their circumference at the root 7½ inches. I did not measure the girth of the body owing to its distention. Its colour was black as coal, with a magnificent tuft at the end of the tail. The hoofs were powerful; the udder not very developed, but the teats on the other hand were large. Thick black fringes of woolly hair hung like draperies down the animal's sides; but there was none under its belly. The bottom jaw was equipped with eight slanting incisor teeth, the upper jaw with a broad horny callosity. The tongue was thickly covered with horny barbs, directed backwards towards the throat. With these the yak plucks up grass, lichens, and mosses, using its tongue more than its teeth and horny upper jaw in grazing.

Finding that yaks were numerous in that neighbourhood, we decided not to take the skin, but wait until we brought a better proportioned animal to the ground. Nevertheless the men chopped out the best pieces of the meat with their axes, as well as the tongue. The latter served me for breakfast for several days, and was excellent eating. The flesh on the contrary was tough, sorry stuff, and had to be boiled several times over before it became anything like tender; but this was also partly the result of the rarefied atmosphere, for water boiled at about 180 Fahr. We also took the tail, and the long fringes of hair, which the men wove into ropes and cords. Further they

A DEAD WILD YAK-COW

arranged some of the hair underneath the front part of their hats to shade their eyes against the sun.

Whilst we were busy with the dead yak, another cow approached within a hundred and fifty yards, then stopped and gazed at us in amazement. Our dogs, ignorant of the noble art of veneric, chased her away, and off she went at a good jog-trot over the hills.

Towards evening we caught sight of a magnificent animal, grazing alone, but near the horses, to which however he seemed to pay no heed. Islam Bai, whose hunter's appetite was now keenly whetted, stalked him like a panther against the wind, and arriving well within range began to blaze away at him. The yak fell at the third shot. But the next instant he was on his legs again, and charging madly down upon the disturber of his peace. He got another bullet, which made him spin right round; but nothing daunted, back he came to the charge. However he fell several times, always struggling to his feet again, till he at length dropped at the seventh bullet, and lay motionless. Thereupon Islam returned to camp triumphant, declaring that no finer skin could be got. The bull, for such it was, lay on the line of march I had planned for the morrow: hence we decided to leave some of the men to flay him when we went past, as well as a camel to carry the skin to our next camp, which would not be very much farther to the east.

Accordingly on September 4th, we once more got under way. Islam remembered precisely where he killed the yak; it was between the hills. Imagine therefore our amazement, when we came to the place, and found the bull had disappeared!

Islam was so thunderstruck that for a long time he was unable to get out a word. When he did find his voice, he swore that the yak *was* dead when he left him the evening before. However the soft moist ground betrayed the fact, that he had recovered, and in spite of his many wounds had managed to get away. His track seemed to show however that he had fallen again and again, at every few yards. All the same, he could not possibly have travelled very far. Following up his spoor, we soon saw him from the top of the hill. He was walking quietly along by the edge of a spring and pool, sniffing the ground. When we approached within a hundred yards of him, he turned round, and stood and watched us, with his head up in the air. Islam planted another bullet in him. That enraged him to such a degree that he rushed towards us in blind fury. We judged it best to beat a retreat; but had barely turned our startled horses round when he was upon us. But luckily he stopped twenty paces away, grunting madly, wildly rolled his eyes, snorted, drew in his breath violently, flung up the sand with his nose and horns, till he enveloped himself in a perfect cloud of it, and lashed his sides furiously with his tail.

At about thirty paces' distance Islam put in yet another shot, which made the yak spin round a good many times. Yolldash made a dash at him; but when the maddened bull advanced to meet him with his horns lowered and his tail in the air, Yolldash instantly turned and fled. The tenth shot broke the bull's left leg, so that it hung loosely when, in the madness of despair, he danced round another two or three times. Finally, at closer quarters, Islam let drive for the eleventh time. The bullet penetrated behind the shoulder, and lodging in a more vital part, put an end to the animal's torment. He fell on his right side. When we approached him, he made a last effort to get up, but could not do so. Shortly after that he died, quietly, without any death-struggle.

I made a couple of sketches of him from different points of view. He was a magnificent animal. His incisors were worn down almost level with his gums, proving him to be an old bull; indeed the outermost two were embedded in the flesh. His horns too were slightly burst open on the inner side, another sign of advanced age. Iskender, one of the Taghliks, who had taken part in many a yak hunt, declared that the bull was about twenty years old. The wild yak, he said, lives on an average six years longer than the tame yak, and the latter at twenty years of age is regarded as worn out.

I took the following measurements of the animal. Length from the edge of the upper lip to the root of the tail, 10 ft. 8 in. Length of the tail, including the tuft at the end, 3 ft. 6 in.; circumference of the tail at the root, 7½ in. Length of head from the base of the horn to the upper lip, 28½ in. Distance between the eyes, 17 in. Length of horn on the outside, 30½ in.; on the inside, 19½ in. From this it will be apparent that the horns were very much curved. Circumference of horn

II.–24

at base, 14 in.; distance between the tips of the horns, 12 in. Circumference of the head, round the muzzle, 24 in.; ditto over the eyes, $44\frac{1}{4}$ in. Girth of the neck behind the ears, 4 ft. 1 in. Girth of body immediately behind the forelegs, 8 ft. $0\frac{1}{2}$ in. Length of hair on flank, $25\frac{1}{2}$ in.; above the foreleg, $21\frac{1}{4}$ in.; under the jaw, 4 to 6 in. Circumference of fore-hoof, $16\frac{1}{2}$ in.; its diameter diagonally, $4\frac{1}{4}$ in.

Its hair was magnificent, thick and even; indeed the long hanging fringes on the sides were so thick that they

THE WILD YAK-BULL

made an actual cushion for the animal to lie on — a sufficient protection against even the rigorous winter climate of Tibet. The hair was a pitch black colour; but the top quarters when seen in a certain light inclined towards dark brown. Along the backbone the hair was very long and black. The eyes were brown, with a black pupil, and very small, the major axis of their opening being hardly $1\frac{3}{4}$ in. The hair round the eyes was thinnest, and as fine as velvet. On the other hand it was thick and tufted on the cheek and between the horns; on the nose it inclined to be grey.

The tongue was set with extraordinarily hard, sharp barbs. Both tongue and gums were tinged a greyish-blue, as in the tame yak. The muzzle was very broad; the nostrils rather longer, flattened, and turned upwards at a slightly oblique angle. The horns were extraordinarily powerful, and formidable by reason of their sharp points. The close woolly hair swept the ground when the animal stood, and, as I have said, made a soft cushion when he lay down. The tail was enormous; the hoofs strong and powerful; and of such the yak has need, to carry his immense weight over rough and stony ground. The two claws of the hoof can easily be drawn very close together, thus increasing the animal's hold upon the ground when climbing slippery rocks or crossing the slopes of loose mountain *débris*. Behind the hoofs proper were a pair of large secondary hoofs; but they did not touch the ground.

When the yak stands upright on its feet, its shoulder forms a conspicuous solid arch, and from it the neck sweeps sharply down towards the head, which the animal always carries close to the ground. In a similar manner the back slopes away, though less abruptly, towards the root of the tail. The height in the pelvic region is thus much less than at the shoulder. An animal which attains the dimensions I have given must evidently be exceedingly heavy. It took a single man all his time to raise the head of Islam's yak bull; and when the men loaded the flayed skin on the back of the kneeling camel it required four of them to lift it; the head however was still attached, that it might be better cured in camp.

It is marvellous that such a huge beast can subsist and develop such enormous muscular strength on the miserable herbage which those highlands afford. In winter the grass is dead and withered, and even in summer so tough and bitter that our caravan animals would only eat it when driven to do so by extreme hunger.

When the yak is pursued, it goes with a heavy clumsy sort of jog-trot, but gets swiftly over the ground; its tail hanging down and its head carried a little higher than usual; whilst its long hair trails on the ground. One advantage the yak always has over its pursuers: it never gets short of breath. When it perceives that danger threatens, it sets off at a gallop, with its head down and its tail in the air. When shot at, it stops; and when wounded, will charge its pursuer. In such a case it is prudent to be well on the alert.

Iskender and the other Taghliks told us, that in Cherchen, Charkhlik, and Achan (places at the northern foot of the Kwen-lun Mountains) there lived *pavans* or hunters who gained their livelihood almost entirely by hunting the yak. Their hunting-grounds are the Arka-tagh and Chimen-tagh in Northern Tibet. Each hunter takes with him two men, and a donkey to carry home the skin. But generally two or more hunters work together, so as to support one another if they are attacked by the yak. They are said to be such skilful and perfect marks-men, that they not seldom bring down their prey at the first shot, which must of course be lodged in the heart. They do not like to fire at more than sixty paces, and aim at a spot behind the shoulder. If the bullet penetrates the pelvic region, the animal will not succumb for two or three days after. If it strikes any other part, the yak troubles himself very little about it. To aim at the head is a mere waste of powder, for no bullet will penetrate the massive bone of the forehead. If a bullet does happen to strike a yak there, he merely shakes his head and grunts. But it is a good thing to break one of the legs, for that enables the hunter to put in his second bullet at close quarters, as well as hampers the animal if he charges. From the story of Islam Bai's many shots at our yak bull, it will be evident, that no bullet is really profitably expended unless it strikes a vital organ. It was, it will be remembered, only at the eleventh shot, which penetrated in the neigh-bourhood of the heart, that the huge monster fell.

The rifles which the Taghlik hunters use are made in the cities of East Turkestan. They are long heavy muzzle-loaders, with flint locks, and when fired are rested on a fork of antelope's horn. With his rifle in his hand, the hunter creeps close along the ground, skilfully availing himself of the slightest scrap of cover. As soon as he gets within range, he rests his long rifle-barrel on the fork, and aims deliberately, and long, before he discharges his piece. As soon as the yak is dead, it is skinned. The skin is divided into three sections, two slits being made along the upper edge of the hair at the sides, the third along the median line of the belly. The best leather is obtained from the section off the back, which, like the top of the shoulder, is called *sirit.* It is employed for making

THE WILD YAK-BULL (FRONT VIEW)

saddles, saddle-girths, bridle-reins, whips, and so on, as well as for the better kind of boots. The other two sections are used for pretty nearly the same purposes, but are not so good in quality. The soft boots (*churuk*) which the Taghliks usually wear are made from the skin of the legs. The tail is generally hung up as a religious offering (*tugh*) at some masar (saint's tomb).

The skins are sold to the merchants of Cherchen, Charkhlik, and Achan, and they carry them to Khotan, where they sell them to the *kunchis*, *i.e.* tanners and saddlers. The skin of the yak is highly valued because of its extraordinary toughness and durability. It is almost impossible to wear it out. The price for the skin of a full-grown yak bull is about 17*s.* 9*d.* But the skin of a cow or calf is much cheaper, and is divided into only two portions, for the sole reason that one donkey could not carry the whole skin.

The Taghliks look upon yak-hunting as a dangerous pursuit, and they are quite right in doing so, and also in hunting in company; for if the brute charges, the native hunter's position, with such a clumsy weapon as that he uses, and the little probability there is of his being able to escape, is anything but an enviable one. If he does have the misfortune to be struck by that thundering mass of solid flesh, with the sharp horns that it drives before it, his fate is irrevocably sealed.

So far extends my experience of this royal monarch of the desolate wilds of Tibet—an animal which excites our admiration not only in virtue of its imposing appearance, but also because it alone of living creatures is able to defy the loftiest altitudes, the bitterest cold, the most violent snowstorms and hailstorms which occur in any part of the earth. To all these things the wild yak is indifferent. He seems rather to enjoy it when the hail pelts down upon his back; and when the snows envelop him in their blinding whirl, he goes on quietly grazing as though nothing were the matter. The only extremity of climate which seems to disturb his equanimity is the summer sunshine. When it gets too warm for him, he takes a bath in the nearest stream, and climbs up the mountains to the cool expanses of the snowfields and the curving hollows of the glaciers, where he finds an especial pleasure in rolling himself and lying down to rest in the powdery snows of the *névés.*

CHAPTER LXXXIV.

LAKES WITHOUT END

FROM camp No. XIX., where we rested a day, we saw in the south-east a magnificent pinnacled mountain-top, covered for two-thirds of its relative height with glittering snows. To that peak, which lifted its head far above all its neighbours, and like a lighthouse was visible from a very great distance, I gave the name of King Oscar Mountain.

On the east of the camp was a large lake, its waters incomparably bitter, but showing the loveliest shades of colour; whilst vast flocks of gulls rocked on its curling waves. It contained no islands; but the delta of one of the small streams which emptied into it stretched out an arm a long way into the lake. As we skirted the northern shore, we were accompanied for above an hour by a herd of yaks; but they took care to keep out of range. Curiously enough, a well-beaten track meandered along the lake-shore, as though it had been made by cattle and horsemen; but the Taghliks asserted, that it was a path used by the wild yaks and asses, and the foot-prints and droppings along it bore out their judgment. Seeing that the wild yak abounded so plentifully in that region, and must surely die some time or other, I confess I was astonished we had not hitherto come across any skeleton. The first we saw were two skulls with some other bones bleached and crumbling, lying beside this lake. Perhaps when the yak becomes conscious of the approach of death, it hides itself in some lonely, inaccessible retreat among the mountains or by the shores of some solitary lake, where the waves wash away its carcass.

After doing nineteen and a quarter miles we halted for the night at the foot of some hills, and near a brook at the east end of the lake. Four khulans, a stallion and three mares, circled round our camp all the afternoon, being apparently greatly astonished at us all. Round and round they trotted, with a short springy step, their heads in the air and turned towards us, and their tails streaming out obliquely. I never grew tired of watching them; they were such beautiful, such graceful creatures.

On September 7th, the country was as monotonous as before. The broad depression or valley between the Arka-tagh and the Southern Range still continued to be divided into a series of self-contained lake-basins without outlet. At the east end of lake No. 15 we descended an imperceptible slope of soft, moist sand to a small threshold or watershed between that lake-basin and the next. The following day however the country improved a good deal; the ground was hard, and the numerous watercourses small, so that we covered eighteen and a half miles. The almost dead level did not tire the animals anything like so much. Our worst enemy was the wind; which visited us daily, thoroughly chilling tent and furs. Camp No. XXII. stood 16,195 feet above sea-level.

On September 9th, we made the splendid record of twenty-four and three-quarter miles, our longest day's march in Tibet. We crossed the low ridge between lake No. 16 and a broad open valley on the other side, which led down to the next lake, beside which we pitched camp No. XXIII. But this forcing of the pace cost us a horse and a donkey. We were often obliged to make longer marches than we liked in order to reach such pasturage as was to be found; but this day we found none at all. We still had sufficient maize to last the animals ten days; but we husbanded the strength of our best horses as much as we possibly could. The days of many of the others were already unmistakeably numbered. The highest altitudes of the Southern Mountain Range were becoming more closely seamed with glaciers; the mountain-sides were sheathed with their icy mail, like the flanks of

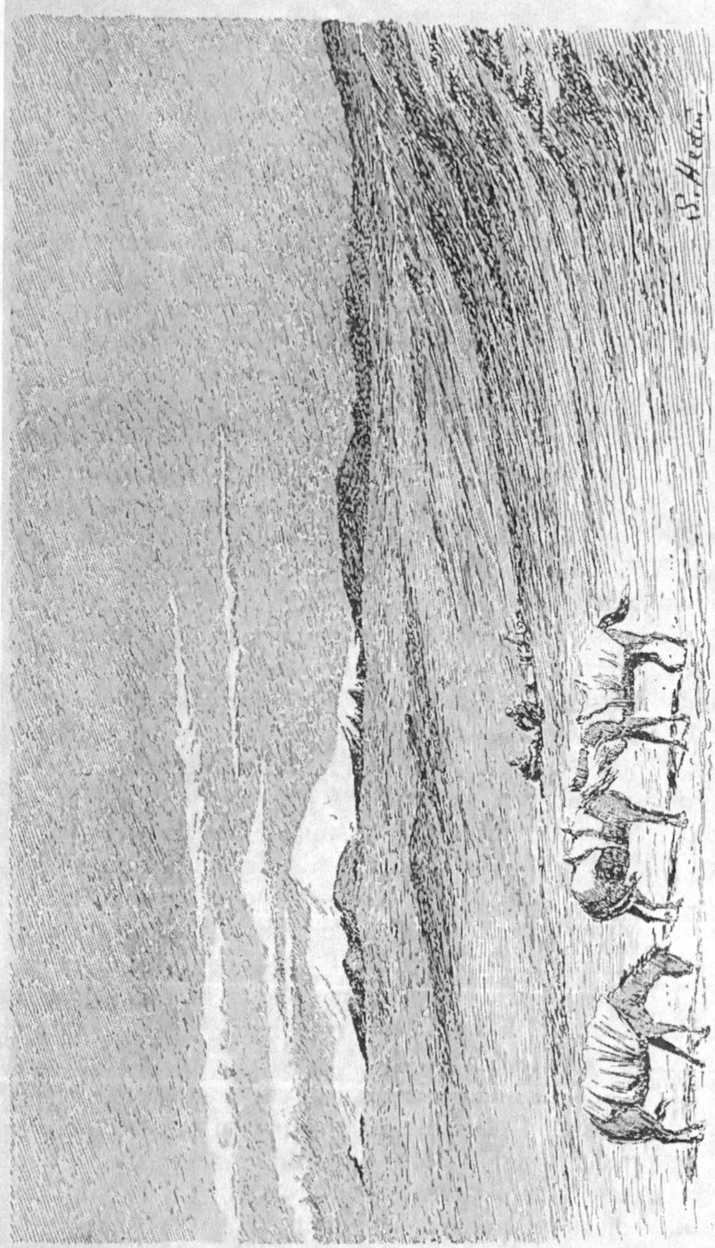

KING OSCAR MOUNTAIN, SEEN FROM THE NORTH

Mus-tagh-ata, although they did not send off any well-developed ice-streams.

September 10th. Our course lay eastwards—always eastwards—along a flat plain, traversed by a stream divided into innumerable narrow channels, which flowed to the next lake, No. 18. Beside this last we encamped; and there, since there was a fair quantity of grass on the neighbouring hills, we also rested a day. And the rest came opportunely, for it was perfectly wintry weather. It hailed and snowed all day long, and an icy wind blew from every quarter. The landscape was enshrouded in thick mist, so that we could not get a single glimpse of our surroundings.

We now took stock of our provision-chests, with the result that we saw it would be necessary to exercise strict economy for the future. We had possibly sufficient bread, flour, and tea to last us a month; but there were eleven of us, and we did not know how far it was to the nearest inhabited district. We had only one sheep left; but if the worst came to the worst, we should have to live upon yak beef. It was six weeks since we left the last inhabited dwelling, and we were all longing to meet with human beings, no matter who or what they were.

It was impossible to do any work all day. I sat on my bed inside the tent, wrapped in my furs, and finished the last sheets of my map, and read. But my fingers got stiff and blue with cold, so that when my tea was brought in, I was glad to warm them against the teapot. I only felt properly warm the first hour or two after meals; then that everlasting wind chilled me to the bone again.

The neighbourhood of our camp was gloomy and lifeless, except for the screaming of the gulls on the lake. Of vegetation there was not a sign, except the grass which already showed its autumn yellow tinge. The wind howled; the hard-grained snow whistled round the tent; the waves beat softly and monotonously against the shore. The shore on the opposite side was hidden by the driving snow, so that I easily imagined I was standing on the brink of the mighty ocean. Oh how ardently did I long for a sight of it! All the more that I was now shut up in the heart of the vastest of the continents, many and many a mile from the eternal sea! The tent with its covering of white snow made a conspicuous object in the midst of the grey lonely scene. Our wearied animals nibbled the scanty grass on the hills near by. Some of the men were asleep in their tent; others sat outside, round the fire of wild-yak dung, which sent up a thick column of black smoke. Night came as welcome as an anxiously expected guest. Once in my fur nest of a bed, I soon became warm; and on the wings of gentle dreams I visited that dear spot of earth towards which my desire grew stronger with every day that passed. But we were still a long, long way from Peking; and thither I *must* go. But once there, I should consider myself at home.

September 12th. At five o'clock in the morning, when we set about getting ready for the start, the ground was everywhere covered with snow, right down to the shore of the lake. The landscape was snow, snow, snow—nothing but snow; so that the icy summits of the Southern Mountains no longer gleamed out so prominently as they had hitherto done. But long before the morning was over, the sun had melted most of the snow, which, as it happened, had been heaped on the slope that looked towards the south and south-east. On the other hand the northern slopes remained white all day long, nor did the ice melt on the lagoons and streams. The temperature was the lowest we had hitherto experienced (10°9 Fahr. or – 11°7 C.), and it continued so until midday; and even after that time it was bitterly cold, in consequence of a persistent wind from the north-west. My hands suffered the most, as I was unable to protect them; I needed them every moment for map-sketching.

Like all the previous lakes, lake No. 18 had an east-west direction, and was one of the largest we encountered: we travelled beside it the whole of the day (sixteen and three-quarter miles). Before us the view was illimitable; on either hand were the giant mountains of the great

THE SALT LAKE AT CAMP NO. XXV.

Tibetan plateau. The irregular shore-line was edged with scum, and the breakers rolled against the slaty gravel with a curious metallic sound, no doubt the combined effect of the attenuated atmosphere and the high specific gravity of the water. It will readily be understood that the extreme rarefaction of the atmosphere must exercise an influence upon the acoustic properties of sound. For example, upon those lofty solitudes we were obliged to speak louder and more distinctly than usual; and I could not hear my watch tick unless I held it close to my ear.

At eleven o'clock in the morning the temperature of the air was still 30°9 Fahr. (–0°6 C.), whilst at the same hour that of the water was 45°1 Fahr. (7°3 C.), a fall of several degrees since the preceding day. Here for the first time we observed the track of a bear; indeed we followed it nearly all day. Further on a fox had come down to the lake. Again we crossed a number of small streams flowing from the Arka-tagh. Most of them formed a delta, more or less developed, with long tongues of sand jutting out still further into the lake; and these were always pointed towards the east or south-east, a fact which must probably be ascribed to the pressure exercised by the west wind.

During the march we lost a donkey. After we encamped we lost two more, also a cream-coloured horse which had done excellent service, carrying my instrument-cases all the way from Korla to Lop-nor, and thence *viâ* Cherchen to Khotan, and finally from Khotan to the present place. Our poor beasts were beginning to show terrible signs of the hard travelling. Not a day passed but we lost one, sometimes more. Their carcasses did not corrupt, but in the pure, cold, attenuated air simply shrivelled up to mummies; and there they now lie as memorials of the road we took through the wilds of Northern Tibet. The difficulties of the journey were greatly increased owing to the pasturage being less frequent, and of inferior quality, to that we met with during the first days of our march through the Tibetan mountains. The plain fact is, horses and donkeys were not suited for such high altitudes. The camels stood the hardships of travel much better; yet even they had grown painfully thinner. The men maintained that the herbage was actually injurious to all the animals. But if so, how is it that the khulans and wild yaks thrive so well on it?

September 13th. This day, although we put seventeen and a half miles under our feet, only one donkey succumbed. The water in the creek at the east end of the lake was so far fresh, thanks to the stream which flowed into it, that the animals were able to drink it. At ten o'clock in the morning its temperature was $49^\circ1$ Fahr. ($9^\circ5$ C.), whilst the temperature of the air was $38^\circ7$ Fahr. ($3^\circ7$ C.). During the course of the morning the wind veered round to the south-west. In consequence of this the scum, which fringed the southern beach, drifted across the lake towards the northern shore like tufts of cotton. The surface of the ground rose imperceptibly towards the east, merging into a level plain, virtually a continuation of the lake-basin. Its marshy ground was very tiring for the animals. But we soon got higher, amongst a tangled labyrinth of low hills; from the top of one of which we obtained a splendid and comprehensive view of the large lake we had just left. Its western extremity was just visible as a faint line along the distant horizon, and above it loomed a row of snow-clad mountain summits.

Having crossed yet another level plain, likewise traversed by a stream making for the lake behind us, and threaded yet another labyrinth of low hills, we reached the saddle which bordered the basin of lake No. 18 on the east. Hour after hour we plodded our slow way through the desolate lifeless scene, the dead silence unbroken by a single sound. At length we reached a small pass overlooking a tiny isolated pool; and beside it I found the tents already pitched when I got down. I hoped, from the broken ground, that we should soon reach a Peripheral region, and come in contact with some of the head-streams and feeders of the mighty Yang-tse-kiang.

Camp No. XXVI. (16,545 feet) was one of the most unfavourable we pitched upon. There was an almost total dearth of grazing, and there was not a single yak discoverable in the vicinity. Before I could get a little water boiled for my tea, I was obliged to sacrifice two or three of the tent-pegs. It was dark when the camels and the last five donkeys crawled into camp. The failure of the animals threatened to put us in a critical position, similar to that which overtook me during my journey across the Takla-makan Desert in 1895. My caravan was gradually melting away in the same way it did then. Then our eyes were constantly turned towards the east, seeking some relief from the unfavourable ground; so it was now. But we did not now suffer from want of water; and even though we lost every animal we possessed, we should still be able to reach some inhabited district on foot.

CHAPTER LXXXV.

TIBETAN STORMS

SEPTEMBER 14th. The death-register was lengthened by the addition of the deaths of a horse and a donkey. A flock of geese passed over our heads, flying north-west in the direction of Lop-nor—a strange spectacle at this season of the year. All day we toiled along between ridges of moderate elevation, down a broad valley, beside a crystal pure mountain-stream. But although the surface sloped very gradually downwards, it did not help the animals much, for the ground was soft and moist like mud, and they sank in over the hoofs at every step. Patches of snow were still left in places, and when they melted, they too saturated the ground.

I hoped that the stream we were travelling beside was the upper course of the Naptchitai-ulan-muren shown on the maps; but eventually we saw a long way ahead of us another large lake. But perhaps it was a freshwater lake? Perhaps the river flowed right through it, issuing again at the farther end? And my hopes rose as the vast area of the lake gradually became unfolded to our view: its surface made a straight line across the distant horizon. At length we reached the lake itself, and pitched our next camp (15,775 feet) between a couple of low hills on its southern shore, after doing seventeen and a quarter miles.

My first concern was to get a tin of water brought up from the lake. The water was bright and clear. I drank a mouthful of it: it was bitter salt. Another self-contained lake-basin then! and still another pass to surmount at its eastern end! Well, well! We had no choice in the matter. We could not strike off to the north or north-east, so as to reach Tsaidam the sooner that way; for the insurmountable wall of the Arka-tagh reared itself up in our path. Besides, our animals were not equal to any real climbing; they would be incapable of climbing over anything more serious than a very low pass.

Towards evening the men sent a deputation to me, asking for a day's rest. Two camels and two donkeys were in a bad way, and unless they got rest would almost certainly succumb on the morrow.

On September 16th we travelled no less than twenty miles without losing a single animal. The lake stretched to an extraordinary length. I began to fancy it would be a worthy rival to the Issyk-kul, which is several days' journey long. But we must have been the victims of an optical delusion or mirage; for at the end of two to three hours' march the hills that lined both shores met together, forming a dark line above the level of the lake. Beyond doubt we had another pass in front of us. This time we were travelling along the southern shore of the lake, and there we found plenty of yak dung, as well as numerous spoor. We also picked up a yak's horn, with the mark of a knife-cut plainly distinguishable near the tip. We likewise discovered some fragments of a clay pitcher—another indication that human beings had some time or other been there before us.

Immediately after noon the clouds flocked closer together all round us, whilst a violent east wind arose, and in a very short time down came the usual snowstorm. It was the most violent storm of snow, and with the heaviest fall, I had experienced since I was on the Mustagh-ata. Clouds of powdery snow as fine as flour swept along close to the surface of the earth, succeeded every now and again by showers of hail—totally blotting out the landscape. The ground became instantly white; indeed we were actually snowed up sitting in our saddles. We seemed however to have left the region in which the west wind was prevalent; for during the last day or two the east wind had been the more general. The storm lasted almost two hours, and then the sun shone out again.

The new lake contracted to a long narrow creek. We turned off from it towards the east-south-east, and slowly made our way over the low hills towards the Southern Mountains, hoping to discover some herbage at their foot. On the right we left a small pool, beside which sat a grey bear in a brown study. Yolldash charged down upon him as bold as you please. But when Bruin looked like waiting for the attack, Yolldash turned tail, and fled back again as swift as an arrow, whilst the bear trotted off amongst the hills.

We did find herbage, some patches of it tolerably good, at any rate the best we had come across since we left Dalai-kurgan; we decided therefore to sacrifice another day for the animals' sakes. As it turned out, it was a wise decision; for hail, snow, and wind disputed for the supremacy from a very early hour in the morning. According to their wont, the men sat in a circle round the fire, and mended their ragged clothes and the saddles, whilst Emin Mirza read aloud to them. One of the camels was galled on the pads of his hind feet. Accordingly one of the men made him a pair of stockings of khulan skin, and sewed them on his feet. After that he got on capitally.

September 18th. The heavy snowfall of the preceding day made it difficult for the animals to find the herbage. One donkey was left in the camp, whilst two more of the horses were unfit for work. They were sent along with the last four donkeys; and of these again only one was able to carry anything like an appropriate load. We had now only eight horses left that were fit for service, and all of them were thin and pined. I, Islam Bai, and Parpi Bai were the only members of the caravan who rode. The rest of the men were obliged to walk. As I have said, two of the camels were not very capital, though the others were still in pretty fair condition. The dogs however were in fine trim; they got many a fat meal from the animals which died in camp.

The weather was splendid, and the ground quite level. We travelled along the base of the Southern Mountains,

OUR CARAVAN IN A HAILSTORM, NORTHERN TIBET

and did seventeen and a half miles before we stopped for the night at camp No. XXIX. There again we rested a day. It was imperative we should husband the animals' strength. About two o'clock in the morning I was awakened by a hurricane of snow, which threatened to rend the tent to pieces; and when daylight came, the snow lay in some places a foot deep. The amount of precipitation seemed to be much heavier in that district than in the regions we had passed through.

At five o'clock in the afternoon I had a hole dug, that I might take the temperature of the ground. At that hour the temperature of the atmosphere was 38°5 Fahr. (3°6 C.). At the depth of 8¼ inches the thermometer registered 37°2 Fahr. (2°9 C.); at 11½ inches 34°7 Fahr. (1°5 C.); at 19½ inches 33°9 Fahr. (1°05 C.); at 27½ inches 32°9 Fahr. (0°5 C.); and at 34½ inches 32°7 Fahr. (0°4 C.). The first four observations were made in fine yellow sand, resting upon blue-black mud and mould, which contained numerous remains of decayed vegetation. The upper layer of the earth used to freeze in the night to the depth of two finger's-breadths, rendering our march somewhat easier of a morning; but it always thawed again as soon as the sun rose.

September 20th. Sixteen miles to camp No. XXX. (15,175 feet). After a tramp of several hours over gentle hills we approached the saddle which bounded lake No. 19 on the east. There I stopped to reconnoitre, so as to ascertain which way to go. The Arka-tagh in the north-east was now lower than it had hitherto been; but we durst not attempt to cross the range with such an exhausted caravan, especially as the Taghliks thought that surmounting the pass would kill all the animals. To the east—yet another lake—yet another self-contained basin destitute of outflow. Was this chain of salt lakes never coming to an end? One thing however was encouraging. The descent from the saddle on which I stood was very much steeper on the east than the ascent had been on the west. We appeared to be approaching lower altitudes than those we had hitherto travelled at. We also met with new species of plants, specimens of which I added to my botanical collection. Yet another donkey gave up; and the surviving three looked as though they would not last very much longer.

September 21st. The object we had before us throughout the whole of the day's march of sixteen miles was to reach lake No. 20. All day we followed the course of a stream which came down from the Southern

LAKE NO. 20, LOOKING EAST

On the shore of which camps No. XXXI.-XXXIV were pitched

Mountains and flowed into the lake ahead, catching up several tributaries on the way, a stream which had a volume of forty-five cubic feet in the second. None of our animals died. The country was still barren and monotonous. But we saw yaks, khulans, antelopes, bears, voles, ravens, larks, wagtails, and gulls, as well as flies and gadflies. At the point where it entered the lake the stream formed an extensive sedimentary delta. This lake too was like a sea, so large that we were unable to perceive its eastern extremity. The two giant mountain-chains gradually approached each other in the far perspective; still there was always a gap left between them, in which lake and sky appeared to meet and touch one another. The lake curved first to the north-west then to the south, and so seemed to bar our advance. We did not know which shore to follow, the northern or the southern; but finally chose the former, a decision which cost us two extra days.

LAKE NO. 20, LOOKING NORTH-EAST

The snowy mountains are the continuation of Arka-tagh

Meanwhile we encamped (No. XXXI.) beside the lake in a spot where there was tolerable herbage. The lake seemed to be deep, for the water was a blue-black colour, and the hills on its western shore came down abruptly towards its margin. It was another self-contained lake without outflow, for its water was bitter salt. We had therefore still another pass to get over at its eastern end. So far as we could see, this was probably the largest of all the salt lakes. But not a sign of human beings.

September 22nd. Our next stage, to camp No. XXXII., was fourteen and a half miles. The ground was the most difficult we had encountered for a long time, consisting for half the way of undulating hills, very much broken, and trenched by gullies and ravines. For some distance however we followed a yak track, which kept at about the same level, although at the cost of innumerable windings and zigzaggings backwards and forwards. The yak, it seems, prefers to make detours rather than constantly go up and down. The hills stood close to the lake shore, and were the northern outliers of a large chain which shut in the lake on the south, and which had hitherto hidden its water from our sight. Hour after hour we rode on towards the west, and yet there was no getting round the lake. We regretted not having chosen the southern shore. Nevertheless we kept pushing on, impelled by the faint hope, that at the western extremity of the lake there might be a glen leading up to a convenient pass over the Arka-tagh. But the farther we advanced towards the west, the lower sank the hills, until at last we were able to ride close along the margin of the water on perfectly level ground. Between us and the lake there was however a chain of freshwater lagoons, each fed by a mountain-stream, and having some invisible connection with the lake.

In addition to the hills, and now the innumerable small brooks, about eleven o'clock the weather took a disagreeable turn. The sky darkened in every quarter, and a hailstorm of unparalleled violence burst over the lake. The clouds drove towards us out of the east like a solid black wall, accompanied by fierce hissings and whinings, like the sound of steam escaping from the boiler of a locomotive. The surface of the lake turned dark grey. The mountains on the shore became lost in the haze; louder and louder waxed the roar of the storm. We could see and we could hear how the drops of water splashed up with a perceptible hiss as the hailstones thrashed the dead smooth surface of the lake. The hail came down in blinding showers; but finally passed over into snow and

LAKE NO. 20, LOOKING NORTH-WEST

A HAILSTORM APPROACHING THE WESTERN GULF OF LAKE NO. 20, LOOKING EAST-SOUTH-EAST

rain. Then the wind changed, and a terrific gale set in from the west. It blew right in our teeth. and nearly froze us to death. The horses literally toiled against it, as though they were struggling up a steep hill. Clots of frothy scum drove against the shore, winding in a sinuous line in and out of the coves and bays. The gulls however seemed to enjoy themselves thoroughly, as they rocked complacently on the crest of the waves.

At length the lake narrowed down to a long creek, pointing west, in which direction the depression was continued by a tolerably broad valley. The north shore was overlooked by the lofty mountains which formed a continuation of the Arka-tagh.

Their ramifying spurs, viewed in perspective, were like gigantic tetrahedra (see p. 1059); as they stood there in a long line, they put me in mind of houses overlooking a corso or marine drive. Upon reaching the end of the lake, the horse-caravan had steered due north, making for the foot of the mountains. We saw the white tents gleaming in the throat of a narrow glen a long time before we reached them. The camping-ground was however ill-chosen, being in the dry bed of a torrent full of stones and gravel; but the perpendicular cliffs at any rate afforded shelter.

September 23rd. Our next camp, No. XXXIII., reached after a march of thirteen and a half miles, was almost exactly opposite to camp No. XXXI., so that the last two days had not brought us a single yard further to the east. We had bad weather all day; first a blinding snowstorm from the east, after that a gale of wind which swept down from the northern mountains. We kept close to the lake shore, having the mountains only about two miles distant on our left. The rocky mountain-wall was broken by a succession of narrow glen-mouths, in which the torrents, now however dry, had formed huge talus slopes of gravel detritus.

Occasionally our route led over very steep hills, on one of which I lost my riding-horse. It was a first-rate animal, and had carried me ever since my summer trip to the Pamirs in the year 1895. But his powers were now exhausted: he was unable to go any farther. I took Emin Mirza's horse, whilst he led mine at a gentle pace. Then I went on by myself, following the caravan through the blinding snow. But I was destined to ill-luck with my horses that day. Emin Mirza's beast came down with me, though without throwing me out of the saddle. I therefore walked into camp, leading him by the bridle. I was very glad to get under the shelter of my tent; but it was a good hour before my frozen hands were sufficiently warm for me to be able to use them. All the afternoon a full-fledged hurricane blew out of the north. My tent was securely fastened down, the side felts being tucked well in under the travelling-boxes; nevertheless it was blown down, and would certainly have been carried clean away, if I had not laid hold of one of the tent-poles and held fast till the men came to my help, and lashed the tent even more securely with extra ropes on the windward side.

Only five camels turned up at camp. The one with the stockings of khulan-skin had succumbed, and been killed. The men brought the best pieces of the flesh with them, a welcome addition to our larder. Here again we were obliged to give the exhausted animals another day's rest.

The first object my eyes fell upon when I stepped outside my tent in the morning was my riding-horse lying dead on the ground. I had ridden him sixteen months, in all sorts of weather, and he had never once stumbled or fallen, in this respect being excellently suited for my mapping work. At Khotan he had a rest of four months in Liu Darin's stable, and when he came out of it he looked as sleek and fit as an English thorough-bred. During the past week or two he had grown thin, and put on a starveling look; his coat had become rough, and his strength failed. The dogs feasted upon the carcass. From this time I rode a little black horse which I bought in Korla, and which had been with me in my Lop-nor expedition.

THE "KITCHEN" AT CAMP NO. XXXII.

Hares were plentiful in the vicinity of the camp; some of them proved acceptable as a variation in our bill of fare.

September 25th. To camp No. XXXIV. (15,565 feet) was a distance of fifteen miles. The greater part of the day we followed the shore-line of the lake. It made an almost straight line, without capes, or bays, or islands, and stretched towards the east-south-east. In one place however our advance was checked by a low ridge; but in compensation its summit afforded a comprehensive view of our surroundings. To the east the country appeared quite open; and beyond lake No. 20, and in the same line with it, I saw two other small lakes. Their relative situations reminded me of Carey and Dalgleish's map, which I had amongst my baggage. They marked the farthest point to which those travellers penetrated; and Parpi Bai, who had been with them, confirmed me in my supposition. South-east, but in the far, far distance, the landscape was closed in by a mighty mountain-range overtopped by snowy peaks. What connection this range had with the Southern Mountains, the chain which we had had on our right ever since we crossed the Arka-tagh, I could not with certainty determine, my line of vision being intercepted by its spurs and outlying ridges. I suspect however that it was the immediate continuation of the range which is known farther east as the Koko-shili (the Green Hills). I thought it very probable, that we were not far from the region in which the river Napchitai-ulan-muren takes its origin.

The next day we rested, waiting for the snowstorm to pass over. My caravan now consisted of five camels, nine horses, and three donkeys, together with eleven men. But several of the animals could not hold out very much longer; and the Taghlik Iskender was ill, so that he was allowed to ride one of the donkeys. Emin Mirza was obliged to walk after his horse became unfit for service. The last time the horses had any maize was at camp No. XXX.; after that we gave them every morning a portion of hard stale bread. This was all they got, except for such wretched grass as they were able to find themselves. For ourselves we baked bread in the shape of cakes twice every day. Fortunately we had no lack of fuel; there was an abundant supply of yak dung everywhere.

CHAPTER LXXXVI.

DISCOVERIES OF INSCRIBED STONES

SEPTEMBER 27th. Stage to camp No. XXXV., seventeen miles. This day promised to bring a welcome change in the monotony of our marches. We hoped to recross the Arka-tagh, and so say good-bye to the highlands of Northern Tibet, with their desolate lake-basins destitute of outflow. We knew as a fact, that there was a practicable pass somewhere immediately to the north of us; for during our last rest-day I sent men to reconnoitre, and they brought back the report, that the road was easy. A couple of hours' riding up a gently inclined valley brought us to the relatively low pass. Nor was its northern approach at all steeper. Taking as our guide a brook crusted with ice, we rode down a valley which gradually widened out into an amphitheatre surrounded by mountain-crests. The brook also acted as a footbath for my men; for they had constantly to leap across it, and in the wider parts sometimes failed to land on the other side. Their feet were encased in pieces of felt, wrapped over with khulan-skin, and upon reaching camp it was always their first concern to dry their "shoes."

Having doubled a projecting promontory of the mountains, we came upon a very discouraging sight, namely a small lake into which all the brooks of the district poured their waters. Plainly we had only stumbled into yet another self-contained basin possessing no outflow. The pass we had just crossed was therefore in all probability not the real pass over the Arka-tagh; that still had to be surmounted, and possibly it would be a much more formidable affair.

At length however we reached the amphitheatre or *cirque* of which I have already spoken, and in which the herbage, such as it was, was not scanty. An exceptionally large herd of yaks were grazing at the foot of the rocks on our right. Islam rode towards them, and took a shot at them. Thereupon the herd divided, the greater part fleeing up the mountains, whilst the others. nearly fifty of them, in a tightly packed drove made straight towards me and Emin Mirza. We were alone and without weapons, and felt we were in a pretty tight fix, for the animals seemed to be charging directly down upon us. The leader of the herd was a well-shaped bull; after him a little calf and five old bulls walloped along as hard as they could put feet to ground; whilst the rear was brought up by Islam on horseback. The yaks were enveloped in a perfect cloud of dust. We could distinctly hear the cracking of their hoofs, and were blindly conscious that in another second or two we should be crushed under the avalanche of their irresistible onrush. It appeared however that they had not yet observed us; for no sooner did the leader become aware of us, which he did at about a hundred paces' distance, than he swerved aside, and was instantly followed by the entire battalion. This gave Islam his opportunity. He hastily dismounted and placed himself in ambush, and fired at a venture right in the middle of the troop. The bullet struck a bull in the foreleg; then the animal, mad with fury, charged straight upon the sportsman. Islam flung himself into the saddle, and set off as fast as his enfeebled horse was able to gallop. The yak however, although running on only three legs, caught him up after two or three minutes' chase; but just as he was on the point of tossing horse and rider on his horns, Islam, who saw the danger he was in, turned in his saddle and took aim. But he was so excited, he could not aim with the cool deliberation that so perilous a moment demanded. However, the yak was so close to him that it was scarcely possible to miss: luckily the bullet penetrated in the region of the heart, and thus put an end to the contest.

The yak was a bull about eight years old. The tongue

"THE YAK WAS ON THE POINT OF TOSSING HORSE AND RIDER ON HIS HORNS"

and meat were especially welcome, since our supplies of rice and flour were fast running out. If Islam's last shot had failed, he would infallibly have been lost. The chase of the wild yak is perilous, and it does not always have such a happy ending as this.

This adventure led to our encamping in a place that was not quite so suitable as usual, for it was a long way from water; and then, in order to get the full benefit of the yak, we were obliged to stay there all the next day. The dogs were tied up, to prevent them from spoiling the meat. For dinner therefore I had soup made from yak beef; it was a dark brown colour, and very nourishing and tasty. For some time this soup formed a portion of my daily diet.

If my dinner was good, my dessert was better. I was just lighting my pipe, when all the men, Islam at their head, came to me in a state of great excitement, crying, "*Biss nishan tappdik*" (We have found a sign!) And down before me they laid four large slates, inscribed all over with Tibetan letter-signs. Each of the slates was whole, and manifestly complete in itself; but two were old, for their inscriptions were partly obliterated.

My curiosity was keenly stirred. What could these dead stones not tell me? Why had such great pains been taken to cut these inscriptions upon them? Perhaps they contained the record of some remarkable occurrence, some historical event? Or perhaps they contained information of great value to pilgrims bound for Lhasa? For, according to my maps, the great pilgrim road from Mongolia to the holy capital of the Dalai Lama bent to the south-west somewhere hereabouts. But the thing which delighted the men most was the indisputable evidence which these inscribed stones afforded, that some time or another human beings had visited the region where we then were.

Before we left, I went to the place where the inscribed tablets had been discovered. It was on the shore of a small lake, whither some of the men had gone to fetch water. I soon made out a square of stones, and the outlines of two or three tents; evidently the place had been inhabited for some time by Tibetan or Mongol nomads, with their herds of yaks. In the immediate vicinity we found eight other stones of a similar character to the first four, all covered with inscriptions. We could not possibly carry them all with us. I selected therefore a couple of well-executed fragments, which were not too thin to stand the rough usage of travel. The others we buried, so as to preserve them; for if the discovery proved to be important, I could return on some future occasion, and fetch them.

Then we continued our journey north-eastwards towards camp No. XXXVI.; and that day covered fifteen miles. Not very long after starting we came to a large stream flowing towards the east, and *out* of the lake. After all, then, lake No. 23 was not a self-contained basin without outlet. For the stream did not flow into, but out of, the lake, and cut its way through the mountain-chain which soared up in front of us. The next notable landmark was an inconsiderable pass, near which we perceived the skull of an arkhari or wild sheep, as well as some herds of yaks and orongo antelopes, and numerous khulans. Every now and again we could make out something like a beaten track; but whether it was made by wild animals or by human beings we could not ascertain. But on the summit of the pass we came across a cairn of stones; *that* at any rate owed its existence to human hands. We descended from the pass into a spacious cauldron-shaped valley, richly supplied with grass, and intersected by several small brooks flowing towards the south-east. It seemed to be a perfect El Dorado for khulans; for they swarmed all over it in such numbers that we counted troops of 80 to 200 individuals, moving like squadrons of cavalry along the mountain-slopes.

In about the middle of the valley we made another discovery—a very remarkable one all things considered, for it consisted of the tracks of three camels and half-a-dozen horses, that is to say, an entire caravan, and it had travelled towards the north-west. According to the Taghliks, the tracks were not more than five days old at the very most. Anyhow, we were once more clearly coming within reach of our fellow-men. This discovery put new life into the men. They kept a sharp look-out for further signs. We might any time now expect to meet Mongols or shepherds.

On the opposite side of the cauldron-shaped valley we ascended between two mountain-spurs to an inconsiderable pass (14,950 feet). There, at the foot of a sand-dune, beside some frozen springs, we pitched our tents. This march cost two more horses their lives.

September 30th. The night was bright but cold. In the morning the country was wreathed in mist, and every blade of grass and every projecting stone was feathered with the long white plumes of the rime-frost. The pass led down into a tolerably broad grassy valley, through which babbled a little brook. A short distance down the valley we caught sight of a black object standing on the left bank of the stream. I took it for a yak lying down and resting; but after we advanced a little nearer, the men asserted that it was a *nishan* (sign, guide-post). We made our way towards it, and were not a little amazed to find in the midst of this wild region an *obo* (religious monument) of such an original and beautiful construction as this was. It had no doubt been built to propitiate the deities of the mountain, and consisted of large slates leaning one against another, covered all over with inscriptions. At last we were getting wind in our sails. The caravan was called in, and up went the tents immediately adjoining the obo; although we had travelled very little more than five miles. There was work here however to keep me busy for two whole days. The grass was better than usual; the brook would supply us with water. A horse and a donkey had, it is true, been left behind in the pass; but that only proved how needful it was to give the animals as much rest as we could possibly spare them.

My first step was to sketch this remarkable structure, and I sketched it from each of its four sides. The ground-plan of the obo resembled the ground-plan of a stable, with three stalls, $1\frac{1}{4}$, $1\frac{3}{4}$, $2\frac{1}{4}$ feet wide respectively. Altogether there were forty-nine slabs of slate, propped up edgewise one against another like a "house" built of playing-cards. The slab at the back was nearly $4\frac{1}{2}$ feet long, and $4\frac{3}{4}$ feet high, and overtopped the others in a picturesque fashion. The portion that projected above the roof of the structure was without any inscription; but every part of it was completely covered with ideographs or letter-signs both large and small. Outside it were other slabs, some as much as 5 feet long. All the slabs were quite flat, not much more than one-third of an inch thick, and of a dark green colour. It was astonishing how they could have been quarried out of the adjacent slate mountains in such a flawless condition. The roof of the "stalls," 2 feet above the ground, consisted of four slabs each $7\frac{3}{4}$ feet long, so that they projected beyond the ten pieces which made the gable-ends. The front looked straight down the valley, that is towards the south-east. The letters or ideographs, which varied from $\frac{3}{4}$ to 4 inches in height, had plainly not been chiselled out, but had been impressed upon the slate with some sharp, pointed instrument; otherwise the brittle tablets—they were only like children's school-slates—would not have stood the process. The letters were a light grey colour, and hence were easily distinguishable against the dark green background of the slates.

Close beside the obo were some soot-blackened stones, together with charcoal and ashes, showing that nomads had been there not long before. Further, we discovered a rectangular tomb and a footpath leading to it; and concluded that the place was probably an object of pilgrimage.

I was again confronted with the same question as before—What was it these silent stones could tell me? In all probability the information they conveyed was of a religious nature. But whatever it was, it would no doubt possess some degree of interest. Perhaps it related some incident which happened there? At any rate the inscriptions must be copied; I could get them deciphered afterwards. We therefore took to pieces the wall that faced south-west, and laid out all the slabs in order on the ground, that we might be able to put them back in their proper places after I had copied them.

The first two that I attacked were small, and I copied them in about half an hour. But shortly after I set to work upon the third, I was struck by the strange uniformity of the lettering, and thought the same signs were repeated with fixed regularity. Upon examining them more closely, I noticed that every seventh letter was

THE "OBO"

always the same. I went out of the tent, and examined the obo. Each and every one of the forty-nine slabs was inscribed with the same seven signs, occurring and recurring again and again precisely in the same regular and uniform order. A light broke in upon me. These mysterious inscriptions could bear only one interpretation. They were repetitions of the well-known Tibetan formula of prayer—"*On manch padmch hum*," *i.e.* "Oh the jewel of the lotus!" I instantly stopped my copying. The animals could very well do without a rest on the morrow.

I contented myself with taking two or three pieces

of handsome stone as specimens, leaving behind those I brought from camp No. XXXVI. We could not of course take the whole structure with us: it would have made three camel-loads. Besides, the only importance of the stones was of an ethnographical character, an importance which did not outbalance their intrinsic solid weight.

I now looked upon the obo, not as a great rarity, but as a ridiculous and idiotic piece of nonsense. It was our first acquaintance with the crass exaggerations of Lamaism. Instead of being an important historical document relating to the great Mongol pilgrim road to Lhasa, which (as I have just said) crossed the border-range of Tsaidam in that neighbourhood, it was merely an empty formula. The most beautiful sentence would become stupid and inane if repeated four thousand times. To write the Lord's Prayer four thousand times would not be a stroke of genius: but to engrave a formula of prayer upon stone that number of times, when each letter demanded a special expenditure of strength, time, and labour—it was unquestionably an idiotic proceeding. But then what else can you expect from fanatics who deliberately strangle the common sense with which Mother Nature thought fit to endow them? I felt somewhat crestfallen over the whole business. Still it had done no harm; I had only gleaned a smaller harvest than I hoped for. One gain was at any rate sure: we had now indubitable proof that we had hit upon one of the great highroads that lead to Lhasa. The obo, the tomb, the footpath, and the cairn of stones on the summit of the first pass, all were indisputable witnesses of the fact. Meanwhile lower down the valley the men lighted upon the trails of two or three camels and of several large troops of khulans. The Taghliks maintained that the khulan persistently shuns inhabited districts, and is never found in the vicinity of human beings. They therefore believed, that at the very least we still had two day's-stages before us to reach the nearest inhabited region.

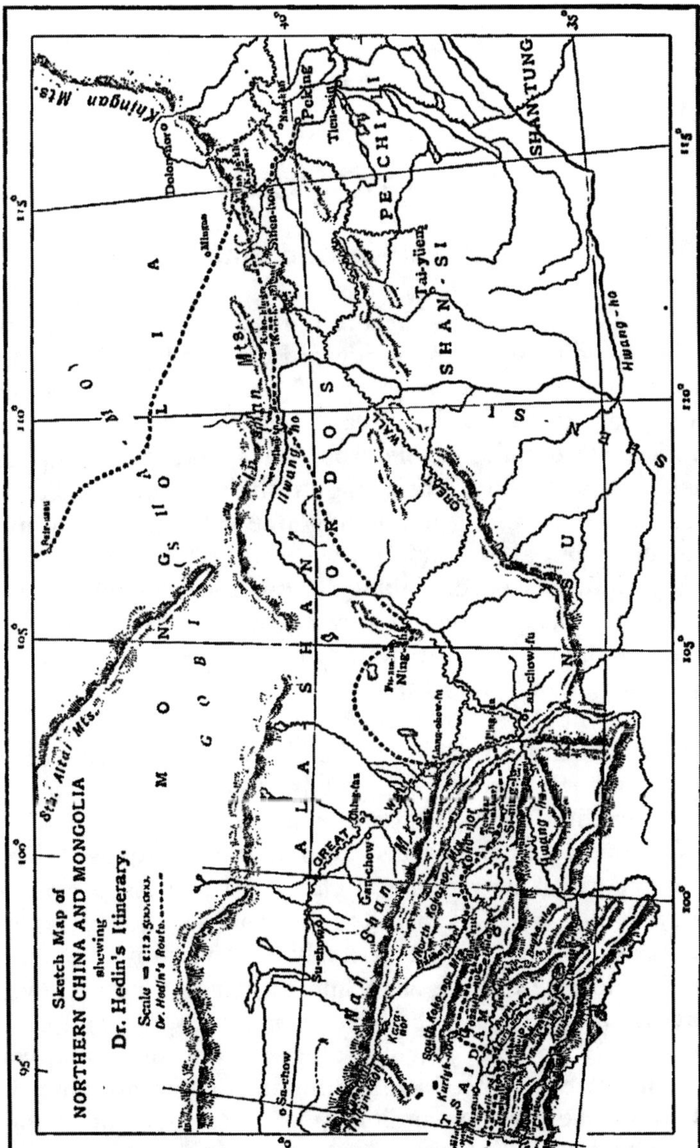

Sketch Map of
NORTHERN CHINA AND MONGOLIA
shewing
Dr. Hedin's Itinerary.
Dr. Hedin's Route.
MONGOLIA
GOBI
ALA SHAN
ORDOS
SHAN-SI
PE-CHI-LI
SHAN-TUNG
KAN-SU
TSAIDAM
Khingan Mts.
Altai Mts.
Nan Shan
Hwang-ho
GREAT WALL
Peking
Tien-tsin
Dolon-noor
Tai-yüen
Ning-hsia
Lan-chow-fu
Kan-chow
Su-chow
Sa-chow
Walker & Boutall sc.

CHAPTER LXXXVII.

INHABITED REGIONS AGAIN

OCTOBER 1st. Accordingly we pursued our way steadily down the straight, broad valley towards the east. Islam shot at a troop of some 120 khulans that were grazing beside the stream, but with no result, except that he started the whole troop in a mad gallop up the mountain-side. In their flight they streamed up the steep slopes in a long undulating line without the slightest difficulty; but after making a wide curve came down again at a breakneck speed, making for our last camping-ground, and finally disappeared in a whirlwind of dust. Near the end of the valley we found two other obos, one of them containing sixty-three slabs of slate; but they were not built up like the first, being merely piled loosely in a heap round a little hill. The letters on the slabs which faced the west were partly obliterated, very possibly by the prevailing winds, which blow from that quarter.

Our valley finally issued into a much broader valley, through which flowed the stream we had passed close to camp No. XXXV. In the angle between the valleys the rocks were again granite. All day long we kept a sharp and anxious look-out for signs of human beings; and we did see another fireplace, together with some tent-pegs and camel dung. Islam Bai, having caught sight of some yaks grazing at the foot of the mountains on the opposite side of the valley, crept cautiously within range, fired three shots without killing anything, then—imagine our surprise! an old woman came running forward, shouting and gesticulating, so that we at once understood the animals were tame yaks, and that we had at length reached the farthest outpost of an inhabited region, after travelling fifty-five days through the wilds of Northern Tibet.

Not long after that we observed the old woman's tent, standing on the right bank of the stream; and beside it we pitched camp No. XXXVIII. Her yaks, goats, and sheep grazed in the vicinity. The last-named made our mouths water terribly.

Our conversation with the old dame may be regarded as a triumphant vindication of the value of the primitive gesture language. She did not of course know who or what we were; and there was none in our party who understood Mongolian. Parpi Bai remembered a single word, *banch* = "there is"; and I knew the three common geographical terms, *ula* = "mountain," *gol* = "river," and *nur* = "lake." But this vocabulary was scarcely rich enough to make the old woman understand that first and foremost, above all things else, we wanted to buy a sheep. I began to bleat like a ram, at the same time showing her two *liang* or Chinese taels (twelve to thirteen shillings); and she understood me.

That evening we enjoyed the rare luxury of fresh mutton for supper.

My men were perfectly enraptured. They had now done with the dreary, lonely, monotonous manner of life they had pursued on the Tibetan highlands. We had no longer any need to put ourselves on short commons and eat tough yak beef; and perhaps we might be able even here to fill up the lamentable gaps which had been made in our caravan since we crossed the Arka-tagh. Further, employment of the language of signs taught us that the old woman's husband had gone into the *ula* (mountains) to shoot *boka* (yaks); but that she expected him home before the *naren* (sun) set. Whilst waiting for the Mongol's return, I, accompanied by Parpi Bai and Emin Mirza, paid a visit to the interior of the old woman's tent. When she saw us approaching, she came to meet us with her eight-year old son by her side. I gave the boy a sweetmeat and his mother a pinch of tobacco, which she instantly stuffed into her long, narrow Chinese pipe, and politely motioned us to enter.

The tent was constructed of an old and very ragged felt carpet, held up by two poles. Each of the long sides was kept back by three horizontal poles fastened, by means of ropes passing through holes in the tent-covering, to upright stakes driven into the ground outside. This made the tent more rounded at the top, and consequently more roomy. In the middle of the roof there was a long, narrow smoke-vent. The poles which supported the tent were of tamarisk wood, and had grown at Hajar in Tsaidam.

A violent snowstorm from the west coming on just then, we went inside the tent and had a look at its furnishings. The most important object was a small cubiform box standing against the short side immediately opposite the entrance. As Parpi Bai justly remarked, it was a *budkhaneh* or shrine to Buddha. After some hesitancy the old woman opened the shrine; it contained Tibetan books, written on long, narrow loose sheets, and each book, or bundle of such sheets, was wrapped in a piece of cloth. The old woman dusted the holy shrine with a yak's tail which lay on the box-lid; and beside the box were a few basins of brass and wood, evidently sacred vessels. The rest of the furniture consisted of a Chinese porcelain bowl, a leather pail, a jug of the same material, an iron cooking-pot, a copper saucepan with a lid, a brass teapot, a bag full of a certain dried plant, which was thrown on the fire to give a fragrant smell, together with knives, bellows, steel (for striking fire), saddles and bridles, ragged clothes, a sheep's bladder filled with yak fat, and a bag of *tsamba* (see pp. 1091–1092). The greater part of the space was taken up with hams, legs, and chines of wild yak beef; others lay piled up in a heap outside the tent, so that we were obliged to keep our dogs tied up. The flesh is left in the air until it shrinks, and turns dry and black, and hard as wood. The old woman took a knife, and cut off a few slices, and roasted them over the fire, and then offered

II.—27

them to us to eat. We subsequently learned, that the family dwelt in the same place all the year round, for the purpose of supplying their fellow-tribesmen in Tsaidam with yak meat.

Three large stones in the middle of the tent supported the cooking-pot, and yak dung, for feeding the fire, was packed up in a circle all round them. When the old woman wanted to make a fire, she caught the sparks from the steel on a handful of vegetable wool or down, which she then placed on the hearth amongst dry, powdered horse dung, and after blowing it alight with the bellows heaped yak dung upon it. The Mongols do not eat the flesh of the khulan. They milk their mares; and the milk tasted like the *ayran* (boiled milk diluted with water, and left to cool and turn sour) of the Kirghiz. A hollow stone, supported by a low tripod, and filled with yak fat, served for a lamp.

Both the old woman and the boy wore sheepskins, with a belt round the middle, and skin boots. Her head was wrapped in a long kerchief, knotted at the back of the neck; and she wore her hair in two long plaits, protected with a piece of cloth. The boy was bareheaded, but wore his hair twisted into three short plaits, which stuck out in different directions like rats' tails.

In the evening, whilst we were having a royal feast of the fresh tasty mutton, the husband, whose name was Dorcheh, arrived home from his yak-hunting. He was not a little amazed to see strangers in his camp; but he was a sensible fellow, and took the matter calmly. A thoroughly typical Mongol, Dorcheh was a little weather-beaten old man, his face furrowed with a thousand wrinkles, his eyes small, his cheek-bones high and projecting, his beard and moustache thin and coarse. He too was dressed in a sheepskin, and wore skin breeches; his feet were sheathed in pieces of felt; and on his head he had a small felt cap or *calotte*.

His knowledge of Jagatai Turki was on a par with Parpi Bai's knowledge of Mongolian. However we managed as well as we could, and soon picked up

TWO MONGOL MEN AND A BOY
Dorcheh at the top

several words. The place where Dorcheh had pitched his tent was called Mössöto, and the stream which flowed through the valley was one of the head-streams of the Naijin-gol. The camel-tracks which we observed two or three days previously were made by the cattle of a camp-mate, who had just transported all his belongings to his winter-camp in Hajar. If we had followed their track, we should have reached Hajar in five days; whereas by our present route it would take us eight days.

One day's journey down the valley there was a settlement of Naiji Mongols. A short time previously they had been attacked by a party of Tangut robbers, who came from the south-east, all armed to the teeth, and carried off everything they could lay their hands on. The unfortunate Mongols were reduced to living exclusively upon yak beef; they sent a deputation to the governor of Si-ning-fu, and he gave them a supply of bread and flour. Dorcheh advised us therefore not to continue in that direction, for we should find nothing at all to eat.

In return for his information, I gave the old man a cigarette and filled his powder-horn; with which he was well pleased. And so that red-letter day came to an end. The constant loneliness had made us somewhat irritable, and "stale." This first contact with our fellow-men freshened us all up, and re-awakened our interests, so that there was quite a new music in the prattling stream, as it rippled amongst the granite blocks which littered its bed.

It was a pure matter of course, that we stayed all the next day beside the first Mongols we came into contact with. Nor were we at all idle. In the first place, we bought three horses of a small breed and in pretty fair condition, as well as two sheep to kill on the road. We also thinned out the worst of our own animals, including two wasted camels. Goats' milk was the only other thing the Mongols had to offer us; but it was most welcome. In return for the milk they were perfectly delighted with a present of a small supply of tea and bread. Whilst we were trafficking beside my tent, a voice called out "A bear!" Off went Islam with his rifle and Dorcheh with his long clumsy flint-lock musket. But Bruin was too quick for them; he turned and disappeared into the mountains.

I was however most diverted by my first lessons in Mongolian. Dorcheh, who taught me, was very amusing in his efforts to understand my gesture-speech. I first learned the numerals, by holding up one, two, three fingers, and so on in succession,—nägä, hoyyer, gorva, dörvö, tavo, surkha, dolo, nayma, yessu, arva, arva-nägä, and so on. It was equally easy to learn the names of such objects as stood round about us, *e.g.* the tent and its several appurtenances, colours, parts of the human body, geographical features, and so forth. By this means I acquired a tolerable vocabulary relating to the commonest objects of daily life; and after my first lesson was able to talk to Dorcheh about simple matters. For instance, "Gorva temen baneh" (We have three camels); "Bamburchi mo" (The bear is an evil beast); and so on in a similar parrot-like fashion, reminding me of the old-fashioned way of teaching Latin—"Columba est timida," "Mensa est rotunda."

The verbs were difficult to get hold of; but I somehow managed to pick up the most essential the first evening, such as the words for "to go," "beat," "ride," "look for," "fall," "snow," "rain," "find," and several others. The picking up of these verbs entailed several feats of gymnastics. Dorcheh looked perfectly amazed when I thumped him on the back, to find out what that action was called in Mongolian.

For a full fortnight Dorcheh was our guide; and during that time my every spare moment was given to lessons in Mongolian. By closely studying his pronunciation and his conversation with other people, I picked up the language remarkably fast. After the first difficulties were overcome, and you have advanced so far that you can put together a few simple sentences, and so in some sort keep up a conversation, it becomes merely a question of extending your vocabulary and acquiring the necessary fluency of speech. I never afterwards needed an interpreter for Mongolian. I lived amongst these people several months, and was able without any intermediary to talk with the Living Buddha in Kum-bum, and with the viceroy of Wang-yeh-fu. In this way I managed to overcome the worst difficulties and inconveniences I expected to encounter in consequence of the loss of my Chinese interpreter Fong Shi.

After measuring, early on the morning of October 3rd, the paces and rate of speed of my new Mongolian riding-horse for the purposes of my map-making, we left Mössöto, but not before another Mongol family, dwelling in a tent higher up the valley, came down to have a look at the strangers.

At first we kept along the left side of the stream, then turned off towards the north up a side-glen strewn with stones, where our appearance put to flight a troop of 150 khulans. The glen gradually widened out, and became broad and fertile; and upon our reaching a little pool, Dorcheh dismounted, and said, that it was Yikeh-tsohan-namen (14,400 feet), and that we were to encamp there. We did so, having covered twelve and a half miles since the morning.

On October 4th our guide led us further up the glen, which gradually curved round towards the north-east and east, at the same time growing much steeper and more obstructed with stones and gravel, which had rolled down from the mountains above. Hitherto the prevailing rock had been a dark green micaceous schist, with a dip towards the north. It now became granite, ranging from red to grey, and granite continued to predominate all day, right up to the pass Yikeh-tsohan-davan (16,320 feet). The ascent was tolerably easy; even our three surviving camels mounted its rounded acclivity without any special difficulty. The view from the summit of the pass was not particularly extensive, the pass being shut in by mountains, which cut off the view. The valley to the east, which curved round towards the north, was likewise encircled by high intercepting mountains. The snow lay very deep on the pass, and was more plentiful on the east side than on the west. The valley to the east, down which we descended through masses of gravel and stones, was likewise more deeply trenched than the valley on the west. The latter had a gentler incline, and formed a sort of step or Transitional offset of the Tibetan plateau. We now perceived that the low pass which we crossed immediately north of lake No. 20 formed an important watershed. South of it the streams drained into the self-contained Tibetan lakes which possess no outflow; whilst north of it they made their way into the salt depression of Tsaidam, which is likewise destitute of an outflow.

The stream which had hitherto coursed along the valley did not accompany it in its curve to the north; but, after picking up a number of tributaries, fell to work upon the herculean task of carving its way through the granite mountains. At present its path is a deep, narrow ravine, with perpendicular walls, and its bottom choked with huge stones. Islam Bai, who still led the way as usual, threaded the ravine with the caravan. But Dorcheh, who rode beside me, to tell me the names of the mountains, valleys, and streams, said, there was a better road up on the top of the left side of the valley, the ground consisting of soft, yellow clay.

From this upper path, which sloped away abruptly to the defile, we heard the stream boiling along at a depth of three hundred feet or more below us. The path was not more than a foot broad, and clung closely to every irregularity of the ground; in places it was actually scooped out of the almost vertical walls, they too being of the same soft material. In consequence of the recent rains the surface was slippery and greasy. Dorcheh rode first, whilst I followed close at his heels, with my heart in my mouth. All at once my horse put his foot a trifle too near the edge of the soft clay path, and down he went.

I had barely time to fling myself out of the saddle, alighting flat on my back on the ground, whilst the horse rolled two or three times over down the steep slope before he was able to stop himself. Dorcheh hurried down after him, and helped him up. If he had not managed to stop himself just as he did, he would almost certainly have gone over the precipice, which was only a yard or two from him; and if I had not thrown myself out of the saddle, I should perhaps have borne him company. After that I prudently walked and led my horse.

The path gradually wound down to the bottom of the defile. There we rejoined the caravan, and made our way zigzag backwards and forwards over the stream, between the countless fragments of rock which littered its channel. It then began to blow from the north, bringing a furious storm of snow, which beat directly in our faces, and prevented us from seeing the country we were approaching. There were still some awkward passages to traverse before we reached the expansion of the valley called Koko-bureh, where there was a plentiful supply of grass on both banks of the river. We had not been down to so low a level for two months; but it was very pleasant to think that we were daily descending to lower and more genial climes. That day we travelled seventeen miles.

CHAPTER LXXXVIII.

AMONG THE MONGOLS OF TSAIDAM

OCTOBER 5th. After leaving Koko-bureh, we still pursued our way down the valley. The bed of the stream continued as full of stones as before, and our Mongolian horses, which were unshod, became rather sore-footed. In an expansion of the valley we met a party of mounted Mongols, all armed to the teeth. Great was the astonishment on both sides. But with Dorcheh's help, I tried to engage them to accompany us. We speedily came to an agreement upon one point. We encamped where we were, in the district of Harato, although we had not covered more than nine and a quarter miles. It was however a splendid camping-ground, with plenteous vegetation. Its altitude was 11,060 feet.

The troop of Mongols consisted of five men and one woman. They were on their way from Yikeh-tsohan-gol to Mössöto, whence they intended to penetrate higher into the mountains to lay in a supply of yak beef for the winter. They expected to be absent fifteen or twenty days; but only carried provisions to last them five or six. After these were consumed, they hoped to live upon yak beef. When they have shot as many yaks as they require, they load the meat on their horses, and themselves make the return journey on foot.

It was the height of the season for yak-hunting; no doubt it is the time of year when the yaks come down to the Peripheral regions in quest of the better herbage. The Mongols hunt on the same plan and in the same manner as the Taghliks. That is to say, two men at least attack each yak, so as to have one or more guns in reserve in case the beast turns upon the hunter.

The yak-hunters were in "fine form," all cheerful and in good humour. It is easy to imagine that this autumn excursion made an agreeable break in their otherwise monotonous life. The season lasts about a month. Each hunting party has its own well recognized hunting-grounds. The hunters live in the open air, without tent, their only encumbrances being the clothes they wear, their saddles,

ROCKS AT HARATO, IN THE VALLEY OF THE YIKEH-TSOHAN-GOL

muskets, and a small supply of provisions in leathern knapsacks.

The men and woman of the party we met encamped in the bushes beside my tent; that is to say, they made a fire between three stones, and hung over it the cooking-pot filled with water. When I stepped into a vacant place in the circle round the fire, I was received with a friendly "*Amir sän?*" (How are you getting on?).

When the water began to boil, one of the older men produced six wooden bowls from a bag and distributed them amongst the party; after that he gave each person a portion of barley-meal, and then added to it a few slices of a sausage made of mutton lard. As soon as that was done, the woman, who had been busy feeding and tending the fire, took a ladleful of water out of the pot, and poured it into the bowls over the barley-meal and mutton lard. Such was *tsamba*, the national dish of the Mongols. After the mess was consumed—and it seemed to go down with great relish—there was still sufficient lard and meal sticking to the bottom of the bowl to require another spoonful or two of hot water. That constituted the whole of their meal. After dinner they produced their pipes, and stuffed them with vile Chinese tobacco, which they took out of a pouch at their side, and were soon puffing away in happy contentment. The entire party appeared to be very much addicted to the weed.

Their clothing consisted of pelt (sheepskin) and breeches, boots, and caps. The pelt was worn next the skin. They seemed to be quite insensitive to cold, for the right arm and right side of the body from the waist upwards were bare. At night they wrapped themselves in their pelts and crept close together round the fire; and when it came on to snow, they made a rude kind of protection with their muskets, saddles, and saddle-rugs. They all wore their hair in plaits; and as they sat, their fingers were busy telling the beads of their rosary, so as to keep count how many times they repeated the prayer "On maneh padmeh hum."

October 6th. The Mongols sold us a couple of their horses. Early the next morning, about an hour after they had started for their hunting-grounds, we discovered that habit had been too strong for the animals: they had gone after their late owners. I sent two of the men on horseback up the valley to fetch them back. Hence it was two o'clock before we were able to make a start; although two of the Taghliks got off hours before that with the three camels. I, Dorcheh, and Yolldash also went on in advance, leaving the horse-caravan to follow after us.

We crossed the stream almost immediately, and for some time kept it on our left hand. The valley expanded; and the granite peaks showed a tendency to a separate existence, independent of one another. On the other side of a last narrow pass or gorge, caused by the stream pressing against the rocks on the right-hand side of its course, we came upon an unusual sight — the horizon forming a perfectly straight line in the far, far distance. After that we quitted the stream; but at the end of an hour or so once more got back into its dry channel. It was now getting not only broader and leveller, but also freer from stones, for it is only in summer that it carries a supply of water. We rode along the dry bed for the rest of the day. The mountain-spurs which bordered the valley of Harato gradually diverged from each other; although their outer ramifications still continued visible in both directions, east and west.

At the end of the valley vegetation ceased nearly altogether. The plain sloped away almost imperceptibly towards the north, and gradually became more and more barren, until finally it passed over into absolute desert, with occasional chains of low sand-dunes, which seemed to have been blown up by the prevailing westerly winds. It was a dreary landscape, utterly destitute of life, with not a trackway to be seen. A death-like silence reigned throughout the length and breadth of the unbounded plain; which was irksome to the eyes after such a long sojourn among the world of mountains in Northern Tibet. Turning in my saddle and looking back, the vast mountain-chain with its snow-clad summits looked as if it were painted on a flat background—the effect of the wonderfully clear atmosphere. I could not even distinguish the exit of the glen out of which we last rode.

The basin of Tsaidam thus possessed many points of resemblance with the basin of the Tarim. In both the oases are separated from the foot of the mountains by a belt of desert; in both, the streams die away in the sand, although in Tsaidam the central parts of the basin are occupied by a series of extensive marshes, leaving room for only a comparatively narrow strip of desert all round them.

Hour after hour we rode on towards the north, overtaking the camels hours before the shades of night began to fall. The belt of desert was replaced by steppe, with tamarisks growing on mounds of their own roots as in East Turkestan. At first they only occurred in thinly scattered twos and threes; but farther on formed continuous and intricate woods. After a good deal of searching about, Dorcheh at length discovered a path. But, saying he was afraid the other men, who followed behind and were without a guide, would never be able to find it, he told me which way to go to reach the next camping-place, and then, before I could offer a word of protest, disappeared in the darkness.

Fortunately my horse was more familiar than I was with the locality, and after riding close upon an hour, I caught a glimpse of fires shining through the bushes ahead. The Mongol dogs gave the alarm, and out rushed a horde of them, barking furiously at my horse and at Yolldash, whom I had caught up and placed on the saddle in front of me. I then saw the tents, and people about them. Riding quietly up to one of them, I fastened my horse outside, and went in. There were half-a-dozen Mongols in the tent. They looked up at me with a stare of amazement. I greeted them with the customary "Amir sän?" and sat down beside the fire and lighted my pipe. I saw a pan with fermented mare's-milk standing in a corner. I got up and took a good drink. It tasted like small beer, and was very refreshing after my long ride of nearly twenty-seven miles. The Mongols still continued to stare at me without uttering a word, though they did not forget from time to time to push more fuel on the fire. Nor had they recovered from their amazement when Dorcheh arrived two hours later, with the caravan. He then explained to them what manner of folk we were. A fire was made in an open space among the Mongol tents, and my tent was pitched so as to enclose it. It was one o'clock in the morning when I got my supper.

This last forced march cost us two more horses and a donkey; so that now we had only three camels, three horses, and one donkey left out of the fifty-six animals

THE AUTHOR ARRIVING AT THE FIRST MONGOL CAMP AT YIKEH-TSOHAN-GOL

with which two months previously we started from Dalai-kurgan.

We stayed over the 11th October with the Mongol community at Yikeh-tsohan-gol, and the rest was not beneficial merely, it was indispensable. At their own request I there dismissed Hamdan Bai and all the Taghliks. They proposed to return home the nearest way, which lay over the Chimen-tagh and the Tokkuz-davan. As a reward for the labours they had undergone, and for their irreproachable service, I gave them double the wages agreed upon, as well as a large supply of provisions, some sheep, and our worn-out animals; but these last were to be allowed to recover their strength a little before they started back.

In their place I set about organizing an entirely fresh caravan. And no sooner did the Mongols realize that we wanted horses than every day, nay every hour of the day, the entrance to my tent was besieged by one or more of them offering horses for sale; nor were the prices they asked at all extravagant. When I resumed my journey towards the east, it was as lord and master over a caravan of twenty first-rate animals. But before we could start, new saddles had to be made for most of them; for the greater part of the old ones had of course been lost along with the animals that died by the way in Northern Tibet. Parpi Bai was a skilful hand at the business. The Mongols provided him with all the materials he required; and the open space in front of the men's tent was converted into a saddle-maker's workshop.

For my own part I was hard at work every day learning Mongolian, and "pumping" the Mongolians as to their knowledge of all that region, its geography and climate, their own ways of life, their religion, and so forth. Most of the men had been to Lhasa (Lassa), and had many interesting things to tell me about that provoking city, and the road to it. As soon as they found out that I took an interest in their *burkhans* (images of Buddha made of terra-cotta and worn round the neck in a small *gawo* or case), they brought them, and sold them to me cheap. But they were more afraid of one another than they were of me. They only came to my tent with them at night, after it was dark, and begged me to keep them closely hidden at the bottom of my boxes. These burkhans are made in Lhasa with masterly skill, and every Mongol I encountered wore one. The case in which the image was carried was very often made of silver, with choice and original engraved designs on the outside, and set with turquoises and coral. The less pretentious gavos were made of copper or brass.

Ere long I stood on terms of cordial intimacy with the inhabitants of Yikeh-tsohan-gol. Whenever I took out my pencil to sketch, they would gather in a circle outside my tent; and when I entered their tents, they were invariably ready to entertain me with tea and tsamba. I failed to discern a trace of either shyness or alarm among them, of either prejudice or superstition; they would sit perfectly still and quiet whilst I sketched them. Some of them even permitted me to take anthropometrical measurements. The only thing they manifested any scruple about was when I wanted to put them with their backs against the tent-pole to take their height. They were always afraid lest I should touch the tops of their heads with my hands. Possibly this was for the same reason that they lift their burkhans to their heads as a sign of reverence: though it may also possibly have been because they had been blessed in Lhasa by the Dalai Lama or some other high dignitary of their faith.

The Mongols of Tsaidam are monogamists; and their women enjoy an incomparably greater amount of freedom than the women do among the Mohammedan tribes of Central Asia. Not only do they share fully in the characteristic gatherings round the fire, and go unveiled, but they are very inadequately clothed. The sheepskin they wear is merely held together by their girdle and at the left shoulder; the whole of the right side of the upper part of the body, down to the waist, is uncovered. The

TERRA-COTTA BURKHANS FROM LHASA

One-half natural size

breasts of even the younger women are anything but well-formed, and hang down loosely in a very unedifying fashion. Whether this undue exposure of the person tends to matrimonial fidelity I will not venture to affirm; I can only say that the Mongols themselves are so thoroughly accustomed to the practice, that to them it is perfectly natural. At any rate, they were not slow to tell me, that morality amongst them stood at a higher level than amongst the Mohammedans; for in their eyes

GAVOS, OR CASES, FOR BURKHANS (SILVER AND COPPER)
One-sixth of natural size

the polygamy which Islam allows the Faithful is proof of a low moral standard.

On the very first day of my stay amongst them Sonum, the chief of Yikeh-tsohan-gol, came to visit me, bringing as gifts of welcome milk, fermented mare's milk (kumiss), and brandy made from the same. The kumiss brandy had a very disagreeable taste; but must have been pretty strong, for Parpi Bai, after a somewhat incautious trial of it, was incapacitated for an entire day. The chief Sonum wore a fiery red mantle, and a Chinese skin cap, with button and long ribbons.

The following day I returned his visit. The little

domestic shrine was set up immediately opposite the entrance to his roomy tent. It consisted of a number of boxes piled one on the top of the other, the whole surmounted by a flat piece of board, along which were ranged a number of dishes and cups containing water, flour, tsamba, and other offerings to the burkhan (holy image of Buddha). I also observed sacred scriptures, prayer-wheels, and burkhans from Lhasa and Tatsilumpo (Tashilunpo). Any person who stops to look at the latter must take his pipe out of his mouth, nor must he breathe upon them. When I inadvertently transgressed against this rule, the burkhan was purified by being held over a brazier, into which fragrant spices were dropped. Nor are the holy images allowed to come in contact with the earth.

In the middle of the tent was the fire, in a sort of iron basket (*tolga*), provided with three upright rods for holding the cooking-pot. The fuel with which the fire was fed consisted of the branches of tamarisks and the roots of other plants. At meal-time the dishes for the guests were placed before them on small stools. In brief, the Mongol tent was better furnished than the Kirghiz tent. They called it in their own tongue *örgö*; it resembled even in dètail the *kara-uy* (black tent) of the Kirghiz. It is very remarkable that tents of this shape are in use throughout such an immense area of Central Asia, and amongst people of different races, between whom there exists no direct intercommunication. But the materials are such as those regions all produce in common; and the shape is the most practical, and furnishes the largest amount of space. The chieftain's tent was indicated by a spear stuck in the ground outside. Round about the encampment were numerous exceptionally fine tamarisks, more like trees than bushes. From them the Mongols obtained materials for the dishes, tubs, saddle-trees, tent-poles, and divers other articles which they made themselves. Other household utensils, together with flour and similar commodities, they obtained from Si-ning-fu.

Our Mongol friends were thorough nomads. As soon

as their flocks and herds have eaten up the pasturage in one place, they move away to another.

Their aul was splendidly situated in the dry river-bed, so that they were able to water their animals of an evening from a well not more than four feet deep. They appeared to devote their attention chiefly to the breeding of horses. The entire neighbourhood echoed with their whinnyings and neighings. In the evening the mares were milked by the women; for the staple drink of the Mongols is kumiss or fermented mare's-milk. They also keep a large number of sheep and camels, and horned cattle. Agriculture is not pursued at all.

All the time we stayed at Yikeh-tsohan-gol we were favoured with magnificent weather. The sky was bright and still, and at noon the temperature rose to 59° Fahr. (15° C.); in fact it was so warm inside the tent that I preferred to sit in my shirt sleeves. On the other hand, the nights were every bit as cold as they were up in the mountains of Northern Tibet. The scenery was often very fine, especially when seen under the colouring of the setting sun. In the purple red glow of the sunset the tents, the tamarisks, the mountain backgrounds, especially the Tsohan-ula (Tsohan Mountains) on the south, stood out with the sharpness of silhouettes in the clear transparent atmosphere. In the evening, when the animals had to be attended to, the encampment presented a very busy scene. The women with their broad felt hats and long plaits of hair bustled about among the fat mares and bleating ewes; whilst the men drove the flocks into the folds, assisted by a troop of black long-haired dogs, who barked tumultuously, making a terrible din. Then my men would stop their day's work, and gather round the fire for supper; and whilst eating it Mirza read aloud to them out of the *teskereh* (chronicles) of Imam Jafer Sadik. The whole scene, with the fires gleaming through the half-open tents of the Mongols, was full of the soft beauty of peace, and I thoroughly appreciated it. After the almost unearthly silence of the mountain wilderness, we seemed to have returned to quite a summery clime; and then we were able to move about and exert ourselves without suffering from shortness of breath, for we were not more than 9240 feet above the level of the sea.

Although my Mohammedan attendants as an actual fact despised the Mongols, looking upon them as savages and heathens, both parties managed to get along very well together, and took pains to try and understand one another. I almost died with laughing to see the hideous grimaces and extraordinary gestures Dorcheh went through, and that with the profoundest gravity, in his efforts to make my men understand what he wanted to say. He shouted at the pitch of his voice, as though they were all stone-deaf, twisted his face about as though it were made of gutta percha, and jumped and flapped his arms as though he had been a cock. And when at length his meaning dawned upon his audience, his delight knew no bounds. He laughed loud and long, and kept on nodding his head like a Chinese porcelain doll with intense self-satisfaction.

CHAPTER LXXXIX.

THROUGH THE DESERT OF TSAIDAM

OCTOBER 12th. At sunrise and immediately after our camp echoed with the noise, bustle, and excitement which invariably attend the first starting of a new caravan. The loads were weighed and arranged in pairs for the different horses, so that the boxes which required more delicate handling might ride on the quietest animals, while the heavier, coarser baggage, such as the tent and provisions, might be put on the skittish. Everybody in the Mongol camp from the chieftain downwards was already up, and eager to supply us with ropes and whatever else we wanted. The women gave us a present of milk, sufficient to last two days. Even after the caravan had got a little distance on the road, we were overtaken by a young man, who had not been able to pluck up courage earlier to offer me his burkhan for sale.

The caravan of about a score of horses made a fine show as they travelled at a rapid pace towards the east under the experienced guidance of Dorcheh. I congratulated myself upon having such a string of fresh, well-conditioned horses. It was quite a relief after the wretched team with which we struggled among the lake-basins of Northern Tibet.

And what a change there was too in the outward appearance of the country! We now rode across a level steppe, covered with luxuriant verdure, and along a well-trodden path, which wound over the plain in easy curves. But on the left we had the boundless ocean of the desert of Tsaidam. The only mountains we could see were the far distant Tsohan-ula, away to the right. The alternations and changes and surprises which kept me busy amongst the mountains now of course ceased, so that I had next to nothing to do. The country was extremely uniform, the ravines and dry beds of the streams being the only diversities of the surface. At Bagha-namaga (the Little Spring) we stopped to water the horses, and after a march of seventeen and a half miles, halted for the night on the steppe of Hojegor, where there was an abundance of water and grass, as well as fuel.

October 13th. A pretty brisk wind sprang up in the west, and loaded the air with dust, as well as hid the mountains. This day we advanced towards the east-south-east, sometimes across rough desert, the soil of which was heavily impregnated with salt, sometimes across steppes dotted with thick beds of luxuriant reeds, crossing numerous dry ravines on our way. Our day's journey of nineteen and a quarter miles ended at Tsakha, an encampment of ten tents, the same number as at Yikeh-tsohan-gol. The chief gave me a friendly welcome and led me into his own tent, where I found the members of his family busy making stirrups out of branches of tamarisk and covering them with leather.

Next day the path inclined more towards the north, and led across some widely extended salt marshes, which were of course just then dry, but none the less tiresome for the horses, because every old footprint had set into a hard and treacherous hole. In the distance we saw every now and again small tent-villages, and flocks of sheep guarded by boys and women. It was sixteen miles to Yikeh-gol, the third branch of the Naijin-gol, so that our camp was made that night beside the same stream which we encountered for the first time at camp No. XXXV.

In the evening we were visited by a party of Mongols, bringing brandy in two or three copper vessels, and cloth from Lhasa, which they were anxious to sell to us. Our visitors and Dorcheh dipped into the copper vessels so industriously that they grew noisy, and challenged my Mohammedans to a wrestling-match, in which the fuddled

MONGOL CAMP IN TSAIDAM

Mongols were a good deal sobered. After that they fell asleep, and slept hard and heavy. Next morning their heads ached, and they begged me to stay the day there; but I refused to accede to their request.

First thing after starting we crossed the broad bed of the Yikeh-gol. It was a good quarter of a mile wide, but contained next to no water. The terraces on each side of it rose however sixteen feet high, indicating that it swells to a very considerable river in the summer. The bed was littered with gravel, and by a multitude of curves wound northwards towards the great central basin of Tsaidam. The country on the other side of the stream presented the same monotonous uniformity as heretofore. Level as the evening sea, silent and desolate, the steppe stretched in every direction; not a creature, tame or wild, to be seen anywhere, not an object to rest the eye upon. Our camping-place (sixteen and three-quarter miles) was called Urdu-tolch, and offered plenty of both water and grass. Contrary to the practice of the Mohammedans, the Mongols turned their horses loose to graze immediately after halting.

On October 16th, we did not cover more than twelve and a half miles, namely to Togdeh-gol (9140 feet). As a general rule, the Mongols of Tsaidam make very short marches, so that it is not difficult to understand how they take two months to travel to Lhasa, and forty-three days to Si-ning-fu.

The night was cold, the minimum registered being 3°2 Fahr. (16° C.). The thermometer dropped much lower than in Northern Tibet; still the continental winter, with its excessive extremes of cold, was close at hand. The day was bright and fine, and in the south we could plainly see the mountain-range called Kharanguin-ula, (the Dark Mountains). The Togdeh-gol flowed at the bottom of a deep narrow gorge, which it occasioned us very great difficulty to get across without a wetting. On the opposite bank we halted among a clump of tamarisks, and made ourselves as comfortable as the circumstances permitted, for I had decided to give the horses a day's rest.

At this point our old friend and guide Dorcheh took his leave, to return to his lonely mountain-home and his wild yak hunting; he was afraid his wife would begin to be anxious at his prolonged absence. In his place I engaged a young Mongol named Loppsen, a big clumsily built fellow, who had several times been to Lhasa and Si-ning-fu, and had an exceptional knowledge of the country we were travelling through. Loppsen (see page 1121) was one of the best followers I ever had. He was always cheerful and pleasant, and freshened up my knowledge of Mongolian. He procured me several burkhans and *tankas*, or temple banners, decorated with portraits of the Dalai Lama and Banching Bogdo. Where he got them from I do not know. Very possibly he stole them from our neighbours, for he was terribly afraid lest they should see them.

October 18th. Our next stage, sixteen and three-quarter miles, was to Toleh. Loppsen came on the next day, having with my permission remained behind in order to furnish himself with provisions and a horse. It was arranged that another man should guide us to Toleh; but of him we never had a glimpse, and set off without a guide. Nor did we really need one, for the path was easy to find. At first we travelled through a belt of tamarisks, so tall and so close set that they resembled a newly planted forest, and in this part of the day's journey we passed a very picturesque obo. Ropes were slung across the road from the branches of the tamarisk thickets on both sides, and to them were stitched pieces of cloth of divers colours, each piece bearing the usual formula of prayer; further the shoulder-blades of sheep, likewise with the everlasting ideographs—"On maneh padmeh hum," hung at intervals amongst the pieces of cloth. The general effect recalled the forest masars of the Mohammedans, only it was more tasteful and decorative.

Upon approaching a pool, we were overtaken by a troop of mounted Mongols, who informed us that that was Toleh, and that for a long day's journey to the

A "TANKA," OR TEMPLE BANNER

east there was not a drop of water to be found. We therefore deemed it expedient to encamp. We also bought from them a sack of barley, which was greatly appreciated by our horses. Grain of all kinds is excessively scarce in Tsaidam. The Mongols buy their wheat in Si-ning-fu. Barley is grown in a few places, though in nothing like sufficient quantity.

Loppsen came up next day, and guided us (sixteen and three-quarter miles) to the deeply eroded stream of Hattar. We now perceived distinctly a mountain-chain on the north also. Loppsen called it Kurlykuin-ula, and gave me to understand that it formed the northern boundary of the Tsaidam depression. That evening we had a talk about my contemplated journey to Si-ning-fu, and Loppsen was of opinion that it would take me thirty days to get there. He said that the Tanguts in the Koko-nor neighbourhood were arrant thieves and robbers, and that whilst passing through their country we should do well to maintain a constant watch. He wondered whether we were sufficiently well armed; but when I showed him our three rifles and five revolvers, he was plainly much easier in his mind. He further warned me, that in the region of the Kurlyk-nor, and further to the east, we must be prepared to find a scarcity of provisions, for the Dungans during their recent revolt had carried off all the flocks of the native population.

On October 20th we had a march of twelve and a half miles to Tenghelik-gol through tamarisk thickets and reed-beds, and across barren desert. The mountains to the south were now called Nomoghin-ula. The Mongols do not seem to have a common name for the range, only a series of local names. The streams at Hattar and Tenghelik, like those of the Bayan-gol, the Khara-ussu, and the Bulunghir-gol, which we crossed later on, all entered the salt lake of Hollussun-nor (the Reed Lake). The Naijin-gol, on the other hand, flowed further west, and entered the lake of Döulätsän-nor, generally called on European maps Davassun-nor. This name is however misleading, for it is merely a general name; almost every

II.—29

lake in Tsaidam that contains salt water being called Davassun-nor (the Salt Lake).

The following day our route inclined a little towards the north, so that the southern mountains grew fainter, whilst those in the opposite quarter became more distinct. The march lay across desert and steppe for seventeen and a quarter miles as far as Ova-tögöruck, where I was as usual received in a friendly spirit by the inhabitants of the few Mongol tents. These people belonged to the important sept or tribe of the Tajehnur Mongols. I was able to get some useful craniological measurements from them.

They wore a big sheepskin tunic, held together by a belt round the waist, but they pulled the tunic up through the girdle in such fashion that it bulged over at both sides like a couple of cushions. These hollow spaces they used as pockets, and on occasion as provision-bags. At their side they also carried in a smaller belt their knife, pipe, tobacco-pouch, and a pair of nippers, with which they pull out their beard if it threatens to grow too thick. Their boots were pointed at the toes. Their hats were pointed or rounded; very often however their head-covering consisted of nothing more than a piece of felt, stretched across the forehead and tied at the back of the neck; sometimes they even go bare-headed. As a rule, they wear the hair short and close, its usual colour being brown or black. Pigtails are much seldomer met with in Tsaidam than amongst the Khalkha Mongols in Mongolia proper. Owing to their constantly living in the open air, their skin is a copper-brown colour, though it must be admitted a good deal of the colouring is due to dirt. Their teeth are small and yellow, but appear to keep sound a long time. Their cheek-bones are high and prominent, their nose is rather flat and small, the head as round as a ball, flattened anteriorly, the beard slow of growth. It is not until a man is past thirty that the fine down develops into a beard, and then the beard is excessively thin.

At Ova-tögöruck we managed to get two or three bags

of corn for the horses, and bought a young mare to carry them. As we had a couple of days of desert travelling before us, the grain was a valuable acquisition. There we rested a day, and Islam Bai seized the opportunity to turn out and take stock of our provision-cases, bringing to light a bag of coffee berries, and a bottle of golden syrup, which Father Hendricks gave me more than a year previously. The coffee was an agreeable change from the invariable tea, and the syrup served for dessert after dinner.

On October 23rd the path inclined towards the north-east. We were about to cross the central desert region of Tsaidam. Vegetation grew thinner and rarer, and finally ceased altogether. The ground was bare and barren, rough and moist, and frequently showed white because of the large impregnation of salt. Once more we were ploughing our way through the dreary desert. Half-way across we expected to ford the Khara-ussu (the Black River). The first of its arms we came to was very small, and the thick dirty water crawled over the muddy bottom with a scarce perceptible movement. Its second arm was dry. Then came the third, so deeply sunk in the ground, and so narrow, that we did not see it until we were close upon it, in fact only a few horse's-lengths away. The banks were of slippery clay, and went steep down to the bottom of the river, so that we had to cut a sloping path in each for the horses to go up and down. Loppsen, who knew where the ford was, rode down first, but the horse had not gone four paces before he sank over the pommel of the saddle in the soft mud, wetting his rider to the waist. Islam tried another place, but with no better fortune. The men rode up and down the bank seeking for a more suitable crossing, but in both directions the river was narrower and deeper, and Loppsen maintained that that was the only ford there was across the Khara-ussu. He was amazed to find so much water in the river, and could only explain it as being due to the unusual warmth of the air during the past few days, combined with a

A MONGOL BEGGAR

copious fall of snow on the Burkhan Buddha, a mountain whose summit gleamed white in the south. After all, the water was not more than three or four feet deep, but unfortunately the horses sank so heavily in the mud, and were even in danger of sticking fast in it. Every packing-case we had would get saturated to the lid. That would never do.

Although we had not covered more than seven and a half miles that day, we had no other choice except to pitch our tents and wait until the water went down. It was very annoying to be stopped by this wretched pretence of a river, not more than forty feet wide at the most, and to be forced to rest in such a howling wilderness, with no other vegetation than a tiny bed of reeds. "Patience!" whispered the west wind as it flaunted restlessly across the wide expanse of the desert. Patience! It was to that west wind we were in no small degree indebted for the delay, seeing that it dammed back the water in its course towards the west.

The tents were put up, the horses turned loose, and a notched stick put down in the stream close to the bank, to show us whether the water rose or fell. By next morning the surface had only fallen three-quarters of an inch, and the bed of reeds was gnawed right down to the roots. I therefore sent Loppsen and two or three of the other men back with their horses to the pastures of Ova-tögöruck. The westerly gale was blowing fiercer than ever. The tent-covering on the windward side was driven in like a half-collapsed bladder, seriously curtailing the space inside. The packing-cases, which had been placed on the turned-in ends of the tent-covering, to hold them fast, rocked and shook, and the tent-poles creaked; every moment I fully expected to see the tent go flying like a kite across the river.

Why had this obstacle come in my way like this? I asked myself restlessly. For I was now waxing impatient to get home, and counted every day's journey as so much ground won. It was now fully a year since last I had news from home. I was quite isolated, and very lonely. For more than three years I had been absolutely alone in the heart of that immeasurable continent of Asia; I thought I should never reach its coast! Every day it afforded me a special pleasure to count how many miles we had rubbed off the score, and subtract them from the hundreds which still stretched between me and my far-distant goal—Peking. From Khara-ussu to Peking was 1260 miles. What an amount of patience I should need before we had traversed all that long distance at the slow rate at which we were crawling along! And what adventures still awaited us ere our tired horses entered the western gate of the famous capital of the Far East? I was growing tired of wandering about like a homeless exile among the half-savage tribes of Asia. I was become fairly familiar with them, and longed to get back among my own people and my own kin. My attendants, their several life-stories, their faiths, their knowledge—I knew them all through and through. I longed ardently for a change of companionship.

At last, on the morning of October 25th, the stream had fallen sufficiently for us to cross. The boxes were tied as high up on the horses' backs as we could get them, and each horse was led across separately. But every animal that crossed churned up the mud afresh, so that those which came last sank in the deepest. However all got over without mishap, and as soon as we were all on the right bank, the baggage was re-adjusted and we went off again.

The path led across a desolate country in an almost perfectly straight line towards the north-north-east. Soon afterwards we crossed the main channel of the Khara-ussu, and then the Bulunghir-gol. The surface was not over and above comfortable to ride on, as it consisted of a hard crumbly clay, of a brownish grey colour, impregnated with salt, and it was full of holes and rough places like a coggled road. But there was an entire absence of drift-sand. Where we crossed it, the basin of Tsaidam was not particularly broad, and after a ride of fifteen and a half miles, we again came in sight of vegetation. But we had no water at our next camping-station, Tsakha-tsak. Loppsen had however warned us beforehand, and we took a supply with us in goatskins.

We still had over 1240 miles to Peking!

CHAPTER XC.

AMONG THE MONGOLIAN LAKES

ON October 26th we travelled the long stage of twenty-four and a quarter miles, and so approached the northern border of the basin of Tsaidam. The country showed no alteration of feature, and we still continued in the same direction. Soon after starting we had to face a "hog's back" of low barren clay hills, thrown together in the most extraordinary shapes and forms, resembling towers, walls, and pyramids. Once only was the solemn desolation and silence of the scene broken by a few starveling tamarisks and saksauls; but how they managed to subsist, God alone knows, for the ground was as dry as tinder, we never saw a single drop of water all day long. We crossed over an entire series of low clay passes. The first was marked by an obo, whilst the "sign-post" which indicated the last consisted of the branches and roots of saksaul lashed together in the shape of arches. At intervals amongst these hills the ground was perfectly flat, and white with salt. Loppsen said that after rain those places were brimming with water.

On the other side of the hills we saw stretching before us, as far as the eye could reach, a level but barren plain, strewn with sand. It was however easy going for our tired horses, which were now urgently wanting water. At length we caught a glimpse of a lake. It was Tossun-nor, a lake embedded amid clay terraces and hills, which fell steeply towards the water's edge. Here our path joined the road which leads from Dsun-sassak to Northern Tibet, and which has been described by Przhevalsky.

Instead of continuing on towards the north-east, which would have been shorter, I preferred to skirt the western shore of the lake, so as to get an idea of its general shape, and examine the mouths of the streams which feed it. We therefore rode down the hill, and followed a narrow strip of level ground close alongside the water; thus we had the whole of the beautiful blue lake immediately on our right. Its surface was diversified with two or three islands, and out on the waters floated a flock of majestic swans, their plumage a dazzling white. The opposite shores were very plainly marked, and at the north-east angle of the lake stood the fine Tsagan-obo (White Mound of Offerings).

The water of the lake was inconceivably salt. Its shores, together with the scanty tufts of grass which grew on them, were powdered with white, as though coated with rime frost. At length we reached a spot where the reeds grew tall and luxuriant amongst the thickets. There we found fresh water. Indeed the place was known as Tsagan-namaga (the White Springs). There we pitched our tents, and a pleasant camping-station it proved to be. I now understood how the lake acquired its name of the Fat Lake. Loppsen explained, that whoever rested beside it found everything he needed—water, grass, fuel, in fact the fat of the land.

What a splendid scene it was, and what a rich variety of colour! As the sun set, the hills and terraces on the opposite shore glowed brick-red across the vivid blue sheet of water, on which the noble swans floated in placid unconcern. Nor did the scene lose anything of its beauty under the magic rays of the moon. The goddess of the night shone with a dazzling splendour amongst the light cloud skirmishers that flecked the sky. Not a breath stirred along the glassy surface of the lake. The tent and tamarisks, ringed round with black reed-beds, stood out in bold and sharp-cut relief, whilst on the shore, down by the water's edge, the salt deposits glistened like new-fallen snow. As I wandered in lonely mood by the brink of the lake, my glance flitted dreamily across it, and my spirit fell captive to its glamorous spell. Why is it those silent Asiatic lakes, with their lone desolate shores, produced such a feeling of familiar strangeness, of mystery, of melancholy in my mind? I know the reason, I know it well. It was because the soft lapping of their waves was the only thing in all that far-off land which echoed the memories of other waves on other shores. But why was it those waves

MY MONGOL GUIDE, LOPPSEN

rocked my mind in the cradle of dreams, and why was it they awakened memories of other shores? I know the reason well. It was because the capricious spirits that sing the songs of eternity through the voices of the winds —it was because they sang there, in the lonely heart of Asia, the same melodies that they have sung for thousands of years among the skerry isles of Sweden, which have not their like on all the earth!

The next day we followed the shore northwards for a

time, but the ground becoming unfavourable down by the lake, we went up on the open level terraces, strewn with coarse sand and gravel. The track crossed a deep dry ravine, which in all probability only carried water during the season of the summer rains. Glancing up it, we caught a glimpse of the Tossun-nor, as it were, through a gateway. Then we approached the broad funnel-shaped depression through which the Holuin-gol entered the lake. But instead of crossing it, we turned up the right bank. The country was however as unfavourable as it well could be—the same complex labyrinth of tamarisk mounds, clay ridges, sand-dunes, and thickets that we had to contend against on the east side of the old Lop-nor. The ford across the Holuin-gol was at Bongkim-obo, a small square "chapel," containing a stone slab with the inevitable formula of prayer carved upon it in relief. The river was 100 feet broad, its maximum depth being not more than three feet, its bottom hard, and its water bright as crystal, so that the animals got over without wetting any of the baggage.

After that the path went almost due east. On the right, but at some distance away, we had the northern shore of Tossun-nor, and on the left, *i.e.* towards the north, the blue expanse of the still larger Kurlyk-nor, also called Khara-nor and Hollussun-nor. The south side of the latter lake was bordered with a wide belt of yellow reeds, almost entirely concealing the place where the Holuin-gol ran out of the lake, to empty itself eventually into the Tossun-nor. On the other hand, the northern shore appeared to be free from reeds, the bare and desolate slopes of the Southern Koko-nor Range sloping straight down to the surface of the lake.

It is an excellent arrangement of Nature to have contrived two lakes in that place instead of one. Into the northern lake, Kurlyk-nor, flowed the rivers Balduin-gol, Bayin-gol, Alikhani-gol, and several small brooks. The current which flowed out of it through the Holuin-gol was relatively sweet, so that the saline matters which the streams carried down with them from the mountains were not deposited until after they reached the more distant lake of Tossun-nor.

After a journey of close upon sixteen miles we came to a halt near the shore of the lake, at the obo of Hlakimto, the handsomest structure of the kind we had yet seen, crowning a barren eminence, and visible to a great distance. It consisted of three cubical monuments resembling altars, built of sun-dried clay, and resting upon pyramidal pedestals. Around it eleven poles, standing upright in the ground, were arranged in the form of an oblong, all laced together by innumerable cords, whilst other cords connected the four corner poles diagonally with a twelfth, which overtopped the central and highest (11 ft. 9½ in. high) of the three monuments. Thousands of little flags or pieces of cloth, of every conceivable colour, as well as the shoulder-blades of sheep, all inscribed with the everlasting Buddhist prayer "On maneh padmeh hum," were stitched to the cords. In the middle monument there was a large square hole, into which Loppsen thrust his arm, and drew out a roll of long narrow strips of paper written all over with Tibetan script. He said there were also burkhans built into the structure, but those he durst not meddle with.

The obo of Hlakimto was built, my men told me, in honour of the *shibbtiks* or *ädsins* of Kurlyk-nor, just as the obo of Tsagan propitiates the shibbtiks of Tossun-nor. Loppsen explained to me that the shibbtiks are spirits or guardian deities, who are alive and resemble men, but to mortal eyes are invisible. There are only good shibbtiks. It is to them that men are indebted for the existence of lakes, rivers, mountains, and so forth. In addition to these spirits, there are also *gadserin-ädsin* or earth spirits, *tengruin-ädsin* or sky spirits, *noruin-ädsin* or lake spirits, and so on. But there are none in the desert; and that is why men find there none of the things they have need of most.

Seen in the moonlight, the obo presented a remarkably picturesque appearance. The three pyramidal structures were like ghosts, and the thousand pennants fluttered in the wind as though they were supplicating, that peace might descend upon some poor soul which had departed this life stained with an awful sin. The stillness of the night was broken by mysterious sounds. Were the spirits of the lake dancing in gladness across its smooth darkling surface? No, it was only the wild-geese calling one to another among the reeds. Two or three ruddy fires gleamed across the darkness of the night from the east end of the lake.

October 28th. The path kept parallel with the lake shore, that is towards the east-south-east. On our left therefore we had Kurlyk-nor, backed on its opposite or northern shore by the Southern Koko-nor Range, and on our right the desolate plain. As we advanced, the lake gradually contracted, and its water was more and more encroached upon by the reeds, which nevertheless left a narrow belt of open water close under the southern shore. We were quite alone in the wilderness, not another creature to be seen, though every now and again we encountered the skeletons of horses lying by the side of the path, proclaiming that people were wont to travel that way. Since leaving Tenghelik we had not met a single mounted Mongol. Loppsen said that the further we advanced towards the east the more unsafe grew the roads by reason of the depredations of the Tangut robbers. At the east end of the lake we saw however in the distance two or three solitary tents. We did not stop, but pushed on to Alikhani-gol (fifteen and a half miles), a stream which because of the thick reed-beds enters the lake unseen. Its banks were marshy and fenny, and the ground treacherous. In one place, which looked perfectly firm, Islam Bai dropped so deep into the soft slushy mud that the men had much ado to save his horse. During that day's march we lost the first of our new horses.

On October 30th we rode across the Barun-kövveh (the southern branch of the Alikhani-gol), and had on our left hand Tsun-ula (the Northern Mountains). The geographical nomenclature in Mongolia is generally as simple

OFFERINGS AT THE "OBO" OF HLAKIMTO

as this. We only had one or two glimpses of the stream, its bed was cut so deeply in the soft soil. The previous night was cold (−8°7 Fahr. or −22°6 C.), so that several sheets of ice tossed on the current, crashing sharply against the banks and against one another. The road to Sorgotsu, a distance of seventeen and a half miles, ran through sandy desert, interspersed with small sand-dunes, reed-beds, and steppes.

Loppsen's cheerfulness had now entirely deserted him. He rode along silent and depressed, his eyes constantly fixed upon the road in front of him, and all day long he kept mumbling, "On maneh padmeh hum." When I enquired what was the cause of this gloom, he shook his head, and replied, we were now coming to a dangerous country. Two Mongols he saw whilst resting at Alikhani-gol told him, that only a few days before Tangut robbers had been to Kurlyk-nor and stolen some horses. He begged us to have our firearms in readiness, for even though we did not meet any of the robbers on the road, they were all the same hiding in the mountains, whence they could watch all our movements. Our fires at night would guide them, and we might think ourselves lucky if we lost nothing more than our horses. I therefore brought out the rifles and revolvers, and distributed them amongst the men of the caravan, at the same time giving each man a supply of cartridges. But Sorgotsu was silent and deserted. We saw no fires, either out on the steppe or at the foot of the mountains, and no signs of human beings. We were quite reassured. All the same, for precaution's sake, the horses were brought back into camp at dark, and turned loose again to graze at daybreak. Our dogs however were excellent night-watchmen. The smallest suspicious sound set them off barking.

The evenings and nights were brilliantly bright, still, and cold. The ink in my pen was frozen as early as four o'clock in the afternoon, and I had to keep thawing it by breathing upon it. I got out my old Kashgar fur coat, which had lain packed away for close upon a twelvemonth. Hot tea was now more welcome than ever, and every evening Islam made me a wheaten loaf. We had brought with us a small stove made of sheet iron, and it now proved very useful, although employed for the first time. Islam put it on the ground inside the tent, and the chimney was fastened with wire to the brass ferrule or socket that held together the two halves of the tent-pole in such a way that it peeped out of the tent-opening. Then he lighted the stove with dry sticks, and it crackled and hissed away beautifully. This was a first-rate idea: it made the tent quite warm and cosy and comfortable—as comfortable as my own study in Stockholm. Yolldash thoroughly approved of the innovation, although he pricked his ears at first, when he heard the dry branches crackling, and the iron prickling under the heat. At night I let the stove die out of itself, and after that the tent grew icy cold. But I cared little about that: I was well wrapped up in my furs, with nothing except my nose peeping out. I always kept a cup of tea from my supper standing by the head of my bed. But in the morning any tea that chanced to be left in the cup was frozen into a lump of ice, and so too was the ink.

The men also were well off. They had a large fire, round which they all gathered. That night at Sorgotsu was the coldest I had experienced for two and a half years —namely – 14°8 Fahr. (– 26° C.), and inside the tent · 9°4 Fahr. (– 23° C.).

CHAPTER XCI.

AN ENCOUNTER WITH TANGUT ROBBERS

ON the last day of October we rode across the steppes to Kövveh-khuduk (the Spring on the Shore), on the southern shore of Khara-nor, a lake which lay in the middle of a small self-contained basin that gathered up the drainage of the surrounding mountains. It was now however quite dry. On the north side, between the lake and the mountains, were a series of yellow sand-dunes; but on the south shore there was plenty of rich herbage. The water of the spring was saltish. But it was a long day's march to the next spring going east, so that, although we had only covered eight and a half miles, we were obliged to encamp where we were.

At that place another enemy threatened our horses. My men detected in the loose soft soil the footprints of bears, which had come down out of the mountains in quest of berries. Loppsen warned us to keep a watch upon our animals, for the bears were wont to lie in wait behind the bushes, and thence attack them and kill them. Here again therefore after the horses had grazed some hours, they were fetched up and tethered amongst the tents.

I now ordered that two men should keep watch every night, and should be relieved every second hour. In order to keep themselves awake, and to let us know they were awake, they were instructed to beat at regular intervals a couple of saucepans—in default of drums. They might also sing as much as they liked, to guard themselves against the attacks of slumber. Often after that, when I awoke in the night, I heard their monotonous, melancholy

Mohammedan songs, echoing like cries of distress around the camp fires. As soon as day dawned, the sentries turned in, trusting to the dogs to give the alarm after that if anything happened.

November 1st. The night passed peacefully. Nothing was heard of either Tanguts or bears, and rifle on shoulder we set off towards the east-south-east. The lake speedily vanished from sight, as we entered a tolerably broad valley, which ascended as we advanced. We then had on both sides moderately high mountain-chains, with jagged tops, and free from snow. The path went up a dry rain-channel, the principal drainage artery of the district, which ran along the middle of the valley among patches of steppe, bushes, and thickets.

We came across the fresh track of a bear going in the direction we were travelling. Islam and Loppsen begged permission to follow him. They soon came pretty near him, and all three disappeared behind the bushes.

The caravan was skirting the mountains on the right. Immediately after passing a projecting shoulder of rock I stopped, with Emin Mirza, to take an observation. The mountains were composed of a violet-black clay-slate, with an inclination of fifty-three degrees towards E. 160° S. Then we rode on after the caravan, and drew near to the middle of the valley.

At the end of about an hour we were rather startled to see Islam and Loppsen come galloping back as hard as their horses could put hoofs to ground, waving their rifles over their heads and shouting, "Tangut robbers! Tangut robbers!" They raced up to us, and close behind them pursued a band of about a dozen mounted Tanguts, enveloped in a cloud of dust. I instantly commanded the caravan to halt. "The baggage animals behind those bushes in charge of one man! Out weapons! Cartridges ready!"

I, Islam, Parpi, and Loppsen, after dismounting and throwing off our furs and pelts, took our station on the top of two clay hills. The Mohammedans fairly shook with anxiety. Parpi had been in conflict with the

"TANGUT ROBBERS! TANGUT ROBBERS!"

Tanguts before, for he was one of Dutreuil de Rhins's party, when that traveller was attacked two and a half years earlier and murdered at Tam-buddha. Przhevalsky and Roborovsky were both compelled to fight in this same neighbourhood, so that I was fully alive to the gravity of the situation. There were twelve of the Tanguts, and Loppsen said that each man would certainly carry a gun. We had only three rifles, besides five revolvers. Their superiority was therefore manifest. Loppsen and Islam were the only two on our side who were anything like good shots, whereas all the Tanguts shoot well, taking long cool aim over their musket-forks, and only firing when they are absolutely sure of hitting. Under these circumstances how would the fight end? Was my caravan going to be routed and scattered and all the labours of my last journey destroyed?

No, things were not so dangerous as they looked. When the band of robbers perceived that we were a pretty large company, and saw our weapons glancing in the sunshine, they pulled up at about a hundred and fifty paces' distance. We could see them distinctly as soon as the dust settled. They crowded together, gesticulating and shouting loudly. The result of their deliberations seemed to be that it would not be advisable to attack until they had ascertained how many we were, and how we were armed. Meanwhile we waited at our posts on the hills. I went on calmly smoking my pipe, and the action had a manifest effect on my men. I also observed the Tanguts through my field-glass, for I always had it at my side.

After about a minute's noisy discussion the Tanguts wheeled away at right angles towards the foot of the mountains on the south. There they divided. Half of them rode up a ravine among the rocks, whilst the other half continued parallel with us, but at the distance of two rifle-shots, for as soon as they turned, we resumed our journey, keeping close together in a body.

The valley began to narrow, contracting to a sort of rocky gateway. Loppsen was apprehensive the Tanguts would hasten on before us, and hide themselves among the rocks, and shoot us down as we went through. There was however no other road, and to turn back was not to be thought of. The best thing we could do therefore was to try and reach the place first, or at any rate pass it before the Tanguts were able to take up advantageous positions. They had however one great advantage over us. They knew every nook and cranny of the mountains, their gorges, ravines, and hiding-places. Moreover our horses were heavily laden, whilst those of the Tanguts were but very lightly accoutred. Hence they easily gained upon us, at the same time gradually closing in upon the road, and finally disappeared in the openings of the rocks.

We hurried on as fast as our horses were able to travel, having the right flank of the caravan covered by those of us who were armed. Then we again caught sight of the Tanguts. They had halted, and did not appear to contemplate an attack. Thus we threaded the extremely narrow defile without misadventure. We rode however with our rifles ready cocked, and our eyes searching the rocks on the right.

On the other side of the defile the valley widened out again, and it was with a feeling of great relief that we debouched into the open. Loppsen believed that the Tanguts had taken a short cut through the mountains, intending to attack us in another place. He was sure they had been on their way to Kurlyk-nor to steal horses, but had turned back in the expectation of finding richer booty in our caravan.

The valley finally opened out into a broad plain, and after a march of twenty-one miles we halted at Kharasharuin-kubb, a place in which there was plenty of good grass, and an open freshwater pool, fed from a spring. We turned the horses loose on the edge of a patch of reeds, and they had a good drink at the pool. Then I set two of the Mohammedans, Kurban and Ahmed, to watch that they did not wander too far away.

As soon as it began to be dusk, the horses were tethered amongst the tents, close to the reeds. We kept the fire over which our supper was cooked purposely low, damped down as much as possible, so that the flames should not betray our position more than could be helped. Loppsen was very anxious with regard to the night, for the Tanguts would easily be able to observe us, whilst keeping themselves concealed in the grass. And Loppsen was right, for no sooner was it dark than we heard them creeping all round the camp, uttering unearthly howls, which I can liken to nothing better than the howling of hyænas or the long-drawn melancholy whine of hungry wolves prowling through the night. It was however a favourite *ruse de guerre* of the Tanguts, adopted, Loppsen said, to find out whether their intended victims had watch-dogs or not. Our dogs gave them no room for doubt, for they barked furiously all night long, and kept dashing out towards the pool, near which, it was evident, the Tanguts had fastened their horses. Loppsen was unable to find words strong enough to express his hatred of the Tanguts. They were not, he considered, one bit better than dogs, and like dogs they sneaked along, crouching close to the ground, rolling up the skirts of their pelts and carrying their guns in their right hands.

However we maintained a vigilant watch, a sentry being stationed at each end of the string of tethered horses, who kept up an almost constant singing and drumming upon the saucepans. Only two men were allowed to sleep at once. The others patrolled unceasingly backwards and forwards between the horses and the tents. Every five minutes or so Parpi Bai would cry: "Khabärdar?" (Are the sentries awake?). Loppsen sat over the fire, silent, warming his hands. But there was not much rest for any of us that night. Every now and again the men stamped up and down, the horses pawed the ground and neighed, and at regular intervals came the cries of the sentries and the banging of the saucepans; in a word, we were regularly besieged. The

Tanguts' intention to attack us unawares was thus thwarted. They did not succeed in stealing a single horse from us.

In this way we made our entry into the country of the Khara Tanguts, with a sharp reminder that we should have to be on the alert. The Tanguts are notorious robbers and thieves, who love to plunder their more peacefully disposed neighbours, the Mongols. When the latter go to the temple-feasts at the monastery of Kumbum, they always ride in large well-armed companies, for their only road lies through the country of the Tanguts.

I am inclined to think it was fear rather than vigilance which kept my men awake. They were instructed to wake me if the Tanguts began to shoot. Once or twice I woke up of my own accord, and on each occasion heard their incessant cries of "Khabärdar? Khabärdar?" and in the intervals between their challenges to one another came the weird melancholy howls of the Tanguts.

At sunrise the Tanguts drew back to a respectful distance. But no sooner did our caravan make a start than they made a rush for the spot where we had encamped the night. The empty match-boxes, ends of candles, and pieces of torn newspaper would prove to them, that they had not simply Mongols to deal with, and that would probably deter them from further pursuit.

On November 2nd we rode almost due east across spacious steppes, between two mountain-chains on north and south, and accomplished no less than twenty-six and three-quarter miles. In several places we crossed the winding tracks of the Tanguts, and my men believed there were several of the robbers lurking in the entrances of the glens that pierced the mountains. The ground was level and easy riding, and we travelled at a good pace, notwithstanding that the strength of some of our horses was beginning to give out. On three separate occasions we saw a large troop of khulans (wild asses), but they all fled up into the mountains. The configuration of the surface was similar to that of Northern Tibet,

"WE MAINTAINED A VIGILANT WATCH AGAINST THE TANGUTS"

in so far as it consisted of a succession of self-contained basins destitute of outflow, but at this time they were all dry. The first depression we came to had a small lake in the middle, the second a long narrow lake. About midway along the shore of the latter, which was called Serkeh-nor, was an obo known as Gadser-udsur.

Lake Serkeh-nor was pretty nearly dry. We only saw water in three places, the rest of the lake bottom being coated with a thick white layer of salt. The Mongols, when travelling to the sacred temple of Kum-bum, are in the habit of taking bags of salt from this place, which they barter in Ten-kar (Donkhur) and Si-ning-fu weight for weight for bags of *taran-gurill* or burnt flour. In summer the lake fills with water, but it is so shallow that, were it not for the mud at the bottom, it would easily be possible to ride right across it. The district around its eastern extremity, called Örtäni, possessed both grass and fresh springs. There our track joined the routes from Dsun-sassak and Nomokhan-khoto, both notable camping-stations of the Mongols in the east of Tsaidam. During the night, for we pitched our tents beside the springs of Örtäni, we kept as vigilant a watch as we had done the night before. But we were not disturbed, nor did we hear an echo of the Tanguts.

Our next stage was fifteen miles and a half to Dulan-yung. On the way the road deflected towards the north-east so as to strike the valley of the Dulan-gol, which was broad and framed in by grassy hills, and traversed by a clear brook, with a good deal of water in it. The mountains on the right were crowned at fairly regular intervals with detached forests, while their slopes were dotted with large herds of sheep. Hundreds of tame yaks ranged up and down the stream. We pitched our tents on its right bank in a splendid neighbourhood, not far from a Tangut tent.

I resolved to let the Tanguts see that we had no fear of them. Two men whom we met on the road clapped spurs to their horses the moment they caught sight of us. But well on towards evening two others, armed with long swords, ventured at length to draw near to my tent.

They were dressed in precisely the same manner as the Mongols, but did not understand a single word of Mongolian. Loppsen however, having four times made the pilgrimage to Lhasa, was tolerably versed in their language—Tibetan, so that through him I was able to converse with them. Seeing that they were received in a friendly spirit, the Tanguts laid aside a good deal of their shyness; all the same, they were not very sure what to make of us. However, they sold us a sheep, and provided us with milk for the evening. Our camping-ground had been deliberately chosen on a sort of island, overgrown with bushes, between two arms of the stream, and commanding a view of the whole of the valley. We had plenty of fuel. The brook prattled vivaciously down its stony channel. I sent the horses to a pasture-ground in the immediate vicinity in charge of two men, mounted and armed, with strict injunctions to keep watchful guard over them all night.

FROM TSAIDAM TO PEKING

CHAPTER XCII.

THROUGH THE COUNTRY OF THE TANGUTS

AT Dulan-yung (the Warm River) we stayed over November 4th and let the worn-out night-watchmen lie and snore all day long. Loppsen still continued to urge vigilance, warning us not to be lulled into a false sense of security by the apparent friendliness of the Tanguts and the cheap price (a liang or tael, worth about 3*s.* 1½*d.*) at which they had sold us the sheep and the milk; he was afraid they meant to recoup themselves by thieving. After a good deal of hesitation he was persuaded to accompany me to the two Tangut tents near to which we had encamped. At first he was far from enamoured with the idea: and my Mohammedans too endeavoured to dissuade me from going. But I failed to see what danger there could be, for I was going quite peaceably and unarmed to throw myself upon their hospitality.

The two tents, both as black as the night, stood close together. We were met just in front of them by half-a-dozen ill-natured black dogs. Then a man came out and drove the dogs away, and after inquiring what we wanted, invited us to go inside his tent. Loppsen told him, I only wanted to see how the Tanguts lived. I accordingly stepped inside, and took a seat beside the fire, where two women were engaged cooking tea, with flour and butter, in a large pot. One of the two was our host's young wife. She looked pleasant and sprightly, and was giving the breast to a noisy infant. All the time I was in the hut she never took her eyes off me. The other was a repulsive old woman, who had a girl of about five by her side. Both women, as well as the man, were dressed in exactly the same style as the Mongols, but had laid aside their sheepskins, leaving only the left arm covered. All the rest of the upper part of the body, down to the waist, was bare. The younger woman was well-shaped and strongly made, and her skin was a copper-brown colour. In general appearance they bore a close resemblance to the Mongol type, at any rate it seemed so to me who saw these people for the first time. Indeed I should have been ready to set them down for Mongols, had it not been for their language, and the peculiar construction of their tent, both of which betrayed a different race. Immediately opposite the entrance, upon a box, was a domestic shrine of the same character as that which I have described among the Mongols. Our Tangut host too wore a gavo (case) round his neck, containing a burkhan (image of Buddha).

We were invited to take tea. Then I noticed the different parts of the tent and inquired their several names, and even wrote them down, to the great disquietude of Loppsen, who urged that the Tanguts might misinterpret what I was doing, and imagine I had come with evil intentions. The two women laughed heartily at my desperate attempts to pronounce the intricate Tibetan words, with their artificial accumulation of consonants at the beginning. They could not for the life of them take their eyes off me. Their hair hung about their dirty heads in a vast number of thin plaits, some of which fell down over their shoulders and back, some in front over the bosom. From the end of the lowest plait behind, as well as from the ends of two others on each side of the head, there hung three heavy gay-coloured adornments, consisting of red and blue ribbons, pieces of cloth, and glass beads of different colours. These pendulous impediments flapped against their backs at every movement, and must have been extremely irksome whenever they moved their heads.

The tent had a four-square ground-plan, giving easily three or four times the amount of space there is in an

A TANGUT TENT AT DULAN-YUNG

ordinary Mongol or Kirghiz tent. On the whole it resembled a low, truncated pyramid, the sides sloping inwards as they went up; but the roof had the shape of a low irregular prism. A row of poles along the middle held up the tent-cloth, which was made of a coarse black linen, which the Tanguts weave themselves, a chink being left along the top for the smoke to escape. The tent-cloth was kept taut by means of ropes from the four corners and from the top of each of the sides, running over a cleft or fork in a pole, and fastened to stakes driven into the ground. The rain-water was carried away by a gutter dug all round the tent. In the middle of the tent was the fireplace, cleverly constructed of flat stones, placed slanting one against the other, with a hollow between for the cooking-pot; there were also holes for the draught. The fuel, consisting of animals' dung, was kept between two rows of similar stones.

Along three of the sides stood rows of sacks, partly made of linen, partly of skin, and containing corn, flour, fat, and salt. These sacks also helped to shut out the draught and prevent it coming in under the folds of the tent-walls. The ragged carpets spread round the fire were littered with a multitude of things—such as furs, copper kettles, wooden bowls, teapots, Chinese porcelain bowls, square flour-boxes, bellows, saddles and bridles—all flung down in picturesque confusion. Several of their belongings, for example the swords, were made by the Tanguts themselves. The religious objects came from Lhasa, and some of the household articles from Si-ning-fu.

November 5th. Raw cold weather, the sky covered with clouds, snow on the ground—quite a rare sight since we came down off the Tibetan plateau. In the morning ten Tanguts came to the camp, each armed with a straight, sharp sword, and dressed in vari-coloured blue and red costumes, with bag-caps, which gave them a certain resemblance to soldiers. They brought us two or three cans of milk, and wanted to sell some horses. But the price they asked was far too high, and so we did no business. Without being impertinent, they examined several of my belongings, and were agreeable and talkative. My revolver inspired them with the profoundest respect after they learned that it was charged with six cartridges at once.

I was anxious to engage a Tangut guide; but they answered that one man could not go with me alone. Nor were they satisfied to take twelve liang each for the journey to Si-ning-fu; they demanded sixteen liang (about £2 10*s.*). After I at length agreed to this, they went on to say that they had no horses. This however was a palpable excuse. The fact was, they were suspicious of us, and were afraid to travel in our company. Fortunately Loppsen had an intimate knowledge of the country, and was moreover the best and most trustworthy guide I ever had.

The valley rose gradually towards the east, between rounded hills covered with soft soil. Half-way up, the slopes were thickly planted with *Coniferæ*, and occasionally the bare rock cropped out above the girdle of forest. The end of every side-valley was occupied by the black tents of the Tanguts, standing scattered about, and wearing a forbidding aspect—ideal lurking-places for robbers and bandits. We counted twenty-five such tents, or, including those at Dulan-yung, some forty in all. Had the inhabitants been so inclined, it would have been an easy matter for them to have stopped our way and overpowered us. But we rode on unmolested, although at every tent the people came out to stare at us.

At last I caught sight of a curious pyramidal object standing in the middle of the valley. It was a cube supporting a cylinder, both made of clay. Loppsen explained that it was a *sovurga*, or sign to indicate that there was a temple close by, and the next instant I caught sight of the walls of Dulan-kitt, the first walled town since we left Kopa. It was a place of a very few houses, but with some tents. The lower parts of the houses were built of stone, the upper parts of clay. The inhabitants were Banga Mongols, a sept in ill-repute for thievery.

The temple (*kitt*) of which Loppsen spoke was a large square house, with a flat roof and windows. This was the residence of the principal lama of the twenty-five septs of the Koko-nor Mongols, namely Khoduktouin-gaghen, himself a Mongol by race, who is said to have lived in Dulan-kitt in successive incarnations for a period of 6100 years. As soon as the lama is sixty-one years old, he lies down and dies, but immediately re-enters life in the person of a little child, who becomes his successor. There are sixty-one lamas of the same rank in Mongolia, Kum-bum, and Tibet.

After a march of sixteen miles we encamped immediately east of Tsagan-nor (the White Lake). The lake was wedged, as it were, into the mountain-side, in such a way that the granite cliffs jutted out in some places in rugged, weathered spurs, descending steeply into the water. By that the forest had dwindled almost entirely away. The last few trees were however so far up the mountain-side that we could not get at them. That evening therefore we had only a scanty supply of fuel.

Loppsen came to me full of trouble. He had lost the pouch in which he carried his provisions, together with ten liang (31*s.* 3*d.*) in silver, with which he had intended buying a camel in Kum-bum. He had had the pouch under his head for a pillow the previous night, and no doubt it had been stolen by one of our worthy Tangut visitors whilst the men were getting the caravan ready to start. I promised Loppsen to make good his loss, if he would procure me some temple flags in Kum-bum. This he promised to do, and after that recovered his spirits.

November 6th. During the night we again heard the unearthly howls from the valley and the neighbourhood. I fully made up my mind that the Tanguts intended to lie in wait for us in the pass at the end of the valley. The dogs barked madly, and the cries of our sentries echoed unceasingly among the tents. But I was tired and slept soundly through it all. In the morning I was told, it was only three wolves, which had crept in as far as my tent, and had a brush with the dogs.

We continued our way towards the north-east and north down the broad grassy valley. Water was entirely absent, and the region was quite uninhabited, although charred wood and ashes, marking the sites of old encampments, proved that it was visited at least occasionally. The mountains were composed of gneiss and a species of quartzite, very greatly weathered.

In the middle of the valley we came across a very curious erection. A sharply pointed fragment of rock, which stood entirely isolated, stuck up out of the ground like a colossal tooth, and against it leaned a rectangular structure, built of blocks of granite, each 2 ft. 6 in. square. The walls were about the height of an average man plus half that height again, and measured some thirty-five to forty feet in length. The floor was paved with slabs of stone, and the place was roofed in with the same materials, each slab having the inevitable Tibetan formula of prayer incised upon it. The walls were hung with tufts of wool, pieces of cloth, and fragments of bone, all marked with repetitions of the same Tibetan ideographs. Entrance to the interior was obtained through a wide gateway. The weathered condition of the stones, and the fact of the wall leaning over at an angle, pointed to a pretty considerable age. The place, which was called Ganchur, was no doubt originally a fort or watch-house, but at the present time was manifestly regarded as an obo, or religious monument, by the inhabitants of the neighbourhood. From the interior there was access to a long and lofty grotto, evidently of natural origin, for the sides were extremely rugged and worn by weathering. They were scribbled all over with Chinese letter-signs.

Khulans (wild asses) were common again in this neighbourhood. We saw one troop of a score, and a little after that another of about eighty, who galloped over the pass in a compact squadron. The valley gradually ascended over soft grassy ground towards the pass, which bore the name of Nökköten-köttel (the Hollow Pass). The summit

A TANGUT BOY

was crowned by a small plain obo, erected to the deities of the Southern Koko-nor Mountains. From the top of the pass, we looked, towards the north-west, down into the broad open valley of the Bukhain-gol, shut in on the north by a range of low hills. The view was very extensive, and the country equally as open as the region of the lake-basins we travelled through in Northern Tibet.

On the other side of the pass we descended the glen of the Nökköten-gol, a brook almost dry, and after a march of nearly sixteen miles pitched our tents beside it. The only fuel we could get was the dung of the wild ass; on the other hand there was plenty of good herbage. At that place we met a caravan of fifty Tanguts from the valley of Dulan. They were greatly surprised to see us, but manifested no sign of hostility. They were all on horseback, and had with them a number of yaks loaded with sacks and other baggage. They said they had been to Ten-kar, to buy flour and other necessaries for the winter.

November 7th. During the night the Tanguts prowled round our camp again, but were unsuccessful in stealing any of our horses, and in the morning they left before we did. All day we travelled nearly due east for a distance of twenty miles. One stream we came to, the Kundelung, although but small, nevertheless occasioned us considerable difficulty to get across it. Islam Akhun from Keriya, who rode one of the pack-horses, was the first to try the soft slushy ice. But the water was so deep that the horse was nearly drowned, and its rider got a cold bath, whilst the packages which the animal carried were splashed all over with water. Parpi Bai made an attempt a little higher up, but with the same result. At length Loppsen discovered a place where the stream was relatively shallow, and the ice could be broken up with axes.

The soft level ground was very much cut up by the holes and runs of voles, and we had to keep a sharp look-out to guard against the horses coming down. Upon emerging from the glen, we turned down beside the Bukhain-gol, and rode through a series of thickets and underwoods. The stream was broad and deep, and its bed littered with gravel. In some places it flowed in one channel; there the water was open. In other places it was divided into several arms; these were frozen. The terraces on both sides of the stream were not less than sixteen feet high. For the space of fully forty minutes we rode across a piece of ground on which, according to Loppsen, some 20,000 Dungan rebels, fleeing from Si-ning-fu, had encamped eight months previously. Signs of their encampment were abundant, for the grass was still trampled down and scorched by their innumerable camp-fires. The skulls and leg-bones of sheep which they had stolen from the Tanguts, besides rags of felt, poles, and such like things, lay scattered about all over the ground. Wherever they went the Dungans devastated the country like a swarm of locusts. In which direction they had turned their steps, Loppsen did not know. They had at any rate not gone to Tsaidam. In all probability they had marched up into the mountainous country of the upper Bukhain-gol.

All day long we met not a soul, saw not a single hut or a single flock. The land was solitary, silent. Khulans, wolves, and foxes roamed over it unhindered, without fear. We saw no wild yaks, although they were said to exist along the upper parts of the Bukhain-gol. In fact, it is from that circumstance the river derives its name of Bukhain-gol, meaning Yak River.

CHAPTER XCIII.

KOKO-NOR

NOVEMBER 8th. Winter had come, laying its icy hand upon the country. The night echoed with the melancholy howling of the wolves, for it was snowing; but as soon as the sun rose, the snow melted rapidly away. Hardly had we quitted our camping-station when a troop of wolves, in utter contempt of our dogs, sneaked into it, to see if we had left anything worth picking up. As for the dogs, they had the good sense not to approach too near to the intruders.

Our next step was to cross the Yak River, an undertaking which proved easier than I anticipated. The stream was 250 feet wide, and had a volume of 600 cubic feet in the second. Beautifully clear and bright, and gliding along without a sound, like a river of oil, the current travelled at the rate of three feet in the second. Beyond the principal stream came six other arms, but they contained nothing except frozen pools and fragments of ice. Beyond these again there was yet another arm, with a volume of 140 cubic feet in the second. Its water was muddy; in all probability it drained off the earthy slopes of the hills to the north.

Meanwhile we had travelled away from the Southern Koko-nor Range, or rather it had fallen away to the east-south-east, skirting closely the southern shore of Koko-nor. We caught occasional glimpses of the black tents of the Tanguts, and once or twice saw mounted Tanguts and their flocks of sheep. Far off in the east the horizon was marked by a straight dark blue line; it was the large lake of Koko-nor. We encamped in a place known as Hadeh-sächi, after doing nearly twenty-one miles. The evening was still and bright, the stars glittered brilliantly, and in the hollows of the mountains around we saw the pale red gleams from the camp-fires of the Tanguts.

November 9th. Soon after starting, one of our horses gave up, and as several of the rest showed signs of exhaustion, we only travelled a short stage. The further we advanced to the east-north-east the more distinct grew the Koko-nor. The steppe sloped gently towards the shore of the lake. The Northern Koko-nor Range, which had an occasional peak capped with snow, was the only mountain-chain visible; it lay to the north-east and east-north-east. The Mongol name for this range is simply Tsun-ula (the Northern Mountains).

At length we heard the waves beating against the shore, and immediately afterwards reached the lake itself, and steered our course beside it. Near the beach the water was not quite clear; this was no doubt owing to the action of the waves. It was also much less salt than the water of the North Tibetan lakes. But the delta of the Bukhain-gol was at no great distance, and no doubt that river tended to keep the water fresh. There was no ice on the surface, and, though the temperature of the air was 35°4 Fahr. (1°9 C.), the temperature of the water was 44° Fahr. (6°7 C.).

We travelled along a rampart of gravel (clay-slate), which the waves had built up along the shore, until we came to the brook Bagha-ulan, where we encamped, and whence I got a truly magnificent view. Right away to the horizon stretched the lake like the boundless sea, its waters a deep blue, changing to green. To right, to left, in the far-off distance, the mountain-chains grew lower and fainter, until they at last faded away into a veil of haze. Their two nearer extremities did not however touch; a wide gap remained open in the south-east. It was glorious to breathe the "sea-breeze" that blew off the lake—glorious, refreshing, inspiring!

At last then we had reached the Blue Lake, the Tso-

A TANGUT

ngombo of the Tanguts, the Koko-nor (Koko-nur) of the Mongols, the Tsing-hai of the Chinese. For three days more we skirted its shores, which were situated at an altitude of 9975 feet above the level of the sea.

Loppsen told me the following legend in explanation of the origin of the lake. In the grey far-off days of old, a great lama dug a vast hole in the ground. Then he took a white root and a black root of some plant, and holding them over the chasm cut the black root into two halves, out of which the water gushed forth in streams, until it filled the lake. If he had cut the white root, the hole would have been filled with milk. It was fortunate he cut the root out of which the water flowed, for otherwise the people who lived in those parts would not have been able to keep sheep, and so would have had nothing to do. After that the lama went up into a high mountain close by, and broke out of it an enormous piece of rock, and cast it into the middle of the lake; and that was how the island was made.

November 10th. At the camp we lost another horse. On the whole the Mongolian horses were after all only moderate animals; still they were very cheap. Most of them at the end of the first month's travel were galled on the back. The Tanguts, who seldom use their horses for anything except riding, take better care of them; but they also ask a higher price—for example, twenty liang or taels (£3 2*s.* 6*d.*) for a good average animal. It might have been expected that the Mongols, who are more dependent upon the breeding of horses than their Tangut neighbours, would produce a better race of animal, but such did not appear to be the case. As a beast of burden, the Tanguts employ the yak instead of the horse. The horses we brought from Khotan stood the fatigues of travel very much better than those we bought from the Mongols at Yikeh-tsohan-gol. It is true, they were better kept, for the Mongol horses were dependent entirely upon such grass as they picked up by the way; whereas in Northern Tibet we fed our horses to a great extent upon corn (maize).

We still continued to travel due east at about a mile or a mile and a half from the lake shore, which glittered a dazzling bright line on the south. All day we had the rocky island in view, rising above the surface of the water like a dromedary's back, and thrown up in dark relief against the scarce perceptible mountains on the south.

To-day we travelled through a less lonely region; for we passed several herds of horned cattle, guarded by women, children, and shepherds, the last invariably armed with a gun or a sword. All the mounted men we met carried a black gun, with its tall fantastic fork, across their shoulder, as well as a sword stuck through their belt and turned horizontally across the front of the body. Their sheepskins were drawn up high through their belts so as to hang over them at the sides. They also wore top-boots with turned-up toes, and close-fitting caps.

After a march of thirteen and a half miles we made our camp beside the brook of Yikeh-ulan, which contained a good deal of water. Curiously enough most of the geographical names in the locality were Mongolian, and they were even used by the Tanguts—for instance, Bagha-ulan and Yikeh-ulan or the Small and the Large Red (Tract) respectively, an allusion to the reddish tinge of the soil.

Immediately above our camp were ten Tangut tents, and we were told there were twenty more in a recess of the mountains on the north. Some of their inhabitants came to visit us, all wearing in their belts naked swords brought from Lhasa. They sold us some milk, a sheep, and a horse; but Loppsen was anxious they should not see too much money all at once. For he persisted in declaring they were all thieves and scoundrels, and that it was simply the fear of our weapons which prevented them from attacking us. The Tanguts used to ask Loppsen, who was my interpreter, whether my packing-cases contained soldiers, and he always replied with stolid gravity, "Yes; the large boxes contained two soldiers, and the small ones one each, as well as a number of guns." My tent-stove, with its strange funnel, they took for a cannon. When

THE NORTH-WESTERN CORNER OF LAKE KOKO-NOR

they inquired why we lighted a fire in it at night, Loppsen told them it was to keep it ready for action. If danger threatened, all we should have to do would be to fling in the powder and balls, and it would at once spit out a murderous rain of bullets.

The Tanguts said it was nine months since the Dungans went past Yikeh-ulan, and they stole 400 of their sheep, besides 140 horses, cattle, and yaks.

They expected the lake and streams would become frost-bound for the winter in about ten or fifteen days, and told me they usually remained frozen three months or so, but that the time varied a good deal according to the severity of the winter. The ice on the lake was however very untrustworthy, for on bright windy days numbers of cracks, "lanes," and holes were wont to be formed in it, and they remained open until calm weather set in again. All the same they said the ice was as thick as a man's arm is long.

On the rocky island in the middle of the lake there was a temple, frequented by pilgrims. But when the ice splits and cracks, the "lanes" or openings prevent the pilgrims from crossing on horseback. They are therefore obliged to walk across, and drag provisions and fuel for three days behind them on sledges, temporarily constructed out of the two wooden ribs which constitute the frame of their pack-saddles. It frequently happens that, when half-way across, they encounter gaps in the ice which they are unable to get over, and so are forced to turn back. Sometimes too they are imprisoned on the island by a thaw, and have to wait until the frost sets in again. But they never go so late in the season as to risk being detained on the island until the following winter. The lamas who live on the island lead a terribly solitary existence, and are exclusively dependent for food and other necessaries upon the offerings which the pilgrims carry to them. My Mohammedans thought that the lamas had a fine time of it, for they were inaccessible. All round the shores of the Blue Lake there was no such thing as a boat to be seen.

The level of the lake is said to vary greatly in different periods. When the lake rises high, it is looked upon as premonitory of an unlucky year; when it sinks, it portends nothing but prosperity. This year the lake rose exceptionally high. No wonder then the Dungans came and inflicted such great losses upon the Tanguts. But if the Dungans had not come, the flocks would have been visited by the plague, the Tanguts themselves by sickness, and there would have been a scanty supply of pasture. The lake, I was told, is always higher in summer than in winter. Although the actual rise and fall of the water is not very considerable, the different levels are very plainly discernible on the shore, owing to the fact that it shelves down so gradually. The year of my visit (1896) the shore-line was said to extend one and a half to two miles farther to the north than usual. It was no doubt this circumstance which led that noble and incomparable man, Father Huc, to believe that Koko-nor was subject to ebb and flow. In this connection he says: "This vast sheet of water really deserves to be called a sea rather than a lake, for, apart from its great extent, its waters are as bitter salt as the waters of the ocean, and like them, they ebb and flow."

At the west end of the lake we passed at a little distance the obo of the Koko-noruin. There was also an obo on the east shore, erected in honour of the deities of the lake, called Tsagan-yempin or Kusha-chulun. It is visited once a year by the chiefs of all the tribes in the vicinity. At other spots along the shore there were several smaller obos. In one place we passed we observed a curious affair, consisting of branches and twigs stuck into the ground, and hung all over with pieces of pelts, tufts of wool, rope-ends, and such like choice treasures. In another place there was a cylindrical stone, in which it was customary to make fires. These two obos possessed the virtue of curing sickness, provided someone interceded for the sick person, by reciting in front of them with sufficient industry the all-efficacious "On maneh padmeh hum!"

A TANGUT BOY

The Koko-nor Tanguts generally spend the winter on the steppes around the lake, the proximity of which tends of course to modify the extreme cold; but in summer they go up into the mountains that lie to the north. The principal chief among the Tanguts was the Gangtse Lama, who acted as intermediary between the governor of Si-ning-fu and the nomads, and was accordingly invested with the *huli* or prerogative of executing justice. When thieves and other criminals are caught, they are carried to Si-ning-fu, and there examined, with the result that they not seldom lose their heads. In the more important cases the Gangtse Lama writes in Tibetan to Si-ning-fu or settles the affair himself. The Chinese are, it is true, the masters of the country, but their administration of it leaves very much to be desired. Neither there nor in Tsaidam are there any Chinese officials. In that respect both regions are very differently situated from East Turkestan, where the Chinese have thoroughly established themselves and organized an excellent system of administration.

The Mongols call their thievish neighbours Khara Tanguts, or Black Tanguts, a name suggested in all probability by their intensely black tents, or by their dark skin and hair, and not, as Loppsen would make me believe, because *khara* was synonymous with *mo*, *i.e.* "villainous" or "bad."

The constant feeling of insecurity which accompanied us made us feel as though we were on the war-path, and any moment might expect an attack. It was a good thing for us that we had moonlight nights, so that our sentries could see well about them. Every night the dogs barked furiously, though generally it was only at the big greyish-yellow wolves, which prowled round our tents.

The Yikeh-ulan-gol is said to increase so much in the summer that it cannot be forded. But now, during the silence of the night, I could hear its crystal clear water echoing melodiously among the stones, whilst far above our heads the beacons of the sky glittered with a vivid brilliance like electric lamps.

CHAPTER XCIV.

FROM KOKO-NOR TO TEN-KAR

AFTER losing our fourth horse, I bought a mule, and on November 12th continued our journey towards the east. Soon after starting, we crossed two frozen marshes, in which reeds, with their tops broken off, pierced through the gleaming sheets of ice, and the ice when struck by the horses' hoofs flew to pieces with a sharp snapping sound. The track turned towards the east-south-east, and at the same time diverged from the lake-shore. The lake, with the dazzling sunshine falling straight upon it, glittered in the south like a brightly-polished sword-blade. Small troops of antelopes were grazing on the steppes; and in a ravine near by we saw half-a-dozen wolves lying in wait for them. But the antelopes were on the alert. The leader of the troop kept glancing keenly about him; and as soon as they scented danger, off they went with a swiftness that was fairly astounding. They cleared the ground in long rapid leaps, and so lightly that they hardly seemed to touch the earth.

We gradually approached the Northern Mountains, in which merely a summit here and there was capped with snow. In the south-east however there was a prominent snow-covered mountain-knot, and between the two, the Northern Koko-nor Range and the mountain-knot, was an indentation, which I was told was the pass of Khara-köttel. The Southern Koko-nor Range was dimly visible obliquely across the lake. But when we looked along the lake from end to end, we could no longer see the mountains on the opposite shores.

After crossing the Harguin-gol, a stream of little account, we came to the more important Hallun-ussun, which was two feet deep. It was covered with soft brashy ice, and on that account was not easy to cross. Here again two or three of the men got wet through whilst trying to find a ford, and afterwards had to dry their clothes at the camp-fire. The tribe of Hargeh-väsu Mongols dwelt beside the lake, not far from that spot. In the beginning of the year they had offered resistance to the Dungans; in retaliation for which the latter seized and beheaded their chief, an old man of ninety.

November 13th. Another twenty miles knocked off the distance from Peking; but there still remained a good thousand miles to travel. The night was cold, the minimum temperature dropping to – 1°1 Fahr. (– 18°4 C.). It was anything but pleasant to get out of bed at sunrise, and wash and dress, with the thermometer at 5° Fahr. (– 15° C.). Our clothes were icy cold, and we did not get warm until we got our coffee down. We ascended the valley of the Ghansega, between mountains of moderate elevation. Everywhere there was an abundance of grass; and at intervals tents, flocks of sheep, and the sites of former encampments. We saw and chased two foxes, and one of them through the cleverness of the dogs was taken alive.

Khara-köttel (the Black Pass) was quite easy to cross over, even for our tired horses. On the other side we entered a broad valley, which sloped gradually to Bayin-hoshun, where we halted beside a brook. The road was now much more plainly indicated, having picked up several side-paths as it came along. The thousands upon thousands of horses and other caravan animals had trampled it into a rather deep furrow. We met a great Tangut chief, wearing a red cloak with a white border, and attended by a troop of mounted men. He told me there was a solitary "Russian" (*Oruss*) lady in Ten-kar (Donkhur), and two or three Russians in Si-ning-fu. I at once suspected they were English missionaries, for in the interior of Asia all Europeans without distinction are called Russians. Later on we met five mounted men, leading some unsaddled horses. Loppsen of course swore that they were horse-thieves. After that again we met a caravan of sixty yaks, laden with all kinds of sacks and bags, and attended by six men on horseback, two of whom were Chinese. They were merchants from Si-ning-fu, carrying corn and flour to sell to the Tanguts of Koko-nor.

November 14th. We followed the brook beside which we had encamped, and which was called the Tsunkuk-gol, for fifteen and a half miles. After being joined by several tributaries, it swelled into a stream of some magnitude, and flowing past Ten-kar and Si-ning-fu, entered the Hwang-ho (Yellow River) immediately above Lan-chow (Lan-chau). As this stream rose on the east side of the pass of Khara-köttel, we had now definitely left the internal drainage regions of Central Asia, and once more come into contact with rivers which issued into the great oceans. The waters of the Tsunkuk-gol were on their way to the Pacific. We were therefore no longer shut up in the heart of the continent; but after a period of three years we were once again in a Peripheral region. What an indescribable feeling of relief!

The valley contracted towards the south-east, where the stream had cleft a deep gorge through the mountains. The mountains on the north were ramifications of the Nan-shan Range. Just where the valley began to narrow, there stood, by the side of the road, an animal hewn out of the granite and resting on a pediment. The place, which rejoiced in the name of Bar-khoto (Tiger Town), was said to mark the site of a former Chinese town.

A short distance further on we met an enormous caravan of Dsun-sassak Mongols, who had been ten days in Ten-kar, laying in their winter supplies; they were now returning home by the same route we had come. It was evident that the late autumn was judged the most suitable season in which to make such a long journey; in summer the road is often stopped by the Bukhain-gol, the Yikeh-ulan-gol, and other rivers. We counted close upon three hundred riders, most of them men, many armed with guns and all with swords; but there were also numerous women in the train, wearing picturesque dresses of dark blue and red, as well as half-grown children. The caravan embraced at least a thousand horses and some three hundred camels; and they were laden with such commodities as flour, macaroni, clothes, utensils, boots, and so forth. The caravan animals marched in closely packed troops of ten abreast, so as not to be too widely spread out in case of an attack. On each flank, and evenly distributed along the whole line, rode the escort of at least 150 guns, eloquent testimony to the extreme insecurity of the roads in the country of the Tanguts. Each troop as it came along raised a light cloud of dust; the ground echoed with a dull rumbling noise, as it was beaten by the multitude of hoofs. The whole made a picture full of life and colour. As one after the other the Mongols caught sight of me, there arose reiterated cries of "*Oruss! Oruss!*" (Russian! Russian!).

Such an enormous caravan must however play havoc with the pastures all along the road; especially as they make excessively short marches and travel very slowly, their pace being regulated by the pace at which the camels travel. One other thing struck me, namely the ridiculously light burdens with which they loaded their animals. The horses carried only two small packages each, equalling in weight about one-third of the burden that would be borne by a moderately laden horse. And not only do the Mongols eat up the grass of the Tanguts whilst travelling through their country; they at the same time spare their own pastures at home.

The stream coursed down its valley through a series of abrupt windings, and as it advanced, the slopes grew steeper, a fact evidenced by the increasing number of rapids and cascades. In one place the current pressed close in against the granite cliffs of the right bank, boiling and hissing with a thunderous roar. There the road was carried across the stream on a sort of threshold or ridge of rock immediately above the foaming rapids. In summer the river is too powerful to permit of a crossing; hence travellers follow a path up above on the cliffs. We had again entered a region inhabited by Mongols; but they used the same kind of black tents as the Tanguts. That evening we pitched our tents in an expansion of the valley, at a place called Murgutsuk, not far from the temple of Shinneh-kitt.

November 15th. The wide but stony road ran along the left bank of the river. By this we had descended a long way below the level of the Koko-nor. We passed various features of interest. For instance, the little secondary pass of Hadda-ulan (the Red Hills), from the top of which we obtained a splendid view of the entire valley, including no less than seventeen obos, planted on every commanding eminence. Then came Tsagan-tokko, a village with clay houses, surrounded by walls of clay, and inhabited for the most part by Chinese. At the temple of Brattsing-kitt the river was spanned by a rickety wooden bridge, the first we had seen for many a day. The villages came more frequently, and were shaded by poplars and birches, larches and spruces, through the branches of which the wind murmured in strangely familiar tones. The traffic too was more lively. We met numbers of horsemen, Chinese, Mongols, Tanguts; and small caravans of donkeys, carrying country produce into the towns. We also saw occasionally two-wheeled carts drawn by mules. The slopes of the mountains were full of cattle and yaks grazing; and almost every projecting crag was crowned by a temple or lonely obo. Everything indicated that we were approaching a large town. Shortly after midday the houses began to stand closer together, and the road assumed something of the appearance of a street. On we rode between the buildings, nor was it long before we saw ahead of us the stone gateway of Ten-kar.

We rode on into the town, along the main street, which was lined with houses having picturesque façades. What a bustling, noisy throng! Unaccustomed as we were to such an animated spectacle, we were well-nigh deafened by the din. Earlier in the day I had sent Parpi Bai on in advance to take my pass to the governor of the town. That dignitary now met us at the gate, bringing a letter from the "Russian lady," with a hearty invitation to share her hospitality. I felt it was rather presumptuous to quarter myself altogether upon a solitary lady. Nevertheless, I decided—perhaps it was curiosity drove me—at any rate to go and pay her a visit. When I reached the house indicated, a good Chinese house with an oblong courtyard, I was met by a bareheaded young lady wearing spectacles and dressed after the Chinese manner. She asked me, in a very friendly tone, "Do you speak English?" I told her, "Yes, I thought so"; and very soon our tongues were going at express speed. She introduced herself as Mrs. Reinhard, an American doctor of medicine. Her husband was the Dutch missionary, Mr. Reinhard, who fully a month earlier had started for Peking with Captain Wellby, who was on his way home from his journey across Tibet.

Mrs. Reinhard was the personification of hospitality and amiability. It was quite a pleasure to talk to somebody whose interests ranged beyond grass and pastures, dangerous passes, wild yaks, cattle and sheep. Her husband's courage in venturing to leave her behind alone among the rabble of Ten-kar truly astonished me. But there was not so much danger perhaps after all; for through her medical knowledge and skill Mrs. Reinhard had won several friends among the native population.

I stayed two days in Ten-kar so as to give the horses a thorough good rest. I paid a visit to the governor of the town, looked over the town itself, and had the rare fortune to make the acquaintance of the ambassador, whom every third year the Dalai Lama sends from Lhasa to the Emperor of China, carrying presents, the only tribute the Tibetans pay to the lord of the Celestial Empire. The presents generally consist of different kinds of cloth, burkhans (images of Buddha), weapons, dried fruits, objects possessing a religious significance, sandalwood, and so forth, to the aggregate value of

5000 liang (about £780). The principal lama in the *cortége*, Garbuin Losang Ghindun, told me that the embassy embraced no fewer than three hundred mounted men, and that the presents for the Emperor were carried by the same number of camels. It takes them three months to travel from Lhasa to Ten-kar; there they make a stay of an entire year, and after that resume

CUP, PRAYER-DRUM, AND PRAYER-WHEELS

Which I bought from the Dalai Lama's Ambassador in Ten-kar

the journey to Peking, which they accomplish in two months. In Peking they stay three months, and rest again four months at Ten-kar on their way home. Garbuin took me to his house and showed me the Imperial presents; and even sold me some of the cloth, idols, silver vessels, and so forth, so that this time the Emperor would not get all that was intended for him. Whilst the bargaining was in progress we drank tea brought from Lhasa near a temporarily arranged temple, that was illuminated by flickering oil-lamps, and in front of which two men intoned prayers and beat gongs.

At Ten-kar I seized the opportunity to replenish our provision-chests, and during the next few days lived a good deal upon eggs. The governor did not take the trouble to repay my visit; whereupon I let his interpreter understand, that his master had thereby failed to observe the rules of both Chinese and European courtesy.

My hostess gave me several particulars of the revolt of the Dungans. She said the rebels invested the town of Ten-kar in the summer of 1895, and that the Chinese themselves provoked them to do so. When the insurrection broke out in the neighbourhood of Si-ning-fu, the Chinese in Ten-kar at once began active preparations for strife, by casting cannon, forging sword-blades, and preparing various other equipments of war. Perceiving this, the Huy-huy, as the Mohammedan Chinese or Dungans were called, concluded that these preparations were directed against themselves. They too revolted, and withdrew to To-ba, a strongly fortified place on the way to Si-ning-fu. There however, after an obstinate resistance extending over several months, during which they subsisted upon the half-starved animals they had in the town, they were in the end so hardly pressed by the Chinese that they were compelled to capitulate. The terms upon which they were willing to yield,—namely, that they should be free to go whither they chose—were tied to an arrow, and shot over the wall into the Chinese camp. The Chinese agreed to the conditions; but demanded that the inhabitants of the place should lay down their arms. Yet no sooner did the latter get clear of the town than they were surrounded by the Chinese, and most of them beheaded. The remnant escaped into the mountains. The number of Dungans who thus laid down their arms was stated to have been 18,000 men.

These occurrences inspired the Dungans who still remained in Ten-kar with a sense of their insecurity.

They sent a deputation to the governor, with assurances of their fidelity, and pledges that they would in no way countenance or assist their revolted co-religionists. Just at this time, when the feelings of both parties were highly strung, a Chinaman beat his wife, who was a Dungan. Thereupon in her exasperation the woman exclaimed, that on such and such a day the Dungans would come and kill all the Chinese in Ten-kar. The husband went and reported the matter to the authorities; and the consequence was, that every Dungan within the town, man, woman, and child, was massacred, till the streets ran with blood.

CHAPTER XCV.

THE TEMPLE OF TEN THOUSAND IMAGES

I SAID adieu to Mrs. Reinhard, and made a short journey to To-ba, the place mentioned in the end of the previous chapter. The road still continued to follow the course of the river Tsunkuk-gol. At first, after leaving Ten-kar, the valley was narrow, and the slopes so steep that the cliffs which overhung the stream echoed continuously with the splashing of the cataracts. In several places indeed the valley was so contracted that it would be quite easy to block it. It is not therefore difficult to understand how it was the Dungan forces were unable to approach within twenty li (six miles) of Ten-kar. Several small villages were perched picturesquely on the cliffs and elbows of rock which jutted out into the loops of the river's windings. Nearly every one of them was protected with walls and towers, their loopholes commanding the valley on both sides. Long strings of camels, with tinkling bells, moved sedately on towards Ten-kar, in which town the Chinese meet the Mongols and Tanguts, and carry on a lively traffic with them by barter.

Every village beside the road had been completely devastated during the recent war, and presented a melancholy appearance.

A man, of whom we inquired in To-ba, assured us there was not a single *deng* (rest-house or inn) left in the town. We therefore encamped in a field outside. The place was indeed simply a heap of ruins. Entire streets were choked with wreckage and *débris*. In a few places, however, but at wide intervals apart, the Chinese had run up a new house or bath. The high rectangular wall of the fortress was riddled with cannon-balls, and from the top fluttered Chinese flags bearing inscriptions, probably some grandiloquent pæan of triumph over the capture of the fort. The courage and warlike skill of the Dungans was not to be despised, seeing that, though armed with no better weapons than lances and swords, they had yet been able to defy the overwhelming forces of the Chinese for such a long period. They were no doubt greatly favoured by the natural strength of the position, which was half encircled by precipitous mountains and protected further by the river, for they took care to destroy the bridge in time.

The walls of the fortress enclosed a handsome Chinese temple, Li-beh-ya, consisting of several small detached edifices, each with the characteristic sagging roof, turned up at the eaves, and ornamented at each corner with a dragon's head and other adornments. The most imposing was however a pagoda-like tower of four stories. All the buildings were faced with green tiles of a tasteful pattern. Heaps of broken bricks and fragments of porcelain showed that the Dungans had done their best to destroy the temple. But even in its damaged condition it presented a remarkably fine appearance, as it rose proudly above the ruins of To-ba, its enamelled plaques glittering in the rays of the setting sun. Within the temple precincts were several Chinese, loading the bricks on the backs of donkeys, to carry them away to make new houses of.

The next day I divided my caravan; sending Parpi Bai in charge of the horses and baggage direct to Si-ning-fu, whilst, with Islam Bai, Loppsen, another Mongol, and four camels, I made a circuit to Lusar (Luksor). Parpi Bai therefore continued to follow the valley of the Tsunkuk-gol; whilst we turned to the south, along a broad valley that gradually sloped upwards. Immediately after entering it, we crossed its stream, which was divided into five arms, and carried a volume of about 880 cubic feet in the second. Then for a short

A LAMA

distance the road was simply a deep trench cut through the loess hills, until we came to a side-valley, whence issued a tributary of the main stream that brought down 210 cubic feet of water in the second. We passed several villages with cultivated fields, the principal being Yuän-sän and Ban-sa.

The fall of the stream rendered it well suited for milling. A canal was led off from the river to the edge of a ravine or hollow in the ground. Thence the water was conducted in a wooden conduit to a position from which it could fall six or seven feet directly upon the float-board of a horizontal wheel, the axle of which projected vertically upwards and supported the millstones. There were several mills of this description along the banks. We could hear the noise of the falling water and the groaning of the mills long before we reached them.

The valley curved round to the north-east. Hence, leaving the stream on our right, we ascended a road carved out of the softly contoured mountain-side, often at a great height above the valley. The town of Lusar clustered on the side of a hill, the buildings rising tier above tier like the rows of benches in an amphitheatre. At first we had the houses on our left hand only; but further on they became visible on our right, or rather their roofs did, for they were several feet below the level of the road. At length we reached a triangular market-place, on one side of which was the rest-house or inn. There I established myself in a small hut on the roof, to which my baggage was hoisted up by means of ropes. Underneath our feet lay the lanes and courtyards of the town, and on the hills to the south-east gleamed the white walls of the renowned temple complex of Kum-bum, or the temple of the Ten Thousand Images, so called from the number of idols it contains.

November 20th. In the morning I and Loppsen paid a visit to the temples. We went on foot; to have ridden along the sacred pathways would have been to expose ourselves to insult or even to stoning. The brook of Lusar flowed towards the east-north-east, that of Kum-bum towards the north, and joined the former at the town of Lusar. Both streams flowed in deep trenches amongst softly rounded, steep-sided hills, on which the vast complex of the temple buildings was ranged in gradually ascending terraces. The path led up the left side of the Kum-bum brook to a gateway, which was topped by a sovurga or sphere, surmounted by a pyramid tapering to a sharp point, and with a stone lion at each corner. Under the gateway sat a number of Chinese petty hucksters behind their small movable stalls, covered with rosaries, gauze kerchiefs, brass bowls, and other articles that play a part in their religious worship, as well as secular objects like pipes, knives, dried fruits, etc., all intended to tempt money out of the pockets of the pilgrims.

We climbed up several steep hills and stone steps to the house of the prior, the "Living Buddha." He was a man of about thirty years of age, with his hair cropped close, but without beard, and dressed in a costume of dark brown cloth, made without sleeves, so as to leave his arms bare. The walls of the room in which he received us were adorned with innumerable idols, standing in carved and painted cabinets, and with temple flags and pennons representing various Tibetan deities. The holy man sat on a divan or bench against one of the walls, telling his beads and gabbling through the eternal "On maneh padmeh hum." Loppsen took off his cap and flung himself prone on the ground at his feet. The holy being graciously extended his hands and blessed his worshipper. Then he had tea brought in for us, and inquired about my journey, and accorded me permission to look over the temple; but warned me that I should not be allowed to make any sketches.

Accordingly we left his holiness the Living Buddha, and went the round of the temple. The heart of the monastery — or rather monkish city — consisted of a labyrinth of sacred buildings, surrounding square or irregularly shaped courtyards. The principal edifice was the temple of Sirkang, with a steep sagging roof, pro-

TEMPLE BANNER, SHOWING LHASA, KUM-BUM, TSUNG KABA, ETC.

Bought in Kum-bum

jecting and up-curving corners, and walls cased with glittering plates of gold. Immediately in front of the entrance, and protected by a wooden fence, stood a now leafless tree, with five stems. This was said every spring to put forth leaves upon which the holy words "On maneh padmeh hum" grow of themselves. The leaves are sold to pilgrims. At the time of my visit there was unfortunately not one left. Father Huc states, that it is from these inscribed leaves that the temple derives its name.

The tree I saw can hardly have been the same tree that traveller described: it seemed to me not to be old enough, and was growing in a different place from the tree Father Huc saw. As regards the inscribed signs or letters Father Huc writes,—"We examined the leaves with very careful and exact attention, and were in the highest degree surprised and amazed to perceive that each separate leaf did bear the Tibetan letters of prayer, and extremely well-formed too. The letters are always green, sometimes darker, sometimes lighter, than the leaf itself. . . . It appeared to us as though the letters belonged to the leaf as essentially as its fibres. . . . We took all the pains we could to discover any deceit that might be practised, but without success. The occurrence was every way perfectly natural." Father Huc is a credible writer; in this case he seems to have been credulous. I myself did not see a specimen of this marvellous nature-writing. When I asked Loppsen if he could account for the lettering on the leaves, he replied, that the lamas themselves printed them. Loppsen was a shrewd fellow.

Along the façade of the temple ran a verandah, its roof supported by six wooden pillars, all sculptured and painted in a way calculated to catch the eye. Some of the planks of the flooring were hollowed into narrow grooves, deep and long. These owed their origin to the worshipping Tanguts and lamas. When they throw themselves prone upon the ground in the act of worship, they let both hands slide along the floor in front of them, till they lie at full length, their forehead touching the ground. After lying in that position for a moment or so, they sit up on their knees, bring their folded arms to their forehead and breast, mumble their prayers, and again prostrate themselves with their arms stretched out in front of them. This performance they repeated time after time, until I grew tired of watching them.

The front wall of the temple was pierced by three doors, handsome specimens of solid hammered brass. The doors stood open, but the doorways were in part closed by curtains. We entered, and found ourselves in

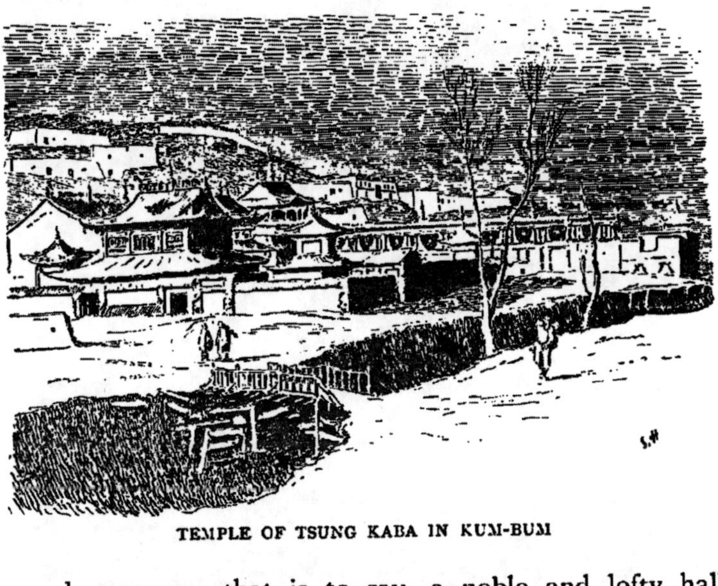

TEMPLE OF TSUNG KABA IN KUM-BUM

a real museum; that is to say, a noble and lofty hall, reaching up to the gilded roof, in which the light was tempered to a deep and mystic twilight, so that I was involuntarily put in mind of the Uspensky cathedral in Moscow, which contains similar gilded images, lighted candles, and a similar dim religious twilight.

In the centre of the hall was a colossal figure of the sublime Tsung Kaba, about thirty feet high, seated, and draped entirely with mantles, except his head and hands. Silently, solemnly, contemptuously the image of the god appeared to gaze down upon the pilgrims who in the sweat

TIBETAN TEMPLE BANNER

of their brows polished the boards with their hard horny hands. Around him were a number of images of less holy deities, each enshrined in his *gavo*, a sort of open cabinet or sentry-box, with ornamental panelling. Five lamps were burning immediately in front of Tsung Kaba, and in front of them again, but on the ground, stood half-a-dozen decorated *jolas*, each a yard high, *i.e.* vessels of brass, in shape resembling drinking-cups, which contained divers eatables, such as rice, flour, tsamba (mutton fat mixed with barley meal), water, tea, etc., all offerings to the god. Each jola was covered with a wooden lid, with a hole in it, so that you could see what it contained. On each of these receptacles there was a lamp burning; all which added to the mystic effect.

The image of Tsung Kaba was surrounded by rows of pillars making a square; and affixed to the capitals of the front row was a rectangular shield, slightly tilted towards the doors, and inscribed with four Chinese letter-signs in gold on a dark background. The effect was remarkably artistic. They told me the inscription signified, that that temple was the home of Edsin Khan, Emperor of China. Rows of shelves or framework, containing innumerable volumes of the Buddhist scriptures, were ranged on each side of the god and along the walls of the temple, that is to say, a vast number of narrow strips of parchment enclosed between two loose boards. The place was in fact a veritable museum; and I was astonished to find so many interesting curiosities collected out there in the wilderness, and found myself eagerly desiring to purloin the entire collection and carry it off home with me.

This temple of Sirkang was encircled by a multitude of similar temples, though without golden roofs. Their walls sheltered a host of more or less gigantic idols, with gilded faces and hands, dressed in handsome and costly robes, and with lamps burning in front of them.

One temple, Tsuggchin-dugun, which stood in the middle of a series of courtyards, was surrounded on every side by colonnades, under which were a number of cylindrical *korlehs* or prayer-wheels, fixed between two rows of horizontal beams, and hung on pegs in such a way that they could be whirled round by means of a handle. The outside of the wheels was beautifully decorated with gilt Tibetan lettering on a blue or green background. Certain of the lamas were appointed to the special duty of perambulating the temple to keep the prayer-wheels spinning. As we approached the spot our ears were saluted with a continuous hum. Thin strips of paper, with the holy words, "On maneh padmeh hum," printed upon them in minute and closely packed lettering, were wrapped round the axles of the wheels, so that at each revolution hundreds of thousands of prayers flew upwards to the knees of the god. Truly a labour-saving business that!

The courtyards swarmed with lamas, all bareheaded, all with their hair cropped close, all beardless—sombre and lean, dressed in a sort of red cloth plaid or toga, folded over the shoulders and twisted round the waist, with the ends hanging down to the feet. With few exceptions, the right arm was always bare. Apart from age, the only difference I could detect amongst this army of temple satellites was that some were dirtier than others. Some of them had their faces as black as sweeps or negroes. Either they belonged to a confraternity of black monks, or else it was their duty to trim the smoky wicks of the lamps. If so, they seldom or never wasted time in ablutions. It disgusted me to see those lazy fellows sauntering about among the magnificent temples doing literally nothing. They were however quite friendly and peaceably disposed; though not willing to give me any explanations. I had perforce to content myself with what Loppsen could tell me. Fortunately he had on several occasions attended the great temple-festivals at Kumbum, and knew every nook and corner of the place, and its every secret.

At the time of the great festivals, when the temples are visited by multitudes of pilgrims, tea and tsamba are prepared for them in a huge kitchen called Mantsa-häsun, in which there is a big brick fireplace with three gigantic pots hanging above it.

A TEMPLE BUILDING AND A GROUP OF LAMAS IN KUM-BUM

A TEMPLE BANNER

After seeing that Buddhist "kitchen," we went out into a courtyard, with cloisters all round it, and its walls painted with a whole series of pictures of the gods. Their wrinkled brows, broad noses, widely expanded nostrils, distorted mouths, screwed up moustaches, and black eye-brows put me in mind of evil spirits rather than gods. But these features were intended to depict the awful and destructive power of the gods.

The Buddhist architecture leaves a peculiar "mythical" impression upon the mind. It conforms to the rules of Tibetan taste; but in the end it becomes wearisome to a European, who is accustomed to the sound and genuine forms of the West. In such interiors you cannot possibly experience that sense of calm serenity and well-being which you feel in a Christian temple. Your eye wanders from one upturned gable, from one florid capital, to another. Whichever way you turn, your glance encounters the same confusion of sculptural forms, the same harsh agglomerations of colour—blue, and green, and violet, all flourishing in peace and amity together. Less than that would be enough to strike you with colour-blindness. Even the legitimate effects of the sometimes imposing interiors of the temples filled me with repulsion, a feeling I never experienced in any Mohammedan mosque I ever was in.

What perhaps contributed to awaken this feeling in me in such an intense degree were the swarms of idle lamas, who did nothing all day long but grovel on their hands and knees, muttering their stupid parrot-like repetitions before those gilded blocks of wood or clay, which they or their fathers fabricated with their own hands. They sat about the cloisters, and yawned, and told their beads. Whenever I stopped to make a sketch or a drawing, they started like rats out of their holes and lurking-places, and swarmed thickly round me, infesting the very air with the ill-savour of their presence. The majority of them were boys between ten and fifteen, who had been sent to the monastery to be trained and brought up as full-fledged lamas. In one place a band of lads were singing with clear, tuneful voices the inevitable prayer, and right pleasant indeed it sounded. All the same, it was a real relief to step outside into the fresh air, and turn my back upon the idle mummeries of idolatry. And yet there was much in all this that is common to Roman Catholicism, with its monks, its images of the saints, soft mystic lighting of its places of worship, its gilded and tinsel-decorated churches, its array of artificial lights, its choirs of singing boys.

A great many houses and walls, all whitewashed, clustered on the hills around and above this complex of temples: seen from Lusar, they looked like long lines of sheets hung out to dry. The town of Kum-bum was bigger than either Ten-kar or Lusar, especially in the seasons when throngs of pilgrims from Tibet, Tsaidam, Koko-nor, and Mongolia flock thither for the great religious festivals.

I stayed in Lusar over the 21st and 22nd November, paying two or three more visits to Kum-bum to sketch various views. After dark some of the lamas, who heard that I was buying temple flags and burkhans, came and offered to sell me some, and those that were not too dear were packed away in my boxes. I also bought several bowls for offerings made of brass, some silver gavos, and a *damaruh* or prayer-drum, made out of the crowns of a couple of human skulls.

THE MAIN STREET AND MARKET-PLACE IN LUSAR

CHAPTER XCVI

SI-NING-FU AND THE DUNGAN REVOLT

ON November 23rd we packed up our baggage, a task which took a long time to do, so that it was midday before we got started for Si-ning-fu. We travelled nearly all day between soft, dusty hills of a reddish tinge, along a road worn down to a depth of twelve to twenty feet by the continuous traffic, so that all the time we were in a sort of tunnel, unable to see a vestige of the country we were journeying through. And for the most part the track was so narrow that it was impossible for two carts to pass. If two vehicles did happen to meet, one of them had to "back" until it came to a wider place. Every brook that crossed the road naturally turned down it, so that the camels repeatedly slipped and slid on the sloppy ground. As soon as the sun set, the water froze, and the road became still more slippery. Hour after hour we rode on, passing caravans, passing villages, crossing brooks. Twilight came on; it grew dark.—as dark as pitch. In fact, it was anything but pleasant to ride along a strange road without being able to see your hand before you. At last our guide stopped in front of a wall, pierced by a gigantic gate. It was Si-ning-fu.

We thundered at the gate with our riding-whips and shouted to a watchman, who was perambulating the wall, rattling a drum. The gates of the city were closed early for fear of the Dungans. I gave the watchman to understand, that if he hastened to the Dao Tai's yamen (palace), and requested permission to admit a European travellér, I would reward him well. He sent a messenger, whilst we waited in the darkness outside the gate. At the end of an hour and a half the messenger came back, to say that the gate should be opened for us—in the morning! There was no help for it. We were obliged to seek out the nearest village, and there after considerable difficulty we succeeded in obtaining shelter.

I was hardly dressed next morning when I was surprised in our wretched deng (guest-house) by the visit of two Englishmen, the Rev. Mr. Ridley and the Rev. Mr. Hunter. Both were members of the China Inland Mission, and wore the Chinese attire, even to the pigtail, so that it was merely their features that betrayed they belonged to the white race. Mr. Ridley came to invite me to his house; and until November 30th he and his wife entertained me with the most generous hospitality, surrounding me with every species of European comfort. I felt quite awkward at having to sleep in an ordinary bed with mattresses and sheets; and I felt it not less awkward to sit on an ordinary chair, and like ordinary folk eat with knife and fork, for I had been accustomed to recline in my furs in my tent, and eat out of the rice dish as it stood on the floor.

Mr. and Mrs. Ridley, and the two assistant missionaries, Mr. Hunter and Mr. Hall, had fitted up a Chinese house, with a large square courtyard, in a snug and comfortable fashion; and they had won the warmest sympathies of the population of the town through the unsparing and devoted assistance they rendered during the Dungan revolt, when they organized and managed a hospital for the benefit of the wounded Chinese soldiers. This disinterested zeal and labour had no doubt paved the way to success in their evangelizing efforts. On the Sunday morning I heard Christian hymns sung in unison by a congregation of Chinese to the accompaniment of a harmonium.

I owe the greatest debt of gratitude to Mr. and Mrs. Ridley, not only for their kindness and generous hospitality, but also for the many great and valuable services they rendered me.

Si-ning-fu was a notable stopping-point on the long red line which marks my journey through Asia. It was there I proposed to dismiss my faithful attendants from East Turkestan, and send them back all the long way to their own homes. There too I intended to re-organize my caravan, so as to adapt it to Chinese conditions of travel. My first object therefore was to call upon the Dao Tai and obtain a proper pass for my men; and this was not difficult, for almost all of them were Chinese subjects. The Dao Tai gave me a pass of gigantic dimensions,

ONE OF THE GATES OF SI-NING-FU

well calculated to inspire the profoundest respect in the minds of all Chinese officials. The men travelled back along the great highroad through the heart of Asia, *viâ* Gan-chow (Gan-chau), Su-chow (Su-chau), Khami, and Korla. Before they started I called them all into my room, and we calculated how much was owing to each man; then to their unspeakable amazement, I doubled the amount that fell to each man's share. And it was by no means too much; for without them I should have accomplished but little. Further than that, I made them a present of the Mongolian horses that survived, with the exception of two, which I and Islam Bai wanted, and sufficient provisions and money to last them the whole journey home. I also allowed three of the men whom Captain Wellby had engaged at Ladak and lost on the way, and whom we picked up at Ten-kar, to go with my men, giving them a horse and provisions. Parpi Bai, who had made the journey before, was chosen leader of the caravan, and I gave him a good revolver, together with a supply of cartridges for it. All the men were satisfied and grateful, and we parted mutually pleased with one another. Then they went their ways; and I hope and trust succeeded in reaching their homes as happily as I reached mine.

After this big hole had been made in my purse, Mr. Ridley calculated and weighed the silver pieces (Chinese coin) I had left. There were 770 liang or taels (about £120), amply sufficient to take me to Peking. There was however still a long stretch of road to travel before I should reach my goal. The post-couriers do the distance in twenty-eight days. It took me fully three months.

Want of space forbids me entering upon any detailed description of Si-ning-fu. Suffice it to say, that the city is enclosed within a square wall, which, according to Asiatic ideas, is well-nigh impregnable. It has been well and carefully built, is thick and massive, and actually affords room for a street along the top, on which the soldiers keep watch. The view from the wall was magnificent and commanding. Looking over the city, you see a rich mosaic of characteristic Chinese roofs, covered with red pantiles, and decorated with dragon arabesques. All the streets crossed each other at right angles, running exactly parallel with the town walls. The main street traversed the heart of the city, and upon it abutted the most important yamens or official dwellings and offices, with their strangely painted signs, their stone lions and dragons, their doors decorated with rich sculpture. A few edifices of a similar imposing character might be found in some of the other streets, having generally been erected in accordance with some wealthy man's will, to perpetuate his name to posterity.

I cannot however leave Si-ning-fu without saying something about the Dungan revolt, of which Mr. Ridley gave me the following account.

The revolt, which, like the first uprising of the Dungans (1861–77), threatened to involve a vast portion of the territory of Chinese Asia in the horrors of civil war, broke out in the district of Salar in December 1894. In that district there existed a dogmatic schism between the two sects of Chinese Mohammedans, the Lao-jao and the Shin-jao, *i.e.* the adherents of the Old Religion and the adherents of the New Religion. The Dao Tai of Si-ning-fu was so imprudent as to meddle in these purely domestic religious differences. He took prisoners five of the leaders of the former, the Lao-jao sect, and had them nailed like dead vermin to the wall of his city. In retaliation the people of Salar fell upon a Chinese force and massacred every man. In reply to that the mandarins affixed proclamations to the gates of the city, saying that the inhabitants of Salar should be exterminated root and branch. The Dungans saw now the doom that impended over them, and resolved to strike the first blow. The revolt spread therefore like wildfire from one region to another. But it was not until July 1895 that the rebels approached Si-ning-fu. The country-folk flocked into the city for safety, bringing their property with them, so that the population increased suddenly from 20,000 to 50,000. Meanwhile the Chinese met their revolted subjects outside the walls, in the valleys which converge upon Si-ning-fu. The wounded soldiers were brought into the town. The temples were converted into temporary hospitals, and Mr. and Mrs. Ridley worked day and night at tending the wounded and binding up their hurts.

For five months the city was closely besieged by the Dungans, and every night four thousand men kept watch on the walls. Every tenth man carried a lantern, so as to be able to see if his comrades were awake, as well as to see if the Dungans approached the walls with their scaling-ladders. On September 1st the large Mohammedan village of Tung-kwan, a suburb of Si-ning-fu, situated outside its eastern gate, revolted, and every Chinaman in the place was slain. Meanwhile famine began to make itself felt inside the city, and various epidemics raged amongst the overcrowded population. Then the fuel ran short. In order to procure fresh supplies of wood, the Chinese began to foray the neighbourhood, always going out in large companies and exercising the utmost caution. But the Dungans were too cunning for them. They placed themselves in ambush and slew all who ventured to leave the shelter of the walls.

The rabble of the town dragged through the streets certain of the mandarins who were suspected of looking with a too favourable eye upon the rebels, and after torturing them in every conceivable way beheaded them. It was only with the greatest difficulty that the governor of the city, the cowardly Dao Tai, managed to save his life. At the end of the revolt he was summoned to appear before the Emperor, to receive the fine silk cord which carries with it the ominous command, "Go home and hang yourself." He did not obey the summons, but put an end to himself in Lan-chow.

Meanwhile it was expected every day that the town would be taken by the Dungans. The Chinese distributed amongst their wives large doses of opium, to be taken the instant the town was invaded, so that they might not fall alive into the hands of the Dungans. But the walls were strong, and the Jen Tai or general in command was a stout-hearted man, and Si-ning managed to hold out until January 1896; when General Ho approached with a reinforcement of 2000 men, who had been fighting the Japanese. General Ho was a very worthy man. He was still in Si-ning-fu at the date of my visit, and I had the honour to make his acquaintance.

It is scarcely possible to conceive the horrors that were perpetrated on both sides. Prisoners were tortured in the most inhuman fashion, and little children were tossed on

AN ORNAMENTAL GATE IN THE INTERIOR OF SI-NING-FU

the points of spears. When General Ho's soldiers returned from a sortie, bringing in Mohammedan prisoners in chains, the populace fairly howled with delight, and swarmed round them in fiendish triumph as they were dragged through the streets to the Jen Tai's yamen to learn their doom. Thereupon they were led away outside the city gate, and their throats cut with blunt knives. After that their chests were opened, their heart and liver torn out, stuck on the points of spears, carried in ghastly procession to the nearest café, roasted, and devoured. This the Chinese did in the belief, that by eating the hearts of their enemies, their courage would pass into themselves.

It is estimated that during the revolt 50,000 Chinese perished, and the same number of Dungans. The latter made brave and capable soldiers, but were wretchedly armed. One instance will illustrate this. When Tung-kwan was stormed, there was one sentry-post on a tower that was fully exposed to the Chinese marksmen, who shot the sentries down one after the other. But as fast as each sentry fell, his place was taken by a comrade. This happened six times in succession; and when the suburb at length capitulated, the Chinese found a sentry still in the tower nailed fast to his post with an arrow.

The Chinese on the other hand were arrant cowards. A large force was besieging a Mohammedan town not far from Si-ning-fu, and for three days on end bombarded the walls, without daring to deliver an assault. When they saw no men on the walls, they feared that treachery was at work. General Ho marched upon the place at the head of several hundred men, and after he had blown up the gates, there came to meet him one blind old woman, the last surviving inhabitant of the town. She told him, all the rest of the people had retired into the mountains several days before, and she wondered what on earth the Chinese were doing outside the walls, making such a din with their cannon.

The position of the English missionaries during those five terrible months was anything but an enviable one. Like the Chinese, they expected every day that some of the besiegers would gain entrance into the city, fling open the gates, and so let in their co-religionists like a horde of ravening wolves, to ruin and destroy everything, and massacre every living being. Amid the unbridled licence of such a time the missionaries would of course have been slain along with the rest of the inhabitants, for they always wore Chinese costumes. The entire five months were a period of painful tension throughout. Again and again when they heard the Chinese running, shouting and screaming, through the streets, they thought that the dreaded moment was come at last. Mr. Ridley would then hasten to the walls, where the sentries were marching up and down with their lanterns and whips, to waken up those who slumbered on their posts. In the daytime they often saw large bands of the Dungans scouring the country around, and the slopes of the circumjacent mountains swarmed with them to such an extent as to seem dotted all over with black spots.

Every Chinese temple outside the wall was reduced to ashes. I visited the ruins of one of these, which had been built only a few years before at the expense of the merchants of the neighbouring province of Shen-si. What a scene of desolation! Heaps of ashes and rubbish, with the mutilated remains of the temple-idols sticking up through them, humiliating memorials of human superstition!

And what awful sights met one in the streets during the period of the siege! Hunger, filth, putrefying corpses, all the concomitants of over-population, gave rise to horrid diseases, every species of privation and suffering. Little children were flung out into the street before they were really dead, to be worried by dogs and devoured by swine. The missionaries however suffered no want, because the Jen Tai kept them supplied with provisions in return for the great services they rendered his soldiers by amputating their limbs, extracting bullets, and nursing the sick and wounded. I myself saw certain ghastly evidences of the revolt. On the gates of the town there were a number of small wooden cages, each with a label affixed, containing the bleached skulls of the leaders of the revolt who had fallen into the hands of the Chinese and been beheaded. Another skull bore an inscription, setting forth that it had belonged to the murderer of Dutreuil de Rhins: although it was impossible to tell which individual it was of the band that attacked him who slew the brave and able Frenchman.

CHAPTER XCVII.

FROM SI-NING-FU TO LIANG-CHOW-FU

ON December 1st, accompanied by my faithful attendant Islam Bai, I left Si-ning-fu and the hospitable English missionaries. As I was unable to engage a Chinese interpreter, Mr. Hall very kindly sacrificed his time and accompanied me as far as Ping-fan. Mrs. Ridley packed me up a boxful of dainties—cakes, tarts, honey, and jam. My new caravan consisted of six mules and three men, whom I engaged for the sum of fourteen taels or liang (nearly 45*s.*) to convey my baggage to Ping-fan. The packages and cases were tied once for all to a bent wooden frame, which was lifted bodily on and off the pack-saddle; so that I only kept out or easily accessible such things as I was likely to want every evening. But the mules were tricky and refractory, and one of them kicked his load off and smashed the packing-frame to pieces. The men were even worse than the mules. They clamoured and swore the whole way, so that I was glad I had not engaged them for longer than six days.

The caravan filed along the streets towards the eastern gate, through a crowd of gaping, curious Chinese, and so on through the ruins of Tung-kwan. A few new houses and shops had been built along the main street; there too we saw some miserable Mohammedans, old men whose eyes had been put out by the Chinese, sitting by the wayside begging. The only inhabitants of the ill-fated suburb were mere ruffians and soldiers. The latter had wedded the women of the Dungans, and they, it was said, accepted the change of husbands with tolerable resignation.

When we reached the open country, the traffic gradually decreased. The valley was wide and open, and bordered by gently rounded hills with a gradual slope, except for a short distance, where it contracted to a narrow defile, into which the sun never shone, and where the sides of the Si-ning, a stream of considerable size, were fringed with ice. In this narrow pass, called Shio-sha, the Dungans kept the road blocked for a long time between Si-ning-fu and Lan-chow, the capital of the province (Kan-su).

That evening it was very dark and cold. We only met one caravan, composed of an immense number of camels. In this part of Asia the camel-caravans only travel by night, for the animals graze during the day. Before reaching the large village of Ping-rung-i we crossed over two brooks, Sa-ku-fueh and Kwen-yin-tang. We had hard work to find a room in the guest-house; every corner being packed with travellers. Before spreading my sleeping-carpets in these places, I always had the bench well swept, to rid it of undesirable intimates of the last person who slept there.

December 2nd. The valley again contracted, forming the narrow gorge of Da-sha (the Great Defile), where the stream (on our left) foamed down a series of cataracts between walls of granite and black clay-slate. But on the other side of the defile the valley once more expanded, and became thickly dotted with villages and cultivated fields. After crossing the river by a ferry-boat, guided by a rope stretched from side to side, we came to the town of Nien-beh. Although it was dark, the town gates were not yet closed.

Our next day's journey took us through a region that was both thickly inhabited and excellently cultivated. The road crossed a number of frozen canals, in which the mill-wheels stood motionless in their icy fetters. Apples, pears, apricots, peaches, plums, and walnuts were grown in the orchards. The fields were being ploughed for the sowing of the next crop of seed.

The road was very deeply excavated in the loess strata,

and both their horizontal and vertical structures could be plainly made out. The roots of former species of vegetation reached down to the level of the roadway. There too the river also cut its way through a similar formation, crumbling it down a great deal at every bend. At Kao-miotsa, one of the largest villages along the road, we stopped for breakfast at an open café. We met numerous caravans of camels conveying packs of wool to Ning-sha or Tien-tsin. We halted for the night at Lo-ya.

On December 4th we still continued to push on towards the north-north-east, leaving on our right the transverse glen through which the Si-ning river made its way to the Hwang-ho, and also a rugged by-path leading to Lan-chow-fu. We ascended to a minor pass through a little glen, at the entrance of which three human skulls were suspended in cages on as many poles. They were the heads of robbers who had attacked, plundered, and slain certain travellers, but who had been afterwards seized and beheaded. Then we climbed the heights of Ping-ko-shan by a winding zigzag path, with excessively sharp turns in it. How I pitied the poor mules that should toil up those steeps with heavy loads on their backs!

Having spent the night in the solitary guest-house of Ping-ko-ko, on the east side of the relatively low ridge we had just crossed, we descended the next day into the wide open valley of the Tai-tung-ho. The river came down from the north-west and traversed the valley in three arms. We crossed the largest of the three with the help of a ferry; it was about 100 feet wide and 5 feet deep. On its left bank were numerous villages; but most of them had been ruined during the Dungan revolt. There was a great deal of traffic on the road. For instance, we met two or three huge companies of Khalkha Mongols on their way to the approaching festivals at Kum-bum; long strings of carts laden with coal, which was dug in the neighbourhood, carts and caravans carrying provisions to Si-ning-fu, to say nothing of individual travellers on horseback and on foot.

On December 6th we journeyed from the village of Shwang-nyu-po to Ping-fan by an easy bridle-path, over yet another pass. It was however a killing road for vehicles, being both steep and narrow, and so deeply excavated, that it was impossible for two carts to pass in the contracted passages. Hence some of the drivers were accustomed to hurry on ahead, uttering loud long-drawn shouts, and in that way kept the road clear till they reached a convenient place to pass. The Ping-fan-ho, which was divided into nine arms, also flowed through a wide, open valley. In summer this river brings down vast quantities of water, as was easy to see from the marks on its banks.

I will hurry over my journey from Ping-fan to Liang-chow-fu; the road is sufficiently well known, having been described by other travellers. On December 9th I said "Good-bye" to Mr. Hall, and made him a present of one of my horses as an acknowledgment of the trouble he had taken on my behalf. Once more I re-organized my caravan. I dismissed the mules and their noisy owners, and in their place engaged two carts of the same shape and appearance as the arbas of East Turkestan. Into one I stowed all my baggage; whilst the other was fitted with a covered roof, straw in the bottom, and carpets. Each vehicle was drawn by a mule between the shafts and two horses harnessed in front of the mule, and the composite teams were driven by two pleasant Chinese, whom I made to understand thoroughly that, if they got me over the ground quickly and without misadventure, I should not forget to give them a handsome tip. It was important to be on good terms with these two men, as I now had no interpreter, but was entirely dependent upon my own not very extensive acquaintance with the Chinese language.

For six days we drove up hill and down dale, over the eastern off-shoots of the Nan-shan Mountains, over rugged passes, over brooks, some frozen, some still running freely, across precarious bridges, and through dark and narrow defiles. The carts rattled and shook, rocked and lurched—it was veritable torture. The drivers went on foot; and in every village we came to, they either had something to say to an acquaintance or they wanted to buy a piece of bread, which they subsequently ate on the way. We started very early in the morning, generally soon after midnight, and took a rest during the middle of the day, when we baited the animals; after that we did another short spell of travelling in the afternoon. It was bitterly raw and cold driving in the middle of the night; in spite of furs and felts I was always frozen through when we stopped. Islam rode on horseback, until he nearly got his feet frost-bitten; after that he preferred to walk. The drivers of the carts kept themselves beautifully warm running beside their animals; and my faithful Yolldash fared first-rate. Two or three times it snowed, and the wind blew icy-cold out of the north-west. In this way we journeyed for six days along the great highroad that skirts the Great Wall north-north-westwards to Liang-chow-fu, passing on the way the villages of Wo-shing-yi, Tha-ku-yi, Lung-go-po, Go-lan-chow, and Cho-dung-po. These were the places we stopped at for the night; between them there were strings of other villages.

We travelled in company with two Chinese, who were taking two cart-loads of miscellaneous wares to Liang-chow-fu. It is a great advantage to travel as large a company as possible on these highways of Northern China; for it is an established rule of the road, that when two parties meet in a deep narrow passage such as I have already described, the smaller party has to give way to the more numerous; also if anything goes wrong with any of the vehicles or animals, all the drivers of the party are expected to lend a hand in righting them. We experienced the advantage of these arrangements at daybreak on the morning of December 10th, when we reached the Shi-ming-ho, which flowed through a wide fertile valley and entered the Ping-fan-ho, making an acute angle with it. The river serpentined backwards and forwards in a broad stony channel, and, with the exception of a few narrow strips of water where the current ran swiftest, was sheeted with ice. But at the

PING-FAN

place where the road crossed it, the river was frozen from side to side, and the ice covered with a sprinkling of sand, so that both horses and caravans were enabled to cross over without the least difficulty.

The two Chinese went first with one of their carts, drawn by three horses. Down they went at full gallop on to the ice; but the wheels had barely made one revolution when they cut into the ice as easily as a razor shears through paper, and the cart stuck fast. The load had to be taken entirely off and carried across to the other side; then after a great deal of labour we succeeded by united effort in hauling out the cart.

The men examined the ice higher up. It was everywhere too thin to bear our heavy vehicles. Then they sought out a wider place, and broke up the ice with their axes, and so made a ford. But the water was a good three feet deep, and full of brashy ice and big floating lumps. My baggage-cart was the next to try its luck. Down it plunged into the water, and stopped—stuck fast. Two other horses were harnessed in front. From the edge of the ice all the four drivers shouted and whooped, and cracked their whips. The poor horses, who were standing up to the girths in ice-cold water, reared, stumbled, and fell, and were very nearly drowned. Then they leapt to one side, and tried to scramble on to the ice; but the men forced them back into the water. One of our two Chinese associates, a young man, who apparently did not know what nerves meant, stripped stark naked, notwithstanding there were fourteen degrees of frost Fahr. (ten Centigrade), and jumped down into the water, and pushed away the ice and stones against which the wheel was jammed, and then unravelled the reins and traces, which the horses had got into a thick tangle. It made me shiver to see him working in the freezing water; for I could actually hardly keep warm in my furs. Meanwhile Islam Bai made a fire among the bushes on the far side of the river, at which the hardy young Chinaman went and warmed himself, whilst the other men, after desperate efforts, succeeded in getting the cart across. The same procedure had to be gone through with each of the succeeding carts; so that it took us four good hours to get them all safely to the other side of the river.

The road we were travelling on was the great highway to East Turkestan, Urumchi, and Kashgar *viâ* Liang-chow. It was bordered the whole way by telegraph-posts with their humming wires, and so imparted a touch of civilization to the desert. I could not help thinking, that the labour would have been better spent, if, instead of building that gigantic wall (which indeed now lies for the greater part in ruins), the Chinese emperors had made a good road and built bridges across the rivers.

On December 12th, we emerged from the mountains into the level plains, which stretched away in every direction to the horizon; and two days later we drove through the fine entrance gateway of Liang-chow-fu. Here again it was my good fortune to be hospitably entertained by English missionaries, the Rev. Mr. and Mrs. Belcher of the China Inland Mission, and to make the acquaintance of their assistants, Miss Mellar and Miss Pickels. These two young ladies lived together in a house situated at some distance from the mission-station, and had none but Chinese servants. But neither was in the least degree apprehensive for her safety.

In Liang-chow-fu I was detained against my will for no less a period than twelve days, which severely tried my patience. The cause of this long wait was the almost absolute impossibility of hiring camels for the journey to Ning-sha. Camels there were indeed in plenty; but none of their owners was willing to hire fewer than forty at once. They refused to divide their caravans; and as Ning-sha lies aside from the great highway, they were afraid they would not be able to obtain transport back again, and consequently demanded double prices.

The days were long and tedious. Still I enjoyed the full sympathy of the missionaries; but their church, in which I was lodged, was bitterly cold. At the time I arrived, Mr. Belcher was absent in Lan-chow; but he

ONE OF THE GATES OF LIANG-CHOW-FU

THE INTERIOR OF A TEMPLE OUTSIDE LIANG-CHOW-FU

came home on the second or third day afterwards. The first day therefore I sat down to dinner with three charming young Englishwomen, dressed in pretty and tasteful Chinese costumes.

The next morning I made my way to the telegraph-office, where one of the clerks spoke English, and telegraphed home to His Majesty King Oscar *viâ* Si-ngan, Han-kow, and Shang-hai, being kindly assisted in the operation by Mr. Boch, Swedish-Norwegian Consul-General in Shang-hai. Seven days later, just right for a Christmas-box, I received a congratulatory reply from His Majesty. The Chinese look upon the telegraph with great scepticism, and have their own explanation of the way messages are carried. They believe that the paper containing the message is rolled into a tiny ball and sent at a stupendous pace along the wires, and that the insulators on the posts are stopping-places under which the pieces of paper find shelter when it rains.

Liang-chow is the second city of the province, ranking next after Lan-chow, the capital, and with its adjacent villages numbers upwards of 100,000 inhabitants. The city is built on the usual rectangular plan, and is surrounded by thick strong walls, pierced by four lofty gates. The main streets are wide, and full of life and colour—carts, caravans, and merchants at every step and turn.

Whilst waiting for a caravan, I spent my time sketching, talking to the English missionaries, who were able to give me much valuable information, visiting some of the mandarins, and making various purchases in the Tien-tsin bazaar, a sort of arcade lined with handsome shops. Amongst other things I bought two *sha-los* or hand-stoves, shaped like teapots, but with grated lids. You fill them with ashes, and put two or three pieces of red-hot charcoal in the middle of the ashes. The sha-lo will then keep warm for a good twenty-four hours. Had it not been for this appliance, I should have got my hands frozen more than once whilst on the way to Peking.

I also paid a visit to a magnificent temple outside the city walls, and took some sketches. Then I went to the mission-station of the Belgian Catholic Brothers at the village of Sung-shu-chwang, situated twenty-five li (seven miles) east of Liang-chow-fu. The bishop had gone to Peking, but was expected home for Christmas. I was however received with great friendliness by three of the Brothers, who offered me red sparkling wine,

THE GOD OF WAR AT LIANG-CHOW-FU

cigars, and cakes. Their church, a noble building, partly constructed in the Chinese style of architecture, and with a high tower surmounted by a cross, was visible from a great distance all round the village. The large window behind the altar was filled with stained glass, and there was an image of the Virgin on the altar, with candles burning in front of it. It was a strange sight, to see a full score of Chinese rustics kneeling on the floor of the

TEMPLE OUTSIDE ONE OF THE GATES OF LIANG-CHOW-FU

nave and offering up their prayers to the God of the Christians. My Belgian cicerones told me that there were families in the place who had been Christians from father to son through seven generations, and that the community then reckoned about 300 members. The people I saw entered the church of their own free will, as they were going past, making the sign of the cross and taking off their caps, and they appeared to repeat their prayers with absolute sincerity of conviction. The Belgian Brothers also carry on schools for boys and girls. I peeped into one of the rooms, and saw a score of boys sitting at their desks, poring over the Bible and the writings of the sage Confucius. The library, which was a large and handsome apartment, was adorned with the portraits of a host of missionaries, amongst whom I recognized the portrait of my Kashgar friend, Father Hendricks. The Belgian Brothers also possess a mission-station in the city of Liang-chow-fu, which they visit to celebrate mass on the high days and festivals of their church.

I was however pained to learn that the Roman Catholic and the Evangelical missionaries do not work amicably together, in fact they ignore one another's existence. Yet it is only natural they should do so, for they preach different doctrines, and what the one body sows, the other does its best to pluck up by the roots. The Chinese may be pardoned if they get confused between the two. Fortunately there is plenty of room for both to work in Liang-chow-fu. Personally I have no complaint to make against either. The Roman Catholic Brothers were quite as hospitable and quite as kind as the Evangelical missionaries.

I spent my fourth Christmas in Asia in Liang-chow-fu, and found comfort in the hope of being able to spend the next Christmas by my own fireside, among the skerry isles of dear old Sweden. Christmas was always a trying time for me, for then, far more than on any other day in the year, I always longed intensely for home. This year too Christmas Eve passed as quietly and uneventfully as its three predecessors had done. I wanted to have a young fir-tree fetched down from the mountains; but the missionaries thought it was a heathenish practice. We sat and talked round the stove, and I retired early to my nest of furs in the cold church. Christmas Day was celebrated with an excellent dinner at Mr. Belcher's, with plum pudding and Christmas presents.

CHAPTER XCVIII.

THROUGH THE DESERT OF ALA-SHAN

AT length, on December 26th, I succeeded in procuring eight camels with three men, and once more had my baggage loaded up for another long stage, the 290 miles to Ning-sha. As ill-luck would have it, it was Saturday, and it was quite evening before the caravan was ready to start. Had the next day not been Sunday, I should have waited until the morning. As it was, I decided to go on to one of the nearest villages outside the walls of the city, and stay the night there. But when we reached the gate, it was already closed, and they would not open it for us. We spent a couple of hours hunting about the dark narrow lanes, and at length succeeded in finding a wretched room in an inn, for I did not of course wish to disturb the Sabbath quiet of the missionaries.

However we got started in earnest early the next morning, but had not advanced further than the open space immediately outside the northern gate of the city when two ragged Chinese came to meet us, and at once began an animated conversation with our camel-drivers. Then one of the men turned to Islam Bai, and in fluent Turki offered to guide us to Ning-sha for fifty taels (about £7 16*s.*). He said he had lived several years in Kashgar and Ak-su, and had nine camels, every way better animals than those we were starting with. An excellent interpreter in addition to baggage-animals—the opportunity was too good to be let slip. We therefore waited in the middle of the road, while the two new-comers fetched their camels, and within an hour the loads were all transferred to the backs of their animals. This stroke of good luck made me forget the twelve days I had lost in Liang-chow-fu. I was not sorry to bid lasting farewell to that sunny disobliging city, and to see its walls and towers vanish from sight in the distance.

Our route to Ning-sha described a long curve through the desert of Ala-shan, first towards the north-east, afterwards towards the south-east, past the following places, wells, and camping-stations, bearing partly Chinese, partly Mongolian names.

Jung-ja-da-ming	17	miles.
Shang-ya-wa	17½	"
Ching-fan	23¼	"
Niu-ba-shing-na-tsa	10¾	"
Bo-to-gai-tsa	12	"
Lei-tsa-kho	19¾	"
Ma-lo-ching	19¾	"
Ka-to-khoa	10¼	"
Lo-cha-ching	5¾	"
Wu-geh-sän	13	"
Koko-möruk	12½	"
Koko-burtu	11¾	"
Ärten-tollga	11½	"
Hashato	18¼	"
Wang-yeh-fu	18	"
Jo-jeh-teh-shang	6	"
Jo-wa	12¾	"
Da-ching	23	"
Ning-sha (the Manchu town)	20½	"
Ning-sha (the Chinese town)	5	"

Each of these names indicates a stopping-place at the end of a day's journey, and the figures which follow it the length of the march. We only passed through two towns—Ching-fan, on the western margin of the desert, 200 li, or 58 miles, from Liang-chow-fu, and Wang-yeh-fu, on the eastern margin of the desert.

Our first day's march took us for the most part due north, past an unending succession of villages, temples, and gardens; while the Nan-shan Mountains on the south, with the scanty patches of snow on their summits, gradually

PAGODA OUTSIDE LIANG-CHOW-FU

faded away as we advanced and left them behind us. The weather was splendid. It was however the lull before the storm, for on December 28th there blew such a tempest from the west that it was impossible to put your face out of your *fanza* (house), which for the matter of that was destitute of both doors and window-panes. The sand and dust drove in whirling clouds across the steppes and along the road, and half filled my wretched cabin.

On the 29th we continued towards the north-north-east. The camels went first-rate, sure of foot and without refractoriness. It was quite a pleasure to be once more riding on the back of one of these hardy and splendid animals. But the ground just suited them, being a hard level, grassy steppe. As we advanced, the population gradually thinned away, the villages grew fewer and fewer; but we still continued to meet caravans of donkeys and ox-carts, carrying country produce into the city. We were rapidly approaching the verge of the desert; already there were low sand-dunes on our right. South of the village of Kho-tung-shing-go we travelled for some hours beside a marsh, crossing a narrow extension of the same on the ice. Half-way across one of the camels broke through and fell into the water. Its load was however prevented from getting wet; but it cost us a good hour to get the poor beast back safe on to firm ground. The sun set among banks of mist, and it turned bitterly cold (minimum, – 1°8 Fahr. or – 18°8 C.) At length we caught sight of the walls of Ching-fan; but the gates were closed, and we were obliged to put up with a rest-house outside.

We stayed one day in the little town, that the camel-owners might provide themselves and their animals with supplies of food sufficient to last them to the other side of the desert. The governor of the place tried to persuade me to take the longer route by the south, where I should find people, towns, and inns. On the desert road I should encounter nothing but sand, besides the risk I ran of being attacked by Mongol robbers. I sent word back to him, that the only annoyance I had had to put up with throughout the whole of my more than three years of travel in Asia had been occasioned by Chinese officials, and I preferred my tent in the desert to being cooped up within the walls of a Chinese guest-house with its undesirable parasites.

Accordingly on 1st January 1897, when I was ready to leave Ching-fan, Mr. Mandarin thought I should not escape him without some evidence of his authority. Two Chinese soldiers came to me, and said they were commanded to escort me through the desert, but they could not get their horses and provisions ready under two or three days. I answered, that I had not asked for an escort, and did not intend to wait a minute for them; and at once ordered my men to load up and get off as soon as they could.

We reached the outside of the gate, but were then stopped by a troop of men from the yamen (official residence of the governor), saying that I must wait until the next day, my Mongol pass was not ready; and if I refused to wait, they were instructed to detain me by force. Bidding the caravan wait outside the gate, I went straight to the yamen; for I was exasperated by this petty official insolence. The governor refused to see me; he was "ill." I was confronted in a filthy room by a dozen clerks, all smoking opium, and all shouting and trying to keep me back at one and the same time. As soon as I could make myself heard, I referred to the passport I had from Peking, and said that if the mandarin prevented me from travelling further, I should report his behaviour to Li Hung Shang through the Russian ambassador, and he would lose both his rank and his position. This impressed the recalcitrant official. His interpreter came back with an invitation to breakfast. I replied with the utmost contempt, that I should do no such thing, and demanded that his master should instantly send me the Mongol pass, and also the two soldiers as an escort. After this the clerks condescended to be polite. They laid aside their opium-pipes; and in a trice both pass and escort were ready. Then we continued our journey, glad that we should have nothing more to do with Chinese mandarins until we reached Ning-sha.

The sandy desert approached quite close to Ching-fan. In fact in some places the people had built short walls to check the advance of the sand-dunes, to protect the roads, their fields, and houses. According to the maps, the protecting bulwark of the famous Great Wall of China ought to have barricaded the Celestial Empire just at this place; but although I tried my utmost to perceive it, I failed, unless the ruins of certain mud walls which we saw in a few places were relics of it.

Before actually entering the desert, we passed a few solitary farms, and met numerous carts laden with dung, which had been gathered off the roads; for the country was very bare of trees, and the people had no other fuel. They dry the stuff in the sun, and in that way get the material for the *kangs* or benches on which they sleep.

On January 3rd we traversed a district that was unusually well cultivated. I was astonished to find that the river of Liang-chow-fu extended so far towards the north-east; it was however at that place called Niu-ning-ho. From it were drawn several canals, which watered a long string of villages, and when it gave out the people had two or three wells to fall back upon.

On January 4th we travelled for the most part across a barren waste, the road bending round towards the east. On our left we had the stream I have just mentioned, but it had now dwindled to a mere ribbon, not of water, but of ice, for it had frozen and the water had flowed away from underneath the crust of ice. Here Yolldash cleverly caught a young antelope as it was endeavouring to escape across the ice. The ice broke under it, and before it could recover its feet, Yolldash seized it and gave it its quietus. Here again we met carts and caravans laden with fuel, not of the same character as before, but various species of steppe plants. On the left too we saw in the distance a low spur of hills, but I was unable to find the lake which is shown on the maps. I was told however, that at its period of summer high water the river forms a temporary lake near the point where it comes to an end. Our camping-station for that day, Ma-lo-ching, consisted of three small huts, which were surrounded by a ring of fuel-carts. The well was 6 feet deep, the water salt, and its temperature 37°4 Fahr. (3° C.).

Next day the country was alternately high sand-dunes, with their steep faces towards the east, steppes, level expanses of salt, and marshes. At dusk we came across two or three Chinese squatting round a fire. They told us it was fifty li (fourteen miles) to the next well and high sand all the way. We therefore halted where we were at Ka-to-khoa, where the well was four and a half feet deep, and its water sweet and good, with a temperature of 33°1 Fahr. (0°6 C.).

On January 6th we got well into the heart of the barren sands, where the dunes were thirty to thirty-five feet high, and the only sign of vegetation an occasional thistle or withered prickly bush. The landscape was such as awakened both joyful and painful recollections of the past two years. When Yolldash ran to the top of a dune and looking towards the east saw nothing but sand, he barked pitifully; no doubt he recollected our toilsome marches beside the shores of Lop-nor. The Desert of Ala-shan was not however so dangerous as the Takla-makan. It did not form one continuous unbroken expanse, like the Desert of Gobi, but consisted of several separate belts of sand, with steppes and marshes between them. All the same, the road was frequently difficult and heavy; the camel is the only animal that could have traversed it. Yet despite its drawbacks we had evidence every day that it was a good deal used. For instance, we met a Chinese caravan of fifty camels conveying divers commodities from Bao-to (on the north of Ordos) to sell to the Mongols of Ala-shan; it had been travelling for forty days. Our two Chinese camel-drivers were both of them first-rate fellows; they looked after their camels and my baggage with zeal and energy, and kept travelling steadily on without a single murmur or complaint.

The country presented the same characteristics during the three following days. The lee side of the dunes still continued to look towards the east, proving that the prevailing winds came from the west. Indeed, every day the wind blew from that quarter, or else from the north-west, with more or less violence. We now began to come across Mongol camps and to see solitary nomads guarding their flocks of sheep. The well of Wu-geh-sän was quite close to the "Five Hills," which had for some days been visible in the distance.

On January 8th the caravan-track wound in and out between the sand-dunes. Sometimes it was not altogether easy to keep it, for the wind had blotted out every trace of the road. But a worse evil was, that the daylight began to fade, and we had not yet succeeded in discovering the well. The twilight deepened rapidly. But at length we reached a small steppe, whereupon our Chinese camel-drivers said they believed we were not very far from the well. They looked for it in every direction, whilst I and Islam stayed with the camels, and made a fire, to serve as a guide to the two searchers. In the east we heard the bells of a caravan quite distinctly; the sound came nearer and nearer, then died away in the west. It was evident we had somehow got off the track. So we waited nearly three hours before the Chinese came back; they had not found the well. During their absence I witnessed the most brilliant display of shooting stars I have ever seen anywhere. A train of meteors of an intensely light green colour shot through the belt of Orion, and for some seconds lit up the steppe so brightly that the fire actually paled before it. Then it seemed to be darker than ever. But after a while the moon rose over the silent waste, and enabled us to see where we were going to. After travelling due east for about a couple of hours, we caught sight of a fire, and thoroughly wearied out, we crept to the well of Koko-möruk, which the Chinese call Cheh-sheh-geh-nian.

Beside the well we found some Mongols, wearing pigtails and speaking Chinese. Strange to say, they had never heard the name of Ala-shan, nor did I succeed in finding out the meaning of the word. They called the sandy desert Ulan-älesu, or the Red Sand, which put me in mind of the Kizil-kum of the Kirghiz, for the words mean the same thing.

The next day we reached, across an absolutely barren desert, the most northerly point of the route, namely Koko-burtu. During that day's march we met only one solitary Mongol, dressed in neat blue furs, a dagger at his side in a silver-mounted sheath, riding a magnificent long-haired male camel, which went along at a grand pace. During the night we again heard the tinkle of camels' bells, and a large caravan came and encamped round the well. The bales and pack-saddles were piled up in heaps, the camels were turned loose to graze, tents were pitched, fires made, and the Chinese shouted and squabbled—on the whole quite a picturesque scene in the midst of the desert and the darkness of the night.

The camel-caravans travelling between Ning-sha and Liang-chow-fu prefer this long route through the desert to the far shorter road on the south, principally to escape the toll-houses, the rest-house (inn) expenses, and other disbursements which are associated with a journey through inhabited regions. Along the more northerly route they are exempt from all these expenses, for they carry provisions with them for the whole of the journey, chiefly large bread-cakes, while the camels provide their own sustenance, browsing upon the hard dry desert plants. As a rule the caravans start about three o'clock in the afternoon, so as to allow the camels to feed as long as it is light; then they travel all night. The men prepare their suppers when they reach the wells; it consisted of tea and *mien*, a kind of soup made of dried meat and vegetables, with bread crumbled into it. During the stage to Ärten-tollga across a gently undulating steppe, we caught the first glimpses of the Ala-shan Mountains in the east. Each well on the route was provided with a wooden trough for the animals to drink out of, and each caravan carried a bucket, made of woven withes, to fill the trough with.

Then we had a broad hard road, winding like a yellow ribbon across the steppe, all the way to Wang-yeh-fu, which we reached *viâ* the well of Hashato on January 12th.

CHAPTER XCIX.

WANG-YEH-FU AND NING-SHA

WE gave the camels a day's rest. I had also other business to do in the little town. First I sent back the two men who had escorted me from Ching-fan: for two others were to accompany me from Wang-yeh-fu to Ning-sha. Then I replenished my stock of provisions, and bought some specimens of Mongol jewellery. Lastly I paid a visit to the Mongol prince Norvo, who was at the time chief of the town, and dwelt in an ordinary Chinese yamen (official residence) inside the walls. He was a *wang* or vassal prince under the Emperor of China. He received me in a very friendly manner in a large plain room with bare walls, in the midst of a group of Mongol notables, dressed in the Chinese manner and wearing pigtails. Norvo was an old man, with a white moustache, and wore a light grey blouse. We had an animated talk together, for I managed to get along pretty well without an interpreter. He was particularly anxious to know what country I came from; and to satisfy him I drew on a large sheet of paper a map showing how Sweden lay with regard to China, whilst one of his secretaries wrote down on the map all the names that were essential to give the true position of my mother-land. But the geographical knowledge of these Mongols was not very extensive. They were only acquainted with the names of two places at a distance, Lhasa and Khotan; and none of those who were present had been to either place, though most of them had paid visits to Kum-bum and Urga. Norvo wondered if the King of Sweden was as powerful as the Tsagan Khan (White Tsar). He remembered Przhevalsky quite well, and called him Nikola (Nikolai Mikhailovitch). He said Nikola had visited him many years ago.

Wang-yeh-fu boasts of a plethora of names. The Chinese also call it Fu-ma-fu and Ding-yuan-ying. The Mongol names for it are Noyin, Ala-shä, Ala-sha-wang, and Yamen-dolo; the last two indicating that it is the residence of the prince. The town lay about a dozen miles from the foot of the Ala-shan Mountains, which stretched from north to south, though they were scarcely visible owing to the clouds and the dust. There was a by-path over them to Ning-sha, but we thought it better for the camels to make the circuit round their southern extremity. The little town was said to have between 2000 and 3000 inhabitants, one-half Chinese, the other half Mongols; but it is not without importance, being the principal emporium of the Ala-shan Mongols, the place where they barter their raw produce for household appurtenances, clothes, jewellery, flour, etc., brought thither by the Chinese.

In the neighbourhood of Wang-yeh-fu the country was rather broken. A stream winding through the hills supplied the town with water, and in the season of flood was said to terminate in a lake. Nobody knew anything about a permanent lake in that part of the desert. The nomads were encamped beside the streams which crossed the steppes in the vicinity of the town. Most of the Mongols I saw in Wang-yeh-fu wore a half-Chinese, half-Mongol costume, that is to say, over their furs they wore coloured Chinese waistcoats, with gilt-plated buttons. The town possessed a handsome Chinese temple built in the usual style. Its pagoda and tower rivalled in height the larches that were planted round about it. The fact of their embowering their temples amid larches says a good deal for the artistic sense of the Chinese, for the broad sweeping branches harmonize well with the hollow upcurving roofs and consequently make an agreeable background.

On January 14th we did a short stage, past several

villages and cultivated fields, to the lonely guest-house of Jo-jeh-teh-shang, which the Mongols call Yikeh-bashingto. During the night I was awakened by the house creaking fearfully, whilst showers of sand and rubbish rained down all over me, and the dust whirled in giddy eddies round the hut. It was blowing a violent gale from the south. Nevertheless the two Mongols whom Norvo sent me from his yamen, to act as my escort, voted for making a start. They rode mules, and were both pleasant fellows, in spite of their decidedly cut-throat appearance, for one of them had a nose like a potato, whilst the other had no nose at all. We travelled south with the storm dead in our faces. At two o'clock the weather underwent an extraordinary change. The wind suddenly moved round to the north, and we were enveloped in a thick blinding snowstorm. I was very glad to have my sha-lo to warm my hands in, perched as I was high up on the back of a camel. When we reached Jo-wa (the Mongol Törgön) camels, riders, and packages—all were smothered with snow.

Beyond that point the road curved gradually to the south-east, keeping alongside the brook of Toli. Then we entered a wide gap in the Ala-shan Mountains, and ascended by long easy gradients to the insignificant pass of Tömur-öden, and descended on the other side down an equally gentle slope to the guest-house of Da-ching. Thence the country fell away at the same easy slope all the way to the Hwang-ho (Yellow River), whilst the road inclined towards the north-east, so that we now had the Ala-shan Mountains on our left hand. After spending the night in the Manchu town of Ning-sha, which was just like any ordinary Chinese town, except that the women were somewhat differently dressed, and had their feet undistorted, we went on, on January 18th, to the Chinese town of Ning-sha, where I steered my course straight for the house of the Swedish missionaries.

It was a real pleasure to meet my own countrymen—Mr. and Mrs. Pilqvist, and three assistants, two of them young men, the other a young lady, as well as to rest two whole days in their hospitable house. What a luxury to sleep in a well warmed room, and actually in a bed! No need that night to cover myself with a heap of furs, to prevent myself from being frozen to death. It was not hard to think I was resting on a piece of Swedish soil in a far distant land.

Missionary enterprise is carried on in Ning-sha with energy and success. There was a community of thirty Christian Chinese, and Bible readings were held both morning and afternoon. The Evangelical Scriptures written in Chinese characters were scattered broadcast, in the shape of fly-leaves, through the streets, and these had tempted many Chinese to the mission-house, in most cases no doubt simply to gratify their curiosity. Mr. Pilqvist rented a hall in one of the principal thoroughfares, and there held services, which passers-by used to stop and listen to. It was grand to watch Mr. Pilqvist preaching of an evening in his own house in the purest Chinese. The congregation were ranged on narrow benches in front of the table at which the missionary sat; and preach he did, with such energy that the very walls shook at the thunder of his voice and the banging of his fist on the table. The Chinese sat like statues, hardly daring to breathe—no fear of *them* dropping off to sleep and not hearing what was said!

Mrs. Pilqvist told me she very seldom met a Chinese woman of twenty who was unmarried. They frequently marry at twelve or fifteen; and even when they are tiny children they beg their parents to cramp their feet, and look forward with eagerness to the time when it can be done. They know perfectly well that no youth will look at them unless they have tiny feet. The operation takes place as a rule when they are five or six years old. An incision is made in the foot between the big toe and its nearest neighbour. Then by sheer strength of hand the four smaller toes are forced back underneath the foot, and there they are kept by strong bandages. The shoes are always made separately for each foot; it is for this reason you never see ready-made shoes in the bootmakers' shops

GATE AT NING-SHA

in China. When a Chinese woman walks, she balances the weight of her body on her big toe, which is driven right into the point of the shoe, and upon the upper sides of her toes turned in underneath her foot, whilst her heel is a long way off the ground. It is impossible to form the faintest conception of the torture which such a monstrous fashion occasions. In some cases for years after the completion of the operation the poor girl is unable to leave her bed, whilst during the night the unhappy victims moan and weep with pain, which becomes ten times worse every time they move. More than that, the nails very often grow right into the flesh; no wonder then the gait of a Chinese lady is the exact reverse of graceful. She waddles like a duck, or rather like a barefooted person walking over pins or stinging-nettles. In consequence of the excessively small amount of exercise they take, the limbs of the Chinese women grow as thin as rods. And all this torture, all this indescribable suffering, simply to get married!

There is another custom which is far more widely spread amongst the Chinese than is commonly believed, that is the exposure of newly-born infants by their parents, when they consider their means will not allow them to rear them. The tiny creatures are usually left in some corner outside the town-wall, where they are devoured by dogs or swine, though it is true they are sometimes drowned. This cruel practice is all the more astonishing, seeing that the Chinese generally treat their children with the most touching tenderness as soon as they are able to walk and talk. Previous to that stage they are looked upon as animals that possess no soul; and if they die, they are not buried in a coffin, but simply put in the ground rolled up in grass.

The missionaries at another Swedish mission-station, which I subsequently visited, were once able to save a newly-born infant immediately after it had been deposited in the moat outside the wall. There lay the tiny creature, crying bitterly. The missionaries picked it up, nursed it, and took care of it, and in the course of two or three years it grew into a very dear little thing. Then came the parents, and begged and prayed the missionaries to give them their little one again; their prayer was of course granted.

In another case an old female servant in a Swedish missionary's family exposed nine of her children one after the other as soon as they were born, and did not keep a single one alive. Possibly this inhuman and barbarous custom is a result of the peculiar social circumstances.

In addition to sowing the seed of the Christian faith, the missionaries tramp many a mile on errands of pure benevolence. An infant life or two saved, and a few young women persuaded to loosen the bandages which so horribly distort their feet, so that they may grow back into their natural position—what are they amid all the vast multitudes of the yellow race? We may reply: "To say the least, the example is ennobling."

How many a time too did I not hear of missionaries using the stomach-pump, and so saving the lives of would-be suicides who had taken an over-dose of opium! More than once, whilst resting in the mission-stations, I have been awakened in the middle of the night by a loud knocking at the gate. In such and such a house a man lay dying. He had just taken a dose of opium. Off went the missionary in hot haste with the stomach-pump, and so saved the man's life. Sometimes the victims were grateful for having been snatched from the jaws of death; but in general gratitude is a virtue which the Chinese do not manifest to any exuberant extent. Suicide by opium is commonest amongst women who are unhappy in their marriage. Sometimes if a man beats his wife or speaks an unkind word to her, it is sufficient to send her to the opium, almost out of sheer spite as it were. The habit of opium-smoking is fearfully common, and quite as much practised by women as by men. The number of children who have died from having crept up on their parents' opium sofa and sucked at their pipes is little short of appalling.

Previous to the first Dungan revolt Ning-sha was a

large town of some 60,000 inhabitants; but the revolt was a serious blow to it, a blow from which it has not even yet recovered, for its present population is only between 12,000 and 15,000. It is only the middle of the town that is occupied; the outer quarters next the city walls are deserted—no inhabitants, no shops, no traffic. The revolt broke out in Ning-sha in consequence of the imprudence of a mandarin. At the time when a large Mohammedan force lay encamped outside the town, a mandarin told his Dungan servant, that on the following day the Chinese intended to slay all the Dungans within the town. When night came, the servant stole out to the camp, and told the Dungan chiefs what he had heard, and then stole back again into the town the same way he had gone out. Then he and his co-religionists inside burst open the gate, and let in the host of the rebels from the camp outside. The invaders found entry through "the little northern gate," which is now walled up to prevent any Dungan from storming Ning-sha that way in future.

The same gate perpetuated another ghastly memory. When the Dungans got inside the town, they raged like wild beasts, slaying every creature they met. Out of the total population not more than two thousand Chinese were left alive; and most of these only saved their lives because they went over to the side of the rebels. The numerous ruins still existing in Ning-sha witness to the destruction that was wrought on that fatal day.

At the present time the feeling between the Chinese and Dungans is, at any rate outwardly, a feeling of repressed hatred. In Ning-sha the Chinese are entirely in the power of the Dungans; for the latter, owing to their capacity and enterprise, have not only possessed themselves of the most profitable occupations, they have got also all the cultivable soil into their hands. It reads like the irony of fate, that the Dungans, who are Mohammedans, should keep vast herds of swine, and grow opium on a more than usually extensive scale, and thus produce two of the standard commodities without which the Chinese can scarcely exist, namely bacon and opium, while they themselves never touch either the one or the other. But then their coffers are full of silver pieces, and they suck the Chinese as dry as oranges.

The district of Ning-sha also yields in great abundance rice, wheat, millet, beans, pease, vegetables, apricots, apples, pears, grapes, melons, and peaches. The gardens are watered by long irrigation-canals, drawn from the left bank of the river. Ning-sha is also an important centre in the lively traffic in wool that is carried on between the interior and the coast. In summer, however, the wool is transported down the Hwang-ho in boats.

CHAPTER C.

TO PEKING AND HOME

THE remaining portion of my long journeyings, namely from Ning-sha to the coast, lay through a country that is tolerably well known. Hence I will merely touch upon one or two incidents, and hasten on to the close. Before reaching China proper I still had another desert to cross. Throughout the whole of my travels in Asia the passage across Ordos was one of the hardest pieces of work I did. I was weary of my loneliness, and of the hardships and fatigues of travel. The 740 miles which still remained to be traversed were done in forced marches: I was going back to civilization, I was going back to rest!

There are several routes from Ning-sha to Bao-to. In summer the most convenient way is to go down the Hwang-ho by boat. During the colder seasons the traveller has the choice between the "longer road," which follows the left bank of the river, and one of the several tracks which cross Ordos, or the region between the northern loop of the Hwang-ho and the Great Wall, a region inhabited by Mongols. The shortest of the routes across Ordos effects a saving of five days, but exposes the traveller to all the inconveniences of a difficult desert journey. The subjoined list of stations and distances indicates the direction and rate of my journey from Ning-sha.

To Li-ngan-fu	14½	miles
„ Ping-lo	18	„
„ Hwang-chu-cho	9¼	„
„ Shi-tsueh-tsa	17½	„
„ Camp No. 1 in Ordos	8	„

To San-yueh-fing	. . . .	13½ miles
„ Camp No. III.	. . . .	16¼ „
„ Bao-yeh-ching	. . . .	16 „
„ Camp No. V.	. . . .	21 „
„ Khara-morch	. . . .	8½ „
„ Borot-chitteh	. . . .	13 „
„ Camp No. VIII.	. . . .	15 „
„ Da-ya-kheh	. . . .	20 „
„ Shwan-shin-gun	. . . .	17¼ „
„ Wä-tä-shian	. . . .	13¾ „
„ Ho-jeh-to	. . . .	21 „
„ Ha-ching-yo-tsa	. . . .	16 „
„ Bao-to	. . . .	7¾ „

Or in all 267 miles in eighteen days.

I started on January 21st, and was accompanied a portion of my first day's journey by the missionaries. The first four days we passed through a string of villages, all standing beside irrigation-canals led from the Yellow River. I still had the nine camels which conveyed me and my belongings all the way from Liang-chow-fu. We crossed the Hwang-ho at Shi-tsuch-tsa, on ice so strong that it never once cracked under the weight of the heavy camels. The river was 374 yards wide, and when we were in the middle of it appeared to be of vast size; but it flowed through an extremely desolate and barren region. For some distance the right bank was bordered by a low chain of hills, the summit of which afforded an unbounded view towards the east.

Our very first stop in Ordos was made in a howling wilderness, where there was no well and not a drop of water to be had; only fortunately we had taken the advice of our Dungan guide, and brought two or three sacks of river ice with us. At nearly every other halting-station however there was a well of excellent water; the wells being bricked round and very deep. For instance, on January 28th we rested at the well of Bao-yeh-ching, 134 feet deep, which contained water with a temperature of 42°3 Fahr. (5°7 C.), though it was no doubt cooled a trifle during the long process of being hauled to the surface. Certain Mongols, who were also staying the night in the same place, affirmed that the well was four thousand years old.

The road was first-rate all the way—hard and smooth and straight, the surface being almost as dead level as the ocean. It bore every indication of being much used, although we met very few caravans; but then, most of the Chinese were at that season at their own homes for the New Year's festivals. Besides, the route we had chosen was by no means the only road across Ordos. One route, somewhat longer than that by which we travelled, was principally used by carts; the others chiefly by camel-caravans.

The northern parts of the country were excessively thinly populated by Mongol nomads. We did not pass more than two or three encampments in districts where there was a little herbage. Northern Ordos is to a great extent desert, and a barren desolation characterized the major portion of the country we travelled through.

It was not however the absence of inhabited and cultivated regions—for of such we were pretty well independent, having brought ample supplies of rice, bread, and mutton with us—it was not this that made the journey across Ordos so extremely trying; it was the abominable weather we experienced. Almost every day without exception a storm raged out of the north-west, and this, combined with the great cold, froze us to the marrow. I do not mean mere gales in the ordinary acceptation of the term; I mean veritable hurricanes, which swept across the wide unprotected plains of Ordos with almost irresistible violence. I frequently felt as though every moment I should be lifted clean out of my saddle, or as though the camel would be blown bodily over. Furs and wrappings afforded very little protection; the wind pierced through everything. Many a time when we came across a few dry steppe plants, we stopped for a few minutes to set a light to them, and in that way thawed our numbed and frozen limbs.

On January 31st it blew the hardest from the west of any hurricane we had yet experienced. Travelling was absolutely out of the question. We happened to be encamped beside the well of Khara-moreh (the Black Horse), in the middle of the open steppe, with not so much as a foot of cover to protect us from the fury of the tempest. My tent blew over; and I feared it would be rent to tatters. The men made a kind of circular rampart of packing-cases covered with felt carpets, and there they sat crouched together all day long. It was impossible to keep warm. Everything was icy cold. If you spilled a few drops of tea down your furs, they instantly froze and became like stearine. My ink was a solid lump; so that I was obliged to enter my notes with a pencil. A violent wind like that we had on February 1st, in conjunction with thirty-one degrees Fahr. of frost (– 17° C.), may easily be dangerous. You have to be careful you do not get frost-bitten. Had it not been for the Chinese hand-stove I have mentioned, I do not know in what condition my hands would have been. In the daytime I carried the stove on my knee on the camel's back; and at night, when I lay down to sleep, I took it in bed beside me. Nor is it any pleasure to wash yourself when the very water freezes on your skin unless you are remarkably quick over it.

The severest cold occurred in the beginning of February. During the night between February 1st and 2nd the minimum was – 22° Fahr. (– 30° C.), and on the following night –27°4 Fahr. (–33° C.); at the same time the minimum inside the tent was – 16°2 Fahr. (– 26°8 C.).

On February 6th we reached Ho-jeh-to, the first village on the northern edge of the desert; and on the following day we crossed the Hwang-ho, at a spot where the river measured 420 yards from side to side. On February 8th we arrived at Bao-to, where I met with a friendly welcome from the Swedish missionaries, Mr. and Mrs. Hellcberg. They had gathered round them a little community of ten baptized Chinese and kept a school for boys, and were devoted heart and soul to their work. I never met pleasanter people anywhere. Along with sixty other Swedish missionaries, they belonged to the

American Society of the Christian Alliance, which maintains a chain of mission-stations all the way from Peking to Bao-to.

But now my patience was utterly at an end; and I fear my readers' too. Leaving my caravan and Islam Bai in trusty hands, I started on February 12th alone, with one Chinese driver, in a little two-wheeled cart drawn by mules, and travelled east through the towns of Sa-la-chi, Dör-chi, and Beh-sia-chi, until I came to Kwei-hwa-chung or Koko-khoto. In each of these places I had the great pleasure of meeting my own countrymen; indeed, in the last-named I found no less than eighteen Swedes, one Norwegian, and one Dane, all members of the American Christian Alliance. Kwei-hwa-chung is the centre of the society, where new aspirants to mission labour learn Chinese before being sent to their several stations.

From Kwei-hwa-chung I drove in eight days through Mei-dar, Cha-kha-bu-lo, No-bo-sha, To-do-go, Wo-ja-wa, and Jo-jeh-chong to Jan-ja-khu or Kalgan, where the Great Wall winds up and down the crests of the hills that shut in the town on both sides. In Kalgan too there were Swedish and American missionaries; but I had no time to stay, I was now within four days of Peking.

At Kalgan I hired a *to-jo* (palanquin or sedan-chair) and two mules to carry it. Then, accompanied by my servant, I travelled through Shwen-hwa-fu, Do-mo, and Nan-kho, halting for the night at each of these places. After that we descended from the Mongolian plateau to the plains which stretch right away to the walls of Peking, threading the border mountains through the valley of Nan-kho. Once down in the lowlands (March 2nd), we passed innumerable villages and temples, crossed over innumerable canals, and met crowds of travellers along every part of the road. I was not insensitive to the peculiar solemnity of that day, the last of my long journeying through Asia. The time dragged with painful slowness; the mules had never moved so sluggishly. "We shall soon be there!" cried my Chinese servant again and again. But fresh villages, fresh temples, fresh gardens kept continually coming into view, and we were constantly losing our way in the long crooked lanes. For more than a thousand days I had been travelling through Asia; but that last day seemed to me longer than all the preceding days put together. At last—at last I caught a glimpse of something between two groups of trees looking out grey in the distance. "Peking!" cried my servant. He was right. It was the great city wall of Peking—the goal and object of my long journey across Asia!

The feelings with which I rode in through the southern gate of the city were such as my pen refuses to describe. For over an hour my mules trotted along the stone-paved road which runs round the western and southern sides of Peh-jin-ching or the Northern Capital, skirting the city walls. Grey and of imposing strength, they reached the height of over forty feet, and compassed the city about four-square. But at length we entered the Chinese town, and approached the "Gate of Heaven," with its massive square projecting tower, and long tunnelled archway, through which a swarm of people, carriages, and animals were going backwards and forwards like ants in an ant-hill.

It was only a short distance from the "Gate of Heaven" to the street of the European Ambassadors, in which I knew there was a French hotel. Owing to the long journey, my clothes showed terrible signs of wear, and my outer man was altogether so unkempt, that I thought it would be wiser to stay in the hotel *incognito* for a few days, until I got myself made presentable. But my palanquin had not advanced very far down the street of the ambassadors, when my eye fell upon a large white-washed gateway, outside which stood a couple of Cossack sentries. I called to them, asking whose house that was. They told me, it was the Russian legation. These words had such an effect upon my ears that I instantly jumped out of the palanquin and went in. At that moment I cared not one jot about my appearance, and that the Cossacks were incomparably better dressed than I was.

THE GREAT WALL BETWEEN KALGAN AND PEKING

I passed my hand hurriedly over my disordered beard, shook off the thickest of the dust, and passed between the astonished sentries. To reach the Russian ambassador's dwelling, I had to cross a garden by a stone-paved path. I rang the bell. A Chinese servant came and opened the door, and asked in Russian: "Whom do you want?" I inquired if Mr. Pavloff, the *chargé d'affaires*, would receive visitors, for I knew that the ambassador, Count Cassini, had recently left Peking. Mr. Pavloff did receive visitors. He received me at once, and with the greatest possible cordiality. He had been expecting me a long time, having been instructed from St. Petersburg, that I was on my way to the Chinese capital. A couple of rooms had been got ready for me, and had been at my disposal for a month past.

This then was my *incognito*—a handsome room, furnished with all the refinements of European luxury—costly carpets on the floor, Chinese silk embroideries on the walls, antique vases standing in niches and on pedestals, and—glorious sight!—actually a bed, in which I did not even dream of the wretched guest-houses in which I had spent the last few nights of my journey. The table in the middle of the room contained a perfect mountain of letters and newspapers from home, the oldest dated fully thirteen months back. How I devoured their precious contents, whilst the English-speaking Chinese tailor measured me for a new suit of clothes!

I subsequently called at the various embassies, and was everywhere received with flattering hospitality. England's representative, Sir Claude MacDonald, the French ambassador M. Gérard, and his secretary the Comte de Sercey, Baron von Heyking, the German ambassador, the American, Mr. Demby, and Mr. Knobel, the Netherlands envoy, whom I had previously met in Teheran—all gave me the friendliest welcome, and congratulated me upon the successful accomplishment of my journey. I also received a congratulatory telegram from King Oscar.

But years of lonely wandering among the savage and semi-savage tribes of Asia cannot fail to have some effect

II.—38

upon a European. I soon grew weary of the gay feastings, and felt awkward and out of place amid the splendid throng. The change from the lonely deserts of Tibet, of Tsaidam, of Gobi was too sudden to suit me.

After a rest of twelve days I said adieu to my many new friends and turned my face homewards. Mr. Pavloff very kindly undertook to look after my baggage, and have it transported right across Siberia free of expense. I had three routes to Europe to choose between. The shortest was *viâ* Vancouver and New York; the most comfortable by the mail-boats touching at India and going through the Suez Canal; the third, the longest and most fatiguing, was the overland route through Mongolia and Siberia. This was nevertheless the route I selected, so that once more I travelled across Asia, though this time it was under very different conditions. I rode in a two-wheeled Chinese cart, at express speed, across the endless plains, deserts, and steppes of Gobi, through Sair-ussu and Urga, to Kiakhta.

The cart was drawn by four mounted Mongols, by means of two ropes fastened to the ends of the cart-shafts. A cross-bar, thrust through loops in the rope near the shaft-ends, was held by two of the men on their knees; whilst the other two men tied the ends of the ropes round their waists; and away we went at full gallop across the steppes, the cart rattling and jolting so that I was almost shaken to a mummy. You can only travel at this express speed under the authorization of a special pass from the Tsung Li Yamen. Couriers are sent on in advance at each stage, so that you always find horses waiting for you. There are twenty mounted men to each stage. As soon as one set of four are tired, another set take their places; and the change is made so swiftly and so deftly that the traveller scarcely notices it, unless he happens to be looking out of the front window at the time. There is no well-defined track, and there are no stations, except the tent-villages of the Mongols. This circumstance, that we were dependent upon the nomads for horses, explains why we were unable to follow any well-known path. Each relay of Mongols rode straight for the next encampment,

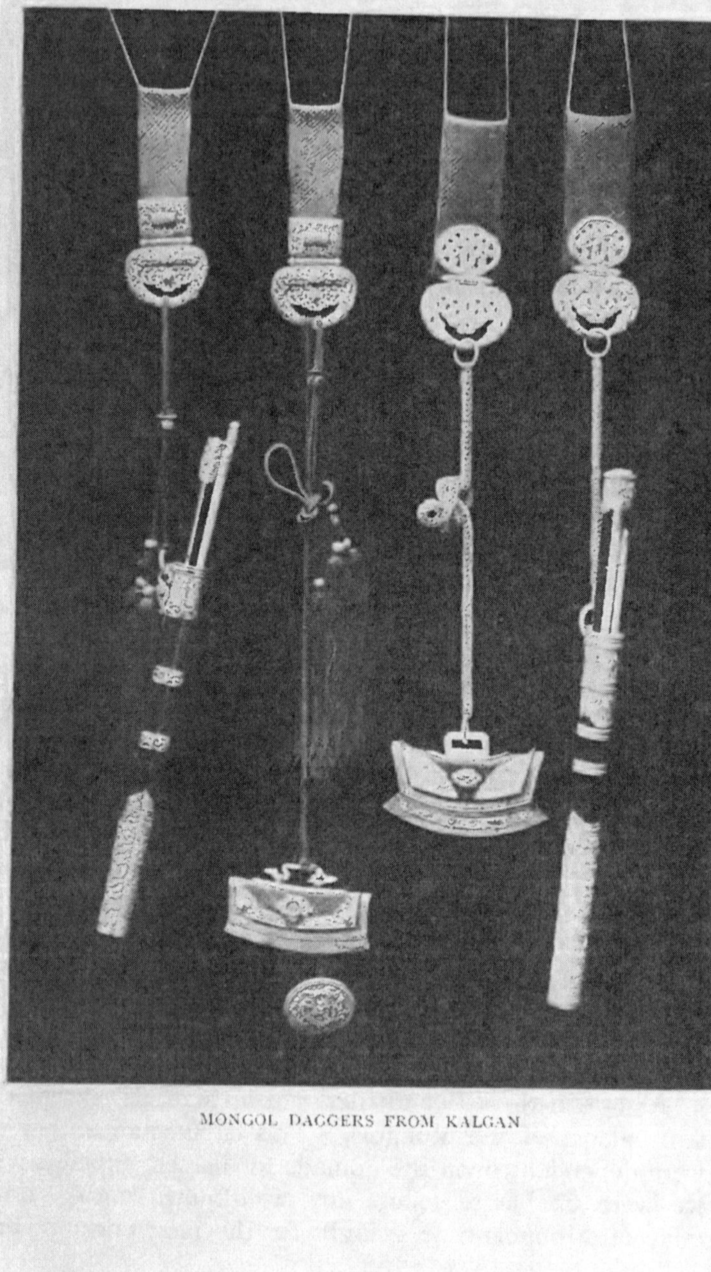

MONGOL DAGGERS FROM KALGAN

across steppes, over ravines, up and down hills. On some of the stages in northern Mongolia the ground was covered with deep snow, so that camels were used instead of horses.

At Urga I paid a visit to the temple of Maidari, the future Buddha. There too I parted from my ever-faithful attendant, Islam Bai, who had travelled across Mongolia in my wake in a second cart. He was very anxious to go home with me to Sweden; but that could not be. It was however hard to part from him. Mr. Luba, the Russian consul in Urga, took charge of him, and for his own safety's sake sent him in the capacity of a Russian post-courier to Uliassutai; thence he travelled *viâ* Urumchi to Kashgar, and thence to Osh in Fergana, where, as I subsequently learned from Captain Saitseff, he arrived safely, and was warmly welcomed by his wife and family.

Thanks to the kind courtesy of Mr. Pavloff, I had an escort of Cossacks all the way from Peking to Kiakhta. From Kiakhta I travelled by tarantass, sledge, and telega through Baikal and Irkutsk as far as Kansk; and from Kansk a nine days' journey by rail took me to St. Petersburg.

It was on the 10th of May 1897 that I at last saw the spires and houses of Stockholm peeping between the islands of the Skärgård. What a thrill of pure, unalloyed pleasure to plant my foot once more on Swedish soil, after travelling for three years and seven months in the heart of the vast continent of Asia!

INDEX

II.—39

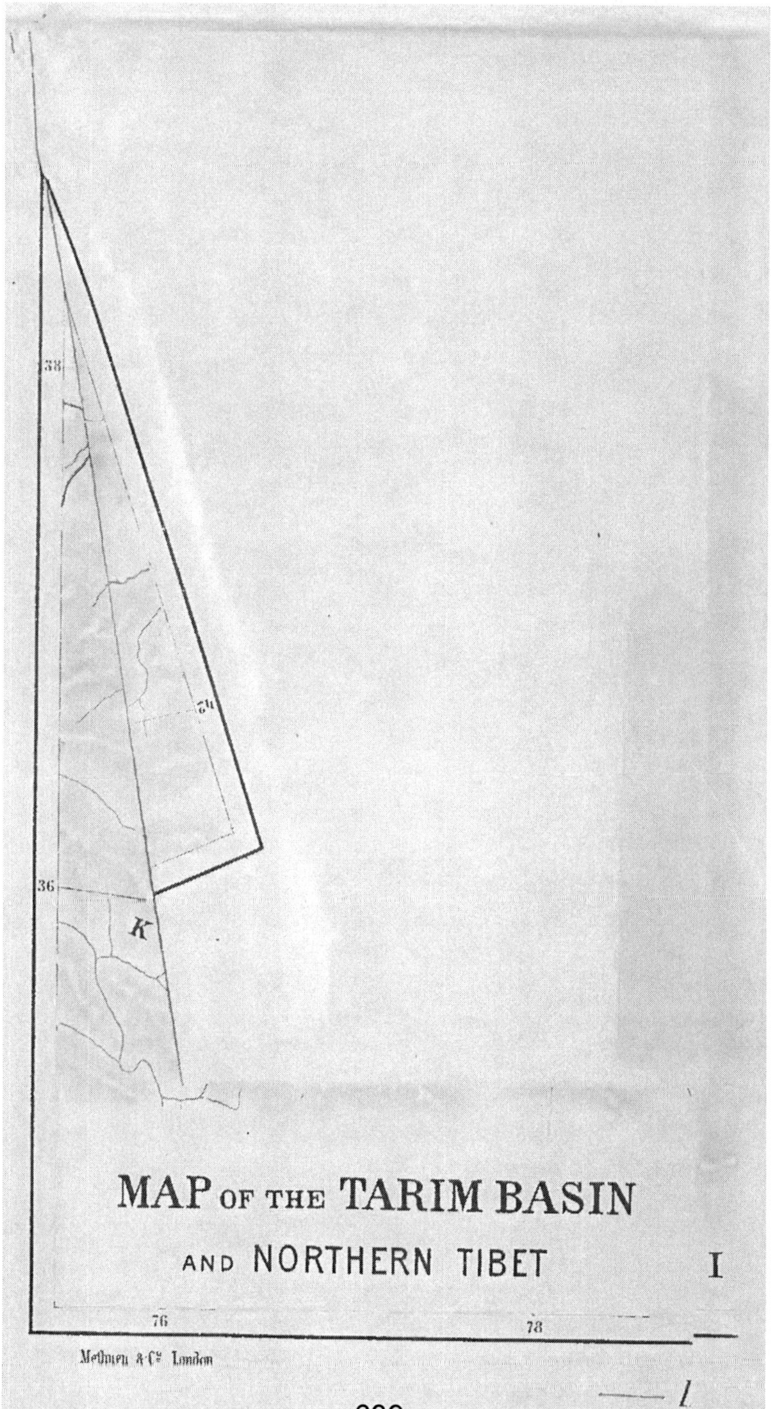
38
36
K
MAP OF THE TARIM BASIN
AND NORTHERN TIBET
I
76
78
Methuen & Co London

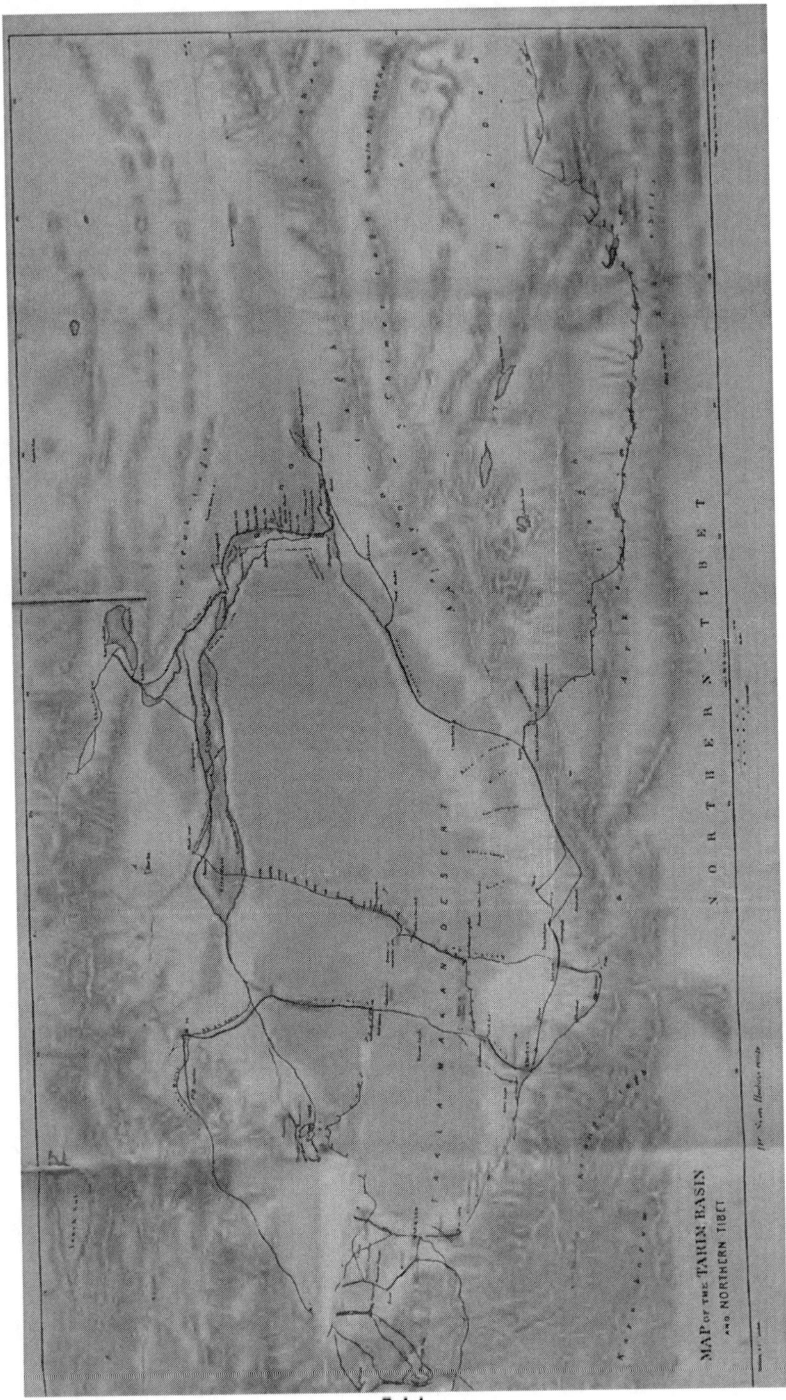
MAP OF THE TARIM BASIN AND NORTHERN TIBET
NORTHERN TIBET
TAKLAMAKAN DESERT